D1642456

READINGS IN THE THEORY

OF

INTERNATIONAL TRADE

THE SERIES OF REPUBLISHED ARTICLES ON ECONOMICS

Volume IV

Selection Committee For This Volume

HOWARD S. ELLIS

LLOYD A. METZLER

The participation of the American Economic Association in the presentation of this series consists in the appointment of a committee to determine the subjects of the volumes and of special committees to select the articles for each volume.

READINGS IN THE THEORY

OF

INTERNATIONAL TRADE

Selected by a Committee of
THE AMERICAN ECONOMIC ASSOCIATION

RICHARD D. IRWIN, INC.

HOMEWOOD, ILLINOIS

1950

PREFACE

The Blakiston Series of Republished Articles on Economics* is the outcome of an agreement between the American Economic Association and The Blakiston Company, in accordance with which the Company has undertaken to publish successive volumes of selected essays upon subjects determined by a standing committee of the Association. Since 1941, when the Series was undertaken, volumes have appeared on Social Control of Industry, Business Cycle Theory, and The Theory of Income Distribution. The present volume is the fourth of the Series.

The primary purpose of the project has been to bring together, field by field, some of the essays and articles which are particularly useful in the instruction of senior and graduate students concentrating in economics. Particularly in the case of advanced instruction, if the student is to be given an opportunity to examine for himself recent doctrinal developments and issues, certain contributions to the economics periodicals are indispensable materials. Yet it is unfortunately true that few or no institutions of higher learning can afford to provide an adequate number of files of the economics periodicals to serve this purpose. The Association believes that the Blakiston Series serves as a partial means of meeting this situation.

It is hoped, however, that these volumes will also serve as a means by which those economists who find themselves constrained usually to specialize in one sector of the subject may inform themselves of progress in related sectors. The annual output of books, articles and essays in economics has become so great that no person can possibly hope to keep abreast of all developments. When, however, advantage can be taken of the work of selection committees of specialists in at least some of the fields, the task of keeping moderately well informed as to the most important contributions in these areas may be more nearly feasible.

---

*Since 1952 this series has been published by Richard D. Irwin, Inc., and is now known as The Series of Republished Articles on Economics.

Although many of the articles included in a volume such as this are necessarily technical in nature, since they are addressed primarily to professional economists, the nonprofessional reader who has no more than an elementary knowledge of economics will find much of the material both understandable and of interest to him. Many of the topics are timely indeed; for example, "The Role of the International Monetary Agreements in a World of Planned Economies," "The Transfer Problem Reconsidered," "Foreign Trade Policy in the Business Cycle," the three essays in the section, Other Aspects of Commercial Policy, and the three essays in the section, The Future of World Trade.

The General Committee on Republications has, in the case of this volume as in the case of its three predecessor volumes, fully delegated the responsibility for the selection of essays to a committee of which Professors Ellis and Metzler have, in this case, served as co-chairmen. Readers of the volume will find it profitable to begin with the explanatory introduction prepared by the co-chairmen.

The extensive use which has been made of the first three volumes of the Series and the encouraging reception accorded the project by economists generally have led the American Economic Association recently to renew the arrangement with The Blakiston Company with a view to continuing the Series. A fifth volume, in the general field of public finance and fiscal policy, is now in preparation, with the editorial responsibility to be borne by Professors Roy Blough and Arthur Smithies. Other volumes are planned for the near future in the fields of price theory and monetary theory respectively.

BERNARD F. HALEY.
Chairman, General Committee on
Republications.

STANFORD, CALIFORNIA
January, 1949.

INTRODUCTION

During the inter-war period economics underwent rapid and striking changes, and this was no less true of international economics than of other specialized branches of the subject. The most spectacular changes, no doubt, were those associated with Keynes and the theory of employment, but far reaching, if less dramatic, innovations occurred also in the theory of value, prices, and production. In particular, the concept of measurable utility was rather generally abandoned in favor of indifference ratios. This substitution had been suggested at a much earlier date by Pareto, Slutzky and W. E. Johnson, but it did not become a widely accepted part of price theory until it was further developed during the inter-war years by Hicks and Allen. The new developments in price theory, as well as those arising out of the theory of employment, were quickly applied to the special problems of international economics, and many of the articles and essays reprinted in the present volume reflect the influence of one or both of these changes.

The theory of employment influenced international economics primarily in its monetary aspects. The concept of the automatic adjustment of the balance of payments, for example, underwent substantial alterations during the inter-war years, largely as a result of the new developments in the theory of the circular flow of income. At the same time, the current items in the balance of payments were related more closely to the circular flow of income than had previously been done; and this in turn made possible a more realistic appraisal of the international spread of business cycles, as well as a better understanding of the conflict between domestic stability and international equilibrium.

If the theory of employment affected international economics principally on the monetary side, the innovations which occurred in price theory during the inter-war years exerted their greatest influence upon the so-called "pure" theory of international trade, *i.e.*, upon that branch of international trade which deals with the Law of Comparative Advantage and with the distribution of the gains from trade between countries. This part of international economics, which was precisely formulated for the first time by Ricardo and later improved somewhat by Mill, went through the remainder of the nineteenth century and a part of the twentieth without essential modification from its original orientation to the labor theory of value. Thus the pure theory of international trade was sorely in need of improvements which would bring it abreast of modern price theory. It is surprising, nevertheless, to find that the improvements in international price theory, when they were finally made during the inter-war years, affected the basic conclusions derived from the classical theory only to a moderate extent. On questions of commercial policy, for example, Mill and Scitovszky are in substantial agreement, even though their methods of analysis and their underlying price theories are considerably different.

The articles reprinted herewith have been classified, as far as possible, in accordance with the distinction drawn above between the monetary and the "real" or "price" aspects of international trade. Thus, the articles in the first four sections deal primarily with various international monetary problems, and in these parts the influence of the theory of employment is most noticeable. The fifth and sixth sections, on the other hand, deal largely with the theoretical and applied aspects of price theory in international economics, and here the inter-war revolution in price theory is most apparent.

Finally, the seventh, eighth, and ninth sections consider various features of commercial policy and of international investment, and the probable future structure of international trade which could not be conveniently classified as either monetary theory or price theory. Although these final parts undoubtedly reflect, to some extent, the changes in monetary and price theory which occurred during the inter-war years, they also reflect something else which has exerted an equally great influence upon international economics, namely, the highly unstable, disturbed and shifting character of international trade and of international economic policies. The years of inflation and fluctuating exchange rates after the First World War, the war debts and reparations, the Great Depression of the 'thirties and the renewed abandonment of the gold standard, the rapid changes in commercial policy, such as the British adoption of a policy of protection and the Central European adoption of numerous and complex exchange controls—these and many other events, painful as they were at the time, had nevertheless the small compensation to the economist that they provided him, as an epidemic provides a medical research worker, with an enormous laboratory for study and experimentation. The influence of actual events upon the theory of international trade is probably most apparent, in the present collection of readings, in sections seven, eight, and nine, but a considerable number of the articles in earlier parts were also affected by the unprecedented events of the inter-war years. The early discussions of the transfer problem, for example, were a direct outgrowth of the German reparations situation.

The general character of the several parts of this book has probably been sufficiently delineated, but it may be advisable to say something about the various articles and essays contained in each of the individual sections. The first section, it is hoped, will provide the reader with a description of the modern theory of adjustment of the balance of payments. The adjustment process is described for a system of fluctuating exchange rates as well as for the traditional case of fixed exchange rates. The essay by Nurkse is, in a sense, a prologue to the others, since it presents a definition of the concept of international equilibrium as well as a discussion of the major elements of the balance of payments. The article by Paish is both an account of the modern theory of adjustment—i.e., the adjustment of the balance of payments through induced changes in income and employment—and a comparison of this modern theory with the classical price-specie-flow mechanism. Despite the excellence of the recent work in the theory of international equilibrium, a great deal remains to be done in this field, for the present and prospective future market conditions in international trade are quite unlike those of the inter-war years. In particular, government participation in foreign trade and in foreign exchange markets has become far more important today than in the past. The final article in the first section, by Mikesell, is an attempt to describe the meaning and significance of international equilibrium in a world of government controls.

The studies in the second section by Mrs. Robinson and Machlup deal, to a considerable extent at least, with the problem of international equilibrium under a system of fluctuating exchange rates. They were included because they appear to be the most lucid accounts of the supply-and-demand technique as applied to the foreign exchange market. It is interesting to note, in this connection, that the discussion of foreign exchange markets was the forerunner of a technique which later became an important tool of general price theory. Since the time of John Stuart Mill, economists have been concerned about the possibility of instability or indeterminateness of foreign exchange rates. Marshall, following Mill, made a tentative investigation of the conditions of exchange stability, and a more precise account was given later (1920) by C. F. Bickerdike. But even with these important antecedents, Mrs. Robinson's study is probably the most illuminating account of the conditions of exchange stability. Be that as it may, the important point, for present purposes, is that all of this discussion of stability and instability in the foreign exchange markets preceded by a considerable period the analysis of general conditions of market stability which later became an important part of price theory. This is but one example of a long list of cases in which the investigation of particular problems in international trade has preceded the formulation of more general principles in price theory.

The third section is devoted primarily to the controversy between Keynes and Ohlin concerning German reparations, and since this controversy is so well known it hardly seems necessary to discuss it in detail here. The transfer problem is of course simply a special case of the more general problem of international equilibrium. But because of its historical importance in the development of international trade theory, the transfer controversy has been made a separate section. The exchange of views between Keynes and Ohlin occurred in 1929, several years before the appearance of Keynes' theory of employment, but the theory presented by Ohlin was closely akin to what was later called the modern theory of the balance of payments. Ohlin's work is perhaps best regarded, in fact, as a sort of steppingstone between the modern theory and the classical. The paradoxical aspect of the controversy is that Keynes, who later laid the groundwork for the modern theory, adopted an extremely classical view in his discussion of German reparations.

The fourth section, dealing with the international aspects of business cycles, contains but one article, the familiar study by Salant on foreign trade policy in the business cycles. If space had permitted, papers dealing with the more technical aspects of international business cycles, such as the work of Robertson and Clark on the foreign trade multiplier and the work of Vining on the concept of a region, might well have been included in this section. In view of the limits placed upon the size of the volume, however, it seemed best to select a single article as representative of modern views on this subject.

The fifth and sixth sections, as noted earlier, are devoted largely to articles which apply modern price theory to international trade. The innovations in price theory which have exerted most influence upon international economics are those related to the theory of consumers' choice and those related to the theory of production. The article by Leontief, for example, is in part an attempt to express the gains from international trade in terms of indifference ratios, and thereby to dispense with the concept of measurable utility. Scitovszky, in the sixth section, applies substantially the same technique to the problem of tariffs. Both Leontief and Scitovszky employ the concept of a collective indifference schedule for the community as a whole, a concept which has frequently been called into question. But whether this affects the validity of their final conclusions is a question which need not detain us here. In any event, the problem of the gains from trade is approached from a slightly different point of view by Samuelson, who presents a criterion of economic gain which dispenses with both measurable utility and collective indifference schedules. Samuelson shows that international trade is preferable to self-sufficiency because international trade makes it possible for all individuals to consume more of every commodity while at the same time performing a smaller amount of work. In other words, his paper represents a generalization of the classical concept of the gains from trade.

The articles by Graham and Williams are well known and little need be said about them here. Although they were written before most of the important inter-war innovations in price theory, they represent a considerable advance beyond the classical doctrines. Graham presents the thesis that the classical argument in terms of two commodities and two countries exaggerates the extent to which the terms of trade are altered by conditions of demand. He argues, further, that when there are several commodities and several countries, the terms of trade are quite rigidly governed by conditions of production, irrespective of demand conditions. His later article of 1932—not published in this volume—recognized that his earlier view was essentially a long-run view, since it assumed a high degree of substitutability in productive processes. In the short-run, therefore, Graham conceded that demand conditions might have a considerable influence upon the terms of trade. But this is a refinement which affects neither the long-run validity of Graham's argument nor the position of his paper in the history of economic thought.

In addition to the innovations in price theory, equally important changes in international economics grew out of the application, during the inter-war years, of the theory of production and distribution to the special problems of international trade. This led to the well-known thesis on the tendency of international trade to equalize the relative returns of various factors of production among different countries. In English-speaking countries the economic theories concerning the relation of international trade to the distribution of income are usually associated almost exclusively with the name of Ohlin, and no doubt there is a good deal of justification for this, since it was Ohlin, more than anyone else, who refined and developed this particular line of thought. Nevertheless, the pioneer work in the field, and a work to which Ohlin acknowledges a debt, was a paper written by Professor Heckscher in Swedish and published in 1919 in the *Ekonomisk Tidskrift*. Because of the language barrier, this paper has been little known in the United States and the United Kingdom. But since it occupies a rather important place in the history of international trade theory through its influence on Ohlin, a translated version is included among the present readings. The translation was undertaken by Professor and Mrs. Svend Laursen, and the editors wish to express their gratitude to both of them for their painstaking work. Apart from the study by Heckscher, the article by Stolper and Samuelson dealing with tariffs and real wages is also indebted to the theory of production. Assuming that production functions are homogeneous functions of the first degree, and that perfect competition prevails, Stolper and Samuelson show that, in a scarce-labor country, protective duties will increase real wages despite the rise in the price of imports. Their paper is essentially a refinement of the work of Heckscher and Ohlin and its application to the problem of tariffs.

The three articles included in the seventh section cover a wide variety of subjects, but all are related to one feature or another of commercial policy. The variety of topics discussed in this section is perhaps simply a reflection of the rapid growth, during the past fifteen years or so, of many different techniques of trade regulation. Taken together, the three articles discuss the economic and political consequences of most of the important types of trade regulation: tariffs, import quotas, and export subsidies are discussed by Mrs. Robinson, exchange clearings and other bilateral devices by Ellis, and state trading by Viner.

The eighth section, consisting of a single article by Polak, represents the broad subject of international investment and the balance of payments. Other articles which might have been included in a larger anthology are the study of A. J. Brown on industrialization and trade, and similar studies by Buchanan.

The final section of the readings presents three papers dealing with the probable development of international trade in the future. Such topics as the influence of industrialization on the gains from trade and the influence of the level of employment on the relative bargaining positions of different countries are discussed in this section. The first of the three articles in the ninth section (by Robertson) was written before the Second World War, the third (by Haberler) was written during the war years, and the second (by Viner) was written after the war had ended. To some extent, therefore, the three papers together may give an indication of the development of economic thought on this subject.

The present volume is a collection of readings in the *theory* of international trade and it is therefore limited in scope to articles which illustrate or develop some general principle of international economics. Although we believe that this limitation is desirable, both because it preserves the uniformity of this series of books and because it tends to give the books more long-run interest than would otherwise be the case, we are also acutely aware that in omitting empirical studies we exclude some of the best work in international economics of recent years. The studies by Folke Hilgerdt and Albert O. Hirschman on the commodity structure of world trade, the statistical investigations by Randall Hinshaw, J. Hans Adler, Rollin F. Bennett and Tse-Cheng Chang of the elasticity of demand for imports and the marginal propensity to import, and the papers by James W. Angell, Arthur I. Bloomfield and Hal B. Lary on the balance of payments of the United States are all articles or essays which would improve the quality of any anthology on international trade.

The method of selection employed for these readings in international economics is substantially the same as that used in the preceding volume, *Readings in the Theory of Income Distribution*. A considerable number of specialists in the field of international trade, perhaps twenty-five in all, were asked to make recommendations of articles to be included. On the basis of these recommendations a tentative list was drawn up and this list was submitted to the same economists for suggestions as to possible deletions or additions. The final list of readings was then compiled by taking into account, as far as possible, the criticisms and suggestions concerning the tentative list.

HOWARD S. ELLIS,
LLOYD A. METZLER,
Co-Chairmen, Selection Committee

January, 1949.

CONTENTS

OTHER ASPECTS OF COMMERCIAL POLICY

INTERNATIONAL INVESTMENT AND THE BALANCE OF PAYMENTS

THE FUTURE OF WORLD TRADE

EQUILIBRIUM OF THE BALANCE OF PAYMENTS

1

CONDITIONS OF INTERNATIONAL MONETARY EQUILIBRIUM*

By Ragnar Nurkse‖ ‡

The purpose of this essay is to consider some of the central issues of international monetary policy in the light both of pre-war experience and of the post-war plans concerning foreign exchange and finance. For the facts of recent history and the conclusions to which they point, our principal source is a League of Nations report entitled *International Currency Experience: Lessons of the Inter-War Period*.[1] For the post-war plans, reference will be made to the agreements adopted at the Bretton Woods Conference.[2]

Our discussion is concerned with relations between independent national currencies. It may be well to state at the outset that the system of relations here envisaged is not of the gold-standard type if that means immutable exchange rates with domestic monetary and economic policies subordinated to the balance of payments. Changes in exchange rates are accepted as a legitimate method of adjustment, and the conditions in which such changes are appropriate will be our first topic (Sections I and II). We shall then comment on "cyclical" fluctuations in the balance of payments for

---

* *Essays in International Finance*, Number 4, Spring 1945. International Finance Section, Princeton University. Reprinted by the courtesy of the International Finance Section, Princeton University, and the author.

‖ Columbia University.

‡ Squared brackets in the present text indicate all substantial additions to or alterations of the original text.

[1] Columbia University Press (International Document Service), New York, 1944.

[2] United Nations Monetary and Financial Conference, *Final Act and Related Documents*, U.S. Government Printing Office, Washington, 1944.

which the method of exchange adjustment is unsuitable (Section III); on the importance of foreign investment for the successful functioning of the international currency mechanism (Section IV); and on the interrelationship of monetary, commercial, and employment policies (Section V). One of our main preoccupations will be to determine the international monetary framework compatible, on the one hand, with the pursuit of national policies for the maintenance of employment and, on the other, with the fullest possible development of international trade.

I. THE EQUILIBRIUM RATE OF EXCHANGE

Let us begin with the concept of the equilibrium rate of exchange. This, to be sure, is a rather hackneyed subject; but it is of considerable practical importance and, despite all the attention it has received, still remains in need of clarification.

A notable feature of the constitution of the International Monetary Fund as drawn up at Bretton Woods is that it provides for agreed and orderly changes in the exchange rates of member countries whenever a change is considered necessary to correct a "fundamental disequilibrium." While certain other terms in the Fund's charter are defined and explained at some length, no attempt is made to give a definite meaning to the phrase "fundamental disequilibrium." From a tactical point of view, it may have been wise to leave the interpretation of this phrase to the managers of the Fund or to the member countries concerned in each particular case; the statutes of the Fund may not be a suitable place for the definition of so abstruse and perhaps controversial a subject. But if the machinery of the Fund is to operate successfully, there should be some more or less generally accepted notion as to what constitutes "equilibrium" or "disequilibrium" in regard to international exchange rates.

At the various monetary conferences after the first world war, the late Gustav Cassel campaigned vigorously for the theory of "purchasing power parity." He and his followers were under the impression that this theory furnished all that was needed for a definition of the equilibrium rate of exchange. Today it is realized that the purchasing-power-parity theory cannot provide a definition of the equilibrium rate; that it can provide only a pseudo-definition in terms which themselves require definition and, indeed, turn out to be incapable of precise interpretation.

The only satisfactory way of defining the equilibrium rate of exchange is to define it as that rate which, over a certain period of time, keeps the balance of payments in equilibrium. This seems very simple. Indeed, for any practical use, it is much too simple. We must carefully examine the component elements of this definition.

Take, first of all, the phrase "over a certain period." What is the length of the period over which payments have to be balanced? Is it a day, a month, a year, or ten years? If, for the purposes of this definition, the balance has to be in equilibrium every hour, every day, or even every week, then we have in effect a constantly fluctuating exchange rate. The rate is left free to vary in order to secure equilibrium in the balance of payments over these very short periods. Now experience has shown that freely fluctuating exchanges are apt to give rise to speculation of a disequilibrating kind, including disequilibrating movements not only of capital but also of commodity exports and imports. Under a system of freely fluctuating exchanges there may be little or nothing to limit people's "elasticity of expectations," at least in the short run. Any change in the rate is likely to create anticipations of a further change in the same direction. Thus exchange depreciation may well occasion a flight of capital, leading to further depreciation, and, if the prices of commodities exported and imported also come to be affected by disequilibrating anticipations, exports will fall instead of rise and imports rise instead of fall, so that the result is still further depreciation. Such self-aggravating processes make it impossible to achieve equilibrium in the balance of payments even in very short periods such as a day or a week.

Moreover, there are reasons why freely fluctuating exchanges would be undesirable even if they *could* secure continuous equilibrium in the balance of payments. For one thing, they create considerable exchange risks, which tend to discourage international trade. For another, they call for constant shifts of domestic factors of production between export and home-market industries, shifts which may be disturbing and wasteful. No country has shown any desire for a system of wholly uninhibited fluctuations in exchange rates, and a prime objective of the International Monetary Fund is to make such a system unnecessary.

The period which we contemplate in the definition of the equilibrium rate of exchange cannot, therefore, be as short as a day or a week. Even if it were a month, exchange rates in most countries would be subject to seasonal fluctuations within each year. The period, therefore, should certainly not be less than a year. But if we make it long enough to eliminate seasonal fluctuations, why not make it long enough to eliminate "cyclical" fluctuations as well? This would give us a period of between five and ten years. If, that is to say, a country's external accounts, at a given rate of exchange, attain an even balance over a period of five to ten years, then that exchange rate would be regarded as an equilibrium rate.

Some countries—especially those exporting primary commodities—have often shown a wide cyclical movement in their balance of payments, and here it is particularly desirable to strike the balance for a period long enough to cover a whole cycle. There are, however, countries (such as France or even England) in which the balance of payments normally shows no very marked cyclical behavior, and, in these cases, it might be safe enough to take the balance over a shorter period—say, two or three years—as an indication of equilibrium or disequilibrium.

But as soon as we turn away from the imaginary system of freely fluctuating exchanges, in which the balance is kept in equilibrium every hour or every day, we must assume that there exists some medium to settle the discrepancies arising within the standard period. To act as such a medium is the most elementary function of the central reserves of international means of payment held by each country in the form of gold, foreign exchange, or international borrowing facilities. Later in this article there will be more to say on the functions of international liquidity. For the present, it is clear that, if we wish, we can alter the wording of our definition and describe the equilibrium rate as that rate at which, over a certain period, there would be no net change in a country's reserve of international means of payment. The longer we make the standard period the larger is the amount that is likely to be needed for settling the intervening discrepancies. As a rule, it takes a larger reserve to even out cyclical fluctuations than it takes to meet seasonal fluctuations. The larger the stock of international means of payment held by any country, and by countries in the aggregate, the less will be the need for changes in exchange rates. It is, therefore, natural that the International Monetary Fund agreement should contain more liberal provisions for exchange adjustments than the British scheme for an International Clearing Union (the "Keynes Plan" of 1943) since the latter proposed to create an amount of international liquidity more than three times as large as the resources of the Fund.

So much for the period over which we consider the balance of payments for the purpose of defining the equilibrium rate. We must now look at the balance of payments itself. What shall we include in the balance of payments for the purpose of this definition? Or rather, is there anything we do not wish to include? There is at least one thing that must be excluded, namely, the transfer of gold or other liquid reserves which may be necessary to balance a country's external accounts. Otherwise these accounts would always be in balance and there would never be any disequilibrium. A net change in any country's international currency reserve is, in fact, our criterion of disequilibrium.[3]

Another item that should be excluded is short-term capital movements. Such capital movements may be of two kinds. They may be of the equilibrating kind, such as used to occur in the gold standard mechanism in response to temporary changes in discount rates or to movements in exchange rates within the gold points. In

---

[3] If there are changes in the world total of international currency reserves (as a result, for example, of new gold production), this criterion should of course be applied not literally but rather in the sense of the *relationship* between the reserves held by the several countries.

that case they merely take the place of—and fulfill the same function as—transfers of gold or foreign exchange reserves.   A country with a deficit in its balance of payments can cover the deficit either by an outflow of gold or an inflow of foreign short-term funds, if it is able to attract such funds by raising its bank rate or otherwise. These funds are equivalent to a loan by foreigners and should be regarded as a draft on the recipient country's stock of international reserves.   Whether there is an outflow of gold or an inflow of foreign short-term loans, the country's net international liquidity will be reduced.   The foreign short-term funds are a liability, can be withdrawn at any moment, and must be treated as a negative gold reserve.

Short-term capital movements of the *dis*equilibrating kind should also be excluded from the balance of payments which we wish to use as a standard of the equilibrium rate.   Such capital movements became very familiar during the 'thirties, in the form of capital flight and "hot money," and were due mainly to fear of exchange depreciation and of war.   They gave rise to large discrepancies in balances of payments which it proved impossible or undesirable to meet by means of adjustments in trade and other normal items and which, therefore, were generally settled by large gold movements.   In considering the balance of payments as a criterion of exchange equilibrium it is desirable, as a rule, to exclude all discrepancies which are due to such abnormal factors. There is now almost general agreement that, in the future, capital movements of this type had better be prevented, or at least curbed, by some form of control.

Apart from international currency transfers and short-term capital movements, no exclusions are necessary or desirable for the purpose of our definition.   We must include all other international transactions entering into the balance of payments.   In particular, we must include all capital movements relating to international investment.   A certain rate of exchange may be an equilibrium rate with a certain flow of foreign investment.   With a different flow of foreign investment, this rate is not likely to be an equilibrium rate. After the first world war, the exchange rates which were established during the 'twenties may have been appropriate so long as there was a certain average annual export of capital from the United States. The fact that during the 'thirties the currencies of many debtor countries depreciated below their previous parities with the United States dollar was no doubt partly due to the complete cessation of capital exports from the United States; some depreciation of these currencies in relation to the dollar may well have been necessary to the restoration of equilibrium in the international accounts under the new conditions in the capital market.

Having examined the "standard period" and the "balance of payments" to be used for the purpose of our definition we come now to a third element that needs clarification. The balance of payments is said to be "in equilibrium" when payments are equal to receipts (apart from the items which, for the reasons given, must be excluded). But payments can be made equal to receipts by artificial restrictions on imports.[4] If a deficit appears in the balance of payments, and the deficit is closed by cutting down imports, are we to conclude that the rate is now at the equilibrium level? The answer is clearly in the negative. To use our definition properly, we must take the structure of trade barriers existing at a given starting-point. If subsequently a certain exchange rate can be maintained, or a balance-of-payments deficit closed, only by means of an increase in trade barriers, then the rate cannot be accepted as the equilibrium rate. The true equilibrium rate is that rate at which payments and receipts are equalized without additional restrictions on trade.

This point has been of great practical importance without having always been clearly apprehended. Germany had no balance-

---

[4] Artificial stimulation of exports by means of subsidies has, for fiscal reasons, been much less common, but it may obviously achieve the same result. We should observe, however, that a *combination* of uniform *ad valorem* import duties with uniform *ad valorem* export subsidies can be exactly equivalent to a devaluation of the exchange. If a deficit in the balance of payments is closed by means of such a combination, then the exchange will, in effect, already have been devalued. In practice, of course, the distinguishing feature of import duties and export subsidies is that they are not uniform but selective and discriminating.

of-payments deficit and suffered no loss of gold after 1934. Nevertheless the reichsmark was rightly regarded as overvalued. At the given exchange rate, Germany's external accounts were balanced only by means of additional import restrictions, which took mainly the form of drastic exchange controls. In the same way France, though failing to close her balance-of-payments deficit, certainly managed to reduce it by means of import quotas.

When a currency is kept far above its equilibrium level, and especially when the country's gold and exchange reserves run out— as they did in Germany—, import restrictions become practically inevitable, and the result is a sharp cut in the volume of foreign trade. A country with an overvalued currency suffers a loss in its competitive power to export and, as exports decline, imports must be cut down correspondingly if the external accounts are to be balanced. The methods by which the cut is brought about are of secondary interest: they may be exchange controls, import quotas, prohibitions, licenses, or merely increased import duties. Exchange control, in particular, was often blamed for the contraction of world trade in the 'thirties. The underlying causal condition was rather the extreme dislocation of exchange rates.

The mere equality of a country's foreign receipts and payments is not, then, an acceptable criterion of the equilibrium rate of exchange if the equality must be enforced by restrictions on imports. There is another important case in which such equality is not a sufficient criterion. It is conceivable that a country may keep its balance of payments in equilibrium by reducing the demand for imports through a depressed level of aggregate domestic money income in relation to productive capacity; and if wage rates and prices are rigid, this contraction in money income will manifest itself in large-scale unemployment in that country. The balance of payments is in equilibrium; yet it is hardly proper to call the exchange rate a true equilibrium rate if it can be maintained only by means of depression and unemployment at home.

Great Britain in the years 1925–1930 affords a good illustration of this point. There was little sign of disequilibrium in the British balance of payments, yet the pound was rightly regarded as overvalued. There was practically no net change in the British gold reserve during that period. An inflow of foreign short-term funds, however, would have been equivalent to an outflow of gold. What happened before 1927 is largely a matter of guesswork, though some inflow undoubtedly occurred, especially as a result of capital flight from France and of speculative anticipation of the pound's return to its former gold parity in the spring of 1925. But for the period from the end of 1927 to the end of March 1931 we have the estimates of the Macmillan Committee, and these show no increase in London's net foreign short-term liabilities.[5] On the contrary, they show a slight reduction which, however, was matched by a slight reduction in the gold reserve, so that, on balance, no change seems to have taken place in Great Britain's international liquidity over those years. If we apply our definition of the equilibrium rate literally, the pound cannot be said to have been overvalued. The British balance of payments was kept in equilibrium, however, only at the cost of depressed conditions at home compared with conditions in the outside world.

Just as the German case led us to conclude that balance-of-payments equilibrium is not a sufficient criterion of an equilibrium exchange rate in the presence of special or additional import restrictions necessitated by the maintenance of the actual rate, so the British case suggests that it is not a sufficient criterion in the presence of a special or additional depression necessitated by the maintenance of the actual rate. At different levels of national income and employment in a given country, equilibrium in the balance of payments can be secured at different rates of exchange. It would seem better therefore to define the true equilibrium rate of exchange as one that maintains a country's external accounts in equilibrium without the need for wholesale unemployment at

---

[5] The fact that the estimates were incomplete can scarcely invalidate the evidence they afford in the present context. For we are concerned with the *movement* in the total over a period of time, and we have no reason to suppose that the amounts not covered by the Macmillan estimates moved in an entirely different manner from the amounts covered, which certainly formed the greater part of the true total.

home.   And if we extend our view from the position of a single country to the whole network of international exchange rates, this would lead us to define an ideal system of equilibrium rates as one that maintains the accounts of all countries simultaneously in equilibrium when all countries simultaneously are free from mass unemployment on the one hand and inflation on the other.

A country which, at a level of full employment, has a deficit in its balance of payments must reduce its national income below the level corresponding to full employment if balance-of-payments equilibrium is to be restored at the existing exchange rate.   Of course, by depressing still further its national income and hence its demand for imports, the country in question may actually produce a surplus in its balance of payments and an increase in its international currency reserve.   But this would be needless self-torture. Even to depress the national income to the point at which the balance of payments is in equilibrium is necessary only if the country's reserve is not adequate to meet the deficit.

One might argue that Great Britain in the late 'twenties should have expanded her domestic income and employment to a normal or satisfactory level; at that level she would have had a deficit in her balance of payments; this deficit would have been conclusive proof that her currency was overvalued; and only after furnishing this proof should the pound have been permitted to depreciate.   This would be an excellent general rule; but it does not work in the case of a country whose margin of international liquidity is so small that it cannot afford to incur a deficit.   The British gold reserve of about 150 million pounds in the late 'twenties was in itself rather a small margin; and if we take into account Britain's net foreign short-term liabilities at that time (about 275 million pounds, according to the incomplete estimate of the Macmillan Committee), there would seem to have been no margin at all.   A lowering of money rates in England might have led immediately to an outflow of foreign short-term funds and a corresponding loss of gold.   This gold would then, of course, not have been available for meeting the rise in imports and the consequent deficit in the balance of payments (exclusive of short-term capital movements) which would have tended to result from Great Britain's domestic expansion.

As a general rule, however, so long as its liquid international reserves are adequate, a country should be expected to make use of these reserves to meet an actual deficit in its balance of payments before a downward adjustment of its exchange rate can be approved. This principle was embodied in the "Keynes Plan," which provided for devaluation only after a country had used up a certain proportion of its quota in the International Clearing Union.

A publicly recognized and recognizable criterion of exchange adjustment has, it is true, the disadvantage that it may act as a signal for speculative capital transfers in anticipation of changes in exchange rates. It may be partly for this reason that such a criterion was not included in the Bretton Woods agreement. But the absence of an objective criterion does not by any means ensure absence of "speculation" and of speculative capital movements. Theoretically such capital movements could be offset, but for this purpose the Fund would need enormous additional resources. The limited resources with which, in fact, it is endowed had certainly better be devoted to the balancing of normal international transactions, including trade, services, and productive investment. Since, in any case, the Fund wisely provides for restrictions on capital movements that might drain its resources for speculative purposes, it is doubtful what force remains in the objection to an agreed and recognizable criterion of exchange adjustment.

II. Principles of Exchange Adjustment

In spite of the qualifications we have discussed, our general conclusion is that the balance of payments must be the chief criterion for any changes in exchange rates. A country with a surplus in its balance of payments should never resort to devaluation; on the contrary, it might be asked to appreciate its currency. Only when a country's balance shows a persistent deficit can devaluation be approved, though in special cases, as we have seen, it may be desirable to permit devaluation even if the balance of payments is apparently in equilibrium.

This simple code is sufficient to regulate the use of devaluation as a means whereby an individual country may seek to influence total demand for its output in the interest of its domestic employment situation. As an anti-depression measure, devaluation can represent either a beggar-my-neighbor policy or a buffer policy. The case of a beggar-my-neighbor policy of devaluation arises when a country that suffers from a depression of mainly domestic origin seeks to cure that depression by improving its balance of payments through devaluation; that is, in effect, by securing for its own national output a larger share of the existing world demand at the expense of other countries. Even without any devaluation such a country is likely to develop a surplus in its balance of payments as an automatic consequence of the fall in its demand for imports and possibly also as a result of a fall in its export prices with a more than corresponding increase in sales. The simple code just mentioned will generally not authorize a country in these circumstances to devalue, since the circumstances themselves will already have given a favorable turn to its balance of payments. Thus the beggar-my-neighbor policy of exchange depreciation would be effectively ruled out. This alone would be a gain, for otherwise any country suffering a depression in its domestic market might claim that such depression constitutes a "fundamental disequilibrium" justifying exchange depreciation. As long as the term is not defined, it may not be easy to reject such a claim. Yet the claim is obviously groundless, since any country that suffers a depression as a result of a fall in domestic investment can and should cure its depression by domestic measures. When depression at home creates a surplus in the balance of payments, there is nothing in the international monetary position to prevent the country in question from adopting a policy of domestic expansion.

The case is quite different when the purpose of devaluation is to act as a protective buffer against a depression originating abroad. If a given country is faced with a depression in one of its foreign markets, this depression will tend to spread to its domestic economy through an adverse balance of payments resulting from a fall in its exports and, if prices abroad are reduced, a rise in the volume of its imports. According to our definition of the equilibrium rate, the deficit in the balance of payments would in this case justify a certain measure of devaluation. Thus it is clear that the definition, if applied in practice, would, on the one hand, exclude devaluation of the "beggar-my-neighbor" type and, on the other, permit the type of devaluation which serves the purpose of a "buffer" policy designed to prevent the spread of depression from country to country.

Devaluation for buffer purposes is defensible, but it should not, in general, be necessary. The first and most desirable method of checking the spread of cyclical depressions is the policy of "offsetting," coupled with the use of international currency reserves for meeting cyclical balance-of-payments discrepancies in a manner presently to be considered. Another possible instrument that might help to insulate a certain area of depression would be the apportionment of scarce currencies, contemplated under the Bretton Woods agreement, which would tend to have the effect of discriminating against the exports of any country that allows its national income, and hence its imports, to decline far below the level corresponding to full employment. The method of exchange-rate adjustment constitutes only a third line of defense. Exchange adjustments for cyclical purposes are likely to be comparatively ineffective. Cyclical shifts in demand schedules may be so wide and violent that it is difficult, or even impossible, to determine precisely what alteration in exchange rates would secure balance-of-payments equilibrium in the short run. Besides, it is generally not worth while to create all the disturbances attending an alteration in exchange rates—including the shifts induced in the structure of production as between export and home-market industries—if the change is required for only short-term reasons; and cyclical factors must certainly be regarded as short-term reasons in this context. As we have seen, the standard period over which the balance of payments is to be balanced as a test of exchange-rate equilibrium should be long enough to permit any cyclical changes to cancel out. This presupposes a volume of international liquidity adequate to settle any temporary deficits within the standard period. It should be the function of international currency reserves, and not of exchange-rate adjustments, to meet cyclical and other short-term discrepancies in the balance of payments.

Exchange-rate adjustments are appropriate mainly in cases of chronic or structural disequilibria in the balance of payments. As a remedy for such persistent strains, they can scarcely fail, given time, to produce the desired effect. It is sometimes objected that the demand for imports on the part of an individual country, as well as the foreign demand for that country's exports, may be so inelastic with respect to price changes that a depreciation of the exchange would increase instead of reduce a deficit in the balance of payments. But even in this case exchange adjustment might still be capable of securing equilibrium though it would then have to take the form of an *appreciation* of the exchange.

III. The Functions of International Liquidity

In a world in which economic activity is subject to fluctuations but in which there is a growing demand for stability, the basic function of international currency reserves is to serve as a "buffer" giving each country some leeway for the regulation of its national income and employment and providing it with a means to soften the impact of economic fluctuations arising outside its borders.

This buffer function of international liquidity can be made clear by a simple example. Imagine a country whose monetary authorities are intent on keeping the national income at a level compatible with good employment at the given wage structure. Suppose a depression occurs abroad. The country's exports will fall as a result of the fall in foreign demand. There will be a loss of income and employment in the export industries. If nothing is done, the depression in the export industries is likely to lead, through the familiar "multiplier" mechanism, to a general and cumulative depression in the home-market industries as well. The depression at home will automatically tend to bring about a reduction in imports to the level of the reduced exports. Equilibrium will have been restored in the balance of payments, but only by rendering the depression general.

In order to prevent the spread of depression, the country we are considering must endeavor to offset the fall in foreign expenditure on its exports by an increase in domestic expenditure. Though a local or partial depression in its export industries may be inevitable, a general and cumulative depression of the whole economy can undoubtedly be averted by such a policy of "offsetting." In so far as the volume of employment depends on total expenditure, it is essential that total expenditure be maintained, which means in this case that the flow of domestic spending must be increased so as to compensate for the decline in foreign expenditure on the country's exports.

This is the policy required for domestic stability; but it does nothing to remove the deficit in the balance of payments resulting from the fall in exports. The deficit will tend to persist so long as the depression abroad continues. The country pursuing an off-setting policy must be prepared to give up temporarily some of its international currency reserve in order to meet this deficit. Only with an adequate reserve of international means of settlement will a country in this situation be able to avoid exchange depreciation or import restrictions.

The policy of offsetting is intended not to raise total expenditure, but to prevent it from falling. Since, therefore, the national income is not raised above its previous level, this policy does not necessarily lead to an increase in imports above their previous level. Yet the amount of imports, and hence the gap in the balance of payments, will certainly be greater than if the country allowed depression to spread to its whole domestic economy. This means that the volume of international liquidity required is larger, with a compensatory national income policy of the type described, than it would be if a country left things to take their "natural" course.

Under the gold standard, not only were things expected to take their natural course but a country in the situation described was expected even to accelerate the spread of depression by pushing up discount rates and contracting credit as gold flowed out. No doubt the gold standard "rules of the game" tended to reduce the loss of gold to a minimum; but they did so only by speeding up the propagation of depressions.

The offsetting procedure described is precisely the opposite of that which would be called for under the gold-standard rules of the game. The essential principle is that any deflationary or inflationary shock entering from abroad and threatening a country's economic stability is to be offset rather than reinforced; and the resulting discrepancy in the balance of payments is to be settled through a transfer of international liquidity. The example just discussed was that of a deflationary shock; but, with the signs reversed, the discussion applies in exactly the same way to the case of an inflationary disturbance.[6]

Even in the best days of the gold standard, the rules of the game were not always very strictly observed. There is some statistical evidence of "neutralization," for example, on the part of the Bank of France and the Bank of England in the nineteenth century.[7] In the inter-war period neutralization of gold movements by central banks became, in fact, the rule rather than the exception. Neutralization of this type was concerned primarily with the cash base of the banking system; any change in a central bank's gold and foreign exchange reserve was usually accompanied by a change *in the opposite direction* in the bank's domestic loans and securities. This tended, no doubt, to stabilize the volume of money in a country. It certainly went some way, though only a small part of the way, towards the more comprehensive policy of offsetting designed to give stability not merely to the money supply but to the national income.

Though neutralization by central banks was very common in the inter-war period it was nearly always frowned upon; it was widely regarded as wicked and disreputable behavior. The hold which the orthodox rules of the game had on people's minds was evidently strong—much stronger than the hold they had in practice. It is time to recognize that for any country aiming at some stability in its national economy, the policy of offsetting—which of course includes "neutralization" in the narrow sense—is the natural method

---

[6] See *International Currency Experience: Lessons of the Inter-War Period, op. cit.,* pp. 214ff.

[7] See Harry D. White. *The French International Accounts 1880–1913* (Harvard Economic Studies, vol. XL, 1933, p. 198); and Elmer Wood, *English Theories of Central Banking Control 1819–1858* (Harvard Economic Studies, vol. LXIV, 1939, p. 216).

of making use of its international currency reserves: it is time to accept it as a normal and respectable procedure.

The main function of the International Monetary Fund will be to create an addition, and quite a substantial addition, to aggregate international liquidity. Without this function, the Fund might still be a useful institution; in particular, it could still serve as a center for international consultations concerning the fixing and adjustment of exchange rates. But even as regards exchange rates, the Fund's effectiveness is likely to rest to some extent on its power to provide countries with additional liquidity.

The additional liquidity furnished by the Fund would no doubt make it easier for countries to pursue what we have called "offsetting" policies in the interests of domestic economic stability. The statutes of the Fund, however, are not very explicit as to the way countries are expected to use the Fund's resources. In regard to the contrast we have discussed between the buffer function of international liquidity and the orthodox rules of the gold standard game, the Bretton Woods agreement gives little or no indication of what will be the attitude in the administration of the Fund, though here again, as in the case of "fundamental disequilibrium," any attempt to lay down a hard-and-fast doctrine would perhaps have been out of place in a document of this kind. In Article I of the agreement there is a general statement of objectives according to which one of the purposes of the Fund is "to shorten the duration and lessen the degree of disequilibrium in the international balances of payments." This may be variously interpreted; but it sounds rather like the orthodox rules which placed all the emphasis on countries keeping in step with one another, and removing as rapidly as possible any discrepancies in the balance of payments among them, no matter what happened to production and employment. In fact, production and employment were left free to move up and down in all countries more or less simultaneously, and a deflationary process in any important country was communicated to the others.

All this is no longer practical politics. In a system of generally stable and unrestricted exchanges the only way to "shorten the duration and lessen the degree of disequilibrium" in balances of payments is to establish close co-ordination between the domestic policies of the different countries with a view to keeping prices in harmony and national incomes at a level corresponding to good employment in all the countries concerned.

Any formal resolution in favor of such co-ordination may not, of course, do much good. Some countries will be less successful than others in maintaining their national economy on an even keel. Occasional breakdowns are likely to occur here and there in the form of either deflationary or inflationary disturbances in particular countries.

Under such conditions any single country pursuing, or at least aiming at, a policy of good and steady employment without inflation will find some reserve of international liquidity indispensable if, without resort to either exchange depreciation or import restrictions, it wishes to offset external disturbances of a cyclical character affecting its balance of payments. What a country pursuing this policy must do is simple; it must endeavor to keep total expenditure on its current national output at a level corresponding as nearly as possible to full employment. But a part of the total expenditure on its output is expenditure by foreigners on its exports. Over that part, the country can have no control. It must therefore be prepared to offset variations in foreigners' expenditure by opposite variations in its own domestic expenditure in order to keep the total flow of spending at the optimum level.

This offsetting policy has its limitations. As stated before, it cannot as a rule prevent booms and depressions in the export industries. It can prevent them only if the export goods are storable and are actually stored by the country in bad years for release in boom years. In this ideal case the compensatory domestic expenditure would be directed to the same goods that are affected by the change in foreign expenditure, so that even local and frictional unemployment would be kept to a minimum. This may not usually be practicable; and just as a road-building program, for example, owing to the imperfect mobility of labor, is not likely to remove all unemployment in, say, the textile industry, so a compensatory increase in domestic spending is not likely to be a complete remedy for depression in the export industries. But the offsetting policy should at least be able to prevent the wide and cumulative fluctuations throughout the domestic economy which might otherwise result from fluctuations in foreign demand.

This seems to be the kind of system for which the world was groping in the inter-war period, and it seems the only one that is compatible at once with a national full employment policy and with a reasonable stability of exchange rates and freedom from severe exchange restrictions.

IV. INTERNATIONAL LIQUIDITY AND FOREIGN INVESTMENT

So far we have spoken as if all countries were economically more or less equal. That is a necessary and common but at the same time a dangerous simplification. There are vast differences in the size, wealth, and economic structure of different countries. Thus the position of the United States with its enormous wealth on the one hand and its cyclical instability on the other, is unique. In the words of Professor Hansen, the United States "could make no greater contribution to the solution of the international political as well as economic problems than that of achieving a high degree of internal economics stability at a level of fairly full employment of labor and other resources."[8] But the position of the United States in international monetary relations, reflected in the "dollar shortage" now frequently discussed, is a rather special subject. Our interest here is more general. From the *function* of international currency reserves we now turn to consider certain general forces affecting their *distribution*.

The global volume of international liquidity must be large enough to permit the settlement of all short-term balance-of-payments discrepancies. Obviously the world total must be distributed among the various countries in accordance with their needs, and the only relevant criterion of need is the size of the dis-

---

[8] Alvin H. Hansen, *Fiscal Policy and the Business Cycle.* (W. W. Norton, New York, 1941, p. 450.)

crepancies to which a country's balance of payments is exposed as a result of cyclical and other short-term factors.   The size of a country's foreign trade, or its share in total world trade, is not a strictly relevant criterion.   In the inter-war period, primary producing countries as well as countries depending heavily on capital imports showed a much wider relative range of year-to-year variation in their balance of payments than did the industrial creditor states.   If international currency reserves had been distributed according to needs, the agricultural debtor nations should have had reserves, on the average, more than proportionate to their share in world trade, while the reserves of other countries should accordingly have been less than proportionate.   In fact, the average reserves held by debtor countries exporting primary commodities were nowhere near the amounts they should have held on the basis of their needs.

In order to account adequately for this disparity between the actual and the appropriate distribution, we must recognize that the objective need for international currency reserves is only one of the factors determining the size of a country's monetary "buffer stock." As in the case of individuals, the optimum or equilibrium amount of liquid reserves which nations endeavor to hold is determined not only by the objective need for such reserves (that is, by the possible or probable range of discrepancies between receipts and disbursements) but also by "the will or inclination to hold them (desire to be protected against emergencies or, more generally, desire for stability)" and, above all, by "the ability to hold them (the level of wealth, the extent to which more vital desires are satisfied)."[9]

The holding of a buffer reserve of international liquidity means that a country must abstain from importing a certain volume of real goods and services.   Just as a poor man, in contrast to a rich, will feel that he cannot afford, and will probably not desire, to hold a large idle cash balance, so a poor country is less likely than a rich

---

[9] See *International Currency Experience, op. cit.*, p. 92.

one to abstain from much-needed imports and to tie up a part of its limited resources in an international cash reserve.

It has been said that, in the course of time, economic progress tends to give rise to a relatively increased demand for economic stability as part of a higher standard of living. This, indeed, may be one explanation for the growing concern with anti-cyclical policies. An obvious corollary of this proposition is that, at any given time, different countries at widely different levels of real income and wealth are likely to attach a different relative importance to stability as compared with greater satisfaction of urgent material needs.[10]

Considerations such as these lead us to conclude that for each country, at any given time, there exists a normal or equilibrium level of international liquidity, a level determined by the various factors governing the need, the desire, and the ability to hold international cash reserves. But here we face the difficulty that the distribution of international reserves appropriate or necessary to the working of a system of free and stable exchanges may not at all correspond to the equilibrium levels of international liquidity from the point of view of the individual countries. Some countries, in fact, given their resources and preference schedules, may feel that they cannot afford to hold the amount of reserves necessary for the maintenance of free and stable exchanges. A reserve which a rich country might consider just sufficient might, to a poor country, seem a luxury beyond its means. Through its central bankers, finance ministers, and other authorities, acting under the pressure of public opinion, political institutions, business interests, demand for credit, and demand for foreign goods, a nation will generally contrive—however imperfectly—to give effect to its scale of comparative necessity.

It is the unequal distribution of wealth and the unequal economic requirements of different nations that largely account for the maldistribution of international currency reserves in the past. It is

---

[10] *Ibid.*, pp. 92–94.

these fundamental conditions that are apt to distort or even wreck any system of international currency reserves aiming at generally stable and free exchanges in the future. If the economic needs of the poorer nations are not met by other means, there will be a strong and perhaps irresistible tendency for those needs to be met by the use of international currency reserves, including such facilities as are to be provided by the International Monetary Fund. Unless, therefore, something is done to change the underlying conditions there may not be much hope of preventing a new distortion or breakdown of the international reserve system and a new maldistribution of liquid reserves.

One way of dealing with the underlying conditions, and in practice perhaps the most important way, is through international investment. In the world as we find it, in a world in which enormous differences exist between the needs and resources of different countries, international investment is thus of crucial importance for the functioning of the international liquidity mechanism.

The equilibrium level of international liquidity in relation to the needs and resources of particular countries is, in normal times, a long-term problem. But after a global war, it presents itself immediately and in a very acute form; for what we have said about the poorer nations in normal times applies equally to countries devastated or impoverished by war. If either an undeveloped or a war-ravaged country is unable to meet its capital requirements by capital imports, then it may be driven to use up whatever international cash reserves it can command, so as to meet at least part of those requirements. International liquidity, which should serve merely as a short-term buffer in the balance of payments, will be used in effect for long-term capital purposes. If international currency reserves are distributed among countries in accordance with needs arising from normal short-term balance-of-payments fluctuations, and if these reserves are in fact expended for capital purposes, then capital will have been distributed according to an inappropriate criterion; that is, not according to capital requirements but according to international liquidity requirements.

There is, of course, no necessary or even probable correlation between the two kinds of requirements.

The upshot of the preceding discussion is clear. The Bank for Reconstruction and Development, set up under the Bretton Woods agreements, is essential to the success of the International Monetary Fund. The Bank could stand without the Fund, but the Fund would have a difficult time without the Bank. Without an adequate volume of reconstruction loans, the Fund quotas of many countries might come to be used up directly or indirectly for capital purposes, with the result that in a few years' time the Fund would be more or less immobilized and the countries concerned would again be short of international liquidity. It should be recalled, however, that the Fund agreement permits countries to maintain exchange control on current payments during the transition period. To the extent that countries rely on exchange control, the provision of—as well as the need for—liquid resources for short-term balancing purposes may, in fact, come to be postponed. It is to be hoped that in the meantime the most urgent relief and reconstruction requirements of the transition period will have been met through UNRRA, disposal of surplus stocks, mutual aid, intergovernmental loans, grants, and other special methods of international reconstruction finance.

Sooner or later, however, the more normal methods contemplated in the plan for the International Bank for Reconstruction and Development will become indispensable. The plan for the Bank attacks the problem of international investment in a central and strategic place by attacking, above all, the problem of risk. There are other factors tending to reduce the international mobility of capital, but the influence of the risk element alone is enormous. The Bank by itself may not be able to do much toward reducing the actual risk factors; many of these will remain outside its control. What it sets out to do—and even that is a great deal—is to pool the risks and equalize the risk premium; and it proposes to do this through a procedure of joint international guarantees and a 1–1½ per cent guarantee commission or "insurance premium." Undoubtedly the Bank represents a novel and promising attack on the troublesome risk problem in foreign lending.   However admirable a piece of mechanism the Fund may be, this mechanism—or indeed any currency mechanism aiming at reasonably free and stable exchanges—would be in danger of getting jammed without some means of securing a steady and adequate flow of international investment.

V. COMMERCIAL VS. MONETARY POLICY

International monetary policy, in the strict sense of the term, falls into two main compartments: (1) that which has to do with exchange-rate adjustments and (2) that which relates to international liquidity.   The former, we have suggested, is appropriate in the case of persistent or structural strains in the balance of international payments, while the latter should take care of all short-term discrepancies.

Other instruments of policy in international economic relations fall more properly under the heading of commercial policy.   This applies especially to exchange control (excepting perhaps the limited form of exchange control designed to restrain abnormal short-term capital movements).   The distinction which has sometimes been drawn between exchange control and trade control on the ground that the former affects *payment* for goods, whereas the latter affects the actual *movement* of goods across national frontiers, is purely legalistic.   In the 'thirties, control of commercial payments proved interchangeable with, and often actually merged into, a system of control of imports.   Exchange restrictions on current transactions are a form of commercial policy on a par with import quotas, licenses, or tariffs.

For this reason the agreement concerning the International Monetary Fund, in so far as it aims at multilateral freedom of transfer for commercial payments, would be pointless if countries were at liberty to evade it by arrangements affecting not the payments for, but the actual movement of, goods.   A distinction between monetary and commercial measures in this connection can have a bearing solely on the legal form and not on the economic substance of policy.   Suggestions to the effect that the monetary scheme of Bretton Woods is compatible with bilateral trade arrangements can therefore scarcely be in harmony with the intent of the Bretton Woods agreement.

Besides, the Bretton Woods scheme is not strictly confined to monetary policy.   That part of it which provides for the apportionment of any currency declared by the Fund to be "scarce" represents essentially a measure of commercial policy.   A hypothetical example will make this clear.   If the dollar were to become a scarce currency under the Fund arrangement, the rationing of dollars which would then come into operation would discriminate against the exports of the United States.   Such rationing would, for example, divert Britain's demand for cotton from the United States to, say, Brazil, even if cotton were cheaper in the United States; and it would similarly divert Brazil's purchases of automobiles from the United States to England, even if automobiles were cheaper in the United States.   In sum, it would divert the effective demand of the outside world away from United States' products in order to make it equal to the United States' demand for the products of the outside world.   In monetary terms, this would mean cutting down the international demand for dollars so as to make it fit the available supply.   The same result of equating demand and supply could be achieved if, in the circumstances considered, the United States were to lower its tariff.   The only difference would be that in this case demand and supply would be equated by increasing the supply of dollars rather than by cutting down the demand for them.

A currency might become "scarce" because of a slump in domestic activity in a certain country and a consequent fall in that country's imports from abroad.[11]   In these circumstances, the

---

[11] [The fact that in the three years since the end of World War II the world dollar shortage has been greater than ever cannot of course be attributed to a slump in the United States; for these were years of unprecedented boom and inflationary pressure in the United States.   Nevertheless the dollar scarcity can be explained in monetary terms, quite apart from war damage and reconstruction needs, by the fact that inflationary pressure abroad was relatively far greater still; and so the effect on international monetary equilibrium was substantially the same as that of a depression in the United States coupled with good employment without inflation in the outside world.]

country in question is likely to develop a surplus in its balance of payments, which will indeed tend to alleviate its depression but only at the cost, or at any rate the danger, of spreading the depression to other countries.   Any measures taken to eliminate the surplus—whether by discrimination against the country's exports or by a reduction in its import barriers—would, it is true, aggravate the slump in the surplus country.   But they would help to arrest the spread of depression to the rest of the world; and, as noted before, there is nothing to prevent the surplus country from offsetting their deleterious effect by a policy of domestic expansion.

The apportionment of scarce currencies in the Bretton Woods plan is clearly intended as a measure of last resort, for temporary use in any emergency—such as a sudden and serious depression in a leading member country—in which a change in exchange rates would be too slow and uncertain a remedy.   Considered as a measure of commercial policy it has this distinctive feature that it is to come into operation only under certain definite conditions agreed upon beforehand among the nations adhering to the scheme.   This element of prior international agreement should render it more palatable to a country against which it might have to be applied, and should, in particular, obviate the danger that the country concerned may retaliate by import restrictions of its own.

It may be vain to expect this measure of international commercial policy to remove any desire of individual countries to resort to individual acts of commercial policy in the form of import duties, quotas, licenses, exchange allocations, or bilateral purchase agreements.   Even if, thanks to the Fund, a country may no longer have to worry about its net balance of payments, it may still worry about its terms of trade, about the volume of its imports and exports, or about the composition of its imports in the light of social priority considerations.   To reach a common understanding on these matters is doubtless far more difficult than to agree on any monetary scheme; yet some minimum code of good-neighborly behavior seems essential in order to prevent commercial policy from degenerating into commercial warfare.

Skeptics may wonder if there is any future at all for international monetary, as distinct from commercial, policy in a world in which they see a persistent trend towards increased state regulation of foreign trade, culminating logically in complete state trading on the Russian model. Would not any international monetary system under such conditions tend to lose its *raison d'être?* It may be that, in a world of state trading monopolies, exchange-rate adjustments would cease to have much significance. But it is by no means certain that "liquidity" would cease to be a necessity, or at all events a convenience, in international economic relations. Even nations trading with one another as units may find it desirable to have, and may consequently agree upon, some medium of international settlement commanding general acceptance and hence capable of serving as a source of liquidity, giving each individual state some protection against the risk of having its foreign-trade budget upset by crop failures, changes in production plans at home or abroad, non-fulfilment of delivery or purchase agreements, or the like. The example of Soviet Russia before the present war may not be conclusive since it relates to a single state-trading unit in a world still operating mainly on private business lines. Nevertheless, the fact is worth recalling that it was not from Soviet Russia that the movement towards bilateral barter originated during the 'thirties. The Russians seldom hesitated to drive a hard bargain; but they found it generally to their interest to sell in the dearest and buy in the cheapest market; and they did not seem to underrate the usefulness of their gold reserves in thus conducting their foreign commercial relations.

Among countries continuing to rely in their foreign as well as domestic trade largely on private price and profit incentives, the regulation of exchange rates must remain an important subject of international monetary policy along with the use and distribution of international currency reserves. Not long ago it was commonly taken for granted that a single country could alter its exchange rates at will, by varying its price of gold or otherwise. Experience has shown, however, that purely unilateral action in regard to exchange rates is not merely undesirable but that it cannot be made effective. An exchange rate, by its very nature, is something that concerns more currencies than one, and any change that one country may wish to make is necessarily subject to the tacit or explicit consent of the others. As we saw in the 'thirties, a change in the price of gold in one country does not produce a lasting change in the exchange rate if other countries follow suit and likewise alter their price of gold. In a system not based on gold, a country's central bank may raise the price at which it is prepared to buy another country's currency; but, if the other country similarly raises its price for foreign currency, then the efforts of the two countries trying to buy up each other's currencies will tend to cancel out without any effect on the exchange rate. In practice, no doubt, it may be possible for an individual country, especially if it is a small country, to change the external value of its currency by unilateral action; so long as other countries feel no strong objection they may condone such unilateral change and refrain from adopting countermeasures. But this does not alter the fact that the change depends, ultimately, on their tacit consent.[12]

The International Monetary Fund Agreement has in some countries been criticized on the ground that it unduly restricts the freedom of national authorities to alter the value of their currencies.[13] This freedom has proved illusory. It is understandable that people in Britain, with the years 1925–1931 still in memory, should feel uneasy about rigidly tying down the pound's external value. It is equally important to remember, however, that in 1936, after the "devaluation cycle" of the great depression, the value of sterling in dollars and other free currencies was practically

---

[12] In the pre-war sterling area, the member countries seemed to be able to set, and to alter, their rates on the pound at their own free will, sometimes in a manner far from agreeable to the United Kingdom. But this was so only because their central banks were prepared to hold sterling, while the Bank of England would not hold their currencies. The limitation on the English monetary authorities was clearly a self-imposed and not an inevitable one. A similar situation prevailed in the United States as a result of the offer of the Treasury to buy gold at a fixed price while other countries could, at will, alter the price they would pay for gold.

[13] See, e.g., The Banker (London), 1944, vol. LXXI, pp. 112–122, vol. LXXII, pp. 15–26, 58–65.

the same as it had been before September, 1931. In effect, Britain was not able to devalue the pound by her own unilateral action; other countries followed suit, so that, before long, something very like the former set of relationships was re-established. The Tripartite Agreement of 1936 was a recognition of the fact that, in the long run, exchange rates cannot be changed without the consent of at least the principal parties concerned. The Bretton Woods plan, if properly carried out, should not result in the "freezing" of a given structure of rates, but should constitute a machinery for mutually agreed adjustments—the only adjustments which, in the last analysis, are possible at all.

Barring inflationary developments in individual countries such adjustments should not be necessary except at infrequent intervals (say, five, ten, or fifteen years) in order to remove chronic or "structural" strains in the balance of payments. The international reserve system should be able to take care of all short-term discrepancies, whether fortuitous or "cyclical." Any such system, however, requires two things for its successful operation: first, a certain minimum degree of domestic stability at high levels of employment in the principal trading nations; and, secondly, a steady and adequate flow of long-term international investment. Needless to say, both are desirable things as such and not merely as prerequisites for a stable international currency system.

The Bretton Woods Conference made a laudable effort to meet the second prerequisite through the Bank for Reconstruction and Development. It did nothing to meet the first, except to issue a general recommendation with a view to "the harmonization of national policies designed to promote and maintain high levels of employment." Such national policies, however, must exist before they can be harmonized. As Professor Graham has emphasized, the maintenance of full employment in any nation is primarily a domestic responsibility.[14]

---

[14] See Frank D. Graham, Chapter on "Economics and Peace," in *The Second Chance: America and the Peace*, edited by John B. Whitton (Princeton University Press, 1944, p. 127).

The conditions which made the nineteenth-century gold standard workable no longer obtain.   In the gold-standard days the correct behavior for each country was to keep on a level with the others —to rise with the tide and sink with the ebb of the general business cycle.   For most, if not all, advanced industrial nations, this sort of behavior is out of the question today.   Rather than float helplessly up and down as the level of world economic activity rises and declines, countries will seek stability by regulating their domestic money income and expenditure with a view to avoiding depression and unemployment on the one hand and inflationary disturbances on the other.   But unless all countries attain such stability, and maintain a steady and active domestic economy without inflation, their balances of payments will perforce be subject to stresses and strains which, if they pass beyond a point, are likely to result in a breakdown of the international reserve system—in a failure, that is, to keep exchanges stable without additional restrictions on foreign trade or payments.

It would be an exaggeration to say that a system of stable and unrestricted exchanges is impossible unless countries maintain absolute stability at home.   The buffer mechanism of international liquidity should certainly be capable of meeting "cyclical" balance-of-payments discrepancies resulting from moderate and temporary deviations from stability in individual countries.   What the liquidity mechanism can hardly be expected to meet is a severe and protracted slump in an important member country, or a situation such as occurred in the early 'thirties.   Obviously the amount of liquidity in the system—the volume of international monetary reserves—determines the maximum amount of strain the system can bear.   With the offsetting policies outlined earlier, the amount of liquidity required is far greater than it would be if countries were prepared to let their entire national income fluctuate at the behest of the balance of payments, though it should also be noted that restrictions on abnormal and speculative capital movements would stop what was perhaps the most serious drain on international liquidity in the 'thirties.

The amount of liquidity to be provided by the International

Monetary Fund, though substantial, is by itself far from adequate. It is true that [in 1944, when the size of the Fund was decided upon, countries outside the United States held, in the aggregate, more gold and dollar reserves than they had ever held before.[15] But a large part of these reserves was subsequently spent on reconstruction requirements. Another large part represented a form of wartime "compulsory saving": the South American republics, especially, were obliged to hoard their gold and dollar receipts during the war because transport difficulties, war-time scarcities, and production controls did not permit them to import the goods they would have liked to import. Their post-war purchases for reequipment and replenishment have drawn down their gold and dollar assets considerably. It is doubtful whether the remaining reserves of these as well as the European countries will be at all adequate for the normal peacetime "buffer" purposes of international liquidity].

The successful operation of post-war monetary mechanisms may therefore come to depend rather closely on the concerted maintenance of stable business conditions at high levels of employment, above all in the major industrial states. If this fundamental requirement is not adequately met, resort to the armory of commercial rather than monetary policy is likely to become the order of the day. Even the entry into force of the Fund's "scarce currency" provisions would, in substance though not in form, constitute a breakdown of the monetary system; and it would probably be optimistic to hope that, in the event of such breakdown, commercial policy could be confined to the concerted and prearranged international measures which those provisions imply.

In the event of severe and protracted departures from the norm of domestic stability in some country or countries, the shifts in effective international demand may be so wide that exchange-rate adjustments would not quickly enough succeed in righting the

---

[15] "It is estimated that by the end of September, 1944, foreign countries had gold and dollar reserves of some 17 billion dollars, as compared with 7 to 8 billion dollars at the close of the 1920's." *Federal Reserve Bulletin*, November, 1944, p. 1043.

balance of payments, or would succeed in righting it only at a level of total trade which is too low for the essential import needs of countries that continue to uphold a steady and active internal economy.   That is why measures of commercial policy, including discriminatory and possibly bilateral arrangements, will be difficult to avoid if the major trading nations are not able to devise appropriate domestic measures for the maintenance of economic activity. Such, at any rate, are the grim lessons of the inter-war period; if they should prove irrelevant in the post-war period, so much the better.

While thus a system of reasonably stable and unrestricted exchanges, under present-day conditions, is possible only on a foundation of domestic stability in the member states, it is equally well to recognize the correlative proposition that, as a rule, the external balance of payments should not require an individual country to depart from domestic stability and to undergo either a general inflation of its price structure or a deflation of money income far below the level corresponding to good employment.   If there is a persistent discrepancy seeming to require adjustment through inflation or deflation, it is the exchange rate that should be changed and not the domestic price or income level.   Ideally, as we have seen, exchange rates should be fixed for long periods in such manner that, when all countries enjoy satisfactory levels of employment without inflation, the international accounts are in equilibrium. It is the business of the buffer mechanism of international liquidity to meet any moderate and temporary departures from this happy state; it is the business of domestic employment policy to prevent severe and protracted departures.

2

BANKING POLICY AND THE BALANCE OF INTERNATIONAL PAYMENTS*

By F. W. Paish‖

The following observations are based largely on the writer's personal experience in South Africa during a period when that country was undergoing violent fluctuations in her balance of international payments. This experience has led to the belief that, in such a country as South Africa, the process of adjusting an adverse balance of payments differs appreciably from that in such a country as Great Britain. It should be emphasized that attention is here concentrated upon the process of adjustment, and that little or no attempt is made to touch upon its effects. The discussion is mainly concerned with quite short-term problems, and supplements rather than amends the work on long-term problems, such as the effects of given changes upon commodity or factor terms of trade, to which the attention of investigators has hitherto been largely devoted. The time scale used here must be measured in months, or even weeks, rather than in years. Nevertheless, it is hoped that the suggestions here advanced may provide some addition to the equipment of those who are investigating the more important long-term problems; while on the immediately practical side it is hoped to develop this method of approach in such a way as to facilitate the making, in certain conditions and for certain geographical areas, of rather more reliable short-term forecasts of business prospects.

---

* *Economica*, Volume III (New Series), November 1936, pp. 404–422. Reprinted by the courtesy of *Economica* and the author, without change from the original text.
‖ University of London.

I

Strictly speaking, every receipts and payments account, whether it be the account of a single individual or firm, of the collective account of many individuals and firms, invariably balances; for every pound that has been paid out has been obtained from somewhere. Nevertheless, it is in accordance with the normal use of terms to say of a man whose money reserves have become depleted during the course of a year that his money payments have exceeded his money receipts—that he has, if we care to use the term, an "adverse balance of payments." This adverse balance is, of course, not necessarily inconsistent with an excess of income over expenditure for the same year and with an improving financial position, for the decrease in his money reserves may be equal to only a part of the debts he has paid off or of the new investments he has made during the year. At the same time, it will, generally speaking, indicate some reduction in the liquidity of his position, of which one possible cause may have been an excess of expenditure over income.

In a country where the great bulk of the money reserves of the inhabitants is kept in the form of bank deposits, any excess of an individual's money payments over money receipts is likely to be reflected mainly in a change in the size of his bank balance, for the total of the cheques he draws during the period exceeds that of the deposits which he makes, and his credit balance is thereby reduced or converted into a debit balance, or his debit balance is increased.

What is true of one individual is equally true of a group of individuals inhabiting any given district. If during any period the aggregate amount of the cheques they have drawn exceeds the aggregate value of the amounts they have deposited, it would be possible to say that, as a group, their money payments have exceeded their money receipts, and that collectively they have "an adverse balance of payments." If the group consists of all the customers of a local bank, this excess of payments will be reflected in this bank's accounts by a fall in its total deposits and/or a rise in its total advances. Any disturbance of the equilibrium of the balance of payments of any given district is thus, in a cheque-using community, primarily a banking phenomenon. The purpose of this article is to discuss, under various conditions, the reactions of the banks to this change in their position, and the effects of such reactions.

It is at once obvious that very different amounts of attention are given to the question of the balance of payments in different geographical areas. No one, for instance, seems to take any interest in the balance of payments of Devonshire, while on the other hand a good deal of interest is taken in the balance of payments of the United Kingdom or Australia. Why is it that the inter-regional balance of payments is regarded as important in one case and unimportant in the other?

The first difference seems to be that the banks in Devonshire are merely branches of large banks whose activities extend over a much wider area. Any excess of withdrawals from Devonshire branches will therefore probably be balanced by an excess of deposits in other branches of the same banks. The only case where this does not hold good is when there is an excess of withdrawals from the system as a whole, due either to an increase in the public's holdings of currency or to a net transfer of funds to outside the system altogether. Apart from this, the chief effect of Devonshire's adverse balance is an increase in the indebtedness of Devonshire branches to other branches of the same banks, or a decrease in the indebtedness of other branches to Devonshire branches. Since banks, generally speaking, have no objection to any amount of inter-branch indebtedness, provided that their total figures for all branches are unaltered and that all advances made are sound, they need take no action to check this process. Indeed, it is well known that certain areas, especially residential areas, habitually lend large amounts to industrial areas through the medium of the banks.

If, however, the banks in Devonshire, instead of being branches of large banks, had been independent banks, or even if some of them had been doing a more important share of the banking business of Devonshire than of the rest of the country, Devonshire's adverse balance of payments would have reflected in a change in inter-bank indebtedness and not merely in inter-branch indebtedness. Such inter-bank debts, whether in the form of deposits, advances, or re-discounts, would hardly be likely to be allowed to rise to anything like the level customary for inter-branch debts, and unless the movement in due course came to an end of its own accord (for reasons which will be discussed later) the Devonshire banks would sooner or later be obliged to take steps to adjust the position.

The time within which such measures would be thought necessary would probably be greatly shortened if there were also present a second difference which usually exists between national and other regional areas—the difference of currencies. The importance of this difference depends mainly on the degree of possibility of any substantial alteration of the rates of exchange; but if there is even a fairly remote chance of exchange fluctuations, no bank can see with equanimity any large margin between its assets and liabilities in each separate currency. This consideration precludes any considerable amount of inter-bank indebtedness not balanced by other assets or liabilities in the same currencies. It would even preclude the existence of large debts between branches of the same bank operating in two separate currency areas.

The third important difference between national and other geographical areas is the existence of different political controls. This factor is of importance rather for its influence on the type of action likely to be taken to restore the balance of international payments than for determining whether or no some sort of action needs to be taken. If there is a separate government, there is a considerable probability that the action taken to restore equilibrium will be of a non-banking character, and that one or more of the familiar expedients of exchange depreciation or devaluation, restrictions of imports or exchanges, repudiation of foreign debts, and so forth, will be resorted to in order to evade the necessity for banking action. In this article the effects of such measures are not discussed.

II

The immediate effect on the banks in any country of the development of an adverse balance of payments is that there takes place a fall in their local deposits or a rise in their local advances or both. This rise in local assets (other than cash) and/or fall in local liabilities have their counterpart in a depletion of the banking system's reserves of gold and/or of external liquid assets, or, less commonly, in a rise in external liabilities. To the banks, therefore, the problem presents itself as a need of restoring the customary ratio of cash and foreign exchange reserves to deposits, or, which is another way of viewing the same thing, of reducing local assets (other than cash) to their customary ratio to local liabilities. If they are forced to take action, this is therefore in the direction of reducing the total of local advances and/or security holdings.

The exact methods used to attain this end will depend partly on local custom and organisation, partly on the form in which the adverse balance is reflected in the bank statements, and partly on the urgency of the necessary adjustment. The best way of ensuring that the reduced volume of advances was available to those who needed them most would be for the banks to raise interest rates equally on all advances, new and old, until the repayments of loans by old borrowers and the reduced demands of new sufficed to reduce the total of advances and to restore equilibrium by the means and after the delays which will be discussed later.

In some countries, however, a general rise in interest rates usually plays only a part, often a minor one, in bringing about this adjustment. Instead, advances are arbitrarily refused or reduced to particular classes of borrowers, and especially to the whole class of new borrowers. Where the movement is reflected mainly in an increased demand for advances, the restriction of new advances may be sufficient in itself. Where the movement takes the form of a fall in deposits, an actual reduction in advances may be necessary. Even in this case, since a proportion of the advances will normally be paid off each week in the normal course of business, a rigorous restriction of new advances will cause the total of advances to fall steadily. Only in extreme cases, where the total of deposits is falling rapidly, will it be necessary to call up existing advances before their normal date of expiration, or to insist on reductions when they come to be renewed. In this case, when the banks' need to adjust their position is urgent, the advances called up are likely to be those which can be repaid in a hurry, that is to say, the safest and best secured, which in normal times the banks would be best pleased to continue.   These measures are tantamount to very large discriminating increases in the rate of interest, for some of those who are refused advances will be obliged to attempt to borrow elsewhere at high rates, while advances not called up continue to pay the old rates.

It may be that, in order to avoid calling up advances, the banks will realise securities.   Such action will have a similar effect of depressing security prices, raising long-term interest rates, and probably causing an increased demand for bank advances which must be refused.   At the same time, by reducing the market value of securities deposited as cover for existing advances, it will cause the banks to reduce certain overdraft limits.   Thus the effect is again that of a rise in bank interest rates, either discriminating or general.   In any case, the effect of the banks' reactions to the adverse balance of payments is a rise in interest rates outside the banks.

Hitherto the case considered has been that of a banking system without a central bank.   The inclusion of the latter complicates but does not fundamentally alter the position.   Instead of the commercial banks holding the whole of the system's reserves of gold and foreign exchange themselves, they hold their cash reserves in the form mainly of notes of, and balances with, the central bank, which in turn holds much of the whole system's reserves of gold and foreign exchange.   When an adverse balance develops, it first causes a fall in the public's deposits with, or a rise in their advances from, the commercial banks, and at the same time either a fall in these banks' own reserves of gold or foreign exchange, or a fall in their holdings of the notes or balances of the central bank, accompanied by a fall in the central bank's holdings of gold or foreign exchange.   If the whole system wishes to return to its old ratios, both the central and the commercial banks must reduce their local non-cash assets until the position is restored.   If, however, the central bank so desires, it can *increase* its local non-cash assets by purchases of local bills or securities at existing prices from the government, the commercial banks, or their customers, thus restoring the commercial banks' balances with the central bank, removing the pressure on the commercial banks, and preventing any tendency for interest rates to rise in order to restore equilibrium. In this case, unless the movement soon comes to an end of its own accord, the central bank's reserves will be increasingly depleted until it may become too late to restore equilibrium by banking measures.

III

In discussing the need for, and the effects of, a rise in interest rates in order to maintain a particular existing exchange standard, it is necessary to take into account three main questions. First, has the balance of payments a tendency to return to equilibrium of its own accord without a rise in interest rates, or will it, if present interest rates are maintained, tend to get progressively further and further out of equilibrium? Secondly, if there is a tendency to return to equilibrium, either spontaneously or in consequence of a given rise in interest rates, how long will it take for the movement away from equilibrium to be reversed and the position restored? And thirdly, are the banks' reserves of gold and foreign exchange large enough to fill the gap in the interval, and if not, how much must interest rates be raised in order to effect adjustment before they are too seriously depleted? No precise answer can of course ever be given in advance to these questions; nevertheless, it is possible to enumerate certain factors, the consideration of which may enable estimates to be less erroneous than they might have been.

Broadly speaking, an adverse balance of payments tends to adjust itself spontaneously (without a rise in interest rates) when it is due to causes which at the same time cause local business to become less profitable. For instance, if there occurs the failure of an important export crop uncompensated by a rise in the world price, the impact effect will be that exporters, in order to meet maturing liabilities and to maintain their customary standard of living, will draw upon their bank accounts, thus decreasing their credit balances or increasing their overdrafts.[1] If the fall in their incomes is moderate and expected to be purely temporary, exporters may wish to maintain their existing standards of living and scales of production, and will therefore continue to draw from their bank accounts more than they deposit. But if the fall is large and likely to be prolonged, sooner or later they will either see the necessity of curtailing expenditure to correspond, or will be compelled to curtail it owing to the depletion of their bank deposits or overdraft facilities. The exhaustion of unused overdraft facilities may be accelerated by reductions of overdraft limits by the banks in consequence of the deteriorating financial position of the customers concerned.

IV

Assuming a tendency towards adjustment, the period taken for it to become fully effective will depend on how rapidly reduced receipts by exporters are reflected in reduced payments by them, and how rapidly these in turn are reflected in reduced payments to foreigners. If the amount by which exporters' expenditure is reduced would have been, for instance, spent wholly on imported goods the demand for these will fall off at once, importers will reduce their new orders, and as soon as existing orders have been

---

[1] During the period during which expenditures of exporters are maintained despite lower incomes, the total of cheques drawn each week on local banks will be maintained while the amounts deposited are reduced, thus reducing the banks' reserves.   The position is slightly more complicated where, as is not unlikely in the example under consideration, deposits fall in comparison with the corresponding month of the previous season rather than with the previous month.   In this case the banks will look, not only at their current position, but at their probable position after the exporting season is over and the period of seasonal import surpluses has to be faced.   The inadequate replenishment of their reserves of foreign exchange during the exporting season may render them unable to finance the former volume of imports during the remainder of the year, and may compel them then to raise interest rates more sharply in order to adjust the position than if the fall in imports had started earlier, while the absolute amount of their foreign reserves was still rising.   In other words, banks must use seasonally adjusted figures for the purpose of determining policy.

filled, imports will decline. Thus the fall in the banks' local liabilities or the rise in their local assets will be checked, and the concomitant fall in their foreign reserves will cease or their expansion be
stimulated.

If, on the other hand, the exporters' economies are made partly
or wholly on locally produced goods or services, adjustment will be a
more prolonged process. Other local residents will now be faced
with a reduction in their money receipts, and will be able to maintain their expenditures only by reducing their deposits with the
banks or increasing their overdrafts. This excess expenditure in
turn must come to an end sooner or later, and economies made,
again on payments either for local or for imported goods and services. If the latter, adjustment is achieved; if the former, a new set
of customers of the local banks tend to decrease deposits and
increase overdrafts until they in turn have to economise. This
process must continue until the original reduction in exports is
reflected in an adequate[2] reduction in the local demand for imports. The length of the process will depend partly on the number
of stages needed, which in turn will depend on the distribution of
economies between local goods and imports at each stage, and
partly on the length of the delay at each stage before reduced
receipts are reflected in reduced payments. The first of these
questions will be considered in a later section. With regard to
the second, the delay at each stage, in the absence of a change in
rates of interest, will depend chiefly on the expectations held about
the future. If people are optimistic, they will delay curtailing
expenditure as long as possible; if they are pessimistic, they will
react much more quickly, or may even reduce their expenditure in
anticipation of a future fall in receipts. The more optimistic the

---

[2] What will be regarded as an "adequate" reduction in imports will depend
upon the attitude which the banks take towards the size of their reserves of gold or
foreign exchange. If they are content merely to check their depletion, monthly
imports need be reduced only by as much as monthly exports. If, however, they
wish to restore their reserves, imports must for a time be reduced more than exports, and only be permitted to recover to their equilibrium level as the banks'
reserves approach their former size.

atmosphere, the slower will be the adjustment. It is however probable that the atmosphere will become progressively less optimistic as the process of adjustment continues, and that the later stages of adjustment will be accomplished more quickly than the earlier ones.

Let us now take an opposite case, where the causes of the adverse balance also bring about, not reduced, but increased profitability of business. Let us suppose, for instance, that increased optimism, or perhaps government loans for public works or armaments, brings about the release of idle balances and a general increase in demand, resulting in an increase in imports, and perhaps a decrease in exports due to the diversion of goods from export to the home consumer. In this case there is no spontaneous tendency towards equilibrium, but rather a progressive disequilibrium. Business is more profitable, business men are more creditworthy, the demand for advances expands at existing rates of interest, not merely temporarily for purposes of distress borrowing, but progressively to finance an increase of business at probably rising prices.[3] Unless some extraneous event occurs, such as a long-term loan from abroad (often the natural solution of the problem), or an internal loss of confidence, due perhaps to an unbalanced budget and fears of higher taxation, advances will continue to rise until the banks' reserves are entirely depleted. To check the movement, they must raise interest rates to a level which will check the further expansion of advances, or even, if they need to replenish their foreign reserves, to one which will induce their repayment. When this occurs, the progress of events will be exactly similar to that described in the previous section, except that since the movement starts in an atmosphere of general optimism, adjustment will probably be very slow in its early stages. It is therefore all the more important that it should be started before the banks' reserves have become seriously depleted.

---

[3] It may be noted that in such conditions the effect on the banks' local accounts is rather to cause a rise in advances than a fall in deposits. It is quite probable that deposits will increase, though more slowly than advances.

It is possible to imagine an intermediate case where the adverse balance of payments is accompanied by no effect at all on internal conditions.   If, for instance, owners of bank balances which would in any case have remained idle elect to transfer them to other banks abroad, all that happens is that the banks' local deposits and their reserves are equally depleted.   The profitability of local business is in no way directly affected, and if the banks have ample reserves they may choose to take no action, for the supply of truly idle balances is limited and if the transfer of balances is carried beyond that limit, local payments are reduced and a depression ensues, which will ultimately tend to correct the position.   If, on the other hand, the banks have reason to believe that their reserves will become dangerously depleted, they must raise interest rates in order to restore equilibrium by checking imports.

V

It is now possible to turn to the discussion of the factors which affect the distribution of any reduction in expenditure between imported and locally produced goods and services, and thus in turn help to determine the length of the time-lag between a fall in incomes and a fall in imports.   It is clear that one of the most important of these is the relation which exists between the demand for the type of goods imported and the demand for the type produced locally.   In a country importing mainly such goods as durable producers' goods and finished consumers' goods of the better qualities—goods for which the demand changes more than in proportion to changes in expenditure—a fall in expenditure will be reflected largely in a reduced demand for imports; it is even possible that there may be a diversion of demand from the more expensive types of goods imported to the cheaper and rougher types made locally, so that the demand for some sorts of locally made goods may actually expand and the profits of their producers be increased.   In this type of country the adjustment of the balance of payments through a reduction in imports will be both rapid and effected with comparatively little difficulty or disturbance.   There seems to be practically no limit in countries of this type to the amount of adjustment which can be brought about by means of a restriction of bank credit.

With the opposite type of country the position is very different. In a country which imports mainly such things as basic foodstuffs and raw materials, perhaps together with the cheaper types of finished goods, the first impact of reduced expenditure is felt mainly upon the demand for local products, while the demand for certain types of cheap imported goods, other than raw materials, may even increase. Local producers in turn reduce their demand mainly for local goods and services, and the depression in internal markets may continue to spread for a considerable time without seriously diminishing the demand for imports. Thus, apart perhaps from the limited effects of a reduction in stocks, there will be no rapid and direct adjustment of the balance of payments. The adjustment will be slow and probably painful, and when it ultimately comes will take one of two forms. Either the effect of the reduced internal demand will be to reduce factor prices and costs of production, in which case adjustment will come through a fall in the local price level, leading to an expansion of exports and to a transfer of demand from some imported goods to the now cheaper local producers; or, if factor or other prices are monopolistically or compulsorily maintained, production will decrease and the demand for raw materials will fall off, while the intensified fall in incomes due to unemployment will decrease the demand for imported foodstuffs and for even the cheapest types of consumers' goods.

Between the two extreme types described above there are, of course, numerous countries in intermediate positions; in fact, it is unlikely that any country stands exactly at either extreme. Nevertheless it seems probable that the countries of the world can mostly be assigned to one or other of two rough groups—those in which the proportion of expenditure at the margin devoted to imports is large and those in which it is small. To adapt a phrase of Mr. Keynes, we may describe the former group of countries as having a high Marginal Propensity to Import and the latter a low one. (To save space, these will in future be referred to as countries having re-spectively a high or low M.P.I.)[4]

In attempting to estimate the M.P.I. of any particular country, two methods of approach suggest themselves. A detailed com-parison of the goods and services produced locally with those imported might be expected to give at least some *prima facie* indica-tion of its M.P.I. This could, in some countries at least, be con-firmed by a study of the sequence of recent fluctuations in its bal-ance of payments, banking statistics, interest rates and imports, though the results would in all cases have to be interpreted in the light of other local and foreign developments, such as changes in tariffs, etc. Further, it would have to be remembered that the M.P.I. of a country might change greatly with changes in the volume of expenditure. In most high M.P.I. countries the M.P.I. would probably alter directly with expenditure, and in low M.P.I. countries inversely, especially if changes in expenditure were accom-panied by changes in the employment of factors. In addition, the whole relationship would naturally alter gradually over a long period of years with changes in the types of goods and services pro-duced and imported. In spite, however, of the obvious difficulties in the application of the conception of the Marginal Propensity to Import to actual conditions, it is believed that the differences between the extreme representatives of each type of country are so great that distinctions could be drawn which would hold good in

---

[4] An alternative phrase, which would have the advantage of fitting in with similar conceptions in other fields, would be "an elastic (or inelastic) Expenditure Demand for Imports." This phrase, however, seems to imply a greater precision of definition than is warranted. It might be justifiable to speak of the Expenditure Demand for Imports of a particular individual, or even of a more or less homo-geneous group under specified conditions over a specified period of time. But for a country in general over an indeterminate period of time the demand for imports might vary, not only with the total expenditure of the population, but according to the precise groups or classes whose expenditures changed, the sources of the funds expended (whether from earnings, hoards, or loans), and the period of time taken into consideration. It has therefore been thought wiser to use the vaguer phrase, which indicates a rough general tendency rather than a precise relationship.

almost all conditions and over periods of many years.   In existing circumstances, it seems probable that advanced "industrial" countries, such as Great Britain, would be found to have a relatively low M.P.I., and the "raw material" countries, such as South Africa or New Zealand, a relatively high one.

VI

Before proceeding to draw further conclusions from the arguments already advanced, it will be necessary to introduce two further considerations.   The first of these is the form in which an adverse balance of international payments is reflected in the banking figures.   Hitherto it has been assumed that the immediate effect of an adverse balance is shown in a fall in the banks' reserves of gold and foreign exchange.   While this has always been true for most countries, and is now more nearly true of all countries than formerly, it is not true of all countries at all times.   Certain countries, generally of the low M.P.I. type, have been, and to some extent still are, international banking centres, where foreign banks are prepared to keep deposits which they regard as the equivalent of cash.   For such countries, therefore, the immediate effect of an adverse balance may be seen, not in a depletion of the banks' reserves, but in an increase in the total of deposits held with them by foreign banks.

This expansion of foreign banks' deposits may arise in one of three ways.   Firstly, the banks of countries which are not financial centres and which themselves have favourable balances may be prepared to keep the additional reserves thus obtained in the form of bank deposits in the centre concerned.   Secondly, quite a small rise in interest rates may be sufficient to induce such banks to transfer their reserves from other financial centres; and thirdly, one effect of the adverse balance may be to cause interest rates in foreign financial centres to fall, thus inducing the transference of funds to the centre in question, even though interest rates are not raised there.

Where the effects on the banks' position of an adverse balance of payments takes this form, it is obvious that the pressure on the banking system to restore equilibrium by restricting credit is much less. If the foreign banks' balances are kept with commercial banks, there is no direct incentive to contract credit, except in so far as the fear that foreign balances are more likely than the balances of local residents to be withdrawn in cash may induce the banks to attempt to increase their cash ratios. Nevertheless, there will still be some tendency towards adjustment from the monetary side, apart from any tendency which may exist owing to a direct decrease in the profitability in local business. Even where the adverse balance is accompanied at first by a trade improvement, the passage of balances formerly owned by local depositors into the hands of foreign banks will first tend to offset the idle balances released by the expectations of improvement, and ultimately reduce the volume of deposits in active circulation. This reduction of effective deposits must in turn lead to reduced purchases of commodities or services, either directly or in consequence of a rise in interest rates due to a shortage of funds available for investment. The process of adjustment will then follow the lines indicated in an earlier section.[5]

It should be emphasised, however, that while the ultimate effect of an accumulation of bank deposits in the ownership of foreign banks is similar to that of the withdrawal of cash from the banks, the pressure towards adjustment will be far more gradual in the former case; for active deposits will then be reduced only by the actual amount of the adverse balance, while a depletion of the banks' cash reserves will (if existing ratios are maintained) compel a reduction in deposits by an amount equal to many times the adverse balance.

Even if the foreign balances are kept with the central bank, the effects on the commercial banks will probably be less severe than if the central bank's own cash reserves were depleted to the extent of the adverse balance. For in the former case the com-

---

[5] This assumes, of course, that the banks do not allow deposits to expand so as to offset the growing amount held idle in the hands of foreign banks; since their cash reserves are assumed to be unchanged, any such expansion of deposits would presumably be strictly limited, even at higher interest rates.

mercial banks' cash reserves will be depleted (even if the central bank does not offset the movement by open market operations) only by the amount of the adverse balance, while in the latter case the central bank, if it is to maintain its existing ratios, must reduce its deposits, including bankers' deposits, by a multiple of its loss of cash.

The deflationary effects of an accumulation of foreign banks' assets in any centre will be mitigated, but not entirely removed, if these assets are held, not in the form of bank deposits, but of investments; though in this case the movement should probably be regarded as an adjustment of the balance of payments by means of loans from abroad rather than as the effect of an adverse balance. If foreign banks were prepared to invest their funds in the same way as local residents, the effect of such an adjustment of an adverse balance would probably be similar to that of an ordinary increase in saving. In fact, however, foreign banks will almost certainly wish to keep these assets in a very liquid form. They will therefore part with their bank balances only if they can obtain suitable short-term investments in exchange for them. Unless the supply of short-term investments increases, or unless existing owners of short-term securities are prepared to invest the proceeds in long-dated securities or loans, the balances thus released by the foreign banks will remain idle in the hands of their new owners; or, if it is the local banks which fail to secure their usual supply of short-term securities, the balances will simply disappear. The final effect of the whole transaction, including the original adverse balance, will be a fall in short-term interest rates, and a fall in the demand for commodities, either directly or in consequence of the rise in long-term interest rates, which will occur in consequence of the transfer of resources from long to short-term investments. Since, however, some addition to the supply of short-term securities and some transfer of funds to longer-term securities may be expected, this tendency towards adjustment is likely to be less marked than that which follows the accumulation of bank balances in the ownership of foreign banks.[6]

---

[6] If the whole of the increase in foreign-owned funds were invested in additional

An offsetting of an adverse balance by an increase in the short-term local assets owned by foreigners other than banks will probably have a very similar local effect to that of an increase of local assets in the hands of foreign banks, though its effects abroad will be very different.

There is also the possibility of a more permanent adjustment of an adverse balance of payments in a low M.P.I. country, which is also a financial centre, by means of a reduction in the volume of its new long-term loans to foreign countries, and the gradual repayment of old loans.   Where there is only one centre lending abroad on a large scale, or, where there are several lending centres, if each supplies capital mainly to its own particular areas, it would probably take a substantial rise in interest rates to check foreign borrowing.   Further, the curtailment of foreign loans by any one country, whether by high interest rates or other means, would reduce the total amount of international lending, cause difficulties in borrowing countries, and probably have the effect of reducing the volume of international trade, including the exports of the country which had curtailed its loans.   In a world, however, in which there were a number of financial centres of comparable importance, competing with each other for the supply of capital to all parts of the world, it would take only a small rise in interest rates in any one centre to divert borrowers, both of new funds and for conversion purposes, to other centres.   If the same causes which had induced a rise in interest rates in one centre brought about a fall in others, there would need to be no net reduction in the total of new long-term international lending and no adverse repercussions in borrowing countries or on international trade.   Such a system would be very different from any which the world has yet seen; but it is at least possible that developments in this direction may ultimately help to solve the difficulties of the adjustment of the balance of payments in low M.P.I. countries.

---

government short-term loans, which in turn were expended, e.g., on unemployment relief or government works, there would be no tendency at all towards adjustment so long as the process could be maintained.

VII

The other important factor, which needs to be taken into consideration in determining the effect on a particular country of its development of an adverse balance of payments, is the effect of its repercussions on other countries. By definition, if one country develops an adverse balance of payments, some other country or countries must simultaneously develop a favourable balance. (This does not, of course, imply anything whatever concerning the balance of direct payments between the countries concerned.) The reactions of a country developing a favourable balance of payments are, in general, the obverse of the reactions to an unfavourable balance, described above. They will be determined partly by the direct effects on the profitability of business, and partly by the indirect effects *via* a fall in the local rate of interest. It should be noted, however, that while a favourable balance resulting from local developments may well be accompanied by a fall in local incomes, a favourable balance resulting from developments abroad will usually be accompanied by a rise.

This direct effect on incomes will be reinforced by the effect on interest rates. The normal effect of a favourable balance is to increase the banks' reserves of gold and foreign exchange, and at the same time to increase the ratio of their local deposits to local advances. If the country concerned is a financial centre, the effect may take the alternative form of transferring to local residents local balances and short-term assets hitherto held by foreign banks. In either case there is a tendency for money available for investment to become more plentiful and for interest rates to fall, though the effect will be more marked in the former case than in the latter.[7]

---

[7] There is one apparent exception to this which it is worth pausing to examine. If a flight from a foreign currency results in an increase in local deposits held by foreigners other than banks, and a simultaneous decrease in local deposits held by foreign banks, the movement will appear to the foreign banks as an adverse balance of payments. To the local banks, however, the position will not have altered; the total of foreign-held deposits has not changed, nor has their ability to make loans been increased. There will therefore be no tendency for the local rate of interest

After a longer or shorter delay, depending partly upon the direct effects of the favourable balance, and partly upon the pre-existing state of business psychology, the fall in interest rates will tend to be followed by increased business activity and rising expenditures. The connection is, however, much less positive than between rising interest rates and falling expenditures; for interest rates can, if necessary, be raised to whatever level is necessary to restore the position, if necessary to infinity by a complete refusal to grant or renew loans.   But they cannot be lowered beyond zero, if as far.

The development of an adverse balance of payments by one country will usually be followed, especially in times of fairly active trade, by a rise, after a longer or shorter time, of expenditures in one or more other countries which at the same time develop favourable balances.   Whether this rise in expenditures elsewhere will help quickly to restore the balance of payments of the country with the adverse balance will depend on two further considerations: firstly, upon the extent to which an increase in expenditures in the countries with favourable balances is reflected in their imports (i.e., upon their M.P.I.), and secondly, upon the time lag, if any, before these increased imports are fully reflected in increased exports from the country with the adverse balance.

VIII

In the light of the foregoing discussion, it seems clear that it is only in high M.P.I. countries that the consequences of an attempt to adjust an adverse balance of payments by means of a restriction of bank credit and a rise in interest rates can be predicted with any

---

to fall.   It is doubtful, however, whether such a movement can be rightly described as entering into the balance of international payments.   The transaction is not one which directly concerns the local banks at all, and may be regarded as a private arrangement between the foreign banks and their customers.   It is exactly analogous to the withdrawal of gold by foreign depositors from their own banks for purposes of hoarding, and will have the same effect of causing a rise in interest rates in their own countries without producing a fall elsewhere.   It will in due course bring about a rise in interest rates in other countries also, as the banks draw gold from abroad or obtain new foreign balances from their former owners.

confidence. In high M.P.I. countries, unless local business prospects are so favourable that expenditures are maintained in the face of a rate of interest high enough to draw sufficient long-term investments from abroad, the balance of payments will be adjusted mainly by a reduction in imports. There need be no fall in local prices or wages, no expansion in exports, and comparatively little increase in unemployment. The whole process of adjustment can be carried through rapidly, at the cost, indeed, of inconvenience to those who have to reduce their expenditures, but without any serious check to local business activity. The time taken to complete the adjustment and the severity of the credit restriction required will depend upon the size of the adverse balance, upon whether expenditures are spontaneously tending to fall or to rise, and upon the adequacy of the banks' reserves of gold or foreign exchange.

For low M.P.I. countries, on the other hand, confident forecasts can be made only in cases where developments are merely the obverse of developments in high M.P.I. countries. To take an extreme hypothetical example, if every low M.P.I. country had an adverse balance of payments, and every high M.P.I. country a favourable one, it would be fairly safe to prophesy that, in the absence of government intervention, adjustment would take place by means of an expansion of exports from low to high M.P.I. countries, even without any restriction of credit in low M.P.I. countries. (This is not to say, of course, that such restriction of credit would be unwise from the long run point of view; for in its absence there might well occur an excessive expansion of credit in the world as a whole, leading ultimately to a serious reaction.) The time-lag in the adjustment would depend partly on whether the banks in the high M.P.I. countries wished to replenish their reserves of gold or foreign exchange before relaxing credit conditions, and partly upon whether incomes and expenditures in high M.P.I. countries were already expanding. If the adverse balance of the low M.P.I. countries had been due to an increase in their imports or in their loans to foreign countries, the adjustment would be likely to be rapid.

So extreme a case as this is hardly likely to occur in fact; but it is possible that an approximation to it exists at the present moment, when in at least three important countries—Great Britain, the United States and France—all of which have probably a fairly low M.P.I., imports have recently been rising fairly sharply, while exports have been rising more slowly in Great Britain and U.S.A., and falling in France. There is some probability that in this case the adjustment will take the form of an expansion of exports from low M.P.I. countries (though not necessarily from all of them). This probability seems to be increased by the fact that in certain other countries whose M.P.I. is probably in normal conditions also fairly low, quotas and exchange restrictions have made the value of imports more or less directly dependent upon the value of exports, so that the foreign trade of these countries reacts in some respects as if their M.P.I. was high.

Where the probable repercussions of developments abroad are so small or delayed as to be negligible, no definite forecast can be made of the results of an attempt to restore equilibrium in the balance of payments of a low M.P.I. country by means of credit restriction. If the country concerned is an international financial centre, adjustment may be brought about by a diversion of long-term borrowing, or more temporarily by an inflow of foreign short-term funds, which, however, may merely mitigate, but not entirely remove, the effects of a rise in interest rates upon internal business activity. In the absence of adjustments through the capital markets, equilibrium can be restored only by a fall in local incomes, either as a direct result of the causes producing the adverse balance of payments or in consequence of a restriction of bank credit, leading in turn either to a fall in internal prices and costs, and to an expansion of exports, probably accompanied by some contraction of imports, or, if the internal cost structure is rigid, to a contraction of imports due to unemployment.

3

THE ROLE OF THE INTERNATIONAL MONETARY AGREEMENTS IN A WORLD OF PLANNED ECONOMIES*

By Raymond F. Mikesell‖ ‡

It is the purpose of this article to discuss certain aspects of the postwar international economic agreements in relation to the economic developments of the postwar world. This analysis will be confined to the credit and exchange policy provisions of the International Monetary Fund together with those provisions of the Anglo-American financial agreement and of the proposed charter for an International Trade Organization which deal with quantitative and exchange restrictions.[1] Although a number of modifications were introduced as a result of negotiations with other governments, the basic structures of these agreements were developed by the technical experts of the United States government. Taken together, the agreements constitute an American program for the restitution of multilateral world trade. They are in large measure postulated on the existence of a world in which trade is conducted by unregimented private enterprise and are designed to assure its

---

* *Journal of Political Economy*, Volume LV (December, 1947), pages 497–512. Reprinted by the courtesy of *The Journal of Political Economy* and the author.

‖ University of Virginia.

‡ Squared brackets in the present text indicate all substantial additions to or changes of the original text.

[1] All references to the Charter will be to the *Draft Charter for the International Trade Organization of the United Nations* (Department of State, September, 1947 [hereafter cited as "*I.T.O. Charter*"]). This draft is based on the articles as drafted at the Geneva meeting of the Preparatory Committee of the International Conference on Trade and Employment, April–August, 1947.

successful operation by correcting the sources of international maladjustment which characterized the 1920's and 1930's.

The increasing socialization of production and distribution and the growing adherence to the philosophy of economic planning raise serious questions regarding the preconceptions upon which these agreements are based.   Whether or not this trend is to be reversed over the next generation or so is hazardous to predict.   It is possible that world economic stability and prosperity will be accompanied by a gradual removal of state controls and a return of international trade to private hands.   International agreements such as the Fund agreement, the Anglo-American financial agreement and the proposed I.T.O. charter may serve to create a more favorable environment for the successful functioning of systems of free enterprise.[2]   But these agreements do not require that trade be conducted by private enterprise, nor do they provide for the elimination of state controls.   International agreements are not likely to alter directly the fundamental structure of production and commerce among the nations of the world.   Developments affecting the pattern of economic controls are rooted in the political and economic philosophies of the individual countries and are generally unaffected by the platitudes and the vague and well-hedged obligations of international conventions.

Without appearing to predict the outcome of current trends, it may be profitable to examine the role of our monetary agreements in a world in which international trade is predominantly subject to state control.   For the purposes of this analysis it makes little difference whether trade is in the hands of state trading organizations or associations of privately owned enterprises whose trading activities are closely supervised by the state or whether control takes the form of a comprehensive system of import licensing.   The essential condition is that decisions regarding what and how much to import

---

[2] It is conceivable that prosperous conditions may favor socialization of industry in some countries.   For example, the Labour government in Britain might be able to move more rapidly in the implementation of its long-range program of socialization in prosperous times than at present.

and export, as well as the origin and destination of trade, are no longer made by private traders operating in accordance with the rules of free competitive enterprise. We will first discuss the objectives and policies stated in our monetary agreements in relation to a world of planned trade, following which we will suggest how these policies and objectives might be modified to serve such a world.

Whatever may have been in the minds of the delegates of the other countries represented at the Bretton Woods conference, it is clear that the American authors of the proposal for an International Monetary Fund predicated their proposal on a postwar world in which international trade would be predominantly in the hands of free private enterprise. The principal considerations on which the Monetary Fund was originally drafted may be summarized as follows:

1. Since the experience of the interwar period shows that exchange rate fluctuations present a serious problem for postwar international trade, the stabilization of exchange rates at appropriate levels and the prevention of competitive exchange depreciation should be part of the first order of business in the restoration of normal world trade.

2. Equilibrium in the balance-of-payments is largely determined by the uncoordinated and unregimented activities of private traders at home and abroad operating in freely competitive world markets for internationally traded commodities and services.

3. Balance-of-payments disequilibriums are normally temporary and self-correcting phenomena. Prolonged deficits may be corrected by appropriate internal fiscal and monetary policies or, in the case of chronic balance-of-payments disequilibriums, by a change in the exchange rate.

4. Although the U.S.S.R. and perhaps a few other countries would have socialistic economies, the bulk of the world's business, internal and external, would be in private hands with a minimum of planning and direct participation by governments. Hence, to restore free and multilateral trade, it is only necessary to remove government restrictions on private traders.

5. The postwar transition period during which most nations would need to maintain exchange and quantitative trade controls in order to protect their balance of payments and to facilitate reconstruction would be relatively short—say, three to five years—following which it would be possible for nearly all countries to achieve international equilibrium and currency stability without the use of exchange and trade restrictions.

The preconceptions outlined above are subject to a variety of modifications depending upon how the monetary agreements themselves are interpreted.   A study of the evolution of these agreements in successive American drafts will, in the opinion of the author, reveal that these considerations dominated the thinking of the American experts.   Let us examine these basic preconceptions in relation to the operation of our monetary agreements under the assumption that the present world trend in the direction of economic planning continues.

EXCHANGE RATE FLUCTUATIONS

The original United States proposal for an international stabilization fund was based largely on the operations and objectives of the United States Exchange Stabilization Fund.[3]   Like our domestic stabilization fund, the primary purpose of the international stabilization fund was the stabilization of exchange rates in a world in which countries were no longer on the gold standard or one in which gold arbitrage could not be counted on to perform adequately the function of keeping rates stable.   Also like its domestic counterpart, the international fund was to be passive in that it would not take a position in a currency on its own initiative.[4]   The parities

---

[3] The first published draft of the American plan, entitled *Preliminary Draft Outline of a Proposal for a United and Associated Stabilization Fund*, was released to the public in April, 1943.   The original drafts of this proposal as developed in the Treasury Department date from January, 1942.

[4] During the period 1936–38 the U.S. Exchange Stabilization Fund supported foreign currencies in the New York market in accordance with the terms of the Tripartite agreement.   However, such purchases were made with a gold guaranty and at rates established by the foreign governments themselves.

were to be determined by international agreement and would not be changed except with the concurrence of both the Fund and the individual member.[5]   Foreign exchange for the support of official parities could be purchased from the international fund by the member with its own currency, a technique which is similar to the method employed by the United States Fund in its stabilization agreements with other countries.[6]

This preoccupation by American experts with international currency values in planning for the postwar world is understandable in the light of the history of widespread currency depreciation following World War I and the cycle of devaluation in the 1930's. Exchange depreciation undoubtedly interfered with the recovery of Europe and contributed to internal inflation in the immediate postwar years.   Likewise, the mad scramble of nations to reduce the pressure of deflation through devaluation during the 1930's was disturbing to international trade.   However, the international economic environment today differs from that of both the 1920's and the 1930's in several significant ways, which greatly alter the position of the exchange mechanism in international relations. Unlike the period immediately following World War I, there is little disposition on the part of countries to get rid of exchange and licensing controls.   Except for a few countries whose currencies are closely tied to the dollar, all countries maintain controls on both capital and current transactions.   Therefore there is no problem of nations being unable to maintain their official rates; nor is there a problem of so-called competitive exchange depreciation so long as there are world-wide shortages of commodities.

Competitive currency depreciation is not likely to take place on a large scale in a world of planned trade for two reasons.   First, imports will be controlled through import licensing and exchange rationing, and currency depreciation will not be required as a

---

[5] This provision was later altered to permit a unilateral change by the member up to 10 per cent of the original parity.

[6] See Arthur I. Bloomfield, "Operations of the American Exchange Stabilization Fund," *Review of Economics Statistics*, May, 1944.

means of reducing the demand for imports.   Second, where lower export prices are considered desirable, there are a number of other means of achieving the same end, e.g., subsidies to private exporters, sales by state trading monopolies at a loss, bilateral arrangements in which losses on exports can be made up by profits from imports, and the use of special exchange rates to encourage exports.   Thus many countries may choose to avoid the political disadvantages of formal devaluation by continuing to employ one or more of these expedients more or less indefinitely as a means of improving their trade balance.   In fact, as international trade becomes more and more a matter of intergovernmental barter arrangements, exchange rates tend to lose their significance.

THE FIXING OF THE INITIAL PARS

The establishment of improper exchange rates following World War I has frequently been cited as contributing to the breakdown of the international currency mechanism of the early 1930's.   One of the most important functions of the Monetary Fund as conceived by its sponsors in the United States was, therefore, the determination through international co-operation of the parities of its members.[7]   In accordance with the provisions of the Fund agreement, it was expected that the Fund would carefully scrutinize the initial pars submitted by its members with a view to determining whether or not such rates were consistent with the maintenance of international equilibrium.[8]   On December 18, 1946, the managing director of the Fund announced the certification of the par values of thirty-two of the Fund's thirty-nine members.   Of the thirty-two par values accepted by the Fund, about half were approximately

---

[7] See, e.g., *Report of the Senate Committee on Banking and Currency on H.R. 3314* (The Bretton Woods Act of 1945 [July 6, 1945]), p. 7.

[8] See *Articles of Agreement, International Monetary Fund and International Bank for Reconstruction and Development* (Treasury Department, 1944 [hereafter cited as *"Articles of Agreement"*]).   Art. XX, sec. 4, provides that the Fund may reject a par value submitted to it by a member if "in its opinion the par value cannot be maintained without causing recourse to the Fund on the part of that member or others on a scale prejudicial to the Fund and to members."

the same or higher than they were in September, 1939, and only one (the French franc) was less than 50 per cent of its September, 1939, parity.   This was surprising in view of the fact that prices in many of the member-countries had increased from 300 to as high as 1000 per cent during the war period.   Each of the par values accepted was identical with the official rates prevailing at the time of the announcement.   The remaining member-countries elected to postpone certification of their rates to a later date, and there is no evidence to show that the Fund rejected any par value which was actually submitted for certification.

Although elaborate balance-of-payments and other studies were made by the technical staff of the Fund and by the United States National Advisory Council, it is evident from the official statement made by the Fund at the time the par values were announced that no attempt was made to establish equilibrium rates.   The following paragraphs taken from the official statement are indicative of the Fund's attitude:

The Fund realizes that at the present exchange rates there are substantial disparities in price and wage levels among a number of countries.   In present circumstances, however, such disparities do not have the same significance as in normal times.   For practically all countries, exports are being limited mainly by difficulties of production or transport, and the wide gaps which exist in some countries between the cost of needed imports and the proceeds of exports would not be appreciably narrowed by changes in their currency parities.   In addition, many countries have just begun to recover from the disruption of war, and efforts to restore the productivity of their economies may be expected gradually to bring their cost structures into line with those of other countries.   Furthermore, for many countries now concerned with combating inflation there is a danger that a change in the exchange rate would aggravate the internal tendencies toward inflation.

In view of all these considerations, the Fund has reached the conclusion that the proper course of action is to accept as initial par values the existing rates of exchange.

Although the author entertains some doubts as to the correctness of the Fund's action,[9] the attitude of the Fund on the initial pars is a

---

[9] See my "Determination of Postwar Exchange Rates," *Southern Economic Journal*, January, 1947.   Although it will be readily admitted that there are many cases at the present time in which no conceivable rate could achieve international

significant indication of the altered position of exchange rates themselves in a world of controlled trade.   Controls on production and distribution of both domestic and internationally traded commodities together with the extensive employment of exchange controls have greatly weakened the influence of exchange rates and exchange-rate changes over the pattern of trade.   In addition, the criterion, established by the Fund agreement, for judging the appropriateness of exchange rates may have little validity in a world in which balances of payments are subject to direct control.[10]   This criterion will be discussed in the following section.

The Concept of International Equilibrium

The concept of international equilibrium as the product of freely competitive forces operating in world markets for com-

---

equilibrium without the aid of controls, gross disparities should not, in the opinion of the author, have been sanctioned by the Fund.   [Even though it may be impossible to prove that a devaluation undertaken by a particular country will substantially improve its balance of payments position in the short-run, the establishment of an appropriate pattern of exchange rates is highly significant for the trade of a trading area such as Western Europe, and ultimately for the trade of the world as a whole.   If production and trade are restored on the basis of an improper rate structure, world trade will not be so large as it would otherwise be, nor will the trade which does take place secure the maximum benefits of international specialization.   Moreover, an unrealistic rate structure may make it impossible to restore trade to private hands even where there is a will to do so. Where domestic price and cost structures in trading countries bear no sensible relationship to one another in terms of existing artificial exchange rates, trade must be largely confined to compensation or barter deals undertaken directly or controlled by the State.]

The argument that rates can be changed after the transition period breaks down for two important reasons.   First, the future structure of production and trade will be developed with reference to the rate pattern of the transition period, and vested interests will have been built up for the retention of existing rates. Second, in the absence of free-exchange markets, there will be little pressure on countries to devalue.   Such pressures as may come from exporters will be more than overbalanced by the political unpopularity of currency depreciation, and existing rates will be continued indefinitely by means of trade restrictions and controls.

[10] According to the *Articles of Agreement*, rate changes are justifiable in the event of a fundamental disequilibrium in the balance of payments of a member.

modities and services is basic to the policies and operations of the Monetary Fund as it was conceived by its authors. The realism of this concept was never seriously challenged in the course of negotiations leading up to the establishment of the Fund, even by the representatives of those countries which may be expected to maintain state control over all or a large part of their foreign trade. The most serious rival to the American proposal for an international fund, Lord Keynes's International Clearing Union,[11] was even more dependent upon the concept of international equilibrium. Under the Clearing Union scheme, a potential creditor country was asked to have enough faith in the mechanism of international equilibrium to be willing to accept an almost unlimited amount of credits from the rest of the world. Under the Clearing Union proposal, credits become available automatically whenever a member experienced a deficit in its current international accounts. These credits at the Clearing Union became transferable and acceptable in payment of international obligations by all members. The United States negotiators rejected this idealistic proposal and proposed, instead, a contributed fund with limited liability for creditor nations. After the general acceptance of the American proposals, the British representatives took the position—both at the Bretton Woods conference in July, 1944, and again at the Savannah monetary conference in March, 1946—that the Fund should grant credits more or less automatically (up to the limit of the member's drawing rights) whenever a member experienced a deficit in its international accounts. Again the American representatives showed somewhat less faith in the fortuitous character of equilibrium and disequilibrium by insisting that extensions of credits by the Fund be reviewed by the executive board of the Fund.

The Monetary Fund was designed to provide international liquidity in the event of balance-of-payments maladjustments of a short-term character. The fundamental requisite for the granting of credits by the Fund is a deficit in the current international ac-

---

[11] *Proposals for an International Clearing Union* (New York: British Information Services, April 8, 1943).

counts of the borrowing member. Although it is explicitly provided in the Fund agreement that the borrowing member shall repay the Fund when its current balance has turned favorable, the mechanism by which the balance is reversed or equilibrium is restored is not made clear. This mechanism obviously does not depend on the effects of gold movements upon price levels since, by the time the Fund was established, it was clear to nearly everyone that monetary authorities in the postwar world would pursue domestic monetary policies independent of the volume of their international reserves. Nor can it be assumed that equilibrium will be restored by permitting trade deficits and surpluses to have a multiplier effect on national income (and hence a corresponding effect upon imports), since it may be expected that most countries will pursue domestic economic policies designed to compensate for the deflationary effects of trade deficits and the inflationary effects of surpluses. A restoration of equilibrium might be expected in the case of temporary discrepancies resulting from seasonal fluctuations, crop failures, national disasters, and short-term cyclical movements. The Fund might also supply foreign exchange in cases where the source of the maladjustment could be traced to an improper exchange rate, an inflationary monetary fiscal policy, or the loss of some important export. In such cases funds might be supplied on condition that the borrowing member took steps to correct the imbalance. But there exists no dependable mechanism by means of which deep-seated maladjustments in the structure of world trade can be removed. For example, it is quite possible that the highly unbalanced condition of world trade in the immediate postwar period may prove to be chronic, and that the so-called postwar transition period, during which an excessive demand for exports from the Western Hemisphere was to be expected, may extend over a generation or more. Under such circumstances the Fund's ability to supply dollars would soon be exhausted if the Fund were to follow the criteria for extending credit outlined in the *Articles of Agreement.*

More significant than the mechanism by which equilibrium is restored is the underlying assumption in the Fund agreement that a balance-of-payments surplus or deficit is not something which is predetermined but is rather the product of a multitude of unco-ordinated transactions arising out of the decisions of individual traders operating in world markets. The Fund agreement does not necessarily presuppose a perfectly competitive world and the absence of all state-controlled trade. What is assumed, however, is that the area of free international dealings is sufficiently large to make the existence of a surplus or a deficit within reasonable limits the product of individual transactions which are free and subject to competitive forces rather than the deliberate operations of the controlled sector of the economy. When all or a major part of a member's foreign transactions are planned, the original basis for the granting of credits by the Fund is destroyed, since the member can determine in advance whether or not it will have a deficit or a surplus. Similarly, the mechanism provided by the Fund agree-ment for repayment loses most of its significance when trade is con-trolled. Instead of fixing a definite maturity for loans granted by the Fund, it is provided that, in years of surplus, borrowing mem-bers must use a part of that surplus to repay the Fund for credits granted in periods of deficit.[12] Fortunately the agreement also provides for interest charges which increase progressively with the amount and duration of the credits. Without these charges (the inclusion of which was fought bitterly by several countries at the Bretton Woods conference on the grounds that they were counter to the principles of the automatic restoration of equilibrium) state trading countries would have little incentive to reduce their in-debtedness to the Fund.

The concept of equilibrium is also basic to the decisions of the Fund relating to the alteration of exchange rates. Members of the Fund agree not to change their rates except to correct a "funda-mental disequilibrium" and, in those cases in which the Fund's permission must be given before a change can be made, the basic criterion is whether or not there exists a fundamental disequilib-rium.[13] Although fundamental disequilibrium is not defined in

[12] See *Articles of Agreement*, Art. V, sec. 7(6).
[13] *Ibid.*, Art. IV.

the Fund's *Articles of Agreement*, it was evident from the discussions which preceded the formal drafting of the agreement that the term refers to a sustained imbalance in a member's current international accounts.[14] Properly interpreted, such an imbalance would be one which was not offset by long-term borrowings and would be accompanied by a sustained loss of international reserves or continued borrowings from the Fund or from other sources of short-term credits. The implication that a change in a member's exchange rate will correct a fundamental disequilibrium depends in large measure upon the existence of world markets and competitive forces which relate prices and costs in different countries. To the extent that internal price systems are insulated from external prices by means of internal price and trade controls, international commodity agreements covering production, prices and marketing quotas, and barter agreements between governments, and to the extent that balances of payments are directly managed by the state, the rationale of the Fund's criterion for alterations in exchange rates breaks down.

Disequilibrium in a member's balance of payments also provides the criterion for the employment of exchange restrictions on current international transactions during the postwar transitional period and thereafter in exceptional circumstances with the permission of the Fund.[15] Similarly the proposed I.T.O. Charter permits members to employ both exchange and quantitative trade controls whenever necessary to safeguard their balance of pay-

---

[14] There has been considerable debate among economists as to what should be the criteria for alterations in exchange rates (see my "Determination of Postwar Exchange Rates," *Southern Economic Journal*, January, 1947). From a study of the unpublished minutes of the pre-Bretton Woods negotiations, however, it is clear that the principal criterion for rate alterations in the minds of the authors of the text of the Fund agreement was the existence of a disequilibrium in the current international accounts of the member requesting a change.

[15] *Articles of Agreement* (Art. XIV, on transitional arrangements) states that "members shall withdraw restrictions maintained or imposed under this Section as soon as they are satisfied that they will be able, in the absence of such restrictions, to settle their balance of payments, in a manner which will not unduly encumber their access to the resources of the Fund."

ments.[16] A serious difficulty with this criterion is that members might maintain controls on current transactions indefinitely simply by pursuing policies which would preclude the attainment of equilibrium in the absence of controls.   Such policies might include the maintenance of an overvalued exchange rate, inflationary monetary and fiscal policies, or large foreign purchases by government purchasing agencies.   Again, where the bulk of the foreign trade is in government hands, the balance of payments becomes largely a matter of governmental decisions.

Finally we come to the role of international equilibrium in the administration of the scarce-currency provisions of the Fund. When the Fund finds that it is about to exhaust its supply of a currency as a result of a world shortage of that currency, it may declare that currency to be scarce and ration its remaining and accruing supply in accordance with the principle of greatest need.   Such a declaration automatically gives other members the right to discriminate in their trade against the scarce-currency country.[17]   A scarce-currency situation could only be brought about in the event of excessive demands for a key currency since demands on the Fund for the currency of a small country could always be met with the Fund's supply of gold and gold-convertible currencies.   Practically, this means that the United States is the only large potential scarce-currency country although, if the United States dollar were declared scarce, a number of other currencies closely tied to the dollar would undoubtedly have to be declared scarce because of increased pressure on the Fund's supplies of these currencies.

The theory underlying the scarce-currency provisions is that there may develop a general disequilibrium resulting from a

---

[16] The *I.T.O. Charter* (Art. 21) states that a member may use import restrictions to the extent necessary "to forestall the imminent threat of, or to stop, a serious decline in its monetary reserves, or in the case of a Member with very low monetary reserves, to achieve a reasonable rate of increase in its reserves"; see my "Quantitative and Exchange Restrictions under the I.T.O. Charter," *AER*, June, 1947.

[17] *Articles of Agreement*, Art. VII.   The I.T.O. Charter and the Anglo-American financial agreement also provide for exchange and quantitative trade restrictions against the dollar in the event that it is declared by the Fund to be a scarce currency.

persistent favorable balance of a key-currency country or area. The Fund agreement provides that, when the Fund finds this situation is threatening to develop, it shall make a report together with recommendations designed to correct the conditions giving rise to the disequilibrium.[18] The implication drawn from the Fund's *Articles of Agreement* by most students is that the cause of the scarce-currency condition will generally be found in the policies of the creditor country. Either that country has failed to maintain full employment, or its trade barriers do not permit sufficient imports, or perhaps its currency is overvalued. However, it would be quite possible for none of these factors to be responsible for the scarce-currency situation if the trade policies of most of the nations of the world are inconsistent with basic assumptions of the theory of international equilibrium. If the volume and direction of trade are in large measure determined by governmental action rather than by free competitive forces, the mechanism for the restoration of equilibrium breaks down. Relative price changes via exchange-rate adjustments may not have the desired effects on trade balances. A world bent on rapid industrialization may choose to expand its exports to the United States in order to import more capital goods, but the desired level of foreign exports may be larger than the United States is willing to buy even at full employment and in the absence of all trade barriers. Lower prices of imports in terms of dollars might expand United States imports somewhat, but recent studies have shown that—in the short run, at least—the price elasticity of imports into the United States is relatively low. Unless price elasticity is greater than unity, no additional dollar exchange would be made available to foreigners by an appreciation of the dollar.[19]

---

[18] *Ibid.*, Art. VII, sec. 3(*a*).

[19] [For an excellent discussion of the limitations on exchange rate adjustments for improving a country's balance of payments position see J. J. Polak, "Exchange Depreciation and International Monetary Stability," *Review of Economic Statistics*, August, 1947. Dr. Polak distinguishes between a balance of payments disequilibrium which is the result of *price disequilibrium* and one which is caused by *structural disequilibrium* in the demand and supply for internationally traded commodities. Rate adjustments are generally applicable only in the case of the former while in the case of the latter they may be of little value.]

In a world of controlled trade, and in the absence of free-exchange markets, when is a currency scarce? The only practical criterion is the Fund's holdings of the currency in question, which, in turn, is the result of the past credit policies of the Fund. But, as was mentioned above, the extension of credits by the Fund cannot properly be the automatic consequence of unfavorable balances in the accounts of its members when balances of payments are the product of deliberate planning by governments. In the absence of free exchange dealings for current transactions, there is little basis for determining whether or not a general scarcity of a currency exists. About all that can be said is that the import programs of the governments of the world at any particular time require more or less of a particular currency than they have on hand or is currently accruing to them.

The Significance of Exchange Restrictions

Before World War II the most important restriction on international trade were tariffs and exchange restrictions.[20] During and since the war comprehensive import and licensing systems have been in effect in most countries along with a growth of state trading and government-sponsored bulk purchase and sale arrangements.[21] Although both the proposed I.T.O. Charter and the British loan agreement deal with quantitative import restrictions, such restrictions are not eliminated by these agreements; they are merely subjected to certain rules of fair dealing and brought under international supervision.[22] Moreover, state trading and bilateral arrangements involving bulk purchase and sale conducted by the governments themselves are not interfered with by any of our international agreements. The door is also left open for intergovernmental commodity arrangements providing for price, production, and marketing quota agreements covering internationally traded

---

[20] An important exception was the extensive use of quotas by France during the 1930's.

[21] For example, it is estimated that more than 60 per cent of Britain's imports come under state-trading or bulk-purchasing arrangements.

[22] See my "Trade Practices under the I.T.O. Charter," *Annals,* July, 1947.

commodities. Let us examine the provisions on exchange restrictions contained in the Fund and British loan agreements to determine just how effective they are likely to be in removing restrictions on world trade under the assumption that the bulk of the world's trade is subject to state control and participation.

The Fund agreement requires that, after the transition period, its members must refrain from imposing "restrictions on the making of payments and transfers for current international transactions"[23] except with the permission of the Fund. What specifically does this obligation mean? Since controls on capital movements are permitted by the Fund, it is clear that members need not permit the operation of free-exchange markets within their borders. What is required is that balances currently acquired by foreigners must be freely transferable anywhere in the world, *provided that such transfers are not contrary to the exchange control regulations of the governments of the nationals holding the balances.*[24] In practice, transfers of foreign balances will be subject to strict government control by most members of the Fund since such transfers may be deemed to be capital movements and hence contrary to the exchange regulations. Most countries imposing controls on capital movements require their nationals to surrender all foreign exchange proceeds to the central authorities. The requirement not to impose restrictions on current payments and transfers may also mean that individuals in one member-country must be free to make payments in their own currency to foreigners provided the payments arise out of current transactions *which are otherwise permitted.* Obviously, a member-country would have no obligation to permit its nationals to make payments to foreigners arising out of illegal transactions, e.g., imports for which a required import license has not been obtained.

---

[23] *Articles of Agreement*, Art. VIII, sec. 2.

[24] *Ibid.*, sec. 2(*b*), provides that transfers of balances by individuals contrary to the exchange-control regulations of members imposed consistently with the agreement shall be unenforceable. Thus, if a French citizen holding sterling were to attempt to sell the sterling to an American citizen in violation of French exchange regulations, Britain would be under obligation not to recognize the legality of the transfer.

In summary, the obligation of members of the Fund not to impose restrictions on payments and transfers arising out of current transactions appears to require that members shall not prevent by means of exchange restrictions current international transactions which are otherwise permitted to take place.

But even the somewhat equivocal obligations which the Fund imposes upon its members are subject to indefinite postponement during the postwar transition period. The principal obstacle to the removal of restrictions on the transfer of foreign-owned balances was Britain's inability to restore the convertibility of sterling. By 1945 it became evident that even the formal establishment of the Fund, to say nothing of the realization of its objectives, was impossible until some disposition was made of the sterling problem.[25] It was reasoned therefore that, if the United States could make Britain financially able to free sterling, the pre-war system of international payments could be largely restored since probably as much as 80 per cent of the world's trade is currently conducted in terms of the dollar and sterling. Under the terms of the Anglo-American financial agreement, therefore, Britain agreed to make currently acquired sterling freely convertible by July 15, 1947.[26] But it is wrong to assume that this action will either restore the sterling area as it existed in the 1930's or that it will necessarily alter materially the pattern of trade among the countries closely tied to the British economy, which has developed since the war.

Before the war the countries of the sterling area did not maintain exchange controls, and sterling balances were largely in private hands. Although a substantial portion of the foreign-held sterling balances are still privately owned, only a small portion of the some $13 billion of foreign-held sterling will become convertible, and freely convertible balances will either be owned by the monetary authorities of the governments themselves or will be closely

---

[25] The first published draft of the American Stabilization Fund proposals (April, 1943) provided for the gradual liquidation of blocked balances. However, these provisions were omitted from the agenda of the Bretton Woods conference.

[26] *Anglo-American Financial and Commercial Agreements* (Department of State, December, 1945).

controlled by them. Sterling balances in the hands of British residents and the residents of British colonial areas and mandates will not be convertible or transferable except for transactions permitted by the British authorities. Convertibility of sterling, therefore, becomes in large measure a matter of the legal option of transferring a particular form of intergovernmental debt. So long as foreign balances are owned or completely controlled by governments, foreign-exchange transactions are little more than intergovernmental clearing. Whether or not a truly multilateral system results from the theoretical convertibility of balances depends upon the underlying trade arrangements and not upon the fact of convertibility itself. So long as sterling balances are controlled by governments and are not at the free disposition of individual traders, what is to prevent Britain from reaching understandings with other governments as to the rate of use of the balances or to the countries in which they will be spent?[27] This is not to say that the agreement with Britain regarding the convertibility of sterling is of no value. The removal of restrictions on the transferability of foreign balances will eliminate an important source of discrimination even in a world of state-controlled trade. But we should not expect to restore free international dealings merely by changing the symbols of international accounting. To accomplish this we would need to restore to free private enterprise the decisions of what and where and how much to buy and sell in the markets of the world.

On August 20, 1947, the British government announced a temporary suspension of general convertibility of currently acquired sterling into dollars. The rapid drain on Britain's dollar resources during the brief period of convertibility, inaugurated on July 15, 1947, was largely a reflection of the overwhelming demand for commodities obtainable only in the dollar area. Under present

---

[27] For example, the recent agreement concluded between Britain and Spain provides that the latter country will undertake *voluntarily* to hold sterling up to the amount of its current surplus with the sterling area (see "Preparing for July 15," *Economist*, May 17, 1947).

circumstances any country which undertakes to maintain convertibility of its currency into dollars is inevitably faced with the likelihood of having the bulk of its foreign payments transferred into dollars. The alternative is for that country to make trade arrangements with other countries which will assure that its trade will not be diverted to the United States. But bilateral arrangements are open to the objection that they direct trade into uneconomical channels and limit total trade. One way of dealing with this problem would be to establish a mechanism by which other countries can restrict their imports from the dollar area within the limits of their available dollar resources while at the same time carrying on multilateral trade among themselves. The scarce-currency provisions of the Fund together with the parallel provisions of the Anglo-American financial agreement provide for such a mechanism, but they cannot be invoked while the Fund has a large supply of dollar resources. Moreover, it was not the intention of those responsible for drafting the Fund agreement that any currency should be declared scarce during the postwar transition period. The agreement specifically prohibits the use of the Fund's resources for reconstruction and rehabilitation, and permits its members to employ exchange controls during the transition period in order to safeguard their balance of payments. The possibility of a system of limited or regional multilateral payments during the transition period will be discussed in the next section.

OPERATIONS OF THE FUND IN A WORLD OF CONTROLLED TRADE

The existence of a world in which international trade is predominantly state controlled does not preclude the Fund's being able to serve useful and important functions, since fortunately its charter is sufficiently broad and its provisions sufficiently vague to permit the adoption of a wide range of policies. The Fund, however, will need to develop policies and programs to deal realistically with the problems arising out of the existing international economic and political environment. It is not likely to create the kind of world it was originally designed to serve.

Let us consider first of all the lending function of the Fund. Because of the doubtful significance of the concept of international equilibrium in a world of planned trade, it is the view of the author that there should not be an automatic right to use the resources of the Fund, or at least that that right should be limited to a certain percentage of the total borrowing privilege of the member. In addition, there should be a definite understanding as to the maturity of loans over and above a minimum drawing privilege. The Fund is not an institution for long-term credits, and borrowing members should give evidence of a definite plan for reducing their indebtedness over a period of, say, three to five years. Unless the Fund plans its loans and maturities, planned balance-of-payments deficits could soon exhaust the Fund's resources of gold and creditor-country currencies even in the most favorable international economic environment. Realism demands that the Fund's lending policies cannot be based on the classical mechanism of international equilibrium.

The credit policy of the Fund is closely related to the scarce-currency problem. As was pointed out above, in a world of planned trade the idea of scarcity in the world's supply of a currency is equivocal and can be defined only in terms of the past credit policies of the Fund. If the Fund were to extend dollar credits up to the limit of the borrowing power of its members, it would be drained of its supply of gold and dollars in about four years.[28] Should the dollar be declared scarce, discrimination against United States trade would be authorized not only under the Fund agreement but also under the terms of the British loan agreement and the proposed I.T.O. Charter. Once its supply of gold and dollars is exhausted the Fund will in large measure be shorn of its power to enforce its decisions with respect to the exchange policies of its members. It would appear advisable therefore that the Fund carefully ration its supply of dollars right from the beginning and not submit this slender reserve to the vicissitudes of the world

---

[28] See Alice Bourneuf, "Lending Operations of the International Monetary Fund," *Review of Economic Statistics*, November, 1946, p. 247.

demand for dollars which is determined more by government fiat than by the operation of competitive forces in accordance with the principles of international trade theory.

What should be the policy of the Fund with respect to the determination of exchange rates? Although exchange rates would not have the same significance as they would have in a world in which international dealings were relatively free, a proper pattern of rates is nevertheless an essential condition for realizing the maximum benefits from trade even in a world dominated by state trading. In such a world the important problem is not the prevention of rate fluctuations or the alteration of parities. The Fund should abandon the negative approach toward exchange rates implied in the *Articles of Agreement*. The policy of the Fund should be a positive one, designed to establish a system of rates consistent with a high level of international trade and a realization of the maximum benefits from international specialization. The implementation of such a policy will require far more than purchasing-power-parity calculations. The Fund will need to make careful studies of the relative costs of production in various countries and detailed balance-of-payments estimates will need to be prepared. These estimates cannot be based on the assumption of free trade in a world in which trade and production are largely planned.

With respect to its policy on exchange controls, the Fund should again not adopt the negative attitude implied in its charter. It should seek to review and supervise existing controls with a view to eliminating inconvertible balances and discriminatory arrangements which tend to reduce total world trade. This does not mean that the Fund should seek to eliminate all bilateral arrangements and to compel all its members to make their currencies convertible during the transition period. The *Articles of Agreement* permit the retention of wartime controls during the transition period since, indeed, to abolish existing arrangements before a workable system of multilateral payments can be re-established would serve to stifle much of the trade which is currently taking place. The Fund should encourage the broadening of existing bilateral-payments arrangements to include several countries and perhaps the establishment of regional multilateral clearing mechanisms which would permit transferability of balances arising out of current transactions between members of a limited group of countries.[29]

It must be recognized, of course, that in the absence of the I.T.O. the Fund's power to deal with restrictions on trade is severely limited, since anything which its members may be precluded from doing under the exchange-control provisions of the Fund agreement can just as readily be accomplished by means of import quotas or licensing.   If and when the I.T.O. is established, the two organizations will need to maintain the closest co-operation.

The Restoration of Multilateral Trade

In dealing with trade practices, the approach of the Fund and the I.T.O. should be positive and constructive.   It is not a question of eliminating government controls but of supervising and modifying them in a manner most conducive to the restoration of multilateral trade.   Multilateral trade is quite possible even in a world of state trading monopolies or of universally planned trade. But, if we are to have multilateral trade under these conditions, it is not enough to state, as does the proposed I.T.O. Charter, that state trading enterprises shall behave like unregimented private traders buying in the cheapest market and selling at the highest prices regardless of any economic or political considerations other than those involved in each particular purchase or sale.[30]   The activities of purchasing and selling agencies are almost certain to be co-ordinated when both are controlled by the same government.   When trade is taken out of the hands of private traders, bilateralism in one form or another becomes inevitable unless the trade arrangements among the governments themselves are multilateral in character. It is in promoting multilateral trade within a system of controlled trade that the Fund and the proposed I.T.O. can make a significant contribution in the postwar world.

---

[29] Proposals for a multilateral clearing arrangement were discussed by the Finance Committee of the Committee of European Economic Cooperation, meeting in Paris during September and October, 1947.

[30] *I.T.O. Charter*, Art. 30.

A successful multilateral trading system depends first of all upon the willingness of nations to abandon political motives in the determination of the character and direction of their trade. Therefore, any comprehensive reconstruction of the world's trade along multilateral lines must await the solution of the world's political problems. However, if we are to have two worlds, politically and economically, limited multilateralism is better than none. A second prerequisite is the elimination of inconvertible balances which can be used only in making payments to a particular country. This is one of the most important services which the Fund can render. The Fund should play an active role in assisting its members in reaching agreements whereby blocked or nonconvertible balances will be funded and gradually released over a period of time along the lines of the provisions of the Anglo-American financial agreement.[31] As was mentioned above, the Fund may find it desirable to encourage limited convertibility of currently acquired balances among a group of countries during the transition period. The fact that most countries are not in a position to permit free transferability of their currencies into dollars or other so-called hard currencies should not preclude their transferability into soft currencies. The opportunity for multilateral clearing in international trade should be as wide as possible even though a world-wide system of multilateral payments cannot, for the present at least, be achieved.

Having established the prerequisites for the restoration of multilateral trade, the main problem becomes one of bringing existing and future trade arrangements under international supervision with a view to giving them a multilateral character. Agreements involving the importation of commodities which shut out or unduly discriminate against other important suppliers should be prohibited.[32] The I.T.O. or some other international organiza-

---

[31] In addition to the sterling balances there are also large inconvertible franc balances held by countries in the franc area and the balances arising out of payments agreements involving some fifteen European countries. These balances will need to be dealt with before multilateral trade can be restored.

[32] During periods of acute dollar shortage, trade discrimination against the dollar area might be permitted in order to enable countries to conserve their

tion might arrange multilateral agreements with all the important suppliers and importers of each category of internationally traded commodities.   Markets should be allocated not on the basis of the amount supplied in a previous representative period but rather on the basis of competitive bidding, with certain safeguards against dumping.   The primary aim of the international organization would be to achieve the maximum volume of trade by promoting multilateral rather than bilateral balancing in agreements covering all or nearly all the commodities in which trade is subject to state control.

It may be objected that such a proposal would tend to bring all international trade under state control and subject to international agreements.   This does not necessarily follow, since the international organization would not encourage trade by international agreement but merely bring all such agreements under its supervision.   There would still be a large area of relatively free international dealings outside the intergovernmental bulk-trading agreements.[33]   Moreover, it is better to accept the world as it is, and to promote as much multilateralism as possible within the existing framework, than to adopt a purely negative approach which merely condemns such arrangements but does nothing about them or expresses a pious hope that state trading will be nondiscriminatory.

Conclusion

It has not been the purpose of this article to criticize any of our existing monetary and trade agreements.   It is not to be expected

---

dollars for commodities obtainable only in the Western Hemisphere.   There will have to be restrictions on dollar purchases in any case, and countries which lack dollars should not be prevented from engaging in profitable trade with one another in order to avoid discrimination against particular commodity exports of the dollar area.

[33] The proposed I.T.O. Charter does provide for intergovernmental commodity agreements dealing with prices, production, and marketing of primary commodities; but the type of arrangement proposed here is much broader since it includes agreements to purchase certain commodities in exchange for agreements covering the sale of other commodities on a multilateral basis.

that the United States government, dedicated as it is to the principles of private enterprise and free international economic dealings, should design an economic program for the postwar world which would best fit the needs of planned and socialized economies. Moreover, it is possible that after the postwar transition period the current trend toward economic planning and socialization of industry and commerce may be reversed. However, we must deal realistically with the world as we find it, and only the most sanguine venture to believe that the United States could alter the fundamental political and economic structures of the nations of the world by means of international conventions and loans.

What has been attempted, therefore, is to indicate how our monetary and foreign-exchange agreements might operate in a world of state-controlled trade. It is concluded that the Monetary Fund and British Loan agreements cannot give us free international dealings or change the basic structure of world trade which must inevitably evolve from socialized and planned economies. At most they could provide a system whereby government-owned or -controlled balances arising out of international transactions would be freely transferable into any currency. Nor would the present programs as represented by these monetary agreements and the proposed International Trade Organization, give us a truly multilateral world if the rest of the world decides in favor of government planning of its internal and external economic affairs. In the absence of a constructive program for making intergovernmental trading arrangements multilateral in character, there would be little hope for the reconstruction of a prosperous world economy.

This does not mean that our existing international economic agreements and institutions would be of no value or that they would need to be replaced in a world such as we have postulated. Fortunately, these agreements were drawn so as to permit a rather wide range of interpretation. It may mean, however, that the economic programs and policies which they represent will need to be revised so as to increase their usefulness in meeting the emerging problems of the postwar world. The postwar transition period may not be a transition to the past!

FOREIGN EXCHANGE RATES

4

THE FOREIGN EXCHANGES*[1]

By Joan Robinson||

I

The exchange rate is determined from day to day by supply and demand of home currency in terms of foreign currency. Each transaction is two-sided, and sales are equal to purchases. Any change in the conditions of demand or of supply reflects itself in a change in the exchange rate, and at the ruling rate the balance of payments balances from day to day, or from moment to moment.

The constituents of the demand for foreign currencies in terms of home currency (or the supply of home currency coming on to the exchange market) may be divided into four groups. Foreign currency may be required (1) in order to pay for goods or services purchased from foreigners (or to make gifts to them), that is, in order to discharge obligations in respect to visible and invisible imports, (2) in order to make loans or purchase securities abroad, (3) for speculative purposes, that is to say, in order to take advantage of an expected reversal in the future course of the exchange rate, (4) in order to remove funds from a country in which political, fiscal or

---

* *Essays in the Theory of Employment*, 2nd ed., (Basil Blackwell, Oxford, 1947), Part III, Chapter 1. Reprinted, without change from the second edition, by the courtesy of The Macmillan Company, Basil Blackwell, and the author, Mrs. Joan Robinson.

|| Cambridge University, England.

[1] The subject-matter of this and the following essay [Chap. 17 of this volume] has been the battle-ground of innumerable controversies, and I have preferred (apart from one or two specific points) to make no references to other writers, rather than to weary the reader with continual acknowledgments and disagreements. It will be obvious that my main endeavour is to elaborate the hints thrown out by Mr. Keynes in his *Treatise on Money*, Chap. 21.

business prospects appear threatening to one in which they seem relatively secure.   A fifth group is represented by official exchange dealings, but, since our object is to discover the influences determining the exchange rate in the absence of official interference, we shall assume that no official dealings take place, except when special reference is made to them.[2]

Interest on foreign capital invested in the home country is most conveniently treated, in the traditional way, as an invisible import, since it represents a payment for the services of foreign funds borrowed in the past.   Day to day fluctuations in the balances of professional exchange dealers may be included in the third group, that is, as speculative transactions, though they do not represent speculation in the popular sense, but are part of the routine business of the exchange market.

If gold is treated as a commodity,[3] and if exchange dealings as an instrument of official policy are ruled out of account, the first four groups cover the whole field.   The third and fourth groups shade into each other, and the second shades into both, for exchange

---

[2] An exchange rate which is considered undesirably high can be corrected by direct intervention in the exchange market.   But while the monetary authorities can always sell an unlimited amount of their own currency they can only buy as much as their holdings of gold or foreign assets permit.   For this reason it is impossible to hold the exchange rate indefinitely above the level determined by a free market without resorting to complete control of all dealings.

[3] In some contexts it is convenient to treat gold movements in a different way (see *General Theory*, p. 335, and *Treatise*, p. 329).   In accordance with our present scheme of analysis an increment to the stock of gold inside the country must be regarded as part of home investment and a decrement as disinvestment.   This has the advantage of putting the gold-producing countries upon the same footing as the rest, and of putting a reduction in the stock of gold upon the same footing as a reduction in the stock of any other commodity.   But no point of principle is involved.   An increase in imports accompanied by an equivalent export of gold taken from stocks may be treated either as a decrease in the balance of trade (foreign investment) without any change in home investment, or as home disinvestment, without any change in the balance of trade.   Exports of newly-mined gold are in either case treated in the same way as exports of any other commodity.

prospects and considerations of security influence foreign lending, while funds removed to a foreign country for security will normally be lent at interest, though they may be used to purchase gold or to make a deposit at a bank.[4] Thus the motives which govern the demand for currency for foreign lending are inextricably bound up with the motives which govern exchange speculation and the panic movement of funds. It is therefore most convenient to distinguish only two major categories in the balance of payments—payments in respect to imports and exports, which represent the income account or *balance of trade*, and payments in respect to lending and borrowing (covering the whole of the last three groups distinguished above) which represent the capital account or *balance of lending*.

Now since the balance of payments always balances it follows that, for any section of time, payments in respect to the balance of trade must be equal and opposite to payments in respect to the balance of lending. Thus when, over any period, the inhabitants of a country have collectively a surplus of receipts from exports over payments for imports (or *positive* balance of trade)[5] they must, over the same period, on balance be lending (in the broad sense) to the inhabitants of foreign countries an exactly equal sum. Similarly a surplus of imports (or *negative* balance of trade) must be matched by

---

[4] It is sometimes supposed that an increase in the prospective earnings of capital in one country will lead to an increased desire on the part of foreigners to lend to it, for instance, that a boom on Wall Street "attracts money" from Europe. But this cannot occur when home and foreign speculators take an equally optimistic view of prospects, for if they do the price of securities will be driven up to such a point as to compensate for the improvement in their prospective yield, and no movement of foreign funds will actually take place. Only if the change in opinion leaves foreigners more bullish than home speculators will it lead to an inflow of foreign funds.

[5] The movement of goods and performance of services do not normally synchronise with the payments which are made in respect to them (cf. Haberler, *Theory of International Trade*, p. 18). This fact is of significance in certain contexts, but in order to avoid a cumbrous degree of exactitude we shall speak in what follows of, for instance, an increase in exports relatively to imports as an increase in the balance of trade.

an equal amount of borrowing. This is merely a truism, but it is a truism which provides the most convenient starting point for the theory of the exchanges.

The same truism can be reached by another route, which it may be instructive to turn aside for a moment to follow. A positive balance of trade is equivalent to investment, from the point of view of the home country, and it has the same influence as investment upon the level of effective demand in the home country. It represents a certain volume of demand for current home output without representing a supply of goods coming on to the home market (for the trade balance represents the home incomes earned by selling to foreigners *minus* that part of home incomes which is expended upon foreigners) and so gives rise to secondary employment. Thus the trade balance is one of the influences which determine the level of income, and consequently the level of saving, in the home country. Since the saving of a community, over any period of time, is equal to its investment for that period, saving is equal to home investment *plus* or *minus* the trade balance. New borrowing at home is equal to home investment, while lending is equal to saving. Therefore foreign lending is equal to the trade balance.

The truism, in the nature of the case, can throw no light upon the manner in which the equality is brought about. It can only tell us that if in fact there is a change in the balance of trade there must be an equal change in the balance of lending. In some circumstances, as we shall find, the two are directly bound together, but in general, though there are always cross-connections between them, they vary in response to independent sets of influences. If I take it into my head to buy a foreign security there is no reason why some compatriot of mine at the same moment should decide to curtail his purchases of imported goods.

The volume of imports and exports is determined by tastes, techniques and resources the world over, and by costs and incomes at home and abroad, which in turn are determined by the levels of money wages and of effective demand. The balance of lending is determined (given wealth and incomes) by relative rates of interest at home and abroad, and by all those considerations which may be lumped together under the heading of "the state of confidence." A fall in the home rate of interest (or a rise in rates abroad) or the growth of dismal expectations about home affairs will increase the desire to lend abroad. It is by such diverse influences that the balance of trade and the desire to lend are determined, and equality between them is preserved not by any natural tendency for the two to vary consonantly, but by the mechanism of supply and demand. The theory of the exchanges may be regarded as the analysis of the manner in which movements of the balance of trade and the balance of lending are equated to each other.

II

A change in the desire to lend abroad will tend to alter the exchange rate. The reaction upon the balance of trade of an alteration in the exchange rate must be examined at some length. Suppose that, after a certain exchange rate has been in force for some time, the amount which the inhabitants of the home country desire to lend abroad increases. At the ruling exchange rate the demand for foreign currency exceeds the supply and the exchange rate consequently falls. This has the effect of making home-produced goods appear cheaper to foreigners and so increasing the volume of exports. If the physical volume of exports increases their home price cannot fall, therefore the value of exports in terms of home currency must increase. But the effect on imports is more complicated. Foreign goods are now dearer at home, and while the physical volume of imports purchased out of a given income will decline, total expenditure upon them may increase. Thus a decline in the exchange rate will not necessarily increase the balance of trade. If the value of imports (reckoned in home currency) increases by more than the value of exports, then a fall in the exchange rate will reduce the balance of trade.

The argument may be treated in terms of four elasticities: the foreign elasticity of demand for exports, and the home elasticity of supply (which is influenced by the home elasticity of demand for exportable goods), the foreign elasticity of supply of imports and the home elasticity of demand for imports (which is influenced by the home elasticity of supply of rival commodities).[6]   For brevity we may speak of the demand for imports as "home demand," the demand for exports as "foreign demand," and so forth.

The actual change in imports and in exports which will come about as the result of a change in the exchange rate will depend partly upon the reaction on the demand for imports, and on the supply of exports, of a change in the balance of trade itself.   For instance, an increase in the balance of trade leads to an increase in home incomes, and consequently to an increase in expenditure upon imported goods; an increase in exports, or in home manufactures rival to imports, may lead to an increased importation of raw materials, while increased expenditure upon home-produced goods may raise the supply curve of exports.   But these effects influence the magnitude, not the direction, of the change in the balance of trade consequent upon a fall in the exchange rate,[7] for the secondary effects follow from the change in home incomes due to the change in the balance of trade, and if the balance of trade does not alter the secondary effects cannot occur.   It is therefore legitimate to discuss the initial effect upon the balance of trade in terms of the four elasticities, abstracting from the change in home incomes.

Let us first consider the export side of the balance sheet.   As we have seen, a fall in the exchange rate leads to an increase in the

---

[6] It is assumed throughout this and a following essay [Chap. 17 of this volume] that elasticities of supply are positive and of demand negative.   Discussions of the magnitude of elasticities must be taken to refer to their numerical, not their algebraical value.

[7] This is not perfectly accurate, for qualitative differences between different types of goods and of expenditure from different types of income may introduce complications into the simple analysis here set out.   For instance, suppose that the initial effect of a fall in the exchange rate is to increase the value of both exports and imports to the same extent, while export goods require a higher proportion of imported raw materials than the home goods whose output declines when expenditure upon imports increases.   Then the initial effect of a fall in the exchange rate is to leave the balance of trade unaltered while the final effect is to reduce it.   The increase in home incomes due to the increase in exports is then less than the reduction due to the increase in imports.

value of exports in terms of home currency. The extent of the increase depends upon the elasticity of foreign demand (which must be reckoned in terms of foreign currency). The increase in the value of exports will be smaller the smaller is the foreign elasticity of demand (given the home elasticity of supply). In the limit, if the foreign demand is perfectly inelastic there will be no increase in the volume of exports and consequently no increase in their value.

Next consider the influence of home elasticity of supply. If home supply is perfectly inelastic the volume of exports does not alter, their foreign price is unchanged and the value of exports increases in proportion to the fall in the exchange rate. If home supply is perfectly elastic, the home price is constant and the price to foreigners falls in proportion to the fall in the exchange rate. If the elasticity of home supply lies between zero and infinity the home price of exports is raised by an increase in their volume, and their price to the foreigner consequently falls less than in proportion to the fall in the exchange rate.

If the foreign elasticity of demand is equal to unity, so that expenditure is constant in terms of foreign currency, the value of exports is independent of the home elasticity of supply and increases in proportion to the fall in the exchange rate. If the foreign demand has less than unit elasticity, the increase in the value of exports will be greater the smaller is the increase in their physical volume, that is, the smaller is their elasticity of supply. Thus, when the foreign demand has less than unit elasticity the maximum possible rise in the value of exports is that which is brought about when their elasticity of supply is zero. The value of exports then increases in proportion to the fall in the exchange rate. So long as the foreign demand has less than unit elasticity any increase in the physical volume of exports means that their value increases less than in proportion to the fall in the exchange rate. On the other hand, when the foreign demand has an elasticity greater than unity, an increase in the volume of exports leads to an increase in the foreign expenditure upon them, and the value of exports increases more than in proportion to the fall in the exchange rate. The increase in the value of exports is then greater the greater is the elasticity of home supply.   In short, a high elasticity of home supply tends to reduce or to enhance the increase in the value of exports induced by a fall in the exchange rate according as the foreign elasticity of demand is less or greater than unity.

The minimum effect of a fall in the exchange rate upon the value of exports is produced when the foreign demand has zero elasticity.   There is then no increase in exports.   The maximum effect is produced when a perfectly elastic foreign demand is combined with a perfectly elastic home supply.   The increase in the value of exports is then indefinitely great.

We must now consider the import side of the balance sheet. The value of imports in terms of home currency will increase or diminish according as the elasticity of demand is less or greater than unity.

If the foreign supply is perfectly elastic, so that the foreign price of imports is constant, then their home price will rise in proportion to the fall in the exchange rate; while if the foreign supply is less than perfectly elastic a curtailment of output will cause a fall in the foreign price, so that the home price rises by less than the fall in the exchange rate.   It can be seen, therefore, that when the home demand has less than unit elasticity, the value of imports will rise by more, and when it has greater than unit elasticity, will fall by more, the greater is the foreign elasticity of supply.

A fall in the exchange rate produces the maximum increase in the value of imports when home demand is perfectly inelastic.   In this case the physical volume of imports is constant, their foreign price is unchanged, and both their price and their value in home currency are increased in proportion to the fall in the exchange rate. The maximum decrease is produced when a perfectly elastic home demand is combined with a perfectly elastic foreign supply.   In this case imports are reduced to zero.

We must now combine the two sides of our balance sheet.   The relations between the various factors in the problem are complicated,[8] but some simple generalizations can be made.   So long

---

[8] The general relationships can be expressed mathematically.   Let I be the

as the home demand for imports has more than unit elasticity, a fall in the exchange rate must increase the balance of trade, for the value of imports falls, while the value of exports is at worst constant. If the home demand for imports has less than unit elasticity, the balance of trade will still increase if there is a sufficient increase in the value of exports, but if the elasticity of foreign demand for exports is not sufficient to compensate for a low elasticity of home demand, then a fall in the exchange rate will reduce the balance of trade.

Before proceeding further, the relative magnitudes of the values of imports and exports must be considered. For instance, if the elasticities are such that a fall in the exchange rate brings about an equal proportional increase in the value both of imports and of

---

quantity of imports, E of exports, p the home price of imports, and q the home price of exports. Let ϵ_h and ϵ_f be respectively the elasticities of home demand for imports and of foreign demand for exports, η_h and η_f the elasticities of home supply of exports and of foreign supply of imports. Consider the effect of a small fall in the rate of exchange in the proportion k. Let the home price of exports rise by δq. Then the fall in the foreign price of exports is:

$$q - (1 - k)(q + \delta q) = kq - \delta q, \ k \text{ being small.}$$

We now have

$$\eta_h = \frac{\delta E}{E} \Big/ \frac{\delta q}{q},$$

and

$$\epsilon_f = \frac{\delta E}{E} \Big/ k - \frac{\delta q}{q}.$$

In the same way,

$$\eta_f = -\frac{\delta I}{I} \Big/ k - \frac{\delta p}{p}$$

and

$$\epsilon_h = -\frac{\delta I}{I} \Big/ \frac{\delta p}{p}.$$

The increase in the balance of trade is $(E\delta q + q\delta E) - (I\delta p + p\delta I)$, which can be reduced to:

$$k \left\{ Eq \frac{\epsilon_f(1 + \eta_h)}{\epsilon_f + \eta_h} - Ip \frac{\eta_f(1 - \epsilon_h)}{\eta_f + \epsilon_h} \right\}.$$

exports, then if imports were equal to exports in the first instance, so that the balance of trade was zero, it will remain zero when the exchange falls. If it was positive in the first instance, it will increase, for an equal proportional increase in exports and imports entails a larger absolute increase in exports if exports exceeded imports in the first instance. If the balance of trade was negative in the first instance it will be reduced by the fall in the exchange.[9] When the balance of trade is zero in the first instance, then if the elasticity of foreign demand for exports is greater than unity, a fall in exchange rate must increase the balance of trade, for the value of exports is increased more than in proportion to the fall in exchange rate, while, in the worst case, where home demand is perfectly inelastic, the value of imports is increased only in proportion to the fall in exchange rate. If the elasticity of foreign demand for exports is less than unity, the balance of trade will still increase provided that the elasticity of home demand is sufficient to compensate for the low elasticity of foreign demand for exports.

It is now clear that the balance of trade may increase with a fall in the exchange rate even if the elasticities of foreign and home demand are both less than unity. In the simple case, where trade is balanced in the first instance, and the elasticities of home and foreign supply are both infinite, the balance of trade will increase or diminish according as the sum of the elasticities of home and of foreign demand is greater or less than unity, that is, according as

---

[9] The effect of inequality between Eq and Ip (in the notation of the foregoing footnote) can be shown most simply in the case in which the elasticities of foreign and home supply are both infinite.

When η_f and η_h are both equal to infinity, the increase in the balance of trade becomes:

$$k\{\,Eq\epsilon_h + Ip\epsilon_h - Ip\,\}$$
$$\text{or } kEq\left\{\,\epsilon_f + \epsilon_h\frac{Ip}{Eq} - \frac{Ip}{Eq}\,\right\}$$

It follows that, for the balance of trade to increase with a fall in exchange rate, it is a sufficient, though not a necessary, condition that the elasticity of foreign demand should exceed the ratio of imports to exports.

the deficiency below unity of the one is more or less than offset by the excess above zero of the other.[10]

The repercussions of a change in the balance of trade upon the home demand for imports and supply of exports must be brought into account when the direction of the change has been discussed in terms of the four elasticities. The final change in the balance of trade, in either direction, will be smaller, the greater are the change in demand for imports and the change in supply of exports brought about by the changes in home activity and expenditure which are due to the initial change in the balance of trade. Further, since foreigners are impoverished or enriched by a decrease or increase in the balance of trade of the world with the home country, there is an additional secondary reaction upon the foreign demand for exports, which also tends to mitigate the change in the home balance of trade.

If, at a given exchange rate, the balance of trade falls short of the balance of lending the exchange depreciates. Under favourable conditions this leads to a sufficient increase in the balance of trade to prevent any further fall in the exchange rate. The most favourable conditions from this point of view are, as we have seen, those in which there is perfectly elastic foreign demand and home supply of exportable goods. These conditions prevail as between countries on the gold standard. In the home country gold is on sale at a fixed price, while transport costs are very low and do not rise, except in extreme circumstances, with an increase in the volume of the commodity handled. Supply is therefore perfectly elastic under normal conditions. In foreign countries demand is perfectly elastic at a fixed price. Any tendency for the exchange rate to fall will therefore lead to an indefinitely large export of gold. Similarly home demand and foreign supply are

---

[10] Cf. A. P. Lerner, *The Economics of Control*, p. 377. In this case not only are η_f and η_h both infinite, but also Eq is equal to Ip, so that the expression for the increase in the balance of trade becomes:

$$kEq\{\epsilon_f + \epsilon_h - 1\}$$

which is positive or negative according as $\epsilon_f + \epsilon_h$ is greater or less than unity.

perfectly elastic, so that any rise in the exchange rate would lead to an indefinitely large import of gold. It is for this reason that movements in the exchange rate cannot occur (beyond the limits set by transport costs) so long as the gold standard is maintained.

Other items in the trade balance have certain peculiar features of their own. Interest on foreign capital which is fixed in terms of home currency represents an export of which the value cannot increase in response to a fall in the exchange rate[11] (though, if debtors are distressed, the reduction in the burden upon them brought about by a rise in the exchange value of their currency may have an important effect in preventing default). For a country in whose total exports this item is an important element, the beneficial effect upon the balance of trade of a fall in the exchange rate is *pro tanto* diminished. From the point of view of a debtor country, interest payments fixed in terms of the creditor's currency represent an import which rises in value in proportion to a fall in the exchange rate,[12] and if such obligations are considerable (and default is not contemplated) exchange depreciation may be extremely dangerous to the balance of trade. Obligations fixed in terms of the debtor's currency represent, from the creditor's point of view, an export whose value rises in proportion to the fall in the exchange rate.[13] They tend, therefore, to make the reaction of depreciation upon the balance of trade favourable. From the debtor's point of view they represent an import which is unaffected by a fall in the exchange rate,[14] and so far as their influence goes, the reaction of depreciation upon the balance of trade is neutral.

A country whose main exports are manufactured goods in which

---

[11] Obligations to the home country fixed in home currency may be regarded from a formal point of view as an export for which the foreign demand is perfectly inelastic.

[12] They may be regarded as an import for which the home demand is perfectly inelastic.

[13] They may be regarded as an export of which the home supply is perfectly inelastic.

[14] They may be regarded as an import for which the elasticity of demand is unity.

it has no monopoly will normally enjoy a fairly elastic foreign demand, combined, except in boom conditions, with a highly elastic home supply. Its exports will therefore respond favourably to a fall in the exchange rate. On the other hand, if its imports consist mainly of food and raw materials which cannot be produced at home, the demand for imports is probably inelastic, while if it does not represent a predominant part of the world market the foreign supply will probably be highly elastic. The effect of depreciation upon imports is then unlikely to be favourable, and the benefit to the balance of trade of an increased value of exports may be cancelled out by an increased value of imports.[15] Moreover, if the balance of trade does tend to increase, the extent of the increase will be limited by the increased importation of raw materials which results from increased activity.

A country which is dependent upon the production of commodities (especially raw materials) of which it provides a predominant part of the world supply will normally find the demand for its exports relatively inelastic, for it has no rivals at whose expense its sales can be increased, and it is faced with the demand for each commodity as such. In this case an inelastic home supply will be a source of strength.[16] Countries of this type normally import manufactured goods for which the demand is likely to be relatively elastic, compared to the demand for foodstuffs. In respect to imports, therefore, the effect of depreciation upon the balance of trade is unlikely to be adverse.

In any given situation, with given wages, there will be, for any one country, a certain rate of exchange at which its balance of trade is at a maximum. This may be called the *optimum* exchange rate.

---

[15] Great Britain in 1931 escaped from the dangers of this situation because her depreciation was mainly *vis-à-vis* rival manufacturing nations, while parity was maintained with countries responsible for a high proportion of her sources of raw materials.

[16] For instance, the remarkable steadiness of Australia's output of wool was an important factor in the benefit which she derived from depreciation in 1931. In default of a naturally inelastic supply monopolistic restriction schemes are widely resorted to by raw-material-producing countries.

It is the "optimum" rate in a strictly limited sense, for a fall in the exchange rate is likely to raise the price of imports relatively to exports, thus reducing real income per unit of output in the home country,[17] so that the rate which maximises the trade balance is by no means necessarily the most desirable rate from every point of view. Moreover, a change in the exchange rate of one of the major countries produces so many reactions upon the rest of the world, and such far-reaching economic and political effects, that it would be absurd to treat it merely in terms of elasticities of supply and demand. But such treatment is a necessary part of the more general discussion of exchange problems, and it is to this narrow sphere that the present analysis is confined.

If the exchange rate stands at the optimum level, any chance fall will precipitate a progressive decline, for each fall in the rate reduces the trade balance and promotes a further fall. In the absence of control, the exchange rate is stable only so long as it stands above the optimum level. But the value of the optimum rate largely depends upon the length of the run which is being considered. From the point of view of very short-period reactions to a fall in the exchange rate, both the foreign elasticity of demand for exports and the home elasticity of demand for imports are likely to be very low (apart from gold), even when over a longer run they would prove to be great, for the fall in the price of the one and rise in the price of the other takes time to produce its effect upon the decisions of purchasers, while, if prices are agreed in terms of the exporter's currency, the force of inertia (and prearranged contracts) delays the rise in the value of exports.[18] Thus it appears at first sight that from the point of view of a very short run the exchange rate

---

[17] See below, p. 401.

[18] If prices are agreed in terms of the importer's currency the short-period reaction of a fall in the exchange rate is favourable. For import prices fail to rise, so that inelastic home demand is innocuous, while, in the first instance, the value of exports rises in proportion to the fall in the exchange rate. When the Belga was devalued exporters were urged to continue to charge the same foreign prices and not to increase their output. The effect upon the balance of trade is the same, in such a case, as though home supply were perfectly inelastic.

can never be above the optimum, and that any country which has abandoned the gold standard must be in chronic danger, no matter how strong its long-period position, that the smallest increase in the balance of lending will precipitate a sudden collapse in the exchange rate.

But against this danger there are two important safeguards. So long as any country in the world adheres to the gold standard there is one commodity for which even the short-run demand is perfectly elastic, while if there is a market in gold in the country whose exchange is falling the supply of this export will be highly elastic, though less elastic than when it is officially on offer at a fixed price.[19] Exports of gold will thus serve as a stop-gap, and prevent the exchange rate from collapsing at a breath.

Further, a fall in the exchange rate which is not expected to last will call professional speculators into action. Purchases of the depreciated currency, representing a form of foreign borrowing, will bridge the gap in the balance of payments and prevent the exchange rate from falling beyond the level at which it is expected later to come to rest. Thus time will be allowed for a moderate fall in the exchange rate to produce its effect upon the balance of trade, and a slight fall will not necessarily lead to an immediate collapse.

On the other hand, as is only too well known, if speculators read a slight fall as a sign that a further fall is to be expected, a violent increase in foreign lending (in the wide sense) will take place and the balance of trade will have no time to react to an initial fall in the exchange rate before a further fall takes place. In this case only official intervention can prevent a sudden collapse.

What happens if there is no intervention, while foreign lending remains constant or increases as the exchange rate falls below the level of the short-period optimum? The rate is then sent hurtling towards zero. But on its way thither it must necessarily pass through a pessimum point (at which the balance of trade is a minimum) and come to rest somewhere below it. For a sufficiently violent rise in the price of imports must ultimately choke demand,

---

[19] See Einzig, *Bankers, Statesmen and Economists*, p. 86.

and even if exports fail to react, in the flurry of the moment, the value of imports must somewhere begin to fall off.

III

A change in the desire to lend abroad can bring about a change in the balance of trade (and consequently in the actual rate of lending) only by way of its effect in altering the exchange rate. But a change in the balance of trade produces a direct effect upon the balance of lending. The rate of saving in the home country exceeds or falls short of the rate of home investment according as the balance of trade is positive or negative. In the normal way a part of the increase in the wealth of individuals in the home country represented by home saving will be used to acquire foreign securities or to make loans abroad. Thus, when the balance of trade increases, and home saving consequently increases, this in itself will lead to an increase in foreign lending. Similarly, when the balance of trade falls off, lending by the world to the home country is directly increased. To look at the same thing in another way, if the balance of trade falls off, there is an increase in the excess of the rate at which home securities (representing borrowing for home investment) are coming on to the market over the rate at which wealth at home is accumulating, while, at the same time, in the rest of the world there is an increase in the excess of the rate at which wealth is accumulating over the flow of new securities, and the world is inclined to buy home securities at a greater rate than before.

If the world capital market were perfect, so that owners of wealth, the world over, were completely indifferent as between home and foreign securities, then, when the home balance of trade falls off, the excess new savings of the world would be devoted to buying the excess of new home securities over new home savings, without any change in relative interest rates, and the rate of exchange would remain in equilibrium in spite of the fall in the balance of trade. This is normally the case as between different parts of the same country.

But the international capital market is not perfect, and, if foreigners are to be attracted to buy home securities at an increased rate, the home rate of interest must rise relatively to the foreign rate. If the home rate of interest does not rise sufficiently, foreign lending to the home country will fail to increase by as much as the balance of trade has fallen, and the rate of exchange will consequently fall.

IV

We must now consider the effect of a change in the home rate of interest upon the rate of exchange. Suppose that a rise in the home rate of interest occurs, other things remaining the same. A rise in the home rate of interest produces its effect upon the exchange in three stages.

The first stage is represented by the additional foreign borrowing (or reduction of lending) which is produced by a rise in the relative rate of interest at home. The increment of borrowing may be divided into two parts, a small increase in the share of world savings devoted to the home country, which will persist (apart from unfavourable reactions upon confidence) so long as the rise in the relative home rate is maintained, and a larger, non-recurrent movement due to the transfer of funds, formerly held abroad, to the home country. Each transfer can only affect the exchange rate as it is made, and to maintain a given volume of transfers over an appreciable length of time the relative rate of interest would have to rise continuously. Thus the balance of payments is not in equilibrium to a given exchange rate and interest rate unless no transfers are taking place.[20]

---

[20] Mr. Sayers ("Japan's Balance of Trade," *Economica*, February 1935, p. 52) suggests that the exchange is in equilibrium when no short-term lending or borrowing is taking place. For practical purposes short-term borrowing provides a useful index of the purely transfer element in the international movement of funds, though the two are not completely identical.

Equilibrium, in the sense that no transfer borrowing or gold movements are taking place, is not the same thing as full equilibrium. Full long-period equilibrium of the balance of payments does not obtain so long as any lending or borrowing is taking place at all. For so long as borrowing is taking place the

There is here a close analogy to gold movements, which also constitute a symptom of disequilibrium in the balance of payments. If the home authorities are subject to the legal obligations of the gold standard or, under influence of more general considerations, desire to maintain a given exchange rate it is the objective of their policy to establish equilibrium in the balance of payments at the exchange rate which they desire to establish, that is to say, to create a situation in which neither gold movements nor transfer lending are taking place at the desired exchange rate.

The second stage in the operation of the rate of interest is its effect upon the balance of trade.   A rise in the home rate of interest will curtail investment and so lead to a decline in activity and incomes in the home country.   Expenditure upon imports will therefore fall off.   Foreign export industries will contract, and the consequent decrease of incomes and expenditure in the rest of the world will reduce the demand for goods exported by the home country. But a part of the reduction in foreign incomes will be subtracted from saving, and even if the supply price of exports in the home country is unaffected it is impossible that exports should be curtailed to the same extent as imports.   Moreover, the supply price of a given volume of exports is likely to be reduced, for exportable goods are partly consumed at home and a reduction in home demand will increase the supply available for export, while services common to all industries, such as transport, are likely to become cheaper to the exporters when the total demand for them is reduced.

---

invisible imports represented by interest payments are mounting up, and as time goes by persistent borrowing will lead, other things equal, to a gradually falling balance of trade. (If, as sometimes occurs, the borrowing corresponds to home investment which would not have taken place without it, other things are not equal, for increased capital equipment will have its reaction upon the other items in the balance of trade.) Full long-period equilibrium is reached only when investment and saving are equal to zero, and imports are equal to exports—a state of affairs which has never been attained in actuality. The present discussion is not concerned with these remote effects, and must be regarded as applying to a length of run within which the accumulation of interest payments is small relatively to current borrowing.

Thus, in spite of the decrease in foreign demand, the volume of exports may actually increase. In short, a decline of effective demand at home tends to decrease imports relatively to exports and so to increase the balance of trade.

Equilibrium with the given exchange rate is reached when, at a constant rate of interest, the balance of trade, excluding gold, is brought to equality with the balance of recurrent lending, and no transfer of funds or movement of gold is taking place. But the position is only attained at the expense of unemployment at home, and any reduction in the rate of interest, by stimulating activity, would set up a tendency for the exchange to fall. The third stage is not reached until increased unemployment has brought about a fall in money wages in the home country.

The effect of an all-round reduction in money wages in the home country upon the balance of trade is precisely similar, apart from obligations which are fixed in terms of home currency, to the effect of a corresponding fall in the exchange rate, for both represent a decline in home incomes and price measured in terms of foreign currencies. The effect upon the value of imports and of exports in terms of foreign currency is the same for a fall in home wages as for a fall in the exchange rate, while the home purchasing power of a given amount of foreign currency increases equally in each case. Obligations fixed in terms of home currency introduce a difference between the two, for while these are unaffected by a fall in the exchange rate, the real burden of payments, and the real value of receipts, are increased by a fall in home wages.[21] There is a further difference between the effect of pressure upon the exchange rate and of pressure upon the level of money wages which is of the utmost practical importance. While a fall in the exchange will have an automatic and equal effect on the relationship of all

---

[21] This applies equally to internal and external obligations, and the increase in the share of rentiers in the national income, brought about by a fall in money wages, may have some reaction upon the demand for imports, which would introduce a further difference between the effect on the balance of trade of a fall in money wages and of a corresponding fall in the exchange rate.

home prices to foreign prices, a fall in money wages is never spread evenly over all industries and relative prices inside the home country are never unaffected by it.   But for the purposes of our present formal treatment we will consider a case in which the unemployment caused by a rise in the rate of interest brings about an equal proportionate fall in all wages rates.

Just as, with given money wage rates, there is an optimum exchange rate, at which the balance of trade is at a maximum, so, with a given exchange rate, there is an optimum level of money wages.   In circumstances in which a fall in the exchange rate would lead to an increase (in terms of home currency) in the value of imports greater than the increase in exports (apart from monetary obligations[22]), an equivalent fall in wages would lead to a decline in the value of exports greater than the decline in value of imports. In such circumstances it is a rise, not a fall, in the level of wages which would redress the balance of payments.[23]   But we may suppose for our present purpose that the pre-existing level of money wages was above the optimum in this sense.   A fall in money wages will then increase the balance of trade corresponding to a given level of effective demand at home.   If the interest rate is maintained at its higher level after wages have fallen the exchange will tend to appreciate; the rate of interest may then be lowered and a recovery of employment allowed to take place.

It is in this way that a tendency for the exchange rate to alter can be offset by appropriate changes in the home rate of interest.

---

[22] A fall in the exchange rate will have a more favourable effect upon the balance of trade (reckoned in terms of home wage units) than a corresponding fall in wages where payments to foreigners fixed in terms of home currency are an appreciable element in imports, and a less favourable effect when receipts paid in terms of home currency are an appreciable element in exports.

[23] If the exchange has once been allowed to fall below its long-run optimum level, the authorities are landed in an extremely awkward situation.   For, while a rise in the rate of interest will produce a beneficial effect upon the exchange at the first stage of its operation and, by reducing employment, at the second stage, its effect at the third stage will make matters worse than ever.   In such a case curtailment of imports (by tariffs and so forth) and of foreign lending, combined with direct intervention in the exchange market, will provide the only remedy.

V

It is now obvious that there is no one rate of exchange which is the equilibrium rate corresponding to a given state of world demands and techniques. In any given situation there is an equilibrium rate corresponding to each rate of interest and level of effective demand, and any rate of exchange, within very wide limits, can be turned into the equilibrium rate by altering the rate of interest appropriately. Moreover, any rate of exchange can be made compatible with any rate of interest provided that money wages can be sufficiently altered. The notion of *the* equilibrium exchange rate is a chimera. The rate of exchange, the rate of interest, the level of effective demand and the level of money wages react upon each other like the balls in Marshall's bowl, and no one is determined unless all the rest are given.[24]

It will be observed that in the foregoing argument the operations of the gold standard are treated in the same terms as the workings of so-called free exchanges. The only difference between the two is that under the gold standard the authorities are committed to one particular exchange rate so that the equilibrium of the balance of payments must be preserved in face of changing conditions entirely by inducing changes in the level of incomes, and not at all by allowing variations in the exchange rate, while under free exchanges the authorities have some measure of latitude in their choice between the two methods of adjustment.

For a country in which money wages do not readily yield to the pressure of unemployment the gold standard can be maintained, in an era of rapid change, only by means of recurrent periods of severe unemployment,[25] and it is the realisation of this fact which has in recent years so much impaired the popularity of the gold standard.

---

[24] One more ball in the bowl is represented by expectations as to the future course of the exchange rate; see p. 97.

[25] The monetary history of Great Britain between 1925 and 1931 is the history of a struggle between the level of money wages and the rate of exchange. It was appropriate that the final collapse of the gold standard should have been brought about by a protest against cuts in pay.

5

THE THEORY OF FOREIGN EXCHANGES*

By Fritz Machlup‖‡

1. Excessive specialisation has led to the disturbing fact that the techniques developed in economic theory are insufficiently employed in the various applied fields. The courses and textbook chapters on Money and Banking, Cycles, International Trade, Transportation, Public Utilities and others—are all cases in point. The beginning student of economics wonders why he had to waste time on the "useless" tools of analysis that were presented to him in Value Theory and which he never afterwards found of service when he came to the applied fields.

One of the objectives of this article is to show how the simple curve analysis can be used to advantage in the theory of foreign exchanges. The presentation here will be an abridged statement of the essentials.[1] An exposition in a textbook or in class would of course have to be less condensed and would have to include numerous illustrations in order to cover the abstractions with realistic dressing.

Another objective of the article is to incorporate into the theory of foreign exchanges relevant results of recent work in monetary economics. New practices of exchange stabilisation funds, on the one hand, new or modernised economic doctrines on the other

---

* *Economica*, Volume VI (New Series), November 1939, pages 375–397, and February 1940, pages 23–49. Reprinted by the courtesy of *Economica* and the author.

‖ The Johns Hopkins University.

‡ The following article is reprinted without significant changes from the original text.

[1] Much of the subject matter presented here is based on Professor Haberler's *International Trade*.

hand[2]—both developed only during the last few years—make it necessary to rewrite foreign exchange theory in significant parts. An attempt in this direction will be made, especially in the later sections of this article.

Section I will lay out the conceptual scheme and some simplifying assumptions for the demand and supply analysis of the foreign exchange market. Section II will discuss the factors that determine the elasticities of supply and demand on a foreign exchange market when transactions result exclusively from commodity trade between two countries with independent currencies. Section III will deal with the effects on foreign exchanges of capital movements, unilateral payments, and payments for services, between countries with independent currencies. Section IV will introduce the assumptions of the gold standard in its old and modern forms, and will discuss the causes and effects of gold flows between the countries concerned. Section V will examine the supply and demand conditions on a foreign exchange market under the influence of private pegging and speculating activities, with special consideration of their effects upon interest rates.

I

2. For the sake of simplicity we shall combine the spot and forward exchange markets, and also the foreign exchange markets at the domestic place (say New York) and at the foreign place (say Paris), into *one* perfect market. These assumptions might be easily dropped at any stage of the analysis, in order to demonstrate the functioning of speculation in spot and forward exchanges, and of arbitrage between the local and foreign markets. Such demon-

---

[2] We refer only summarily to the contributions by J. M. Keynes, *The General Theory of Employment, Interest and Money;* Arthur Gayer, *Monetary Policy and Economic Stabilisation;* G. von Haberler, *Prosperity and Depression;* Jacob Viner, *Studies in the Theory of International Trade;* F. A. von Hayek, *Monetary Nationalism and International Stability;* P. Barrett Whale, "International Trade in the Absence of an International Standard," *Economica,* 1936, "The Work of the Pre-war Gold Standard," *Economica,* 1937; F. W. Paish, "Banking Policy and the Balance of International Payments," *Economica,* 1936; Thos. Balogh, "Some Theoretical Aspects of the Gold Problem," *Economica,* 1937.

strations would prove that the merger of all these partial markets into a single foreign exchange market with the one currency as the "commodity" and the other currency as "money" assumes little away from the facts of the real world.

It is not difficult, for example, to translate the demand for dollars on the Paris market into a supply of francs on the combined foreign exchange market, and likewise the supply of dollars on the Paris market into a demand for francs on the combined foreign exchange market.[3]

To simplify further we shall speak of two countries only. The abstraction from the existence of more than two countries could be immediately dropped if the device were adopted to treat the "rest of the world" as the second country and some composite of the various currencies as *the* foreign exchange. It is, however, less confusing to discuss matters first with reference to two countries only.

3. In good analytical fashion we shall examine the various sources of supply and purposes of demand, one by one. Let us thus take commodity trade between the two countries as the first thing to be isolated.

If commodity exports are to be the only source of supply of foreign exchange, and commodity imports the only purpose of demand, we must abstract from the gold standard in its various forms. Sales of gold would constitute a supply of foreign exchange,

---

[3] It is a good undergraduate exercise to practice such a translation: starting from a demand curve for dollars in terms of francs the amounts of dollars are shown by the horizontal axis (x), the amounts of francs offered in exchange for these dollars are shown by the rectangle (xy); this gives a supply curve of francs for dollars where the abscissae correspond to the values of the rectangles in the original demand curve, while the ordinates on the new supply curve, i.e. the prices of francs in terms of dollars, correspond to the quotient of the abscissae divided by the values of the rectangles $\left(\dfrac{x}{xy}\right)$ of the original demand curve. The analogous calculation has to be done in order to transform the original supply curve of dollars in terms of francs into a demand curve for francs in terms of dollars. This sounds complicated—yet every sophomore ought to be able to do it, or he has never grasped the meaning of demand and supply curves.

and gold purchases demand for foreign exchange. Gold movements will be introduced only at a later stage of the analysis.

If commodity trade is to be the only factor behind supply and demand on the foreign exchange market, we must abstract, furthermore, from the supply out of old stocks (foreign balances held by individuals, banks or official funds) and out of new debts (due to foreigners), and from the demand for foreign exchange for purposes of accumulating new stocks of foreign balances and of reducing old debts. In short, foreign lending and borrowing, i.e. the acquisition and diminution of foreign balances and debts, are ruled out at this stage; they will be introduced later.

It goes without saying that foreign long-term investments, unilateral payments, and the exchange of invisible services are all assumed away if commodity trade is to be studied in isolation.

4. It is clear that the equality of exports and imports follows logically from these assumptions. If foreign lending and borrowing (and the other non-commodity transactions) are ruled out entirely, export surpluses or import surpluses cannot exist even in the shortest run.

It would, of course, appear too unrealistic to assume that the goods imported and exported cross the border at exactly the same moment. And it would be difficult to see how an increase in the demand for imports should make for a *simultaneous* increase of imports and exports if the moments at which the goods pass the frontier or the customs house were regarded as the relevant points of time.

This slight difficulty disappears if we take as relevant the moment at which the export orders are given and received and if simultaneously with each order the importer buys foreign exchange and the exporter sells foreign exchange. This assumption corresponds, incidentally, to the actual practice of wholesale trade: at the time the business is concluded, the importer covers on the forward exchange market the foreign exchange needed for payment for the orders given, and the exporter sells the foreign exchange expected for the order received.

If every importer buys the foreign exchange at the time when he gives the order, and if he cannot buy the foreign exchange (directly or indirectly) from anybody but an exporter, it follows that imports cannot exceed, or fall short of, exports, in the sense defined, for even the shortest instants of time.

The volume of imports and exports, however, will depend on the foreign exchange rate at which the amounts of exchange demanded and supplied are equal.

5. A rise in the foreign exchange rate[4] makes imported commodities more expensive in terms of dollars, and exported commodities cheaper in terms of the foreign currency. A fall in the foreign exchange rate makes imported commodities cheaper in terms of dollars and exported commodities more expensive in terms of the foreign currency. This explains why the importers' demand curve for foreign exchange will usually (abstracting from speculative transactions) have a downward slope from the left to the right, and why the exporters' supply curve of foreign exchange will usually have an upward slope from the left to the right. Exceptions will be discussed presently.

Every demand and supply curve must refer to a certain period of time which is allowed for the depicted changes and adjustments to take place. Curves which do not allow any time for market reactions to take place are usually called "instantaneous curves." Apart from these we should for our purposes distinguish at least three sets of curves. The *shortest period* allows only for the effects of the change in foreign exchange rates upon import and export orders, with domestic prices in the two countries unchanged. These effects are too provisional to be of much analytical value, because changes in the quantities of goods to be ordered will affect, with little or no delay, the prices at which the various producers are willing to sell, or the various distributors are willing to buy.

The *short period* allows, therefore, for both reactions to take place: it shows, for example, how the quantities of foreign exchange supplied by exporters will react upon a rise in the foreign exchange

---

[4] Throughout this article the foreign exchange rate is assumed to be expressed in terms of the amount of domestic currency exchanged per unit of foreign currency.

rate after the export industries have adapted their selling prices in dollars to the increase in business.

In other words, the short period demand and supply curves of foreign exchange are not drawn on basis of "given commodity prices" in the two countries, but on basis of "given demand and supply conditions" in the commodity markets of the two countries. These given conditions are the traditional short period curves which assume given tastes of consumers and given fixed equipment of producers.

The *long period* curves on the foreign exchange market are based on long period conditions in the commodity markets of the two countries; the main adjustment of supply, for example, which is allowed to take place in the long run is, of course, that of plant capacity. It is understood that an increase in exports which is expected to be lasting may induce producers to expand plant capacity and to supply their products, after this adoption, in increased quantities or at lower prices. Consequently, the long period curves of the foreign exchange market will be more elastic than the short period curves.

In what follows we shall be concerned with a *short-period* analysis.

6. The argument that short run supply implies *some* lapse of time until the reaction to a change in price takes place does not restrict the validity of the statement that, under the enumerated conditions, exports and imports must balance for any interval of time. Assume that DD' and SS' (Fig. 1) are the short period curves for the foreign exchange market. Exports equal imports at the foreign exchange market. Exports equal imports at the foreign exchange rate OQ. A sudden change in tastes makes for an increased demand for foreign exchange for increased imports. At the given rate, OQ, the amount demanded would be ON, an amount which is, of course, not to be had. Therefore the exchange rate will rise. Under the assumption that the short-run reaction of supply takes time but no time is allowed, it will rise to OT. At this increased rate, the quantity of foreign exchange demanded (OM) will be no greater than before, which is obvious as long as the "instantaneous supply" is assumed to be perfectly inelastic.

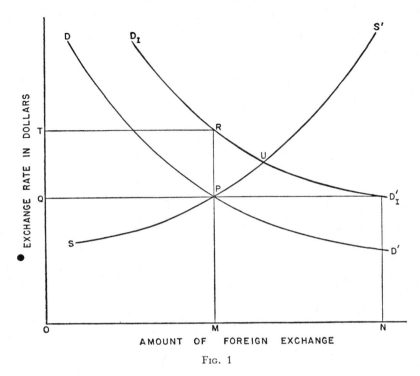

FIG. 1

It need hardly be mentioned that exports equal imports both in terms of foreign exchange $(OM = OM)$ and in terms of dollars $(OMRT = OMRT)$. The volume of exports and imports has increased in terms of dollars $(OMRT > OMPQ)$ and remained unchanged in terms of the foreign currency $(OM = OM)$.

The described situation based on a zero elasticity of the instantaneous supply corresponds to Professor Taussig's "*impact theory*" of foreign exchange rates under dislocated currencies. (*International Trade*, pp. 344–345.)

It corresponds more to the conditions of reality if we assume that the reactions on the supply side begin to take place after a trivial lapse of time: If it is not misplaced concreteness to transform operational time into clock-time, one may assume that the reactions on the part of exporters will start after no more than a few minutes—because at the higher exchange rates much money can be made by arbitrage in international commodities. More and more of the short-run elasticity of supply will come into play the more minutes, hours or days we allow to pass. A theory which does not concern itself with minute-by-minute oscillations of the market will neglect the instantaneous inelasticities and proceed to the elasticities of the short period.

II

7. The study of the elasticities of supply and demand is, thus, the core of the theory of foreign exchange rates. If, under our present assumptions, commodity imports are the substance behind the demand for foreign exchange, and commodity exports the substance behind the supply of foreign exchange, we have to turn to the conditions of the domestic demand for, and foreign supply of, our imports, and to the conditions of the foreign demand for, and domestic supply of, our exports.

Let us begin with the *supply of foreign exchange*, that is, the export of commodities. What determines the increase (or decrease) in export which is brought about by a certain rise (or fall) in the foreign exchange rate?

To be quite modern in the emphasis placed upon regulations, we may list in the first place the foreign restrictions which are directed against an increase in imports. If a quota had been established by foreign nations for all possible import articles and if the quota had been completely exhausted in all articles, it is clear that a rise in the foreign exchange rate cannot bring about any rise in our exports, and hence in the amount of foreign exchange. The elasticity in the foreign demand for our exports, that is to say, the elasticity of supply of foreign exchange, would be zero (or negative) above a certain rate. Below this rate the supply of foreign exchange would not be perfectly inelastic, because our exports can certainly fall below the limit set by quotas; below the critical rate there would then be numerous articles in which the foreign import quotas were not exhausted and, hence, in this range our exports would be allowed to rise and to fall as the foreign exchange rate rises or falls.

Tariffs at a given level play a different role. If a certain quantity of goods were sold under the given tariff and at a certain foreign exchange rate, a larger quantity could be sold if a rise in the foreign exchange rate made the goods cheaper for foreign buyers. If a considerable portion of the price paid by the foreign buyer in terms of his currency consists of a specific import duty, a rise (or fall) in the exchange rate will reduce (or raise) the price paid by the buyer only by a smaller percentage. The foreign demand for our exports will thus become less sensitive to changes in the foreign exchange rate. The role of the tariff is analogous to the role played by the foreign cost of transportation and distribution. The higher these costs the less sensitive is the demand to exchange rate fluctuations.

8. Foreign import restrictions are, as we have seen, factors influencing the elasticity of foreign demand for our exports. It does not need any detailed explanation when we state next that *the elasticity of supply of foreign exchange will be higher, the higher is the elasticity of the foreign demand for the articles which we export.*

But this is not all. The same or similar products may be produced also in the foreign country. The price of our exports is reduced (raised) for foreign buyers as the exchange rate rises (falls). The increase (decrease) in our exports will then depend, in part, on the reduction (increase) in output by the foreign producers. If the foreign supply, which competes with our exports, is very elastic, that is if their output falls (rises) much as our exports are offered at reduced (increased) prices in terms of their currency, our exports will increase (decrease) by relatively more. We can thus state that *the elasticity of supply of foreign exchange will be higher, the higher is the elasticity of supply of foreign products which compete in the foreign market with our exports.*

This second factor is rather important. It is this factor which may be decisive in making the elasticity of supply of foreign exchange a positive value (i.e. in giving the curve an upward slope from the left to the right) in cases where the foreign demand for the articles which we export happens to possess an elasticity smaller than unity. With an elasticity of demand less than unity the quantity of goods demanded would increase as the goods become cheaper, but it would not increase by the same percentage; the amount of foreign money spent on the goods would thus decrease.

The elasticity of supply of foreign exchange would then be negative (i.e. the supply curve would be backward-rising from the right to the left). But if the lower price (in terms of foreign currency) at the same time reduces the supply from foreign competitors, enough business might accrue to our exporters to raise the amount of foreign exchange received for our exports. In short, even when the elasticity of demand, on the foreign market, for the *articles* which we export is smaller than unity, the elasticity of demand for *our* exports may be greater than unity if the supply by foreign rival producers is sufficiently elastic.

We must add that in all probability the elasticity of foreign demand for our exports ("our" stands for almost any one country) is greater than unity. This is, at least, likely (*a*) where the export industry is in strong competition with foreign production (which would appear to be almost certain if the second country were the rest of the world) and/or (*b*) where goods which had not been exported become exportable at a higher exchange rate. This, naturally, means a "high" elasticity of demand between certain price ranges since, in those articles, sales increase from zero to a positive figure. Such articles are likely to exist everywhere—so that it would be quite mistaken to estimate the elasticity of demand for our exports by confining oneself to the actual export articles and neglecting the potential ones.

9. In order to export more the export industry must be capable of increasing the quantities supplied to foreign buyers. This will depend, in part, on the capacity of our export industry to expand its output, and, in part, on the willingness of domestic buyers of the exportable articles to forego their consumption as they rise in price. Thus, to the two propositions stated previously we add a third, namely that *the elasticity of supply of foreign exchange will be higher the higher is the elasticity of supply of exportable articles*, and a fourth, that *the elasticity of supply of foreign exchange will be higher, the higher is the elasticity of our domestic demand for the goods whose surplus production is exported.*[5]

---

[5] To understand better the relationship between the last two statements, let us suppose, for a minute, that the supply of the commodity, part of which is exported, is absolutely inelastic. This means that no more can be produced, however high

10. As we have stated, it is not likely that (barring trade restrictions of a certain type) the elasticity of foreign demand for our exports is smaller than unity; hence, it is not likely that the supply of foreign exchange is of negative elasticity within any "practical" range. (By "practical" I mean under conditions which are likely to be encountered in reality.)

Nevertheless, it is interesting to examine what would be the consequences of such a negatively elastic supply of foreign exchange. Let us compare the effects of an increased demand for imports under conditions of a positively inclined supply curve with those under conditions of a *negatively* inclined supply curve of foreign exchange. This is done in Fig. 2, where the supply curve SS'' turns backward from a certain point on.[6]

Before the increase in demand for imports the foreign exchange rate is OQ; exports and imports amount to OM in terms of foreign exchange, and to $OMPQ$ in terms of dollars. If the supply curve is "normal," i.e. positively inclined (SS'), the increase in demand (from DD' to D_1D_1') raises the foreign exchange rate to OT, and raises exports and imports both in terms of foreign exchange (from OM to ON) and in terms of dollars (from $OMPQ$ to $ONRT$). If, however, the supply curve is "abnormal," i.e. negatively inclined, the exchange rate rises to OV; exports and imports fall in terms of foreign exchange (from OM to OL) and rise in terms of dollars (from $OMPQ$ to $OLUV$).

Exports equal imports, of course, whether calculated in terms

---

its price rises. The part bought by domestic consumers, however, will probably diminish as the price rises; it will diminish much upon a modest rise in price, if the elasticity of demand for this product is high. The exports of this good may thus increase even if its production cannot be increased.

[6] The curve cannot rise backward more sharply. The slope of the negative inclination must at every point be greater than that of the rectangular hyperbola passing through that point. This is clear when we consider that, as the foreign exchange rate rises, the price of our exports is lowered only in terms of foreign currency, but not in terms of dollars. The dollar prices of the exports will rather be higher than before. The increased quantities exported may thus fetch reduced proceeds in terms of foreign exchange while the proceeds in terms of dollars are certainly increased.

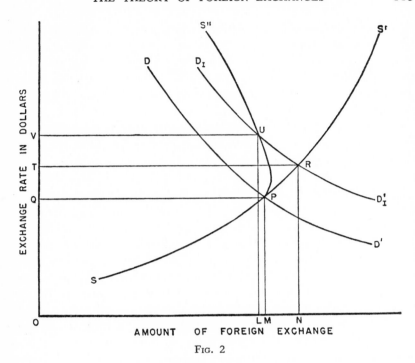

Fig. 2

of dollars or in terms of the foreign currency. But while both exports and imports rise in terms of dollars, they fall in terms of the foreign currency if the supply of foreign exchange is of negative elasticity.

11. In sub-sections 7 to 10 the conditions of supply of foreign exchange from commodity exports were examined. We turn now to an examination of the conditions of *demand for foreign exchange* for commodity imports. Most of the statements which will have to be made concerning the elasticity of demand for imports will be analogous to those made about the supply side.

The role of quotas is obvious. With quotas for all possible import articles and with all quotas exhausted, the demand for imports, and, thus, the demand for foreign exchange, must become perfectly inelastic below a certain exchange rate. Above this exchange rate demand will be of elasticities greater than zero.

The role of tariffs is no different than before. The greater the portion which specific customs duties are of the selling price of imported articles, the less sensitive will demand be to changes in the exchange rates. Hence the higher the tariffs the less will the quantities of foreign exchange demanded fall as the foreign exchange rates rise and *vice versa*.

Four fundamental rules linking supply and demand conditions for the imported articles to the elasticity of demand for foreign exchange can be stated as follows.

(1) *The elasticity of demand for foreign exchange will be higher, the higher is the elasticity of the domestic demand for the articles which we import.*

(2) *The elasticity of demand for foreign exchange will be higher, the higher is the elasticity of supply of domestic products which compete in the domestic market with our imports.* As, for example, the foreign exchange rate falls (because of an increase in the supply of foreign exchange, owing perhaps to an increased foreign demand for our products), foreign products become cheaper in terms of dollars. If domestic rival producers will greatly reduce their output as prices fall, i.e. if their supply is very elastic, imports will rise even if the domestic demand for the articles concerned is (very or perfectly) inelastic. Likewise, even with an inelastic demand for the articles concerned, imports will fall sharply as the foreign exchange rate rises, if the domestic rival producers expand output readily as domestic prices rise.

(3) *The elasticity of demand for foreign exchange will be higher, the higher is the elasticity of supply by foreign producers of the articles which we import.* If, for example, a fall in the foreign exchange rate tends to reduce foreign prices in terms of our currency, imports would not be able to rise, in spite of our elastic demand for them, if foreign supply were perfectly inelastic. The selling prices of these foreign products in terms of their own currency would rise so much as to offset the price reduction which the lower exchange rate would imply for our buyers in terms of our currency. Statement (3) has, however, to be qualified by the fourth rule.

(4) *The elasticity of demand for foreign exchange will be higher, the*

higher is the elasticity of the foreign demand for their own products.   If, for example, foreign producers are not capable of expanding their output, as our demand rises, and if therefore the prices of their products in terms of foreign currency rise, this may induce foreign domestic buyers to forego the purchase of these goods, thus releasing them for our disposal.   Our imports can therefore increase even if foreign production cannot, since a fall of foreign consumption can provide the goods whose production seems to be fixed.   Conversely, even with an inelastic supply by the producers of the articles concerned, imports will fall sharply as the foreign exchange rate rises, if foreign home consumption expands readily as prices in their country fall.

12. The reader with a sense for symmetry will now expect a digression on the possibility of negative elasticity of demand, i.e. of a backward falling demand curve.   Nothing of this sort is in order, unless we wish to enter into perfectly absurd theorising about imports being sufficiently affected by prestige values of imported luxuries.

The lack of symmetry is only a seeming one, resulting from the properties of our curve analysis.   That the foreign demand for our exports is inelastic means that the amounts spent, *in foreign currency*, for our exports fall, as these exports rise in physical quantities owing to a higher exchange rate.   That our demand for imports is inelastic means, in contrast, that the amounts spent, *in our own currency*, for our imports fall, as these imports rise in physical quantities owing to a lower exchange rate.   Since our curves depict amounts of foreign currency by the values of the abscissae, a fall in these amounts, as the exchange rate rises, has to be shown by a backward rising supply curve.   Since, in contrast, amounts of our own currency are depicted by the rectangular areas produced by abscissae and ordinates, a fall in these amounts, as the exchange rate falls, has to be shown by no "backward" turn of the demand curve but simply by a slope which is steeper than that of rectangular hyperbolae passing through the same points.

As to the question whether the demand for foreign exchange for import purposes is likely, in reality, to be of an elasticity smaller than unity, we must recall what was said above (in 8), on the analogous problem. One point which was emphasised there was the degree of competition. Elasticity of demand from the point of view of any particular *seller*, or selling country, is a function of the number of sellers, or selling countries, which compete for higher shares of the market. If the other country is larger than the own country, or, if the other "country" is the rest of the world, then it is highly probable that the share of our exports in the foreign market is small, and, hence, the elasticity of foreign demand for our exports is very high.

These considerations are not applicable to the problem of elasticity of demand from the point of view of any particular *buyer*, or buying country. Whether the domestic demand for an imported article is elastic or inelastic is not a function of the number of sellers; here we are concerned with the total market demand, the elasticity of which depends on "tastes," consumption habits, income, income distribution, etc. Even if the importing country is smaller than the other, or even if the other "country" is the rest of the world, there is nothing which would make us expect our demand for imports to be highly elastic.[7]

The other point used in the argument in favour of a high elasticity of foreign demand for our exports was the existence of potential export articles. This point is valid also in a consideration about the elasticity of our demand for imports. There are undoubtedly a number of goods which at a given exchange rate are not among imported articles but which might become imported

---

[7] One might think that the proposition advanced in the text hinges on the definition of "commodity" or "imported article." If these terms were narrowly applied so as to regard special types, brands, qualities, etc., as separate articles, the demand for each "article" would naturally be more elastic the greater the number of near substitutes. This is, however, not the same thing as the elasticity of the market demand as dependent or not dependent on the number of sellers of each "article." Whereas demand as seen by each seller possesses greater elasticity the greater the number of sellers of the article, market demand as the aggregate of the buyers' demand schedules possesses an elasticity which is independent of the number of sellers of the article.

articles if the foreign exchange rate were lower. Whether or not this circumstance is sufficient to make total demand for imports of an elasticity greater than unity, cannot be answered in general theory.

III

13. Commodity trade has been assumed to be the only source of demand and supply of foreign exchange up to this point. Imports of goods have been the substance behind the demand, exports of goods the substance behind the supply. We proceed now to including unilateral payments or long-term capital movements into our analysis. We still rule out invisible services, gold movements, and short-term capital movements.

Let us assume that a series of large payments is to be made from our country to the foreign country, so that there emerges a demand for foreign exchange which is not arising from a demand for imports. The purpose of the payments may be investment in the foreign country, or settlement of old debts, or a war tribute, or something of the sort. In order to obtain the aggregate demand for foreign exchange, we have to add the demand for foreign exchange of those who wish to make these payments, to the demand for foreign exchange of those who wish to import commodities. (That the latter demand is not likely to be the same as it would be without the non-trade payments will be discussed later.)

The purpose of the payments will, of course, have a bearing on the elasticity of the demand for foreign exchange. If it concerns the payment of a debt contracted, or a tribute imposed, in terms of our own currency, so that a fixed amount of our currency has to be used for purchasing foreign exchange, then the demand for foreign exchange arising from this payment has an elasticity of unity, i.e. the demand curve is a rectangular hyperbola. If it concerns the unpostponable payment of a debt contracted, or a tribute imposed, in terms of foreign exchange, so that a fixed amount of foreign exchange has to be purchased, then the demand for foreign exchange arising from this payment has an elasticity of zero, i.e. the demand curve is a vertical straight line—at least up to some point above which an increase in the price of foreign exchange would surpass the good faith or solvency of the payers in terms of their own currency.

The amount of the payments is not fixed in either terms in case of investments in the foreign country. Apart from changes in expectations due to changes in the foreign exchange rate, it seems certain that the elasticity of demand for foreign exchange for purposes of long-term foreign investment is more than zero, and it may be also more than unity.

14. Let us assume provisionally that the emergence of the demand for foreign exchange for purposes of investment abroad ("capital export") leaves demand and supply of foreign exchange arising from demand for imports and supply of exports unchanged. What are the probable changes in exchange rates, in imports, in exports?

For the accompanying graph (Fig. 3), the exchange rate would be MP or OQ, if demand and supply of foreign exchange were exclusively due to demand for imports and supply of exports. ($D_M D'_M$ and $S_X S'_X$); imports, in this case, would equal exports in terms of foreign exchange ($OM = OM$) and in terms of the own currency ($OMPQ = OMPQ$). If now the demand for foreign exchange of "capital exporters" (investors) is added to the demand for foreign exchange of the commodity importers, an aggregate demand curve ($D_{M+I} D'_{M+I}$), to the right of and above the first demand curve, would make an exchange rate of OQ impossible: the exchange rate will be driven up to NR or OT, where the quantities demanded and supplied are equal (TR or ON).

At this increased exchange rate capital exporters buy less foreign exchange than at the lower rate ($UR < PJ$), commodity importers buy less than at the lower rate ($TU < QP$), and commodity exporters sell more than at the lower rate ($TR > QP$). Who provides the foreign exchange (UR or LN), which the capital exporters take from the market? It is provided through an increase in the amounts supplied by commodity exporters (VR) and through a decrease in the amounts demanded by commodity importers (UV).

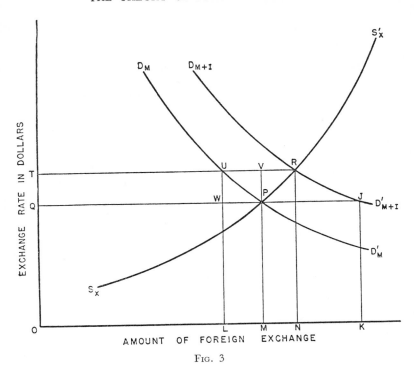

Fig. 3

We see, then, that the capital export brings with it a decrease in commodity imports and an increase in commodity exports, all calculated in terms of foreign exchange.   Capital export *equals* Fall in commodity imports *plus* Rise in commodity exports, i.e.,

$$LN = LM + MN$$

If these quantities are calculated in terms of our own currency, instead of in foreign exchange, the result is different in so far as the imports may not fall but rise, if the demand for imports is of an elasticity smaller than unity.   In our graph imports in terms of dollars, at the higher exchange rate, are higher than at the lower exchange rate ($OLUT > OMPQ$).   We are therefore confronted with the fact that in consequence of the capital export, commodity imports may show an increase in terms of dollars but a decrease in terms of foreign currency.   Statisticians, trying to "verify" a fall in imports due to increased capital exports, should beware of this trap.

On the other hand, the change of the trade balance to an export surplus occurs in terms of both the own and the foreign currency. Commodity exports *equals* Commodity imports *plus* Capital exports

i.e. $$ON = OL + LN$$
and $$ONRT = OLUT + LNRU$$

The above results follow logically from our assumptions.   If there are among the international transactions no (invisible) services rendered or received, and if there are no movements of gold or short-term balances, the balance of trade is uniquely determined by the balance of capital movements.   The so-called "favourable" trade balance must be equal to the net capital export, and the so-called "adverse" trade balance must be equal to the net capital import.

15. "Invisible" exports and imports, that is the balance of services or "current items" other than commodity trade in the balance of international payments, can be introduced into our analysis without any difficulties.   Demand and supply of foreign exchange arising from these services received from, or rendered to, residents of foreign countries, might be treated graphically exactly as we have just treated the demand for foreign exchange arising from capital exports.

We can easily imagine a demand curve for foreign exchange for foreign travel.   The aggregate demand curve for both visible imports (commodity) and invisible imports (tourists' expenditures abroad) might look exactly like the aggregate demand curve in Fig. 3.   The result of our considerations would, of course, be analogous.   For example, if foreign travel were the only service item, the export surplus in the trade balance would be equal to the net "deficit" in the balance of tourist expenditures; or, conversely, the import surplus in the trade balance would be equal to the net "gain" in the balance of tourist expenditures.   And again, an increase in the demand for foreign travel would lead to an increase in commodity exports and a decrease in commodity imports, in terms of foreign currency; and to an increase in commodity exports and a decrease or increase in commodity imports, in terms of our own currency.[8]

It may be mentioned that some of the service items are complementary, while others are competing with exported and imported commodities; furthermore that supply and demand of foreign exchange arising from these current service items may be of all possible elasticities, ranging from less than zero to more than unity.

Some examples may be instructive.

(a) "Immigrants' remittances" to their relatives in foreign countries may be solely dependent on the remitters' budgets, or, on the other hand, solely dependent on the beneficiaries' needs; the respective demand for foreign exchange would be fixed in dollars, that is of unit elasticity in the former case, and fixed in foreign exchange, that is of zero elasticity in the latter. The elasticity would be between zero and one, if both factors bore on the size of the remittances.

(b) Interest and dividends received from foreign securities involve a supply of foreign exchange. If the amounts are fixed in foreign money, the respective supply of foreign exchange is perfectly inelastic; if, on the other hand, the amounts are fixed in terms of our own currency (which can be the case with special bonds only), the respective supply of foreign exchange is negatively elastic, that is to say, it is exactly minus one.[9]

(c) Payments for freight and shipping services sometimes bear a complicated relationship to the commodities imported and exported. If it is assumed that the foreign country has no merchant marine and that both exports and imports have to be transported in our ships, the supply of foreign exchange arising from

---

[8] If the possibility of a backward rising supply curve is to be accounted for, the last statement should read: "An increase in the demand for foreign travel would lead to an increase or decrease in commodity exports and a decrease in commodity imports in terms of foreign currency; and to an increase in commodity exports and a decrease or increase in commodity imports, in terms of our own currency."

[9] In other words, the supply curve would look just like a demand curve of unit elasticity (i.e. a rectangular hyperbola).

these shipping services must necessarily tend to make our balance of trade "adverse." (Would that we might get rid of these nonsensical terms "adverse" and "favourable"!) If all commodity prices are fixed f.o.b. our ports, every import gives rise to a demand for foreign exchange, in payment for the goods, and a supply of foreign exchange, in payment for their transportation; and every export gives rise to a supply of foreign exchange received for the goods exported and another for their transportation. In deriving a supply curve of the foreign exchange which proceeds from shipping services, one is then faced with the difficulty that any change in the exchange rate may increase transportation in one direction but decrease it in the other. The supply of foreign exchange from shipping services is of positive elasticity only if the services of our marine compete with those of the other country (or, that is, of the rest of the world). In this case, a rise in the foreign exchange rate implies a relative cheapening of the services of our merchant marine in terms of foreign currency, and this would (in the case of competition sufficient to produce an elastic demand for the services of *our* merchant marine) bring our marine sufficiently increased business to secure increased proceeds in terms of foreign exchange, unless competing fleets lowered their prices to American ports.

16. It is now time to drop our provisional assumption that the emergence of a demand for (or supply of) foreign exchange for purposes other than commodity imports (or exports) leaves the importers' demand and the exporters' supply unchanged. It may be well, however, to warn here against the possible confusion between demand (in the schedule sense), on the one hand, and quantity demanded, on the other.

The fall in commodity imports (in terms of foreign money) which was found above to be the necessary consequence of a new demand for foreign exchange by capital exporters, did not constitute a fall in the commodity importers' demand for foreign exchange, but merely a fall in the amount of foreign exchange demanded by commodity importers. The amount of foreign exchange demanded by commodity importers fell because of the rise in the foreign exchange rate which was caused by the capital exporters' demand for foreign exchange. It represented a shift *along* the commodity importers' (unchanged) demand curve.

Now, we have to examine whether there may not be also a shift *of* the commodity importers' demand curve (and commodity exporters' supply curve) resulting from a new demand for foreign exchange for payments of any sort—such as capital exports, unilateral remittances, or payments for foreign services bought.

Let us assume an increase in demand for foreign travel. The persons who plan to spend an increased amount for their trip to the foreign country plan of course to spend a decreased amount of their budget for other things. Among these other things may be imported articles. (Instead of consuming imported foodstuffs here, the tourists will consume them abroad; thus less may be demanded to be imported.) What happens then is a shift of demand from imported articles to touring abroad. The increase in the demand for foreign exchange arising from tourists' expenditures abroad may, in this case, be partly offset by a decrease in the demand for foreign exchange arising from commodity imports. The offsetting is only in part, because the consumers' expenditures for the imported articles would have included payments for domestic services of distribution (services of the importers, wholesalers, transporters, retailers). Thus, not all of the amounts spent by the consumers on the goods in question constitute demand for foreign exchange, whereas after the switch of these expenditures over to foreign travel the whole sum goes into purchasing foreign exchange.

Some of the consumers' purchasing power devoted to foreign travel may have been withdrawn from buying goods which are exportable. The diminution of the domestic demand for exportable goods may easily induce the producers to look for more outlets in the foreign market, or, in other words, it may cause the supply of exports, and, under certain conditions, the exporters' supply of foreign exchange to increase. This would constitute a shift of the supply curve to the right and downward.

What has been said of the influence of the tourists' demand upon the importers' demand for, and exporters' supply of, foreign exchange, is similarly valid for other sources of demand for foreign exchange. We have to ask from what markets the purchasing power of those who now demand foreign exchange is withdrawn. In the case of capital export, where would the money funds have gone, had their owner not decided in favour of foreign investment? Have the funds come from an increase in voluntary saving, or from the usual flow of voluntary savings, or from disinvestment (omitted replacement) in home industry? Or have they come, perhaps, from idle hoards, or from bank credit expansion, in which cases no other demand is reduced by the increased capital export? This last possibility shall be ruled out for the movement. Only later shall we allow changes in the monetary circulation to be related to international transactions.

17. The shifts of the importers' demand and exporters' supply curves due to the increase in tourists' or capital exporters' demand for foreign exchange, must not be confused with those famous shifts due to a "transfer of purchasing power" from the paying country to the receiving country. These are different matters which do not come into the picture before we get to international movements of gold and short-term balances. At our stage of the analysis monetary circulation is assumed not to be affected by international transactions. Thus, an increased demand for foreign exchange by tourists does not involve a withdrawal of purchasing power from circulation but merely a change of the flow of purchasing power through the national economic system.[10]

Let us look again at our Fig. 3 and ask ourselves where the money spent by capital exporters for foreign exchange (*LNRU*) comes from and where it goes. The question "where it comes from" is, however, very loosely expressed; it should not mean the channels through which it has reached the capital exporters, but

---

[10] The assumption that monetary circulation is not affected by transactions such as foreign investments is admittedly unrealistic, even if international movements of short-term balances are ruled out. Improved investment opportunities abroad would lead to dishoarding and to increased borrowing from banks. And even apart from this the change in the money flow would most likely involve some slight change in the income velocity of circulation. However, a clean analysis must first abstract from all these complications.

rather the directions into which it *does not go* because of the switch toward foreign investment.   There will be one answer in the case of increased saving, in which the money is diverted from the market of (domestic or imported) consumers' goods; and another in the case of maintained saving, in which the money is diverted from the market of (domestic or imported) producers' goods.   The other question, "where the money goes," can be accurately answered: it goes to exporters of commodities.

Without capital export or any other demand for foreign exchange by others than importers, commodity exporters get no more and no less than the amount spent on foreign exchange by commodity importers ($OMPQ$ in Fig. 3). When a demand for foreign exchange by capital exporters becomes effective, a greater part of the total money flow goes to commodity exporters. They get what is spent on foreign exchange by capital exporters plus what is spent on foreign exchange by commodity importers, though the latter amount may be greater or smaller than it was prior to the export of capital.

This reshuffling in the distribution of purchasing power in the national economic system makes it highly improbable that the original importers' demand and exporters' supply curves remain unchanged.   The final direction of the shifts cannot be ascertained *a priori*.   Although we have argued above that the increase in demand for foreign exchange by tourists or capital exporters or the like *may* lower the demand for foreign exchange by commodity importers, the contrary may be true just the same.   The factors of production employed by the busy export industries may be willing to spend much more for imported articles than the tourists or capital exporters would have done—had they not become tourists or capital exporters.   Thus the capital export may result in an increase in the commodity importers' demand for foreign exchange, whereas it can, of course, never result in an increase in the amount of foreign exchange demanded by commodity importers.

18. Before we proceed to introduce movements of gold and short-term balances into our analysis, a word on the "purchasing power parity theory" seems to be in order.   This theory claims

that the foreign exchange rate is determined by the ratio between the real purchasing power of the two currencies; the price levels in the two countries would thus be the independent variables, the exchange rates the dependent variables of the relationship.

We have avoided a discussion of the concept of "price levels" in our analysis so far, and we shall try to do without it for the rest. We emphasised, however, from the beginning that commodity prices must not be assumed as "given" because they may be affected by the international transactions themselves.   Even for the simplest considerations not *actual* prices but *potential* prices, that is to say, supply and demand conditions served to explain the determination of foreign exchange rates.   And we saw that without "inflation" or "deflation" in any of the countries concerned, the exchange rates between them could be changed through a number of events.   The degree of the change, however, is always determined by the potential commodity prices, i.e. by the supply and demand conditions on the two markets.

Nothing is more capable of altering supply and demand conditions and, thus, the exchange rate of a country, than inflation. While changes in tastes, changes in productivity, changes in capital movements, etc., can change exchange rates somewhat (or even by substantial percentages), inflation in one of the countries can change the rates by huge multiples.   It is for this reason that the explanation of very great changes in the exchange rates has to turn to the increase in monetary circulation, and to the subsequent changes in supply and demand conditions (loosely expressed: to the change in "price level") as the causal factors.   There cannot be a minute's doubt that the "balance-of-payments" theory was all wrong and the "inflation" theory essentially correct when the vast movements on the foreign exchange markets was discussed in the first part of the twenties.   The greatest possible increase in the demand for imports plus the greatest possible fall in the supply of exports plus the greatest possible flight of capital would not be able to produce the conspicuous exchange depreciations of that period —had it not been for the inflations; for these inflations a measure was devised in the form of "purchasing power parities."

In this historical perspective, the purchasing power parity

theory must be given full credit. It was important, at the time, to pronounce tersely: "Don't be so ridiculous as to hold the 'need for imports' responsible for the exchange depreciation, if it is only inflation which can account for the effective demand for these imports." But this must not blind us to the fact that changes in the foreign exchange market—less conspicuous, but significant enough—may take place without any preceding change in the monetary circulations and purchasing power parities of the countries concerned.

IV

19. As long as commodity trade, exchange of services, long-term investments and unilateral payments are treated as the only sources of supply and demand of foreign exchange, as long, therefore, as international movements of gold and short-term balances are excluded, the analysis can be said to deal with "independent currencies."

As soon as international movements of gold (and other monetary metals) and short-term (bank) balances are introduced as sources of supply and demand of foreign exchange, the analysis proceeds to currency systems whose effective circulation is not independent of international transactions. Inflow and outflow of gold, and acquisition and disposal of foreign bank balances, may change the effective monetary circulation of the countries concerned. That gold and foreign bank balances can be bought and sold at fairly fixed prices, constitutes the essence of the gold standard.

Leaving international movements of bank balances for the last step of our analysis, we introduce first international gold movements and make the assumption that the monetary authorities of both countries are prepared to buy and sell gold at fixed prices or pairs of prices. This assumption, i.e., the assumption of the gold standard maintained in both countries, implies that at a certain exchange rate the supply of foreign exchange becomes infinitely elastic, and at another (somewhat lower) exchange rate, the demand for foreign exchange becomes infinitely elastic.

Under an "orthodox" gold standard system, it is not the

monetary authorities themselves which offer to sell or to buy foreign exchange. They buy and sell only gold.[11] On the other hand, the people who wish to make payments abroad are not those who themselves would buy gold from the monetary authorities. The ancient textbook story about the business man who has to make a payment abroad and finds, when the foreign exchange rate rises above a certain point, that it is cheaper to buy gold and ship it to the foreign country, is unrealistic without necessity. It is more correct and no less simple to refer to the gold *arbitrageurs* who buy gold from the monetary authority, ship and sell it abroad, and supply the foreign balances thus obtained to the foreign exchange market. It is, furthermore, easy to understand that this business works under fairly constant marginal cost and that the supply of foreign exchange is infinitely elastic, as soon as the respective rate—the gold export point—is reached, and as long as the monetary authorities in the two countries maintain their preparedness to sell and buy gold at the fixed prices.

For analogous reasons, the gold *arbitrageurs'* demand for foreign exchange is infinitely elastic, as soon as the exchange rate falls to the gold import point. They are willing to buy every amount of foreign balances at this price, since they can use them to buy gold in the foreign country and import and sell it to the monetary authority.

The gold *arbitrageurs* are dealers in gold and foreign balances. In order to postpone movements in foreign balances to the next step of our analysis, we simply assume here that the gold *arbitrageurs* do not change the size of their stocks in foreign exchange. This assumption implies merely that they use any amount of newly obtained foreign balances immediately, either for selling them to final buyers, that is, to people who wish to make foreign payments, or for buying foreign gold to import it. Likewise, they replenish immediately any amount of foreign balances which they have disposed of from their "stock," either by buying foreign exchange

---

[11] In some gold standard countries, however, the "modern" system of exchange stabilisation funds was already practiced in the 19th century.

from final sellers, that is, from people who have received payments from abroad, or by buying gold from the monetary authority to export and sell it abroad.

20. An example of the functioning of the foreign exchange market in gold standard countries is illustrated in Fig. 4. It is assumed that initially commodity trade is the only source of international payments. $D_M D'_M$ is the commodity importers' demand for foreign exchange, $S_X S'_X$ the commodity exporters' supply of foreign exchange; OM is the amount of foreign exchange bought and sold at the equilibrium rate MP. Exports amount to OM in terms of foreign currency and to $OMPQ$ in terms of dollars; imports are of course equal to exports.

Capital export appears and increases the demand for foreign exchange to $D_{M+I} D'_{M+I}$. We know from previous considerations

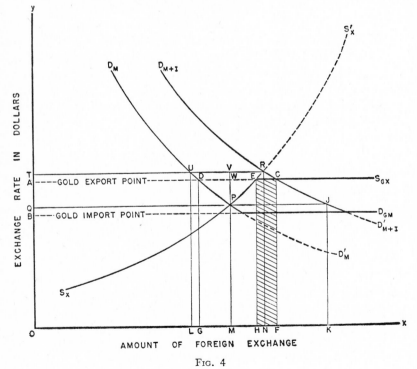

Fig. 4

that the commodity importers' demand for foreign exchange is likely to be affected by changes in the distribution of the income stream which accompany the capital export. However, since we cannot know *how* the import demand will change, we assume it to be unchanged. (For certain problems we might assume instead that $D_{M+I}D'_{M+I}$ already takes account of all concomitant changes in the demand for foreign exchange.)

In absence of the gold standard the foreign exchange would rise to the rate OT or NR, exports would rise to ON, imports would fall to OL. Under the gold standard the exchange rate cannot rise to OT, which is above the gold export point OA. At the exchange rate OA the supply of foreign exchange becomes perfectly elastic, the supply curve sharply turning parallel to the X-axis. The commodity exporters' supply curve breaks off at E and is replaced by the gold exporters' supply curve (S_{GX}) of infinite elasticity.

This supply curve is intersected by the aggregate demand curve ($D_{M+I}D'_{M+I}$) at C. The exchange rate FC is of course equal to OA, the gold export point. At this rate the amount of foreign exchange demanded by capital exporters is DC or GF and the amount demanded by commodity importers is AD or OG. Of the total amount demanded, AC or OF, commodity exporters contribute AE or OH, and gold exporters contribute EC or HF.[12]

We see, thus, that the capital export brings with it a decrease in commodity imports ($OG < OM$), an increase in commodity exports ($OH > OM$) and a net gold export (HF), all calculated in terms of foreign exchange. Capital export *equals* Fall in commodity imports *plus* Rise in commodity exports *plus* Gold exports, i.e., $GF = GM + MH + HF$.

A calculation in terms of our own currency may, again, lead to different results if the elasticity of the import demand is smaller than unity. In this case imports in terms of dollars would rise rather than fall. In Fig. 4 the importers' demand is, in the relevant

---

[12] The repercussions which a concomitant reshuffling in the distribution of purchasing power may have on the original supply and demand conditions are neglected here for the reasons given above in 18 (p. 127).

range, of an elasticity slightly above unity so that imports fall also in terms of dollars ($OGDA < OMPQ$) when the exchange rate rises from OQ to OA. The change of the trade balance to an export surplus will be realised in terms of our own as well as in terms of the foreign currency. The commodity export surplus is GH in terms of foreign exchange and $GHED$ in terms of dollars. Only if the former equilibrium exchange rate had been just at the gold export point would the emergence of a new demand for foreign exchange for capital exports lead first merely to gold exports instead of directly to an export surplus.

For our new situation shown in Fig. 4 the "balance of payments" can be written as follows:

Commodity exports *plus* Gold exports *equal* Commodity imports *plus* Capital exports, i.e., $OH + HF = OG + GF$ and $OHEA + HFCE = OGDA + GFCD$.

In the absence of the gold standard commodity exports would be greater (by HN) and commodity imports would be smaller (by LG) than under the gold standard; the export surplus would be equal to capital exports. The gold standard allows this commodity export surplus to develop more slowly. But develop it will, because the equilibrium pictured above is distinctly unstable.

21. The inherent tendency to change in the situation described above is connected with the destiny of the dollars paid to gold exporters. This money goes another way than the money paid to commodity exporters. Commodity exporters pay the proceeds from their sales ($OHEA$ in Fig. 4) chiefly to the producers of export commodities; and the producers pass the money on to producers of intermediate products and to factors of production, etc. Gold exporters, on the other hand, turn the proceeds from their sales of foreign exchange ($HFCE$ in Fig. 4) less their commission and transport charges over to the monetary authorities in payment for gold. Thus most of the money passes out of existence.

Provided no policy of "offsetting" is pursued by the monetary authorities, this contraction of circulation alters not only the distribution but also the amount of money income in a decided direction: money income falls. The fall in money income, in turn, affects demand and supply of foreign exchange in a definite way:[13] the demand, both by commodity importers and by capital exporters, falls, and the supply by commodity exporters rises. That is to say, the demand curves shift to the left, the supply curve to the right.

This increase in supply and decrease in demand may not be sufficient, at the first stroke, to bring the market rate of foreign exchange down below the gold export point. Then another dose of gold exports will further reduce domestic circulation. The income deflation, resulting from a gold outflow without offsetting, cannot help eventually leading to a diminution of demand for foreign exchange and to an increase in the supply of foreign exchange. If the shift in demand and supply curves takes place only after a considerable time lag, then a more complete reversion of the situation is likely to occur: the delayed reduction in importers' demand and increase in exporters' supply may then, when it finally arrives, push the foreign exchange rate down to the gold import point, thus causing the gold *arbitrageurs'* infinitely elastic demand for foreign exchange to become effective. Gold *arbitrageurs* would pay out to commodity exporters dollars newly created by the monetary authorities in payment for the imported gold, and domestic circulation would rise again.

While the reduction of demand for foreign exchange cannot fail to take place if incomes fall in consequence of a gold outflow, the increase in supply of foreign exchange may, under rather exceptional circumstances, fail to appear. The same "abnormal" conditions which are capable of making for a negative elasticity of the supply curve (see 8) may, in concurrence with other factors, make also for a perverted shift of the supply curve to result from income deflation. To recall it shortly, inelasticity of foreign demand for our export articles and inelasticity of foreign supply of substitutes for our export articles are the conditions in point; conditions which cannot be realised if our exports compete heavily with foreign products, and if we produce goods which are not actually but

---

[13] Subjective to qualifications set forth subsequently.

potentially exportable.   The perverted shift is, however, still more "extremely unlikely" than the perverted elasticity if it is assumed that the gold inflow into the foreign country is not offset there by official sterilisation or private hoarding.   With the gold inflow allowed to have its effects on foreign money incomes, *price-elasticity* of foreign demand for our exports can be ever so small without preventing our commodity exporters' supply of foreign exchange from rising, if only the *income-elasticity* of foreign demand for our exports is not negligible.   It would be almost absurd to assume that both price-elasticity and income-elasticity of demand are so small that neither higher incomes of foreign buyers nor lower prices charged by our sellers would lead to increased exports measured in terms of foreign currency.

The shift to the right of the foreign demand for our exports, as is known from the famous controversy about the transfer problem of reparation payments, may result in an increase in the commodity exporters' supply of foreign exchange even without any price reductions on the part of our exporters.

22. It may be desirable at this stage to summarise in a convenient catalogue all the factors which may concur in bringing about an export surplus as the result of an export of capital or of any other payment to the foreign country.

(1) Domestic purchasing power used for making the remittance may have been withdrawn from buying imported goods; hence the demand for foreign exchange for our commodity imports may fall.

(2) Domestic purchasing power used for making the remittance may have been withdrawn from buying exportable goods; hence the supply of foreign exchange from our commodity exports may rise.

(3) The foreign exchange rate is raised; hence the amount of foreign exchange demanded for our commodity imports falls.

(4) The foreign exchange rate is raised; hence the amount of foreign exchange supplied from our commodity exports may rise.

(5) Domestic purchasing power used for buying gold is wiped out; hence the demand for foreign exchange for our commodity imports falls.

(6) Domestic purchasing power used for buying gold is wiped out; hence the supply of foreign exchange from our commodity exports may rise.

(7) Foreign purchasing power is created through gold exports; hence the prices of foreign products may rise and the demand for foreign exchange for our commodity imports may fall.

(8) Foreign purchasing power is created through gold exports; hence foreign demand for our exports rises and the supply of foreign exchange from our commodity exports rises.

Factors (1), (2), (3) and (4) can be effective under the gold standard as well as under independent currency systems; factors (5), (6), (7) and (8) can function only under the gold standard. Factors (1), (2), (5), (6), (7) and (8) represent shifts *of* the supply or demand curves, factors (3) and (4) represent shifts *along* the supply and demand curves of the foreign exchange market. Factors (1) and (2) do not function reliably; factors (5) and (6) can function only if no "offsetting" policy, or dishoarding, is at work in the paying country; factors (7) and (8) can function only if no "sterilisation" policy, or hoarding, is at work in the receiving country; factors (4) and (6) may refuse to function under "abnormal" conditions (i.e., factor (4) if the price-elasticities, factor (6) if both price- and income-elasticities of foreign demand for our exports are very small); factor (7) may refuse to function (or may function perversely) if the elasticity of domestic demand for foreign products is smaller than unity.   Under normal market conditions and under normal gold standard management factors (3), (4), (5), (6), (7) and (8) can all be expected to function; the more of these forces are at work the less will be the disturbances; the fewer of these forces are at work simultaneously, the heavier may be the possible disturbances connected with a sudden change in the flow of capital or unilateral payments.

It must be mentioned that the "normal gold standard management" mentioned above does not imply the necessity of credit expansion in case of gold inflow, or the necessity of credit restriction in case of gold outflow.   In other words, it is not necessary for the functioning of the described mechanisms that monetary circulation increases or decreases by some multiple of the gold in- or out-flow. The "automatic" increase in circulation through a gold purchase by monetary authorities (or banks in general) or the "automatic" decrease in circulation through a gold sale by monetary authorities (or banks in general) are all that is needed.

23. No change in our analysis is required when we substitute the assumption of a more "modern" gold standard system for the assumption of an orthodox one. We may drop the assumption of legally guaranteed gold sales and purchases by the monetary authorities (to and from gold *arbitrageurs* or the public in general) and substitute the assumption of an Exchange Stabilisation Fund which undertakes to stabilise the foreign exchange rates within relatively narrow margins.

The infinitely elastic demand for foreign exchange was, under the old system, the demand by gold *arbitrageurs* who bought (at the lower gold point) foreign balances in order to import gold and to sell it to the monetary authorities. Under the new system, there is the infinitely elastic demand for foreign exchange on the part of the Exchange Stabilisation Fund, which buys all foreign balances offered at the low point below which the exchange rate is not to be allowed to fall. The infinitely elastic supply of foreign exchange was, under the old system, the supply by gold *arbitrageurs* who sold (at the upper gold point) foreign balances obtained by the export of gold which they bought from the monetary authorities. Under the new system, there is the infinitely elastic supply of foreign exchange by the Exchange Stabilisation Fund, which sells all foreign balances demanded at the upper point above which the exchange rate is not to be allowed to rise.

If the Exchange Stabilisation Fund does not carry varying amounts of foreign balances but rather uses all foreign balances acquired to buy gold, and furnishes all foreign balances needed by selling gold, on the foreign gold market, and if, furthermore, the fund sells the gold it acquires to the central banking system, and buys the gold it needs from the central banking system—then the Exchange Stabilisation Fund is nothing else but a large-scale gold *arbitrageur*, acting exactly as do the gold *arbitrageurs* in our orthodox gold standard case above.   The legal framework under which all these actions take place is of small significance from a purely economic point of view.

The Exchange Stabilisation Fund may, instead of selling gold to and buying gold from the monetary authorities, keep the gold on its own account (on "inactive account").   In this case we must ask out of what funds of domestic money the foreign balances bought are paid for.   The Exchange Stabilisation Fund itself is ordinarily not authorised to create money.

The Fund may have been endowed with a sufficient amount of domestic money—so far back in the past that we need not inquire now whence the money came; the Fund then "dishoards" (i.e., pays out idle balances) when it acquires gold, and "hoards" (i.e., sets idle the balances received) when it sells gold.   If this is so, the analysis holds as laid out in previous sections.   Effective domestic circulation is increased, as foreign balances are offered to the Fund, by dishoarding rather than by creating domestic balances; effective domestic circulation is decreased, as foreign balances are supplied by the Fund, by hoarding rather than by wiping out domestic balances.

The Fund may, on the other hand, not have sufficient working balances in domestic money; it may obtain the domestic balances, which it needs for purchasing foreign balances offered to it, by borrowing from the banks; likewise it may use the domestic balances, which it receives for foreign balances sold, to repay its bank debts.   In this case we find that our analysis still holds, provided the banks have enough excess reserves (i.e., so high reserve ratios that the banks' supply of credit is infinitely elastic for a certain range).   The expansion of bank loans for the purpose of financing the Fund's purchases of foreign balances, and the liquidation of bank loans by means of the proceeds from the Fund's sales of foreign balances, produce precisely the changes in domestic circulation which would result from the working of the "automatic" gold standard.

24. The situation is different if the Exchange Stabilisation Fund finances its purchases by borrowing from the public rather

than from the banks, or by borrowing from banks which have no ample provision of excess reserves; and, as to the converse movement, the situation is different from the analysed ones if the Fund uses its sales proceeds for repaying loans to the public rather than banks, or to banks which have been short of excess reserves.   In these cases the purchases and sales of foreign balances by the Exchange Stabilisation Fund will not increase and decrease effective circulation by the full value of the foreign balances bought or sold.

Assume that capital import sets in (Fig. 5) and that the Exchange Stabilisation Fund buys, as is necessary in view of the adopted policy, *HFCE* dollars' worth of foreign balances (or gold), raising the *HFCE* dollars by borrowing from the public. · If the public had just become more thrifty and furnished the *HFCE*

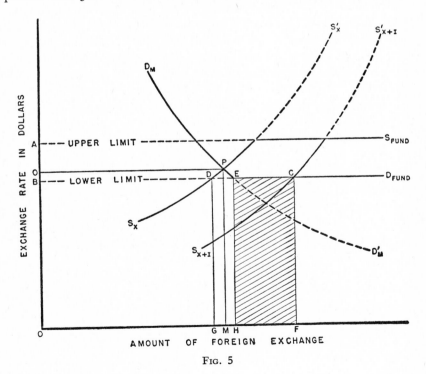

Fig. 5

dollars out of new voluntary savings, then the balances of the savers would be transferred *via* the Exchange Stabilisation Fund to the sellers of foreign exchange, i.e., to the capital importers. Hence no increase in circulation would result from the capital import and the foreign exchange purchases of the Fund.

The assumption of an increase in thriftiness simultaneous with the "favourable balance of payments" is, of course, rather arbitrary. Let us assume instead that the Exchange Stabilisation Fund tries to borrow from a public whose propensities to save have not changed. The total demand for loanable funds increases to the extent to which the infinitely elastic demand for foreign exchange on the part of the Exchange Stabilisation Fund becomes effective (i.e., by *HFCE*). In simpler words, the Fund seeks liquid funds to buy foreign balances or gold, and the money market may become stiffer.[14] Increased interest rates will induce some holders of idle balances to dishoard them: so, while the greater part of the money raised by the Fund will be withdrawn from other employments, a portion will come from hitherto inactive balances. Only a small part of the *HFCE* dollars paid out by the Fund to the sellers of foreign balances will thus constitute an increase in effective circulation. The larger part will constitute previously active money that merely changes the channels of its flow. That is to say, the gold acquired by the Fund has been "sterilised."[15]

Much the same result will follow if banks participate in financing the Fund's purchases, but if the banks have no ample excess reserves (i.e., no extraordinarily high ratio of reserves to deposits). In this case some slight net expansion of bank credit may take place under the inducement of increased interest rates, but the bulk of the loans to the Fund (mostly in form of purchases of Treasury bills) will be at the expense of other loans and investments. Only if the

---

[14] About this (temporary) rise in interest rates due to capital imports see below, sub-sections 30 and 31.

[15] It should be recalled that, according to our present assumptions, it makes no difference whether we say that the Fund buys foreign balances or that the Fund buys gold. If the Fund buys foreign balances it is only to use them for gold purchases; if the Fund buys gold it is (indirectly) using foreign balances.

supply of bank credit is perfectly elastic can effective circulation be increased by the full amount which the Exchange Stabilisation Fund borrows in order to finance its perfectly elastic demand for foreign exchange. If the elasticity of supply of bank credit is less than infinity, only a part of the amount borrowed by the Fund constitutes an expansion of monetary circulation.

Vice versa, if a capital export leads to sales of gold (or foreign balances) by the Fund, and if the Fund uses the proceeds from these sales to pay off bank debts (i.e., to buy back Treasury bills), the full amount will disappear from circulation only if the banks have ample excess reserves. But if the banks have been nearly loaned up, they will be able to make other loans and investments when their earning assets and demand deposits diminish through the Fund's repayments.[16] Hence only a part of the amount which the Fund received from the capital exporters and returned to the banks will constitute a contraction of monetary circulation.

Let us look back at our graph Fig. 4 and assume this time that it is the Exchange Stabilisation Fund which provides the amount HF of foreign balances (by selling gold) and receives for them $HFCE$ dollars. Assume, furthermore, that the $HFCE$ dollars are used by the Fund for repaying bank loans, that is to say, for purchasing from the banks $HFCE$ dollars' worth of Treasury bills. The deflationary effect of this transaction depends then chiefly on the elasticity of supply of bank credit. If the banks have been completely loaned up, and their credit supply is of zero elasticity, *none* of the $HFCE$ dollars will be wiped out (except for a negligibly short interval) because the banks have other uses for these funds. (If this implies slightly lower interest rates, a small fraction of the amount might be hoarded under the inducement of the lower interest.) If the banks have had abundant reserves, and their credit supply is of infinite elasticity, *all* of the $HFCE$ dollars will be wiped out. If the supply of bank credit is of more than zero and less than infinite elasticity, the amount of deflation will be between nil and $HFCE$.

---

[16] Certain qualifications concerning the reverse situation (see below, sub-sections 30 and 31) apply also to this case.

It should be mentioned that the effects of capital and gold flow may be completely perverted if capital importers wish to hold inactive bank balances and if capital exporters have been holding inactive bank balances.   In these cases, with the supply of bank credit less than perfectly elastic, the inflow of foreign funds may be deflationary and the outflow inflationary.

25. Most of the existing Exchange Stabilisation Funds avoid carrying large amounts of foreign balances.   They use, as we have assumed so far, foreign balances acquired for buying gold, and they obtain foreign balances needed by selling gold.   It might, however, be otherwise.   The Stabilisation Funds might be willing to carry any amount of foreign balances.   They might increase their "stocks" of foreign exchange by buying, and decrease them by selling.   Movements in foreign balances held would then be substituted for international gold movements.

Let us introduce these assumptions to the situations discussed in connection with our graphs Fig. 4 and Fig. 5. No gold is then exported, but the Exchange Stabilisation Fund reduces its holdings in foreign balances by HF (Fig. 4) when it sells foreign exchange to capital exporters.   No gold is imported, but the Exchange Stabilisation Fund increases its holdings in foreign balances by HF (Fig. 5) when it buys foreign exchange from capital importers.   One change in our conclusions which is certainly called for by the change in assumptions, concerns the balance of international payments.

In 20 we stated that the capital export (GF of Fig. 4) was equal to a fall in commodity imports (GM) plus a rise in commodity exports (MH) plus a net export of gold (HF), all calculated in terms of foreign exchange.   Now, under the changed assumptions, we have to state that the capital export (GF) is equal to a fall in commodity imports (GM) plus a rise in commodity exports (MH) plus a net reduction in foreign short-term balances (HF).   A reduction of balances due from foreign banks is, of course, a repayment of debts by foreigners, and thus, in technical language, a movement of short-term capital from the foreign country to our country.

We arrive therefore at this restatement regarding the changes in international transactions:

Long-term capital export equals Fall in commodity imports plus Rise in commodity exports plus Short-term capital import, i.e., $GF = GM + MH + HF$.

The balance of payments for the period during which the curves remain unchanged as in Fig. 4 reads now as follows:

Commodity exports plus Short-term capital import equals Commodity imports plus Long-term capital export, i.e., $OH + HF = OG + GF$, and $OHEA + HFCE = OGDA + GFCD$.

That this cannot be a position of stable equilibrium is clear. It is not necessary to prove this by refering to the fact that the stocks of foreign short-term balances must be exhausted sooner or later, just as it was not necessary to prove the instability of the gold export situation by referring to the limited gold stock.   What makes for the instability of this temporary equilibrium is the deflationary effect of the "short-term capital import."   This short-term capital import is a not very descriptive term for the underlying phenomenon: the disposal of balances held with foreign banks by the Exchange Stabilisation Fund.

The extent of the deflationary effect depends, as shown before, on the use which the Fund makes of the proceeds from the sale of foreign exchange.   The deflationary effect causes eventually the supply curve of foreign exchange to shift to the right and the demand curves to shift to the left.   The stable equilibrium[17] of the balance of international payments will then show (increased) commodity exports equal to (decreased) commodity imports plus (decreased) long-term capital exports.

The discussion of the converse case, that of long-term capital imports, can be brief.   The provisional change in the balance of payments as shown in Fig. 5 would be this:

Long-term capital import equals Fall in commodity exports plus

---

[17] "Stable" describes this equilibrium position only if the capital export is regarded as a *datum* for our problem.   From another point of view the incentive to export capital diminishes, of course, as the cumulative sums exported grow.

Rise in commodity imports plus Short-term capital export, i.e., $GF = GM + MH + HF$. The "short-term capital export" of this balance is, of course, nothing else but the purchase of foreign exchange, or more concretely, of foreign bank balances by the Exchange Stabilisation Fund. By acquiring claims against foreign banks the Fund "exports" short-term capital which takes up a part of the import of long-term capital. "Export of short-term capital" is again not a very descriptive term for the phenomenon designated, i.e., for the purchase by the Fund of balances with foreign banks.

This transaction has an inflationary effect, the extent of which will depend on the methods employed in financing the Fund's purchases of foreign exchange. The inflationary effect will cause a decline in the supply of foreign exchange, both from commodity exports and capital imports, and an increase in the demand for foreign exchange for commodity imports. The result of these shifts will be a stable equilibrium with (increased) commodity imports equal to (decreased) commodity exports plus (decreased) long-term capital imports.

V

26. In the preceding section, since we dropped the assumption of independent currency systems, we have carried on our analysis on the assumption of organised exchange rate stabilisation. This stabilisation of foreign exchange rates was first (19–22) the result of an "orthodox" gold standard system with legally guaranteed gold sales and purchases; later (23–25) it was the result of a "modern" gold standard system with sales and purchases of gold or foreign balances by an Exchange Stabilisation Fund.

To drop the assumption of organised exchange stabilisation is not equivalent to returning to the assumption of flexible exchange rates or, still less, to returning to the assumption of independent currencies. Exchange stabilisation, firstly, may be the result of persistent pegging by commercial banks and foreign exchange dealers. Secondly, movements in foreign short-term balances, whether the exchange rate is fixed or flexible, involve ordinarily changes in the monetary circulation, thus removing the criterion of an "independent" currency.

Persistent pegging by commercial banks and foreign exchange dealers could be motivated by open or tacit agreements among them, or by their general belief in the permanence of the value of the currencies, or, most plausibly, by their confidence in the existence of some organised stabilisation scheme or in some latent stabilisation policy of the monetary authorities. The last of these motives may render it possible that the actual stabilisation of the exchange rates is achieved through the stabilising purchases and sales of foreign balances by commercial banks and dealers without the existing (or only imagined) official stabilisation machinery ever being put into operation.

The range over which the demand for foreign exchange at a certain low rate, and the supply of foreign exchange at a certain high rate, are perfectly elastic is, of course, smaller if this demand and supply are thus based solely on the voluntary pegging activities of commercial banks and dealers. If the monetary authorities stand behind the voluntary pegging in that they offer their ever ready organised stabilisation machinery (orthodox or modern), then we may interpret the infinite elasticities of demand and supply of foreign exchange as resulting, for a certain range, from private pegging and, for another range, from official stabilising. In the absence of effective organised stabilisation the supply curve would resume its usual upward direction, and the demand curve would resume its usual downward direction, once the readiness or the forces of private pegging are exhausted. Private pegging would have exhausted its power to supply foreign exchange when all the holdings in foreign balances had been disposed of and new foreign credit could be had only at increased cost. Private pegging would have exhausted its power to demand foreign exchange, when the institutional limits of credit expansion had been reached and domestic funds could be raised only at increased cost. Fig. 6 depicts this situation.[18]

---

[18] Fig. 6 shows that dealers would be willing to sell an amount EV of foreign exchange before the exchange rate could rise above OA, and that dealers would be willing to buy an amount RT (or $R'T'$) of foreign exchange before the exchange rate could fall below OB. The combined demand curve (of importers and deal-

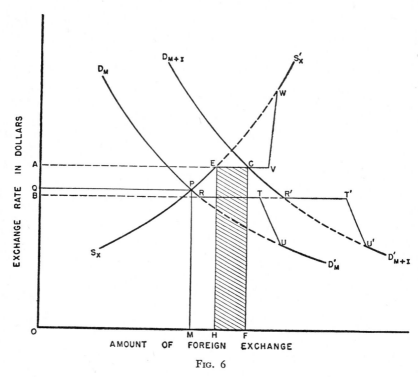

FIG. 6

It is, however, quite possible that the range over which private
pegging can effectively secure perfect elasticities of supply and
demand at a pair of exchange rates is large enough for most
practical situations.   (In Fig. 6 the supply by dealers is sufficient
to meet the increase in demand.)   This will be more probable the
more inflationary and deflationary are the effects of foreign exchange purchases and sales by the pegging banks and dealers.   For,
if these purchases of foreign balances increase domestic circulation
and if these sales of foreign balances decrease domestic circulation,

---

ers) is $D_M RTUD'_M$, the combined supply curve (of exporters and dealers) is
$S_X EVWS'_X$.

If the appearance of a demand for foreign exchange for purposes of capital
export raises the aggregate demand for foreign exchange from $D_M D'_M$ to D_{M+I}
D'_{M+I}, the exchange rate rises from OQ to OA and dealers sell EC from their

then the "correcting" shifts of market supply and demand curves take place before the forces of private pegging are exhausted. We should examine, therefore, the extent to which purchases and sales of foreign exchange by commercial banks and dealers affect the monetary circulations of the countries.

27. If it is commercial banks that do the pegging of exchange rates, then it is obvious that their purchases immediately increase, and their sales immediately decrease, monetary circulation (i.e., check deposits). The only question is whether or not their purchases of foreign balances prevent them from acquiring other assets, and whether or not their sales of foreign balances give them occasion for the acquisition of other assets. If the purchase of foreign exchange prevents the banks from making loans which they otherwise would have made, then the purchase cannot be said to cause a net expansion of monetary circulation. And if the sale of foreign exchange gives the banks occasion to acquire other assets which they otherwise would not have acquired, then the sale cannot be said to result in a net contraction of monetary circulation. Is this likely to be the case?

The answer depends on two circumstances: first, on the flexibility of the banks' ratios between reserves and deposits, and on the flexibility of their "borrowed reserves"; second, on whether foreign balances are counted among the reserves. If foreign balances are counted as reserves, the inflationary effects of their acquisition and

---

holdings of foreign balances. They receive $HFCE$ dollars from the capital exporters.

The graph is, however, open to objections on methodological grounds. Firstly, the assumptions concerning expectations of future exchange rate changes are of one type in the case of the exporters' and importers' supply and demand, and of a totally different type in the case of the dealers' supply and demand. This problem will be alluded to later on in 33. Secondly, the exporters' and importers' supply and demand refer to a *flow* of foreign exchange (e.g., exporters sell AE per month) whereas the dealers' supply and demand refer to a *stock* of foreign exchange (e.g., dealers sell EC in the first month but would not sell more than EV in the aggregate). The combination of all these curves and parts of curves in one graph is, I believe, legitimate for a short period (e.g., for the *period* of one month if the other curves represent *rates* per month).

the deflationary effects of their disposal are beyond doubt; indeed, these effects are magnified because even secondary expansions and restrictions of credit may be induced by these "changes in reserves." In the United States the law confines the concept of reserves of member banks to balances held with the Federal Reserve banks; foreign balances, therefore, are no reserve; their acquisition, by creating demand deposits, reduces the reserve ratio, and their sale, by wiping out demand deposits, raises the reserve ratio. Hence, in the United States, it is the first of the above-mentioned circumstances which determines our question.

If the ratio of reserves to deposits were absolutely constant, purchases of foreign balances by commercial banks would be at the expense of other loans and investments, unless the banks borrow from the central banks. The member banks which are "loaned up" but wish to purchase foreign balances and to hold them until foreign exchange rates rise from their low level, can do so only if they have a part of their bill-portfolio rediscounted or a part of their investment-portfolio taken over by the Reserve banks. If the banks are not "loaned up" but have a high reserve ratio (i.e., high excess reserves) and are willing to see the reserve ratio reduced, they can buy and carry foreign balances without obstacles. Hence, flexibility of the reserve ratio or flexibility of the amount of reserves are the conditions which make for inflationary effects of foreign exchange purchases by commercial banks.

Likewise, sales of foreign exchange by commercial banks are deflationary, if the banks are willing to see their reserve ratio (i.e., their excess reserves) increased or if they have a part of their reserves "borrowed" and can now repay them. If none of their reserves were borrowed and the reserve ratio were to be kept constant, so that the banks would have to acquire immediately other assets as soon as they sell foreign balances, then no deflationary effects would ensue from these sales.

Looking at present-day practice we find that the reserve ratios of member banks are sufficiently flexible to allow exchange purchases and sales by commercial banks to have inflationary and deflationary effects.

28. If not banks but private dealers are engaged in foreign exchange pegging, we have to ask what funds are used by these dealers for their purchases of foreign balances.   If they use borrowed funds and arrange for bank loans in order to purchase foreign exchange, and repay bank loans when they sell foreign exchange, then the situation is almost the same as described before. The banks acquire the foreign exchange dealers' bills instead of the foreign exchange directly.   The banks' bill-portfolio rises when the dealers buy and falls when the dealers sell foreign balances.

Had the dealers the habit of disbursing and accumulating idle balances whenever they bought and sold foreign exchange, the inflationary and deflationary effects would be a matter of dishoarding and hoarding (and would show through velocity, rather than volume, of circulation).   If neither dealers' idle balances nor created bank funds were available for the dealers' purchases so that the necessary funds would have to be sought on the open market from non-banking sources, then the inflationary effect of their purchases would be trivial: it would be confined to the dishoarding induced by slightly increased interest rates.   Likewise, the deflationary effect of dealers' sales of foreign exchange would be confined to the hoarding induced by slightly reduced interest rates if the dealers had no bank funds but only private business funds borrowed for carrying their foreign balances.

The more common practice is certainly that the dealers finance their transactions through bank loans.   Hence, again, the conclusion seems warranted that dealers' purchases of foreign balances have the inflationary effects, and dealers' sales of foreign balances have the deflationary effects, which we have discussed several times; so that the effects of ordinary transactions by foreign exchange dealers approach the effects of the gold movements under an orthodox gold standard.

The sharp line which many writers have drawn between the international gold standard and other monetary systems proves to be without justification from a purely economic point of view. The time-honoured theory of foreign exchange under the gold standard has, for example, a more appropriate application to a case of legally flexible exchanges where speculators sell foreign balances and repay debts to highly liquid banks, than it has to a case of a legally simon-pure gold standard where the central bank sells gold but allows at the same time commercial bank deposits to remain unchanged.

29. Contemporary writers on the subject have expressed the view that movements of foreign short-term bank balances "differ radically" from international gold movements as far as their effects on incomes and prices are concerned. This view is correct only if writers think of the *secondary* expansions and restrictions that are invited by gold movements under the fractional reserve system: a movement of a certain amount of gold might call forth a multiple amount of bank credit creation in the one country, and a multiple amount of bank credit destruction in the other. We said, however, above (in 22) that the secondary creation and destruction of bank credit is not necessary from the point of view of international equilibrium theory. From this point of view we consider as an essential part of the mechanism only the "transfer" of such purchasing power as is equivalent in amount to the international payment which gives rise to it.

If it is, thus, not expected that a certain gold flow wipes out in the one country and creates in the other country, more than an equivalent amount of purchasing power, then it makes, in principle, little difference whether gold flows or whether bank balances move. To return to our example of Fig. 4, the flow of gold is expected to reduce circulation in the paying country by *HFCE* dollars and to increase circulation in the receiving country by *HF* units of its currency. Assume now that no gold is exported but that the amount *HF* of foreign balances is bought (by capital exporters) from domestic banks. In the paying country *HFCE* dollars of domestic bank deposits are wiped out through this transaction. In the receiving country *HF* units of its currency are transferred from the idle accounts of foreign banks to the (probably) active account of the persons from whom the capital exporter buys securities. The amount wiped out in the one country corresponds to the amount which is "activated" in the other country.

The deflationary effect in the paying country takes place, in this case, through a reduction in the volume of circulation; the inflationary effect in the receiving country takes place through an increase in the velocity of circulation.

In which country the amount and in which country the velocity of bank deposits change depends on the method of payment. One might send a check drawn on a bank in one's own country (i.e., a dollar check) and the foreign bank to which the payee sells the check may then carry an increased dollar deposit. In this case V' changes in our country while M' changes in the foreign country. On the other hand, one might buy, as in the previous example, from one's bank a draft on a foreign bank which the payee abroad deposits in his bank account. In this case M' changes in our country while V' changes in the foreign country.

To employ Fig. 5 once more, we see that foreign bank checks in the amount of HF units of the foreign currency may be sold to our banks. Our banks thus create $HFCE$ dollars of new deposits. In the foreign country the amount of HF units of its currency is transferred from the probably active accounts of the remitters to the idle accounts of our banks which buy the foreign checks from the payees. This time, the deflationary effect in the paying country takes place through a reduction in velocity of circulation; the inflationary effect in the receiving country takes place through an increase in the volume of circulation.

30. One important difference between exchange stabilisation by central banks (or with central bank funds) and exchange stabilisation without central bank funds bears on the rate of interest. If central banks buy foreign exchange or gold, the reserves of member banks are increased. The same is true if an Exchange Stabilisation Fund buys foreign exchange and obtains the necessary means from the central bank, for instance through the issue of gold certificates. The ensuing increase in excess reserves of banks and in the liquid balances of firms and individuals has the tendency to ease the money market and to lower interest rates.

If, on the other hand, commercial banks buy foreign exchange, or if dealers and speculators buy foreign exchange with funds borrowed from commercial banks or in general on the money market, the excess reserves of banks and the liquid balances of firms and individuals are reduced.   The same is true if an Exchange Stabilisation Fund buys foreign exchange and obtains the necessary means by borrowing from commercial banks or on the open market, for instance, through the issue of Treasury bills.   Except in the case of an infinitely elastic supply of bank credit, a tendency to stiffen the money market and to raise interest rates is the result of the inflow of foreign payments.

The reverse, of course, is true for an outflow of gold or foreign exchange.   If central bank funds are liquidated by the outflow, excess reserves and liquid balances are reduced.   If commercial bank funds or private funds are liquidated by the outflow of foreign exchange, excess reserves and liquid balances are increased. A tendency towards higher interest rates follows from the former situation, a tendency towards lower interest rates may follow from the latter situation.

Thus, if no central bank funds are engaged in exchange stabilisation transactions, a flow of capital may lead to temporarily reduced interest rates in the country from which the capital is withdrawn, or to temporarily increased interest rates in the country to which the capital is sent.   This sounds paradoxical but it is nevertheless true.   If we imagine that English capitalists buy American securities we invariably associate with this the idea that interest rates in the American markets are reduced.   According to our customary reasoning, the transaction involves an increased demand for American securities, hence increased security prices which are equivalent to reduced long-term interest rates.   Yet this reasoning is valid (abstracting from changed expectations on the part of domestic investors) only if the supply of pound sterling in New York (or demand for dollars in London) leads to a purchase of the pound sterling or of gold by the American monetary authorities and to a creation of American excess reserves and liquid balances. It is different if the Exchange Stabilisation Fund, pursuing a policy of offsetting, has first to raise on the open market the dollars with which to buy the pound sterling, before the English capitalist can buy American securities; or, similarly, if an American dealer or speculator has first to borrow dollars with which to take over the pound sterling, before the increased demand for securities can become effective.   In these cases an increased demand for investible funds precedes the increased demand for securities; the demand for securities is thus nothing but the (immediate) re-supply of the investible funds raised by the buyers of foreign balances.

31. A simplified picture of this situation can be gained by the following description: an English capitalist desires to hold American securities and offers English bank balances. By offering the English balances at a low dollar price, he makes an American dealer desire to hold English bank balances and offer his promissory notes. By offering promissory notes at a reduced price, i.e., at a higher discount—it is assumed that the supply of bank credit is not perfectly elastic—the dealer makes an American investor desire to hold promissory notes instead of securities, and instead of idle cash. So the American investor will get the foreign exchange dealers' promissory notes, the English capitalist will get the American securities formerly held by the American investor, and the foreign exchange dealer will get the English balances from the English capitalist. Since the impulse to these transactions starts with the offer from the English capitalist and is continued by the offer from the foreign exchange dealer, the prices of pound sterling balances and of promissory notes have to recede.   The decline in the price of promissory notes is, of course, identical with an increase in the short-term rate of interest.

In the absence of frictions the increased demand and higher interest rate for liquid funds would make the holder of both securities and cash balances desire to switch some of his securities and some of his liquid balances into holdings of short-term credit instruments. Frictions of psychological and institutional nature, however, will often arrest any tendency towards security selling and turn the whole impulse into dishoarding and bank credit expansion. But inasmuch as the supply of bank loans is less than perfectly elastic the increase in short-term interest rates is sustained.

Security prices did not have to fall (or only a trifle or for only a short period) in the foregoing example, partly because of the induced dishoarding and credit creation; chiefly, however, because the possibly increased willingness to part with securities on the side of American investors, which was prompted by the attractive terms for short-term loans, was met by the increased demand for American securities by the English capitalists.   If, however, the increased supply of English balances (or gold) had been due not to increased English capital exports to the United States but to increased English commodity imports from the United States, or to any other English payments to the United States, then American security prices might have receded more noticeably.   The supply of English balances would have, as in the other case, led to an increased demand for American short-term funds by the buyers of the cheap English balances (foreign exchange dealers, speculators, or the Exchange Stabilisation Fund) without these funds being used afterwards for the purchase of the securities offered by American investors.   The funds would have gone to those who had to receive payments from the foreign remitters, for instance, to American commodity exporters.

It is thus clear that a rise in interest rates may result from a so-called favourable balance of payments if the increased supply of foreign balances (or gold) is purchased out of funds other than newly created central bank money.   Conversely, a fall in interest rates may result from a so-called adverse balance of payments if the increased demand for foreign balances (or gold) is satisfied by sales which liquidate funds of individuals, firms and commercial banks instead of wiping out central bank money.

A qualification is in order concerning the situation in which the supply of commercial bank credit is perfectly elastic.   In this situation, of course, short-term interest rates would neither fall nor rise.   This would be, therefore, the intermediate case between that where central bank funds are created and wiped out, and that where other funds are employed and released, when foreign balances are acquired and disposed of.

32. Organised exchange stabilisation and private pegging (based chiefly on a *belief* in the existence of a stabilisation policy)

have allowed us to assume the existence of a supply and demand of foreign exchange on the part of those who are willing to draw on, and to add to, their existing foreign balances. This supply and demand would be precarious and absolutely indeterminate in the absence of any definite policy of the monetary authorities and of any definite expectations concerning such a policy. Under these circumstances this private supply and demand would be based on ever-changing expectations which make the respective supply and demand curves shift so rapidly, erratically or unpredictably that it becomes meaningless to "assume" any such supply and demand curves even in a short-period analysis.

In the absence of any definite policy of the authorities (i.e., when the policy is indefinite even for the shortest period), the least illegitimate assumption will be that over a longer period of time nobody will want to carry an appreciably increased or decreased amount of foreign (credit or debit) balances. This assumption implies that the analysis of the foreign exchange market is reduced again to the other (less erratic) sources of supply and demand such as commodity trade, exchange of services, regular payments, etc. "Speculation" may then at any moment result in a somewhat different exchange rate than would follow from the other factors in the market, but it cannot lead to perpetually one-sided deviations of the actual rate from the "equilibrium-rate." This follows logically from our assumptions: if speculation has a persistent influence in a certain direction, then speculation is based on definite expectations and allows us to assume the shape of the respective supply or demand of foreign balances. If, on the other hand, speculation is erratic, so that none of the foreign credit balances acquired for speculative purposes are held for a long time, and none of the foreign debit balances arranged for speculative purposes are left unsettled for a long time, then speculation has no lasting net influence on the foreign exchange rate.

33. Expectations concerning future changes of the foreign exchange rate shape supply and demand of those who are willing to draw on, and add to, their foreign balances (banks, dealers, speculators). But expectations as to future rate changes may enter

also into the determination of supply and demand of other groups. Commodity importers will have an increased demand for foreign exchange when they expect a rise in the foreign exchange rates,[19] and a decreased demand when they expect a fall. Commodity exporters' supply of foreign exchange will decrease when a rise in foreign exchange rates is expected, and increase when a fall is expected. These changes in supply and demand would not be due to *direct* speculation in foreign exchanges; if they were, the respective transactions would have to be included in the supply and demand of those who sell foreign balances which they have held, and buy foreign balances which they will carry. The demand for foreign exchange by commodity importers (in their capacity as commodity importers) rises because they actually intend to import more at the time being when they expect that later the imported goods would cost them more and would sell higher. In a sense they speculate in goods, not in exchange.

The importers *qua* importers do not increase their holdings of foreign balances but they increase their commodity stocks. And when they expect a fall in exchange rates, they do not sell foreign balances but they diminish their commodity stocks by postponing further import orders.

An actual rise or fall in exchange rates may cause principally three types of anticipations: (1) that the exchange rates will rise or fall still further; (2) that the exchange rates will fall or rise again to their former level; (3) that the exchange rates will remain at their new level. Only the last type of anticipation is fully consistent with the usual assumptions under which supply and demand curves (of final sellers and final buyers) are drawn. If a fall or rise in exchange rates arouses expectations of type (1) or (2), this is usually depicted by a shift of the supply and demand curves. Should now *every* change in the exchange rates give rise to some unpredictable change in expectations of type (1) and (2), then short-run analysis of the usual type would break down completely. The changes in expectations would cause the whole curves to shift

---

[19] Foreign exchange rates are assumed to be expressed in terms of the amount of domestic currency exchanged per unit of foreign currency.

as often as the rate changes; hence shifts *along* the old curves (and, thus, elasticities) would become irrelevant.

Short-run analysis becomes thus impossible if rapid, erratic and unpredictable changes in expectations make almost everybody a speculator. Theoretical analysis is then more or less confined to the long period; and it loses, of course, some of its significance: its immediate applicability to currently observable facts is gone.

Changes in expectations are, by and large, eliminated as determining factors in long-period analysis. The postponement or advancing of orders by buyers, as well as the withholding or pressure-selling by sellers, are supposed to cancel out in the long run. In long-period analysis the complications introduced by erratic changes of expectations are avoided, although several qualifications would have to be added to the statements of a long-run theory of the foreign exchange market. We shall not expatiate here on these problems.

34. One of the most naive misunderstandings in the theory of foreign exchanges is the idea that the balance of international payments shows the supply and demand of foreign exchange and can explain the movements of the foreign exchange rates observed in the market. Where this idea errs can be best seen by recalling something we were taught in first-year economics.

If 125 quarts of strawberries were sold at a price of 24 cents we know that 125 quarts were demanded and 125 quarts were supplied at 24 cents, but we know neither the demand nor the supply of strawberries. If during the next period 125 quarts are sold at a price of 22 cents, we do not know whether the demand for strawberries has decreased (with a perfectly inelastic supply), or whether the supply of strawberries has increased (with a perfectly inelastic demand), or whether both a decrease in demand and an increase in supply have concurred in bringing about the result. The matter is fundamentally the same if quantities change rather than prices, or if both change. Every teacher of economics is apt to become impatient when a student confuses demand with quantity demanded and supply with quantity supplied.

The balance of international payments can never show more

than one point on the demand and supply curves; but even this is not true if one looks at the balance of payments for any given year, because the transactions during a period of a year may be the result of several changes in the supply and demand situation. And if the statistics show that imports have increased from one year to the next, this does not tell whether the increase in imports was brought about in consequence of an increase in the demand for imports, or in spite of a decrease in the demand for imports, or with an unchanged demand for imports, etc. The balance of international payments does not reveal which of the changes were "spontaneous" and which were "induced," either directly by changes in the exchange rate or more indirectly by the effects upon circulation of other items in the balance.

An attempt to analyse the foreign exchange market with the tools and in the terminology of general price theory helps in avoiding pitfalls into which one is easily led by the often confusing terminology in which foreign trade and foreign exchange theory is usually treated.

THEORY OF INCOME TRANSFERS AND REPARATIONS

6

THE GERMAN TRANSFER PROBLEM*

By J. M. Keynes‖

The Dawes Committee divided the problem of the payment of German Reparations into two parts—into the *Budgetary* Problem of extracting the necessary sums of money out of the pockets of the German people and paying them to the account of the Agent-General, and the *Transfer* Problem of converting the German money so received into foreign currency.

As time has gone on, opinion has become even more sharply divided than it was on the question whether this dichotomy has theoretical and practical significance. The view has been widely expressed that the Transfer Problem is of quite secondary importance and that, so long as the Budgetary Problem is solved, the Transfer Problem will, in the main, solve itself. The following note is directed to a theoretical discussion of this issue.

Those who think that the Transfer Problem is secondary argue thus. The German people receives its income in return for its current output of goods and services. If an appropriate part of this income is sequestrated, there will be no buyers for a corresponding amount of goods, which will therefore be available (in addition to what would be available otherwise) to expand exports or in diminution of imports. Since not all the consumption of goods and services, which the German people are compelled to forgo, is suitable for export, there will have to be a certain amount of change-over in the character of production. There is, however, no reason to suppose that ordinary economic forces will not bring this about within a reasonable space of time. Thus—according to this school—the real question is, how much cash can the German

* *Economic Journal*, Volume XXXIX (March, 1929), pages 1–7. Reprinted by the courtesy of the *Economic Journal*, without change from the original text.
‖ King's College, Cambridge, England, until his death on April 21, 1946.

Government raise by sound financial methods and pay over to the Agent-General. Once this is settled, we can be sure that a way will be found of looking after the Transfer Problem.

Now I do not doubt that there are sets of premises from which this conclusion follows. For example, there is one very simple set from which it obviously follows. For let us suppose that the German factors of production produce nothing but exports and consume nothing but imports; in this case it is evident that there is only a Budgetary Problem and no Transfer Problem;—or rather the Transfer Problem is removed from the shoulders of Germany and becomes a problem as between the recipients of reparation and the countries from which Germany previously drew her imports.

But, on the other hand, if we suppose that Germany is already exporting all the goods which she has facilities for producing on any terms on which the rest of the world will buy them—suppose, for example, that, not so unlike Russia to-day, her exports are limited to caviare and platinum, of which the output cannot be increased—then the Transfer Problem is paramount and, indeed, insoluble. Or, again, let us suppose that, whilst, as before, Germany's exports are limited to caviare and platinum, she is, this time, in a position to increase their output, but unfortunately the demand of the rest of the world for these articles has an elasticity of less than unity. In this case the more she exports, the smaller will be the aggregate proceeds. Again the Transfer Problem will be a hopeless business.

The first question to consider is, therefore, a question of fact —whereabouts between the two extremes exemplified above is present-day Germany situated? In other words, our first question is, whether there exists an ideal distribution of Germany's factors of production as between different uses which, if it could be arranged, would solve the Transfer Problem?

When this question has been dealt with, there remains a second question,—How completely and by what train of causation is the machinery of the Dawes scheme capable of bringing about this ideal distribution?

I

(1) If £1 is taken from you and given to me and I choose to increase my consumption of precisely the same goods as those of which you are compelled to diminish yours, there is no Transfer Problem. Those who minimise the question of transfer seem sometimes to imply that the above is a fair representation of the present facts. To the extent that high taxation causes German consumers to buy less foreign goods, it is a fair representation. But clearly only a proportion of their abstention from consuming will be in respect of foreign goods, and, so far as one can judge at present, not a very large proportion. Moreover, the German balance of trade *already* has most of the benefit of this, inasmuch as individual Germans are already paying enough, or nearly enough, taxes to solve the Budgetary Problem, and are, therefore, already reducing their personal consumption to the requisite extent.

(2) For the last two or three years the Transfer Problem has been temporarily solved by Germany borrowing abroad for capital purposes at home, cash which she does not bring home in the shape of imports. She has been using this cash to buy back from the Agent-General the proceeds of taxes paid over to him, out of which she then pays the wages of German workmen employed on capital improvements within Germany. Clearly this process of borrowing from abroad cannot go on indefinitely. When it comes to an end, it will be necessary to divert the labour which it now employs to producing for export.

Thus it will not be—in the main—a question of reducing German consumption. In so far as the Budgetary Problem has been already solved, the necessary reduction of consumption is already effective. When the foreign borrowing comes to an end, it will be a question, not of reducing current consumption in Germany, but of transferring labour from capital works in Germany to the export trades. Only in so far as additional savings within Germany take the place in future of foreign loans will there be any surplus of resources which were previously directed to supplying German consumers. On the other hand, where the output of capital improvements, financed by foreign loans is not in an exportable form (and much of it will not be in such a form), the diversion of production out of other employments into the export trades (or to produce goods previously imported) will have to be on a greater scale than is required by the payment of Reparations alone, since it will be necessary to provide also for the interest on the foreign loans.

(3) I conclude, therefore, that the solution of the Transfer Problem must come about, in the main, not by the release to foreign consumers of goods now consumed by Germans (*e.g.* wheat, sugar, cotton), but by the diversion of German factors of production from other employments into the export industries.[1]

(4) Now, what prevents Germany from having a greater volume of exports at the present time?   Is it that the export trades cannot attract more labour at the present level of remuneration? Or is it that they cannot sell an increased output at a profit unless they can first reduce their costs of production?   The available facts seem to indicate that the first, namely, inadequate supplies of labour at the present rates of remuneration, plays little or no part, and that the second is the real explanation.

That is to say, the solution of the Transfer Problem requires a reduction of German gold-costs of production relatively to such costs elsewhere.   There are three ways of bringing this about. Either German industrialists must increase their efficiency faster than industrialists elsewhere; or the rate of interest in Germany must be lower than elsewhere; or the gold-rates of efficiency-wages must be reduced compared with elsewhere.   Since German industrialists are reputed to be already at a fairly high level of efficiency relatively to those of other countries, I do not know why we should assume that they will outstrip us yet further.   For it is not enough that they should increase their efficiency (that they will doubtless do); they must increase it faster than others increase their efficiency. Nor is there any prospect of relatively cheap money for Germany; though there may be some future gain from a fall of German interest

---

[1] For brevity, I include in these in what follows the production of goods previously imported.

rates below their present high level. It follows that the Transfer Problem requires a reduction in the present gold-rates of efficiency-wages in Germany relatively to efficiency-wages elsewhere.

That is the first point to establish. The expenditure of the German people must be reduced, *not only* by the amount of the reparation-taxes which they must pay out of their earnings, but also by a reduction in their gold-rate of earnings below what they would otherwise be. That is to say, there are two problems, and not—as those maintain who belittle the difficulties of transfer—one problem. Indeed, a short way of putting the case is this. The *Transfer* Problem consists in reducing the gold-rate of efficiency-earnings of the German factors of production sufficiently to enable them to increase their exports to an adequate aggregate total; the *Budgetary* Problem consists in extracting out of these reduced money-earnings a sufficient amount of reparation-taxes. The *Budgetary* Problem depends on the wealth and prosperity of the German people; the *Transfer* Problem on the competitive position of her industries on the international market.

(5) If x is the percentage by which German efficiency-wages in terms of gold have to be reduced in order to develop an excess of exports sufficient to pay for Reparations, x—we may say—is the measure of the gravity of the Transfer Problem.

So far we have no experience to guide us as to the value of x. Nor shall we, so long as the Reparations payments are provided by borrowing abroad. It is quite certain that this must come to an end some day. But when, no one can say. Meanwhile the new Committee, now sitting in Paris, has very little more evidence to guide it as to the value of x than the Dawes Committee had five years ago.

In round figures German exports (including deliveries in kind) now stand at about £600,000,000 per annum. It looks—again in round figures—as if their excess over imports would have to increase by about £150,000,000 (perhaps even by £200,000,000) in order to balance the account without borrowing. Since German industry is largely dependent upon foreign sources for raw materials, this means a still larger increase in the gross figure of exports. The Agent-General concludes that Germany must look mainly to an increase in her exports of finished goods, which came to a total of £434,000,000 last year. Very roughly, therefore, Germany has to increase the value of her exports of finished goods by (say) 40 per cent. It is a formidable task.

Now, a reduction in the money-rate of efficiency-wages does not help her, and may injure her, in the following cases:

(i) Where the output, *e.g.* personal services or buildings, cannot be exported anyhow;

(ii) Where the world's demand for Germany's goods has an elasticity of less than unity, *i.e.* where a reduction in price stimulates demand less than in proportion, so that the greater quantity sells for a less aggregate sum;

(iii) Where Germany's foreign competitors fight to retain their present trade connections by reducing their own rates of wages *pari passu;*

(iv) Where Germany's foreign customers, reluctant to allow this more intensive competition with their home producers, meet it by raising their tariffs.

Moreover, if a reduction in price of 10 per cent. stimulates the volume of trade by 20 per cent., this does not increase the value of the exports by 20 per cent., but only by 8 per cent. ($1.20 \times 90 = 108$).

Two points should be noted in passing. The reduction in real wages would be by no means so large as the reduction in money-wages, since the prices of home-goods for home consumption might be expected to fall.[2] It does not follow, however, that it would be any the easier to reduce money-wages, as we have found in this country in the last four years. On the other hand, such reduction in real wages as does occur may reduce efficiency, in which case a still greater reduction in money-wages per head would be necessary to secure a given reduction in efficiency-wages.

In the light of these considerations, what reduction in the

---

[2] For the reverse phenomenon see the figures quoted on the next page, from which it appears that the recent increase in money-wages has caused the cost of living to rise by more than half the amount of the increase in money-wages.

money-rates of German wages will be required to increase German exports of finished goods by 40 per cent.? I do not venture to guess—except that I should expect it to be substantial. Only those who believe that the foreign demand for German exports is very elastic, so that a trifling reduction in German prices will do what is required, are justified in holding that the Transfer Problem is of no great significance apart from the Budgetary Problem.

My own view is that at a given time the economic structure of a country, in relation to the economic structures of its neighbours, permits of a certain "natural" level of exports, and that arbitrarily to effect a material alteration of this level by deliberate devices is extremely difficult. Historically, the volume of foreign investment has tended, I think, to adjust itself—at least to a certain extent—to the balance of trade, rather than the other way round, the former being the sensitive and the latter the insensitive factor. In the case of German Reparations, on the other hand, we are trying to fix the volume of foreign remittance and compel the balance of trade to adjust itself thereto. Those who see no difficulty in this—like those who saw no difficulty in Great Britain's return to the gold standard—are applying the theory of liquids to what is, if not a solid, at least a sticky mass with strong internal resistances.

Meanwhile—so far from a start having been made in reducing wages—the breathing space allowed by foreign borrowing has weakened Germany's competitive position by allowing German wages to rise again from the very depressed position which they occupied in 1924 after the Great Inflation. Mr. Parker Gilbert reckons that money-wages in Germany have risen by 40 per cent. since 1924 and real wages by 23 per cent., with the result that real-wages are now estimated at 8 per cent. higher than they were before the war.

II

Thus the Transfer Problem involves a reduction of x per cent. in the rates of gold-wages in Germany relatively to rates elsewhere, the value of x being determined by the factors outlined above.

The next question is—How does the Dawes scheme propose to bring about this reduction of wages? The answer is that it makes almost no contribution to the solution of this problem.

The easiest method would be to allow the exchange value of the German mark to fall by the amount required to give the necessary bounty to exports and then to resist any agitation to raise money-wages. But it is precisely this method which the Dawes scheme's device of "transfer protection" expressly forbids. Nor—as I read the Dawes scheme—is there any compulsory deflation when the "transfer protection" comes into play and the proceeds of the reparation-taxes accumulate within Germany, since these proceeds are to be invested in the short-loan market.

If, however, we suppose that, by agreement with the Reichsbank, deflation is enforced, how will this help? Only if, by curtailing the activity of business, it throws men out of work, so that, when a sufficient number of millions are out of work, they will then accept the requisite reduction of their money-wages. Whether this is politically and humanly feasible is another matter. Moreover, an attempt by foreign financiers to withdraw some part of their vast short-term loans to the German Money Market, estimated at £300,000,000, might be a by-product of a violent political and economic struggle aimed at the reduction of wages in the interests of foreign creditors.

The comfort of Germany's position under the Dawes scheme is this. The surplus, furnished by exports and foreign loans, will be duly remitted up to the amount of the annuity. But if in any year exports and foreign loans fail to furnish a sufficient surplus —and the mere fact that the annuity has been collected by taxation is no guarantee whatever that this surplus will be sufficient— then the Dawes scheme provides no effective means of pressure to increase the surplus. One may assume, therefore, that the German Government will be extraordinarily reluctant to forgo "transfer protection"—at any rate until there is more evidence than exists at present as to the amount of the surplus which exports left to themselves are likely to furnish.

But the retention of "transfer protection" may be desirable from other points of view than Germany's. Addressing the shareholders of Barclay's Bank last January, Mr. F. C. Goodenough said:—"It will be of great importance that the amount to be fixed should be not only acceptable to the Allies, but such as will obviate, as far as possible, forcing Germany into excessive industrial competition with the rest of the world through compelling her people to accept too low a standard of living." If Mr. Goodenough is right, some measure of "transfer protection" should be retained.

7

THE REPARATION PROBLEM: A DISCUSSION*

By Bertil Ohlin ‖

Transfer Difficulties, Real and Imagined

I

Mr. Keynes' article on "The German Transfer Problem" in the March number of this JOURNAL represents a forceful summing-up of the arguments of those economists who maintain that a transfer of the annuities fixed in the Dawes plan is beyond practical possibilities. His reasoning ignores, however, one very important side of the problem. In attempting to set forth why consideration of this neglected element must modify the practical conclusions I intend to imitate as far as it is within my power the brevity and clarity of Mr. Keynes' most elegant treatment.

Let me begin with a quotation: "If £1 is taken from you and given to me and I choose to increase my consumption of precisely the same goods as those of which you are compelled to diminish yours, there is no Transfer Problem. Those who minimise the question of transfer seem sometimes to imply that the above is a fair representation of present facts. To the extent that high taxation causes German consumers to buy less foreign goods, it is a fair representation. But clearly only a proportion of their abstention from consuming will be in respect of foreign goods, and, as far as one can judge at present, not a very large proportion" (p. 163).

This is the first part of a trend of reasoning which seems to me

---

* *Economic Journal*, Volume XXXIX (June, 1929), pages 172–173. Reprinted by the courtesy of the *Economic Journal* and the author, without change from the original text.

‖ Graduate School of Business, Stockholm.

to be of fundamental importance in any discussion of international capital movements.   It is a pity that Mr. Keynes has not followed it up, but has even failed to draw the consequences of the part of it he has stated in this passage.

He continues: "Moreover, the German balance of trade *already* has most of the benefit of this . . . "   Evidently, no account is taken of the fact that, if Mr. Keynes has given me £1 and I have returned £2 to him, the effect on our trade balances must be the reverse of what it would be, if only the first transaction had taken place.   Germany has paid half a dozen milliards of marks in reparation payments, but has borrowed twice as much.   Thus, the German trade balance has not had the "benefit" of a reduction in total buying power,[1] but the "disadvantage" of an increase to the amount with which borrowings have *exceeded* reparation payments.   This increased buying power must have tended to swell imports and reduce exports.

This fact, that the total buying power has been increased, not reduced—and that consequently experience tells nothing concerning the efficiency of a transfer of buying power in creating a German export surplus—is ignored also in the following passage, which forms the starting-point for the whole reasoning in the rest of Mr. Keynes' paper:

"Now, what prevents Germany from having a greater volume of exports at the present time?   Is it that the export trades cannot attract more labour at the present level of remuneration?   Or is it that they cannot sell an increased output at a profit unless they can first reduce their costs of production?   The available facts seem to indicate that the first, namely, inadequate supplies of labour at present rates of remuneration, plays little or no part,

---

[1] In a country, which neither borrows from nor lends to other countries and which maintains equilibrium on its capital market, "buying power" is identical with "aggregate of money earnings."   Foreign borrowing, however, increases and loans reduce buying power.   Similarly, inflationary credit policy increases and deflationary policy reduces it.   In the former case new buying power is created by the banks; in the latter, money which is earned and saved is not lent by the banks to others,—it vanishes and buying power falls off.

and that the second is the real explanation. That is to say, the solution of the Transfer Problem requires a reduction of the German gold-costs of production relatively to such costs elsewhere"[2] (p. 164).

Nothing is said about the influence of the German borrowings, which—being far greater than the reparation payments—seem to me to be the real explanation why the excess of imports into Germany is what it is. They also largely explain why Germany's productive resources have to such an extent been used for production of capital goods for the home market and have not increased the output and marketing of export goods.

These borrowings, in so far as they have exceeded the reparation payments, have not only increased the buying power in Germany and thus its importation of foreign goods; they have also reduced the buying power in the lending countries and, thus, their importation of German goods. It is true that the *direct* influence in this latter direction may not have been very great—as indicated in the first of the passages I have quoted—but indirect effects cannot be ignored.

Let us consider the nature of these indirect effects of a transfer of buying power.

II

A and B are two countries with normal employment for their factors of production. A borrows a large sum of money from B this year and the same sum during each of the following years. This transfer of buying power directly increases A's demand for foreign goods while it reduces B's. Thus, A's imports grow and its exports fall off.

If the sum borrowed is 100 mill. marks a year, the excess of imports in A brought about in this direct manner may be 20 mill. marks. For in large countries only a small part of demand turns

---

[2] In the business world the impression prevails that at any given moment sales cannot be increased, except at the cost of price reductions. Every firm sells as much as it can, at present! Surely, neither *this* fact nor the existing unemployment justifies the conclusion in the text. What other facts are available? Compare the end of Section II of this paper.

directly to foreign goods or to export goods.   The rest, 80 mill. marks, increases the demand in A for home market goods.

Evidently Mr. Keynes and the school of economists who share his view think that this is the end of these 80 mill. marks.   As they do not directly increase the excess of imports, they can have no effect whatever on the balance of trade.   They can be left out of the reasoning altogether.

I venture to suggest that, on the contrary, this amount of borrowed buying power deserves special attention.   It sets in motion a mechanism which indirectly calls forth an excess of imports in A of about the same magnitude.   Just as the loss of this buying power indirectly creates an export surplus in B; or, rather, these changes in buying power bring about at the same time an excess of imports in A and of exports in B.

The increased demand for home market goods in A will lead to an increased output of these goods.   In a progressive country this means that labour and capital, that would otherwise have passed to export industries and industries producing goods which compete directly with import goods, now go to the home market industries instead.   Output of these "import-competing" goods and of export goods increases less than it would otherwise have done.   Thus, there is a relative decline in exports and increase of imports and an excess of imports is created.

A corresponding adjustment takes place in B.   Home market industries grow less as a result of reduced demand for their products, and the labour and capital turns in greater proportion to export industries and industries manufacturing goods which compete directly with import goods.   The outcome is an excess of exports. B finds a widened market for its goods in A as a result of the adaptation of production which takes place in that country.   Thus, the readjustment of production is the consequence of the change in buying power in the two countries.

The monetary mechanism which brings about the change varies with the organisation of the monetary system.   In all cases of fixed foreign exchanges, however, there is an increase in monetary buying power in A and a decrease in B, which may be much larger than the 80 or 100 mill. marks. A secondary "inflation" and "deflation" may be necessary to bring about the adaptation of production and trade quickly enough. The more sudden the readjustment has to be, the greater this inflation in A and deflation in B, and the greater the changes in sectional price levels that are called forth.

The character of these price changes must be discussed briefly. Home market prices tend to rise in A and fall in B, relative to prices of export and import goods and prices of the goods which compete with import goods. The readjustment of production is partly, but partly only, the consequence of this change in "sectional price levels." (Production has a tendency to expand in the same way as demand, *i.e.* as the development of "markets," even without the stimulus of considerable price changes.)

It is not necessary that A's *export* prices should rise and B's fall. Thus, B need not offer its goods on cheaper terms of exchange to induce A to take a greater quantity of them. Indirectly, however, it is probable that a certain shift of the terms of exchange will take place. The increased buying power in A will to some extent affect also the prices of its export goods and its "import-competing" goods in an upward direction, while the corresponding classes of goods tend to become cheaper in B. In that way the readjustment of the balance of trade is made easier.

Note that these price changes are quite different from those assumed by the classical barter theory, which seems to underly Mr. Keynes' analysis. Mill and after him Edgeworth, Taussig[3] and many of their followers would say that *B must offer its goods on cheaper terms of exchange in order to induce A to buy more.* Thus, the primary price change is one between the prices of import and export goods in both countries, not between prices of these international goods and of home market goods, as explained above. This erroneous conclusion is reached because of the fact that the

---

[3] Professor Taussig seems to me to present two different and incompatible theories: (1) the barter theory of Mill; (2) a theory of the monetary and price mechanism, which has been further developed by Professor Viner, with whom I am in substantial agreement.

shift in buying power is ignored, except in so far as it *directly* affects demand for international goods.   It is left out of account that the demand conditions—the demand curves in an analysis *à la* Edgeworth in the ECONOMIC JOURNAL of 1894—are changed not only by the 20 but also by the 80 mill. marks.

If the mechanism I have endeavoured to indicate briefly above corresponds to reality, evidently a sufficient adjustment of the balance of trade may take place without any considerable reduction in B's export prices or increase in A's.   It seems, therefore, very misleading to represent the increase in B's exports as due entirely to a reduction in its export prices.

Of course, a discussion of the elasticity of demand for B's export goods, which tacitly assumes demand conditions to be unchanged, must reach the conclusion that considerable increases in the value of its exports are impossible.   As Mr. Keynes points out: "if a reduction in price of 10 per cent. stimulates the volume of trade by 20 per cent., this does not increase the value of the exports by 20 per cent., but only by 8 per cent. (1.20 × 90 = 108)" (p. 166).   An increase by 20 per cent. as a result of a 10 per cent. price reduction may appear as a very great elasticity of demand, and yet the value of exports grows only by 8 per cent.   How violent, then, must the price reduction be, if export values are to increase by 40 per cent. as in the German case, when the borrowings have ceased and reparations have to be paid by means of an export surplus.

The impression becomes quite different if it is remembered that the mechanism of adjustment indicated above will be at work and that exports from the lending (indemnity-paying) country will, therefore, grow even if export prices are not reduced at all relative to prices of international goods in other countries.   In this connection it should also be noted that—even regardless of changed demand conditions—the volume of exports of a country is not a function solely of its export prices relative to prices abroad.   More or less capital and labour may be used for the building up and support of marketing organisations with corresponding effects on sales abroad.   If it were not for these and other similar circumstances, it would be difficult to see, for instance, how import duties can reduce the export trade considerably and, reversely, how a return to free trade, which in many cases would reduce costs in export industries only a little, can substantially increase the volume of exports. Remember also that many German goods which lay on the border line of "exportability" may be sold in large quantities if their prices fall 10 per cent. With this background an increase of exports by 30, 40 or 50 per cent. does not seem impossible.

III

Of course, the assumption made above concerning A and B, that their productive factors are normally employed, does not apply to post-war conditions in Germany or all the Allied countries. In my opinion this fact does not, however, invalidate the conclusions. If the period of transition, during which Germany is to create an export surplus, is not less than five or six years, it will almost certainly contain a year or two of fairly full employment of the labour and capital which is not for some special reason immobilised (as many English miners seem to be at present).

I suspect that one of the reasons why most people are inclined to exaggerate the difficulty in creating a German export surplus is the impression of the "practical" business man, who has already a large export trade, that it is difficult for him to increase his sales abroad. This impression, however, is misleading, as it is based on a tacit assumption of unchanged demand conditions and fails to take into account the fact that many firms may pass from exporting practically nothing to considerable sales abroad during a period of five or six years.

Another fact to which little attention has been given in the recent discussion is that the present reorganisation of production, partly with the aid of foreign capital, has not yet had time to show its full effect on German competitive power and sales in other countries.

Let me add that experience speaks very strongly in favour of the conclusion that adjustments of trade balances go much easier and even quicker than the orthodox theory would have it. To take the latest example only: is it not surprising that one has heard so little of transfer difficulties during the last five years, when one single country has had a net import of capital (over and above its own payments to other countries) of six or seven milliards of marks?

That country is Germany.

It is not, of course, my intention to deny that a transfer of sums of the same magnitude as the Dawes annuities may meet considerable difficulties. If the policy of protection and of preference to home-made goods, which has been growing so much after the war, is intensified when German exports begin to grow, and is used consistently to prevent such exports, then the reparation payments may become virtually impossible. There can be little doubt that if Great Britain turns to protection and other countries are thereby led to raise their tariffs, the chances of substantial reparation payments are considerably reduced.

It is also clear that the rise in German wages and home market prices in recent years has been, although probably unavoidable, yet very unfortunate, as in the future it will almost certainly be necessary to deflate wages and prices to some extent, particularly in home market industries, if an export surplus is to be created. Possibly this difficulty may be partly evaded if rationalisation continues at a rapid pace and thus the effectiveness of production is raised, while monetary wages are kept constant.

IV

Granted, however—for the sake of argument—that an *automatic* transfer of several milliards of marks may be impossible, can the conclusion be defended that reparation payments of this magnitude are impossible? Is there anything in the reasoning of economists upholding the former thesis which proves that deliveries in kind of a similar size would also be impossible?

The answer seems to me to be in the negative. Whatever the possibilities of automatic transfer, there can be no doubt that deliveries in kind, *i.e.* an *organised shifting of demand*, can bring about an export surplus from Germany of the size and value envisaged in the Dawes plan. German taxation can make a sufficient quantity of German factors of production available for this purpose. Such a policy, like one of automatic transfer, assumes a readjustment of production in the countries which are to receive the indemnity payments. As everybody knows, this is not Great Britain or Italy, but partly France, partly and largely the United States (reparations being used to pay the inter-allied debts). Almost certainly, however, the United States will continue to export huge sums of capital to South America. It may be argued, therefore, that the ultimate recipients of the reparation amounts are France and South America. In principle, the safest and simplest way of organising the reparation payments would be a policy of deliveries in kind from Germany to France and the South American nations, which require imports of many commodities German industry is well able to produce.

Unfortunately, such a policy is outside the range of practical possibilities. The inevitable opposition of powerful American and British export industries to any such plan is one of the real obstacles, perhaps the greatest of them all, which lie in the way of an organised solution of the reparation problem.

8

THE TRANSFER PROBLEM RECONSIDERED*

By Lloyd A. Metzler‖ ‡

The analysis of capital movements has been characterized in recent years by increasing complexity. Few economists today would defend the adequacy of the orthodox theory of price-level adjustments induced by gold movements; and yet the theories which have been substituted for this simple doctrine are so eclectic as to allow for almost any conceivable type of reaction. We are told, for example, that a transfer of purchasing power from one country to another may move the terms of trade in favor of either country[1] or, again, that real income in the receiving country may either increase or decrease as a result of the transfer.[2] In short, an element of truth is found in almost every theory.

Unfortunately, discussion has been confined largely to special cases in which the possibility of a particular reaction is demonstrated. Hence, although it is known that a capital transfer may produce a great variety of results, very little may be said with precision about the conditions necessary for the occurrence of a particular set of reactions. This unsatisfactory state of affairs will no doubt continue until a manageable general equilibrium theory of capital transfers has been developed. Such a theory must be sufficiently simple, on the one hand, that properties of the system

---

*Journal of Political Economy, Volume L (June, 1942), pages 397–414. Reprinted by the courtesy of the Journal of Political Economy and the author.

‖ The University of Chicago.

‡ Squared brackets in the present text indicate all substantial additions to or alterations of the original text.

[1] Carl Iverson, Aspects of the Theory of International Capital Movements (London, 1936), passim.

[2] W. W. Leontief, "Note on the Pure Theory of Capital Transfer," in Explorations in Economics (New York, 1936), p. 88.

may be examined and sufficiently complex, on the other hand, to include the relevant factors of adjustment.[3]

Equilibrating factors usually considered are changes in relative price levels, modifications of resource distribution, movements of interest and exchange rates, and changes in sectional price levels. Of these, the first two have undoubtedly received the greatest amount of attention. It is now generally recognized, however, that shifts of monetary purchasing power may change not only prices and factor allocations but also levels of total employment and hence real incomes. A completely general theory must include these output adjustments, as well as the types of change enumerated above. Since the difficulties of such a general analysis are so formidable I have attempted the more modest task of isolating the influence of real income adjustments alone.[4]

To discuss this problem I have set up a simplified model of trade between two countries, in which changes of prices, interest rates, and exchange rates are impossible. The assumptions of unemployment, rigid monetary wage structures, competitive industries, and constant returns are sufficient to insure that changes of monetary demand will affect levels of output rather than prices. Monetary assumptions necessary to isolate real income effects are (1) the maintenance of constant interest rates in both countries and (2) the maintenance of fixed exchange rates. With the fixed-exchange-rate assumption, the currency unit of either country may be used as a unit of measure in both. Henceforth, all figures of income,

---

[3] Most general equilibrium theories satisfy the second criterion but not the first. Cf., e.g., B. Ohlin, *Interregional and International Trade* (Cambridge, 1935), Appen. I, pp. 553–62. On the other hand, cf. T. O. Yntema, *A Mathematical Reformulation of the General Theory of International Trade* (Chicago, 1932).

[4] Although my conclusions are strictly applicable only to economies conforming to a rather rigid set of assumptions, I believe that much can be said to justify the real income approach. In the first place a partial analysis may considerably improve one's intuition and make "guessing" about the general problem more intelligent. Second, the results even for this simple case are so numerous as to defy broad generalization. Finally, impediments to movements of prices and monetary costs frequently make it extremely useful to know whether real income adjustments alone can create for a debtor country the required export surplus.

consumption, etc., will be given in the currency of the paying country.

Under the simplified conditions set forth above, total income in each country will be determined by the amount of net investment and the character of consumption functions. The definition of income is the usual one of consumption *plus* net investment. But net investment now comprises two parts: (1) the net increase of producer's goods (and stocks), which will be called "domestic investment," and (2) the increase (decrease) of indebtedness abroad, arising from a favorable (unfavorable) trade balance. This second item of investment is simply the difference between exports and imports.[5]   Since total consumption for a given country consists of its consumption of domestic goods *plus* its imports, it follows that income may be measured by the sum of consumption of domestic goods, domestic investment, and exports.[6]

We may assume that initially the system is in equilibrium in the sense that any difference between exports and imports of one of the two countries is offset by private-capital movements.   Suppose that an international transfer amounting to 10 monetary units disturbs this equilibrium.   The mechanics of the monetary transfer will not be discussed.   It will be assumed either that foreign balances of the paying country are drawn upon or that gold is shipped or that banks of the receiving country extend loans to those of the paying country, the proceeds of which are used to make payment.   In any case, as long as interest rates and exchange rates are not altered, the effects of the transfer upon incomes are independent of these financial arrangements.[7]   The income effects

[5] [More accurately, it is the difference between foreign receipts and expenditures on current account.   In what follows, the so-called "invisible" items in the balance of payments on current account are assumed to be included among the exports and imports.]

[6] I have introduced here the simplifying assumption that imports in both countries are for consumption purposes.   If the period of time considered is sufficiently long, so that investment is independent of the level of output, my simplification will not alter the final outcome.

[7] Invariance of exchange and interest rates implies a flexibility of bank policy which probably does not exist among any of the modern banking systems.   I have

depend entirely upon the fiscal policies of the two countries. [If governmental budgets are exactly balanced in the two countries both before and after the transfer, or if the size of the budget surpluses or deficits remains unchanged, the transfer necessarily involves a direct reduction of money income in the paying country and a corresponding direct increase of such income in the receiving country. That is, in order to prevent the transfer from influencing its budget, the government of the paying country must collect the transferred sum in the form of increased taxes. On the other hand, in the receiving country taxes must be *reduced* to prevent the accumulation of a budget surplus. Under these circumstances the transfer is equivalent to a direct transfer of money income from the one country to the other. It cannot be assumed, however, that the transfer will always affect income in the two countries in precisely this manner.] The government of the receiving country, for example, may simply build up a surplus with the transfer sums. In this case the only income adjustment is that attributable to taxation in the paying country. Likewise, the debtor country may pay from the proceeds of a bond issue, in which case the sole income adjustment arises from tax reduction in the receiving country. Thus there are three cases to consider: (1) a transfer accompanied by increased taxes in the paying country and reduced taxes in the receiving country; (2) a transfer accompanied by increased taxes in the paying country but with no change in tax rates in the receiving country; (3) a transfer accompanied by reduced taxes in the receiving country but with no change in taxes in the paying country.

The original changes of monetary incomes brought about by changes in taxes should not be confused with secondary movements of consumption and investment, in subsequent periods, induced by the initial purchasing-power shift. I shall refer hereafter to the initial change as a "direct" or "primary" income effect to distinguish it from "induced" or "secondary" changes. Solution

---

assumed that gold movements and movements of international balances leave lending terms of the central banks unchanged, not because I regard this as a realistic assumption but because I wish to isolate the influence of real income adjustments alone.

of the transfer problem, for my simple model, reduces to analysis of the manner in which secondary effects alter incomes and the balance of trade of the two trading countries. Such secondary changes will obviously vary according to the time sequence of income receipt and expenditure; consequently, it is necessary to specify a dynamic system. For this purpose it will be assumed, throughout, that consumption of income lags one period behind its receipt. Likewise, it will be assumed that induced private investment in a given period depends upon income of the previous period. With this dynamic system in mind, interpretation of Tables 1, 2, and 3, where the analysis is set forth, is a simple matter.

Each of the tables is divided into three parts. In Part I the transfer is assumed to affect income directly in both countries; that is, money incomes are expanded in the receiving country and contracted in the paying country by exactly the amount of the transfer. In Part II, on the other hand, contraction in the paying country is the only direct effect of the transfer; the government of the receiving country is assumed not to pay out the proceeds to its citizens. Finally, in Part III of each table direct income effects are limited to reduced taxation in the receiving country; the debtor government is assumed to make payment either from an accumulated surplus or from the proceeds of a loan.

Since the construction of all the tables is the same, it will suffice to explain one of them. Consider the first line of Table 1. In the first period the income of the paying country is reduced by 10 and that of the receiving country increased by the same amount. These changes react upon consumption and investment of subsequent periods in the manner indicated. A marginal propensity to consume domestic goods of 0.2 in the debtor country means that consumption of these goods in the second period is 2 units less than it would have been in the absence of the transfer. Likewise, imports are 2 less and domestic investment 1 less, since marginal propensities to consume foreign goods and to invest are 0.2 and 0.1, respectively. Similar considerations explain the deviations of consumption and investment from equilibrium levels (in the second period) in the receiving country.

It was shown above that income in each country may be ex-

TABLE 1.   TRANSFER EFFECTS WHEN BOTH COUNTRIES ARE STABLE IN ISOLATION

(*International Transfer = 10 Units*)

	In Paying Country	In Receiving Country
Marginal propensity to consume domestic goods	0.2	0.3
Marginal propensity to consume foreign goods	0.2	0.1
Marginal propensity to invest	0.1	0.1

Part	Changes in Paying Country				Changes in Receiving Country			
	Consumption of Domestic Goods	Consumption of Foreign Goods	Investment	Income	Consumption of Domestic Goods	Consumption of Foreign Goods	Investment	Income
	(1)	(2)	(3)	(4)	(5)	(6)	(7)	(8)
I......	..	..	−10.0	−10.0	..	..	10.0	10.0
	−2.0	−2.0	− 1.0	− 2.0	3.0	1.0	1.0	2.0
	−0.4	−0.4	− 0.2	− 0.4	0.6	0.2	0.2	0.4
	−0.08	−0.08	− 0.04	− 0.08	0.12	0.04	0.04	0.08
	−0.016	−0.016	− 0.008	− 0.016	·0.024	0.008	0.008	0.016
	−0.0032	−0.0032	− 0.0016	− 0.0032	0.0048	0.0016	0.0016	0.0032
	.	.	.	.	.	.	.	.
	.	.	.	.	.	.	.	.
	.	.	.	.	.	.	.	.
	−2.5000	−2.5000	−11.2500	−12.5000	3.7500	1.2500	11.2500	12.5000
II.....	..	..	−10.0	−10.0	..	..	..	..
	−2.0	−2.0	− 1.0	− 3.0	..	..	..	− 2
	−0.6	−0.6	− 0.3	− 1.1	−0.6	−0.2	− 0.2	− 1.4
	−0.22	−0.22	− 0.11	− 0.47	−0.42	− .14	− .14	− 0.78
	−0.094	0.094	− 0.047	− 0.219	−0.234	− .078	− .078	− 0.406
	−0.0438	−0.0438	− 0.0219	− 0.1063	−0.1218	−0.0406	− 0.0406	− 0.2062
	.	.	.	.	.	.	.	.
	.	.	.	.	.	.	.	.
	.	.	.	.	.	.	.	.
	−3.000	−3.000	−11.5000	−15.0000	−1.500	−0.500	− 0.500	− 5.000
III....	..	..	..	..	..	..	10.0	10.0
	..	..	..	1.0	3.0	1.0	1.0	4.0
	0.2	0.2	0.1	0.7	1.2	0.4	0.4	1.8
	.14	.14	.07	0.39	0.54	0.18	0.18	0.86
	.078	.078	.039	0.203	0.258	0.086	0.086	0.422
	0.0406	0.0406	0.0203	0.1031	0.1266	0.0422	0.0422	0.2094
	.	.	.	.	.	.	.	.
	.	.	.	.	.	.	.	.
	.	.	.	.	.	.	.	.
	0.500⁻	0.500	0.250	2.500	5.250	1.750	11.750	17.500

pressed as the sum of consumption of domestic goods, exports, and domestic investment. Deviations of income from equilibrium may therefore be obtained by addition of the deviations of these three items. Thus the quantity -2 in the income column of the paying country (for the second period) is found by adding the items in line 2, columns 1, 3, and 6, while the excess income of the receiving country for this same period represents an addition of the items in line 2, columns 2, 5, and 7. Changes of income in the second period then react upon consumption and investment of the third period and so on. In this manner the time sequence of income and trade adjustments following a single transfer may be computed for as many periods as desired. The systems outlined in the tables are all stable, so that, in the absence of further payments, incomes of the two countries return eventually to their original positions.

Discussions of the transfer mechanism usually distinguish between two problems: (1) analysis of time sequences (such as those discussed above) which follow a single payment and (2) comparison of the old equilibrium with the one which eventually prevails when transfer payments are regular. The distinction is the familiar one between dynamic analysis and comparative statics.

The behavior of dynamic adjustments is obvious from the tables, but it is perhaps less obvious that the same tables may be used to compare a new equilibrium with an old one. For the cumulative effect upon income (let us say) in the nth period after regular payments are begun is simply the sum of the first n terms in our income columns. That is, the total effect of the n regular payments is the sum of the effects of single payments made $n-1$, $n-2$, . . . , 2, 1, 0 periods previously. But the effect (in the nth period) of a payment made $n-1$ periods previously is given by line n, while the effect of a payment made $n-2$ periods previously is given by line $n-1$, etc. Hence the sum of the first n lines represents the total influence (in the nth period) of all previous payments. The process of addition may be continued indefinitely, but eventually the sums will approach limits. When this point is reached, a new equilibrium has been established. Displacements of the new equilibrium from the old are then measured by the column totals.[8]   In other words the totals may be interpreted alternatively as the sums of income adjustments in all periods to a single payment or as the eventual displacement of equilibrium which will result from a series of regular payments.

The upper part of Table 1 shows that, with a periodic payment of 10 units affecting income directly in both countries, the new equilibrium level of income is 12.5 less in the paying country and 12.5 greater in the receiving country than without the transfer.[9] Collection of the transfer sums has depressed the level of output in the debtor country, while the spending of the same sums has stimulated output of the creditor.   These changes, in turn, have reduced imports of the paying country by 2.5 per period and have increased her exports by 1.25 per period.   Income adjustments induced by the shift of purchasing power have thus made available 3.75 units of foreign exchange per period—an amount obviously inadequate to make the entire payment.

When the direct effects of the transfer are limited to its collection in the paying country (Table 1, Part II), real income of each country is reduced, that of the paying country by taxation and that of the receiving country by lower exports to the paying country. Thus both exports and imports of the debtor country decline.   But her imports decline more than her exports so that 2.5 units of foreign exchange per period are freed for making the actual transfer.

Finally, Part III of Table 1 shows that, if the transfer affects income directly in the receiving country but not in the paying country, real incomes of both countries rise.   The higher income of the former is attributable to tax reduction induced by the transfer, that of the latter to greater exports to the receiving country.   Both exports and imports of the paying country are increased, and again foreign exchange is freed for making the actual

---

[8] Totals given in the tables are not the actual ones but the limits which the sums in each column approach (cf. appendix).

[9] It is only an accident of the particular numerical example chosen that reduction of income in the paying country is exactly equal to the rise of income in the receiving country.

payment, since exports rise more than imports.   Once again, however, the foreign exchange set free is inadequate to make the entire transfer.

It appears from Table 1 that adjustments of real income brought about by a transfer of purchasing power are capable of creating a part, but not all, of the necessary export surplus for the paying country and that the surplus will be greater if both countries allow incomes to be affected directly than if only one does so.   A glance at Tables 2 and 3, where the same problem is worked out for different marginal propensities to consume and invest, shows, however, that the results obtained in Table 1 are not general.

Consider Part I of Table 2.   Despite increased taxation in the debtor country, income has risen there, as well as in the creditor country.   Increased exports to the receiving country have exerted a more important influence on the income of the debtor country than has reduced consumption arising from collection of the transfer sum.   Hence both her exports and her imports have increased. But exports have risen much more than imports, and the foreign exchange set free in this manner is more than sufficient to make the actual transfer.

Part II of Table 2 presents a situation analogous to the Keynes dilemma over German reparations.   Contraction in the paying country being the only direct income effect, real income naturally declines in both countries.   As a consequence both exports and imports of the debtor country are reduced.   Her exports however, decline more than her imports.   In other words, taxation has moved the balance of trade against the paying country—a result quite contrary to usual expectations.   No amount of contraction in the debtor country will, in this case, create an export surplus. It follows that the transfer imposes an impossible burden upon the paying country unless the receiving country will co-operate in expanding her citizens' money incomes.

On the other hand, if direct income effects are limited to expansion in the receiving country (Part III, Table 2), the real income adjustment is sufficient in this case to make the actual trans-

TABLE 2. TRANSFER EFFECTS WHEN THE RECEIVING COUNTRY IS UNSTABLE IN ISOLATION

(International Transfer = 10 Units)

	In Paying Country	In Receiving Country
Marginal propensity to consume domestic goods	0.1	0.1
Marginal propensity to consume foreign goods	0.1	0.8
Marginal propensity to invest	0.1	0.3

Part	Changes in Paying Country				Changes in Receiving Country			
	Consumption of Domestic Goods	Consumption of Foreign Goods	Investment	Income	Consumption of Domestic Goods	Consumption of Foreign Goods	Investment	Income
	(1)	(2)	(3)	(4)	(5)	(6)	(7)	(8)
I	..	..	−10.0	−10.0	..	..	10.0	10.0
	−1.0	−1.0	−1.0	6.0	1.0	8.0	3.0	3.0
	0.6	0.6	0.6	3.6	0.3	2.4	0.9	1.8
	0.36	0.36	0.36	2.16	0.18	1.44	0.54	1.08
	0.216	0.216	0.216	1.296	0.108	0.864	0.324	0.648
	0.1296	0.1296	0.1296	0.7776	0.0648	0.5184	0.1944	0.3888
	.	.	.	.	.	.	.	.
	0.500	0.500	− 9.500	5.000	1.750	14.000	15.250	17.500
II	..	..	−10.0	−10.0	..	..	..	..
	−1.0	−1.0	− 1.0	− 2.0	..	..	..	− 1.0
	−0.2	−0.2	− 0.2	− 1.2	−0.1	− 0.8	− 0.3	− 0.6
	−0.12	−0.12	− 0.12	− 0.72	−0.06	− 0.48	− 0.18	− 0.36
	−0.072	−0.072	− 0.072	− 0.432	−0.036	− 0.288	− 0.108	− 0.216
	−0.0432	−0.0432	− 0.0432	− 0.2592	−0.0216	− 0.1728	− 0.0648	− 0.1296
	.	.	.	.	.	.	.	.
	−1.500	−1.500	−11.500	−15.000	−0.250	− 2.000	− 0.750	− 2.500
III	..	..	..	..	..	..	10.0	10.0
	..	..	..	8.0	1.0	8.0	3.0	4.0
	0.8	0.8	0.8	4.8	0.4	3.2	1.2	2.4
	0.48	0.48	0.48	2.88	0.24	1.92	0.72	1.44
	0.288	0.288	0.288	1.728	0.144	1.152	0.432	0.864
	0.1728	0.1728	0.1728	1.0368	0.0864	0.6912	0.2592	0.5184
	.	.	.	.	.	.	.	.
	2.000	2.000	2.000	20.000	2.000	16.000	16.000	20.000

fer. As in Table 1, Part III, income rises in both countries, and higher incomes increase both exports and imports of the paying country. But unlike Table 1, Part III, the rise of exports in the present case is sufficiently greater than the rise of imports to move the trade balance in favor of the paying country by an amount greater than the transfer.

It is clear from Table 2 that, for the propensities to consume and invest there postulated, the co-operation of the receiving country is absolutely essential; contraction in the paying country only makes matters worse. But if monetary income in the receiving country expands by the amount of the transfer, it makes no difference whether or not the paying country's income is reduced in its collection, for in any case the change of the trade balance arising from expansion in the receiving country will be sufficient to make the actual transfer.

A third set of possible results is given in Table 3. Contraction of purchasing power in the paying country and its expansion in the receiving country (Part I) serve here to reduce real incomes in both countries. The lower income of the former is attributable to the transfer collection; the latter's income is reduced because the secondary effects of reduced exports to the paying country are more important than the original expansion of purchasing power. Imports of the debtor country decline more than her exports, and the shift of the trade balance is greater than the amount of the transfer. With both countries co-operating, therefore, the income adjustments alone are adequate, but neither party gains, since incomes of both are reduced. Likewise, when the paying country contracts income in collection of the transfer sum, but the receiving country does not expand (Part II), incomes of both countries are again reduced, and once more the reduction of the debtor's imports is sufficiently greater than the reduction of her exports to make the transfer possible with no further adjustments. But again the transfer is detrimental to both countries. Finally, expansion in the receiving country unaccompanied by contraction in the paying country (Table 3, Part III), while increasing incomes in both, moves the balance of trade in a direction unfavorable to the debtor

TABLE 3. TRANSFER EFFECTS WHEN THE PAYING COUNTRY IS UNSTABLE IN ISOLATION

(*International Transfer = 10 Units*)

	In Paying Country	In Receiving Country
Marginal propensity to consume domestic goods	0.1	0.1
Marginal propensity to consume foreign goods	0.8	0.2
Marginal propensity to invest	0.2	0.1

	Changes in Paying Country				Changes in Receiving Country			
Part	Consumption of Domestic Goods	Consumption of Foreign Goods	Investment	Income	Consumption of Domestic Goods	Consumption of Foreign Goods	Investment	Income
	(1)	(2)	(3)	(4)	(5)	(6)	(7)	(8)
	..	..	−10.0	−10.0	..	..	10.0	10.0
	−1.0	−8.0	−2.0	−1.0	1.0	2.0	1.0	−6.0
	−0.1	−0.8	−0.2	−1.5	−0.6	−1.2	−0.6	−2.0
	−0.15	−1.20	−0.30	−0.85	−0.20	−0.40	−0.20	−1.6
	−0.085	−0.680	−0.170	−0.575	−0.160	−0.320	−0.160	−1.000
I.......	−0.0575	−0.4600	−0.1150	−0.3725	−0.1000	−0.2000	−0.1000	−0.6600
	.	.	.	.	.	.	.	.
	.	.	.	.	.	.	.	.
	.	.	.	.	.	.	.	.
	−1.500	−12.000	−13.000	−15.000	−0.250	−0.500	9.750	−2.500
	..	..	−10.0	−10.0	..	..	..	..
	−1.0	−8.0	−2.0	−3.0	..	..	..	−8.0
	−0.3	−2.4	−0.6	−2.5	−0.8	−1.6	−0.8	−4.0
	−0.25	−2.00	−0.50	−1.55	−0.40	−0.80	−0.40	−2.80
II......	−0.155	−1.240	−0.310	−1.025	−0.280	−0.560	−0.280	−1.800
	−0.1025	−0.8200	−0.2050	−0.6675	−0.1800	−0.3600	−0.1800	−1.1800
	.	.	.	.	.	.	.	.
	.	.	.	.	.	.	.	.
	.	.	.	.	.	.	.	.
	−2.000	−16.000	−14.000	−20.000	−2.000	−4.000	−2.000	−20.000
	..	..	..	..	..	..	10.0	10.0
	..	..	..	2.0	1.0	2.0	1.0	2.0
	0.2	1.6	0.4	1.0	0.2	0.4	0.2	2.0
	0.1	0.8	0.2	0.7	0.2	0.4	0.2	1.2
III.....	0.07	0.56	0.14	0.45	0.12	0.24	0.12	0.80
	0.045	0.360	0.090	0.295	0.080	0.160	0.080	0.520
	.	.	.	.	.	.	.	.
	.	.	.	.	.	.	.	.
	.	.	.	.	.	.	.	.
	0.500	4.000	1.000	5.000	1.750	3.500	11.750	17.500

through an increase of her imports (4.000) which exceeds the increase of her exports (3.500). In this case no part of the actual transfer may be completed through income adjustments of the creditor country.

In discussing Table 2 it was noted that the transfer could not be completed through income adjustments without co-operation of the receiving country and that contraction in the paying country only aggravated the situation. Table 3 represents, in some respects, the converse of Table 2. For now it appears that income adjustments will not suffice unless the paying country is willing to contract income in collection of the transfer sum and that expansion in the receiving country makes the balance of trade unfavorable to the debtor.

Study of our three tables reveals that purchasing-power shifts incident to an international transfer may either increase real income of the receiving country while decreasing that of the paying country (Table 1, Part I) or increase real income of both countries (Table 2, Part I) or decrease real income of both countries (Table 3, Part I). The tables also show that the trade balance may move in favor of the paying country by more than the transfer or by less than the transfer or that it may even move against the paying country. The diversity of results may appear to preclude the possibility of useful generalization. If, by altering marginal propensities to consume and invest, such pronounced differences as those noted are obtained, it is conceivable that still other types of solution might be obtained with other propensities to consume and invest. Fortunately, this is not the case. It may be shown that, for the dynamic system postulated, the three tables are typical of the only solutions which are consistent with stable equilibrium. Hence, if we can summarize the tables, our answers will be general.

It is desirable, first, to note the essential differences between the tables. I have selected marginal propensities to consume and invest in such a way that certain stability conditions are fulfilled. Suppose for a moment that the entire consumption function of each country refers to domestic goods only and that each country is isolated.   Call the sum of the marginal propensity to consume domestic goods and the former marginal propensity to consume imports the "marginal aggregate propensity to consume."   It is easily shown that an isolated country is in stable equilibrium (in the sense that, after small displacements, the variables of the system tend to return to their old equilibrium positions) if the marginal aggregate propensity to consume *plus* the marginal propensity to invest is less than unity.   If, for example, spendable income is increased by 10 in a country whose marginal aggregate propensity to consume is 0.5 and whose marginal propensity to invest is 0.1, the income of the next period will be $5 + 1 = 6$ higher than otherwise, because of the induced consumption and investment.   Likewise, income of the second period after the spending begins will be $3 + 0.6 = 3.6$ higher than without the spending, because of the consumption and private investment induced by higher income of the previous period.   Thus the sequence of differences between the equilibrium level of total income and the actual level will be a convergent series of the form 10, 6, 3.6, 2.16, 1.296, etc.   On the other hand, if the marginal aggregate propensity to consume is 0.8, while the marginal propensity to invest is 0.5, the same reasoning as above shows that a spending program will set in motion a series of increasing differences between the actual and equilibrium levels of income.   No tendency exists, in this latter case, for a return to the old equilibrium position.

In summarizing the tables a country will be called "stable in isolation" if its marginal aggregate propensity to consume *plus* its marginal propensity to invest is less than unity; otherwise it will be called unstable in isolation.   The three tables may now be distinguished readily according to this stability criterion.   In Table 1 both countries are stable in isolation; in Table 2 the paying country is stable in isolation while the receiving country is unstable; finally, in Table 3 the receiving country is stable in isolation while the paying country is unstable.   Although in Tables 2 and 3 one of the two countries is always unstable in isolation, the world-economies in each case are none the less stable because of the low propensities to consume and invest of the stable country.   The obvious fourth case—of two countries which are both unstable in isolation —is excluded because it is inconsistent with stability of the world-economy.

A brief summary of our results may facilitate examination of the tables. Transfers affecting income directly in both countries (Part I of all three tables) will modify the system as follows:

1. When both countries are stable in isolation, income will fall in the paying country and rise in the receiving country. The decline of imports and the rise of exports of the paying country will create a surplus of exchange which is inadequate to make the actual transfer; hence some further restriction in the paying country or expansion in the receiving country will be necessary.

2. When the paying country is stable in isolation while the receiving country is unstable, total income will rise in both countries. The exports of the paying country will rise by more than her imports, and the favorable change in her balance of trade will be larger than the amount of the transfer.

3. Conversely, if the paying country is unstable in isolation while the receiving country is stable, total income will fall in both countries. Imports of the paying country will fall by more than her exports, and again the favorable change in the trade balance will be greater than the amount of the transfer.

If the paying country permits the transfer to reduce income directly while the receiving country uses it to accumulate a government surplus, we may expect the following:

1. Total income will fall in both countries regardless of stability conditions.

2. In the normal case—in which both countries are stable in isolation—imports of the paying country will decline more than her exports, but the surplus of bills thus created will not be sufficient for the entire transfer.

3. With the paying country stable in isolation and the receiving country unstable, the decline of exports of the paying country will be greater than the decline of her imports. In other words, increased taxation in the paying country will turn the balance of trade against her and make payment more difficult than before.

In this case no amount of income reduction in the paying country will create a surplus of bills of exchange.

4. In the converse case—in which the paying country is unstable in isolation while the receiving country is stable—imports of the former will decline more rapidly than exports, and the surplus of bills will be greater than the amount of the transfer.

The following changes will occur if the transfer affects income directly in the receiving country only:

1. Total income will rise in both countries, regardless of stability conditions.

2. If both countries are stable in isolation, the rise of exports in the paying country will exceed the rise of imports, but the exchange surplus will be smaller than the amount of the transfer.

3. An exchange surplus will likewise be created when the receiving country is unstable in isolation while the paying country is stable. Moreover, the excess of the rise in exports over the rise in imports will, in this case, be larger than the amount of the transfer.

4. On the other hand, if the paying country is unstable in isolation and the receiving country is stable, the rise of imports of the paying country will exceed the increase of her exports. Thus direct expansion of income in the receiving country will serve only to aggravate the situation.

The multiplicity of results summarized above may seem, at first glance, rather bewildering. Even with a system as simple as the one with which I have dealt, no very broad generalizations may be demonstrated. Nevertheless, we are now beyond the stage of analysis in which literally "anything may happen," for it is possible to state precisely the conditions necessary to bring about a particular result. The conclusions, moreover, are not so complex as they first appear. Their systematic character may be examined most readily in Table 4 where, for purposes of comparison, I have tabulated them according to stability conditions and direct income effects.

We are now in a position to evaluate the importance of real income adjustments, induced by shifts of purchasing power, in creating a favorable change in the trade balance of the paying

TABLE 4. SUMMARY OF TRANSFER RESULTS

	Income Affected Directly in Both Countries	Income Affected Directly in Paying Country Only	Income Affected Directly in Receiving Country Only
Both countries stable in isolation	1. Income falls in paying country, rises in receiving country	1. Income falls in both countries	1. Income rises in both countries
	2. Trade balance moves in favor of paying country by less than amount of transfer	2. Trade balance moves in favor of paying country by less than amount of transfer	2. Trade balance moves in favor of paying country by less than amount of transfer
Paying country stable in isolation, receiving country unstable	1. Income rises in both countries	1. Income falls in both countries	1. Income rises in both countries
	2. Trade balance moves in favor of paying country by more than amount of transfer	2. Trade balance moves against paying country	2. Trade balance moves in favor of paying country by more than amount of transfer
Paying country unstable in isolation, receiving country stable	1. Income falls in both countries	1. Income falls in both countries	1. Income rises in both countries
	2. Trade balance moves in favor of paying country by more than amount of transfer	2. Trade balance moves in favor of paying country by more than amount of transfer	2. Trade balance moves against paying country

country. It is clear that such adjustments will not produce a sufficient surplus unless (a) one of the two countries is unstable in isolation and (b) the unstable country permits the transfer to affect its income directly. Empirical evidence is inadequate to determine how often such a situation may be encountered. Most investigations of consuming and importing habits have revealed marginal aggregate propensities to consume considerably less than unity. It seems likely, therefore, that few countries will have marginal propensities to consume and invest large enough to place them in the unstable class. In other words the "normal" case—of stability in both countries—appears to be the most probable one. If this is true, real income movements induced by shifts of purchasing power may be expected to create only a part of the surplus required for capital transfers.

APPENDIX

The propositions set forth above may easily be verified analytically. Let $y = u_1(y) + v(y) + u'_2(y')$ represent income of the debtor country, where $u_1(y)$ is her consumption of domestic goods, $v(y)$ her domestic investment, and $u'_2(y')$ her exports, assumed to depend upon income of the creditor country. Likewise, income of the creditor country may be represented by $y' = u'_1(y') + v'(y') + u_2(y)$. The balance of trade of the paying country is then given by $b = u'_2(y') - u_2(y)$. The three equations of our static system are sufficient to determine the three unknowns y, y', and b:

$$\left. \begin{aligned} y &= u_1(y) + v(y) + u'_2(y') - \theta - \tau, \\ y' &= u'_1(y') + v'(y') + u_2(y) + \theta' + \tau, \\ b &= u'_2(y') - u_2(y). \end{aligned} \right\} \quad (1)$$

Parameters θ, θ', and τ of equations (1) represent, respectively, transfers which affect income directly in the paying country only, transfers which affect income directly in the receiving country only, and transfers which affect income directly in both countries. By differentiating equations (1) partially with respect to these parameters it may be shown that

$$\left. \begin{aligned} \frac{\partial b}{\partial \theta} &= \frac{u_{2y}(1 - v'_{y'} - u'_{y'})}{\Delta} \equiv 1 - \frac{(1 - v_y - u_y)(1 - v'_{y'} - u'_{1y'})}{\Delta}, \\ \frac{\partial b}{\partial \theta'} &= \frac{u'_{2y'}(1 - v_y - u_y)}{\Delta} \equiv 1 - \frac{(1 - v_y - u_{1y})(1 - v'_{y'} - u'_{y'})}{\Delta}, \\ \frac{\partial b}{\partial \tau} &= \frac{u_{2y}(1 - v'_{y'} - u'_{y'}) + u'_{2y'}(1 - v_y - u_y)}{\Delta} \\ &\equiv 1 - \frac{(1 - v_y - u_y)(1 - v'_{y'} - u'_{y'})}{\Delta}, \end{aligned} \right\} \quad (2)$$

where

$$\Delta \equiv (u_{1y} + v_{1y} - 1)(u'_{1y'} + v'_{y'} - 1) - u_{2y}u'_{2y'},$$
$$u_y \equiv u_{1y} + u_{2y},$$

and

$$u'_{y'} \equiv u'_{1y'} + u'_{2y'}.$$

Letter subscripts, of course, indicate differentiation. "Income effects," obtained in the same process of differentiation, are given by equations (3).

$$
\left.
\begin{aligned}
\frac{\partial y}{\partial \theta} &= - \frac{(1 - v'_{y'} - u'_{1y'})}{\Delta}, & \frac{\partial y'}{\partial \theta} &= - \frac{u_{2y}}{\Delta}, \\
\frac{\partial y}{\partial \theta'} &= \frac{u'_{2y'}}{\Delta}, & \frac{\partial y'}{\partial \theta'} &= \frac{1 - v_y - u_{1y}}{\Delta}, \\
\frac{\partial y}{\partial \tau} &= - \frac{(1 - v'_{y'} - u'_{y'})}{\Delta}, & \frac{\partial y'}{\partial \tau} &= \frac{1 - v_y - u_y}{\Delta}.
\end{aligned}
\right\} \tag{3}
$$

I have shown elsewhere that, for the dynamic system postulated, stability of the world-economy requires that Δ be positive and that both $u_{1y} + v_y$ and $u'_{1y'} + v'_{y'}$ be less than unity.[10] Further, the paying country is stable or unstable in isolation according as $u_y + v_y$ is less than or greater than unity, while the receiving country is stable or unstable in isolation according as $u'_{y'} + v'_{y'}$ is less than or greater than unity. With these restrictions in mind, all the conclusions of Table 4 may be established from equations (2) and (3).

---

[10] The proof is obtained from solution of a set of difference equations of which the system (1) is a limiting case. Cf. L. A. Metzler, "Underemployment Equilibrium in International Trade," *Econometrica*, April, 1942, pp. 97–112.

BUSINESS CYCLES AND INTERNATIONAL TRADE

9

FOREIGN TRADE POLICY IN THE BUSINESS CYCLE*

By William A. Salant|| ‡

When resources are fully employed, the economic problem is to use them as efficiently as possible. When they are only partially employed, it is to raise the quantity of employment as well as to maximize its efficiency. Because of this difference in the nature of the problems, policies that are appropriate under conditions of full employment may be inapplicable when resources are unemployed.

Much reasoning about foreign trade policy, based as it is on the assumption of full employment, becomes fallacious when misapplied to conditions of unemployment. This essay is a discussion of the relation of international trade to domestic prosperity under conditions of partial and fluctuating employment. The first section contains an outline of the analytical framework which underlies the remainder of the paper, the second a discussion of the part played by foreign trade in the transmission of cyclical fluctuations between countries, and a statement of the issues of policy that arise. The final section is an examination, with respect to these issues, of several countries and, in particular, of the United States.[1]

* *Public Policy*, Volume II (Cambridge, Mass., 1941), pages 209–231. Reprinted by the courtesy of the Graduate School of Public Administration, Harvard University, and the author. Copyrighted, 1941, by the Harvard University Press.

|| Department of State.

‡ Squared brackets in the present text indicate all substantial additions to or alterations of the original text.

[1] I have profited greatly from discussions with Professor Alvin Hansen and Mr. Emile Despres.

EXPORTS, IMPORTS AND NATIONAL INCOME

The national income of a country can be defined as the net value of goods and services produced, including those sold to foreigners as well as those marketed at home.   If the value of the product destined for the domestic market remains unchanged, a rise in exports[2] will involve an equal rise in the national income. But the increase in exports will itself influence domestic consumption.   Exporters and all those who assist in production for export will find that their incomes have increased.   They will spend either all or a part of the increment on home-produced consumption goods, thereby raising the incomes of producers of those goods. These producers will in turn increase their expenditures.   The question arises, how far will the increase in incomes go?

Saving and Investment Excluded

To arrive at an answer which will suffice for the needs of this paper, it will be convenient to assume at first that in the country in question neither saving nor investment,[3] positive or negative, takes place.   All goods and services produced are either immediately consumed at home or sold abroad; all income is spent either on imported or on home-produced consumer's goods.

---

[2] Throughout this paper I have used the terms "exports" and "imports" to refer respectively to total receipts and payments on current international account, including the exchange of services and interest and dividend payments as well as merchandise trade, except where statistics are used.   The more inclusive and accurate terms are too cumbersome, and any possible misunderstanding could do damage, since any statement made about "exports" or "imports" in the paper applies equally to merchandise transactions or to all current receipts or payments. It is true that some of the service items in the balance of payments may be relatively fixed or may vary for special reasons, but the same might be said of many types of exports and imports.   Furthermore, merchandise trade usually constitutes the bulk of the international income account.   Hence the gain in convenience far outweighs the disadvantage of the looseness in terminology.

[3] Saving may be defined briefly as the difference between current income and current consumption, investment as the value of additions to the stock of goods in the country (home investment) plus the increase in claims on foreign countries and in gold holdings (foreign investment).   The numerous problems connected with these definitions lie outside the scope of this paper.

Under these conditions exports must equal imports, for an excess of exports could be financed only by foreign lending or the purchase of gold from abroad, either of which requires saving, while an import surplus would involve foreign borrowing or the sale of gold, and negative saving.[4]   Furthermore, we will assume that when a person's income and consumption rise, he increases his purchases both of imported and of home-produced goods.

In such a country, a rise in exports will increase both income and imports, and the rise in income will stop at the point where imports are equal to the new level of exports.   If only a small part of the additional income is spent on imports, the rise in income will be large, but if most of it is spent on imports, the rise will not be much greater than the original increase in exports.   If we call that fraction of a small increment in income which is spent on imports the marginal propensity to import, and its reciprocal the multiplier, the increase in income consequent on a small increase in exports will be equal to the product of the rise in exports and the multiplier.

The fraction of total income spent on imports at any level of income is the average propensity to import, and the whole schedule of related values of income and imports is the propensity to import function.   The level of income can be altered by changes either in exports or in the average propensity to import.   If, for example, with unchanged exports there is a shift in demand from imported to domestic goods, incomes will rise to the point where imports are restored to their former value.

Both the average and the marginal propensity to import are determined by a multitude of factors.   The division of an individual's expenditure between imports and domestic goods is influenced by the schedule of his preferences for different goods, relative prices at home and abroad, and the size of his income, while for the community as a whole it is also affected by the distribution of the national income between individuals of different tastes and different incomes.   The important point for our purposes is that the level of income is one of the principal factors in

---

[4] Strictly speaking, this statement requires the additional condition that both home and foreign investment as well as total investment should be zero.

determining imports, higher incomes being generally associated with higher imports and lower incomes with lower imports.

It may be noted that it makes a great deal of difference whether or not resources are fully employed. If they are, an increase in foreign demand for exports will result in higher prices at home, which will in turn cause a shift to imported goods. Money incomes will increase, but employment will not. If, however, there is widespread unemployment of resources, prices may remain unchanged while output expands, real and money incomes will rise together, and imports will increase because of the higher level of income. Or the outcome may be intermediate between these two cases, both prices and output increasing. In the remainder of this paper we shall assume that an increase in demand results in some expansion of output, either with or without an accompanying rise in prices.

Saving and Investment Taken into Account

The foregoing analysis is, of course, merely a translation of the familiar multiplier concept into foreign trade terms. If investment is substituted for exports and saving for imports, the analysis can be applied almost *verbatim* to a closed economy in which saving and investment take place. If we consider an economy with foreign trade and saving and investment, the two analyses must somehow be combined. For our purposes the most satisfactory method of effecting the combination is to consider investments and exports as the autonomous factors, changes in which have a multiplied effect on income. The multiplier is the reciprocal of the marginal propensity to save plus the marginal propensity to import.[5] With a given propensity to save, the higher the marginal

---

[5] This formulation is used in Colin Clark and J. G. Crawford, *The National Income of Australia* (Sydney and London, 1938), pp. 90–103. Perhaps the most familiar formulation is that in which the multiplier is the reciprocal of the marginal propensity to save, and the export *balance* (i.e. exports less imports) is added to investment as an autonomous factor. The disadvantage of this formulation, as Colin Clark points out (cf. "The Determination of the Multiplier from National Income Statistics," *Economic Journal*, Sept., 1938, pp. 438–39) is that it includes

propensity to import the smaller the multiplier. In any open economy the multiplier is smaller than in a closed economy with the same propensity to save.

Other Links Between Exports and Imports

This form of the multiplier emphasizes the effect of changes in investment and exports, through the medium of incomes, on saving and imports. But the export-income-import sequence is not the only line of connection between exports and imports. If it were, foreign investment or disinvestment in the form of gold or capital movements would have to take place freely to cover any surplus or deficit of exports that might arise, and this gold or capital movement could not independently affect exports or imports. In fact, however, this is not the case. In order that the use of the multiplier analysis should not be misleading, it will perhaps be advisable to mention at this point the other lines of relation between exports and imports, although to discuss them would involve a digression into the theory of international adjustment.[6]

---

imports among the autonomous factors whereas it is often better to regard them as a function of income. The formulation used in the text, on the other hand, is defective in that it diverts attention from relations between exports and imports other than the export-income-import sequence, as is pointed out below.

Any formulation is formally correct, though not necessarily useful, if the product of the autonomous factors and the multiplier is equal to the change in income, assuming that the functions do not shift. A convenient symbolic presentation may be found in D. H. Robertson, "Mr. Clark and the Foreign Trade Multiplier," *Economic Journal*, June, 1939, p. 354. The formulation used here is Professor Robertson's (iii). For other discussions of the multiplier in an open economy see R. F. Harrod, *The Trade Cycle* (Oxford, 1936), pp. 145–158, R. W. Jastram and E. S. Shaw, "Mr. Clark's Statistical Determination of the Multiplier," *Economic Journal*, June, 1939, p. 358, F. W. Paish, "Banking Policy and the Balance of International Payments," *Economica*, Nov., 1936, p. 404, and A. F. W. Plumptre, "The Distribution of Outlay and the 'Multiplier' in the British Dominions," *Canadian Journal of Economics and Political Science*, August, 1939, p. 363.

[6] [The multiplier approach to the analysis of income is used in this paper as a convenient method of focussing attention on those aspects of the relations between exports, imports, and income which are examined in the second and third sections of the paper. The content of those sections could be translated into terminology

1. In gold standard countries, gold flows may cause interest rate changes which alter both incomes and relative prices and costs of domestic and foreign foods.

2. In paper standard countries, movements of the exchange rate may alter relative prices and costs of domestic and foreign goods.

3. In exchange control countries, the entire balance of payments, and therefore the relation of exports to imports, is directly subject to administrative determination. In other countries, tariffs and quotas may be imposed to protect the balance of payments or they may be removed when strain on it disappears.

4. Any of the above adjustments taking place in other countries in response to a change in one country's balance of payments will affect the balance of payments of the first country. For example, if country A increases its imports from country B, B may, for any of the above reasons, increase its own imports, and A's exports will share in the increase.

All these factors must be considered in a discussion of the balance of payments. Nevertheless, it was well to emphasize the importance of the multiplier and the marginal propensity to import on the simplest assumptions because that particular relation has not, until recently, received much attention. Furthermore, for free exchange countries with relatively stable exchange rates, it is the most automatic, and, in the short run, perhaps the most important form of adjustment.

FOREIGN TRADE IN THE BUSINESS CYCLE

In analyzing the part played by exports and imports in transmitting fluctuations in economic activity from one country to

which does not refer to the multiplier without effect on the analysis, although it is believed that the exposition would be more difficult and cumbersome. The multiplier terminology tends to divert attention from other important aspects of the inter-relations between foreign trade and the domestic economy which lie, for the most part, outside the scope of the present article.]

another, we shall proceed in two stages. In the first we assume that only the pure multiplier effect operates, that is, that the relation between imports and income is given, and that exports are determined only by changes in foreign demand. In the second stage we drop this assumption and consider the interrelations between exports and imports mentioned above.

Only the Multiplier Effect Considered

On the simplified assumption, the role of foreign trade is easily described. The larger a country's exports relative to its total national income, and the greater the fluctuations in exports, the larger will be their influence in initiating fluctuations in income. The greater the marginal propensity to import, the smaller will be the effect on home incomes of a given change in exports or home investment.

At this stage there is but one complication to consider. It may best be brought to light by assuming that there are only two countries, A and B. If A decreases its imports from B, B's income will be reduced, and its imports as well. But since A supplies all of B's imports, this means a reduction in A's exports and a fresh decline in its income. Hence a decline in A's imports affects exports and income.[7]

In the actual world, of course, the situation is complicated by the existence of a large number of countries. A decline in A's imports from B will affect B's imports not only from A, but also from C, D and E. These countries in turn will import less, and part of the burden will fall on A's exports to them. If world trade were evenly distributed, that portion of the decline in total imports falling on A's exports would be equal to A's share in world exports. But trade is not evenly distributed in this sense. For

---

[7] The multiplier in B determines the ratio of the decrease in income to the original drop in exports, the marginal propensity to import that of the reduction in imports to the decrease in income. Since the marginal propensity to import is itself a determinant of the multiplier, the relation between the reduction in imports and the marginal propensity to import is somewhat more complicated.

example B may supply 25 per cent of A's imports though it supplies only 5 per cent of total world imports. If A reduces its imports from B, the reaction on its own exports will be greater if B buys mainly from A than if B's imports are obtained from C, D, and E.[8] The repercussions on a country's exports of a change in its imports will be greater, other things being equal, if the countries which supply most of its imports are also the principal customers for its exports.

Summarizing, we may conclude that the reaction of a change in a country's imports on its exports will be greater:

1. The greater are the marginal propensities to import and the multipliers of the countries from which it imports.
2. The greater is its share in world trade.
3. The more heavily are its exports concentrated on those countries from which it imports most.

Action to Alter the Balance of Payments Considered

It has been assumed up to this point that only the pure multiplier effect has been allowed to operate, that is, that the operation of the multiplier provides the only causal connection between exports and imports and that home investment is independent of both. Proceeding to the second stage of the analysis, we drop that assumption. The discussion falls into two parts, the response of a country to a change in its exports, and the effect of a change in domestic conditions on imports and exports.

When a country's exports fall off, the effects on it are twofold. Not only does the reduction in exports have a multiplied effect on income, but in addition the balance of payments is subjected to pressure because although a decline in imports will take place, it must be smaller than the original loss of exports if the marginal propensity to save is greater than zero.[9]

---

[8] This will be true even if A sells heavily to C, D, and E, because reduction in their exports to B will probably be greater than the resulting fall in their imports.

[9] We are ignoring the possibility that the decline in income will cause a second-

In this situation, a country can allow the multiplier effect to operate freely or it can take any of three lines of action:

1. The traditional gold standard behavior is to deflate at home in order to restore equilibrium in the balance of payments. Such a policy would further reduce money incomes and probably real incomes as well.
2. Another choice, directly antithetical to this, is to offset the effect on incomes on the loss of exports by using monetary and fiscal measures to stimulate home activity. While sustaining home incomes, such a course will aggravate the tendency toward a deficit in the balance of payments.
3. Finally, it can alter the balance of payments by allowing the exchange rate to depreciate in response to the original drop in exports, or by employing tariffs, export bounties or other devices designed either to stimulate exports or reduce the propensity to import or both. Action of this sort has the double effect of forestalling both the decline in money income and the pressure on the balance of payments (although it cannot offset the decline in real incomes caused by the adverse change in the terms of trade).

All three of these policies are directed at the immediate situation created by the decline in exports. In the long run, however, still another policy is possible. The country can attempt to insulate itself from fluctuations originating in other countries by reducing its dependence on foreign trade in general, diverting expenditure from imports to home-produced goods and selling more of its production at home and less in the export markets. Such a policy may be adopted because the domestic economy is considered freer from cyclical fluctuations than the export markets, or it may be a prelude to a comprehensive program designed to eliminate fluctuations. In either case, if the policy is to be justified, it must be shown not only that the domestic market must prove more stable than the export markets, but also that the gain in

---

ary reduction in home investment, which in turn will result in a further decline in income and imports.

stability outweighs any loss in efficiency that may result from the reduced volume of international trade.[10]

A less drastic method of insulation is to join several countries into an economic bloc and endeavor to maximize trade between members of the bloc at the expense of trade with the outside world. Here again, the bloc may be formed because it is thought that business cycles in the member countries are comparatively mild, or it may be a prelude to a joint effort to control them.

Where domestic factors initiate an increase in home income and in imports, a country is confronted with much the same choices. By deflating it can protect the balance of payments at the cost of choking off the domestic expansion. By depreciating or employing protectionist measures it can enjoy the full effects of the domestic expansion and avoid the strain on the balance of payments. Finally, it can allow the multiplier effects on income and imports to operate freely. Such a policy will be possible, for example, if receipts on current account were originally greatly in excess of payments, so that the effect of the expansion is only to turn a large surplus into a small one, or if there are substantial reserves of gold and foreign assets, or if the country is able and willing to borrow abroad. Under such a policy, some of the stimulating effect of the domestic expansion will be spilled over to foreign countries.

A fourth possibility is to expand at home, but conserve the stimulating effect on income and protect the balance of payments by bilateral trade policies. It has been stated above that change in a country's imports may react upon its exports. Ordinarily this reaction will be quite small. The objective of bilateralism is greatly to increase it, to insure that the full amount of the rise in imports is reflected back on exports. This end can be achieved by a commercial policy that provides for a close balance of bilateral trade by means of barter and clearing arrangements.

We have seen that a single country may employ exchange depreciation or protective measures of some variety as a supple-

---

[10] Military and other non-economic considerations may be even more important than the economic factors mentioned here in determining what degree of self-sufficiency is desirable.

ment to a program of internal expansion. Under those circumstances I think depreciation would generally be regarded as justifiable if not carried too far, since its unfavorable effects on other countries are offset by their gains from the expansion program, leaving their balances of payments and national incomes on balance unaffected. But there is another situation in which depreciation would be just as generally condemned: when it is used, not as a supplement to, but as a substitute for the stimulation of internal activity. Instead of raising home investment, a country can restore its income by stimulating exports and restricting imports, and the latter course may appear the more expedient. When undertaken for this purpose, depreciation is branded as a beggar-my-neighbor policy, since it enables the depreciating country to obtain a larger share of total world income without increasing that total.[11]

Once we attempt to distinguish between justifiable and unjustifiable depreciation, however, we raise the whole issue of equilibrium in the balance of payments and the equilibrium exchange rate. When a country depreciates, its rivals will attack its action as an unjustified attempt to gain at their expense and will call for retaliatory measures. The depreciating country in turn will often reply that it is merely restoring its balance of payments to an equilibrium which has been upset at some previous time. In the ensuing controversy, relative costs and prices receive much attention. Without going into the problem, I wish merely to point out that whatever "international equilibrium" may be, relative income levels enter into it as well as relative costs and prices.

To summarize, a country can attempt in its foreign trade policy to influence:

The *balance* of trade. By increasing exports and diverting demand from imported to home-produced goods, it can expand money income and, to a smaller extent, real income. In a world

---

[11] This statement requires qualification. If the multiplier has different values in the depreciating country and in the countries which suffer from the depreciation, or if the shift in trade affects investment, total incomes will change, but the movement may be in either direction, depending on the particular circumstances.

of unemployed resources, improving the trade balance is one way, though perhaps not the best way, to raise employment. But a country may be unable to improve its balance if others are simultaneously attempting to improve theirs, or if they retaliate against any action it takes. Furthermore, there may be better ways of increasing employment, so that action of this sort may be both difficult and unnecessary.

The *amount* of trade. Even if a country is powerless to alter its foreign balance, it may still be able to influence the total amount of its foreign trade, increasing or decreasing exports and imports together. A country that is subject to violent cyclical fluctuations might try to increase its trade relations, one with only moderate swings to reduce them. The amount of trade is likely to be subject of long-term policy, the balance a matter of the short run.

The *direction* of trade. A country might direct its trade into more or less bilateral channels for much the same reasons as would lead it to increase or decrease the total amount of trade.

Both depreciation (or other measures to improve the balance of trade) and bilateralism provide the freedom of action for internal expansion, the former by creating a surplus in the balance of payments, the latter by minimizing the deficit when the expansion materializes. By themselves, however, neither supplies the motive power for an expansion of world income. If they are not implemented by an aggressive domestic monetary or fiscal policy, bilateralism will result only in a less efficient use of resources and reduced real income, depreciation in some improvement in the home country at the expense of the rest of the world.

Foreign Trade and National Income in the United States and Other Countries

In the previous sections we have reached some conclusions with respect to the relations between the national income and foreign trade. Our present task is to apply these conclusions to the United

States.   In doing so, we will have occasion to discuss the position of other countries as a basis for comparison.

It is, of course, well known that foreign trade plays a smaller part in the economy of the United States than in that of most countries.   Table 1, which shows the percentage of exports to national income for selected countries, will serve to give a rough indication of the magnitude of the differences.   It should be noted, however, that this table gives the percentage for exports alone, not for the total of income received from the sale of goods and services to foreigners.   The figures range all the way from 4 per cent in the United States to 36 per cent for New Zealand in 1936.

TABLE 1.   EXPORTS OF SELECTED COUNTRIES AS PER CENT OF NATIONAL INCOME

Country	1929	1932	1936
United States	6	4	4
United Kingdom	17	10	9
Germany	18	13	7
Sweden	24[a]	15	18
Canada	23	18	21
New Zealand[b]	27	28	36
Denmark	46	33	33

[a] 1930 figure.

[b] Figures are for years beginning April 1.

Sources: National income figures from League of Nations, *World Economic Survey*, 1938–39, p. 84.   Export figures from statistical yearbooks or abstracts of each country except figures for Denmark which are from League of Nations *International Trade Statistics*.

For countries in widely differing positions different monetary and foreign trade policies are appropriate.   For example, a program of domestic expansion unaccompanied by any action to protect the balance of payments will result in a large increase in home incomes and a small adverse change in the balance of payments (leaving purely domestic factors out of account): (1) if the marginal propensity to import is small, and (2) if the reaction on exports of a given increase in imports is great.

Incidentally, this proposition enables us to give more precise meaning to the common but unsatisfactorily vague statements that a "large" country has greater monetary autonomy than a "small" one. The statement is correct if a "large" country is one whose imports are a small portion of its own national income, but whose exports are a large fraction of world exports, for one would expect the marginal propensity to import in such a country to be low, and the reaction on exports of a change in imports to be high. In general, we may say that a country may pursue an independent monetary policy without regard to the balance of payments if foreign trade plays a small part in its economy, but its foreign trade is a sizeable portion of world trade.

It is obvious that no country meets these conditions nearly so well as the United States. American merchandise exports are larger than those of any other country (though total receipts on current account are exceeded by those of England) while the ratio of imports to income is smaller than that of any important country. In the year 1936 they were only 4 per cent of income, compared with 16 per cent in Great Britain and 6 per cent in Germany, the only other countries whose exports compare with those of the United States.[12]   An additional reason why the United States can pursue an independent policy of expansion is that the size of our gold reserve enables us to regard a substantial deficit in our balance of payments with equanimity.

---

[12] These percentages correspond to what we have called the average propensity to import, whereas it is the marginal propensity that is relevant here.   The marginal propensity, i.e., the ratio of a small change in imports to the change in income that caused it, is difficult to measure because in fact imports are affected by other factors than income.   There is no stable relation between imports and income in Great Britain.   For the United States, annual changes in total payments on current account were in general about one-tenth as large as annual changes in income in the period 1926–1939, and this relation seems to hold fairly consistently throughout the period.   Although that fact does not justify the conclusion that the marginal propensity to import in the United States is one-tenth, it supplies partial evidence that it is comparatively small.   It is of interest to compare the American figure with the value of .25 which Clark and Crawford found for Australia for the period 1930–1938 (*National Income of Australia*, p. 100).

Some Foreign Experiences

A country less favorably situated than the United States can usually carry through an internal expansion if adequate measures are taken to protect the balance of payments.[13]   A remarkable example of the use of bilateralism to protect the balance of payments is provided by the experience of Germany in the period 1933–1939.[14]   In the absence of drastic measures of some sort to protect the balance of payments, Germany was in no position to effect an expansion.   Imported raw materials were essential to any increase in production and particularly in the sort of production that dominated the German expansion—production for military purposes.   Gold reserves were negligible and it was impossible to borrow abroad except by a novel device—the accumulation of debit balances in clearing accounts with other countries.   Hence the necessary imports could be obtained only by a simultaneous expansion in German exports.   A policy of aggressive bilateralism coupled with export subsidies was adopted as the method of securing the expansion of exports.   As a result of this policy, an increase in German imports from any country insured a corresponding increase in purchases by that country from Germany.   The demand for German exports was thus closely tied to Germany's demand for imports.

If circumstances are favorable, a small country producing largely for export will be able to carry through an internal expansion if it takes adequate measures to protect the balance of payments.   But under adverse conditions, such an expansion may prove impossible.   Just how serious are the limitations imposed by the balance of payments under such conditions is illustrated by a comparison of the experiences of Denmark and Sweden between

---

[13] This does not mean, of course, that it can offset all the effects of a decline in the demand for its exports, for such a decline will lead to a more or less serious reduction in real income no matter what internal policy is adopted.   It can, however, sustain money income and perhaps employment.

[14] I am indebted to Mr. Emile Despres for this interpretation of German commercial policy.

1932 and 1935.[15]   It is true that foreign trade bulks considerably larger in the Danish economy than in the Swedish, exports representing in 1932 33 per cent of the Danish national income as against only 15 per cent of the Swedish, but this fact will not materially affect the comparison.

Early in 1932 both Sweden and Denmark initiated easy money programs.   In both, the central bank discount rate was reduced in successive stages from 6 per cent at the end of 1931 to 2½ per cent in 1933.   The Swedish government, in addition, launched a public works program in 1933.   The rapidity and completeness of Sweden's recovery has so often been described that there is no need to repeat the story here.   The only point that need concern us is that the balance of payments position was highly favorable.   Exports increased considerably because of the depreciation, and later the British building boom created a demand for Swedish timber while German rearmament required large quantities of Swedish iron ore.   At the same time, there was a large inward capital movement with the result that reserves of gold and foreign exchange rose continuously.   (In fact it may be that the easiness of money was due at first to the expansion of the Riksbank's foreign assets rather than to any deliberate policy.)

Denmark's experience was far less fortunate.   The stimulus of easy money was concentrated largely on construction activity. Since the bulk of building materials is imported, more construction requires considerably higher imports—the marginal propensity to import is abnormally high.   But the international position did not permit any increase in imports.   Since gold and foreign exchange holdings were small, and there was no reserve of foreign securities to draw upon, more imports could be obtained only by increasing exports.   Great Britain, which took over 60 per cent of Danish exports, was by far the principal customer for Denmark's intensive agriculture, while Germany, with 13 per cent, was in second place. Special circumstances restricted Danish exports to both these

---

[15] This section is based almost wholly on Carl Iversen, "The Importance of the International Margin," in *Explorations in Economics* (New York, 1936).

countries.   Where Sweden had the good fortune to produce the raw material for German guns, Denmark supplied only butter (and other pork and dairy products), of which Germany was consuming as little as possible, while, as Table 3 below shows, part of the British market was lost to New Zealand as a result of empire preference.   Nor could depreciation be invoked to assist exports, since both German and British demand was inelastic.   If Germany had obtained butter at lower prices, she would have used the savings to purchase still more guns, not more butter.   England subjected her imports from Denmark to direct quantitative limitation in the form of quotas.   Furthermore, it was impossible to finance a deficit on current account by the liquidation of foreign assets.   While the Swedish gold and foreign exchange reserves rose steadily between the end of 1931 and the end of 1935 from 500,000,000 to 1,250,-000,000 kroner, Danish holdings shrank from kr. 150,000,000 to kr. 25,000,000 in the same period.[16]   Nor did Denmark have any stock of foreign long-term securities, such as Sweden possessed, to draw upon.

Even a thorough-going system of import controls instituted in 1932 to insure that only essential materials were imported did not suffice to overcome the difficulties, according to Iversen.[17]   In spite of the low official discount rate, the yield on government securities never fell much below 4 per cent, although in Sweden it dropped to 3 per cent.[18]   The easy money program was finally abandoned early in 1935, the central bank raising its discount rate to 3½ per cent in that year and to 4 per cent in 1936.   Apparently the balance of payments responded to the reversal of policy; the import surplus was reduced from kr. 114,000,000 in 1934 to 62,000,000 in 1935, and the entire balance on current account shifted from a deficit of kr. 38,000,000 to a surplus of 40,000,000.[19]   Where a

---

[16] *Ibid.*, p. 75.

[17] The objective of control was not only to limit the total but to shift the distribution of imports in favor of Great Britain, in order to reduce the export surplus and consequent weak bargaining position with respect to that country.

[18] League of Nations, *Monetary Review, 1938*, pp. 138–140.

[19] It is impossible to tell without further study how great a part the change in

favorable balance of payments situation reënforced the program of internal expansion in Sweden, the unfavorable course of the balance of payments defeated the Danish program.

In the British recovery of 1932–37, international and domestic factors are intertwined in a complicated manner.[20]   On the domestic side, easy money and the housing boom contributed heavily to the completeness and promptness of the recovery.   But it is questionable how effective they would have been in the absence of depreciation, the tariff, and the Ottawa agreements.   Each of these measures operated in a different way to improve the international position.   Depreciation acted as a stimulus to exports and a check on imports, except to the extent that it was offset by counter-action in competing countries.   The Ottawa agreements, by giving Great Britain preferential treatment in the dominion markets, stimulated exports, although the stimulus was in part offset by retaliation by other countries.   The tariff substituted home production of manufactured goods for imports.   Its effect is strikingly brought out by Table 2.   Imports of manufactured goods were reduced from 31 per cent of total imports in 1931 to 22 per cent in 1932, but this fact is not conclusive because the percentage later recovered to a figure not far from its 1924–1929 average, and because the classification "manufactures" includes a large number of semi-manufactured materials that are not competitive with British products.   But when we turn to the imports of goods most highly competitive with British products, shown in Table 2, there is no mistaking the effects of the tariff.   Imports of iron, steel, cotton, and woolen manufactures and clothing declined drastically after 1931.   Only iron and steel imports regained their former level, and that was because of a domestic shortage in 1937 which resulted in a reduction in some of the duties.   The shift of expenditure from

monetary policy had in this shift.   Iversen implies that it was largely responsible. *Op. cit.*, p. 76.

[20] For a more extended discussion of the British recovery, see George Jaszi, "The Budgetary Experience of Great Britain in the Great Depression," in *Public Policy* (Cambridge, 1940).

imported to domestic goods must have contributed a substantial stimulus to the British economy.

The British recovery was due primarily to expansion of the home market, and in fact there was a rather remarkable reduc-

TABLE 2. BRITISH IMPORTS OF MANUFACTURED GOODS 1942–1937

			Selected Manufactures		
Year	Total Manufactures	Iron and Steel	Cotton Products	Woolen Products	Apparel
	(1931 = 100)				
1924–28 average	145	130	111	108	90
1929	142	125	122	123	100
1930	121	115	111	100	95
1931	100	100	100	100	100
1932	82	45	22	15	32
1933	78	30	22	15	37
1934	85	45	22	15	37
1935	88	45	22	15	37
1936	98	60	33	23	37
1937	119	100	33	31	47

Source: *Statistical Abstract of the United Kingdom, 1913 and 1924 to 1937*, pp. 402–407.

tion in the role of foreign trade.   Exports, which averaged 17 per cent of national income in the period 1924–1929, fell to 9 per cent in 1933–1938, while the average for imports dropped from 26 per cent to 17 per cent.   Nevertheless, the improved foreign trade position brought about by depreciation, the tariff, and empire preference was probably indispensable to the domestic expansion.

All three of these measures acted in a straightforward manner both to improve the international position and to provide leeway for an internal expansion.   But the Ottawa agreements had an additional effect.   They favored imports from the dominions, which obtain a large fraction of their imports from Great Britain, at the expense of non-British countries which buy a considerably smaller portion of their imports in England.   For example, the agreements resulted in a shift of British purchases of dairy products away from Denmark, which in 1931 took only 15 per cent of its imports from England while sending 60 per cent of its exports there, in favor of New Zealand, in whose imports the British share was 50 per cent in 1931, and which sold 88 per cent of its exports to Great Britain.[21]   This shift is reflected in Table 3.   The result was to in-

TABLE 3.   UNITED KINGDOM IMPORTS FROM DENMARK AND NEW ZEALAND, 1924–1937

Year	Imports from Denmark (In millions of	Imports from New Zealand pounds sterling)	Imports from New Zealand as Per Cent of Imports from Denmark
1924–29 average	50.5	40.5	81
1930	53.6	40.3	75
1931	46.2	33.7	73
1932	40.3	33.2	82
1933	35.2	31.9	91
1934–37 average	33.5	37.8	113

Source: *Statistical Abstract for United Kingdom, 1913 and 1924 to 1937*, pp. 378–9.

crease the demand for British exports which would result from any future rise in imports.   By increasing the interdependence of Great Britain and the empire, empire preference added to Britain's monetary autonomy.[22]

As Table 5 shows, this tendency toward the formation of economic blocs, in most cases based on imperial relations, is by no means confined to the British countries.   There can be no doubt that it is closely associated with world depression and that it enhances the opportunities of individual countries to raise themselves

[21] League of Nations, *International Trade Statistics*.

[22] I do not mean to imply that the negotiators sought this result; on the contrary, they were probably interested only in the purely protective aspect of the agreements.   Another by-product of imperial preference was an increase in British exports to the countries that were unfavorably affected.   In order to secure more favorable treatment for her exports, Denmark increased her purchases in Great Britain from 15 per cent of her total imports in 1931 to 38 per cent in 1937.   As Table 4 shows, this shift was made at the expense of Germany and the United States.

TABLE 4. DISTRIBUTION OF DANISH IMPORTS BY PRINCIPAL COUNTRIES, 1932–1937

Year	United Kingdom	Imports from Germany (As per cent of total imports)	United States
1929	14.7	32.9	13.3
1931	14.9	33.5	10.5
1932	22.3	25.1	7.7
1937	38.1	24.1	5.2

Source: League of Nations, *International Trade Statistics.*

above the general level by their own action, at the same time increasing the chance that they will be pushed below it by the action of others. If all countries recover in unison, such an opportunity is not necessary, but in fact recovery from the great depression was very uneven.

TABLE 5. TRADE OF CERTAIN COUNTRIES WITH THEIR ECONOMIC "BLOCS"

Country	Economic Bloc	Trade with Bloc As per cent of total trade					
		Imports			Exports		
		1929	1932	1938	1929	1932	1938
United Kingdom	British Empire	30	36	42	44	45	50
United Kingdom	Other sterling countries[a]	12	13	13	7	10	12
France	French Empire	12	21	27	19	32	28
Japan	Japanese Empire[b]	20	33	41	24	30	55
Germany	6 countries of Southeast Europe[c]	5	6	12	5	4	13

[a] Sweden, Norway, Finland, Denmark, Egypt, Iraq, Esthonia, Latvia, Portugal, and Siam.
[b] Korea, Formosa, Kwantung, and Manchuria.
[c] Bulgaria, Greece, Hungary, Roumania, Turkey, and Jugoslavia.
Source: League of Nations, *Review of World Trade*, 1938, pp. 34–35.

The Position of the United States

Returning to the United States, we have already seen that exports represent a comparatively small fraction of total production. Table 6 shows that home investment is not only considerably larger but also that it is subject to far wider fluctuations, both absolutely and relative to its average value, than receipts on international account. In the decade 1929–1938, gross capital formation averaged about $11,000,000,000, and the mean deviation was almost $5,000,000,000, or 45 per cent of the average, while the average for receipts on international account was only $4,000,000,000, with a mean deviation of just over $1,000,000,000 or 28 per cent.

TABLE 6. NATIONAL INCOME, RECEIPTS ON CURRENT INTERNATIONAL ACCOUNT AND
GROSS INVESTMENT IN THE UNITED STATES, 1929–1935

(In billions of dollars)

Year	National Income	Receipts on Current International Account	Gross Capital Formation
1929	82.7	6.9	20.3
1930	69.1	5.4	13.7
1931	54.2	3.5	8.5
1932	40.1	2.4	3.0
1933	42.5	2.3	3.6
1934	50.6	2.9	5.2
1935	55.8	3.3	9.5
1936	65.2	3.5	14.1
1937	71.9	4.6	17.5
1938	64.0	4.3	12.0

Sources: National income from *Survey of Current Business*, June, 1939. Receipts on Current Account from *Balance of International Payments*. Gross Capital Formation 1929–31 from Simon Kuznets, *National Income and Capital Formation*, p. 40, 1932–1938, from Kuznets, *Commodity Flow and Capital Formulation in the Recent Recovery and Decline*. (Bulletin No. 24 of National Bureau of Economic Research), p. 2. Figure for 1932–1938 is gross capital formation less net addition to claims against foreign countries.

Furthermore, the American economy has in the last decade functioned at an unsatisfactorily low level. As long as the fluctuations are violent and the level low, our relative independence of foreign trade is, from the cyclical point of view, no asset but a positive liability. The more our economy is isolated from the outside world, the more intense are the effects of fluctuations originating within it, and the less the repercussions of outside fluctuations. The decision as to what volume of trade is desirable must take into account the probable relative levels of economic activity and the probable violence of fluctuations at home and abroad in the future. Past performances would indicate the desirability of economic internationalism, though current trends may well point in the opposite direction.   In any event, there is no necessary presumption in favor of insulation.

It is often said that the demands of domestic prosperity should not be sacrificed to the maintenance of an international standard. There is nothing in the preceding argument to controvert this proposition: on the contrary, it is precisely domestic prosperity that we have been considering.   But the proposition is usually followed by the argument that we should, by means of variable exchange rates or economic isolation, protect the economy from outside fluctuations, particularly deflationary tendencies.   This argument ignores the fact that internal as well as external forces may be responsible for fluctuations; if they are, fixed exchanges and the closest possible economic relations with foreign countries will cushion their impact on the domestic economy and divert it to the world outside.   Furthermore, policies designed to combat a depression are hampered by international factors only when recovery in the home country is outdistancing that in the rest of the world, a situation which is by no means inevitable.

The 1937–38 depression illustrated the part that foreign trade can play under exceptionally favorable circumstances.   At the peak of the 1937 recovery, our merchandise balance was negative by some $50,000,000 a month and the entire current account was probably about in balance.   In the autumn we suffered one of the most precipitous downswings of activity in our history, the Federal Reserve Board's index of industrial production dropping from 117 in August to 80 in January 1938.   As Table 7 on page 224 shows, the down-turn was clearly reflected in imports, which dropped by one-third from 1937 to 1938.   Exports, however, were maintained not far from their 1937 levels and the export surplus remained close to $100,000,000 a month from October 1937 through the greater part of 1938.   In its origin, the depression was almost entirely an American phenomenon; to the extent that activity in other countries declined it was mainly as a result of deflationary forces originating in the United States.   Of course, there was a special reason for the maintenance of activity in the other industrial countries, the intensification of rearmament.   The fact remains that the pressure on the American economy was somewhat relieved by the sharp drop in imports.   If the United States had been a closed economy with no imports, the full force of the decline in expenditure would have been concentrated on home activity; if imports had been larger, still more of the burden would have been shifted.

TABLE 7.   INDUSTRIAL PRODUCTION AND FOREIGN TRADE OF UNITED STATES, 1937–39

Period	Industrial Production	Imports	Exports
	(seasonally-adjusted indexes, 1923–25 = 100)		
1937—1st quarter	116	82	64
2nd "	117	87	78
3rd "	114	81	78
4th "	91	67	75
1938—1st "	80	50	74
2nd "	77	46	72
3rd "	87	52	65
4th "	101	54	62
1939—1st "	99	52	63
2nd "	94	57	68
3rd "	105	57	71
4th "	124	72	77

Source: Department of Commerce, *Survey of Current Business*, 1940 Supplement.

Although the place of foreign trade in the American economy may be small as compared with its position in most countries, our trade is an important component of the total trade of the world. Our imports are exceeded only by those of the United Kingdom. Since imports are largely determined by home incomes, the level of economic activity in the United States is of the highest importance to the rest of the world.   A billion dollar increase in the national income of the United States may be accompanied by a smaller increase in our imports than an equal rise in, say, the Swedish national income, but a 10 per cent rise in American incomes will have a far greater absolute effect on our imports, and therefore on the exports of other countries, than a 10 per cent rise in Sweden, or for that matter in any other country except the United Kingdom or Germany.[23]

The importance of American demand in world markets was clearly demonstrated in the 1937–38 depression referred to above. According to the *Review of World Trade*, "the United States accounts for nearly one-third of the total decline in world imports and for about half the decline in the trade in raw materials between 1937 and 1938."[24] The resulting adverse shift in the balances of payments of the raw material countries forced them to sell gold and foreign exchange on a large scale, to depreciate their exchanges, or to reimpose or tighten exchange controls.[25]

The United States is a highly important market; if it is also an unstable and depressed market, that fact must exert a strong influence toward world instability and depression. Many countries resort to exchange control and trade restriction in their attempts to resist the impact of depressing forces either on their balances of payments or their incomes. Like so many other economic problems (those of inflexible prices and low farm income suggest themselves), that of economic nationalism is in part simply a facet of the broad problem of depression. This is not to say that economic nationalism would disappear with prosperity, but only that its magnitude would be considerably reduced, and that it would no longer be much cause for concern on purely economic grounds.[26]

---

[23] Of course our import demand is not spread uniformly over all countries and all commodities. There is no reason for describing in detail the distribution of trade, except to point out that the producers of certain raw materials such as rubber are particularly dependent on American demand and that our trade with the British empire takes a triangular form, since we ordinarily have a large excess of imports in our trade with the colonial empire and India and a large export surplus with respect to Great Britain, while Great Britain's sales to its colonies plus its income from colonial investments are greater than its purchases from them.

[24] League of Nations, *Review of World Trade*, 1938, p. 19.

[25] For discussions of the impact of the American depression on the raw material countries, see *Federal Reserve Bulletin*, June, 1938, pp. 427–430, and League of Nations, *World Economic Survey*, 1937–38.

[26] Political and military considerations would still be operative, but they are another matter.

The growth of restrictions on trade is deplored in many circles and the administration is committed to an effort to reverse the trend. There can be no doubt that the American depression of the 30's is to a considerable extent responsible for the tendencies that are regarded as undesirable. Where trade barriers are raised to stimulate employment the situation is eminently suited to bargaining because a reciprocal reduction of trade barriers may be in the interest of both parties where unilateral action would not. It will presumably not injure employment, since each country gains a share in the other's market while giving up a portion of the home market, while it will bring about a somewhat more efficient use of resources. Nevertheless, the possibilities of such action seem to be distinctly limited, and it is questionable whether much more remains to be done. Any further relaxation must await the revival of prosperity.[27]

The conclusion is not that we should secure domestic prosperity—that is already obvious. It is rather that *unless* we achieve prosperity, we cannot expect to free foreign trade from the regimentation which we find so distasteful on political grounds. Furthermore, we shall be disappointed if we hope to use foreign trade to achieve prosperity, either through reciprocal agreements or by unilaterally pushing our exports.[28] If, however, we succeed in obtaining a high level of national income, resulting in higher imports, we will have a good chance of securing some relaxation of trade restrictions and of obtaining favorable treatment for our exports.[29] Failing in our domestic program, we may expect a continuation of the tendency toward controlled foreign trade and bilateralism.

---

[27] These remarks do not apply to the present war-time situation. They were relevant to the pre-war world; whether or not they will be relevant to the post-war world depends on the economic and political organization of that world.

[28] I do not mean to exclude the possibility of a strong war or post-war demand for our exports, or to deny that we can sell our goods abroad if we extend loans to finance them.

[29] This statement applies particularly to many Latin American countries, which would greatly increase their purchases in the United States if they had sufficient dollar exchange.

PRICE THEORY AND INTERNATIONAL TRADE

10

THE USE OF INDIFFERENCE CURVES IN THE
ANALYSIS OF FOREIGN TRADE*

By Wassily W. Leontief‖ ‡

The recent developments in analysis of international trade have made it difficult to handle all the various theoretical cases by the traditional means of numerical examples. The following graphic application of indifference curves may provide a comparatively simple and handy tool of representation and analysis for the problem involved.

The theoretical tools applied are those of Marshall, Edgeworth, Pareto, but they are used in such a way as to enable us to disclose the intimate connection between the "national" and the "international" elements of economic equilibrium.

Fig. 1 illustrates the elementary case in which the possessor of the quantity b of commodity B is exchanging a part of it against another commodity, A, the terms of exchange being given. Representing the given rate of exchange (the "terms of trade") of B against A by the slope of the straight line bP_1, we find that the possessor of B will attain an equilibrium position by exchanging a quantity (bC_1) of B for P_1C_1 of A and retaining OC_1 of B; P_1 being the point where the exchange line is touching the "highest" indifference curve and consequently secures him the maximum utility. If there is movement away from this point (P_1) in either direction, by stopping the exchange nearer to b, or by pushing it further along

---

* *Quarterly Journal of Economics*, Volume XLVII (May, 1933), pages 493–503. Reprinted by courtesy of *The Quarterly Journal of Economics* and the author. Copyrighted, 1933, by the Harvard University Press.

‖ *Harvard University.*

‡ The following article is reprinted without significant change from the original text.

the exchange line in the opposite direction the total utility of both commodities in his possession would be reduced. Another—more favorable—exchange line bP_2 will bring about a different equilibrium point, P_2. This new position is marked by a larger quantity of both commodities exchanged and by a "higher" indifference curve; hence a greater total utility is attained.

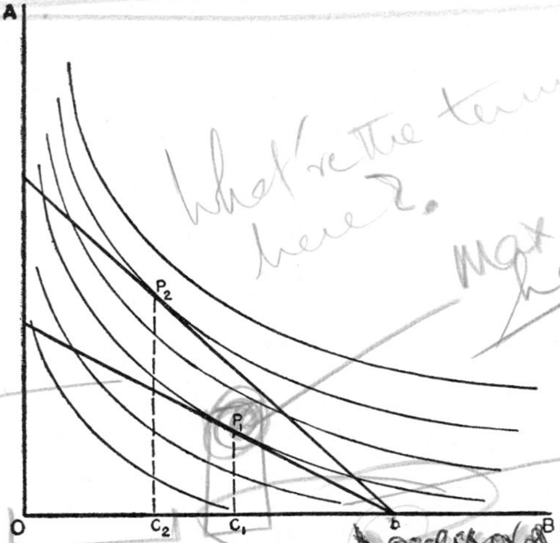

FIG. 1

The response of the quantities to a given change in the terms of trade depends entirely upon the shape of the indifference curves. Fig. 2 shows how the equilibrium point of a country shifts when the exchange line changes its slope.[1] The curve bP_1P_2 indicates that from b to P_1 the demand is elastic; an improvement in the terms of trade between the two limits raises both the exports and the imports. After this point is passed the demand becomes inelastic; any further betterment of the terms of trade is still accompanied by increasing import but leads to a reduction of export.

Evidently, under the assumption of constant opportunity costs, the same diagram can illustrate the distribution of a given amount

---

[1] This diagram leads directly to the demand-supply curves of Marshall and Edgeworth.

of productive forces of a country between two alternative branches of industry. The opportunity costs of B in terms of A and vice versa, will remain constant when each of the two commodities concerned is produced at constant cost.[2] In this case, Ob (Fig. 1) represents the possible total output of B if this good only were pro-

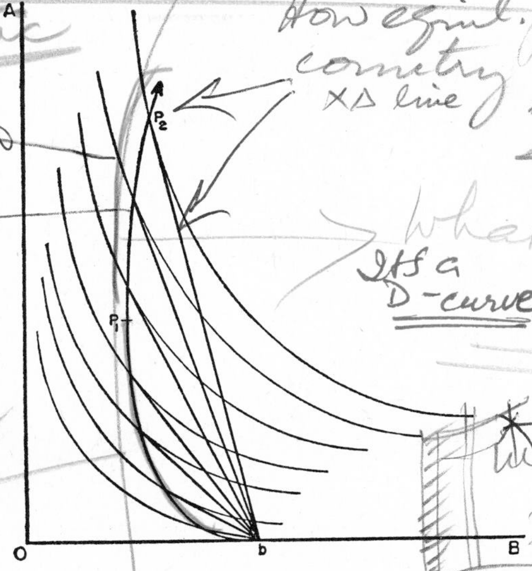

FIG. 2

duced. The slope of the line bP_1 indicates the possible results of diversion of productive forces into the other industry. In complete analogy with the previous case, the equilibrium will be attained in P_1 or P_2 respectively.

If both industries are subject to decreasing returns, the production curve will be concave toward the axes as indicated in Fig. 3.

Given the choice between diverting the production into the B

---

[2] For the sake of theoretical completeness, the exceptional case may be mentioned in which a combination of increasing costs in one branch of production and decreasing costs in the other may result in a constant opportunity cost relation between the two commodities.

industry along a given (straight) production line and providing the same commodity by trade moving along a given path of exchange (bP_2), the preference will be given to the line of the steeper slope, which in any case will lead to a "higher" indifference curve. However, in most cases the production path will be of a curved type as represented in Fig. 4. In this case some of the B-stuff will be produced and some will be acquired in exchange for A-stuff.

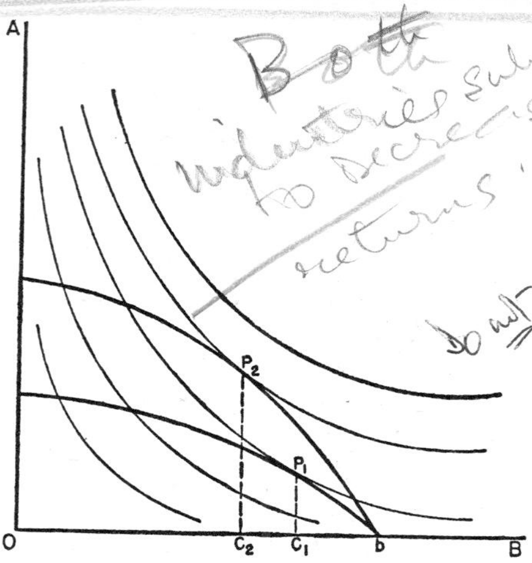

FIG. 3

The maximum utility will be attained by moving along the production curve to the point K, and then proceeding along the exchange line to P_1. Analytically defined, K is the point at which a line with a given "exchange" slope $\left(\dfrac{P_1R}{RK}\right)$ will touch as a *tangent* the fixed production curve.

In the equilibrium position, Kg ($= RC$) of the total quantity CP_1 of A is produced at home and P_1R is imported from abroad. The total production of B amounts to Og; Oc of which is retained at home and Cg sent abroad. Evidently a change in the terms of trade will alter the whole situation, shifting the point K either to the right or to the left. At K_1 (which corresponds to P_1 in Fig. 3) the country will evidently discontinue its foreign trade and reach a state of self-sufficiency. But should the slope of the exchange line, P_1K, decrease even more and move the point of tangency to the left of K_1, an "inverse" trade will start. It will become profitable to export A and to import B. Fig. 5 represents this situation. In complete analogy to Fig. 4, the quantity nq of B will be produced, an additional quantity, fP_2, of the same commodity will be exchanged "along" the qP_2 line for a quantity, nm of A. The dis-

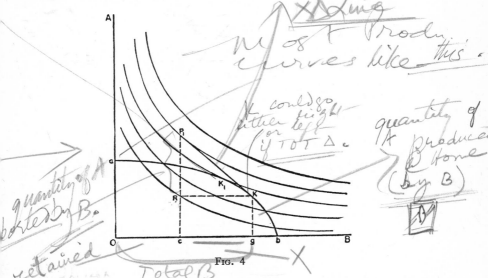

FIG. 4

tance, mO, will represent the amount of A which is retained in the country after the new equilibrium is reached.

Fig. 6 combines Figs. 4 and 5 in one system of coördinates, and gives a complete picture of balanced trade relations between two countries. So long as the analysis referred to only one country, the "terms of trade" represented by the slope of the exchange lines were considered as given. Now only the indifference curves and the cost curves of the two countries are considered as "data." In Fig. 6 both countries have the same system of indifference lines; but the following analysis could be equally well applied if two different systems of indifference lines were charted. The terms of trade and the quantities produced and exchanged can be deduced. The two conditions of equilibrium are: (1) both countries are dealing on the same terms of trade, i.e. the exchange lines are parallel, and their slopes are equal; and (2) the imported and exported quantities of each commodity are equal,

$$qf = P_1R \text{ and } fP_2 = RK.$$

The same condition can be expressed more simply by

$$qP_2 = P_1K,$$

i.e. both countries have to proceed equal distances along their respective paths of exchange.

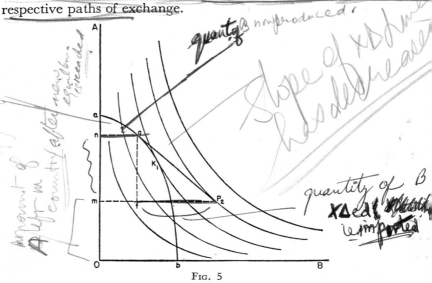

Fig. 5

Without trying to make a point against the spirit of the theory of comparative costs, it may be interesting to observe that two countries with costs of production which are equal not only comparatively, but even absolutely, will start an exchange of their products if their systems of indifference lines, i.e. their relative demands are different. In Fig. 7 the case is represented graphically. The curve ab is the common opportunity cost line of the two countries. The two sets of indifference lines represent the different utility systems of the two countries. The indifference lines with the steeper slopes apply to country A, those with the lesser slopes apply to country B. In a state of self-sufficiency, country A would reach its equilibrium point in P_1, producing and consuming the quantity P_1C_1 of A-stuff and P_1D_1 of B-stuff. The other country has its point of self-sufficiency in P_2 with P_2C_2 of A and P_2D_2 of

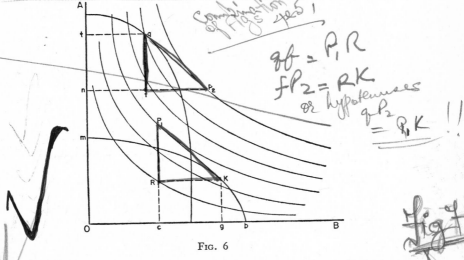

FIG. 6

B-stuff produced and consumed. Applying our previous reasoning, we find that both countries will profit by exchanging part of their products. Each will produce, after the international equilibrium is reached, NK of B-stuff and MK of A-stuff, respectively. But according to their different needs, they will redistribute their equal products by mutual exchange. Country A will attain its highest utility point P_1' by moving along the exchange line from K to P_1', while country B will proceed an equal distance in the opposite direction, from K to P_2'. The trade between the two countries will consist in exchanging $P_2'R_2(= KR_1)$ of A-stuff against $P_1'R_1(= KR_2)$ of B-stuff. The case is not as artificial as it may appear at first sight. It may partly explain the highly developed interchange of commodities between countries with similar industrial structure.

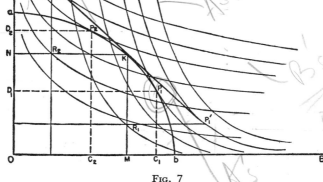

Fig. 7

The influence of an import duty is illustrated in Fig. 8: the curve MP_1D_2b represents the "demand curve" (the same curve as the demand curve in Fig. 2). Under conditions of free trade, P_1 is the equilibrium point if P_1b represents the path of exchange. Imposition of a duty means that a certain part of imported goods or an equivalent amount of the B-stuff has to be surrendered to the customs officials. If P_1D_1 is the amount of the tax (which is supposed to be ad valorem), D_1 represents the new (reduced) utility point of the consumer under the fictitious assumption that the amount of trade is not altered. The net exchange line is bD_2D_1 the slope of which represents the domestic terms of exchange between A-stuff and B-stuff. This utility point can be displaced in either direction along the $b_1D_2D_1$ line by a corresponding contraction or expansion of foreign trade.

The new maximum utility position is indicated by D_2 which is the cross point of the demand curve MP_1D_2b with the net exchange line bD_2D_1. Should the whole (proportionally reduced) amount of the duty be paid in A-stuff, the external equilibrium point would be P_2; P_2C_2 representing in this case the total imports, P_2D_2 the quantity of A-stuff surrendered to the customs and D_2C_2 the remainder "on hand." The same utility point, D_2, could be attained if the total trade would be reduced to P_2' but the amount of the tax which, estimated in A-stuff, is now equal to $P_2'D_2'$ would be

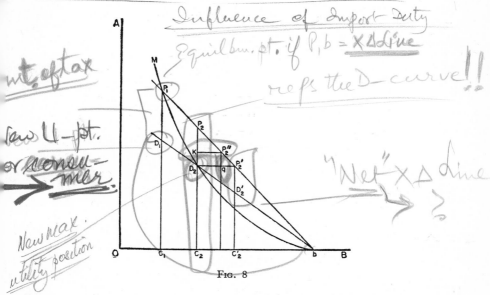

FIG. 8

actually paid in an equivalent quantity, D_2P_2' of the home-made B-stuff.

Between these two marginal cases many intermediate ways of discharging the duty are possible. Stopping at P_2'' the movement along the exchange line bP_1, it is possible to discharge the duty by surrendering $P_2''K$ of B-stuff and $P_2''q$ of A-stuff, so that D_2 will still indicate the "net" position of the consumer. In a monetary economy the "distribution" of the duty between the two kinds of goods is equivalent to the question how the government spends the money collected. The effect of the duty evidently depends to a large extent upon the form of the demand curve, MP_1D_2b.

The same method of approach can be directly applied to a case where an opportunity cost curve is introduced.

When speaking about the ultimate utility point attained, we have of course to distinguish D_2 and P_2'' (or P_2, or P_2'). D_2' represents the utility attained directly by the consumer, P_2'' (or P_2 or P_2') indicates the "total" utility position of the country, including the market value of goods collected in payment of the import duties (estimated on consumers indifference curves).

The previous analysis was conducted on the assumption that the slope of the exchange line is fixed.

This limitation can be removed, and a complete picture of all the interrelations obtained, by taking into account the other country. The reduction of imports which results from the new tax will eventually shift the terms of trade. The character of the shift as well as the resulting change in the quantities of imports and exports depend upon the cost curves of the two countries and their respective lines of indifference.

This method of treatment can be readily extended. Another commodity can be introduced by adding a third dimension. More "countries" with their respective indifference lines and cost curves may be included in the same diagrams. Capital movements and the general transfer problem can also be analyzed by the method. The monetary side of the problem can be attacked by the introduction of special "monetary indifference curves"; but these are not treated here because they would call for a fundamental discussion of the theory of money and credit.

11

THE GAINS FROM INTERNATIONAL TRADE*

By Paul A. Samuelson‖ ‡

[1] In a recent paper[1] the thesis was advanced that while it is not possible to demonstrate rigorously that *free* trade is better (in some sense) for a country than *all* other kinds of trade, it nevertheless can be shown conclusively that (in a sense to be defined later) free trade or some trade is to be preferred to *no* trade at all. I should like here to amplify these remarks with respect to the last point, that some trade is better than no trade.

This is by no means a novel proposition. Indeed, it can be traced back to the beginnings of the Classical theory of international trade. It has become associated, however, quite unnecessarily in my opinion, with a labour theory of value, or a "real cost" theory of value, or more recently, with an opportunity cost theory of value. All of these have come in for considerable criticism in recent years as restrictive special cases of the so-called theory of general equilibrium. Those writers who have insisted on the need for a modern theory of value for a positive description of behaviour in international trade have in general ignored the normative aspects of international trade, presumably in the belief that as soon as one gives up the inadmissible special theories indicated above, nothing

---

* *Canadian Journal of Economics and Political Science*, Volume V (May, 1939), pages 195–205. Reprinted by the courtesy of the *Canadian Journal of Economics and Political Science* and the author.

‖ Massachusetts Institute of Technology.

‡ The following article is reprinted without significant change from the original text.

[1] P. A. Samuelson, "Welfare Economics and International Trade" (*American Economic Review*, June, 1938).

can be said concerning this problem.[2]   It will be argued here that this is a mistake, that from the most general theories of equilibrium all valid normative propositions can be derived.

[2] It is well to indicate clearly the assumptions under which our analysis is to take place.   We shall consider a single economy consisting of one or more individuals enjoying a certain unchanging amount of technological knowledge, so that we may take as data the production functions relating the output of each commodity to the amounts of inputs devoted to its production.   Any number of commodities is assumed; there may also be any number of inputs or productive services.   These are not necessarily fixed in amount, but may have supply functions in terms of various economic prices. Moreover, for our purposes the differentiation of the factors of production can proceed to any degree; thus, labour services of the same man in different occupations are not regarded as the same factor of production unless the provider of these services is indifferent as between these two uses.   Similarly, in order that the productive services rendered by different individuals may be considered the same service, it is necessary that in every use they be infinitely substitutable.

In order to ensure that perfect competition is possible, we rule out increasing returns, and assume that all production functions show constant returns with respect to proportional changes of *all* factors.   Each individual acts as if he were a small part of the markets which he faces and takes prices as given parameters which he cannot influence by changes in his own supplies or demands. It is assumed that for each individual there exists an *ordinal* preference scale in which enter all commodities and productive services, and that subject to the constraints of fixed prices he always selects optimal amounts of each and every commodity and every productive service (some zero in amount).   Each individual is better

---

[2] A recent exception is provided by P. T. Ellsworth's *International Economics* (New York, 1938). However, the problem is posed, not settled. Professor Haberler in his *The Theory of International Trade* (London, 1936) does not employ a full general equilibrium approach.

off if he receives more of every commodity while rendering less of every productive service. No attempt is made to render the "utilities" and "disutilities" of different persons comparable.

[3] Under these conditions, for any assumed set of prices there will correspond definite demand and supply reactions on the part of every individual. Moreover, the total outputs of each commodity will be determined, and the total amounts of productive factors necessary to produce these outputs will be determined. If the economy is isolated, it will be necessary as conditions of equilibrium that prices of commodities and factors of production be such as to equalize the amounts produced and consumed of each and every commodity, and to equalize the amounts supplied and demanded of every productive factor.

Under assumed conditions of ownership of the factors of production and assumed scales of preference for commodities and productive services on the part of every individual, there will result in general (waiving possible multiplicities of equilibrium raising problems not peculiar to international trade) unique equilibrium quantities of consumption goods and productive services for each and every individual. It is unnecessary to write down mathematically these equations to deduce the familiar fact that not enough has been assumed to be able to deduce the absolute level of commodity and factor prices, but that these are determined except for a factor of proportionality; i.e., relative commodity and factor prices are determined. Let us write as follows the equilibrium set of prices, determined to within a factor of proportionality, which will be established for our economy when isolated,

$$p_1^0, p_2^0, \ldots, p_n^0, w_1^0, w_2^0, \ldots, w_s^0,$$

with corresponding equilibrium total quantities of the respective commodities and productive services,

$$x_1^0, x_2^0, \ldots, x_n^0, a_1^0, a_2^0, \ldots, a_s^0.$$

The total amounts produced of the respective commodities will be indicated by the barred letters,

$$\bar{x}_1^0, \bar{x}_2^0, \ldots, \bar{x}_n^0,$$

equal respectively in the isolated state to the quantities (unbarred) consumed.

[4] Before introducing possibilities for trade into our system, it will be useful in view of the later discussion first to develop certain relations which must hold in the field of *production*. Confronted with given factor prices, firms will combine factors of production in such proportions as to produce any selected quantity of consumers' goods at the lowest total money cost. In consequence of this, certain marginal conditions of equality will be attained (or at least certain inequalities with respect to finite movements). Although the proof is not given here, it can be shown that this places restrictions on the possible combinations of factors of production and commodities which can occur. Indeed, it will be found that the totals of commodities produced and the totals of productive services must obey an implicit "production possibility" equation of the following form:

$$\phi[\bar{x}_1, \bar{x}_2, \ldots, \bar{x}_n, a_1, a_2, \ldots, a_s] = 0. \qquad [1]$$

This is capable of the following interpretation: for preassigned values of all productive services and all but one commodity, this equation gives the *maximum* amount of the remaining commodity which can be produced with the given state of technology. Moreover, with preassigned amounts of all commodities and all but one productive service, this shows the *minimum* amount of this one productive service which is necessary.

Utilizing the well-known law of variable proportions, the following remarkable theorem can be established. Consider any set of commodity and factor prices

$$p_1', p_2', \ldots, p_n', w_1', w_2', \ldots, w_s',$$

such as might prevail in competitive equilibrium. Since each entrepreneur is trying to maximize his profits, there will result an optimal set (not unique) of commodities produced and productive services used, indicated by

$$\bar{x}_1', \bar{x}_2', \ldots, \bar{x}_n', a_1', a_2', \ldots, a_s',$$

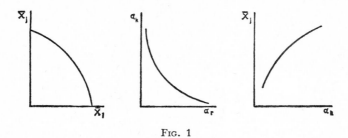

Fig. 1

satisfying, of course, equation [1]. Our theorem says that *for such possible equilibrium prices the resulting optimal quantities of commodities and productive services maximize for the economy as a whole the algebraic difference between total value of output and total factor cost, as compared to any other commodity and factor combinations satisfying equation* [1]. This is equivalent to the following inequality:

$$[p_1'\bar{x}_1' + p_2'\bar{x}_2' + \cdots + p_n'\bar{x}_n']$$
$$- [w_1'a_1' + w_2'a_2' + \cdots + w_s'a_s']$$
$$\geqq [p_1'\bar{x}_1 + p_2'\bar{x}_2 + \cdots + p_n'\bar{x}_n]$$
$$- [w_1'a_1 + w_2'a_2 + \cdots + w_s'a_s], \quad [2]$$

where the unprimed x's and a's represent *any* point satisfying equation [1]. This inequality merely places certain curvature restrictions on the production possibility surface represented by equation [1], for the various ratios between respective prices correspond in a well-known manner to the respective slopes (when they exist) of this surface.[3] In figure 1 are presented typical shapes for various cross-sections of this surface. In the first diagram is shown the amount that must be given up of one commodity, $\bar{x}_j$, in order to get more of another, $\bar{x}_i$, with all other variables held constant. This substitution curve must be concave to the origin. The next diagram shows the amount of one input, a_k, which must be added to compensate for withdrawals of a_r, all other variables being held

---

[3] The equality sign can hold if all the x's and a's are respectively proportional (or equal) to the primed x's and a's. In the singular (and rare) case where technology and the preassigned factor prices are such that all factors of production are used in equal proportions by all commodities, it is possible for the equality sign to hold. This constant cost case does not essentially modify the analysis.

constant. The last diagram shows the amount of commodity, $\bar{x}_j$, that can be secured with additional amounts of a_k, with constant levels for the remaining outputs and inputs.

The above inequality can be written symbolically

$$\Sigma p'\bar{x}' - \Sigma w'a' \geqq \Sigma p'\bar{x} - \Sigma w'a, \qquad [2]$$

where it is always understood that the summations are over the respective n commodities and s productive services. Of course, a similar inequality holds for any other possible set of equilibrium prices.

[5] Trade can be introduced very simply into our system without explicitly dealing with any new country or countries. This is done by the useful device of supposing that there exists an outside market in which there prevail certain arbitrarily established (relative) prices at which this country can buy or sell various commodities in unlimited amounts without changing those quoted prices. It does not matter for the present purposes how, in fact, such prices would be established in this outside market or source, but rather we are interested in the effects upon this country of the existence of such quoted prices.

The fact that this outside market will both buy and sell at the new quoted prices will compel the prices of respective goods in the domestic economy to assume equivalent ratios, or else corrective arbitrage movements would take place. Obviously, therefore, we have introduced new forces to determine some of the prices. It is necessary, then, to drop some of our previous conditions. In particular, we must dispense with the condition that the amounts of commodities produced domestically and consumed domestically must be equal. Instead we have the single condition that the total value of imports must equal the total value of exports, or the total value of consumption must equal that of production,

$$\Sigma px = \Sigma p\bar{x}. \qquad [3]$$

It is clear that for any preassigned prices of internationally tradable goods there will result certain equilibrium values for all the other variables: quantities produced and consumed, productive services supplied, and prices of non-tradable commodities and services.

For one set of prices, namely those proportional to the set $[p_1{}^0, p_2{}^0, \ldots, p_n{}^0]$ which would prevail if the economy were isolated, no trade will result;[4] for these particular prices are such as to equalize the domestic production and consumption of each and every good. For any other set of prices, some trade will result, and there will emerge new equilibrium values for all of our unknowns. By assigning appropriate values to our outside prices, we can obviously reproduce all possible conditions of trade which could conceivably arise. This is the justification for introducing a simplifying device which enables us to ignore the existence of outside economies. Of course, if we were trying to explain the *actual* prices with which our economy will be confronted, it would be necessary to consider outside conditions.

[6] I first apply our analysis of the effect of introducing relative prices, different from those which would be established if our system were isolated, to a simplified case in which all members of our economy are identical in every respect. That is, the same ordinal preference schedule relating commodities and productive services is assumed for every individual, and also the same ownership in the means of production. This does not mean that the utilities of different individuals are comparable. Indeed, since all individuals are identical, if one is bettered (in an ordinal sense) by the introduction of trade, then all will be bettered, and there will be no necessity for making any welfare comparisons between individuals.

In these circumstances, the following theorem can be established: *the introduction of outside (relative) prices differing from those which would be established in our economy in isolation will result in some trade,*

---

[4] A trivial exception is provided by the constant cost case mentioned in the previous foot-note. Here at the isolated state prices there might be an unimportant possibility of neutral equilibrium as recognized in the Classical theory of international trade. I adopt the convention of defining trade to exclude this possibility.

and as a result every individual will be better off than he would be at the prices which prevailed in the isolated state. The truth of this has been intuitively apprehended by a great many economists, but I do not believe that there exists anywhere in the literature a rigorous proof of this proposition.

To illustrate the difficulties which must be encountered in establishing this theorem I present a table showing some possible re-

TABLE I

	p	x	p	$\bar{x}$	w	a
Case I—no trade.........	1	10	1	10	4	5
	2	15	2	15	2	20
	1	20	1	20		
Case II.................	3	11	3	20	9	4
	2	17	2	15	3	18
	1	23	1	0		
Case III................	3	8	3	20	6	5
	2	17	2	15	3	20
	1	32	1	0		
Case IV................	3	8	3	20	6	4
	2	17	2	15	3	22
	1	32	1	0		

sults of the introduction of trade. In the first two columns are respectively the prices and quantities consumed of three commodities; in the next two columns, the prices and quantities produced of the same three goods; in the last two columns, the prices and quantities of two factors of production. Case I gives a hypothetical set of prices which would prevail in the isolated state with equal production and consumption of all commodities. The amounts corresponding to each individual would be some constant fraction of the total quantities. Although actual prices are given to avoid the asymmetry of using any one good or service as *numéraire*, only relative prices are of importance.

If a new set of relative prices are imposed from without, new equilibrium values will be appropriate. Cases II, III, and IV indicate possible sets of equilibrium values which might emerge, depending on the particular make-up of tastes of the individuals in question.[5]   In Case II after trade is established, it will be noted that more of every commodity is consumed, while less of every productive service is provided.   Obviously, Case II is an instance of our theorem.   But what can be said of Case III?   Here, the same amounts of all productive services are provided, but not more of every commodity is consumed.   More of commodities x_2 and x_3 will be consumed, but less of commodity x_1.   In Case IV things appear to be still worse.   Not only does the quantity of some commodity decrease, but also more of the productive service a_2 is provided.   Is it possible to say in the general case that the new situation is better than the old, or is our theorem false?

It is obvious that a labour theory of value cannot be of any aid in the analysis of this problem, since two factors of production have been assumed.   The opportunity cost doctrine as presented by Professor Haberler could be applied only to Case III, where the total amounts of the various factors of production remain unchanged after trade has taken place.   Contemplation of the behaviour of the terms of trade would suggest that an improvement has taken place, but it would be easy to construct examples for which this test would give a spurious result.   None of the usual methods throws any light on the question as to whether Case IV represents an improvement over the condition which would prevail in the absence of trade.   And yet there can be no doubt that the situation represented in Case IV is the typical case when trade occurs.   If we assume that in the real world there are innumerable commodities and productive services, it is scarcely conceivable that after trade takes place more of each and every commodity and less of each and every productive service will result.   The introduction of trade would be expected to result in less of one or more commodities and more of one or more productive services.

Still, if the theorem given above is valid, it must follow that we can very definitely show that all the given cases in which trade takes

---

[5] Cases II, III, and IV are alternative and mutually exclusive possibilities. Hence, although each is consistent with Case I, they are not necessarily consistent with each other.

place are better than the original situation illustrated by Case I. It remains only, therefore, to prove our theorem, after which all the illustrative examples will emerge as special instances.   It will be noted that the proof to be given depends only on the elementary operations of arithmetic: addition, subtraction, equality, inequality, etc.

To ensure generality, consider any initial set of prices prevailing in the isolated state,

$$p_1{}^0, p_2{}^0, \ldots, p_n{}^0,$$

and the corresponding equilibrium values of the remaining variables,

$$x_1{}^0, x_2{}^0, \ldots, x_n{}^0, \bar{x}_1{}^0, \bar{x}_2{}^0, \ldots, \bar{x}_n{}^0, a_1{}^0, a_2{}^0,$$
$$\ldots, a_s{}^0, w_1{}^0, w_2{}^0, \ldots, w_s{}^0.$$

Now consider any new set of prices leading to trade,

$$p_1{}', p_2{}', \ldots, p_n{}',$$

and the corresponding new equilibrium values

$$x_1{}', x_2{}', \ldots, x_n{}', \bar{x}_1{}', \bar{x}_2{}', \ldots, \bar{x}_n{}', a_1{}', a_2{}',$$
$$\ldots, a_s{}', w_1{}', w_2{}', \ldots, w_s.$$

From the production inequality of equation [2] we know that

$$\Sigma p'\bar{x}' - \Sigma w'a' \geqq \Sigma p'\bar{x}^0 - \Sigma w'a^0. \qquad [4]$$

But from the condition that the total value of imports must equal exports, or that the total value of goods produced must equal the total value of goods consumed, a similar inequality will hold if we leave the bars off the x's and consider goods consumed instead of goods produced.   This gives

$$\Sigma p'x' - \Sigma w'a' \geqq \Sigma p'x^0 - \Sigma w'a^0. \qquad [5]$$

I now assert that this condition (barring the unimportant case of equality sign mentioned in foot-note 4) assures us that each of our identical individuals is better off in the second case than in the first.

Imagine an individual confronted with commodity and productive service prices $[p_1', p_2', \ldots, p_n', w_1', w_2', \ldots, w_s']$. Subject to these prices, his most preferred position with respect to consumption and the providing of services is shown by his behaviour to be $[x_1', x_2', \ldots, x_n', a_1', a_2', \ldots, a_s']$. By considerations similar to the economic theory of index numbers as developed by Pigou, Haberler, Konüs, Staehle, Leontief, Frisch, *et al.*, it can be shown that this combination is preferred in an ordinal sense to $[x_1^0, x_2^0, \ldots, x_n^0, a_1^0, a_2^0, \ldots, a_s^0]$.[6] If at the primed set of prices the individual would have bought the original combination of goods $[X^0]$, and provided the original amounts of productive services $[A^0]$, the total algebraic cost would have been less than that of what he actually bought and sold $[X', A']$. In addition, therefore, something more could have been bought of every commodity, and a little less of every productive service supplied. This proves that $[X', A']$ is better than $[X^0, A^0]$; for if this were not so, why did not the individual actually choose $[X^0, A^0]$, and perhaps a little more of every good and a little less of every service, in preference to $[X', A']$? If the individual was in a true maximum position at the primed prices, it must necessarily follow from our inequality that $[X', A']$ is better than $[X^0, A^0]$. Thus, our theorem is proved.

To appreciate the true meaning of this theorem and its proof, the reader may make the experiment of dropping one or more of our premises to show how the proof will break down or have to be modified. Such an exercise is provided by the well-known Graham's decreasing cost paradox.

No modification in the proof is required by the assumption that there exist domestic consumers' goods which cannot be traded under any circumstances. With slight modification transportation costs could be introduced into the analysis without affecting appreciably the results. It will be noted that the proof is still valid in the case where there exist no resources transferable between different production uses. Indeed, if the commodities are not pro-

---

[6] For many reasons I regard the index number approach as a clumsy device for solving the problem at hand. A more convenient test as to the ordinal desirability of two situations is presented in my "Note on the Pure Theory of Consumers' Behavior" (*Economica*, March, 1938).

duced at all, but fall from heaven in fixed amounts per unit time, the theorem still applies. Moreover, the introduction of discontinuities requiring modifications of the usual marginal analysis is already covered in our theorem.

[7] If, as I have shown, the introduction of outside prices different from those which would prevail in the isolated state betters all of our identical individuals, a possible generalization suggests itself. Is it possible to state that the more prices "deviate" (according to some appropriate convention) from those of the isolated state, the better off all individuals will be? The answer is in the affirmative. In order not to complicate the present exposition, I withhold the rigorous proof of this proposition until a future occasion.

[8] Before going on to consider more realistic cases where individuals are not all alike, I should like to point out two interesting special cases covered by the previous theorem. The limiting case of an economy in which all individuals are exactly alike is that of a single household or Robinson Crusoe economy consisting of but one unit. Also, from a formal point of view a completely unified economy under perfect control of some central authorities interested in maximizing some ordinal preference scale is like a one individual economy. For such single individual economies, pretending to play the game of perfect competition is one possible way of arriving at optimal equilibrium values. If self-sufficiency is not an end in itself, it follows from our previous theorem (and even under less stringent assumptions) that for an individual or unified economy trade is always preferable to no trade, although it is not necessarily true that free trade is the best trading policy.

[9] I now drop the assumption that all individuals are alike with respect to tastes, abilities, ownership of the means of production, etc. The introduction of changed prices leading to trade cannot, of course, be expected always to better each and every individual. After trade, the prices of items chiefly consumed by a particular individual may have risen making him worse off than

before. (It is not possible, however, for every individual to be made worse off.)

In order to evaluate the resulting situation, it would be necessary to have some scale which would take into account comparisons as between different individuals. For some type of weighting of the fortunes of different individuals, the result might be judged an improvement. For some other, such as an egocentric evaluation on the part of those rendered worse off, the resulting situation might be judged to be worse than that which prevailed in the isolated state. If nothing more than this could be said, the problem of the benefits from trade would be of limited theoretical and practical importance.

Fortunately, definite results which do *not* depend upon the comparisons of the real incomes of different people can be derived. Although it cannot be shown that every individual *is* made better off by the introduction of trade, it can be shown that through trade every individual *could* be made better off (or in the limiting case, no worse off). In other words, if a unanimous decision were required in order for trade to be permitted, it would always be possible for those who desired trade to buy off those opposed to trade, with the result that all could be made better off.[7] This can be deduced from the fact that as a result of trade larger (or in the limiting case, equal) amounts of every commodity can be secured with smaller (or equal) amounts of every productive service. Without trade the range of possible commodities which are available with pre-assigned amounts of all productive factors is given by the implicit equation [1]. If outside prices are introduced, it will always be desirable for production policy to be aimed at maximizing the total value of output at the outside prices, with any preassigned amounts of each and every productive factor. For this will yield a larger money sum than any other production policy, and with a larger sum of money more can be bought of every commodity than with a smaller one. As a result, each of the following three statements is true: [1] more can be had of every commodity as of the same totals

---

[7] See Professor Viner's interesting remarks in his *Studies in the Theory of International Trade* (New York, 1937), pp. 533–4.

of all productive services; [2] of the same preassigned quantities of all consumers' goods, less of every productive service need be rendered; [3] after trade, more of every commodity can be secured with less of every productive service. This ensures us that by Utopian co-operation everyone can be made better off as a result of trade.[8]

I shall make no attempt to construct a numerical index of the gains of trade. In the simplest case of a single individual, only an ordinal preference scale is assumed so that only better or worse comparisons can be made. Such constructs as consumers' surplus are in general inadmissible. Even in the singular cases where they are able to be employed, they are perfectly arbitrary and conventional, adding nothing to the analysis.

[10] In conclusion, I should like to point out that in the above exposition an attempt has been made to demonstrate rigorously with little reliance on intuition the truth of the theorems advanced. Whether or not this should be done is, of course, a matter of taste. Much more important than the carrying through of the formal steps of the argument is the realization that the theorems are true consequences of the premises, and do not rest on *presumption* or *probability*. For in pointing out the consequences of a set of abstract assumptions, one need not be committed unduly as to the relation between reality and these assumptions. On the other hand, in advancing a presumption in favour of an undeducible proposition, the suggestion is conveyed that the difficult task of interpreting reality has already been performed.

---

[8] Mathematically, subject to preassigned outside prices and with preassigned quantities of all productive services, there will result optimal production quantities which are functions of the preassigned variables and satisfy the production limitation of equation [1]. These optimal production quantities will sell for the largest possible total in the outside market, and hence the expression $\Sigma p'x$ is maximized subject to equation [1] and fixed amounts of productive factors. The resulting money sum will be sufficient to permit consumption of goods obeying the condition that all imports must be paid for by exports, or $\Sigma p'x = \text{maximum } \Sigma p'\bar{x}$. Because production is optimal, the result is more (or equal) consumption of every good. Moreover, for sufficiently small reductions of all production services, it will still be possible to have more of every commodity, and hence the truth of the third statement follows.

12

THE THEORY OF INTERNATIONAL TRADE RECONSIDERED*

By John H. Williams‖

I

The purpose of this paper is to offer some criticism of the English classical theory of international trade and to suggest some other lines of analysis. That theory has always rested mainly upon the distinction made by Ricardo between external and internal mobility of economic factors. It abstracts too, for simplicity's sake, from cost of transport. Less obviously, perhaps, it assumes for each trading country fixed quanta of productive factors, already existent and employed, and asks how, subject to the assumptions, these may be most effectively applied under conditions of free international trade.[1] On this foundation it builds its famous doctrines of comparative cost and reciprocal demand, working, in a money economy, through the medium of international gold flow, and expressing themselves in unequal divisions of benefit from international trade, as displayed by persisting income and price differences between the trading countries.

My present concern is not primarily with the correctness of this analysis, taken on its own ground, but with the limitations which its premises have imposed upon it. It is one question whether these

---

* *Economic Journal*, Volume XXXIX (June 1929), pages 195–209. Reprinted as Chapter XII in J. H. Williams, *Postwar Monetary Plans and Other Essays*. 3rd ed., (New York: A. Knopf, 1947); from which it is here reprinted, without change, by permission of the *Economic Journal*, Alfred A. Knopf, and the author.
‖ Harvard University.
[1] See especially Schüller: *Schutzzoll und Freihandel* (1905), Chap. ii.

conclusions follow logically from these premises.[2]   It is a more important question whether these are the premises best calculated to illuminate the subject-matter.   The classical theory assumes as fixed, for purposes of the reasoning, the very things which, in my

---

[2] Professor Taussig's *International Trade* (1927), is our most complete statement of the classical theory of international trade; it aims particularly at verification of theory, especially of the analysis of the mechanism of trade adjustment under conditions of gold standard and inconvertible paper; to this end it reviews the studies in verification made by his former students and presents the results of his own recent investigations.   Edgeworth, though fundamentally in agreement with the classical analysis, offered keen criticism on particular points of doctrine.   Marshall accepted without reservation the assumptions, but pointed out that comparative costs are subject to change under the play of reciprocal demand (*Money, Credit and Commerce*, Appendix J).   F. D. Graham has made the same point independently and in more detail (*Quarterly Journal of Economics*, November 1923).   E. S. Mason (*Quarterly Journal of Economics*, November 1926) cites the economists' (particularly Marshall's) recognition of the facts of industrial and occupational friction and of the variation of productive factors, and contrasts their rejection on these grounds of labor cost doctrine in domestic value theory with their acceptance of it in international value theory.

On assumptions essentially the same as the classical, Bertil Ohlin, in a book to be published in the Harvard Economic Studies, rejects comparative costs and presents an analysis in terms of the principle of variable proportions.   Comment on this analysis, which I had opportunity to discuss in detail with Professor Ohlin during his visit to Harvard in 1923–24, must await the appearance of the book. Cliffe Leslie accepted the fact of imperfect mobility of productive factors, but would apply it both to international and domestic trade.   French and German writers, such as Cournot, Nogaro, List, Schüller, have exhibited a marked unwillingness to accept either the premises or the conclusions of the classical theory.

Since I am not here primarily concerned with the mechanism of trade adjustment, it is unnecessary to discuss the recent literature of that subject, which contains such outstanding studies as Viner's *Canada's Balance of International Indebtedness*, which presents a view sympathetic to the classical explanations of the trade adjustment mechanism, though the facts presented seem to me less corroborative than the author feels them to be; and Angell's *The Theory of International Prices*, which includes an admirable summary of the literature and current views.   I may mention also my own doctoral thesis *Argentine International Trade under Inconvertible Paper Money: 1880–1900* (Harvard Economic Studies, 1920).

(I have made no effort to bring this footnote on the literature down to date. The book by Ohlin referred to is his *International and Interregional Trade*, 1933.)

view, should be the chief objects of study if what we wish to know is the effects and causes of international trade, so broadly regarded that nothing of importance in the facts shall fail to find its place in the analysis.

It is my view:

1. that the premises are inaccurate in sufficient degree to raise serious question of the soundness of the theory, or at least of the range of its useful application to the trade of the world;
2. that the relation of international trade to the development of new resources and productive forces is a more significant part of the explanation of the present status of nations, of incomes, prices, well-being, than is the cross-section value analysis of the classical economists, with its assumption of given quanta of productive factors, already existent and employed;
3. that the international movement of productive factors has significance relative to comparative prices, incomes, positions of nations, at least equal to that of the trade in goods, and that the study of these movements tends to be minimized in a theory which abstracts from them as much as possible, and for the strictly logical support of its conclusions should abstract from them entirely; even today, in most treatments of international trade theory, capital movements are discussed mainly in connection with the balancing of payments, being limited to their currency ("purchasing power" or "substitutes for gold flow") functions in connection with trade adjustment mechanism, and are not discussed as transfers of productive power; and international movements of labor are scarcely discussed at all;
4. that international trade in goods, cost of transport, and mobility of economic factors—externally and internally—continually react upon each other; and by investigating these interactions —in this actual, growing, changing world—we may hope to throw light upon the causes and effects of international economic contacts—upon market and productive organization, upon prices and price processes, upon incomes and general

well-being, and finally upon the wisdom or unwisdom of international commercial, financial, and labor policies.

II

Viewed from this standpoint, the question whether we have, have ever had, or are ever likely to have the same mobility of factors between as within trading countries ceases to be *the* question on which the entire analysis must turn, and takes its proper place as one, only, among a number. In discussions of this sort the point most often made is that the persistent differences of incomes and prices in different countries—higher in the United States than in England, higher there than in Italy, higher there than in China— is striking proof of the international immobility of productive factors, *and therefore of the correctness and adequacy of the classical theory of international trade.* This remark is often regarded, indeed, as a signal to adjourn the discussion; nothing more remains to be said. I hasten, therefore, to disclaim intention to disprove so familiar a fact, though I shall have more to say about it at a later place.

Indeed, it is not Ricardo's *immobility* premise that stands most in need of defense, but rather his *mobility* premise, the assumed free movement of factors *within* countries. Perhaps no reminder is necessary that this assumption, no less than the other, is essential for the validity of the comparative cost principle. Bagehot, in the *Postulates of English Political Economy*, discussed in penetrating fashion the relativity of economic concepts, set forth the conditions necessary for free domestic movement of factors, and concluded that value theories based on this hypothesis could not apply to any country in the world prior to the English classical period itself, and then only to the conditions of the "large commerce" upon which England, in advance of other countries, was embarked. Indeed, up to the middle of the eighteenth century, at least, the only "large commerce" had been international; nor is it mere coincidence that productive factors appear then to have moved more freely between countries than within them.

One wonders, moreover, how correct this particular assumption was for the Ricardians' own time, or even later. International

friction in the movement of capital and labor there doubtless has
been, and international differences of incomes and prices.   As
Professor Taussig has said: "The same phenomenon, less striking as
regards the differences in real and money wages (than those between England and India), but more striking as regards the close-
ness of the contact, appears on a comparison between Great Britain
and continental Europe . . . in the latter half of the nineteenth
century. . . . The Anglo-French treaty of 1860 led to a . . .
range of import duties so low that it could have been no appreciable
factor in maintaining differences in wages and prices.   Yet these
differences persisted."[3]   But there is abundant evidence that such
differences have persisted also *within* the trading countries.   This
was a phenomenon which especially interested Cliffe Leslie, who
found within England, France, Belgium, and Germany local
diversities of all sorts, some which had persisted for centuries and
some which were the product of the new nineteenth-century economic activity, in which foreign trade played a major part.   In
agricultural wages the diversities were "prodigious."   "The real
movement of agricultural wages throughout Europe will be seen
to be in striking contradiction to generalisations, such as the
tendency of wages to equality, which have passed with a certain
school of English economists for economic laws: . . . generalisations, one may add, which were once useful and meritorious as first
attempts to discover causes and sequence among economic phenomena, but which have long since ceased to afford either light
or fruit, and become part of the solemn humbug of 'economic
orthodoxy.'"[4]

On the other hand, Brassey, the railway contractor, found the
price of labor of equal efficiency in railway construction (which involved international migration of labor and capital) nearly on a
level throughout the railway-building countries, and was led to
wonder whether labor did not move more readily from country to

---

[3] *International Trade*, Part II, Verification, p. 154.

[4] Cliffe Leslie: "The Movements of Agricultural Wages in Europe"; *Essays,*
2nd edition, 1888, p. 379.

country in the same employment than from occupation to occupation at home (another tempting generalization, as dangerous perhaps as the one it attempts to supplant).   It is unnecessary to offer elaborate proof of the existence of much local and sectional difference of prices and incomes in Europe. Any casual American tourist, without getting far off the beaten track, soon becomes aware of the striking diversity of economic conditions, of prices and incomes, even as between near-by places, in any of the European countries.   Even for England one has only to compare the north with the south, the east coast with the west, or the Scottish Lowlands with the Highlands, though in each case distances by rail or road are short.

The United States presents, in comparison, a case of high internal mobility, one reason for which I believe to be the relatively greater importance (and greater freedom from restriction) of the domestic market than the foreign, and the consequently greater growth of and closer connections between trade, transportation, and movements of productive factors. Yet even here we are far from realizing an approximate equality of either wages or prices, or return to capital, as between different parts of the country.   In fact, the marked heterogeneity of economic conditions, of stages of economic development, of point of view, the diversity of economic interests, the "sectionalism" of the United States are quite as familiar and have proved almost as significant in economic and political ways as has the phenomenon of a large, highly-organized, competitive home market, with comparatively high internal mobility of goods and productive factors which that condition signifies.   These two sets of facts doubtless account for the confusing statements made by the same writers, though not in juxtaposition: first, that the trade between our East, South, and West closely resembles international trade; and second, that the high mobility of economic factors within the United States is a striking proof of the validity of the Ricardian theory of international trade and the premises on which it rests. That there are great disparities of incomes and prices between North, South, and West is familiar observation.   An obvious case in point is that of white textile workers in the Carolinas and Massachusetts. A *Bulletin* of the U. S. Bureau of Labor, July 1907, gives comparisons of wages in some fifty occupations in 1906 for the North Atlantic, South Atlantic, North Central, South Central, and Western states, and compares wages in twelve leading occupations in the United States and European countries. Wages in the North, South, and West differ strikingly in all occupations covered. The nearest approach to equality is between North Atlantic and North Central states, but even here the discrepancies run to as high as 40 per cent and are distinctly greater than those shown for Germany and France. Shadwell, in *Industrial Efficiency* (1906), concluded that in general German wages were about four fifths and American wages seven fifths of English wages; but the American data cited show that for blacksmiths, Western wages were 1.44 of Southern, bricklayers' wages 1.46, carpenters' 1.44, painters' 1.47, plumbers' 1.57, lino-type operators' 1.36, street laborers' 1.64. It is true there are explanations of these differences, such as "poor white" and Negro labor in the South, concentration of immigrant labor in the North-east, and principally, I suspect, the unequal economic develop-ment of the several regions. But these explanations do not help the case, since they lie quite outside the assumptions of the classical theory. Indeed, as to immigrant labor, it is a noteworthy fact that its students emphasize both its enormous inflow from abroad (leading finally to restriction) and its very imperfect, un-"free" internal distribution; and some go so far as to assert that the immi-gration problem is primarily that of more effective distribution of the new labor rather than its exclusion. In any case, both aspects of the problem run singularly counter to the classical assumptions.

But of course the whole problem of geographic mobility in rela-tion to the comparative cost principle is complicated still further by the facts of industrial and occupational friction within countries. Professor Taussig devotes a chapter of his recent book, *Inter-national Trade*, to the difficulties which "non-competing groups" raise for the Ricardian analysis: "Are we to conclude that the more simple analysis with which we started, resting on the assumptions of homogeneity in labor groups and uniformity of wages, become quite inapplicable where there are heterogeneous social and indus-trial conditions and wide diversities of wages in any one country? The answer depends not so much on the existence of non-competing groups in the several countries as on the similarity or dissimilarity of their make-up. . . . If the groups are in the same relative positions in the exchanging countries as regards wages—if the hierarchy, so to speak, is arranged on the same plan in each—trade takes place exactly as if it were governed by the strict and simple principle of comparative costs. . . . Now, in the Occidental coun-tries—those of advanced civilization in the Western world—as a rule the stratification of industrial groups proceeds on the same lines."[5]

If one accepts this generalization for the advanced Western world (though perhaps all would agree that it raises just the sort of question on which economists desire more knowledge than is now available), it apparently has the effect of limiting the application of the comparative cost principle to the industrial countries of the West, and excluding not only Asia, Africa, South America, but also Russia, most of the Mediterranean countries, and some at least of the Scandinavian; and Professor Taussig's analysis would suggest exclusion of the German chemical industry before the war, as resting on special cheapness and abundance of chemists and their assistants, and of some American industries in so far as they have benefited peculiarly from the use of cheap, unskilled immigrant labor, or "poor whites" in the South (not to mention the Negroes)— industries of the Southern states, the steel industry and the textile industries in the North. England's "parasitic trades," products of slum labor or other specially low-paid labor, would doubtless com-prise another list of exceptions. As to American immigrant labor, it is important once again to observe external mobility of labor pro-ducing internal immobility.[6]

The expression "advanced countries" suggests another major limitation upon the classical theory. Its premises do not, apparently, apply to the comparative internal and external *geographic* mobility of productive factors in countries of unequal economic advancement.

---

[5] Taussig: *International Trade*, Chap. vi, pp. 48, 55, 56.

[6] Ware: *The American Foreign-born Workers* (p. 10), gives the following percent-

Inferior organization of capital and labor in the more backward country, inferior domestic banking, inferior internal means of communication, inferior perception of economic opportunity—these are obstacles to free movement which far outweigh those commonly cited as impediments to the movement of factors from the more advanced countries. The movement of capital, and to a less degree of labor, is therefore likely to be more free from a more advanced to a less advanced country than is the internal mobility of factors in the latter. This is part of the explanation of great cosmopolitan seacoast cities, foreign trading centers, nearer to Europe in their economic and cultural contacts and characteristics than to their own interiors, and relying upon Europe for finance, transport, and management; of the presence of large-scale foreign enterprise, mainly in the extractive industries; of the existence of problems of immigration or emigration, in countries and continents otherwise comparatively primitive, "pre-economic," to use Bagehot's phrase.

Even for the advanced countries the facts remain complex and generalizations about them not unfraught with some danger. This group contains some young countries and some old ones. As already stated, it contains countries which differ widely in their internal geographic mobility. It contains countries of essentially small-unit enterprise and others of large-scale industry; countries which differ widely in productive technique, in the proportion of capital goods applied to land and labor, even in enterprises of similar sort. It contains countries which have pursued a policy of self-sufficiency and others which have sought the widest possible development of international economic relations. It contains

---

ages of foreign-born workers in American basic industries:

Iron and Steel	58
Bituminous Coal	62
Slaughtering and Meat Factory	61
Woolen and Worsted	62
Cotton Goods	62
Clothing	69
Leather	67
Furniture	59
Oil Refining	67

countries which have exhibited markedly varying degrees of liberality and conservatism as to import duties, a circumstance which would itself account in part for international differences of prices and incomes.   It contains countries, like the United States, as yet comparatively inexperienced in the export of capital, in which foreign bond issues must bear yields distinctly higher than domestic; and others, like England before the war, which have specialized in international finance, with effective marketing machinery, special knowledge of foreign countries to offset risks of distance, ignorance, and inertia, the major part of whose organized distribution of new annual capital is external rather than domestic, and which enjoy in consequence special economies of large-scale enterprise in capital exportation compared with domestic distribution.   One is reminded of Bagehot's cosmopolitan loan fund and his prediction that the economists' distinction between internal and external mobility of capital would be found to rest on no enduring foundation.   That some capital is internationalized and moves freely from country to country in response to slight changes in prices, exchange rates, or interest rates is evidenced by the wide recognition of security movements, of both long and short term, as a substitute for, and preventive of, international gold flow.[7]

Whether for countries so diverse one can make *any* assumptions, applicable to all, regarding comparative mobility of economic factors is a question not easily answered.   One cannot say, for example, whether capital moves more freely within such countries than between them (with sufficiently greater freedom, that is to say, to constitute a difference in kind for the purposes of value analysis) until one has considered also the nature and importance of industrial and other barriers to its free internal movement. That an entrepreneur is frequently apt to think in terms of his industry rather than of political geography was observed by List, and also by Adam Smith.   It is increasingly true as industry and trade have become larger in scale.   Oil, copper, gold, steel, tex-

---

[7] I must add, though space forbids discussion, that I am not content with the gold-flow explanation of trade adjustment, even when thus qualified.

tiles, rubber, chemicals, automobiles, telephone and telegraph, electric power, agricultural machinery, the match industry provide an impressive and ever increasing array of basic industries which have expanded in disregard of political frontiers. They represent in some cases the projection by one country into others of its capital, technique, special knowledge along the lines of an industry and its market, as against the obvious alternative of home employment in other lines. They represent, in other cases, an international assembling of capital and management for world enterprises ramifying into many countries.[8] They suggest very strikingly an organic interconnection of international trade, movement of productive factors, transport, and market organization.

Logically followed through, the classical doctrine of international trade contradicts itself; its conclusions contradict its premises. It is a theory of benefits from territorial division of labor. If, before trade, England and Portugal produce cotton cloth and wine, after trade is opened England will produce cloth for both and Portugal wine. This means national specialization for the wider market. Specialization is thus the characteristic feature and the root idea of international trade. But specialization is the antithesis of mobility, in this case of domestic movement of productive factors. The point may be illustrated with the aid of Mill's famous objection to Adam Smith's "vent for surplus" principle of foreign trade, which he characterized as a "surviving relic of the Mercantile Theory":

"The expression, surplus produce, seems to imply that a country is under some kind of obligation of producing the corn or cloth which it exports; so that the portion which it does not itself consume, if not wanted and consumed elsewhere, would either be produced in sheer waste, or, if it were not produced, the corresponding portion of capital would remain idle, and the mass of productions in the country would be diminished by so much. Either of these suppositions is erroneous. . . . If prevented from exporting this

---

[8] They represent, in some cases, the response of industries to tariffs and patent laws, providing one class of cases in which impediments to the flow of goods produce a flow of productive factors.

surplus it would cease to produce it, and would no longer import anything, being unable to give an equivalent; but the labor and capital which had been employed in producing with a view to exportation would find employment in producing those desirable objects brought from abroad; or . . . substitutes for them. . . . And capital would just as much be replaced, with the ordinary profit from the returns, as it was when employed in producing for the foreign market."[9]

It is to be doubted whether Mill today, or indeed the Mill of his later years, the writer of the chapter on the "Tendency of Profits to a Minimum," would care to stand by this passage in reference to England. There is no mention of an alternative in capital and labor outflow, although the Mill of the later chapter, not then concerned with Ricardo's theory of international trade, was quick to see that possibility and to assess its relation to England's economic development. England provides us today with the best illustration of the ultimate logical effects of international trade upon national economic organization. Through specialization in production for world markets, fostered by export of capital and labor from early colonial times down to the war of 1914, and by a free trade policy, she has been able to concentrate capital and labor on a small amount of land in "increasing return" industries, and to buy the products of "increasing cost" industries from abroad. By such specialization she has achieved, of course, enormous advantages of territorial division of labor; but in so doing she has no less clearly committed herself to a particular organization of her productive effort. International trade is her *raison d'être*. If cut off from foreign markets, it is difficult to see how "the labor and capital which had been employed in producing with a view to exportation would find employment in producing those desirable objects which were previously brought from abroad," and this without loss of capital or profits. What Mill overlooked was the entire absence, under assumptions of predominant foreign trade, of comparable alternatives in purely domestic production; for by the very fact of spe-

---

[9] Mill: *Principles*, Book III, Chap. xvii, pp. 579–80.   Ashley ed.

cialization for foreign trade such alternatives could not logically exist. He failed to see, indeed, that but for specialization in world trade such concentration of labor and capital on little land would not be possible. What is more significant, perhaps, he failed to see the relation of international trade to national economic development, spread over time. For him the problem was one of cross-section value analysis upon particular assumptions about mobility of factors. He failed to see that England's capital and labor were *products* (results) of international trade itself, but for which they would not have existed in any comparable degree. Having been created by international trade they stand committed to it, the only alternatives being, (1) a shift from some lines of international trade to others, (2) an international migration of productive factors, and, (3) as a temporary stopgap, support from the public revenues. Looked at from this standpoint, Mill's principle appears less true and more naive than "the surviving relic of the Mercantile Theory."[10]

III

The classical theory of international trade dates from the first half of the nineteenth century. Since some modern economists recognize the relativity of economic doctrines to the circumstances of their times, the theory of international trade is sometimes referred to (though surprisingly little such comment has come from specialists in the literature of the subject) as sound for its time, sound in its fundamentals even yet, but in need perhaps of some modification with the changing conditions of the world. To my own mind, the main assumptions of the theory bear little evidence of careful observation of the current and antecedent phenomena of the times out of which the theory emerged. This fact should appear from a brief survey of the earlier history of foreign trade.

---

[10] An implicit alternative is a loss of real income. For a more hopeful view of the possibilities of substituting domestic for international trade, see Sir Henry Clay: "Britain's Declining Role in World Trade," *Foreign Affairs*, April 1946.

The questions here raised are of course highly relevant to the debate now going on in Britain and elsewhere with respect to bilateral versus multilateral trade, and the problems of external-internal economic adjustment.

In the Middle Ages and the early modern period international trade was peculiarly associated with progress. Communication was easiest by water, and this fact found expression in the rise successively of the Italian city states, the Hanseatic League, Portugal, Spain and Holland. Progress in industrial technique and market organization was greater in international trade industries than in the purely domestic.[11] The trade involved, too, a considerable international diffusion of capital and enterprise, at a time when internal mobility was slight indeed. Thus the merchants of the Italian city states and the Hanseatic League spread their capital and themselves resided, throughout western Europe and the Levant. The League merchants promoted agriculture in Poland, sheep-rearing in England, iron-production in Sweden, and general industry in Belgium.[12] On the decline of the League its capital and its merchants emigrated to England and Holland. Adam Smith observed this fact, recognized the relation between international trade and capital migration, and in that connection made his famous remark about the mobility of merchants: "A merchant, it has been said, very properly, is not necessarily the citizen of any particular country. It is, in a great measure, indifferent to him from what place he carries on his trade, and a very trifling disgust will make him remove his capital, and together with it all the industry which it supports, from one country to another."[13] It was partly by reason of this instability of mercantile and industrial capital that Smith, who was a nationalist of nationalists, objected to the encouragement of international trade and industries dependent thereon; in a "natural" order capital would go first into agriculture at home and become planted in the soil: "No part of

---

[11] "If the putting-out system appeared in England on any considerable scale only in modern times, this was because of the relative backwardness of that country. A similar form of organisation had been common in the mediaeval towns of the Low Countries and Italy which manufactured for export," M. M. Knight: "Recent Literature on the Origins of Modern Capitalism," *Quarterly Journal of Economics*, May 1927, p. 524.

[12] List, *National System of Political Economy*, Book I, Chap. ii, p. 100.

[13] *Wealth of Nations*, Book III, Chap. iv.

it [capital] can be said to belong to any particular country till it has been spread as it were over the face of the country, either in buildings or in the lasting improvements of lands. No vestige now remains of the vast wealth said to have been possessed by the greater part of the Hanse towns."

International trade prior to the nineteenth century strikingly displays a movement of the factors of production underlying, requisite to, and proceeding out of the anticipation of profits to be made by international extension of markets and raw material resources. There was general recognition among writers and statesmen, including Adam Smith, that the same profits motivation which moved goods could move also the labor and capital requisite to produce them effectively. The Whigs in the eighteenth century, like the Manchester School in the nineteenth, were inclined to disparage the movement. Like the distant trade of the East India Company, the American trade seemed to divert labor and capital that could be usefully employed on English soil, without conferring any compensating advantage. This objection was stated and effectively answered by William Penn[14] and others who dilated on the superior advantages to capital and labor in the New World and the benefits to England of their transfer. The slave trade found favor with many because it would prevent the draining off of Englishmen and lessen the danger of establishment of competitive industry.[15]

In this field, as always, Adam Smith was a close observer of facts. Though in his view home employment is nationally more advantageous than foreign, and in a "natural" order capital and labor will go first into home industry—capital export, equally with

---

[14] *The Benefit of Plantations*, in *Select Tracts relating to Colonies* (Brit. Mus., 1029, e.16).

[15] The slave trade was, of course, quite literally international trade in men, an exchange of men for goods; the migration of free men and of capital was an essentially similar process based on essentially similar motivation. Present and prospective profits from trade did not buy free men and translate them into the production which created the profits, but it offered prospect of high wages and return to capital and induced their movement.

goods export, being in the nature of a surplus—he is careful at all times to say that domestic application of factors will be preferred only on "equal or nearly equal profits." If under natural conditions (i.e., in the absence of special monopolies) the rate of profits were higher in foreign (colonial) trade, that would indicate the trade was understocked, productive factors would flow into it, costs of foreign goods would fall, to the benefit of home production and consumption, English exports would increase, and in this way the domestic application of labor and capital would be increased.[16]

Mill was struck with the significance of the same set of facts as Smith observed in the colonial trade: "There is a class of trading and exporting communities on which a few words of explanation seem to be required. These are hardly to be looked on as countries, carrying on an exchange of commodities with other countries, but more properly as outlying agricultural or manufacturing establishments belonging to a larger community. Our West India colonies, for example, cannot be regarded as countries with a productive capital of their own. If Manchester, instead of being where it is, were a rock in the North Sea (its present industry continuing) it would still be but a town of England, not a country trading with England; it would be merely, as now, a place where England finds it convenient to carry on her cotton manufacture. The West Indies, in like manner, are the place where England finds it convenient to carry on the production of sugar, coffee and a few other tropical commodities. All the capital employed is Eng-

---

[16] Nicholson cites Smith's recognition of the international mobility of capital as one of his significant "lost ideas": "In what may be called the pure theory of foreign trade it is assumed that between different economic nations there is no mobility of capital or that the mobility is so imperfect that for theory it may be neglected. Adam Smith, on the other hand, held the view confirmed by experience (and it may be said in harmony with the 'modern' principle of continuity) that foreign trade can only be carried on by sending a certain amount of capital out of the country. . . . These lost ideas have again been forced on the public attention by two significant facts: first, the enormous investments of British capital in foreign states; and secondly, the increasing tendency in recent years in the commercial policy of other nations towards the protection of native industries." J. S. Nicholson: *A Project of Empire*, p. xiii.

lish capital; almost all the industry is carried on for English uses.
. . . The trade with the West Indies is therefore hardly to be considered as external trade, but more resembles the traffic between
town and country, and is amenable to the principles of the home
trade. The rate of profit in the colonies will be regulated by English profits: the expectation of profit must be about the same as in
England, with the addition of compensation for the disadvantages
attending the more distant and hazardous employment; and after
allowance is made for those disadvantages, the value and price of
West India produce in the English market must be regulated . . .
like that on any English commodity, by the cost of production."[17]

In attempting to ascertain the precise range of application of
this suggestion of Mill's, so strikingly in contrast with his general
theory of international trade, I find it a matter of the utmost
difficulty where to draw the line. Though he mentions several
peculiarities of the case of these colonies, the decisive ones, clearly,
are that England finds it convenient to produce certain goods there
(as is indeed true of all international trade), and that this convenience actuates the movement of English productive factors,
tending to produce an equality of profit "after allowance is made
for the disdvantages" of distance and risks. This applies certainly
to very much of English trade in the nineteenth century. On these
precise principles, England has found it convenient to produce
wheat and meat (and for that purpose to export capital) in Argen-
tina, gold and wool in Australia, minerals and food products in
Africa, raw materials and foods in the United States and Canada
through the greater part of their history; nor was her nineteenth-
century trade with western Europe devoid of these same characteristics, though there the goods trade and the movement of capital
were not so directly and obviously linked together. Once again we
find the suggestion that the same profits motivation that moves
goods tends to move factors of production, and that foreign trade
tends to produce an extension of productive factors over the expanding market area. It is true that this applies with special force

---

[17] *Principles*, Book III, Chap. xxv. §5, pp. 685–6.

to the development phase of international trade, and particularly to trade between unequally developed areas; but how much of foreign trade, first and last, escapes from these limitations? It is one question whether, under conditions of an approximately uniform development of nations, the factors do not move more freely within than between them, and whether (which is a different and a more important question) we cannot for purposes of value theory abstract in our analysis of goods trade from the movements of factors which do in fact occur under these conditions. But given a lack of uniform development, an uneven world apportionment of capital and labor and managerial skill to land and to economic potentialities, and given an uneven development of communication, external and internal, the traditional "obstacles" to movement must be measured against the "pull" of economic incentive if our interest in foreign trade is to discover and assess what really happens, rather than what ought to happen under particular assumptions. And the negative fact that even under these conditions incomes are not made uniform internationally is not a sufficient excuse for avoidance of a more positive analysis than the economists have given us of the economic effects of the enormous and increasing drift of capital and labor over the world's surface.

To understand the industrial revolution a sense of continuity is indispensable. While it is never possible to ascribe complex economic changes to simple or single causes, it is increasingly the view of historians that the industrial revolution was primarily a phenomenon of expanding markets. There followed a geographical and social, as well as an industrial, transformation of internal productive effort. Industries moved to new sites, employers cried out against old legal and customary restraints, while laborers sought to resist change and movement by invoking them, and economists (particularly the lesser lights, out-doing as always the creative thinkers) set forth as infallible and universal economic law new doctrines of economic liberty which were, like other changes mentioned, the product of the times and circumstances. For us, the theoretical question raised is the adequacy of a method of analysis which, taking a cross-section view in that moment of time, to fit those conditions so created, assumes as a first fact national entities, economically organized, internally mobile and coherent, and then attempts to study contacts between them on the assumption that international mobility of factors is so imperfect that for value purposes it may be ignored.   British economic development to their time, including the domestic economic organization which they were analyzing, suggests that the economists' foreign trade assumptions ignored organic elements of the problem.

13

THE EFFECT OF FOREIGN TRADE ON THE DISTRIBUTION OF INCOME*

By Eli Heckscher||

Prefatory Note

When the editors of the present collection of reprints of articles on international trade did me the honor of asking for permission to include the following article from the Swedish *Ekonomisk Tidskrift* of 1919, it was clear to me that if such a reproduction should be required, it must be on account of the place held by the article in the development of thought in the field of theory of international trade.

As mentioned in its opening sentence, the article owes its origin to Knut Wicksell's criticism of an earlier book of mine. Wicksell had a great influence on the minds of his younger Swedish colleagues—especially during the later years of World War I and the beginning of the interwar period—until his death in 1926. This, however, does not mean that Wicksell either agreed with or differed from my approach to the theory of international trade; it remained rather alien to his thought. But my then pupil, Bertil Ohlin, followed up my attempt and reshaped it, especially through an application of the general price theory of Walras, in the form it had received at the hands of Gustav Cassel. Ohlin's results were first published in his doctoral dissertation in Swedish, *Handelns Teori* (Theory of Trade, 1924), and afterwards, far more fully, in his well-known book in the Harvard Economic Series, *Interregional and International Trade* (1933). My previous treatment, in the article here reproduced, does not, in the eyes of its author, contain much of any value over and above Ohlin's books, while the latter have removed numerous blemishes in the earlier treatment and—still more important—have brought the theory into connection with actual conditions and problems of the interwar period. This, however, does not prevent my attempt from being one of the first to combine foreign trade with distribution of income or, perhaps better, with the prices of the agents of production.

If, after an interval of upwards of thirty years, I should attempt to rewrite my article in accordance with my present views both of the problem and of its best

---

* *Ekonomisk Tidskrift*, Volume XXI, 1919, pages 497–512. Reprinted, by the courtesy of *Ekonomisk Tidskrift* and the author, in slightly abridged form.

||University of Stockholm.

treatment, the result would be rather different from my early text. But for this I lack both leisure and inclination. That the approach is a good one still remains my opinion.

Professor and Mrs. Svend Laursen very kindly have undertaken the trouble of translating my Swedish text into English, and I thank them heartily for their pains.

ELI F. HECKSCHER

The origin of the following remarks can be traced back to a review which Professor Wicksell was kind enough to write, nearly a year ago, of my book, *Swedish Production Problems*.[1] Although I have reached a different conclusion from Wicksell's on at least one important point, I have nevertheless profited greatly from his criticism in a number of different ways. It is not my intention, however, to follow Professor Wicksell's article too closely, since it seems to me that the problem may be discussed, with better results, in more general terms. The importance of the subject as well as the surprisingly scant attention so far paid to it in the theoretical literature tend to make a theoretical study of it both useful and tempting; very likely it may be possible to explain the actual nature of foreign trade and its effects more fully than has heretofore been done. Even in the best case, however, this article cannot pretend to be more than a first, purely theoretical orientation, since the subject is not only difficult but also very broad in scope. If the following sketch inspires others to continued study of the subject, my goal will have been reached, even though it may be shown that I have been mistaken in some respects, a possibility which is by no means out of the question.

I

The effect of foreign trade on the distribution of income is closely related in a number of ways to its effect on the total national income, and this latter problem thus cannot be excluded from consideration. On the other hand, however, it is sufficient to study the problem of income as a whole simply in its context

---

[1] In the weekly *Forum*, 1919, Nos. 2 and 3.

with the original problem of income distribution, and this first section must therefore be regarded only as the basis for certain conclusions to be developed later, and not as a complete picture of the effects of foreign trade on the national income.

The following assumptions underlie the argument throughout the entire paper. Changes induced by foreign trade in the nature of the factors of production ("dynamic" changes) are completely disregarded, and so are the disturbing effects resulting from the difficulties of transition from one position to another. Moreover, no attention is paid to the advantages one particular country may achieve, by means of protection, in altering the relation between supply and demand of a certain commodity and thereby wholly or partly letting the "foreigner pay the duty"; since this problem has been discussed so widely, and since it is not relevant in the present connection, it seems unnecessary to discuss it here. The value of money is considered throughout to be constant in the sense that a unit of currency always corresponds to the same amount of goods; although this formulation is not very definite it is enough so for the present purpose.

It is more important, however, to emphasize two assumptions which are not valid for the entire paper, but only for its earlier parts. First, a *numeraire* is chosen as a unit of measure, and the national income is measured according to its market value in terms of this *numeraire* without regard to differences in subjective value among different individuals. When considering the distribution of income at a later stage of the argument, this assumption clearly must be relaxed. The second assumption is the one which provides the basis for the generally accepted theory of foreign trade as it was originally formulated by Ricardo, namely, the assumption that the quantity of the factors of production within a country is given.

If one initially employs *all* of the above assumptions—an important reservation—it follows from the nature of barter that trade will create the maximum satisfaction of wants or the maximum national income. Exchange will only be agreed upon or continue insofar as it offers the traders a higher gain than if it did not occur.

This is in full accordance with List's point of view, since his criticism of the "school" was directed only at the dynamic factors.   Nevertheless, it is a proposition which has to be briefly demonstrated.

If a country can produce a number of different goods, but the possibility opens up of obtaining a few or several of these goods through exchange, there is still no reason for the country to alter its economic system to that end unless the total satisfaction of wants (in the sense that this term was used above) is thereby increased. Such a gain in total satisfaction arises whenever the law of "comparative costs" operates, *i.e.*, whenever a want is more easily satisfied in an indirect way, through the production of another commodity which can be exchanged for the commodity desired, than by producing the latter directly.   If a country, for example, can obtain grain more easily by producing wood pulp in excess of its needs and exporting the latter, than by producing grain directly, this means that by allocating the country's given resources in part to the production of exportable wood pulp, the country can increase its welfare in one of three different ways: more grain may be available for home consumption without any smaller consumption of other commodities, *or* more of other commodities may be available without any smaller quantity of grain, *or* the consumption of both grain and other commodities may be increased.   If the same supply of means of production which was formerly used for grain production is now used for the new export, more grain for consumption will be obtained as a result; and if consumers do not want this additional grain, some of these means of production will be free to produce other things which could not be produced before; finally, in between these two cases lies the case where the quantity of grain is somewhat increased and, at the same time, some of the means of production are freed to produce more of other goods.

The only doubtful case arises when foreign trade results in a decrease in the consumption of some commodities and an increase in others; in the example above, for instance, the lower cost of obtaining grain might reduce the consumption of some other type of food.   In this case it is difficult to find general measurements for the decrease in some commodities compared with the increased value of others.   Exact figures are not necessary, however, since the case in question is only possible insofar as it results in a gain. Moreover, if the terms of trade are used as a measure, it is not difficult to show that the various possibilities discussed above all lead to the same type of gain for the country as a whole.[2]

II

Our main concern, however, is not with the influence [of foreign trade] on the national income as a whole, but with the influence on the distribution of this income and more specifically with the separate factors of production.

The problem is formulated in this way to show that we are interested primarily in the distribution of income between land, capital, and labor.   The other side of the problem of distribution, which deals with the allocation of national income among individuals, is omitted because foreign trade can hardly be expected to operate in any consistent manner with respect to this type of distribution.   In what follows, a certain given distribution of the factors of production among different individuals is taken for granted; and since this distribution is not uniform, it follows that a change in relative prices of the factors of production will alter the distribution of income among individuals.   This assumption is

---

[2] *Cf.* fil. kand. F. von Koch's article "Om Frihandels-och Tullskyddsteorier" [On Theories of Free Trade and Protection], *Ekonomisk Tidskrift*, 1918, Part II, pp. 73 ff.   The confusion on this point has been caused mainly by Sidgwick's example in his *Principles of Political Economy* (Book III, Chapter V, Section 2a, London 1887, pp. 496 ff.).   The confusion is not attributable to any mistake in the example but simply to its presentation, in which different aspects of the subject are included without discussion of the relation of each to the result.   Sidgwick's conclusion that "the *aggregate* wealth of the persons living *in this country* may be reduced by the change" depends entirely upon his assumption that the production group squeezed out by the change emigrates or dies from starvation.   As a rule no attention is paid to this fact either by those who agree or by those who disagree with Sidgwick's theories.   Owing to the special assumption, his proof remains outside the premises of the present discussion.

natural in a society where the total income is not equally distributed, but it is nevertheless pointed out because the theory of foreign trade which built upon the classical theory seemed to take the opposite view.

Our primary purpose, then, is to discover the influence of foreign trade upon the prices of the factors of production.   It will soon be clear that this question leads to some of the fundamental assumptions in the theory of foreign trade.   The first of these fundamental assumptions concerns the *reasons for differences in comparative costs among countries*.   It is most surprising that this basic issue in Ricardo's still valid theory of foreign trade has thus far received so little attention.   If Ricardo's assumption of immobility of factors of production between countries is dropped, it can easily be seen that the determination of factor prices has an important bearing upon factor movements.   At the beginning, however, we shall retain Ricardo's assumption of immobility, and on this basis the reason for differences in comparative costs will be discussed.

If we say, initially, that the same relative scarcity of factors of production exists in two countries, then, assuming the same efficiency in both countries, the most natural outcome will be that both countries use the same technique in all branches of production.   The only possible exception would be differences in the absolute size of markets which might lead to differences in the size of units of production and thus to differences in technique.   This possibility is considered at a later point of the present paper.   If, for the moment, such differences in size are neglected, it follows that, with the same relative scarcity of factors of production and the same techniques, both countries will have the same comparative costs for all goods.   Since the relative prices of the factors of production are the same in both countries, substituting one factor for another in the first country but not in the second would be impossible; and, since all factors of production are combined in the same proportions in the production of a given commodity in both countries, while at the same time relative factor prices are the same, comparative costs in one country cannot possibly differ from those in the other. Foreign trade between the countries will thus be impossible.[3] If the prices of arbitrarily chosen units of the factors of production land, capital, and labor are called l, c, and w respectively, and if we assume that $l = c = w$ in both countries, it can immediately be seen that a given quantity of the factors of production will produce the same results in each country regardless of whether the factors are used to produce a commodity directly or to produce it indirectly through exchange with the other country. If, for example, one commodity requires $l + c + w$ for a unit of output, while another one requires $l + 10c + 20w$, and the assumption that $l = c = w$ is still valid in both countries, the ratio between the value of the two commodities will be 3:31 in both countries. In the absence of transportation costs, exchange of commodities between countries will thus result in neither a gain nor a loss. Where transportation costs exist, the impossibility of initiating trade between the countries becomes obvious, for new exchange would result in a loss.

A difference in the relative scarcity of the factors of production between one country and another is thus a necessary condition for a difference in comparative costs and consequently for international trade. A further indispensable condition is that the proportions in which the factors of production are combined shall not be the same for one commodity as for another. In the absence of this second condition, the price of one commodity, compared with the price of another would remain the same in all countries regardless of differences in relative factor prices.

The prerequisites for initiating international trade may thus be summarized as *different relative scarcity, i.e., different relative prices of the factors of production in the exchanging countries,* as well as *different proportions between the factors of production in different commodities.* The second of these prerequisites is a given condition of production and does not require further explanation. It must be remembered, however, that the failure of this condition to be satisfied may well explain why

---

[3] It will be shown later that trade between the countries may well occur even when comparative costs are equal, and, indeed, that trade may be the cause of equality in comparative costs.

the exchange of certain commodities does not occur.   The presence or absence of the first prerequisite, on the other hand, is of the utmost importance.   It must be stressed at this point that the term "factor of production" does not refer simply to the broad categories of land, capital, and labor, but to the different qualities of each of these.   The number of factors of production is thus practically unlimited.   International trade may be attributable to a particularly fertile soil in one country, compared with another, or to a particularly skilled population, as well as to a disproportionate distribution of land or workers "in general."   It is only with respect to free capital or savings that the question of differences in quality does not arise.   It must be remembered throughout the remainder of this paper that when prices of the same factors of production in different countries are compared, the comparison always refers to the prices of the *same qualities* of the given factors.   The problem of why a worker in one country earns more than a less efficient worker in another hardly requires an explanation.   And yet in the theory of international trade it is interesting to observe how readily just this type of problem *is* discussed.

III

In studying the influence of international trade on the price structure of the factors of production, it is necessary to recall the basic principles of trade.

As long as the value of exports is equal to the value of imports, we may begin the discussion with either exports or imports without altering the final result.   Exports decrease the amount of certain factors of production available for production for the domestic market, *i.e.*, those factors used to produce the export commodities. On the other hand, imports which are the payment for exports, make available for domestic markets those factors of production which formerly were used to produce the goods now imported.[4] Foreign trade thus creates, on the one hand, an increased scarcity

---

[4] It is hardly necessary to explain that exports and imports include all services to or from the foreign country.   It must be pointed out, however, that in this basic discussion extension of credit and transfer of real capital are neglected.

and, on the other hand, a decreased scarcity of the different factors of production available for domestic-goods production.

Obviously the question before us is whether the increases and decreases in scarcity of factors, taken together, result in an equilibrium, or rather, whether or not the old equilibrium is disturbed. In order to answer this question, we may assume that both the commodity produced domestically and the imported one replacing it are of the same type, *i.e.*, that *no substitution between different kinds of commodities takes place through foreign trade.* The only substitution, in this instance, is a replacement of domestic goods with the *same kind* of commodity produced outside the country. At this point, the conclusions reached at the end of the preceding section may be employed. In order for trade to take place, there must be a difference in comparative costs between import and export goods in the two countries, and this means, according to Section II, a difference in the relative amounts of the factors used in the production of those two commodities. Since the imported commodity and the domestic good which the imported commodity replaces are the same, it follows that those factors of production whose scarcity is increased by exports must be different from the ones whose scarcity is reduced by imports. Thus the relative scarcity of the various factors of production for the economy as a whole is altered.

Before proceeding further, it seems desirable to draw attention to a tacitly made assumption, especially since the presence or absence of this assumed condition may modify the result. This assumption is that *the same technique is used to produce a given commodity* in different countries. Even if the relative prices of the factors of production are the same in the trading countries, there is still the possibility, mentioned earlier, that differences in technique may arise as a result of differences in the sizes of enterprises. It is much more interesting, however, to take as the starting point the condition, previously regarded as the necessary condition for international trade, of differences in the relative prices of the factors of production between one country and another. The possibility of substitution among the factors of production then creates the possibility, or rather the likelihood, of differences in technique between the countries.   In this case the imported commodity employs the factors of production according to a different yardstick than is true of the same commodity when produced in the importing country. It is then possible, although always accidental, that the imported commodities may free the factors of production in the importing country in exactly the same proportions as they are employed in exports.   In this event, international trade would result in no change whatsoever in the relative scarcity of the factors of production in the importing country, although it might well have that result in other countries.

The preceding argument may be clarified by means of a numerical example.   Suppose that arbitrarily chosen units of two products, textiles and machinery, can be produced by using the same quantity of the factors of production, i.e., by $l + 2c + 3w$. Suppose, further, that the relative prices of the factors of production in the "home country" (C) are $l = c = 2w$, and in the "foreign country" (F) these relative prices are $2l = c = 3w$.   To determine the absolute level of money prices and costs in both countries, let the price of capital in C be $c = 1p$, and in F let $c = 3q$; l and w will then be determined according to the preceding ratios, and in country C both commodities will cost $4.5p$ while in F both will cost $10.5q$.   We may now assume that in the case of machinery, but not in the case of textiles, it is possible to substitute labor for capital at the rate of one unit of capital against two units of labor.

This substitution will obviously pay in F, where a unit of capital is three times as expensive as a unit of labor, and if it is assumed that half of the needed capital can be replaced by labor in the production of machinery, the cost of a unit of machinery in F will be $l + c + 5w = 9.5q$, as against $10.5q$, before the substitution occurred.[5]   Since textiles in F remain at the price of $10.5q$, the ratio between the price of machinery and the price of textiles has changed to $9.5:10.5$.   If a corresponding substitution were possible for textiles as well, comparative costs would remain unchanged.

---

[5] This substitution will no doubt increase the price of labor and decrease the price of capital, and thereby somewhat alter the numerical result; but no particular purpose is served in discussing this refinement here.

With the figures chosen here, there would be no purpose in substitution in country C, but with other price ratios between the factors (*e.g.*, $l = c = w$), substitution in the opposite direction to that in F would pay if it were technically possible.   But if no additional substitution is possible, then, according to the law of comparative advantage, machinery will be exported from F to C and textiles from C to F.   This exchange alters the relative scarcities, and hence the relative prices, of the factors of production in F but not in C.   Country C almost completely stops producing machinery, but the factors of production thereby freed have the *same* relation to each other as those used by the country's new textile export.   Country F, on the other hand, reduces its output of textiles, and in this process more capital and less labor becomes free than is needed in the new export of machinery.   Thus the distribution of income is altered in F but not in C.

If the above example is correct, it shows how difficult it can be to anticipate the effects of foreign trade. . . . [Nevertheless], it demonstrates that foreign trade almost always results in a new distribution of income.

At this point it seems desirable to alter one of the assumptions upon which the foregoing argument was based, and to examine the consequences of this change in assumptions.   Throughout the preceding discussion it has been assumed that foreign trade does not result in substitution among different types of commodities [but simply replaces domestic output with the *same* type of product made abroad].   The question now arises whether foreign trade will affect the distribution of income if the *opposite* is assumed, *i.e.*, that the imported commodity is not exactly the same as the domestic product which it replaces.

Some influence upon the distribution of income is possible in this case, and, indeed, is far more likely than in the former case, but the result will not, in the long run, at least, be the usual one. No longer is the problem one of replacing home-produced cotton textiles, *e.g.*, with imported cotton textiles; with the new assumption, we may suppose, instead, that imported cotton products replace home-produced woolen textiles.[6] This leads to several possible results not thus far considered.   We know that the imported commodity, cotton textiles, employs factors of production in a different proportion than does the exported commodity, machinery. Nevertheless, if the imported commodity replaces a somewhat different domestic commodity such as wool textiles, it is conceivable that the production now terminated may have employed land, capital, and labor in the same way as does the new export commodity, machinery.   The immediate effect of this new exchange will no doubt be a surplus of the factors of production tied up completely or partly in the now superfluous domestic industry.   It is not unlikely, as a result, that the country will now export the unwanted commodity formerly sold on the home market.   Consider, for example, a country without international trade using woolen clothing exclusively.   If this country now has the opportunity of importing cotton clothing, the raising of sheep, which formerly made possible the woolen production, may possibly lead to the export of wool.

Whether it can be assumed that this immediate situation will last is quite a different question.   In order that the export of wool shall continue, or that other exports shall be developed in which the relative importance of the factors of production is the same as in sheepraising, the country must have a more than normal supply of those factors of production employed in the enterprises squeezed out by foreign trade.   While this condition is possible, it is not certain and perhaps not even probable.   In more general terms, it was the condition of demand, i.e., the demand for clothing on the home market, which caused the factors of production to be used in the old way, at the old relative factor prices; it therefore seems likely that the new and altered demand will change the relative scarcity and the relative prices of the factors of production.   In

---

[6] It is shown later that the imported good actually need not replace any domestic output at all; i.e., the imports need not make any domestic output superfluous; in order not to make the problem more involved, however, this possibility is omitted from the present discussion.

other words, it is possible that the demand conditions prevailing before trade was opened may have led to an extraordinary scarcity of certain factors of production.   In the example discussed above, it is more likely that sheep were raised because of the need for textile materials than that consumers chose woolen clothing because the country possessed unusually good pasture land for sheep. And even if this latter point of view had some influence in the choice of a type of clothing, this merely shows that in choosing a textile raw material the conditions of production within the country were taken into consideration.   It does not in the least indicate that, when international trade begins, it will be more advantageous to raise sheep than, *e.g.*, to forge iron or saw wood.   It is predominantly this latter shift in production that decides what exports will be used to pay for new imports.

It remains only to study the [behavior of] factors of production released by trade.   Such a release usually occurs since the direct and indirect returns from the factors of production make up the gain without which trade would never have materialized.   With respect to these forces as well as to the changes in economic life resulting from the altered relative prices of the factors of production, both will tend to some extent [as we shall see later] to counteract the original change in prices.   Since the secondary reactions are a consequence of the change in prices, however, they will not eliminate the price changes entirely.

If the foregoing is correct, changes in the distribution of income must be considered the normal effects of expanding or contracting international trade.

IV

Having established that foreign trade has an influence upon the distribution of income, we must next inquire about the direction and limits within which this redistribution takes place.

At the outset, one can see that it would be most unlikely for international trade to change the distribution of income in the same direction in all countries and under all conditions.   A general increase of interest rates, *e.g.*, or a general increase in wages throughout the world would be a most improbable consequence of international trade.   International exchange, like exchange in general, must, under most circumstances, have opposite effects upon the two participants, although always in such a manner that both parties gain; a general change in a given direction is therefore unlikely. The scarcity of a particular factor will increase in some countries, as a result of trade, and decrease in others, and since each country tends to export commodities using relatively large amounts of its abundant factors, the primary question is under what conditions, how, and to what extent *foreign trade evens out the scarcity of the factors of production among countries;* obviously this is a question of the tendency of trade to create the same economic conditions in different countries.

When a country changes from isolation to international exchange, the effects depend in part upon the mobility or immobility of the factors of production. Ricardo assumed complete immobility of factors, and Edgeworth, in his well-known article on the theory of international trade in the *Economic Journal* (1894), said that international trade *means* exchange on the basis of immobile factors of production. I do not intend to discuss here whether this assumption is a realistic one. Naturally much depends upon individual conditions. Generally speaking, the assumption appears to be partly valid for capital, even more so for labor, and valid without limitation for land. The position of the doctrine of immobility in the theory of international trade, as well as its relation to reality, makes it imperative that the present problem be discussed under the assumptions of both mobile and immobile factors of production.

At the outset, the factors of production may be regarded as completely immobile between countries. More than this, we shall assume that the quantities of the factors of production within each country are given and unchangeable, so that the domestic supply of a factor is not influenced by its price. We have seen above that, with the same technique of production in all countries, a difference in the relative scarcity of factors of production was a necessary condition for an expansion of international trade. The question before us now is, how far will this process of exchange go? In other words, will not all differences in relative factor prices lead to an expansion of trade?

If the conditions of production are the same in all countries, this question must be answered in the affirmative. Each difference in the relative prices of the factors of production will make it profitable to get, by trading, any commodity which requires relatively more of a relatively scarce factor of production, for another commodity in which a relatively more abundant factor is predominant. Thus trade must continue to expand until an *equalization of the relative scarcity of the factors of production among countries* has occurred. As long as the relative scarcity of the factors is not the same between one country and another, trade will continue to expand. When relative scarcities are finally equalized, the trade already entered upon, which was a condition of the equalization, will continue, but no further expansion will occur. Thus it can be seen that a difference in comparative costs between countries will *create* trade but such a difference is not necessary for the continuance of already established trade; on the contrary, the differences in comparative cost are doomed to disappear as trade expands. Differences in the relative prices of factors of production thus nullify themselves even in the absence of movements of the factors. Before drawing conclusions and enumerating limitations, these propositions may be illustrated by the following example.

Assume that an exchange between country C and country F has begun and has led to a partial equalization of the relative prices of the factors of production as follows:

(1) Originally: In C, $l = c = w = 1p$
                    In F, $l = 3c = 4w = 3q$

(2) After trade has commenced:

                    In C, $l = 1.5c = 2w = 1p$
                    In F, $l = 2c = 3w = 3q$

Assume further that for two commodities, meat and machinery, the cost of production in both countries is $l + c + w$ and $l + 3c + 4w$ respectively. Obviously C produces meat, since this commodity requires relatively less of c and w, both of which are relatively expensive in C; country F, for the opposite reason, produces machinery.   As C reduces the output of machinery and substitutes meat, the relative scarcity of capital and labor declines in that country.   In F, on the other hand, the intensified production of machinery increases the scarcity of capital and labor.   As a result, relative factor prices change as shown in (2) of the above example. Equalization will not stop here, however, for with the relative prices shown by (2) it is still profitable in both countries to expand foreign trade further.   The exchange will thus continue until equalization is complete.   It is necessary again to point out that costs of transportation and other trade barriers limit the equalization.

With fixed supplies of the factors of production and the same techniques of production in all countries, we have seen that the final effect of international trade, with unimportant reservations, is the equalization of the *relative* prices of the factors of production. We must next inquire whether the equalization will be *absolute* as well as *relative*, *i.e.*, whether rent, wages, and interest for the same qualities of the factors of production will *amount* to the same real return in all trading countries.   This proposition has not thus far been demonstrated, but it is an inescapable consequence of trade.

The generally accepted explanation may be formulated as follows: since a certain factor of production, *i.e.*, land, exports its own product, wheat, this factor must receive in return, when equilibrium prevails, as much of the other country's product, textiles, as that same factor of production, land, receives within the second country for the same product, and *vice versa*.   The consumers of wheat will pay the same amount regardless of whether their wheat is domestic or imported, and the same is true of the buyers of textiles; the price of one country's exported wheat and the other country's domestic wheat thus will be the same, and this is also true of textiles.   Obviously export goods and the same type of goods sold on the home market must be priced the same, and wheat prices and textile prices are thus the same in both countries.   More important, however, is the conclusion that, with the same technique and the same prices of products, the absolute returns to the factors of production must also be equalized.   Since a certain commodity in both countries is priced at $l + c + w$, another one at $l + 3c + 4w$, a third at $l + \frac{1}{2}c + 15w$, etc., and since these prices are the same for each commodity in both countries, it is inevitable that l, c, and w each must have the same value in the two countries.

The preceding argument is entirely dependent upon the assumption that both countries have the same technique of production, and the full meaning of our conclusions becomes clear only when this assumption is closely examined.

The same given technique in both countries obviously means that a substitution among the factors of production cannot take place in one country without an identical change taking place in the other. But we know that international trade alters the relative scarcity of factors of production in two trading countries in opposite directions, and any factor substitution which occurred in one country would therefore occur in a sense opposite to that which took place in the other; *i.e.*, the factor substitutions in the two countries would lead to differences in technique. In the foregoing discussion this type of substitution is neglected. Perhaps the most important consequence of the assumption of fixed proportions of the factors of production is that international trade may make one or more of the factors of production superfluous. If trade leads to curtailment of production in one field and to an increase in another, this is due to the fact that the proportions in which the factors are employed in the two fields are different, and since the factors, by hypothesis, cannot move out of the country, one or more of them may become redundant. If the curtailed field of production has the proportions $l : 3c : 4w$, for example, while the field enlarged has the proportions $l : c : w$, then part of c and w will be made superfluous by the shift in output.

This does not mean that international trade inevitably leads to unemployment of some factors of production, for substitution may occur on the side of consumption even when it is impossible among the factors of production. The argument may be illustrated by an example which resembles the situation of the United States in the middle of the nineteenth century. Suppose a country has plenty of land for growing wheat but a small supply of workers for producing textiles.   Before international trade begins, we may suppose that two units of wheat correspond in value to one unit of textiles. This is assumed to mean that the ratio of prices of the factors of production is $l = \frac{1}{2}w$, leaving capital out of consideration to simplify the problem.   International trade is now opened, with the result that textile prices, and consequently wages, go down to one-half their former level, *i.e.*, to $l = w$.   Half of the wheat which the landowners formerly had to pay their countrymen for textiles will now be available for exports, and this is what is paid for the imports of textiles.   Both groups produce the same as they did before, but half of the wheat formerly consumed by the textile workers is now exchanged abroad for textiles.

What happened here was a tremendous shift which occurred *without any part of the home production becoming superfluous.*   Prior to the development of trade, the relatively high price of textiles was caused by the disproportion between land and labor, compared with the situation in the rest of the world.   When the effects of this disproportion are offset through trade, and the land in this particular country (*i.e.*, the United States) is given the opportunity to support the same relative population as is supported by the same quality of land in other countries, then the wage of American workers decreases to the same level as the wage of workers of the same quality in other countries.   When trade is begun, there will thus be no difference between "rich" and "poor" countries in regard to the price of each unit of a factor of production of a given quality. The difference between countries will rather be in the greater or smaller *amounts* of special factors of production which they possess.

Under the assumption of the same technique in all countries, it follows that nothing is lost either in the individual country or in the world as a whole by the fact that the factors of production remain where they are.   This, incidentally, shows that mobility of factors of production between countries would not necessarily mean a gain for the transferred factors.   [In the absence of mobility] the different kinds of production will be located where the necessary factors of production are present.   Each unit of each individual factor has to satisfy the same part of the demand from the world's population as any other unit of the same factor, no matter where the factors are located.   It is all very much like the ideal case of economic liberalism, which Carlyle disdainfully called the "ragman's millennium."   Exactly for this reason, it is necessary to point out that trade is not unpatriotic, but is consistent with an unaltered location of all the factors of production.   The case might better be called a harmonious state of equilibrium.

It can readily be seen, however, that in general such a state is unimaginable.   If the case discussed above actually existed, this would mean that the distribution of the world's population was without economic significance and that a movement of factors of production, as a consequence of economic motives, was out of the question.   Where, then, is the limitation to the case as discussed above?

It is not too difficult to see that the limitation lies in the assumption of the *same technique* in different countries, or in other words at the point where substitution between factors of production becomes possible or desirable.   At that point there is more of one and less of another factor of production than is required for the most economic combination in different branches of production.   The result is that, insofar as possible, a scarce factor of production is replaced by one more abundant.   This *partly* offsets the effect of the rather inconvenient proportions between the factors of production within the country and of the corresponding relative factor prices which do *not* correspond to the world price situation.   Since, however, these unusual proportions and prices are necessary conditions for the substitution to occur, it is impossible for such substitution to equalize relative factor prices within the country with those in the rest of the world.   If substitution is technically impossible although economically desirable, [on the other hand,] the factors of production will not be used fully and the disproportion will apparently increase. Situations such as this explain a great deal of the economic life of the world, a point which may be made obvious by a concrete example.

The situation of the United States in the period before the large European immigration may be considered once again, but this time the case will be treated in closer accord with reality than in the previous illustration.   The country had enormous riches of good arable land but a very small population.   When trade with Europe became possible through improved transportation, it was obvious that exports of products using land would be exchanged for imports of products using labor.   The scarcity of labor in the United States was so great that there were not sufficient workers to cultivate all of the land which could have been used advantageously for the export of wheat to Europe; even to the extent that the land was cultivated, this was done largely by the substitution of land for labor, *i.e.*, to use a common phrase, by extensive cultivation.   As a result, rents were low and wages were high in the United States, compared with the rest of the world, and trade alone could not level out these discrepancies.   Apart from costs of transportation, trade must equalize the prices of a given product throughout the world. But when a given product is produced by *different* quantities of each factor of production in the United States and Europe, then it is not only possible, but necessary, that *the relative and absolute prices of the factors of production must differ in the two exchanging countries.*   Just as it is certain that, under free exchange, the same technique leads to the same prices for the factors of production in all countries, so it is equally certain that differences in technique lead to differences in factor prices.

On this basis the emigration of Europeans to the United States is easily explained.   It must be emphasized that without the change in the proportions of the factors of production which occurs as a result of migration or population growth, differences in factor prices in various countries will continue, and factors of production of the world as a whole will not be used to their best advantage.   The natural resources within a country must be accompanied by *at least* enough labor to permit the proportions of factors in each branch of production within the country to correspond to the "normal" or world situation.   Otherwise, world output will be less than with some other distribution of the factors, and some of the factors could gain by migration.   In a country such as England, on the other hand, labor must have enough natural resources so that an analogous substitution of workers for natural resources does not occur, for such substitution would be inefficient from a world point of view, and would result in emigration of workers. The foregoing argument with respect to land and labor is, of course, equally valid for capital.

"Harmonic" equilibrium demands, in other words, that each country must have enough of its most scarce factor so that the proportions of factors in each branch of production can be the same as the corresponding proportions in other countries.

It is usually supposed that foreign trade has a much greater effect than would be indicated by this harmonic equilibrium. As a rule it is supposed that foreign trade will increase the demand for a country's plentiful factor of production to such an extent that its scarce factor is made superfluous and either emigrates from the country or is extinguished. To return to the previous example, the idea has been that the world demand for American wheat, and indirectly the demand for American land, would make American workers superfluous. While it is certain that foreign trade decreases the relative return to American labor, it makes no sense to think that workers in the United States will thereby be made superfluous. When American wages have decreased to the world level, American workers can compete as much as they formerly did; moreover, there is no possibility that the increased demand for land will result in American wages falling below the world level, for this would mean that the originally *too* scarce labor is now *less* scarce than in other countries. If that were the case foreign trade would have passed its equilibrium and would necessarily have to be reversed. In the previous example, such a large decrease in the wages of American textile workers would result immediately in a textile export, since the price of textiles would thereby have decreased below the world level. But with the export of textiles, wages would increase to the world level. As previously shown, it is the *scarcity* of workers in the United States which prevents the same relative use of labor in the production of American wheat as in the production of European wheat and thus keeps wages higher, and rents lower, than in Europe.

V

It now remains to be seen to what extent the result above will change if the elasticity or price sensitivity of the factors of production is considered. In other words, in the present section the assumption of a fixed supply of the factors of production will be dropped, while the assumption of immobility is retained. Since price sensitivity is out of the question with regard to land, supply reactions can be considered only with respect to capital (savings) and labor (more or less total population).

If the same elasticity of supply is assumed for a given factor of production throughout the world, changes in the world supply of a given factor as a result of trade will tend to cancel each other. The increase in interest rates which international trade brings about in a country with a plentiful supply of capital, for example, will increase savings in that country; the corresponding effect in a country with little capital will be an increase in wages and a decrease in the rate of interest as well as a decrease in savings. There might be cases, of course, where the increased supply of a factor in one country would not exactly offset the decrease in another, but it would be futile to discuss such refinements here.

The foregoing argument points to the rather paradoxical result that, when supply reactions are taken into account, foreign trade tends to increase the relative differences in the supply of factors of production in different countries. This, of course, is only a tendency and may be counteracted either through changes in population or through the increase in national income which results from international trade. If these complications are overlooked, however, the conclusion above is valid. A particularly frugal population, such as the French, is freed by international trade from some of the unfavorable effects to the savers themselves of their great savings, and savers as a whole are induced, by the increase in the rate of interest, to save even more than before. A less frugal population, such as the Swedish, on the other hand, is tempted to spend even more than before because foreign trade reduces interest rates in Sweden. Similar effects occur with respect to the supply of labor; wages do not decline as much in countries with large increases in population, or increase as much in countries with stationary or decreasing populations, as would have been the case without international trade. This, indeed, is only a natural effect of the tendency of trade to equalize relative factor scarcity between trading units.

VI

We have now reached the point where our last assumption may be dropped, and full mobility of the factors of production may be assumed.

In principle, the effect of mobility is simple: apart from costs of transportation, the absolute prices of the factors of production tend to be equalized throughout the world. This result is obviously beyond the scope of Ricardo's model; with full mobility, the theory of international trade in its conventional sense is put aside, and prices or costs in different countries are compared directly. Any deviation from full conformity in absolute prices would immediately result, under such conditions, in a movement of the factors of production, and a disturbed equilibrium would immediately be adjusted. Factors of production would be distributed in accordance with the needs of production, and these needs would accordingly govern the localization of such factors. If we adhere literally to the assumption of full mobility of all factors, a case which is impossible since the factors include natural resources, it follows that production will be distributed in accordance with the preferences of individuals to live in various parts of the world. All international trade, under such conditions, would cease, since the factors of production always would go to the places where they were needed. This impossible situation has been described not only to show exactly what full mobility means but also as a useful point of departure for an important practical question of policy within the framework of the present discussion.

The question concerns the measures that should be adopted to retain within a country more of a completely mobile factor than would otherwise remain. The answer, clearly, is to increase the demand for this particular factor within the country itself. Assuming that the country cannot be made a more attractive place to live, the increased demand can be brought about only by increasing the production of goods which use that factor more than proportionally; this means protective tariffs or other means of preventing the import of such goods, or perhaps export subsidies.   With full mobility, the price of the particular factor must of course [ultimately] be the same in all countries; by increasing the demand for or the scarcity of the factor within the country, however, an increased supply or a diminished rate of efflux will result.

Thus far only part of the problem has been described.   To complete the discussion, suppose that an increased supply of a particular factor is drawn into a country [by a tariff or similar measure].

Apart from the additional products produced by the incoming factor, it is clear from Section I that the tariff will *reduce* the country's national income.   Moreover, since the price of the factor which receives the benefit of protection is [temporarily] increased above the world price, a double burden falls upon the other factors of production in the form of a reduced national income and a higher cost of the protected factor.   Later, when the higher price of the protected factor brings in additional amounts of this factor, its price will of course decrease to the world price again.   But this does not offset the decline in national income which falls upon the other factors.   The protected factor of production obviously yields less than what corresponds to its world price, for if it had yielded as much it would of course have come into the country without the inducement of protection.   And since the average world price has to be paid to the *whole* amount of the protected factor, there is no doubt that the economic loss is borne by the other factors of production.   Assuming these other factors to be completely mobile, it is clear that they will tend to leave the country; thus *the increase in the amount of one factor of production within a country decreases the amounts of the other factors.*[7]

---

[7] This point is later illustrated by a numerical example.   Although the changes in other countries have been neglected in order to simplify the exposition, it is clear that such changes will be exactly opposite to those discussed above.

Of considerably greater interest than the extreme case of complete mobility is the more realistic situation in which some factors—the material resources—are assumed to be immobile while others are assumed mobile. Under these conditions, free trade clearly results in the mobile factors' being distributed throughout the world in such a way that they combine most productively with the immobile factors.

It is important to find out how protection or any hindrance to free trade will work when there are both mobile and immobile factors. This is easily done. In the earlier case, where all factors were mobile, an increase in the supply of one of the factors without a decrease in its price led to an efflux of the other factors. If these other factors are immobile, however, such an efflux cannot occur. Thus *capital, as well as labor, if completely mobile, might be increased within a country, without a lowering of their prices, by means of protection at the expense of rent.* This is probably the strongest possible argument for permanent protection; whether it is sufficiently strong is another question to which I shall return in Section VIII. In any event, it can be seen that the argument is valid only for protection of those products which require a more than proportional amount of labor and capital; it does not apply to those fields where natural resources are used a great deal.

The essence of this section and the one preceding it may be summarized in the following manner. *Free trade* only guarantees, under certain conditions, the *same* relative prices of the factors of production in different countries; *the mobility of the factors of production* guarantees the same [absolute] prices of the factors in different countries, not proportionality among the amounts of these factors; free trade and full mobility taken together assure proportionality among the amounts of the factors.

VIII[8]

In concluding the present paper, it is necessary to consider once again the influence of international trade upon total national in-

---

[8] Section VII, dealing with a controversy between Professor Heckscher, on the one hand, and Professors Sidgwick and Wicksell, on the other hand, has been

come, a subject which was discussed in Section I.   In that section it was concluded that, with a fixed supply of the factors of production, free trade maximizes both total national income and average income per capita.   The problem which remains to be considered is how this conclusion will be modified if there is a change in the supply of some, but not all, of the factors of production.   It will soon become apparent that this problem is somewhat complicated.

After what has been said earlier, it is not necessary to amplify the argument that national income as a whole may theoretically be increased by protection.   This result may be reached by premiums upon mobile factors of production which expand the supply of such factors at the expense of the immobile factor, land.

With respect to average income per person the outcome is less simple, and depends upon whether the mobile factor which benefits from protection is capital or labor.   A protective policy which benefits capital at the expense of some immobile factor may well increase income per person.   Protection which benefits labor, on the other hand, will undoubtedly decrease average income per person, for the simple reason that such protection adds more to the population than to the national income.   It should be added that, with full mobility of capital and labor, neither wages per worker nor returns per unit of capital can be increased, by protection, above the world level.[9]

Although the preceding arguments are not difficult to understand, it may be well, nevertheless, to illustrate them with a numerical example.   Let arbitrarily chosen units of land, capital, and labor be denoted by L, C, and W, respectively, and suppose that a particular country possesses $1,000L$, $1,000C$, and $1,000W$.   The total laboring class consists of 5,000 persons, $i.e.$, five persons per active worker, while landowners and the capitalist classes comprise

omitted from the translation because it is largely of interest to contemporaries of the period when Heckscher wrote the paper, and is less general in scope than the remainder of the paper.

[9] It must be added that only static conditions are considered, and changes in industriousness, intensity of work, etc., as a result of changes in population are not taken into account.

a total of 500; the country's total population thus numbers 5,500. Although it implies a tremendously uneven distribution of income, the simplifying assumption is here adopted that the prices of the factors of production are $L = C = W = 10p$. The national income is consequently $1,000L + 1,000C + 1,000W = 30,000p$. The average income per person is then $5.46p$. Suppose that initially protection reduces the national income to $28,000p$, but that subsequently the supply of capital is doubled, without a corresponding increase in the number of capitalists. It is assumed that each additional unit of capital increases the national income by $8p$, so that total national income rises to $36,000p$. Since the prices of C and W remain unchanged and the premium must be covered entirely by a decrease in the price of L, the new situation is as follows: $1,000L + 2,000C + 1,000W = 36,000p$; $C = W = 10p$; $L = 6p$; the average income per person is now $\dfrac{36,000}{5,500} = 6.55p$, as against $5.46p$ before protection.

Suppose, now, that protection results in a premium on labor instead of capital, and that the size of the working class is doubled as a result. If national income increases, as before, to $36,000p$, this income must be distributed among 10,500 individuals, compared with 5,500 before protection. Average income per person thus declines to $3.43p$. Income per person falls because, by hypothesis, the rise in population brings about a less than proportional rise in income. In the preceding example, the new capital likewise increased income less than proportionality, but income per person nevertheless increased because the total population remained the same. Because labor and capital are fully mobile, wages and interest rates are both unchanged, and the entire change in income per person is absorbed by the landlords. It is assumed throughout that rent is able to make this adjustment without becoming negative.

From the preceding analysis, and perhaps most simply from the summary in Section VI, it is evident that international trade guarantees nothing with respect to the distribution of income. This is true whether one considers the distribution of individual incomes or the functional distribution among the factors of production; measured in either way, the inequality in the distribution of income may be either increased or diminished by international trade.   Thus, when the factors of production are immobile, foreign trade does not inevitably assure either maximum wages per worker or a maximum total return to the working population as a whole. When labor is assumed mobile, the wage rate is given since it must be the same in all countries; a premium on labor in this case increases the absolute and relative amount of wages as a whole but reduces average income per person.

Whether any arguments for or against free trade can be found in the preceding results is a question which it is impossible to neglect.   The above investigation is not well suited, however, to provide a definitive answer to such a question, for the assumptions throughout have remained extremely abstract; the question has been taken up at the end of the paper primarily in order to reject conclusions which might be drawn by a reader who did not see the limitations in this abstract formulation.   It seems to me, however, that an unambiguous and conclusive answer can be given in a few words.

Protection and other obstacles to trade are unreasonable means to ends which could not be considered unreasonable; this is true whether the factors of production are mobile or immobile.   The various aspects of this essay all lead back to changes in the distribution of income, or, if the factors of production are mobile, to changes also in the total national income and income per person.   If it is desired to avoid that distribution of income which would result from free trade, and to reach another distribution which increases either wages or population, this may be done in ways more economically advantageous than by restricting international trade— through a tax on rent, for instance.   Taxation has the advantage over protection that it does not result in economic losses for the country as a whole, such as the changes in production and reduction of trade which are the inevitable consequences of protection. When the factors of production are immobile, protection leads to a decrease in the total national income as well as in the average income per person, while taxation has neither of these effects.   If the factors of production are mobile, protection again reduces the productivity of the factors of production within the country, but taxation does not. With mobility of the factors, the newly acquired amounts of the factors will yield a smaller return not only as compared with the factors already in the country but, what is worse, as compared with their yield in the place where originally employed; and this is true whether the factors are attracted by protection or by some form of taxation. A loss to the world as a whole is thus unavoidable with such a move of the factors of production. But the world economic loss will be smaller if the movement is a result of taxation of rent than if it is a consequence of protection; and for the *individual country* the gain through taxation is the highest possible.

The economic thesis of the present essay may be summarized as follows: Under an old-fashioned liberal regime, it is possible to raise objections to free trade from the point of view of the distribution of income, particularly if taxation is proportional to income. Nevertheless, free trade, if combined with a deliberate redistribution of income, is better than any other commercial policy because it creates the *possibility* for maximum satisfaction of human wants, however this term may be defined—a possibility that does not exist under any other commercial system.

14

THE THEORY OF INTERNATIONAL VALUES RE-EXAMINED*

By Frank D. Graham‖ ‡

No part, perhaps, of John Stuart Mill's synthesis of the political economy of his time has come through the succeeding three-quarters of a century of criticism with fewer scars than mark his theory of international values. This, Mill's outstanding original contribution to economic science, has shown itself at least as robust as any of the ideas he adopted from his predecessors. Professor Edgeworth, writing in 1894,[1] repeatedly speaks of Mill's chapters on the subject as "stupendous," and Bastable's standard work on the *Theory of International Trade* is an express "attempt to restate, in a more complete form, the doctrines of the classical English school."[2] that is to say, so far as international values are concerned, the doctrines laid down by Mill. In spite of the weight of sanction, both express and implied, which it has thus commanded, the classical theory of international values seems to the present writer to be open to grave objections, objections which, while they do not subvert its foundations, nevertheless call for a substantial modification of its conclusions.

The reader will recall that Mill, "for the sake of simplicity," restricts his initial consideration to trade between two countries

---

* *Quarterly Journal of Economics*, Volume XXVIII (November, 1923), pages 54–86. Reprinted by the courtesy of the *Quarterly Journal of Economics* and the author. Copyrighted 1923, by the Harvard University Press.

‖ Princeton University.

‡ The following article is reprinted without significant change from the original text.

[1] *Economic Journal*, Volume IV, pp. 35, 424, 606.

[2] Preface to First Edition.

only and in but two commodities, and supposes that these commodities are capable of being produced in any quantity at constant
effort cost,[3] and of being transported without any cost whatever.
This paper will attempt to show that this is an overabstraction
which, far from clarifying the actual situation, in reality obscures
it, and that it has led Mill and his followers to quite unjustifiable
conclusions upon the nature of international trade.   It will indeed
be no part of our present purpose to question the assumptions of
constant cost of production or of costless transportation.   The
danger of generalizations from the former of these assumptions has
already been pointed out in the present writer's article on "Some
Aspects of Protection Further Considered,"[4] while the effects of cost
of transportation are not essentially different from those of the
varying costs which are there examined.   It is to the assumptions
of trade between two countries only and in but two commodities
that attention will here be drawn in an endeavor to show that to
construct a theory of international values in this piecemeal way is a
method so faulty as to have issued in wholly unwarranted inferences.

"Suppose," says Mill, "that 10 yards of broadcloth cost in
England as much labor as 15 yards of linen, and in Germany as
much as 20. . . . The problem is, what are the causes which
determine the proportion in which the cloth of England and the
linen of Germany will exchange for each other?"[5]   In his analysis
of this situation Mill assumes a state of reciprocal demand which
will bring about equilibrium on some terms of interchange well
within the limits of 15 and 20 yards of linen for 10 yards of broadcloth, and this he regards as the typical case, tho he says:

It is even possible to consider an extreme case, in which the whole of the advantage resulting from the interchange would be reaped by one party, the other
country gaining nothing at all.   There is no absurdity in the hypothesis, that, of
some given commodity, a certain quantity is all that is wanted at any price; and

---

[3] This is implicit in Mill's treatment.   In Bastable's "restatement" it is express; see *Theory of International Trade*, p. 23.

[4] *Quarterly Journal of Economics*, Volume XXXVII, pp. 119 *et seq.*

[5] *Principles of Political Economy*, Bk. III, chap. xviii.

that, when that quantity is obtained, no fall in the exchange value would induce other consumers to come forward or those who are already supplied to take more. Let us suppose that this is the case in Germany with cloth.[6]

Mill then shows that the English demand for linen might be so strong as to force up the price of linen to 10 yards of cloth for 15 of linen, in which case Germany would gain the whole of the advantage arising from the trade and England would be exactly as she was before the trade commenced.   Conversely, if the demand for cloth were similarly strong, *England* would secure the whole gain from the trade.

So far from this being an extreme and barely conceivable case, logic will compel the conclusion that on Mill's assumptions it is the normal one.   As a condition precedent to the conclusion that one of the countries will obtain the whole of the gain from the trade, and the other none of it, it is by no means necessary to assume an absolutely inelastic demand for one or the other of the commodities concerned.   All that is necessary is that the total consumption by either of the countries of that commodity in which it is at a comparative disadvantage shall, on any terms of exchange within the limits set by comparative cost, be incapable of an equilibration in value with its export of the commodity in which it is comparatively efficient.   This will happen whenever a large country trades with a small one in commodities of approximately equal total value, or when two countries of approximately equal economic importance trade in commodities the total values of which show a considerable disparity.   It will be noted that Mill selected for his exposition countries of approximately equal size, and commodities (in his illustration at least) of approximately equal total values.   Let us see what would happen (1) if, instead of England and Germany, he had supposed trade between England and Denmark in cloth and linen, and (2) if, instead of cloth and linen, he had supposed trade between England and Germany in cloth and, let us say, matches, assuming in the one case that the commodities are of approximately equal economic importance

---

[6] *Loc. cit.*

while the countries are not, and, in the other, that the countries are, while the commodities are not.

Taking the first case and paraphrasing exactly Mill's assumptions, with the substitution of Denmark for Germany, let us suppose that trade is initiated at the exchange rate of 10 yards of cloth for 17 of linen.   Such a trade must cause a rapid shifting of English production from linen to cloth, and of Danish production from cloth to linen, and, under the assumed conditions, nothing can stop this shifting until it has completely eliminated either the Danish production of cloth or the English production of linen.   Since we are supposing that the total value of linen and cloth is in approximate equality, Denmark, as the smaller country, will be completely specialized in linen production while there are, perhaps, nine-tenths of the English linen producers still left in that business, the specialization by the Danes being sufficient to drive only one-tenth of the English linen producers into the making of cloth.   In these circumstances the terms of interchange of cloth for linen must move to the extreme most favorable to Denmark, that is to say, 10 cloth for 15 linen; for a supply of linen adequate to the English demand is not obtainable on any better terms, the terms which the English linen producers require if they are to continue their operations.

Let us go now to the second case in which we shall suppose England and Germany, countries of approximately equal importance, to possess a comparative advantage in cloth and matches respectively, 10 yards of cloth exchanging for 15 crates of matches in England, and for 20 in Germany.   The opening up of trade on the basis of 10 yards of cloth for 17 crates of matches will quickly put the English producers of matches out of that business and into the making of cloth.   But the Germans will never be able to find in England a market for matches large enough to pay for their whole consumption of cloth, and they must therefore continue to produce cloth at home.   Such a situation will mean that the terms of interchange of cloth for matches will move to the extreme most favorable to England, that is to say, 10 yards of cloth for 20 crates of matches; for a supply of cloth adequate to the German demand is not obtainable on any better terms, the terms which the German cloth producers require if they are to continue their operations.

On Mill's assumptions, then, the establishment in international trade of any stable equilibrium other than at one of the extremes of the possible terms of interchange is dependent upon the simultaneous elimination, in both the trading countries, of the industry of comparative disadvantage. The chance of this happening is negligible; this is the extreme, the barely conceivable, case, not, as Mill alleged, the normal one; while that which he regarded as abnormal, namely that the terms of interchange should go to one or other of the points which mark the limits of advantage, must (again on his assumptions) prove to be the reality unless the dice are loaded by assuming trade in two commodities of approximately equal total consumption-value and between two countries of approximately equal economic importance.

Bastable, in his restatement of Mill, recognizes this difficulty so far as it applies to trade between a small and a large country,[7] and attempts to minimize its importance by declaring (without proof) that the competition of other nations would have a tendency to deprive the smaller country of this special advantage.   In the end, however, he rather weakly concludes that "the probability is that a small country gains by opening up trade with a large one." This alleged probability will be critically considered presently. For the moment it is enough to assert that the conclusion is unjustifiable,[8] to list it as (1) the first of several questionable inferences to which Mill and his disciples are led by the nature of their exposi-

---

[7] *Theory of International Trade,* 4th ed., p. 43.

[8] Except in the case of a single very small country trading with a large one and subject to no competition in the sale of its exports in the large country's markets. This may be what is meant, but it has little applicability to actual conditions. Bastable must, of course, mean that a small country tends to secure the *major share* of the gains from trade with larger countries.   His statement is otherwise just so many words since the probability is that *any* country gains by opening up trade with any other.

tion of international trade doctrine, and to note, in addition, others as follows:

(2) That the richest countries, *ceteris paribus*, gain the least by a given amount of foreign commerce: since, having a greater demand for commodities generally, they are likely to have a greater demand for foreign commodities, and thus modify the terms of interchange to their own disadvantage.[9]   Much depends here upon the content of the phrase *ceteris paribus;* but at any rate it will be demonstrated that the wealth of a country has no direct bearing on the percentage gains it may realize from international trade.

(3) That, but for cost of carriage, every commodity would (if trade be supposed free) be regularly imported or regularly exported; and that a country would make nothing for itself that it did not also make for other countries.[10]   Bastable, it is true, questions this statement, but on the ground of varying costs of production within the country.   So far as Bastable's treatment of the subject goes, it would, however, be a perfectly valid inference from Mill's implied, and Bastable's express, assumption of constant costs.   But it will be later shown that, even on the assumption of constant costs, it is erroneous.

(4) That the more varieties of goods a country can "offer for export," the better is its position in trade.[11]   It will be pointed out, in due course, that the variety of a country's exports is not a cause but an effect of the terms of interchange, and that those terms are more likely to be unfavorable to a country with a wide variety of exports than to one whose exports are few in number.

It will be convenient to deal with these inferences in reverse order and for the moment to hold to the assumption of trade between two countries only, but in several commodities.   We shall be using familiar terms if we take Bastable's assumptions[12] that:

---

[9] Mill's *Principles*, Bk. III, chap. xviii, paragraph 8.

[10] *Loc. cit.*, paragraph 3.

[11] This is not specifically stated in Mill, tho it is implicit in his treatment, and Professor H. G. Brown, in his *Principles of Commerce*, Part II, Chap. ii, p. 26, cites Mill as his authority for the statement as given above.

[12] *Theory of International Trade*, p. 36.

Country A with one unit of productive power can produce	and	Country B with one unit of productive power can produce
$10x$		$10x$
or		*or*
$20y$		$15y$
or		*or*
$100z$		$90z$

It will be recalled that the commodity z is introduced by Bastable *after* trade between A and B has been established on the basis of $10x$ for $16y$. "B is now able," says Bastable, "to offer to A not x only, but also z, and it will be to A's interest to take some of the commodity z at $17y = 90z$, as there would be a gain of $5z$ by the transaction, since, in A, $1y = 5z$ ∴ $17y = 85z$. . . . B's position as a trader will be improved."[13] All of this is sound enough if we admit the logic of the method of introducing commodities one by one. But, taking the three commodities together at the start as part of a single trading situation, it is clear that z could be an export of either A or B according to the terms of interchange of x and y. With the terms $10x$ for $16y$, B can export z to A, as Bastable points out; but, with the terms $10x$ for $19y$, A can export z to B, for A can produce $95z$ as easily as $19y$ and it will be to B's interest to take anything above $90z$ for $10x$. At anything less than $18y$ for $10x$, B can export z in addition to x; at anything more than $18y$ for $10x$, A can export z in addition to y. In other words, the comparative advantage in z shifts from one country to the other according to the shifting in the terms on which x and y are exchanged; and this may be generalized in the assertion that any commodity, except those two which mark the limits of the greatest difference in productive power between the exchanging nations, are potential exports (or imports) of either.

This will be clearer if, with Bastable, we take into consideration

---

[13] *Theory of International Trade*, p. 36.

a fourth commodity, w, relative productive powers being assumed to be:

In A	In B
$10x$	$10x$
$20y$	$15y$
$100z$	$90z$
$50w$	$40w$

"Here," says Bastable, "if the ratios of exchange be, as would follow from the last case, $10x = 17y = 90z$, it will be A's interest to offer $45w$ for $10x$, since it thus gains $5w$; it is, too, for B's advantage to accept these terms, as it will also gain a similar amount."[14] The fact is, however, that if A can get $10x$ for $17y$, it will *not* be to its interest to offer $45w$, which in A is the equivalent of $18y$, as it would be better to continue to offer y.[15] A would, however, instead of $17y$, be willing to give up to $42\frac{1}{2}w$ in exchange for $10x$, and anything over $40w$ would be acceptable to B. B might, on the other hand, use w for export if the terms of interchange of x and z for y should fall below $16y = 10x$ or $90z$. B could then give something more than $40w$ for $16y$, and this would be acceptable to A, where $16y$ is equivalent to $40w$. The export of w, then, is not to be regarded as a resource peculiar to A, nor z as one peculiar to B. The fact is that y is an inevitable export of A, and x an inevitable export of B, because these are the commodities which mark the limits of the greatest difference in productive power between A and B; or, to put it more familiarly, y is the commodity in the production of which A has a comparative advantage as against all other commodities, and x the commodity in which B has. But w and z may be exports of either A or B according as the terms of interchange of

---

[14] *Loc. cit.*

[15] To offer $45w$ would, moreover, controvert Bastable's assertion (*Theory of International Trade*, p. 23) that, in the premises laid down, commodities produced in either country will exchange in that country on the basis of cost of production. A will presumably not sell w abroad on any different terms than at home; but, if Bastable's statement is correct, $17y$ would exchange for $45w$, which is not in accord with their costs of production in A.

x and *y* move one way or the other.   For, according to the assumed conditions:

> For 15*y*, B will give a maximum of 10*x*, 90*z*, or 40*w*, while, for 15*y*, A will take a minimum of 7½*x*, 75*z*, or 37½*w*.

Commodities *x*, *z*, and *w* are therefore all potential exports of B and potential imports of A.

On the other hand:

> For 10*x*, A will give a maximum of 20*y*, 100*z*, or 50*w*, while, for 10*x*, B will take a minimum of 15*y*, 90*z*, or 40*w*.

Commodities *y*, *z*, and *w* are therefore all potential exports of A and potential imports of B.

Similarly it could be shown that every commodity but one is a potential export from any given country,[16] every movement of the terms of interchange increasing the number of commodities capable of export by the country to which the movement is unfavorable and diminishing the number capable of export by the country to which the movement is favorable.   The fact that a country is able to offer a wide variety of goods for export raises, therefore, no presumption whatever that the terms of interchange will be favorable to that country, but rather leads to the conclusion that they *have* been unfavorable; such a situation is, in short, not a cause of favorable but an effect of unfavorable terms of interchange.[17]

---

[16] Cost of transport, it will be remembered, is abstracted.

[17] It may of course happen that a country, A, has a great number of goods in the production of which its comparative advantage is but little less than in that commodity in which its comparative advantage is greatest; and as each commodity, as it becomes available for export, will, in the assumed conditions, represent a transfer from the export list of the foreign country to that of A, the movement of the terms of interchange against A, which is due to A's excess of demand for imports over the foreign country's demand for A's exports, cannot proceed very far until it is checked by the advent of equilibrium, in which case the terms of interchange will be fairly favorable to A.   But when a country shows a wide variety of exports there is no reason to suppose that this, rather than its opposite, is the case.

This transfer of exports from one to the other of two trading countries furnishes the check to the movement of the rates of interchange against a country for whose original exports the foreign country's demand shows an elasticity of less than unity, since it automatically diminishes the number, and therefore the total value, of the foreign country's exports, and increases that of the home country's. For this situation, of a demand of less than unitary elasticity, the classical economists furnish no solution. They merely dismiss it as improbable, tho everyday facts show that it would be by no means out of the question in the premises they themselves set up.

From the statement thus far made it will be clear that, under the assumed conditions, so long as a country imports more than one commodity (or exports a variety of commodities at least two less in number than it consumes), it must obtain some share of the gains arising from its international trade,[18] for the terms of interchange could move still further against it until the penultimate import was supplanted by home production, and even then it would be deriving some slight advantage from the remaining import. It is well-nigh impossible that a country should, with trade free, fail to import more than one commodity; and the true reason for Mill's statement that it is barely conceivable that one of two trading countries should obtain all the advantages of the trade between them, and the other no advantage at all (except, perhaps, so much as would be requisite to provoke the demand for imports as against the domestic production of the commodities of comparative disadvantage), is that which is given above, not the quite untenable reason which Mill actually gives, that, to deprive a country of any gain from international trade, its demand for the imported goods must be absolutely inelastic. The truth of Mill's statement is, indeed, dependent upon the assumption of trade in more than two commodities and, as has been shown, cannot be demonstrated when exchange is confined to two commodities only, as in Mill.

---

[18] Unless, indeed, in the highly improbable event that its comparative disadvantage in its several imports be identical each with the other.

The line dividing national comparative advantage and disadvantage is a moving line, its position at any moment being determined by the then present rate of interchange of international products. If we should arrange in a column the names of the commodities consumed by any given country, placing at the top and at the bottom, respectively, the two commodities in which the country showed the widest difference in productive power when compared with the foreign trading world in general, then, taking the commodity last on the list as a base, and measuring in the same way, should set down in the order of diminishing difference in productive power all the commodities lying between the two originally selected, we should have a list in which that country would have a comparative advantage in the production of any commodity on the list over all the commodities which succeeded it, and a comparative disadvantage, therefore, with regard to all the commodities which preceded it. But the line dividing national comparative advantage and disadvantage might settle anywhere between the two extreme commodities, and would shift from time to time as the terms of exchange of international products moved in one direction or the other.[19]   The logic of the situation is this: if trade be opened up between two countries which at the start trade only with each other, and exchange but two commodities, those commodities would presumably be the two at the extremes of the lists prepared as above (for the list of one country needs only to be reversed to provide that of the other); and, if the amount and intensity of demand of country A for the goods it was importing should cause A to require a greater value of import than B, A must offer better terms, and will continue to do so, if necessary, until some other commodity presents as good an opportunity of profit on export by A as did the original commodity.   This second commodity will then be exported along with the first.   If both together are inadequate to meet the value of the import which A requires from B, they will both be offered on better terms (the price of both falling together so as to keep a constant ratio to cost of production),

---

[19] See on this point Marshall, *Money, Credit and Commerce*, Appendix H.

until some third commodity becomes available for export, and so on until a balance of values is achieved.[20]

Tho the foregoing is the logic of the situation, in actual fact several commodities would probably be exported and imported by both countries immediately on the opening up of trade, and the commodities in which the respective countries possessed the greatest comparative advantage would be exported in increasing volume by both countries, until their price fell so far in the importing country as to leave no greater profit than would be realized on the exports in which productive comparative advantage was not so great. Since this adjustment is a matter not of *inter-* but of *intra*-national competition, the classical economists are, on their own premises, bound to assume that the prices of all exported goods, measured in any commodity not imported, will ultimately correspond to cost of production (tho, as we have seen, Bastable here falls into a contradiction); and, since constant cost is assumed, the prices of exports must preserve the same relation to each other after, as before, international trade is opened up. It is in the prices of imports that the gain will make itself manifest.

The inevitable conclusion is that the export of second, third, and later commodities is forced upon a country by the volume and intensity of its demand for imports, and that, as this process develops, its gains per unit diminish from those which are realized on its product of greatest comparative advantage to those realized

---

[20] This principle has some application to a protective policy. Protection is usually invoked to cover commodities which, in the list of goods consumed, would be not far below the line of comparative advantage at the moment. Such protection cuts down on those imports which, of all the goods imported, cost least to make at home, and it also cuts down on the exports which, of all the goods exported, cost most to make at home. The result is to secure those goods as imports which would cost a very great deal more to produce at home than to import, and to secure them with exports which cost less per unit of import than before the protection. The *ratio* of gain from international trade will thus tend to increase, the total gain may or may not. This is simply another form of the old doctrine that duties may change the terms of interchange of goods in favor of the levying country, tho it is more applicable, as the old doctrine was not, to protective than to revenue duties.

on its second, third, and later commodities of originally inferior comparative advantage, the diminution in gain being spread over the whole trade and not merely over that part of it most recently entered upon.   The greatest ratio of gain from international trade will probably therefore be obtained by the country which can secure all its imports by the export of one commodity only, for this commodity will be that which the given country can produce with the greatest comparative ease.   The more commodities exported, the further must one go down the gamut of comparative advantage, and the smaller will be the difference between the cost of exported goods and the cost which would be necessary to produce at home the imported commodities which are obtained in exchange for them.   This conclusion is sufficiently attested by experience. Chile with nitrates, East India with rubber, Cuba with sugar, procure the bulk of their respective imports.   Surely it will not be denied that recourse to other exports on the part of any of these countries (technological conditions remaining unchanged) would mean that the gains from their principal export had declined so far that it had become as profitable to export other things as to export the original staple, and that the latter condition of these countries would then be worse than the former.   This was shown clearly enough during the late war (World War I) by Brazil, when its market for coffee was suddenly, in large part, swept away.   In her distress Brazil developed a considerable variety of exports which she had not sent out in the period of her prosperity; but no one supposes that this situation was an improvement on the former status of that country.

So much for the doctrine that a wide variety of exports makes for favorable terms of exchange.   Let us now proceed to an examination of the statements that, but for cost of carriage, every commodity would be regularly imported or exported, no country making anything for itself that it did not also make for other countries; that the richest countries gain the least from a given amount of foreign commerce; and that small countries gain the larger share of trade with large ones.

Instead of taking, as above, two countries and four commodities, let us take four countries and two commodities, the countries A, B, C, and D being in economic importance in the ratio 1:2:3:4. Suppose that for one unit of productive power (not necessarily identical in the several countries) there can be produced:

In A	*In B*	*In C*	*In D*
10 cloth	10 cloth	10 cloth	10 cloth
or	*or*	*or*	*or*
15 linen	21 linen	30 linen	18 linen

Suppose A offers 10 cloth for 16 linen. B, C, and D will all want to sell linen for cloth on these terms, and, as all are larger than A, the price of cloth must move in A's favor. How far will it move? Let us try 10 cloth for 18 linen. At this rate of interchange D will have no interest in buying or selling abroad, but B and C will still want to exchange linen for A's cloth, and, as both are larger than A, the terms of interchange must, from A's point of view, continue to improve. But as soon as they go beyond 18 linen for 10 cloth, D joins A as an importer of linen and an exporter of cloth. A and D together represent a productive and consuming capacity approximately equal to B and C, and this is therefore a situation which promises stability. Further, if the price of cloth in linen should rise to 10 cloth = 21 linen, B will drop out as an importer of cloth and exporter of linen, leaving C alone in that capacity, while both A and D will still be importers of linen and exporters of cloth. Their combined productive and consuming capacity being greater than C's, their competition must drive the price of cloth down to something less than 21 linen for 10 cloth, when B will again enter the field as a buyer of cloth and seller of linen. The range within which the terms of interchange of cloth for linen must fall is therefore 10 cloth = 18 to 21 linen, the play of reciprocal demand fixing the exact terms within those limits. Let us suppose the terms to settle at 10 cloth = 19.5 linen.[21] At this price, C, the second larg-

------

[21] This, tho a conceivable, is not a very probable, ratio of interchange. It depends on a nice balance between the productive powers of A and D, taken together, and those of B and C, taken together. In my book on *The Theory of International Values* it is called a "limbo" ratio.

est country, makes the greatest gain, since it can produce 30 linen as easily as 10 cloth and has to give but 19.5 of them to secure 10 cloth. A, the smallest country, makes the next largest gain, as it obtains 19.5 linen for 10 cloth, whereas it could itself produce but 15. B, and D, respectively the next to the smallest and the largest countries, make an equal small gain. There is here shown no tendency for small countries to secure a paradoxical lion's-share of the gains from trade with larger ones. What actually happens is that the play of international competition fixes a fairly narrow range within which the terms of interchange of traded commodities must move, and that the greatest gains from international trade are secured by those countries in which the rate of interchange of the commodities concerned would, in the absence of international trade, be farthest away from the rate actually established, while the smallest gains are secured by those countries in which the rate of interchange of the commodities concerned would, without international trade, approximate that which is actually established when that trade is carried on.

This point will be brought out more clearly, and other points will be established, if a third commodity be introduced, when we shall be dealing with a situation which approximates actual conditions and avoids the errors arising from the artificiality of the method employed by the classical economists, which failed to take into account competition among countries or the possibility of one country taking up the production and export of more than one commodity.

Let us suppose, then, that there are four countries, A, B, C, and D, which trade in three commodities, cloth, linen, and chairs. Let it also be assumed that, before international trade is opened up, each country devotes one third of its resources to the production of each of the three products, and that each country increases its home consumption of these three products, proportionately, as it secures gains from international trade. Let the productive power of these four countries, measured in terms of cloth, be in the ratio 1:2:3:4. Then, let one unit of productive power yield:

In A	In B	In C	In D
10 cloth	10 cloth	10 cloth	10 cloth
or	or	or	or
19 linen	20 linen	15 linen	28 linen
or	or	or	or
42 chairs	24 chairs	30 chairs	40 chairs

and let it be assumed that on a non-specialized basis, without international trade, there would be produced in a given time:

In A		In B		In C		In D	
10,000 cl.	(10)	20,000 cl.	(10)	30,000 cl.	(10)	40,000 cl.	(10)
19,000 l.	(19)	40,000 l.	(20)	45,000 l.	(15)	112,000 l.	(28)
42,000 ch.	(42)	48,000 ch.	(24)	90,000 ch.	(30)	160,000 ch.	(40)

What will be the terms of interchange under international trade? Let us try 10 cloth = 19 linen = 42 chairs. At this rate of interchange B, C, and D will all want to buy chairs with cloth or linen, while A will find no motive in trade. The price of chairs must rise rapidly. Suppose it rises to the point where the terms of interchange of products are 10 cloth = 19 linen = 30 chairs. At these prices A will specialize in chairs, B in linen, C in cloth and chairs, and D in linen (since on these terms D has a greater advantage in linen than in chairs). With B and D specializing in linen the price of that commodity must fall, since their total production would be 3 × 40,000 plus 3 × 112,000 = 456,000 linen,[22] an amount far in excess of the total requirement of linen, by all four countries, on the assumption that each country expands its demand for linen in proportion to its gains from trade. How far will the price of linen fall? Suppose it falls to 10 cloth = 22 linen = 30 chairs.[23] At

---

[22] Without specialization equal resources are devoted to each of the three products. With specialization each country can therefore produce three times its production of any one commodity under the non-specialized regime.

[23] It will be well in indicating price changes to keep 10 cloth as a constant base, and to show a rise or fall in cloth relative to linen or chairs, and of linen and chairs relative to each other, by changing the number of units of linen or chairs offered for 10 yards of cloth.

these prices A will specialize in chairs, B in cloth, C in cloth and chairs, and D in chairs (for at these new prices D has a greater advantage in chairs than in linen). Under these circumstances the supply of linen will rapidly decline, since no country finds its comparative advantage in that line.

On the terms 10 cloth = 19 linen = 30 chairs, then, too much linen tends to be produced, while, on the terms 10 cloth = 22 linen = 30 chairs, there is no tendency to produce linen at all. When, in other words, D specializes in linen, the price of linen declines; but when, as a result of that decline, D specializes in chairs, the supply of linen tends to fall off to zero, since B, as a result of the same decline in price, tends to go in for the production of cloth rather than linen. The price of linen will therefore move upward from the 10:22:30 ratio. No stability can be reached while D specializes exclusively in either linen or chairs, and the only solution is to have D produce both of these commodities. The terms of exchange which will accomplish this are 10 cloth = 21 linen = 30 chairs; for, on those terms, D has an equal comparative advantage in linen and chairs and will therefore do as well in one as in the other. The ratio of 21 linen to 30 chairs (7 linen to 10 chairs), which gives D an equal comparative advantage in linen and chairs, could of course be preserved with an exchange rate for each against cloth very different from that here laid down, but, with any other than the terms 10 cloth = 30 chairs, C, a large country, would specialize in either cloth or chairs exclusively, according as one or the other sold on better terms, and, along with A's chairs or B's cloth, would flood the market with its specialty and would force a readjustment in price. 10 cloth must therefore exchange for 30 chairs, and 21 linen must exchange for 30 chairs. The rate of interchange 10 cloth = 21 linen = 30 chairs is consequently the only rate which will show any stability, and it is stable because, under it, both C and D, the two large countries of the four, tend to diffuse their productive resources, rather than concentrate them upon a single product, and thus to keep a balance of production which is impossible when they devote their efforts to the production of but one commodity.

But it must not be supposed that C and D will divide their productive resources equally between the products they manufacture, tho in a non-specialized regime they would have done so. How much of each they will produce, when stabilized conditions are attained, will depend upon the preceding play of prices, which will have encouraged a greater production in one line than in the other according to the relative supplies which were forthcoming from other centers of production. It we take the figures of production on a non-specialized basis and adhere to the supposition that, after international trade is opened up, the gains which each country derives from that trade are spent so as to keep the same proportionate consumption of each of the commodities as prevailed under the non-specialized regime, it is possible to determine with a high degree of exactness just what the trade would be.[24]

We have seen that the terms of interchange will be 10 cloth = 21 linen = 30 chairs, and that on these terms A will produce chairs, B cloth, C cloth and chairs, and D linen and chairs.[25] When A specializes exclusively in chairs it can produce in the given period 126,000 chairs (3 × 42,000). To preserve the original proportions in A's consumption of cloth, linen, and chairs (viz., 10:19:42) A will retain 53,370 of these chairs, and will export 72,630 in exchange for 12,710 yards of cloth and 24,150 yards of linen.[26]

---

[24] To avoid ridiculous fractions, however, results will be presented in whole numbers only.

[25] The exposition will be followed more easily if reference is made as required to the table (p. 321).

[26] It will be found that the margin of error in these and the following proportions is not more than one in four thousand. It would be possible to make them absolutely accurate, but this would involve the use of long and clumsy fractions. It seemed better to deal in round numbers (see note 24). The method adopted for obtaining the desired proportions is as follows. Take the proportions in country A—10:19:42. At the rate of interchange finally established

$$10 \text{ cloth} = 30 \text{ chairs}$$
$$19 \text{ linen} = 27\frac{3}{7} \text{ chairs}$$
$$42 \text{ chairs} = 42 \text{ chairs}$$

(Adding) 10 cloth plus 19 linen plus 42 chairs = 99⅗ chairs.

When B specializes exclusively in cloth, it can produce in the given period 60,000 yards of cloth (3 × 20,000). To preserve the original proportions in B's consumption of cloth, linen, and chairs (viz., 10:20:24) B will retain 21,800 yards of cloth, and export 38,200 yards in exchange for 43,596 yards of linen and 52,320 chairs.

C produces both cloth and chairs. If its whole productive power were concentrated on cloth, it could produce in the given period 90,000 yards of cloth (3 × 30,000); if on chairs, it could produce 270,000 chairs (3 × 90,000). Taking either as a base, it will be found that to preserve the original proportions in C's consumption of cloth, linen, and chairs (viz., 10:15:30), C must use 33,158 yards of cloth, 49,735 yards of linen, and 99,474 chairs.

D is the only country producing linen. A, B, and C must all, therefore, obtain their linen from D. We know how much linen each will consume (24,150; 43,596; and 49,735 yards respectively), and therefore how much linen will be exported by D (117,481 yards). In the same manner as for C we may find that to preserve the original proportions in D's consumption of cloth, linen, and chairs (viz., 10:28:40), D must use its productive power to secure 43,636 yards of cloth, 122,182 yards of linen, and 174,548 chairs. Having the amount of linen exported by D (117,481 yards), and the amount consumed at home (122,182 yards), addition will give us the total production of linen in that country, viz., 239,663 yards. The rest of D's productive capacity, devoted to chairs, will yield 137,624 units of that product; but, as D requires 174,548 for its own consumption, it must import, from A or C, 36,924 chairs.

We have now obtained the figures of production in A, B, and D; C, it will be remembered, produces cloth and chairs. B is the only other country producing cloth. We know how much cloth B produces (60,000 yards), and how much B itself consumes (21,800

But by concentrating on the production of chairs, country A, for the same effort that will yield 10 cloth plus 19 linen plus 42 chairs, can produce 126 chairs. The consumption in A of the respective commodities under a trading regime will therefore be to the consumption under the non-trading regime in the proportion of 126 to 99¼, since the productive efficiency of A is increased in that proportion.

yards).   Subtraction will then give us how much cloth B exports (38,200 yards).   We know also how much cloth A and D import (12,710 and 43,636 yards respectively).   This is greater than B's export by 18,146 yards, and this amount must therefore be obtained from C.   Add this to C's own consumption of cloth and we get C's production of that commodity, viz., 51,304 yards.   The rest of C's productive capacity is devoted to chairs, of which it will produce 116,088.   Its own consumption of chairs is 99,474 and it thus has for export 16,614.   These together with A's export of 72,630 chairs will just be adequate to meet the demand of B and D.

The table on the following page will show the whole situation clearly.[27]

Let us now consider the proposition that the richest countries gain the least from a given amount of foreign commerce.   If we assume, as has not been necessary hitherto, that a unit of productive power is identical in all four countries, then the wealth (per capita)

---

[27] The data from which this trading situation was developed were random selections, and similar results would have been achieved with practically any figures one might take.   Yet the results are quite at variance with the conclusions on international trade which have been drawn by Mill and his followers.   Thus, tho Mill claimed that, under the conditions we have assumed, no country would make anything for itself that it did not make for other countries, we find country D not only making chairs but importing them; moreover it is absolutely essential that D should do so if any stability is ever to be reached or retained in the trade between A, B, C, and D.   For, if D should at any time produce enough chairs for its own consumption, or even increase its production slightly, the supply of chairs from A must be sold at such low prices as to make it unprofitable for D to continue in that line; while, if D should go out of chair manufacture altogether, or even diminish its production of that commodity slightly and turn its productive powers to the making of linen, the increased supply of linen would so lower its price as to make it unprofitable for D to continue to manufacture linen.   The play of prices will therefore cause D to produce both chairs and linen, chairs in a supply inadequate for D's own needs, linen in a supply sufficient for D's needs and for the needs of the other three countries as well.   Similarly the play of prices will set C producing both cloth and chairs; but, unlike D, C will export both of these commodities in exchange for imported linen.   There is no *inherent* reason why a country, in the premises laid down, might not produce exactly its own consumption of any or all commodities, and neither export nor import, tho the chances of this happening are extremely small.

TABLE OF TRADE RELATIONS BETWEEN COUNTRIES A, B, C, AND D

Terms of Interchange of Goods: 10 cloth = 21 linen = 30 chairs

	Units of Cloth				Units of Linen				Units of Chairs			
	Production	Exports	Imports	Consumption	Production	Exports	Imports	Consumption	Production	Exports	Imports	Consumption
Country A. Productive Capacity in cloth = 1	None	None	12,710	12,710 (10)*	None	None	24,150	24,150 (19)*	126,000	72,630	None	53,370 (42)*
Country B. Productive Capacity in cloth = 2	60,000	38,200	None	21,800 (10)*	None	None	43,596	43,596 (20)*	None	None	52,320	52,320 (24)*
Country C. Productive Capacity in cloth = 3	51,304	18,146	None	33,158 (10)*	None	None	49,735	49,735 (15)*	116,088	16,614	None	99,474 (30)*
Country D. Productive Capacity in cloth = 4	None	None	43,636	43,636 (10)*	239,663	117,481	None	122,182 (28)*	137,624	None	36,924	174,548 (40)*
Totals (All Countries)	111,304	56,346	56,346	111,304	239,663	117,481	117,481	239,663	379,712	89,244	89,244	379,712

EXPLANATION OF THE TRADE

A produces 126,000 chairs. It imports 12,710 cloth for which it must export 38,130 chairs, and it imports 24,150 linen for which it must export 34,500 chairs; a total export of 72,630 chairs.

B produces 60,000 cloth. It imports 43,596 linen for which it must export 20,760 cloth, and it imports 52,320 chairs for which it must export 17,440 cloth; a total export of 38,200 cloth.

C produces 51,304 cloth and 116,088 chairs. It exports 18,146 cloth for which it obtains 38,106 linen, and it exports 16,614 chairs for which it obtains 11,629 linen; a total import of 49,735 linen.

D produces 239,663 linen and 137,624 chairs. It imports 43,636 cloth for which it must export 91,635 linen and it imports 36,924 chairs for which it must export 25,846 linen; a total export of 117,481 linen.

Total exports and imports and total production and consumption of each article of course correspond.

* The figures in parentheses (read crosswise) represent the ratios in which the three commodities were consumed in the several countries before trade was opened up, a ratio of consumption which has been assumed to have remained constant after the development of trade.

of A, B, C, and D, before the opening up of international trade, might reasonably be supposed to be in proportion to their general productive powers. If one unit of productive power (identical in the four countries) yields 10 cloth in each of them, then per capita wealth will depend upon the relative productivity of the several countries in the other commodities. Inspection will show that D will be the richest country, A second, B third, while C will be the poorest of them all. How do they share in the gains from international trade? These can be determined by comparing the consumption of any one of the three commodities in the several countries before and after international trade has been established. This is shown on pages 316 and 321. It will be found that the percentage gains from international trade are as follows: A, 27.1; B, 9.0; C, 10.53; D, 9.04. There is certainly no correlation here between poverty and large percentage gains from international trade. Ranged in order of poverty the countries are C, B, A, D; ranged in order of percentage gains from international trade, they are A, C, D, B.[28]

As to the allegation that a small country tends to secure the larger share of the gains arising from international trade it turns out that A, the smallest country, makes the highest percentage gain. This will presently be shown to be fortuitous, but meanwhile it is pertinent to point to the fact that B, the smallest country aside from A, makes the lowest percentage gain, while the large countries C and D are in an intermediate position. Thus, the two smallest countries are found at opposite ends of the percentage scale.

That A's large gains are due merely to the special situation, and that a large share of the gains accruing to the smallest of several trading countries is not a constant result of international commerce, may be shown by taking new data. Suppose that a unit of productive power will produce:

---

[28] It is interesting to note that the country with the highest percentage of foreign to domestic trade gains the least from its foreign trade. B's foreign trade is a larger proportion of its total trade than is the case for any of the other countries, yet its gains (per cent) are the smallest of all. This is doubtless merely a coincidence, but it serves to refute a popular superstition.

In A	*In B*	*In C*	*In D*
10 cloth	10 cloth	10 cloth	10 cloth
or	*or*	*or*	*or*
27 linen	28 linen	15 linen	35 linen
or	*or*	*or*	*or*
30 chairs	24 chairs	27 chairs	40 chairs

and that in a given time there can be produced:

By A	*By B*	*By C*	*By D*
20,000 cloth	30,000 cloth	30,000 cloth	30,000 cloth
or	*or*	*or*	*or*
54,000 linen	84,000 linen	45,000 linen	105,000 linen
or	*or*	*or*	*or*
60,000 chairs	72,000 chairs	81,000 chairs	120,000 chairs

that is to say that B, C, and D are, in productive power (measured in cloth), all in the ratio of 3:2 to A. Experiment will show that the only terms of exchange which will give stability are 10 cloth = 27 linen = 30 chairs, or something very close to this ratio. Thus, if linen temporarily rises or falls above this ratio, a transfer of productive power into or out of the manufacture of linen will go on until equilibrium is restored, and the same is true of chairs. This will be evident if we take figures just on one side or the other of the 10:27:30 ratio.

10 cloth = 26 linen = 30 chairs	10 cloth = 28 linen = 30 chairs	10 cloth = 27 linen = 29 chairs	10 cloth = 27 linen = 31 chairs
A will produce linen	A will produce cloth and chairs	A will produce chairs	A will produce cloth and linen
B will produce linen	B will produce cloth and linen	B will produce linen	B will produce linen
C will produce cloth	C will produce cloth	C will produce cloth	C will produce cloth
D will produce linen	D will produce chairs	D will produce chairs	D will produce linen
. . Linen must *fall* in price	. . Linen must *rise* in price	. . Chairs must *fall* in price	. . Chairs must *rise* in price

But with the rate of interchange 10 cloth = 27 linen = 30 chairs, B will produce linen, C cloth, D chairs, and A all three, and a stable condition of trade can be established.   Working this trade out on the lines already indicated, at a ratio of interchange of 10 cloth = 27 linen = 30 chairs, we shall find the situation shown on page 323.

Country A, the smallest country of the four, will, when equilibrium is reached, be receiving no gain at all from its international trade, the terms of interchange in the international market being precisely those which would prevail in A if it carried on no foreign trade.   The classical economists would have said that in these circumstances A would do no foreign trading.   But this is not so. *For, so long as the terms of interchange of cloth, linen, and chairs show any deviation from the 10:27:30 ratio,* A will push the production and export of the commodity which that deviation favors, and this specialization will of necessity mean a *pro tanto* withdrawal from the production of some other commodity, or commodities, and consequent import. *But the terms of interchange will inevitably shift from the 10:27:30 ratio if A attempts to be self-sufficing;* for D's productive power in chairs is so great as to make it impossible to sell that commodity, on the 10:27:30 basis, if B and C are the only foreign markets available.   In this situation the price of chairs must fall, and it will then pay A to import them, sending out cloth and linen in payment.   But after the requisite number of chair producers in A have been driven into other lines by the fall in the price of chairs, the terms of interchange will tend to stabilize at the 10:27:30 ratio, leaving some chairmakers in A but not enough fully to supply A's consumption of that commodity.   If the withdrawal from chair production in A should be overdone, the price of chairs would rise, and a reverse movement would take place, leading to the reestablishment of the 10:27:30 ratio with A producing about one sixth of its consumption of chairs (as indicated on page 325).

If A were a still smaller country, say one-third instead of two-thirds as large as B, C, and D (measured in the production of cloth), all of A's producers of chairs would be driven out of business, by D, before D's production could be absorbed on the 10:27:30 basis, and the terms of exchange must shift to a ratio which will enable

TERMS OF INTERCHANGE OF GOODS: 10 CLOTH = 27 LINEN = 30 CHAIRS

	Produces	Exports	Imports	Consumes	Would Produce and Consume Under a Non-specialized Regime without International Trade
COUNTRY A	32,611 cloth 64,806 linen	12,611 cloth (= 37,833 chairs) 10,806 linen (= 12,007 chairs)		20,000 cloth (10)* 54,000 linen (27)*	20,000 cloth (10)* 54,000 linen (27)*
	10,160 chairs	(= 49,840 chairs)	49,840 chairs No gain from international trade.	60,000 chairs (30)*	60,000 chairs (30)*
COUNTRY B	252,000 linen	159,885 linen	32,898 cloth { (= 88,825 linen) 78,956 chairs { (= 71,060 linen) (= 159,885 linen) 9.66% gain from international trade.	32,898 cloth (10)* 92,115 linen (28)* 78,956 chairs (24)*	30,000 cloth (10)* 84,000 linen (28)* 72,000 chairs (24)*
COUNTRY C	90,000 cloth	53,348 cloth	54,977 linen { (= 20,362 cloth) 98,959 chairs { (= 32,986 cloth) (= 53,348 cloth) 22.173% gain from international trade.	36,652 cloth (10)* 54,977 linen (15)* 98,959 chairs (27)*	30,000 cloth (10)* 45,000 linen (15)* 81,000 chairs (27)*
COUNTRY D	360,000 chairs	227,755 chairs	33,061 cloth { (= 99,183 chairs) 115,714 linen { (= 128,572 chairs) (= 227,755 chairs) 10.203% gain from international trade.	33,061 cloth (10)* 115,714 linen (35)* 132,245 chairs (40)*	30,000 cloth (10)* 105,000 linen (35)* 120,000 chairs (40)*

* Figures in parentheses represent the ratio of consumption of the three commodities in each country, a ratio assumed to remain constant after the opening up of international trade.

D to produce some other commodity to as great advantage as chairs. Trial will show that this ratio will be 10 cloth = 27 linen = 30⅔ chairs. On these terms of interchange A will produce cloth and linen, B linen, C cloth, D chairs and linen, and the trade will then be carried on as shown on page 327.

From these examples it is clear that the alleged tendency of a small country to secure the greater portion of the gains arising from its trade with larger countries is without scientific foundation in a trading world which consists of many countries and deals in many commodities. The scintilla of truth in the idea lies in the fact that a small country may be able to specialize exclusively on a single commodity, in which it possesses a very great comparative advantage, and obtain all its imports through the export of this one commodity. But, were this condition realized, it would run directly counter to another of the classical propositions, viz., that a variety of exports makes for favorable terms of interchange. We have seen rather that *un*favorable terms of interchange make for a variety of exports, and it is interesting to note that, in the cases given above (tho this was not the point at issue), the countries with the greatest variety of exports are invariably in a relatively bad position, so far as their percentage gain from international trade is concerned, and are usually in the position absolutely the worst.

In refutation of the doctrines of the classical school—doctrines based upon an overabstraction the results of which cannot be imported into a more complex trading situation—it has been shown that:

(1) International trade may be carried on by a country which obtains no advantage whatever therefrom, the play of prices forcing a distribution of productive powers which will result in such a country producing more than its own demand for some commodities and less than its own demand for others.

(2) A great variety of exports is not a cause of favorable, but an effect of unfavorable, terms of interchange of the products of any given country for those of other countries.

(3) Even abstracting cost of carriage, and assuming constant cost of production, a country may produce a commodity without

TERMS OF INTERCHANGE OF GOODS: 10 CLOTH = 27 LINEN = 30⅔ CHAIRS

	Produces	Exports	Imports	Consumes	Would Produce and Consume in the Absence of International Trade
COUNTRY A	22,753 cloth 19,567 linen	12,660 cloth	7,689 linen (= 2,848 cloth) 30,280 chairs (= 9,812 cloth) (= 12,660 cloth) Gain from international trade 0.93%	10,093 cloth (10)* 27,253 linen (27)* 30,280 chairs (30)*	10,000 cloth (10)* 27,000 linen (27)* 30,000 chairs (30)*
COUNTRY B	252,000 linen	159,158 linen	33,158 cloth (= 89,526 linen) 79,579 chairs (= 69,632 linen) (= 159,158 linen) Gain from international trade 11.053%	33,158 cloth (10)* 92,842 linen (28)* 79,579 chairs (24)*	30,000 cloth (10)* 84,000 linen (28)* 72,000 chairs (24)*
COUNTRY C	90,000 cloth	52,972 cloth	55,543 linen (= 20,572 cloth) 99,977 chairs (= 32,400 cloth) (= 52,972 cloth) Gain from international trade 23.429%	37,028 cloth (10)* 55,543 linen (15)* 99,977 chairs (27)*	30,000 cloth (10)* 45,000 linen (15)* 81,000 chairs (27)*
COUNTRY D	17,734 linen 339,733 chairs	209,836 chairs	32,474 cloth (= 100,206 chairs) 95,926 linen (= 109,630 chairs) (= 209,836 chairs) Gain from international trade 8.247%	32,474 cloth (10)* 113,660 linen (35)* 129,897 chairs (40)*	30,000 cloth (10)* 105,000 linen (35)* 120,000 chairs (40)*

* See note on page 325.

exporting it, and may import a commodity which it also produces. Compare this with Mill's dictum that, but for the cost of carriage, every commodity would (if trade be supposed free) be either regularly imported or regularly exported, and that a country would make nothing for itself which it did not also make for other countries.

(4) Rich countries are at no disadvantage in international trade, and poverty is no security against unfavorable terms of interchange.

(5) Small countries are at no advantage in international trade unless they can specialize to the extent of devoting their whole resources to the production of one or two commodities for export in exchange for imports which, to produce at home, would have cost them much more than the exports with which they bought them. To the degree, of course, that any country, small or large, can do this, its gains from international trade will be great. This is a matter of soil, climate, natural resources, situation, and many other factors, of which size is one.

So much for the negative aspects of the present analysis. The positive conclusions may be set down in the following propositions:

(1) Competition is as significant in the theory of international values as in that of domestic; and, just as in domestic trade the abstraction of all but two individuals and two commodities from a market, and the later introduction of new commodities and new traders, would give us results very different from those which would issue out of a consideration of the market as a simultaneous whole, so does a similar method in the theory of international trade result in conclusions that have no application to reality.[29]

(2) Quite apart from changes in the conditions of production, the comparative advantage of any given country is not a fixed but a shifting thing, moving according to the alterations which take place in the rate of interchange of the traded commodities. A movement of the terms of exchange against any country is accompanied by an increase in the number of commodities capable of

---

[29] See Marshall, *Principles of Economics*, Appendix F.

export by that country and a diminution in the number of commodities capable of import.

(3) The shifting of commodities from the export to the import side, or *vice versa*, as the rate of interchange of goods moves in one direction or the other, prevents a precipitous movement in that rate such as, without this check, would take place whenever the phenomenon of an elasticity of demand less than unity should appear, a demand, that is, which diminishes less than proportionately to a rise in price.[30]

(4) A country secures a smaller or larger share of the gains arising from international trade according to the degree in which the rate of interchange of commodities which secures equilibrium in international trade varies from the rate which would prevail in the exchange of the commodities concerned, within the country, were that country on a self-sufficing basis. So far as the share in the gains is concerned, it makes no difference whether this variation is due to great superiority in the production of the goods which are exported or to great inferiority in the production (were any produced) of the goods which are imported.

(5) A country may, as a supplement to home production, import a commodity in which it has a comparative advantage as great as in those commodities which it is exporting. (See, for example, the case of country D in the production of chairs, page 321.)

(6) The distribution of productive resources within a country (with trade free) is determined not only by the principle of comparative advantage but also by the general trading situation, and may result in very unequal relative development of two industries which, at a given rate of interchange of their products, offer equal opportunities of profit.

(7) In international trade the fluctuations in the rate of interchange of such commodities as are produced at approximately constant cost, and such fluctuations in the rate of interchange of

---

[30] See Marshall's interesting discussion of this and related topics in his *Money, Credit and Commerce*, Appendix J.

other commodities as are not due to changes in the cost of production of one or more of them, will, if those commodities be produced in several countries, be confined within a rather narrow range. This is attributable to the fact that any alteration in the rate of interchange will affect the margin of comparative advantage of some country in the production of some one of the commodities concerned, will bring that country in as an exporter where formerly it was an importer or as an importer where formerly it was an exporter (according as the terms of interchange move one way or the other), and, by the affected country's addition to the supply or demand side, will keep the terms of interchange from moving far from their original position. There would thus seem to be but slight opportunity of seriously affecting the terms of international interchange of products by duties or otherwise.

TARIFFS AND THE GAINS FROM TRADE

15

PROTECTION AND REAL WAGES*

By WOLFGANG F. STOLPER‖ AND PAUL A. SAMUELSON‡

INTRODUCTION§

Second only in political appeal to the argument that tariffs increase employment is the popular notion that the standard of living of the American worker must be protected against the ruinous competition of cheap foreign labour. Equally prevalent abroad is its counterpart that European industry cannot compete with the technically superior American system of production. Again and again economists have tried to show the falaciousness of this argument. Professor Taussig, for example, stated that "perhaps most familiar and most unfounded of all is the belief that complete freedom of trade would bring about an equalisation of money wages the world over. . . . There is no such tendency to equalisation."[1] And Professor Haberler classifies the argument that wages

---

* *The Review of Economic Studies*, Volume IX (November, 1941), pages 58–73. Reprinted by the courtesy of the *Review of Economic Studies* and the authors.

‖ Swarthmore College.

‡ Massachusetts Institute of Technology.

§ The following article is reprinted without significant change from the original text.

[1] F. W. Taussig, *International Trade*, p. 38. The statement might have been made equally well with respect to real wages, since in the classical formulation the prices of internationally traded goods cannot diverge in different countries by more than the cost of transfer. In his *Principles* there is a passage which might be interpreted in the opposite direction. "Under certain contingencies, it is conceivable that protective duties will affect the process of sharing and so will influence wages otherwise than through their effect on the total product." 4th ed., p. 517. But the phrasing is not quite clear and refers probably to the share in national income rather than to the absolute size. We have not found any similar

might suffer from international trade among those "that do not merit serious discussion. . . . An equalisation of wages comes about only if labour is mobile [between countries]."[2]

More recently, however, the writings of Ohlin seem to suggest that a re-examination of this accepted doctrine might be fruitful. It is the intention of the present paper to show that definitive statements are possible concerning the effects of international trade upon the relative remunerations of productive agencies, and more important, upon their absolute real incomes. That this is possible is surprising since the voluminous literature appears to contain only statements of possibilities and presumptions rather than of necessities. Indeed, in the beginning we expected to do no more than delineate factors which would indicate a likelihood in one direction or another, and only in the course of the investigation did we discover that unambiguous inferences were possible. It may be illuminating, therefore, to follow in the exposition our original sequence of thought rather than attempt the most direct derivation of theorems.

The Effect of Trade upon Relative Factor Prices

According to the train of thought associated with the name of Ohlin, differences in the proportions of the various productive factors between countries are important elements in explaining the course of international trade. A country will export those commodities which are produced with its relatively abundant factors of production, and will import those in the production of which its relatively scarce factors are important.[3] And as a result of the

---

passage either in *The Tariff History of the United States*, in *International Trade*, or in *Free Trade, the Tariff, and Reciprocity*.

[2] G. Haberler, *The Theory of International Trade*, pp. 250–251, bracketed expression ours. See also the preceding sentence on p. 251 where Haberler expressly denies that movement of goods will lead to an equalisation of factor prices. However, as will be discussed below, he does in another place introduce important qualifications to this denial.

[3] Professor Viner has shown that this line of reasoning was not unknown to the classical economists. See his *Studies in the Theory of International Trade*, pp. 500–507.

shift towards increased production of those goods in which the abundant factors predominate, there will be a tendency—necessarily incomplete—towards an equalisation of factor prices between the two or more trading countries.[4]   Although partial, the movement in the direction of equalisation is nevertheless real and can be substantial.

Assuming, as we shall throughout, that the total amounts of the factors of production remain fixed, it is clear from the Heckscher-Ohlin theorem that the introduction of trade must lower the relative share in the real or money national income going to the scarce factor of production.   For the total return to a factor equals its price times the amount employed, and since we assume full employment before and after trade, the total returns to the factors are proportional to the rates per unit.   This argument seems to have relevance to the American discussion of protection versus free trade. If, as is generally thought, labour is the relatively scarce factor in the American economy, it would appear that trade would necessarily lower the relative position of the labouring class as compared to owners of other factors of production.

So far we have dealt only with the relative shares of the various factors and have not gone into the effect upon absolute shares. Before entering upon this latter problem, it is of considerable interest to mention the most important currently held viewpoints.

Some Existing Views

Nobody, of course, ever denied that the workers employed in the particular industry that loses a tariff could be hurt in the short-

---

[4] B. Ohlin, *Interregional and International Trade*, Chapter II and elsewhere.   This appears to be a novel theorem largely unknown to the classical economists, or at least completely unmentioned in Viner's masterful review of doctrine.   Perhaps the earliest clear enunciation of this doctrine is that of E. Heckscher in a 1919 article in the *Ekonomisk Tidskrift*, cited by Ohlin.   [This paper appears as Chap. 13 in the present *Readings* volume under the title of "The Effect of Foreign Trade on the Distribution of Income."]   Heckscher apparently gives no prior references.   Unfortunately, this important contribution is in Swedish, and we are indebted to Mr. Svend Laursen for a paraphrasing of its contents.   Because of its extensive development at the hands of Ohlin, we shall refer to it as the Heckscher-Ohlin theorem.

run, but according to the classical theory, in the long-run there would be an increased demand for those commodities in which the country had a comparative advantage, i.e. where labour is more productive.[5]   Although money wages might fall, the removal of a tariff would result in a still larger reduction in price levels so that the real wage must rise.   In the words of Taussig, "The question of wages is at bottom one of productivity.   The greater the productivity of industry at large, the higher will be the general level of wages."[6]

How can this argument be reconciled with the Ohlin type of discussion?   If there were only one commodity produced, then indeed the marginal productivity of labour would depend simply on the relative quantities of labour and capital as a whole.   And the same would be the case with more than one commodity if labour and capital were combined in the same proportions in the production of each.   A balanced movement of the factors of production from one employment to another would then leave the marginal productivities of labour and capital unchanged.

Now, it is true that under the assumptions of pure competition— homogeneity, and perfect mobility of labour—the value of the marginal product of labour (expressed in terms of any commodity) must be the same in each occupation; it nevertheless does not follow that this will depend simply on the proportion of labour and capital as a whole.   For in so far as capital and labour are combined in different proportions in each occupation, any change from one production to another will change the "value marginal productivity" of labour (however expressed), even though it will, of course, still be equal in all occupations.   In this sense the value marginal productivity of labour as a whole may be considered to depend upon a kind of weighted average of the effective demands for the various producible commodities.   It is the essence of the argument

---

[5] "The free-trader argues that if the duties were given up and the protected industries pushed out of the field by foreign competitors, the workmen engaged in them would find no less well-paid employment elsewhere."   F. W. Taussig, *Principles of Economics*, 4th ed., Vol. 1, p. 516.

[6] Ibid., p. 517.

of the previous section that international trade in accordance with the principle of comparative advantage so shifts production and the relative effective derived demands as to produce the Heckscher-Ohlin effect.

It is not surprising that the classical argument should not have touched upon the problem of relative and absolute shares since for most purposes the older economists implicitly assumed a one factor economy or an economy in which different factors of production were applied in a dose whose proportions never varied. It is to their credit as realists that again and again they relaxed these assumptions, but they were not always able to weld into a synthesis these excluded effects.[7]

Among more modern writers, who are nevertheless in the classical tradition, it has long been recognised that a small factor of production specialised for the production of a protected commodity might be harmed by the removal of tariffs.[8] This has received particular attention in connection with the problem of non-competing groups in the labour market. Certain sub-groups of the labouring class, e.g. highly skilled labourers, may benefit while others are harmed. Thus, Ohlin holds that it is quite possible under certain circumstances for free trade to reduce the standard of living of the manufacturing labouring class. "If manufacturing and agricultural labourers form two non-competing groups, high protection of manufacturing industries may raise the real wages of the workers in these industries at the expense of the other factors."[9] Similarly, Haberler remarks that " . . . in the short-run, special-

---

[7] A good case can be made out that even Ricardo did not adhere narrowly to a labour theory of value, but this is not the place to enter into controversy on this subject. See, however, John Cassels, "A Re-intepretation of Ricardo on Value," *Quarterly Journal of Economics*, Vol. 49, pp. 518 ff.

[8] "It is perfectly clear that the imposition of a prohibitive tariff on the import of raw silk into the United States would increase the rents of the owners of land suitable for the growth of mulberry trees and the earnings of workers, if there be such, completely specialised in caring for silkworms." M. C. Samuelson, "The Australian Case for Protection Re-examined," *Quarterly Journal of Economics*, November, 1939, p. 149.

[9] Ohlin, op. cit., p. 306.

ised and immobile groups of workers, like the owners of specific
material factors, may suffer heavy reductions in income when for
one reason or another they are faced with more intense foreign
competition."[10]   Once the principle that no factor can benefit from
a tariff has been broken, one is tempted to ask whether similar
results are not possible for a large factor of production even if only
two factors are assumed.   For the logic of the case seems the same
whether two classes of labour are considered to be non-competing
or whether the "non-competing" factors are labelled "capital"
and "labour" respectively.

In treating this problem Haberler expresses doubt that a large
and mobile factor such as labour can be harmed by unrestricted
international trade.   "We may conclude that in the long run the
working-class as a whole has nothing to fear from international
trade, since, in the long run, labour is the least specific of all factors.
It will gain by the general increase in productivity due to the international division of labour, and is not likely to lose at all seriously
by a change in the functional distribution of the national income."[11]
This is not a dogmatic necessity, but rather regarded as the most
probable situation.   For lower on the same page Haberler recog-
nises explicitly a possible qualification.   If labour enters more im-
portantly in the protected industry, it might possibly be harmed by
free trade.[12]

Viner criticises Haberler's conclusion, maintaining that there
appears to be "no *a priori* or empirical grounds for holding this to be
an improbable case."[13]   In this connection Viner is concerned
primarily with the *relative* share of labour in the national money
income.   In his discussion he introduces as an element in the
problem the prices which consumers must pay for commodities,
particularly imports and exports with and without protection.
Thus, he says, "But even if labour on the average had low occupational mobility and were employed relatively heavily in the

---

[10] Haberler, op. cit., p. 195.
[11] Haberler, ibid., p. 195.
[12] Similar views are attributed to Wicksell, Carver, Nicholson, and others.
[13] Viner, op. cit., p. 533.

protected industries, its real income might still rise with the removal of tariff protection . . . if it was an important consumer of the hitherto protected commodities, and if the price of these commodities fell sufficiently as a result to offset the reduction in money wages in the new situation."[14]

Ohlin and other modern writers raise this problem, but it can also be found in the older literature. Bastable, for example, in good classical fashion points out that free trade may force a food exporting country "to bring worse soils into cultivation, and to raise the value of food, thus permitting of an increase in the amount of agricultural rent. In this instance, the labourers, and possibly the capitalists, may suffer while the landlords gain."[15]

We may sum up as follows: (1) In the narrowest classical version the problem of the effect of trade upon the relative and absolute shares of various productive factors could hardly arise since only one factor is assumed. (2) Outside the confines of this rigid system it has long been recognised that the relative and possibly even the absolute share of a small specific factor of production *might* be increased by protection. This received particular attention in connection with the problem of non-competing groups. (3) With reference to large categories, opinion is more divided. Almost all admit the possibility of a decline in the relative share of a large factor of production such as labour as a result of free trade. Many even admit the possibility of a decline in the real income of a large factor of production. But all writers consider highly improbable a decline in the absolute shares, and many believe the same with respect to the relative shares. Some take the position that no *a priori* presumption is possible in connection with the last problem. (4) The vast majority of writers take it as axiomatic that a calculation of effects upon real income must take into consideration the behaviour of prices of commodities entering into the consumer's budget. Thus, if the owners of a factor of production consume only

[14] Viner, ibid., p. 533.
[15] C. F. Bastable, *The Theory of International Trade*, 4th ed., p. 105.

the exported good (in Professor Pigou's terminology this is the wage good), a different result will be reached than if the wage good were imported.   And since in the real world consumption is diversified so that the concept of a wage good is an oversimplification, a difficult index number problem would appear to be involved.

It is the purpose of the present investigation to show that under rather general assumptions definite conclusions can be derived concerning the absolute share of a factor (a) even when there is perfect domestic mobility of factors of production and a complete absence of specificity, (b) even if we are dealing with as few as two large factors of production, and (c) without any recourse to the index number problem or to the concept of a wage good.

Assumptions of the Analysis

For purposes of the analysis we shall start out with rather simplified assumptions, considering subsequently the effect of more realistic modifications.   In order to keep the number of variables down to manageable proportions we assume only two countries. This involves no loss of generality since the "rest of the world" may always be lumped together as Country II.   For the sake of exposition and diagrammatic convenience, only two commodities are considered, labelled respectively "wheat," A, and "watches," B.   To accord with the Ohlin assumptions the production functions of each commodity are made the same in both countries and involve only two factors of production identified for convenience as labour (L) and capital (C).[16]

Moreover, by means of a simple device it is possible to avoid detailed consideration of the second country since all of its effects upon the first operate via changes in the price ratio of the two traded commodities.[17]   We shall call this price ratio of wheat to watches

---

[16] It might possibly give rise to less confusion if instead of capital the second factor were called land because of the ambiguities involved in the definition of capital.   The reader who is bothered by this fact is invited to substitute mentally land for capital in all that follows.

[17] For an example of the use of this device see P. A. Samuelson, "The Gains from International Trade," *Canadian Journal of Economics and Political Science*, May, 1939.

P_a/P_b. It is irrelevant for our argument just why the exchange ratio of the two commodities is different after international trade is established; it is sufficient that it does change.[18]

The effect of international trade upon the shares of the productive factors can now be analysed by varying P_a/P_b as a parameter from its value as determined in the absence of trade, or with a given amount of protection, to its new value after free trade is opened up. Throughout we follow the conventional method of comparative statics, disregarding the process of transition from the old to the new equilibrium.   Full employment of both factors is assumed to be realised before and after the change, and each factor is assumed to have perfectly complete physical mobility.[19] Throughout pure competition is assumed.   The following symbols are used:

The amount of labour used in producing A.............. L_a
The amount of labour used in producing B.............. L_b
The amount of capital used in producing A.............. C_a
The amount of capital used in producing B.............. C_b
The total amount of labour used in producing both A and B L
The total amount of capital used in producing both A and B C
The marginal physical wheat productivity of labor........ MP_{L_a}
The marginal physical wheat productivity of capital....... MP_{c_a}
The marginal physical watch productivity of labor........ MP_{L_b}
The marginal physical watch productivity of capital....... MP_{c_b}

It is assumed that regardless of trade the total amounts of each factor of production remain unchanged.   Therefore, we have the following obvious identities:

---

[18] In the limiting case P_a/P_b would be unchanged.   Also, in the classical constant cost case of a large country facing a smaller one, trade may take place, but to an extent insufficient to result in complete specialisation on the part of the large country, and hence P_a/P_b may be unchanged.   This exception is touched upon later.

[19] We should like to emphasize that in our argument there is no dependence upon imperfections in the labour market such as form the basis for the Manoilesco type for defense of a tariff.   See M. Manoilesco, *The Theory of Protection and International Trade* (1931).

$$L_a + L_b = L. \dots\dots\dots\dots\dots\dots\dots\dots\dots\dots\dots\dots\dots\dots\dots (1)$$
$$C_a + C_b = C. \dots\dots\dots\dots\dots\dots\dots\dots\dots\dots\dots\dots\dots\dots\dots (2)$$

The production functions relating each good to the inputs of the factors allocated to its production can be written respectively as:

$$A = A\ (L_a,\ C_a). \dots\dots\dots\dots\dots\dots\dots\dots\dots\dots\dots\dots\dots\dots (3)$$
$$B = B\ (L_b,\ C_b). \dots\dots\dots\dots\dots\dots\dots\dots\dots\dots\dots\dots\dots\dots (4)$$

Because we are concerned with proportions and not with the scale of the process, these functions are assumed to be homogeneous of the first order.

It is a well-known condition of equilibrium that the ratio of the marginal productivities of the two factors must be the same in each occupation, because otherwise there would be a transfer from lower to higher levels. Symbolically this can be expressed as follows:[20]

$$\frac{MP_{L_a}}{MP_{C_a}} = \frac{MP_{L_b}}{MP_{C_b}}. \dots\dots\dots\dots\dots\dots\dots\dots\dots\dots\dots\dots\dots\dots (5)$$

We are still lacking one condition to make our equilibrium complete. If we add as a known parameter the value of P_a/P_b, that is, the price ratio between the two goods, wheat and watches, all our unknowns will be completely determined: the amounts of each factor of production allocated to the various commodities (L_a, L_b, C_a, C_b), the amounts produced of each good (A, B) and most important for the present investigation, the marginal physical productivities of each factor in terms of each good (MP_{L_a}, MP_{C_a}, MP_{L_b}, MP_{C_b}).

But what is the meaning in terms of all of the above magnitudes of labour's real wage? This is not an easy question to answer if, as is usually true, labour consumes something of both commodities. In principle it is of course possible to determine whether a given individual's real income has gone up or down if one has detailed knowledge of his (ordinal) preference field. But we cannot gather

---

[20] Of course, this holds only if something of both commodities is produced, that is, if trade does not result in complete specialisation. The effect of this qualification is treated below.

such knowledge simply from observation of the price changes which take place.   Possibly an index number comparison of the type associated with the names of Pigou, Haberler, Könus, Staehle, Leontief, and others could serve to identify changes in real income. But we shall later show that this is unnecessary.   At this point, purely for reasons of exposition, we shall consider the highly restrictive case where labour consumes only one of the commodities, that is, where there is a single wage good.   In this case the real wage in terms of that good is an unambiguous indicator of real income[21] because of the proportionality between occupations indicated in condition (5).   It is the marginal physical productivity of labour in the production of the wage good.

The effect of international trade upon the real wage (thus defined) could now be determined mathematically by varying P_a/P_b, the price ratio of the two goods, and observing how the marginal physical productivity of labour in the wage good industry is affected.   One could perform this purely mathematical computation by differentiating our equilibrium equations with respect to P_a/P_b, treating as variables all the unknowns listed above.   The result of this procedure, not shown here because of its purely technical character, would be found to involve a sum of terms of necessarily different sign, and without introducing further economic content into the problem, we would not be able to achieve a definite result, but would be forced, like the older writers, simply to indicate that all things are possible.   However, by introducing further economic content of no less generality than theirs, we shall find that definite results can be derived.

The Elimination of the Index Number Problem

With the assumptions made so far it is hardly surprising that no more definite results have been reached.   For no assumption has as yet been made as to which country is relatively well supplied with

---

[21] It is true that we have been talking about the real wage rate and not about the total amount of real wages, but as we have assumed full employment before and after any change and unvarying total amounts of the factors of production, it follows that the real wage sum will always be proportional to the real wage rate.

capital or with labour. To begin with we make two assumptions. The first is that the country in question is relatively small and has no influence on the terms of trade. Thus, any gain to the country through monopolistic or monopsonistic behaviour is excluded. Secondly, it is assumed that the removal of the duty will not destroy the formerly protected industry, but only force it to contract.

Now in equilibrium the value marginal productivity (expressed in terms of any *numéraire*) must be the same in all occupations, and so must be the wage. Therefore, whatever wage labour receives in the wage good industry it must also receive in any other employment. Moreover, any change in the value marginal productivity and, therefore, the wage rate of labour in the wage good industry must mean a corresponding change in the wage rate in all other employments. It follows that we can tell what will happen to real wages (rates as well as sums) of labour as a whole by investigating what will happen to wages in the wage good industry. Since the relevant value marginal productivity, and hence the wage of labour in the wage good industry, is in terms of the wage good, and since labour gets the same wage in all occupations, a decline of the marginal productivity of labour in the wage good industry means a fall in the real wage rate and the real wage sum of labour as a whole.

In other words, whatever will happen to wages in the wage good industry will happen to labour as a whole. And this answer is independent of whether the wage good will be imported or exported, and can be reached without any discussion of what will happen to prices of the commodities as a consequence of international trade.[22]

Assume, for example, (*a*) that the country in question is relatively well supplied with capital, and (*b*) that the proportion of labour to capital is lower in the production of wheat than in the production of watches. There is nothing restrictive about these assumptions because in terms of our previous assumptions one of the countries must be relatively well supplied with a given factor, and through our postponement of the constant cost case for later

---

[22] In connection with a slightly different problem the same point is made by F. Benham, "Taxation and the Relative Prices of Factors of Production," *Economica*, N. S. Vol. 2, 1935, pp. 198–203.

discussion the importance of labour must be greater in the production of one of the commodities. And since the names "wheat" and "watches" are arbitrary, by re-naming the variables all possible cases could be expressed in the formulation given above.

Two alternative cases must now be considered. (1) The good in whose production capital is relatively important (wheat) is also the wage good. (2) The good in whose production labour is relatively important (watches) is the wage good. Each of these possibilities must be considered in turn.

(1) The introduction of trade will shift production in the direction of the good with "comparative advantage." According to the Ohlin analysis—even though he would not employ the previous term—this will be wheat which uses much of the abundant factor. Its production will expand, and part of it will be exported, while watch production will contract, and part of the watch consumption will be satisfied by imports. This shift in production will be accompanied by a transfer of *both* labour and capital from the watch industry to the wheat industry. But by a reduction in the production of watches more labour will be set free than can be re-employed at the same rates in the production of wheat. This is because the amount of capital released, while sufficient to employ a worker in watch production, is insufficient to employ him in wheat growing at the old wage rate. Hence wage rates have to go down in wheat growing, and it follows from the changed factor proportions that the real wage must also decline. It would be clearly incorrect to argue—as one familiar with the orthodox theory of international trade would be tempted to do—that in addition to this decline in productivity due solely to changed factor proportions, there must be added a further loss to the worker *qua* consumer resulting from the inevitable price rise of the exported wage good.

(2) We turn now to the case where watches are the wage good. On the face of it this case would seem to admit only of an ambiguous answer, since any definite conclusion in the productivity sphere would have to confront a necessary fall in the (relative) price of the wage good. Fortunately, that is not so. This case admits of no less definite an answer than the previous one.

The introduction of trade will increase the production of wheat and decrease that of watches. As shown in the previous case, this will entail a movement of both labour and capital. But just as labour has less capital to work with in wheat production than formerly, so does labour now have less capital to work with in the production of watches. This is brought about by the change in relative remunerations of the factors necessary to result in the reabsorption of the otherwise redundant labour supply. Therefore, regardless of the behaviour of consumer's goods prices, the lowering of the proportion of capital to labour in the production of watches must adversely affect the marginal physical productivity of labour there, and hence, along now familiar lines, the real wage.

We see, therefore, that the seemingly opposite cases lead to exactly the same result. *International trade necessarily lowers the real wage of the scarce factor expressed in terms of any good.* It follows that we are now in a position to drop the assumption of a single wage good. For if the real wage declines in terms of every good, real income must suffer regardless of the tastes and expenditure patterns of the labourers as consumers. Not only can we avoid making index number comparisons, but it is also unnecessary to make the assumption of uniform tastes of all workers which such comparisons implicitly presuppose.

DIAGRAMMATICAL TREATMENT

It may be useful to illustrate the above arguments graphically. In Fig. 1 we plot the familiar substitution curve (production possibility or transformation curve) between the two commodities in the given country. Before trade, equilibrium will have taken place at M with a price ratio corresponding to the slope of the tangent there. International trade will change the price ratio of the two goods, and a new equilibrium point may be taken as N with more wheat production, less watch production, and a higher price ratio between wheat and watches. This diagram represents the result of a fairly complicated economic process by which the given fixed amounts of productive factors are optimally allocated between the two commodities in accordance with marginal productivity conditions that guarantee a maximum amount of one commodity for preassigned given amounts of the other. For many international trade problems this "short-circuiting" is an advantage; but it omits the essential features of the present problem, and so we must go back of the substitution curve to the underlying production relations.

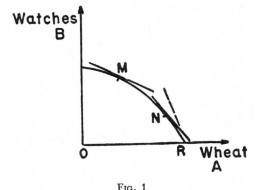

Fig. 1

This is done in Fig. 2 which consists of a modified box diagram long utilised by Edgeworth and Bowley in the study of consumers' behaviour. This rather remarkable diagram enables us to represent the relations between six variables on a two dimensional figure. On the lower horizontal axis is indicated the amount of capital used in the production of wheat. On the left-hand vertical axis is indicated the amount of labour used in the production of wheat. Because the amount of each factor which is not used in the production of wheat must be employed in the production of watches, the upper horizontal axis gives us, reading from right to left, the amount of capital used in the production of watches. Similarly, the right-hand vertical axis, reading downwards, gives us the amount of labour used in the production of watches. The dimensions of the box are, of course, simply those of the unchanging given total amounts of the two productive factors. Any point in the box represents four things: measuring from the lower left-hand corner the amounts of labour and capital used to produce wheat, and measuring from the upper right-hand corner the amounts of labour and capital used in the production of watches.

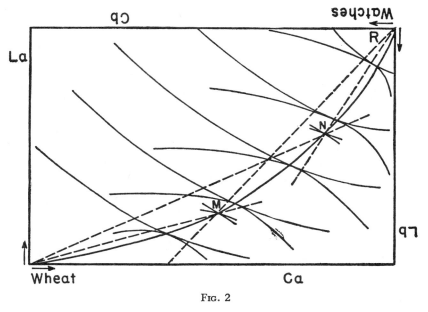

Fɪɢ. 2

Disregarding for the moment the other commodity, watches, it is clear that every point in the box corresponds to a given production of wheat, and hence lies on a uniquely determinable "isoquant" or "equal-product" contour line of the production surface. There is a one-parameter family of such curves with the shape as indicated by the lines, convex to the lower left-hand corner. Turning now to the production of watches, there also exists a one-parameter family of equal-product curves convex to the upper right-hand corner, and indicated in the diagram by a second family of curves.

We are now in a position to derive the substitution curve. Any point in the box taken at random corresponds to given amounts of watch and wheat production, but not necessarily to a point on the substitution curve. Only those points which reflect an optimal allocation of resources according to the marginal productivity relations stated earlier correspond to points on the substitution or opportunity cost curve. The locus of points representing optimal positions is clearly given by joining all the points of tangency of the two sets of contour lines.   It corresponds geometrically to Edge-worth's *contract curve*, and although the present study does not deal with bargains between contracting parties, we shall retain this descriptive title.   If we hold the production of one good constant and thus move along a given isoquant, we will only stop when there is the maximum possible amount of the other good, or when we have reached the highest possible isoquant of the other family.   This will be so only at a position of tangency where the ratios of the marginal productivities of the two factors are the same in each line of production.

Under the assumption of "linear and homogeneous" production functions in two inputs, the contract curve must have the shape indicated in our figure.   On the contract curve we have indicated points M and N corresponding to the situation before and after trade.   It can now be shown graphically how the following some-what paradoxical statement can be true: even though the proportion of total capital to total labour remains the same in both lines together, nevertheless the introduction of trade lowers the proportion of capital to labour in each line; and the prohibition of trade, as by a tariff, necessarily raises the proportion of capital to labour in each industry.   Although it seems intuitively anomalous, it is graphically clear from the diagram that a movement from N to M raises the proportion of capital to labour in watches, the total proportions remaining unchanged as indicated by the box.   The proportion of labour to capital in the production of wheat with trade is indicated by the slope of the angle of the dotted line going between N and the wheat origin.   A similar dotted line between the same origin and M shows the proportion of labour to capital in the production of wheat after trade.   Its being less steep than the other makes it clear that the ratio of capital to labour has increased. Utilising similar dotted lines between the watch origin and the points M and N, it is likewise seen that the abolition of trade in-creases the proportion of capital to labour in the production of watches.

How can we reconcile the graphical result with our numerical intuition which tells us that when each of two quantities goes up, an average of them cannot remain constant? An examination of the exact relationship between the proportions of capital to labour in each line and the proportions in both at once dispels the paradox. The proportion in both is found to be not a simple average but a weighted arithmetic mean of the proportions in each as indicated by the following identity:

$$\frac{L_a}{L}\frac{C_a}{L_a} + \frac{L_b}{L}\frac{C_b}{L_b} = \frac{C}{L} \dots\dots\dots\dots\dots\dots\dots\dots\dots\dots\dots\dots \quad (6)$$

The weights are simply the proportions of the total labour supply used in the respective industries. The abolition of trade raises the proportion of capital to labour in each line, but at the same time through the reverse operation of the principle of comparative advantage automatically gives more weight to the industry which uses the lesser amount of capital to labour.

Thus, we have shown conclusively that a restriction of trade will increase the proportion of capital to labour in both lines. It follows necessarily that the real wage in terms of each commodity must increase regardless of any movements of prices of the consumer's goods. For within each industry, increasing the capital which co-operates with labour raises the marginal productivity of labour expressed in physical units of that good. Not only are the labourers of that industry better off with respect to that good, but by the equivalence of real wages everywhere (expressed in terms of any good) labour in general is better off in terms of that good. If the real wage in terms of every good increases, we can definitely state that real income has increased. This is one of the few cases in economic analysis where a given change moves all relevant magnitudes in the same direction and obviates the necessity of a difficult, and often indefinite, index number comparison.

Under the assumed conditions—(a) two commodities, (b) produced by two factors of production, and (c) where trade leaves something of both commodities produced but at a new margin— it has been unequivocally demonstrated that the scarce factor must be harmed absolutely. This is in contrast to the accepted doctrine which may be fairly represented as saying that trade *might* conceivably affect adversely the relative share of a factor, but cannot be expected to harm absolutely an important factor of production. Not only is the latter possible, but under the posited conditions it follows necessarily.

THREE OR MORE COMMODITIES

If the above conclusion held only for two commodities, its interest even for theory would be limited.   It is of interest to show, therefore, that the introduction of any number of commodities in no way detracts from the validity of our conclusions.   Of course, no simple graphical device can be used to portray this because of the increased number of variables.

One method of approaching the problem might be to arrange the commodities in a sequence according to the relative importance of labour in each.   This is not unlike the ordering of commodities long used by Mangoldt,[23] Edgeworth, and others to explain which commodities will be imported and which exported when more than two commodities are introduced into the classical theory of comparative advantage.   In our case, however, costs are not constant and are not expressible in a single homogeneous unit of a factor or in a given composite factor.

For the present purpose one need not rely upon such a construction, but need only realise that the introduction of trade will increase the production of those commodities which use relatively much of the abundant factor, and will lower the production of the commodities using relatively little of the abundant factor.   Accompanying this, there will be the familiar Heckscher-Ohlin tendency towards partial equalisation of factor prices in the two countries, the price of the scarce factor falling in relationship to the price of the abundant factor.   By itself this tells us nothing concerning the absolute burden or benefit from trade, but deals only with the effect upon relative shares.   We cannot simply infer from this anything concerning the behaviour of absolute shares.   For it is not as if international trade leaves the total amount of real national

---

[23] J. Viner, op. cit., p. 458; G. Haberler, op. cit., pp. 136–140.

income unchanged so that the more one factor receives, the less there will be left for the other. On the contrary, it has been shown elsewhere that trade must increase the national income under the conditions here postulated.

It is nevertheless true that the introduction of trade will harm absolutely the scarce factor of production. To demonstrate this we must recall the fact that at the new higher relative price of capital to labour there will inevitably be a *relative* substitution of labour for capital *in each line* of production. In exactly the same way a restriction upon trade will raise the price of the scarce factor, labour, relative to the abundant factor, capital. There is nothing paradoxical in the fact that the ratio of capital to labour can increase in every line, while the ratio of total capital to total labour remains constant. The explanation given in the two commodity case whereby the weights in the arithmetic mean change in an appropriate fashion holds without modification when there are any number of commodities.

It is now a simple matter to show that the physical marginal productivity of labour in each line must increase, and because of the equalisation of wages in all lines, expressed in terms of any commodity, it immediately follows that restriction of trade increases the real wage of workers expressed in terms of each and every commodity. This obviates the necessity for any index number comparison or for any consideration of the worsening of the terms of trade.

THE CASE OF COMPLETE SPECIALISATION

The reader of the above argument will have realised that its remarkable simplicity springs from the fact that we may infer the real wage of workers in terms of a given good from the real marginal physical productivity of those workers who produce that good. This requires that before and after trade some finite amount, however small, be produced of every good. In a world where technological conditions are conducive towards the maintenance of the state of pure competition implicit in all our previous argument, and where regional factor endowments are not too dissimilar this is perhaps not too unrealistic an assumption. However, it is still desirable to see what remains of the argument when this assumption is dropped. This is even more so because in the course of the argument it will be shown that the classical theory was not so much incorrect as limited in scope.

Provided that costs are not constant, and that something of both goods was previously consumed, price changes brought about by international trade will at first shift the margin of production, but will still leave some production of both commodities. At one crucial price ratio corresponding to the slope of the tangent at R in Fig. 1 the production of one of the commodities will cease completely, and further changes will not alter the specialisation. Up until the critical price ratio is reached, the introduction of trade worsens the position of labour according to the previous arguments. But what happens after this critical price ratio?

There is no essential loss of generality in considering the two commodity case. For the commodity which is still produced, the real wage is determined as before by the physical productivity of the workers in that line. Up until the critical price ratio at which complete specialisation takes place, the scarce labour factors have been shown to lose. Beyond this critical price ratio their physical productivities remain unchanged. It is clear, therefore, that the real wage in terms of the export good using little labour is necessarily harmed by the introduction of trade.

With respect to the imported commodity the matter is more complicated, and the final result is indeterminate. Up to the critical price ratio we know that the real wage in terms of this commodity must fall. But after specialisation, the level of real wages can no longer be determined by the productivity of workers in this line since there are no such workers. One cannot avoid bringing into the analysis the price ratio between the two consumers' goods, that is, the terms of trade. Given this price ratio, it is possible to convert real wages in terms of one commodity into real wages in terms of the other. It becomes apparent that beyond the critical point the real wage in terms of the non-produced, imported good must begin to increase. This is to be balanced against the earlier loss of real wages in terms of this same good taking place before the critical point was reached.   Whether the result will be on balance favourable or unfavourable cannot possibly be determined on *a priori* grounds, but rests upon the technological and economic features of the countries in question.   Even if in a limited number of cases we could determine that the real wage in terms of the imported good would increase, there would still be involved a problem of weighing against this the demonstrated loss in real wages expressed in terms of the good in which the country has a comparative advantage.   Here again the final result would be indeterminate, although in favourable cases an index number comparison might be decisive.

Applying this same line of reasoning to the constant cost case of the classical theory of international trade, it is seen that theirs is one of the special unambiguous cases.   Either a single factor of production or a never varying composite dose of factors is assumed. Because of constant costs the slightest change in the price ratio of the goods will lead instantaneously to complete specialisation. There results no shifting of the proportions of the factors, and hence no deterioration of wages in terms of either good.   On the contrary, in terms of the imported good there must be an improvement in real wages with a consequent increase in real income.   This is made intuitively obvious from the consideration that trade necessarily increases the real income of a country, and in the classical case the proportion of income going to the respective factors cannot be changed by trade.   It is the latter feature of the classical theory which constitutes one of its important short-comings.

More than Two Factors

One by one we have been able to drop our various restrictive assumptions with only slight modifications of results.   Still there remains the problem of introducing into the analysis more than two productive factors.   Unfortunately, this entails more serious consequences.

In the first place, the definiteness of the Heckscher-Ohlin theorem begins to fade.   With three or more factors of production it is certainly not necessary that the result of trade is to make the ratios of factor prices in the respective countries more closely approach unity. Some may do so, but others may diverge depending upon complicated patterns of complementarity and competitiveness.[24] Whether on balance the movement towards equalisation exceeds the tendency towards diversification is not a meaningful question until a non-arbitrary method of weighting these changes is specified. Furthermore, even the concepts of scarce and abundant factors lose their sharpness of definition.

The fact that the Heckscher-Ohlin theorem breaks down when many factors of production are involved affords an explanation of its failure to account for the facts *if the production functions in the two countries differ, or if the factors of production of different countries are not identical.* By appropriate terminological conventions it is always possible to attribute differences in the production functions to differences in amounts of some factors of production (knowledge, available free factors, etc.). Similarly, if the factors of production of different countries are regarded as non-comparable and incommensurable,[25] this can be classified as an extreme case of factor disproportionality, but there must be more than two factors. We conclude, therefore, that the Heckscher-Ohlin theorem does not necessarily hold in the case of constant costs or multiple factors of production.

It does not follow that our results stand and fall with the Heckscher-Ohlin theorem. Our analysis neglected the other country completely. If factors of production are not comparable between countries, or if production functions differ, nevertheless, so long as

---

[24] See Ohlin, op. cit., pp. 96–105 and passim. [In 1946 the junior author, P. A. S., changed his mind on this point, coming to believe that *so long as something of each good is produced in every region, the Ohlin analysis asserts complete equalization of all factor prices, regardless of the number of commodities, regions, or factors.*]

[25] If the extreme classical assumption of immobility of labour between countries were valid, then over time the working populations of the various countries would become differentiated culturally, genetically, and in the limit cease to be of the same species. But those in the narrower classical tradition are least in a position to bring this up as an argument against the Heckscher-Ohlin theory, for in expositing the comparative cost doctrine they repeatedly (and sometimes unnecessarily) compare labour (costs, productivities, hierarchies, etc.) in various countries.

the country has only two factors, international trade would necessarily affect the real wage of a factor in the same direction as its relative remuneration.[26]   The only loss to our analysis would be the possibility of labelling the factor which is harmed as the "scarce" (relative to the other country) one.

However, we must admit that three or more factors of production within a single country do seriously modify the inevitability of our conclusions.   It is not only that the relatively scarce factor can be defined only circularly as the one whose price falls most after trade, but even if we do know the behaviour of relative factor prices, i.e. relative shares in the national income, it seems that we cannot infer unambiguously that the physical marginal productivities move in the same direction.   Even though these continue to depend only upon the proportions of the factors in the respective industry, diverse patterns of complementarity and competitiveness emerge as possibilities.   It is outside the scope of the present paper to attempt a catalogue of the various conceivable permutations and combinations.

This lack of definiteness in the more complex case is typical of attempts to go beyond the level of abstraction current in economic theory.   We have resisted the temptation to lump together diverse factors into two composite factors and thereby achieve the appearance of versimilitude, although others may care to do so for some purpose.

CONCLUSION

We have shown that there is a grain of truth in the pauper labour type of argument for protection.   Thus, in Australia, where land may perhaps be said to be abundant relative to labour, protection might possibly raise the real income of labour.[27]   The same

---

[26] This is in contrast to the problem of the effect of a technological innovation to which Professor Haberler (op. cit., p. 195) has compared the effects of trade: Technological change shifts the production function, and no inferences concerning the new marginal productivity relationships are possible.   As we have shown, trade leads to definite effects.

[27] See D. B. Copland, "A Neglected Phase of Tariff Controversy," *Quarterly Journal of Economics*, 1931, pp. 289–308; K. L. Anderson, "Protection and the

may have been true in colonial America.   It does not follow that the American working man to-day would be better off if trade with, say, the tropics were cut off, because land suitable for growing coffee, rubber, and bananas is even scarcer in America than is labour. The bearing of the many factor case will be obvious.

We are anxious to point out that even in the two factor case our argument provides no political ammunition for the protectionist. For if effects on the terms of trade can be disregarded, it has been shown that the harm which free trade inflicts upon one factor of production is necessarily less than the gain to the other.   Hence, it is always possible to bribe the suffering factor by subsidy or other redistributive devices so as to leave all factors better off as a result of trade.[28]

Historical Situation: Australia," *Quarterly Journal of Economics*, November, 1938, pp. 86–104; M. C. Samuelson, op. cit., pp. 143–149.

[28] Viner, op. cit., p. 534; P. A. Samuelson, op. cit., p. 204.

16

A RECONSIDERATION OF THE THEORY OF TARIFFS*[1]

By TIBOR DE SCITOVSZKY‖

The theory of tariffs, the most fertile field of economic speculation in the days of the classical economists, has for some time lain barren. Historically, it was the origin of the modern subjective theory of value (in the doctrine of comparative costs), it was earliest in emphasising the importance of demand in determining relative prices (J. S. Mill's reciprocal demand), and it has provided the analytical tools, Marshall's offer curves, from whose application to the problem of exchange between persons the general theory of perfect competition has been developed. Unfortunately, however, the analogy between countries and persons was considered irreversible. Our theory of the individual's rational economic behaviour was not applied to problems of international trade because of our supposed inability to draw community indifference curves. Hence, we have no theory of the rational behaviour of a single country, and even less do we know what would be the result of such behaviour on the part of all countries.

Free trade can be shown to be beneficial to the universe as a

---

* *The Review of Economic Studies*, Volume IX (Summer, 1942), pages 89–110. Reprinted, without significant change from the original text, by the courtesy of the *Review of Economic Studies* and the author.

‖ Stanford University.

[1] I propose to give this name to that part of the theory of international trade which deals with the problem of tariffs and the gain from trade. We shall not be concerned here with the problem of international capital transfer.

I am indebted to Miss Anne M. Aickelin for her valuable suggestions concerning the presentation of this article and for much of the reasoning and results of sections VI and VII.

whole but has never been proved to be the best policy also for a single country. That, however, is not always realised; and "strange to say, a confusion between ideas so different as part and whole pervades many of the arguments in favour of Free Trade." Edgeworth, who made the above remark, was conscious of the need for remedying the shortcomings of the theory of tariffs, and took a step in the right direction when he made use of indifference curves in his "Pure Theory of International Trade."[2] But either he was unaware of the difficulties attending the use of community indifference curves, or he did not deign to justify what to him may have seemed a perfectly legitimate commonsense approach, treating countries as individuals. In any case, his approach was abandoned and condemned as inadmissible. Later economists either persisted in the error pilloried by Edgeworth or adopted the following somewhat defeatist attitude. They declared that owing to the impossibility of interpersonal utility comparisons it was impossible to choose among alternative trade policies from the point of view of a single country. Since, therefore, national interest gave no directives concerning international trade, and because free trade was known to be beneficial for the world as a whole, it was concluded that free trade was the most rational policy (for want of a better one, so to speak) also from the point of view of single countries.

It is the aim of this article to attempt to get out of this *impasse*. To that purpose we shall have to modify somewhat the meaning of the classical welfare propositions. That will enable us to draw community indifference curves to serve as a standard of reference, against which we can compare the national welfare to be gained from various trade policies. These welfare propositions, however, assume full (or a given level of) employment and, as will be seen below, only appraise a country's efficiency at making use of its strategic advantages in exploiting the foreigner. Since welfare also depends on the degree of utilisation of resources, we shall also have to consider the effect of tariffs on employment. Which of

---

[2] *Economic Journal*, vol. 4 (1894); reprinted in F. Y. Edgeworth, *Papers Relating to Political Economy*, London, 1925, vol. ii.

these two considerations was more important in swaying international trade policies in the past I do not feel competent to decide.
In the future, welfare considerations in the classical sense may well
acquire predominance.   For it is likely that after the war governments will generally have to assume responsibility for maintaining
employment and the stability of economic life, which would render
the classical assumption of full employment legitimate.   Finally,
we shall analyse the infant industry argument and try to give it a
more exact interpretation than it has hitherto received.

I

A tariff usually favours some and prejudices other inhabitants
of the country imposing it.   Hence, its appraisal from the point of
view of that country must, among other considerations, include a
value judgment of the redistribution of welfare occasioned by it.
That, being a question of social justice, is outside the economist's
domain; which is the reason economists give when they refrain
from appraising tariffs from the point of view of a single country.
In so doing, however, they seem to ignore that the classical economists' welfare propositions also have to share with considerations
of social justice when serving as a guide to economic policy—a fact
which does not diminish their usefulness.[3,4]

The classical argument in favour of perfect competition and free
trade is not that they would improve everybody's and every country's welfare, but only that they create a situation in which it would
be impossible to increase anybody's welfare without diminishing
someone else's.   Perfect competition and free trade are economically
more efficient than imperfect competition and tariff-ridden trade
respectively, because they would make everybody and every coun-

---

[3] Cf. however N. Kaldor: "Welfare Propositions of Economics and Interpersonal Comparisons of Utility," *Economic Journal*, vol. 49 (1939), p. 549; J. R.
Hicks: "Foundations of Welfare Economics," *Economic Journal*, vol. 49, p. 696;
and N. Kaldor: "A Note on Tariffs and the Terms of Trade," *Economica* (N.S.),
vol. 7 (1940), p. 377.

[4] Cf. my "A Note on Welfare Propositions in Economics," *Review of Economic
Studies*, November, 1941, for a more detailed statement of the following argument.

try better off for any distribution of welfare among them *if* that were the same in the alternative situations. Actually, the transition from one situation to the other generally redistributes income so as to make some better off and others worse off than they were before. This fact may raise problems of equity, which cannot be ignored, but it does not render the criterion of economic efficiency nugatory.

The classical welfare propositions appraise the efficiency of a closed system. They state that a given change increases or diminishes the economic efficiency of a community that comprises *all* the people affected by the change. But just as we can say that, considerations of equity apart, free trade is beneficial to the universe as a whole; so we should also be able to tell whether free trade or protection is better from the point of view of a single country, ignoring the fact that some of its inhabitants may prefer the former and others the latter situation. We do not suggest that considerations of equity should be disregarded. On the contrary, they should always be weighed against considerations of efficiency. But for purposes of analysis they must be kept strictly apart.

In the following we shall only be concerned with problems of efficiency. We propose to apply the criterion of efficiency underlying the classical welfare propositions—or rather a slight modification of it—to the problems of an open economy; and we shall appraise the efficiency or inefficiency of tariffs from the point of view of the country imposing them. In this way we shall be able to make fairly general statements, which must be qualified by considerations of equity in particular instances. Equity is a matter of ethics and has nothing to do with economics; hence we shall not be concerned with it any further. But the reader is reminded once more that all our statements concerning national welfare are subject to modification by considerations of social justice.

It is well known that when the foreigners' reciprocal demand for a country's exports is inelastic, a suitable tariff will increase the quantities available for home consumption both of imports and of exportable goods. Hence, such a tariff will improve the welfare of the country imposing it in exactly the same sense in which perfect competition improves that of a closed community.   For, although it may actually make some people better and others worse off than they were before, it *could* make everybody better off for any given distribution of welfare.[5]

When the elasticity of the foreigners' reciprocal demand is greater than unity, a tariff will increase the quantity of retained exportable goods but diminish that of imports.   In such cases, propositions of the generality of the classical welfare propositions cannot always be made, because it is possible that for some hypothetical welfare distributions the tariff would increase while for others it would diminish our country's welfare.

It seems unnecessarily strict, however, to confine welfare propositions to alternatives where one would be better than the other for *all* hypothetical welfare distributions.   A whole range of welfare distributions has no practical importance; and strictly speaking, it is only the welfare distributions actually obtaining before and after the contemplated change that really matter.   It is suggested, therefore, to extend the scope of welfare propositions by restricting their range to these two actual distributions, and, in a probability sense, to the distributions of welfare intermediate between them. The test suggested for determining whether or not a given change, say the imposition of a tariff, is desirable, is as follows.

We must first see whether the people benefited by the change could fully compensate those prejudiced by it and still be better off than they were before the change.   It will be convenient to express this by saying that we make sure whether the people who would benefit by the change could profitably bribe those harmed into accepting it.   Secondly, we must make sure that the people who are against the change would be incapable of bribing those in favour to vote against it, without thereby losing more than they would if the change were carried.   The profitableness of the first bribe indicates that everybody would prefer the tariff to its alter-

---

[5] Because if there is more of some goods without there being less of others, everybody can be given more and made better off, whatever the initial distribution of income.

native (free trade or another tariff) in the hypothetical case that
the distribution of welfare after its imposition were similar to what
it was before.[6] The improfitableness of the second bribe shows
that the tariff would also be preferred in the hypothetical case that
the distribution of welfare before its imposition were similar to what
it is to become after it. In this case, therefore, we shall say that
the tariff increases national welfare; especially since everybody's
preference for the tariff in these two hypothetical situations makes
it probable that it would also be preferred for intermediate welfare
distributions. In cases where its alternative is preferred in both
situations (and presumably in intermediate situations); that is,
where the second bribe is possible but the first impossible, we shall
say that the tariff diminishes national welfare. If both bribes are
possible or both are impossible, that indicates that the tariff would
be preferred on the basis of one welfare distribution and its alternative on the basis of the other. In such a case we shall refrain
from making a welfare proposition or say that the two situations
are equally good.

The significance of welfare propositions based on this double
criterion is exactly the same as that of the classical welfare propositions. They do not state that one situation is actually preferable to
the other from everybody's point of view; but only that it *would* be
so preferred *if* the distribution of welfare were similar in the two
situations. They differ from the classical welfare propositions in
that they make this statement not for all hypothetical welfare distributions; but with certainty only for those actually obtaining
before and after the change, and with a high degree of probability
for all intermediate welfare distributions as well.

In the following we shall make ample use of this criterion and
adjudge trade policies by it as rational or irrational. In contrast
to the classical welfare propositions, it estimates a country's efficiency, not at allocating its given resources among alternative uses,

---

[6] That this is so, will become clear to the reader when he considers that the
bribing always tends to reproduce the welfare distribution of the situation that it
seeks to avoid.

but at making use of its strategic advantages for exploiting foreigners and at maximising its share of the world's resources. The analogy so frequently drawn between tariffs and excise taxes may mislead some readers into thinking that we should appraise tariffs also for their effect on allocating efficiency. It can easily be shown, however, that a tariff on international trade leaves the allocating efficiency of single countries unaffected.[7] The allocating efficiency of an economy is at its optimum when the relative prices of all commodities are the same for all members of the community. An excise tax interferes with allocating efficiency, because it makes the relative price of the taxed commodity different for different members of the community—producers being interested in the price net of the tax, and consumers in the price including the tax. A duty on international trade resembles an excise tax in that it makes relative prices different for inhabitants of different countries; thereby reducing the allocating efficiency of the universe as a whole. It does not, however, affect that of each country taken separately. For the prices relevant for any person always include his own country's tariffs and exclude those of all other countries, irrespective of whether he is a producer, a consumer or an export-import merchant.

II

We can now proceed to construct community indifference curves that are to serve as a standard of reference for appraising the desirability of a given change by our above criterion. In a Cartesian plane whose axes measure physical quantities of two commodities, say bread and wine, designate by p_0 the amounts of these goods possessed by the community and assume that they are distributed among its members in a given way (Fig. 1). Assume next that the community is induced by a rise in the price of bread to give up a certain quantity of it, say $b_0 b_1$.[8] Then it is possible exactly to

---

[7] Provided that it is not accompanied by an excise tax on home produced import substitutes and does not further the formation of monopolies.

[8] If we think of our plane as a cross-section along the bread and wine axes in an n-dimensional diagram, compensatory changes in other prices, equating supply

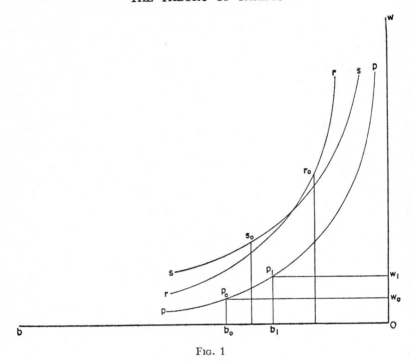

Fig. 1

compensate everybody for his loss of satisfaction by distributing a certain quantity, say $w_0 w_1$, of wine. p_1 therefore is a point of indifference to p_0, in the sense that it represents for each member of the community the same welfare that he enjoyed at p_0. In a similar way, we can draw all points of the community indifference curve going through p_0.

It will be noticed that there is not one but an infinite number of community indifference curves going through p_0, corresponding to different distributions of welfare (i.e. of bread and wine) among members of the community. This is so, because the exact quantity of wine needed to compensate for a given loss of bread depends: first of all, on the distribution of the total loss of bread ($b_0 b_1$) among

---

and demand in all other markets, will be necessary. It is simpler to think of bread and wine as the only two commodities.

individuals; and secondly, on the average rate of substitution between wine and bread at which each person has to be compensated for his loss.[9]   In their turn, both these depend on the
distribution of welfare.   The first, because it is the distribution of
welfare that determines people's relative reaction to a given change
in market price; the second, because the average rate at which people
have to be compensated with wine for their loss of bread depends
on the quantities of the various commodities already possessed by
them.

Once the distribution of welfare is given, the shape of the community indifference curve is uniquely determined.   Conversely,
while a point in the plane may correspond to an infinity of welfare
distributions, a community indifference curve uniquely determines
the welfare of each member of the community.   Since each community indifference curve represents a given welfare distribution,
they have the same geometric properties as individuals' indifference
curves.   (Negative slope and convexity towards the origin.)   The
relationship between different community indifference curves,
however, need not obey the rules of the individual's indifference
map, because they need not represent the same distribution of welfare.[10]   In other words, they may intersect one another!

Assume now that we want to compare two situations, P and R,
which are represented in Fig. 1 by points p_0 and r_0, and their respective indifference curves.   The indifference curves indicate the
level and distribution of welfare, the points on them show the
quantities of commodities possessed, in the two situations.   The

---

[9] In equilibrium everybody's marginal rate of substitution is equal to the relative prices of bread and wine; but the *average* rate of substitution for a finite quantity will in general be different for everybody.

[10] It may be worth pointing out that owing to the impossibility of measuring
satisfaction we cannot draw community indifference curves for the same distribution but different levels of welfare.   We could not, for example, draw a community indifference curve and then draw another one representing 10 per cent
more welfare for everybody, because we can attach no sense to "10 per cent more
welfare."   Yet, this seems to be the only possible interpretation of some earlier
attempts of drawing community indifference curves.

fact that p_0 lies below and to the left of the community indifference curve rr indicates that the quantities of commodities available in situation P would be insufficient for reproducing the welfare situation R.   Conversely, r_0 lying above and to the right of the community indifference curve pp means that the quantities of commodities possessed in situation R would be more than sufficient to reproduce the welfare situation P; and could, if properly redistributed, make everybody better off than he was in situation P. In other words, people favoured by and hence in favour of situation R could bribe those benefited by P, but these could not afford bribing the former.   Therefore, situation R is preferable to situation P on the basis of our double criterion.   We can state as a general rule that of two situations one is better than the other if it lies on a higher indifference curve and if the two indifference curves do not intersect between their relevant points.   If they do intersect, as is the case between r_0 and s_0, then each situation is worse (or better) than the other for its own welfare distribution; and according to our convention we must regard the two situations as equally good.

The likelihood of two community indifference curves intersecting is the greater, the more the change (e.g. the imposition or abolition of a tariff) affects the distribution of welfare between different social classes; that is, between *people with significantly different tastes*.   It also depends on the relative position of the relevant points, and hence on the factor or factors that determine their position.   If, for instance, one point is above *and* to the right of the other point, the indifference curves on which they lie cannot possibly intersect between those points, however different their shapes may be, because each indifference curve must have a negative slope.

III

In the foregoing two sections we have adopted a definition of welfare and constructed the community indifference curves corresponding to that definition.   We can now proceed to make use of our new concepts for drawing an analogy and applying to communities our knowledge of the rational behaviour of persons. Readers who feel uneasy about what has been said so far are well advised at this stage to forget about sections I and II altogether. They may then, as a first approximation, adopt the commonsense approach of personifying countries, and regard what follows as a theory of monopolistic competition, which applies to persons without qualification and to countries with whatever qualifications they may regard as necessary.

No one trained in general economic theory can fail to be struck by the perfect parallelism between tariffs and monopolistic price determination when he first examines the literature of the theory of tariffs. That this obvious analogy, which has been emphasised before,[11] has not yet gained general acceptance may be due, partly to the historical accident that duties are usually imposed on imports and not on exports,[12] and partly to the convention in the theory of production that imagines the monopolist as restricting his output and then letting the price to be determined by demand. In reality, producers exploit their monopolistic position by adding to their costs a monopolistic profit margin, which is an obvious and exact parallel to an export duty.

According to the traditional theory of production, the producer aims at maximising his money profits, and in this he differs from the tariff imposing government, which aims, or should aim, at maximising not the total tariff revenue, but the welfare of the country as a whole. But to represent the entrepreneur as maximising his money profits is to give an inaccurate though simplified interpretation of rational behaviour. To the extent that he is the owner of

---

[11] Cf. A. P. Lerner: "The Diagrammatical Representation of Demand Conditions in International Trade," *Economica*, N.S., vol. 1, 1934; and N. Kaldor: "A Note on Tariffs and the Terms of Trade," *Economica*, N.S., vol. 7, 1940. In fact, the argument of this section is little more than a repetition of what they, and especially Mr. Kaldor, already said more succinctly. Nevertheless, this was necessary because of the incomplete nature of their definition of community indifference curves.

[12] Cf. A. P. Lerner: "The Symmetry between Import and Export Taxes," *Economica*, N.S., vol. 3, 1936, for a proof that the economic effects of export and import duties are identical.

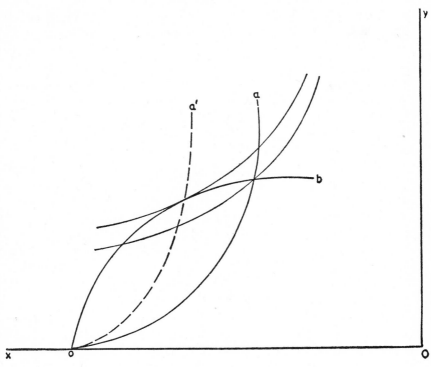

FIG. 2

productive resources, for whose use he pays himself wages, rent and/or interest, the entrepreneur's most rational behaviour would not be to maximise profits but to equate his marginal net revenue to the marginal cost of the use of his own productive factors.

This argument can be illustrated with the aid of the entrepreneur's indifference map (Fig. 2), showing his relative valuation of his own productive services (x) on the one hand, and of money income (y) on the other. In this indifference map we can draw as an independent datum the entrepreneur's total net revenue curve, ob, which is derived from the total demand curve confronting his firm, and which can also be interpreted as the community's total demand curve for his services. The offer curve or total cost curve, oa, of the entrepreneur's own factors can be derived geometrically from the indifference map. The entrepreneur will maximise his welfare by producing the output and utilising his private resources to the extent that brings him to the point of tangency of the total net revenue curve (*ob*) with one of his indifference curves. He will achieve this aim by adding to the cost of his services a monopolistic profit margin that so distorts his offer curve as to make it intersect the total net revenue curve at that point. The magnitude of this margin depends on the elasticity of demand for his services, and becomes zero as that approaches infinity.

This, as the reader will have noted, is just the application of Marshall's and Edgeworth's foreign trade diagrams to illustrate the behaviour of the entrepreneur or of any other owner of productive resources. The argument remains the same when we reinterpret the axes as measuring imports and exports, and the Marshallian curves as showing the foreigners' reciprocal demand for and the country's offer of exports in terms of imports. The monopolistic profit margin will now be called protective tariff, whose rate determines the point on the foreigners' reciprocal demand curve at which international trade takes place. The indifference curves will now show the country's collective appraisal of the relative advantages of exports and imports; and since that depends on the distribution of welfare—itself a function of the degree of protection—we must be careful to draw the requisite community indifference curves through each point of the foreigners' offer curve.[13] The optimum tariff will be that to which the community indifference curve tangential to the foreigners' demand curve belongs. If the foreigners' reciprocal demand is infinitely elastic, free trade will be the optimum policy on this criterion.[14,15]

---

[13] i.e. the indifference curve representing that distribution of welfare which corresponds to the degree of protection bringing trade to that point.

[14] It is not always realised that the (terms of trade) elasticity of the reciprocal demand curve would be equivalent to the price-elasticity of the foreigners' demand for exports, *only* if imports were the *numéraire*. Otherwise, the elasticity of reciprocal demand, τ, is given by the expression:

$$\tau = \frac{\epsilon\eta + \eta}{\epsilon + \eta}$$

We must remember, however, that community indifference curves may intersect one another. If the indifference curve tangential to the foreigners' offer curve intersects another indifference curve between its point of tangency and the latter's point of intersection with the foreigners' offer curve; we must, according to our convention, regard the corresponding trade policies as equally favourable to national welfare. Thus, it is possible that instead of one optimum tariff we should get a whole range of optimum tariffs, which in an extreme case may even include a zero tariff; that is, free trade.

The probability of community indifference curves intersecting is the greater, the more the change in trade policy redistributes income between different social classes; and it diminishes as the foreigners' offer curve, whose slope determines the position of the relevant points, rises less steeply. It becomes an impossibility if that is horizontal or even falling, because each indifference curve must have a negative slope. That proves the statement that a suitable tariff *always* improves national welfare if the foreigners' reciprocal demand has unit or less than unit elasticity. If that elasticity is greater than one, it is only probable that a suitable tariff will improve national welfare; the probability diminishing as the elasticity of reciprocal demand increases. But while it need not be worse, *in no case will free trade be better than protection,* short of the foreigners' reciprocal demand curve becoming infinitely elastic.

Economists sometimes assert that tariffs are always erected without regard to national welfare, solely on the instigation of sectional interests directly profiting by them. It cannot of course be denied that people who stand to gain most from a given change will be its

---

where ϵ is the price-elasticity of the foreign supply of imports, and η is the (absolute value of the) price-elasticity of the foreigners' demand for exports. It is evident from the formula that if ϵ is positive (upward sloping supply curve), $\tau \gtreqless 1$ as $\eta \gtreqless 1$, independently of the value of ϵ. The condition for τ tending to infinity, however, is that both ϵ and η should tend to infinity. For, if $\epsilon \to \infty$, $\tau \to \eta$; and if $\eta \to \infty$, $\tau \to (\epsilon + 1)$. Thus, τ cannot exceed the value of the expressions: η and $(\epsilon + 1)$; and will generally be smaller than either of them.

[15] Cf. Edgeworth, Collected Papers, vol. II, p. 39, and Kaldor, op. cit.

most ardent advocates.   But that in itself is no proof that the change will not increase national welfare.   In fact, sectional interests, representing an industry or group of industries, are unlikely to achieve their aim unless they succeed in convincing public opinion that their interest coincides with the national interest.   Their frequent appeal to the terms of trade argument shows that public opinion *is* concerned with national welfare as defined above, and that such considerations do play an important part in determining international trade policy.   For the terms of trade argument can be regarded as a rough-and-ready way of presenting our welfare argument.   If the imposition of a tariff affects the terms of trade very much, that is a sign of the foreigners' reciprocal demand not being very elastic.   That, in its turn, makes it plausible that the tariff has brought the trading point[16] onto a higher community indifference curve, and that that indifference curve does not intersect the lower indifference curve corresponding to the previous situation.

IV

So far we have been concerned with a problem of partial equilibrium: the rational behaviour of a single country trying to maximise its national welfare.   We now propose to consider a problem of general equilibrium: the mechanism of the interaction of various countries' trade policies.

Let us draw a pair of Marshallian offer curves and call the countries whose trading terms they represent A and B (Fig. 3). Free trade would result in the exchange of the two countries' produce at p_0, the point of intersection of the two curves.   That would be a situation most advantageous from the point of view of the two countries taken together, because their community indifference curves going through that point and corresponding to their distributions of welfare under conditions of free trade are tangential one to another.

From the point of view of each country separately, however, it

---

[16] By trading point we mean the point in the diagram at which trade actually takes place.

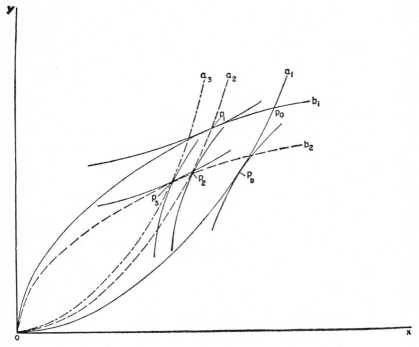

FIG. 3

would be more advantageous to impose a tariff that brings it to a higher indifference curve of its own. That will be possible for either country, if its relevant community indifference curves do not intersect between their relevant points, and if the other country's offer curve is not a straight line (i.e. infinitely elastic). Which of the two countries will reap this advantage (which is not open to both of them simultaneously!) depends on the promptness of their actions. Assume that country A is more alert and imposes an optimum tariff, which so distorts its offer curve as to make it intersect B's offer curve at p_1. Country B will now have forfeited its own opportunity of imposing an optimum tariff (which would have brought it to p_b), and it will also be worse off than it was under free trade; facing the new less favourable terms on which country A is now willing to do trade, and which are represented by oa_2, A's new tariff-distorted offer curve. Nevertheless, B will be able to recover some of its lost advantages by imposing a tariff of its own that so distorts its offer curve as to bring its point of intersection with oa_2, onto a higher one of its (B's) community indifference curves. Then it will be country A that will face new, less favourable trading terms, represented by B's distorted offer curve, ob_2; but also A may be able to regain some of its lost advantages by raising its tariff still higher and distorting its offer curve to, say, oa_3.

At each successive step, the welfare of the two countries taken together will have diminished. Nevertheless, each time one country has raised its tariff, the other country will be able somewhat to improve *its* welfare by further raising its own tariff, if it can thereby reach a higher one of its community indifference curves. That is always possible after the first tariff has been imposed[17] and may be possible after several subsequent tariff raises. The "competitive" raising of tariffs will continue until equilibrium is reached at the point where the two tariff-ridden offer curves are both tangential, each to one of the other country's community indifference curves. At that point, which need not be unique, neither country can hope to increase its national welfare by further raising its tariff. It need not but probably will be reached before international trade is completely eliminated; and its position and the number of successive tariff raises necessary to reach it depend on the shape and relative position of the two countries' community indifference curves.

Fig. 3 has been drawn in such a way that the equilibrium point, p_3, should be reached in three steps of optimum tariff raises. It is likely, however, that in general the number of steps would be greater; and in no case can they be under two. The argument is conditional on the same country's community indifference curves not intersecting. The probability of this condition being fulfilled

---

[17] This follows from the rule for the derivation of offer curves. B's relevant community indifference curve at p_1 must be tangential to the straight line connecting p_1 with the origin. A's tariff-distorted offer curve, oa_2, is bound to have a greater slope at p_1, whence it follows that country B can reach a higher community indifference curve by imposing a tariff that makes its offer curve intersect oa_2 somewhere below p_1.

increases with each step.   (We assumed it for the initial step.)   For
as tariff is piled upon tariff, trade diminishes and becomes confined
to goods whose demand is least elastic.   Since it has been shown
above that the probability of a country's community indifference
curves intersecting diminishes with the elasticity of the foreigners'
reciprocal demand curve (and becomes an impossibility when that
falls to or below unity); it follows that the probability of the raising
of tariffs improving national welfare increases with the height
they have already reached.

Exception may be taken to our above argument on the ground
that long before they have reached equilibrium, the two countries
will have recognised the causal connection between the raising of
their own tariff and retaliation by the other country, and come to
some agreement.   In other words, it may be argued that if protection is the monopolistic behaviour of a collectivity, two countries
raising tariffs against each other are bilateral monopolists—and we
know that bilateral monopoly results in the two parties coming to
some working agreement, whose terms depend on their bargaining
skill and are analytically indeterminate.

That, indeed, would be the case if there were two countries only.
When, however, there is a large number of countries, and each
trades with many of the others, any single country will be justified
in neglecting the danger of retaliation to its own tariff policy.   We
must, therefore, reinterpret our diagram so that one of the Marshallian curves should stand for the offer curve of the several single
countries in succession, and the other represent the reciprocal
demand for that country's exports of the rest of the universe; i.e.
of all other countries taken together.   No single country will have
scruples in establishing or raising its tariff; knowing that its own
reciprocal demand for foreign produce contains only a negligible
fraction of the total foreign demand facing any other single country,
and that therefore changes in it are unlikely to influence the latter's
policy.   As all countries act on this principle and raise their tariffs,
the universe's reciprocal demand curve facing each of them will
get distorted just as much as if tariffs had been raised against it by
the rest of the world acting in unison.   To call the raising of tariffs

on these assumptions irrational, would be similar to calling competitive behaviour irrational. There, each producer's quest for higher profits tends to eliminate the profits of all; here, the attempt by each country to increase its own advantage from trade diminishes the advantage of all. The theory of perfect competition and the above argument, which may be named the theory of heterogeneous competition (polypoly), are based on identical assumptions in that they both assume a sufficiently large number of independent economic units for each of them to neglect the reaction of others to his own actions. They differ in so far that perfect competition does while our above argument does not assume that the produce of various units is perfectly interchangeable. That the two assumptions have nothing to do with each other is well known; and the importance of keeping them strictly apart has recently been emphasised.[18] The difference—real and supposed!—between a country's produce and its foreign substitutes determines the elasticity of the foreigners' reciprocal demand, and hence the size of the optimum initial tariff and of subsequent tariff raises. The more perfectly identical are in the estimation of foreigners their substitutes for our country's produce, the more elastic will be their demand for its exports, and the smaller will be the tariff it can profitably impose upon foreign trade. If foreigners produced perfect substitutes, their reciprocal demand would be perfectly elastic[19] and the optimum tariff rate would be zero, and would remain zero even after other countries have imposed tariffs of their own. Perfect competition refers to this limiting case alone.

At this stage we may attempt to sketch a long-period theory of international trade. Imagine an initial situation where trade is free, or at least tariffs are low and the most-favoured-nation clause is in vogue; and where each country trades with most of the others, and there is some triangular trade. Countries that believe themselves to be sufficiently small to erect or raise tariffs unpunished

---

[18] Cf. Robert Triffin: *Monopolistic Competition and General Equilibrium Theory*, Cambridge, Mass., 1940.

[19] We assume that the price-elasticity of the world's supply of any single country's imports approaches infinity.

will do so as soon as they discover that they can thereby increase their national welfare. When a number of countries have followed this course, those still on a free trade basis will find themselves monopolistically exploited and will be perfectly justified in saying that they are being *forced* into erecting tariff walls too. That they can thereby improve their position we have shown above; and this should be as obvious as that a monopolistically exploited consumer can improve his position by charging monopolistic prices in his capacity of producer.

When tariff walls have been erected all around, those who started the process will find some of their initial advantage gone; but they are also likely to find that they can improve their position by raising tariffs further, even if initially they made full use of their monopolistic position. As tariff walls rise, conferences on international trade may be called to arrest the process, which is obviously harmful to all concerned. Yet, as long as it remains in the individual interest of each country separately to raise tariffs, such collective attempts are bound to be ineffectual if not backed by international sanctions; just as cartel agreements are ineffectual if there is not a large producer with enough authority to enforce them.

As tariff walls mount and international trade dwindles, the number of countries each country trades with will diminish. That will tend to destroy the atomistic nature of international trade and lend increasing reality to the danger of retaliation. In other words, it will lead to the realisation of the interdependence of the various countries' tariff policies. That may cause the most-favoured-nation clause to fall into disuse and tariffs to be determined by bargaining, before equilibrium had been reached. If, on the other hand, equilibrium is reached, so that no country can improve its welfare by raising tariffs further, in that case also bargaining will appear as the only way in which national welfare can still be increased. So in either case, heterogeneous competition leads through the rational behaviour of each competitor to "paucilateral" and bilateral monopoly; and tariff autonomy will, in time, give way to tariff clubs and bilateral trade agreements.

V

Bilateral trade agreements are a matter of higgling and bargaining and have little interest for the economist. Nevertheless, it may be worth our while to make a short digression and discuss barter agreements, a special form of them, which has recently acquired some importance. Barter trade agreements not only set the terms on which indefinite amounts of goods are to be traded for each other, but also fix the exact amounts to be exchanged. They have been introduced by Nazi Germany in her trade with South American and South-East European countries, and declared by a Nazi spokesman to be the principle on which trade in Hitler's "New Order" would be based. Since by their very nature they overrule all existing tariffs, it is to be expected that they should be able both to improve and to worsen the situation they replace. We set out to prove that barter agreements may be to the mutual advantage of countries whose trade was previously conducted across tariff walls; but that at the same time they are a convenient way of exacting tribute from conquered or intimidated countries.

Let us draw a pair of Marshallian offer curves belonging to countries A and B, and assume that owing to the existence of trade barriers between them, their trading point is not at the intersection of the offer curves but, say, at point p_1 (Fig. 4). We shall not bother to draw the two tariff-distorted offer curves that intersect at that point. The two countries' community indifference curves going through p_1 and corresponding to their distributions of income brought about by this particular set of tariffs intersect one another, as shown in the figure, since they could not be tangential under any combination of tariffs. That means, however, that a new trade agreement bringing the trading point within the area enclosed by the two indifference curves would be likely to be beneficial to both countries.

The qualification "likely" is that accompanying all arguments based on community indifference curves. For, if the new trade agreement resulted in a very drastic redistribution of income as between social classes in either or both countries, either or both of the indiffer-

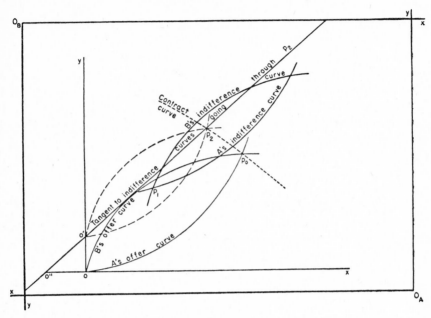

Fig. 4

ence curves pertaining to the agreement might intersect the corresponding indifference curve or curves going through p_1, and therefore not signify an increase in national welfare.   After this last warning we shall leave it to the reader to make the qualifications incumbent on the use of community indifference curves and proceed for the rest of this argument pretending that each country is a single person. That will simplify the argument considerably, without qualifying its results more than turning them from certain into probable statements.   We also wish to emphasise once more that the intersection of community indifference curves cannot reverse a statement based on the assumption that they do not intersect.   That is, it cannot turn "better" into "worse" but only into "no better."

We know that no further raising of tariffs could bring the trading point within the area between the indifference curves, since that could only move it leftwards and downwards; that is, away from the contract curve, which we can now draw into our diagram.   An agreement between the two countries mutually to lower their tariffs could improve both their welfare; but only to a limited extent. For no combination of tariffs could bring them onto the contract curve,[20] while free trade would take them to p_0, the intersection of the offer curves, which in our particular example lies outside the indifference curves going through p_1. The two countries can, however, reach a point on the contract curve within the indifference curves going through p_1 by concluding a barter trade agreement that overrides all existing tariffs and directly fixes the physical quantities to be exchanged in such a way as to bring them to, say, p_2.[21]

From the definition of the contract curve it follows that there must be at least one initial distribution of resources between A and B wherefrom free trade would lead to p_2.[22] Anyone acquainted with the derivation of offer curves from indifference maps will see at once that the tangent to the two indifference curves going through p_2 is the locus of all such initial situations; for it is the locus of the origin of all pairs of offer curves that intersect in p_2. It follows from this that the barter agreement leading to p_2 is equivalent in its effect to free trade between the two countries, after the payment of a tribute from A to B that brings them from the origin of the barter diagram to any point of the tangent drawn through p_2. In the figure, the new offer curves are drawn (broken line) from o' as origin, assuming that the tribute is paid in terms of y. But the tribute could just as well be paid in terms of x, bringing the origin of the offer curves—still intersecting in p_2—to o''; or it could be paid in any combination of x and y, as long as the rate of transformation between them remained equal to the slope of the indifference curves

---

[20] Ruling out "negative tariffs."

[21] It has been pointed out to me by Mr. N. Kaldor that the same result could also be reached by having additional trade duty free.

[22] In Fig. 4 the intersection of the axes of the two indifference maps gives the total quantity of the two goods jointly possessed by A and B, while the origin of the barter diagram itself shows their initial distribution between A and B. Cf. A. L. Bowley: *Mathematical Groundwork of Economics*, Oxford, 1924, for the best description of such a diagram.

tangential to each other in p_2. Barter trade agreements, therefore, represent the exploitation of one country by the other, just as tariffs do; but with the difference that to the extent that they bring the trading point nearer the contract curve, they are more efficient.

So far we have only considered barter trade agreements that are voluntarily entered into and therefore do not increase the exploitation of one country by the other but only render existing exploitation more efficient. If, however, one of the countries can bring political or military pressure to bear on the other country, it can force it into a barter agreement that brings them onto a trading point outside the area enclosed by the indifference curves going through the point reached under existing trading conditions (p_1). In an extreme case, a barter agreement may bring the trading point outside the indifference curves going through the origin of the barter diagram (not drawn in the figure), indicating that trade under such circumstances would be worse for the exploited country than no trade at all.[23] Barter agreements, of course, need not necessarily be efficient in the sense of leading to the contract curve. They do, if after their conclusion the relative prices of the bartered goods are the same in the two countries[24]; and *the conformity of that price ratio in the two countries is an index of the efficiency of the agreement.*

To sum up the above argument, barter trade agreements are a method for one country to exploit another, more efficient potentially than tariffs. They are equivalent to free trade *plus* the payment of a tribute from one country to another, if efficient.[25] A barter agreement may be to mutual advantage if it supersedes protective tariffs, provided that it does not increase already existing exploitation but merely makes it more efficient. To the extent that it increases the degree of exploitation, it may be regarded as a method of turning political ascendancy to economic account by

---

[23] In a happier age, Edgeworth and Marshall have not even drawn the contract curve beyond these limits.

[24] We are referring to the ratio of market prices and not to that of the purely fictitious prices that usually figure in such agreements.

[25] If inefficient, they can be represented by the payment of a tribute *plus* trade under a tariff.

exacting tribute from defeated, conquered or intimidated countries. As such it is more efficient than, say, the reparations imposed in the Versailles treaties were, because it presents no transfer problem. On the other hand, it imposes tribute in a veiled form, and is therefore less open to the critical scrutiny of public opinion.

VI

So far we have been concerned with the theory of tariffs on the classical assumption of full (or a given level of) employment. We now proceed to consider the effect of tariffs on employment; such effect to be added to or subtracted from the effects of tariffs on national welfare hitherto discussed. For an increase in employment increases national welfare in exactly the same way as a tariff does when the foreigners' reciprocal demand is inelastic. It increases the quantity of all goods except that of involuntary idleness, and thus makes it possible for everybody to be better off than he was before, whatever the distribution of welfare. Before examining how tariffs affect employment, however, it will be necessary shortly to recapitulate the theory of employment in a closed community.

It is generally agreed to-day among economists that it is most convenient to think of the level of employment as being determined by the equality of investment and saving. If we consider investment activity in the short period as a datum—a convention based on the consideration that capital equipment, having the longest gestation period, is the commodity whose rate of production is least dependent on present and most irrevocably determined by past decisions—employment and income must be such as to make saving equal to investment. The function showing the proportion of income the community saves out of each level of income is called the propensity to save function. If its form is approximately linear, the process by which additional investment generates additional income can be illustrated by an infinite geometric progression, well known as the theory of the multiplier.

In a closed community saving must equal investment in short-period equilibrium, because that is the condition for the equality of anticipated and realised receipts in current production. In an open economy, the condition for short-period equilibrium is still the equality of anticipated and realised receipts in domestic current production. But since in the latter case there are two alternatives to spending on home produced goods: saving, and spending on imported goods; and the receipts of domestic producers originate not only in domestic expenditure but also in exports, it follows that, in an open economy, the condition for short-period equilibrium is the equality between the sum of imports and saving and the sum of exports and investment. In other words, an open economy has no inherent short-run tendency to equate either saving with investment or exports with imports; but only to make the discrepancies in these two equal to each other.[26] Only to the extent that the central bank allows changes in its reserves (caused by the export or import surplus) to influence its interest rate policy, and to the extent that this affects investment activity, will there be a tendency towards the equality of saving and investment and of exports and imports separately.

After this digression we can conveniently list the factors through which a change in trade policy can influence the level of employment. They are: (1) the value of imports net of tariffs; (2) the value of exports; (3) the shape of the propensity to save function; and the two determinants of the level of investment activity; (4) the rate of interest; and (5) the marginal efficiency of investment.

(1) The imposition or raising of tariffs always diminishes the *net* value of imports, and on that count *always* increases employment and income. It increases them to the extent that is needed to raise the community's saving, and expenditure on imports (net of the tariff), by the amount of the initial fall of imports. The ratio between the value of additional income and the primary fall of imports may be called the foreign multiplier. Its value is equal to that of the investment multiplier in the same economy.

(2) The impact effect of tariffs to create an export surplus is

---

[26] Cf. M. Bronfenbrenner: "The Keynesian Equations and the Balance of Payments," *Review of Economic Studies*, vol. 7, 1939–40.

sometimes said to be of short duration only.   If it is based on the belief that exports automatically tend to be equal to imports, that statement is wrong, as has been shown above.   While trade is relatively free, that statement is also wrong if it is based on the consideration that one country's export surplus is the import surplus of other countries, who may retaliate.   For the argument of section IV about the danger of retaliation holds good here just as much as it did there.   If during a world depression a country imposes tariffs to diminish its imports, and if subsequently its export surplus is eliminated by a diminution of its exports, that may be due not so much to retaliation as to the existence abroad of the same motive to diminish imports (i.e. other countries, also suffering from depression, might have thought of the same way of relieving it).   This argument also shows that our long-period theory of tariffs is not dependent on the assumption that trade policies are determined by welfare considerations of the kind discussed in section I.   If the desire to increase employment and to stop import surpluses and resulting depression were the sole motive force behind rising tariff walls, it would still be true that the rational behaviour of each country, aiming at fuller employment and greater internal prosperity, tends to defeat that aim and only results in ever-mounting tariffs.

(3) The form of the propensity to save function depends on the distribution of income; for rich people generally save a larger proportion of their income than the poor.   Hence, we can say that the more unequal is its distribution, the greater the proportion of the national income which will be saved.   A change in trade policy, therefore, will on this account tend to raise or to lower the level of employment according as it makes the distribution of income less or more unequal.   This is a purely economic argument in favour of trade policies that tend to make the distribution of income more equal.

(4) Since tariffs always diminish the value of imports and do not directly affect that of exports, they always enhance the liquidity of the banking system—or at least alleviate the drain on its reserves. Increased protection, therefore, will always lead to lower interest

rates, provided that the banking system allows its interest rate policy to be at all influenced by its liquidity. But too much importance should not be attached to this as a factor stimulating employment. Our preoccupation with the rate of interest is probably explained by the fact that for a long time in the past it was the only lever through which our economic system could be controlled; and that it was a powerful tool then, is probably due more to its influence on short-term international capital movements than to its effect on industrial investment.[27]

(5) The marginal efficiency of investment is defined as the ratio of the flow of expected net receipts from operating capital equipment to the latter's cost of construction. It is therefore an increasing function of the price of the industry's output, and a diminishing function of the price of capital equipment and co-operating factors. Tariffs will affect the marginal efficiency of investment if they alter the relationship of these prices. The prices relevant here are those including the tariff. Hence, an import duty raises the prices of the goods on which it is imposed. To a lesser extent, it also raises those of their substitutes and lowers the prices of their complements. An import duty, therefore, will increase the marginal efficiency of investment in industries producing goods identical with or similar to those hit by the duty; it will diminish the marginal efficiency of investment in industries that *make use* of such goods and that produce goods complementary to them. This argument, therefore, together with that of paragraph (3) of this section, does not enable us to make *general* statements about the effect of tariffs on national welfare, though it is very important in considering the effects of *particular* tariffs.

VII

The preceding argument, concerning the effect of duties on the marginal efficiency of investment, has an important bearing also on the secular aspects of the free trade *versus* protection controversy. First of all, it provides an economic explanation of why England

---

[27] Cf. P. B. Whale: "The Working of the Pre-War Gold Standard," *Economica*, N.S., vol. 4, 1937.

was for such a long time the champion of free trade. In eighteenth and nineteenth century England free trade, by lowering the price of labour[28] and raw materials, meant a higher rate of profit in industry, greater investment opportunities, more prosperity, and fuller employment. It depressed agricultural production; but possibilities of expansion being more restricted there, it increased national prosperity and income on balance. In all other countries the situation was the reverse during the same period: it was protection that raised the marginal efficiency of investment in industry and, may be, depressed agricultural production.[29] This is so, because free trade favours whichever line of activity is already best established in a country. If we believed that the division of labour among nations is the outcome of inherent and unalterable national and geographical characteristics, that would be an argument in favour of free trade. If however we recognise, as I think we should, that specialisation among countries is to a large extent a matter of historical accident, we would have to draw a different conclusion.

Since the progress of our material welfare depends mainly on technical advance, our civilisation offers the greatest rewards to industrial skill and technical ingenuity, and the nations specialising in these fields will inevitably lead, and agricultural nations lag behind. Hence, the best long-run policy a nation can pursue is to create an atmosphere favourable to industry and technical progress. But, it may be asked, if industry is more profitable than agriculture, why does it need special stimulus? The answer to that question can best be put in the language of external economies. The produce of industry consists of goods and services sold for money, and

---

[28] *Via* cheapening foodstuffs, the primary wage good.

[29] I am doubtful about this last statement, because historically, the transition from agricultural to industrial production was invariably accompanied by drastic institutional changes, which probably gave a stimulus to agricultural production more important than the depressing effect taken account of by more formal analysis. Such a stimulant, for instance, must have been the transition from barter to a money economy. By introducing the new habit of expressing welfare in terms of money, and thereby minimising the importance of those elements of welfare that cannot be so expressed (leisure, a comfortable life, etc.), it must have stimulated farmers to produce more for the market.

of benefits for whose use no charge can be made by their very nature, but which nevertheless contribute to the social product. These benefits are called external economies from the point of view of those benefited: they consist in the training of workers, the creation of a labour market and of markets for bye-products, the stimulus given to transport facilities, the arousing of interest in science and engineering, and the like. In an industrial community, a new firm or industry will not only contribute to, but also benefit by, the external economies already in existence. The free benefits he makes use of *repay*, so to speak, the entrepreneur for his free contribution to the community's welfare. No free benefits compensate the first firm or industry to be established in an agricultural community for the advantages it confers on the firms and industries to follow. Yet, those advantages may be very important and valuable from society's point of view, and should be accounted for when calculating the firm's or industry's marginal productivity. A firm's or industry's economic right to live, therefore, should be based not on its private but its social marginal productivity, which takes account of intangible factors[30] and products. In an industrial community these two are likely to cancel each other out, making private and social marginal productivity approximately equal. In an agricultural economy the difficulties of beginning may make an industrial firm's private marginal productivity significantly lower than its social marginal productivity; and to make up for the difference, protection or the payment of subsidies is economically justified.

This is, I think, what writers like Carey, List, and Schüller really meant. The above argument shows that to extend public assistance to infant industries is economically fair and proper, provided it does no more than equate private to social marginal productivity. Tariffs are the cheapest way of giving such assistance from the point of view of the country imposing them, which adds yet another rational reason for imposing tariffs, at least in the special case of industrially backward countries. This, of course, is not incompati-

---

[30] Only those that have an opportunity cost.

ble with the fact that from the universe's point of view, direct subsidies, paid out of general taxation, would be a more efficient way of doing this.

Protection, in this restricted and true sense of the word, was probably the main factor motivating the first tariffs of capitalism. One gains that impression not only when perusing the writings of early Continental and American writers on the subject; but also from the fact that the export duties of the mercantilist era should have been replaced by import duties. For these are more suitable for affording protection in the above defined sense; while those would have been more natural and more efficient had the monopolistic exploitation of foreigners been the primary aim.[31] In more recent times, changing the terms of trade and creating employment were probably more important considerations with public opinion and legislative bodies in determining tariff policy.

VIII

We have tried to show in the foregoing that to impose tariffs on international trade is generally in the rational interest of single countries for more than one reason. This does not conflict with the fact that free trade is the best policy for the universe as a whole. For just as each entrepreneur's competitive behaviour diminishes the profits of all entrepreneurs, so each single country's effort to increase its national welfare tends to diminish the welfare of all.

Free trade leads to the best allocation (most efficient utilisation) of the world's resources, provided that full employment is somehow ensured. It leads to a distribution of welfare among nations that, if ethically neutral, is at least based on historically and geographically determined inequalities and not on inequalities of political and military power. Any corrections of this distribution that may be considered necessary or just, are better made openly (preferably in kind), in the form of payments of tribute or assistance, than surreptitiously, under the cloak of tariffs or barter

---

[31] This is in apparent contradiction with footnote 12, p. 368. But Mr. Lerner's demonstration that the effects of import and export duties are identical in all respects only holds good of duties that are levied at a uniform rate on all commodities.

agreements. That is a better guarantee of economic efficiency and justice.

But it is not enough to declare the desirability of free trade and trust that enlightenment will bring it about; nor is it enough to create initial conditions favourable to it: it must be imposed and enforced. Whether this should be done with the aid of the more effective sanctions of a new League of Nations, or through the political prestige of a British Empire, or in any other way, is beyond the economist's competence to decide. We can only tell that some form of compulsion is necessary to ensure free trade. The truth of this statement is attested by the past history of international trade as much as by our rationalisation of it. Both show that independent states, in possession of their full sovereignty, will keep on erecting and raising tariffs in order to increase their share of the world's resources, to achieve fuller employment, and to protect their growing industries. Of these three aims only the last is likely to be realised; the second will generally defeat itself as tariffs are erected all round; whereas the first will not only defeat itself but every country will actually be impoverished as they all raise their tariffs. It is to guard against this general impoverishment that free trade must be enforced and each country kept from seeking more than its share of the world's resources. Employment can be maintained and infant industries subsidised by other means than protection. This, from a single country's point of view, is probably the cheapest way of achieving those aims; but it is against the general interest to let one country do what would be detrimental to all if generally practised.

The enforcement of free trade, of course, would not in itself solve all problems of international economic co-operation, on the contrary. Since freer trade means more trade, problems of a satisfactory international standard, of international co-operation in maintaining a stable level of employment, and the like, would become greater in proportion. I believe, however, that post war reconstruction would lead to better and more stable results if free trade were enforced and a constructive attempt made at solving attending problems, than if undue faith in the principle of laisser faire resulted in a repetition of past mistakes.

OTHER ASPECTS OF COMMERCIAL POLICY

17

BEGGAR-MY-NEIGHBOUR REMEDIES FOR UNEMPLOYMENT*

By Joan Robinson‖

For any one country an increase in the balance of trade is equivalent to an increase in investment and normally leads (given the level of home investment) to an increase in employment.[1]   An expansion of export industries, or of home industries rival to imports, causes a primary increase in employment, while the expenditure of additional incomes earned in these industries leads, in so far as it falls upon home-produced goods, to a secondary increase in employment.   But an increase in employment brought about in this way is of a totally different nature from an increase due to home investment.   For an increase in home investment brings about a net increase in employment for the world as a whole, while an increase in the balance of trade of one country at best leaves the level of employment for the world as a whole unaffected.[2] A decline in the imports of one country is a decline in the exports of other countries, and the balance of trade for the world as a whole is always equal to zero.[3]

---

* *Essays on the Theory of Employment*, 2nd. ed., (Basil Blackwell, Oxford, 1947), Part III, Chapter 2.   Reprinted, without change from the second edition, by the courtesy of The Macmillan Company, Basil Blackwell, and the author, Mrs. Joan Robinson.

‖ Cambridge University, England.

[1] See below, p. 396, note, for an exceptional case.

[2] Unless it happens that the Multiplier is higher than the average for the world in the country whose balance increases.

[3] The visible balances of all countries normally add up to a negative figure, since exports are reckoned f.o.b. and imports c.i.f.   But this is compensated by a corresponding item in the invisible account, representing shipping and handling costs.

In times of general unemployment a game of beggar-my-neighbour is played between the nations, each one endeavouring to throw a larger share of the burden upon the others. As soon as one succeeds in increasing its trade balance at the expense of the rest, others retaliate, and the total volume of international trade sinks continuously, relatively to the total volume of world activity. Political, strategic and sentimental considerations add fuel to the fire, and the flames of economic nationalism blaze ever higher and higher.

In the process not only is the efficiency of world production impaired by the sacrifice of international division of labour, but the total of world activity is also likely to be reduced. For while an increase in the balance of trade of one country creates a situation in which its home rate of interest tends to fall, the corresponding reduction in the balances of the rest tends to raise their rates of interest, and owing to the apprehensive and cautious tradition which dominates the policy of monetary authorities, they are chronically more inclined to foster a rise in the rate of interest when the balance of trade is reduced than to permit a fall when it is increased. The beggar-my-neighbour game is therefore likely to be accompanied by a rise in the rate of interest for the world as a whole and consequently by a decline in world activity.

The principal devices by which the balance of trade can be increased are (1) exchange depreciation, (2) reductions in wages (which may take the form of increasing hours of work at the same weekly wage), (3) subsidies to exports and (4) restriction of imports by means of tariffs and quotas. To borrow a trope from Mr. D. H. Robertson, there are four suits in the pack, and a trick can be taken by playing a higher card out of any suit.

Before proceeding any further it is necessary to make a digression, for it has sometimes been denied that the restriction of imports will increase home employment.[4] This view appears to arise from

---

[4] See *General Theory*, p. 334. Mr. Keynes offers himself as a sacrifice. But (*pace* Sir William Beveridge) it was never the orthodox view that a tariff cannot lead to an increase in employment in the short period; see Pigou, *Public Finance*, p. 224.

a confusion as to the nature of the classical argument for free trade. The classical argument states that (with certain well-known exceptions) the pursuit of profit will bring about the specialisation of resources and the distribution of trade between nations in such a way that the maximum of efficiency is achieved. Any arbitrary interference with the channels of trade will therefore lead to a decline in efficiency, and a reduction in the amount of output obtained from a given amount of resources. This argument, on its own ground, is unexceptionable. But in the nature of the case it can throw no light upon the division of a given total of employment between nations. It tells us that, with given employment, output per head will be higher when trade is free. It cannot tell us that when one country increases its share in world employment, at the expense of reducing output per unit of employment, its total output will be reduced. Still less can it tell us that employment in any one country cannot be increased by increasing its balance of trade.[5] Indeed it is obvious to common sense that a tax upon imported goods will lead to an increase in the output of rival home-produced goods, just as a tax upon any commodity will stimulate the output of substitutes for it.

The popular view that free trade is all very well so long as all nations are free-traders, but that when other nations erect tariffs

---

[5] The argument is backed up by the contention that 'exports pay for imports,' see, e.g., Beveridge and others, *Tariffs: the Case Examined*, chap. vi. It is admitted that in some circumstances imports may be curtailed without exports falling to an equal extent, but this entails an increase in foreign lending, and it is argued that if foreign lending increases, home investment must decline (*loc. cit.*, p. 57). Now when the imposition of a tariff increases the balance of trade the increase in foreign lending which is required to prevent a rise in the exchange rate is brought about by a fall in the home rate of interest, and this is calculated to increase, not diminish, the volume of home investment. The flaw in the argument consists in overlooking the fact that an increase in home income will increase saving, so that increased foreign lending is not made at the expense of lending at home.

The classical, as opposed to the neo-classical, argument is usually set out upon the assumption that full employment is the normal state, and in the classical system of analysis the question of a beggar-my-neighbour increase in home employment does not arise.

we must erect tariffs too, is countered by the argument that it would be just as sensible to drop rocks into our harbours because other nations have rocky coasts.[6] This argument, once more, is unexceptionable on its own ground. The tariffs of foreign nations (except in so far as they can be modified by bargaining) are simply a fact of nature from the point of view of the home authorities, maximum of specialisation that is possible in face of them still yields the maximum of efficiency. But when the game of beggar-my-neighbour has been played for one or two rounds, and foreign nations have stimulated their exports and cut down their imports by every device in their power, the burden of unemployment upon any country which refuses to join in the game will become intolerable and the demand for some form of retaliation irresistible. The popular view that tariffs must be answered by tariffs has therefore much practical force, though the question still remains open from which suit in any given circumstances it is wisest to play a card.

Exchange depreciation and a reduction in the level of money wages lead to an increase in the balance of trade, in the manner which has already been discussed,[7] provided that each stands above the optimum level.[8] A subsidy to exports will increase the balance of trade provided that foreign demand has an elasticity greater than unity,[9] while restriction of imports by quotas will increase the balance of trade provided that home demand has an elasticity greater than unity. These four expedients are thus all limited in their scope. A tariff reduces the volume of imports, and tends to reduce their foreign price, even when home demand is inelastic.

---

[6] Beveridge, *op. cit.*, p. 110.

[7] See page 87.

[8] See p. 95.

[9] When the foreign demand is inelastic a tax on exports (as in Germany in 1922) or restriction of output (as in many raw-material-producing countries in recent years) will increase the balance of trade (cf. p. 95), while at the same time reducing the amount of employment in the export industries, and increasing the ratio of profits to wages in them. In these circumstances, therefore, an induced increase in the balance of trade may be accompanied by no increase, or even a decrease, in the level of employment.

Total expenditure by home consumers upon imports, including tax payments, may increase, but the payment to foreigners must be reduced. Tariffs thus provide an expedient for increasing the balance of trade which can still be used when all else fails.

We must now consider the effect upon home employment of an increase in the balance of trade brought about by each of the four expedients. To simplify the discussion we may postulate that the funds necessary for a subsidy are raised, or the receipts from import duties expended, in such a way as not to interfere with the distribution of income or to alter thriftiness in the home country.[10] Each expedient must be supposed to produce its own full effect. For instance, it must not be supposed that the influence of a fall in the exchange rate on the balance of trade is counteracted by a rise in money wages, or that a tariff leads to a rise in the exchange rate.

A fall in the exchange rate, or in money wages, causes a primary increase in employment in export industries, and in industries producing goods rival to imports.[11] For a given increase in the value of exports (in terms of home wage units) the increase in employment will be greater the greater is the elasticity of supply, and for a given decrease in the value of imports it will be greater the greater is the elasticity of foreign supply and the greater is the elasticity of supply in the rival home industries.[12] It is possible that an in-

---

[10] The manner in which funds are raised or receipts expended is, of course, of the utmost importance, but analysis of the effects of changes in fiscal policy on employment can easily be superimposed upon the analysis here set out. For instance, if receipts from import duties are paid into a sinking fund, or used to relieve taxation on the rich in such a way as to increase their savings, there will be an increase in thriftiness which will counteract the effect upon employment of increased foreign investment.

[11] If the elasticity of demand for imports is less than unity, there will be a primary decrease in employment in these industries, since additional expenditure upon imports will be made at their expense, but in this case a given increase in the balance of trade must entail so much the greater increase in exports.

[12] This generalisation can be made applicable to the exports and imports represented by foreign obligations if the elasticities concerned are treated in the manner suggested in the footnotes to p. 94.

crease in the balance of trade may lead to no primary increase in employment. For instance, suppose that the elasticity of home supply of export goods is zero and the elasticity of demand for import goods unity. Then a fall in the exchange rate will lead to a proportional increase in the value of exports, without any increase in their volume, and consequently without any increase in employment in the industries producing them, while the value of imports and the output of rival commodities will be unchanged.

In the case of a subsidy the primary increase in employment is in the export industries alone,[13] while in the case of a tariff the primary increase is in the industries rival to imports[14] and in the industries benefited by the expenditure of the receipts from duties.[15] In the case of quotas the primary increase is in the rival industries alone.

In each case, the increase in incomes due to the increased balance of trade will lead to secondary employment. Thus even when there is no primary increase in employment at all, total employment will increase as a result of the increased balance of trade. The lower are the elasticities of supply in the industries primarily affected the greater will be the increase in profits, relatively to wages, in them, and the smaller the increase in expenditure coming from them. Thus the secondary increase in employment is likely to be smaller the smaller is the increase in primary employment.

We must next consider the effect of the various expedients upon real income per unit of employment. Output per unit of employment normally falls off as employment increases. For a given increase in employment the decline in output per unit of employment will be greater in the case of subsidies, tariffs or quotas than

---

[13] While there may be a primary decrease in employment in industries whose costs are raised as a result of the increase in output of export goods or whose receipts are reduced by the collection of funds for the subsidy.

[14] While there may be a primary decrease in employment in the industries whose costs are raised.

[15] In general, the more elastic is the demand for imports the larger will be the increase in the output of the rival industries and the smaller the proceeds of the duties. Cf. above, p. 397, note.

in the case of exchange depreciation or a fall in wages, since advance is being made upon a narrower front.   This is merely another way of stating the classical argument that the mal-distribution of resources due to an artificial stimulus of particular industries leads to a decline in output for a given level of employment.

The change in income per unit of employment will also be influenced by the effect of the various expedients upon the terms of trade.   An improvement in the terms of trade, that is, a rise in the price of exports relatively to the price of imports represents an increase in incomes, per unit of employment, earned in export industries, relatively to the cost of imported commodities.   If the total value of imports and of exports is more or less commensurate an improvement in the terms of trade will therefore bring about a rise in the average real income per unit of employment for the country as a whole.

A fall in money wages, which affects all industries equally, is equivalent, as we have seen, to an equal proportional fall in the exchange except in respect to obligations fixed in terms of home currency.[16]   Abstracting from them for the moment, we may conduct our discussion in terms of exchange depreciation alone, the argument being made applicable to a fall in wages by means of reckoning prices and incomes in terms of home wage units.

A fall in the exchange rate, which stimulates the output of export goods and reduces the demand for import goods, leads to a fall in the world price of both types of goods, and a rise in the home price.   Since the prices of both types of goods move in the same direction it is impossible to say out of hand what the effect will be upon the terms of trade.

The fall in the world price of export goods in the first instance will be greater the less elastic is the foreign demand for them, and the more elastic is the home supply; while the fall in the price of import goods will be greater the more elastic is the home demand and the less elastic is the foreign supply.   It can be seen that if the elasticity of foreign demand for exports is equal to the elasticity of

---

[16] See p. 101.

foreign supply of imports, while the elasticity of home supply of
exports is equal to the elasticity of home demand for imports, the
initial effect of a fall in the exchange rate will be to move both sets
of prices to the same extent, so that the terms of trade are unchanged. Further, if the foreign elasticity of supply exceeds the
foreign elasticity of demand in the same proportion as the home
elasticity of demand exceeds the home elasticity of supply, the
terms of trade are unchanged.[17]

In general, each country is more specialised in respect to the
goods which it produces than in respect to the goods which it consumes, so that any one country plays a more dominant role in the
world supply of those goods which it exports than it plays in the
world market for those goods which it imports. In general, therefore, the world demand for the exports of one country is less elastic
than the world supply to it of those goods which it imports. So far
as the foreign elasticities are concerned, there is thus a strong presumption that a fall in the exchange rate will turn the terms of
trade in the unfavourable direction.

Each country imports a large number of commodities which
cannot be produced at home, so that the elasticity of demand for
imports tends to be low. The elasticity of supply of exports will
depend upon the particular types of goods in question, and upon
the general state of trade. In slump conditions, such as prevail
when the game of beggar-my-neighbour is most in vogue, the elasticity of supply of all commodities, except certain agricultural
products, is likely to be high. It is thus only in exceptional cases
that the home elasticity of demand can exceed the home elasticity
of supply to a sufficient extent to compensate for the excess of the
foreign elasticity of supply over the foreign elasticity of demand,
and in general a fall in the exchange rate must be expected to cause
a deterioration in the terms of trade.

---

[17] Using the notation of p. 91, note, the adverse change in the terms of trade is
$\frac{\delta p}{p} - \frac{q}{q}$, which is equal to $k \left(\frac{\eta_f}{\epsilon_h} - \frac{\epsilon_f}{\eta_h} \right)$. Thus the change in the terms of trade is
adverse or favourable according as $\frac{\eta_h}{\epsilon_h}$ is greater or less than $\frac{\epsilon_f}{\eta_f}$.

An exceptional case would occur if the home supply of exportable goods were perfectly inelastic. There would then be no fall in the world price of exports, while unless either home demand for import goods is perfectly inelastic or the foreign supply of them perfectly elastic, there will be some fall in the price of imports, and the terms of trade will become more favourable when the exchange rate falls. Thus, as we have already seen,[18] for an agricultural country which produces a considerable proportion of the world supply of some commodity, the drawbacks of an inelastic world demand for its exports may be overcome by a sufficiently inelastic home supply. A country for which an inelastic foreign demand is combined with a highly elastic home supply will suffer a serious deterioration in the terms of trade as a result of exchange depreciation.

The importance of the home country in world markets will also affect the result. The change in world prices brought about by exchange depreciation will in general be smaller the smaller is the country concerned, and the narrower will be the range of the possible changes in the terms of trade. A large country is likely to suffer a greater deterioration in the terms of trade, when its exchange depreciates, than a small country, but at the same time it is only for a very large country that a favourable movement in the terms of trade can possibly occur, for it is only a large country which can exercise an appreciable influence on the world prices of the goods which it imports.

The effect upon the terms of trade of a fall in money wages differs from the effect of depreciation in so far as there are foreign obligations fixed in terms of home currency. These are unaffected by a fall in the exchange rate, while a fall in wages raises the cost of payments and the value of receipts in terms of home wage units. Thus, in so far as payments fixed in terms of home currency are an appreciable element in invisible imports, the deleterious effect of a fall in wages upon the terms of trade will be greater than the effect of a corresponding depreciation in the exchange, while a given increase in the balance of trade, in terms of wage units, will require a

---

[18] P. 95.

larger fall in wages, and so entail larger changes in the prices of other imports and exports. In so far as receipts fixed in terms of home currency are an appreciable element in invisible exports, the deleterious effect of a fall in the exchange rate will be greater.

A subsidy to exports leads to a fall in the world price of export goods which will be greater the less elastic is foreign demand and the more elastic is home supply. In so far as the price of import goods is affected at all, it must be raised. The output of export goods is increased, and their price in the home market, in which they are not subsidised, is raised,[19] so that the price of imports which are rival in the home market to exportable goods may be raised. A subsidy to exports therefore causes an unfavourable movement in the terms of trade.[20] In this respect a subsidy is necessarily more deleterious than exchange depreciation or a fall in money wages.

A tariff leads to a fall in the world price of import goods, which will be greater the less elastic is foreign supply and the more elastic is home demand.[21] In so far as it affects the price of exports it must raise them. Raw materials entering into export goods may be subject to duties, while the increase in the output of home goods which are substitutes for imports may raise the price of the exportable goods. A tariff therefore has a favourable effect upon the terms of trade.

Neither a tariff nor a subsidy can normally be applied to the invisible exports and imports (with the exception of shipping services). Where it is possible to increase the invisible balance by means of exchange depreciation without any adverse effect upon the terms of trade (for instance when the main invisible export

---

[19] Services such as transport must be regarded as exports in so far as they enter into the production of export goods.

[20] Income per unit of output in the export trades is not reduced, but real income per unit of output for the country as a whole is reduced by the levy of funds to pay the subsidy.

[21] This is known as 'making the foreigner pay the tax.' If foreign supply is perfectly inelastic, price to the home consumer is not raised by the import duty at all and 'the foreigner pays the whole of the tax.'

consists of receipts fixed in terms of foreign currency), the advantage of a tariff, as opposed to exchange depreciation, is *pro tanto* diminished, and the disadvantage of subsidies increased.

The restriction of imports by means of quotas does not have the same effect upon the terms of trade as a tariff, since it leads to a rise in the home price of import goods, while preventing the restriction in home consumption from lowering the foreign price. A quota upon imports has much the same effect as an increase in the degree of monopoly amongst foreign suppliers. It leads to a deterioration in the terms of trade, while the benefit from the raised price to the home consumer, which goes to the exchequer under a tariff, goes to the foreign producers under a quota.

We have so far considered the terms of trade only in the light of the elasticities of home and foreign supply and demand. Any increase in the balance of trade, by whichever expedient it is brought about, will lead to an increase in home incomes and activity. It will therefore raise both the demand curve for imports and the supply curve of exports.[22] But the effect of increased incomes in raising the demand for consumable imports, and the effect of increased activity in raising the demand for raw materials, will normally be far greater than the effect of increased home consumption in reducing the supply of goods available for export. Increased activity is therefore likely to have a larger effect in raising the price of imports than in raising the price of exports, and therefore tells in the direction of worsening the terms of trade. The presumption that the terms of trade will deteriorate as a result of a fall in the exchange rate or of wages is therefore increased, the deterioration due to a subsidy or to quotas is enhanced, and the improvement due to a tariff mitigated, by the effect of increased activity.

The effect of changes in the terms of trade upon income per unit of employment must be combined with the effects, discussed above,[23] of the distribution of home activity between different

[22] See p. 88.
[23] P. 398.

groups of industries. The beneficial effects of a tariff upon the terms of trade may offset the deleterious effects of concentrating output in a narrower group of industries, and in favourable circumstances may even lead to an increase in income per unit of employment. Exchange depreciation and wage cuts occupy the intermediate position on both counts; while subsidies and quotas are the most deleterious, on both counts, of all the expedients for increasing the balance of trade.

The change in real wages which is brought about by the various expedients is not necessarily commensurate with the change in real income per unit of employment, for wage earners may consume goods of various types in different proportions from the average for the country as a whole, while, in the case of a tariff, the benefit to wage earners of the expenditure of tax receipts is not necessarily, or usually, commensurate with the contribution which they make to them. For a given increase in the balance of trade, the rise in the home price of export goods is greatest in the case of a subsidy, and the rise in the price of import goods, and of home goods which are rival to them, greatest in the case of tariffs, while a fall in the exchange rate or in money wages has an intermediate effect upon both sets of prices (prices being calculated in wages units, in the case of a fall in money wages). Thus for a country whose export goods are an unimportant element in the consumption of wage earners the fall in real wages will be least for a subsidy, greater for depreciation, and greatest for tariffs, while for a country which exports food-stuffs and imports the luxuries of the rich the order of preference is reversed. Quotas, which are commonly applied to agricultural commodities and so raise the price of food-stuffs, and which make no contribution to fiscal revenue, bring about the largest fall in real wages of all the expedients for increasing the balance of trade.

The various expedients have important effects upon the distribution of income and activity between industries within the home country. An increase in the balance of trade is accompanied by a rise in the home price of export goods, or of goods which are rival to imports, or of both together, so that an increase in the balance of trade increases not only activity, but also income per unit of output, in the industries concerned in producing these goods. Now, when the game of beggar-my-neighbour is being hotly played, these industries suffer a decline in incomes relatively to the industries which are not subject to foreign competition,[24] and an improvement in their situation may be regarded as desirable for its own sake, apart from any increase in the total of activity and incomes of the country. This consideration is of particular importance in so far as it affects agricultural commodities, since the agricultural community is in general poorer than the industrial. Any policy which is designed to increase the exports, or reduce the imports, of agricultural commodities has the effect of turning the terms of trade between agriculture and industry inside the home country in favour of agriculture, and so of reducing the inequality in their earnings. Such policies are widely held to be beneficial, in spite of the fall in the average of real wages which they necessarily bring about.[25]

Certain special considerations apply to each of the four expedients. We have treated a reduction in wages as being in general equivalent to a fall in the exchange rate, but there is one difference between the two which is of the utmost importance. Even if obligations to foreigners fixed in terms of home currency are unim-

---

[24] Even in a country so greatly dependent upon foreign trade as Great Britain these industries occupy much less than half the working population, while the Multiplier appears to be normally something in the neighbourhood of 2. Thus a given decline in employment in the foreign trade industries causes an almost equal absolute, and therefore a smaller proportionate, decline in employment in the home trade industries. This is known as 'the problem of the unsheltered industries.'

[25] A fall in the exchange rate, or an all-round reduction in wages, will benefit the export industries even when they bring about no increase, or even a decrease, in the balance of trade, while quotas will always benefit the home industries protected by them, and subsidies the industries which receive them. These expedients may therefore be resorted to in certain circumstances entirely for the sake of the industries concerned, without regard to their effect upon the general level of activity, while tariffs are often designed for the benefit of particular groups without much regard to their incidental effect in improving the balance of trade.

portant, internal indebtedness still has to be considered. A cut in wages leads to a redistribution of real income in favour of the fixed-income classes, and an increase in the burden of indebtedness within the home country. For this reason a cut in wages is undesirable so long as any other expedient will serve, even if it can be brought about smoothly without the distress and wastage of industrial disputes, and even if it can be made equal in all industries so as to avoid arbitrary redistribution of income and activity between them.

Depreciation of the exchange rate has the disadvantage of being regarded as a breach of international good faith, while the apprehension of a fall may have serious effects upon the international financial position of the home country.

Tariffs and subsidies bring well-known political evils in their train, from which the more general, automatic and inhuman mechanism of exchange depreciation is comparatively free, while tariffs foster monopoly by violently reducing the elasticity of demand for home goods formerly subject to foreign competition, and so making the gains of monopolisation more tempting to the home producers. Tariffs, it is true, have the advantage that they are selective, and may be devised in such a way as to bring about the minimum decrease in real wages for a given increase in employment, but actually they are not always devised with this end in view.

All expedients are subject to the objection that they are calculated to promote retaliation; indeed this is the very nature of the beggar-my-neighbour game. Which expedient is the least dangerous from this point of view will depend upon general political considerations.

When a nation, hard pressed in the game, is determined to take a trick, the decision as to which suit it is wisest to play must be taken in the light of all the considerations set out above, as they apply to the particular situation of the nation concerned at the particular moment when the decision is taken.

From an un-nationalist point of view all are equally objectionable, since each is designed to benefit one nation at the expense of the rest. But there are circumstances in which a limited indulgence in them cannot be regarded as a crime. First of all, they may be justified by the plea of self-defence, and secondly they may be used merely to cancel out a benefit to the rest of the world that would otherwise result from the policy of one nation. An increase in home investment in one country tends to increase activity in the rest of the world, and measures designed to protect the balance of trade when home investment increases merely cause a larger share of the reward of virtue to fall to the virtuous nation, while measures which protect the balance of trade when money wages rise at home merely prevent the rest of the world from gaining an advantage, and leave it no worse than before.

18

BILATERALISM AND THE FUTURE OF INTERNATIONAL TRADE*

Howard S. Ellis‖

I. Introduction

The chief peril to a large volume of free multilateral trade in the post-war world may be bilateralism, and the chief problem of international commercial and economic comity may be the effective curbing of this tendency. There are many devices by which government authority or private monopoly can interfere with the course which international trade would take if left to the free choice of individual producers and consumers. These range from the venerable method of protective tariffs to the newer and more versatile methods of under- or over-valued exchange rates, multiple (or discriminatory) exchange rates, direct quantitative control of imports, and sometimes of exports, through exchange control, quotas, clearing and compensation agreements, cartels, and finally, as a sort of culmination, state trading.

An examination of the operation of each of these methods of interference with private commodity and capital transactions will reveal that, as they have actually operated, the device most restrictive upon the volume of international exchange is bilateralism in its common forms of clearing and compensation. A further inquiry into the prospective post-war scene will reveal the multiplicity of situations which may induce or thrust countries into a policy of bilateralism.

---

* *Essays in International Finance*, Number 5, Summer 1945. International Finance Section, Princeton University. Reprinted, by the courtesy of the International Finance Section, Princeton University and the author, without change from the original text.

‖ University of California, Berkeley.

II. Limits upon the Restrictiveness of Devices Other than Bilateralism

In a mechanical and static sense, in which the condition of *ceteris paribus* is strictly imposed, any one of the familiar devices for "regulating" trade can be carried to a point to produce the same quantitative limitation upon trade as any other.[1] However, as has been frequently observed, there exists a sharp contrast between protective tariffs and exchange rate manipulations, on the one hand, and direct quantitative regulations, such as exchange allocation, quotas, categoric prohibitions, and time-period embargoes, on the other. Interference by means of tariffs and authoritarian setting of exchange rates still permits readjustments in the price systems of both selling and buying countries. These work in the direction of permitting a larger flow of goods to hurdle the tariff or exchange rate obstacle than was possible upon the first imposition of the barrier. But all the direct quantitative limits, being absolute, permit no such adjustment of the comparative price structures to offset them, even in part.

On the score of partial offset through price adjustments, bilateral arrangements lie somewhere between the extremes of quotas and tariffs. For while the condition of a 1:1 balance (or any other arbitrarily chosen ratio) imposed upon the mutual trade of the two countries persists as absolutely as a quantitative import or export quota, nevertheless the prices of individual commodities—whatever the ratio chosen—can still show a certain interdependence between the two economies.

But on other, institutional, grounds there are good reasons for believing that no device portends more restriction of international trade in the post-war setting than bilateral trade arrangements. This conclusion comes from a piecemeal analysis of the operation of each of the main trade-regulation devices.

---

[1] *See* Kurt Häfner, "Zur Theorie der mengenmässigen Einfuhrregulierung," *Weltwirtschaftliches Archiv*, Vol. 40, No. 2, pp. 18–61, Vol. 41, No. 2, pp. 190–223.

1. *Under- and Over-valued Exchange Rates*

The most common reason for undervaluing national exchange rates has been the desire to defend or expand domestic employment by increasing exports and decreasing imports; and it may confidently be expected that the temptation to cut exchange rates below an equilibrium level will recur with countries experiencing cyclical or chronic balance-of-payments difficulties after the war. But the very fact that the gain in employment is in two respects temporary prevents it from exercising a *cumulative* downward effect upon international trade. Prices, and eventually wages, rise under the influence of the increased cost of imports, and this begins to eliminate the bonus to exports. But, in the second place, retaliation by other countries, particularly through devaluations, undermines the original export differential. Having experienced such a cycle, countries are more apt to resort to other devices than to launch upon the same course again.

Overvaluation of a country's exchange rate, under ordinarily valid assumptions as to elasticities of demand for exports and imports, secures more advantageous terms of trade than an equilibrium rate of exchange. But the cost of the favorable terms is a penalty upon exports; and, in countries short of totalitarianism, export interests are usually sufficiently vocal, and the adverse effect upon employment is sufficiently clear, to make an adherence to the overvaluing rates practically impossible. Thus, by the latter part of the 'thirties, nearly all countries with nominally overvalued rates were conducting their trade, in fact, at near-equilibrium rates concealed by a multitude of devices. The chances of *real* and persistent overvaluation are meager because of the political effectiveness of export interests. But it should not be overlooked that the persistence of merely *nominal* overvaluation perpetuates exchange control, and the exchange control in turn is the prolific source of bilateral trading arrangements.

As long as it persists, *real* overvaluation, on the other hand, is attended by a shortage of other countries' exchange in the overvaluing country. This shortage typically gives rise to a resort to clearing and barter, which enable the country to command a certain volume of purchases abroad without monetary wherewithal, much as "book credit" permits a prospective private buyer without cash resources to obtain goods against his eventual payment "in kind." But once launched upon bilateral balancing for a fair share of its trade, a given country may find no single juncture at which its reserves of free foreign exchange seem to be strong enough to permit it to risk a return to multilateral free payments.

This may be true even if considerable progress has been made toward reducing the overvaluation by means of adjustments in the clearing rate. For these rates now appear to be an integral part of the whole clearing system: to abandon bilateral balancing seems to entail sacrificing also the rates which have rescued exports from the incubus of over-valuation. Thus the enduring drag upon the volume of international trade is less apt to be over-valuation than the bilateralism which it engenders.

2. *Multiple Exchange Rates*

Where the authorities controlling a country's foreign trade "charge what the traffic will bear" by exacting higher rates of exchange for the country's currency for some exports than for others, or carry discrimination still further by differentiating exchange rates not only by export category but *also* by buying country, we encounter the phenomenon of "multiple currencies" or "multiple exchange rates." While the practice is commoner for exports, it is by no means unknown for imports when the importing country dominates the world demand and in some fashion is able to isolate one set of sellers from others.

Though multiple exchange rates may on balance involve either under- or over-valuation of a country's currency, the primary purpose of the plurality of rates is less apt to be an artificial departure from exchange rate equilibrium than it is to be an artificial *raising of the country's equilibrium rate* by means of discrimination imposed upon foreign buyers or sellers. Underlying such discrimination there must, of course, be monopoly or at least downward inflexibility of prices. Perhaps a private monopoly already exists within the country and the central trade authority merely adds to it the discriminatory feature. But, if competitive firms supply the foreign market, the state must create the monopoly by fostering private cartels, or must itself monopolize sales for export, since otherwise competitive firms would be induced by the windfall profits to expand output and cut prices. Thus the additional income temporarily secured by differentiated exchange rates would disappear through competitive firms' quoting such domestic prices as would, when converted into terms of foreign currency, be uniform for all buyers.

The restriction imposed upon international trade by multiple currency or multiple rate practices is more severe than that which attends a uniform exchange rate which is above or below equilibrium. For, while overvaluation is apt to be *temporary* for the bulk of a country's trade, and undervaluation is *offset* to the degree to which foreign countries follow suit, neither is true of discriminating rates. One country proceeds to exploit the potential monopoly or monopsony discrimination for particular countries or for particular commodities, and then other countries emulate its example. Since, within the very widest limits, monopoly restriction in one direction can be added to monopoly restriction in another, the shrinkage of world trade proceeds cumulatively.

The success of discriminating monopoly or monopsony depends, however, in international trade as elsewhere, upon the isolation of foreign buyers or sellers into non-communicating markets. The very extent and diversity of world markets make the international field a more intractable subject for monopolization upon either the supply or demand side than a single country. International cartels have, of course, been able for longer or shorter periods to surmount these difficulties. But if we are concentrating attention upon what a *single country* can accomplish by means of differential exchange rates (chiefly upon its exports) it would be difficult to find cases of successful discrimination which depended solely upon that device. Actually the cutting of the market into non-communicating segments is the handiwork of *bilateral clearing or payment agreements*, and the multiple exchange rates simply exploit the monopoly power created by these devices. Cases in which multiple rates unsupported by a clearing system have rested simply upon a national monopoly or quasi-monopoly are indeed rare.

3. *Exchange Control and Quotas and the Quantitative Limitation of Imports*

In the present context we look aside from the aspects of exchange control which are already treated under under- and over-valuing and multiple exchange rates, and concentrate attention upon the direct regulation of exports and imports. In this respect, exchange control can achieve much the same results as quotas except for those minor differences arising from the fact that exchange control operates indirectly through stipulation with respect to the means of payment in place of direct stipulations as to the physical quantities of imports or exports. The chief difference is that, if foreign sellers are willing and allowed to vend their wares on credit, imports in excess of a physical quota can proceed unimpeded. But this can easily be eliminated by forbidding imports for which payment in foreign exchange has not already been officially approved.

In a setting of general depression and unemployment, there is no theoretical limit to the shrinkage of international trade which could be brought about by the various monetary instruments for restricting imports. For precisely this reason, unless the general prescription of the International Monetary Fund against the *monetary* devices of restriction and discrimination is complemented by a *commercial policy* agreement limiting the use of tariffs, quotas, preferential systems, bulk purchases, and the like, for similar ends, the Fund will be reduced to nugatory significance.

Economic welfare in the immediate post-war period will, however, be less jeopardized by impending unemployment for many important regions than by a scarcity of men, resources, and capital. For England, this is becoming increasingly apparent, as revealed by the London *Economist's* series of articles under the title of "A Policy for Wealth."[2] For rebuilding the nation's housing, rational-

---

[2] Under dates of August 19, 26, September 2, 9, 16, 30, October 7 and 14, 1944.

izing industry, increasing man-hour output, restoring and redirecting the export trades, England will require a selection rather than a reduction of imports.   Indeed, in the aggregate, imports should increase if post-war planning for Britain actually succeeds.   No extended argument should be necessary to show that the same situation should prevail for the large areas of Europe ravaged by war.   Even the industrial aspirations of Latin America, China, and India need not betoken more than control of the character of imports, not a reduction of their volume.   All arguments supporting the desirability of large foreign loans by the United States rest upon a similar supposition, that during the—conceivably quite protracted—transfer period, the outside world will on balance be importing.   In these circumstances exchange control and quotas will be used to screen out sumptuary imports and imports which compete directly with the infant industries of the borrowers, but not those which contribute to restoration or the creation of industrial equipment.   The regulation of imports may thus operate chiefly upon the composition of trade and only incidentally, or even negligibly, in a restrictive fashion.

4. *International Cartels and State Trading*

Private and government monopoly in international trade in the forms respectively of cartels and state trading and bulk purchasing by governments may conceivably lead to a restriction of the volume of exports and imports conformable to the theoretical maximization of profits under simple or discriminating monopoly. Future developments are conditioned by manifold political and economic factors.

In the non-ferrous metals, chemicals, and electrical equipment fields, private cartels before the war undoubtedly substantially limited output and international trade.[3]   Without direct government support, and indeed without inter-governmental collabora-

---

[3] *See* T.N.E.C. Hearings, Part 25, *Cartels;* and Corwin D. Edwards, *Economic and Political Aspects of International Cartels*, Kilgore Committee, Monograph No. 1, Washington, 1944.

tion, persistently successful cartels are not common in fields where producers are numerous; and thus there exists a certain "natural" limitation. But in oligopoly situations—where the number of producers is so small that each producer attempts to take account of the effect of his own price and output policies upon other producers—the outcome can be as restrictive as in simple monopoly. In many cases, cartels have gone sufficiently far in this direction as to constitute an importunate case for international intervention. In the past the intervention of national governments has frequently *supported* monopoly in the field of foreign trade. A multilateral convention would be less apt to fall victim to producer interests, though this risk would still be present.

In the post-war situation an equally serious threat to free and mutually profitable trade may come from state trading, which does not depend upon international action for its existence. While a really exhaustive monopoly of foreign trade does not exist outside of Soviet Russia, extreme forms of exchange control approached this condition, as in pre-war Germany. State trading in particular commodities was carried on in Switzerland, Norway, Czechoslovakia, and elsewhere. Bulk purchasing also can be made a powerful instrument of the state in foreign trade. Undoubtedly the war has given a strong impetus to nationalism and collectivism. Whether state trading, either explicit or concealed, exhaustive or partial, will flourish, and, if prevalent, whether it will be primarily an instrument of expansion or contraction, would seem to hinge primarily on whether effective organs of collective security and international economic collaboration will or will not be forthcoming after the war. But bilateralism, as will later appear, may flourish because of the peculiarities of the post-war situation even under a fair degree of international accord.

III. The Restrictive Effects of Bilateralism

1. *The Character of Bilateral Arrangements*

Just as with any one of the common restrictive devices which we have already reviewed, the aggregate influence of bilateralism will depend partly upon how widespread the practice will be. But in advance of assessing these possibilities after the war, we should look more closely into the character of bilateralism. A trading arrangement is bilateral when it involves an effort to achieve a predetermined quantitative ratio of the exports of country A to country B to the exports of country B to country A. Since the underlying price and exchange rate relationships are rarely such as actually to achieve the contemplated ratio, the definition must run in terms of the approximate goal. In many arrangements a 1:1 ratio has been the norm; but if interest payments, the amortization of outstanding obligations, or the making of new loans are incorporated into the agreement, a ratio deviating from simple equality may be contemplated with the export balance of the one country being applied to the payment of interest, old debts, or to the making of new loans.

The commonest devices for securing bilateral balance in the trade between two countries have been compensation and clearings. The former signifies a continuous and piecemeal equation of each parcel of exports from A by an equivalent value in exports from B; one-sided balances cannot then pile up nor, by the same token, can capital be transferred either as a loan or as a payment of existing claims. To obviate the nuisance and restriction upon trade involved for an exporter in ferreting out a suitable and available import from B for each parcel of exports from A,[4] clearing accounts have more

---

[4] Compensation in international trade, while not improperly conceived of as barter, has a less restrictive influence upon trade than if the condition of barter were imposed on *all* transactions, including those purely domestic. If the latter still proceed under a free monetary exchange economy, the "double coincidence" required by a foreign barter transaction can potentially be satisfied by *any* good in the entire economy which can be had for money, for with the money the necessary good for export or import can be had. Of course the exporter must still go to some trouble in looking up the available commodity to match his own deal. Aside from this, however, the "double coincidence" means only that the transaction has to be settled, with no outstanding debts, with each "batch" of goods purchased or sold. Compensation thus differs from clearing, not in restricting still farther the range of commodities, but in precluding capital transfers. It should be noted, however, that in Germany a somewhat "impure" type of compensation required

frequently been used.   All importers in B from A pay local currency
into a common account, managed by an organ of the state; and
all exporters in B to A receive payment from this common account
as fast as funds become available through importation.   If exports
from A to B exceed exports from B to A, the difference piles up as a
credit balance of country A: exporters in A then have to wait their
turn to be paid from the lagging importations from B, or else look
to other markets for their wares.   Equilibrium can be produced:
(1) by an inter-government arrangement as to the accumulated
credit balance, for example, by application to outstanding obligations of A, funding B's debt, etc.; (2) by the government's direct
intervention to limit the "excessive" exports from A to B or to
stimulate exports from B to A; (3) by an arbitrary stopping of
exports from A until B has paid off the balance; or (4) by a downward adjustment of the value of A's currency in terms of that of B
until bilateral exports balance.   These devices may be used to
secure a simple 1:1 ratio or a ratio which transfers capital from A
to B at a rate agreed upon by the contracting states.

2. *The Peculiar Restrictiveness of Bilateralism*

Whatever the ratio and *whatever* the method employed for enforc-
ing it, clearings must, for the individual traders concerned, cause a
reduction in the volume and profitability of foreign trade over what
would be realized for them collectively with free multilateral trade.
This follows from the fact that exporters in each country are no
longer free to sell in the best market, but must now sell to those
countries which buy enough from the home country to give the
exporter an opportunity of receiving payment.   On the import
side, it is no longer the cheapest country but the country for which
a clearing balance is available that now secures the trade.   Under
certain situations, particularly if clearing is accompanied by discriminatory exchange rates, a given (discriminating) *country* can
increase the profitability of its foreign trade; but such a gain is

that the transaction produce a certain fraction of the sale price in free foreign
exchange.

always purchased at a higher cost to other countries and the net effect upon world trade must be restrictive.

Now there are several characteristics of bilateralism which cause it to be more restrictive in its practical operation than other interferences in foreign trade. In the first place, clearing is more or less inevitably contractive in that practical considerations usually counsel the complete omission of certain items from the clearing process; and, once adopted, clearings are usually the only legally sanctioned method of conducting trade. To prevent "padding" of the clearing with fictitious items, the partner country requires physical evidence of the particular export or import item; and since this is difficult for most *services* outside the tourist trade, they simply cease to be bought and sold across national borders. The same is true of the transit trade. International trade thus comes to be confined to visible exports and imports, with the possible— though by no means universal—exception of travel.

In the second place, the institution of clearing does not, like over-valuation, tend to "play out" because of the resort to the same device by other countries. Bilateralism, on the contrary, propagates and augments itself. When a particular country finds, for example, that because its trading partners have instituted clearing it is beginning to lose its inflow of free exchange for the purpose of commanding necessary raw materials, it may consider itself constrained to impose clearing upon those countries selling the raw materials. The process thus tends to work in a vicious spiral.

Furthermore, instead of contrasting logically with systems of under- or over-valued exchanges, clearing necessarily involves in the achieving of bilateral balance *ad hoc* exchange rates, with each partner, which have no mutual consistency. The clearing country's exchange rates are necessarily over- or under-valued, depending upon the accident of the particular bilateral balance with its partner, *when compared with a unified rate in a free market.* By the same token, and upon the same basis of comparison, exchange rates under clearing are necessarily discriminatory between trading partners. To this inevitable sort of discrimination involved in clearings there may, of course, be added all sorts of outright discrimination through the rigging of rates of exchange, prices, availability of exports, and other such measures.

It is worthy of equal emphasis that the ratio of exports of A and B, adopted in a clearing or payments agreement, is always more or less arbitrary; and by consequence the volume and direction of not only current trade but also capital movements are more or less alien to the ordinary processes of economic maximization. Conceivably a given country could strive to incorporate into its clearing agreements such a ratio of trade with each partner that the "natural" or free multilateral balances would not be disturbed. Initially the import-export ratios of the clearings would scarcely distort trade at all; but with the lapse of time, unless these ratios were constantly revised, the system would lose contact with relative costs and prices in each pair of countries as well as with the clearing rate of exchange. Actually, however, such constant revision is foreign to the nature and even to the purpose of clearing, for if it were carried through with complete success the result would be the same as if free multilateral trade obtained; and thus clearings—even from the beginning—would lose their *raison d'être*.[5]

3. *Monopoly Power as the Motive of Bilateralism*

Let us therefore explore somewhat further the purposes which animate a resort to clearing. The purpose cannot be simply the *stabilization* of exchange rates, for this can be achieved through other features of exchange control without resort to the dividing of foreign trade into arbitrarily balanced segments. Nor can it be the mere *selection* of imports for purposes of national defense or consumer welfare, since this also can be imposed by import controls without bilateral balancing with each partner country. The same can be asserted with regard to the prevention of unwanted capital movements.

Since bilateralism *consists* in the breaking up of a country's external market into a series of isolated segments, we shall not go

---

[5] If clearings were divested of the contractive features which have been noted, and were used only to even off seasonal inequalities in trade, they might actually exercise a stabilizing and expansionary influence.

far astray if we discover its long-run *purpose* in this very isolation;[6] and isolation amongst groups of buyers or sellers gives to the other party to the market the power of monopoly or monopsony. The institution of monopoly or monopsony inevitably reduces the gain from trade derived by the party subjected to monopoly or monopsony exaction. Hence we may fairly deduce that bilateralism in its common forms of barter, clearing, and payment agreements are in general *imposed* by one country upon another. Though the second country may still derive substantial gains from the bilateral trade, what the first country derives, in *additional* gain from imposing bilateral balancing, the second country in general loses. Of course situations are imaginable in which both the first and second countries gain at the expense of third countries.

If we look back one step to discover the power which enables one country to impose bilateral trade arrangements upon another we find that the most common source has been the threat of a debtor country in current bilateral trade to stop payment unless conditions suitable to its purposes are met, amongst them repayment of outstanding obligations owed to the current-account debtor. It should be sharply emphasized that this power of the current-account debtor in a given bilateral relation cannot be brought to bear upon a particular country *unless* the bilateral trade of the two is separated from the rest of its trade. The current-account debtor in this particular relation may be a current-account creditor in relation to other countries; indeed, because of the long-run tendency of a country's aggregate imports to be balanced by exports, a country will typically have no current account debtor position to use as a club to secure repayment on old obligations. But, *even if its total*

---

[6] In the short-run—for a few months, let us say—clearing permits some trade to go on where none would be possible because a complete shortage of foreign exchange exists. But after the emergency, the same basic factors which provide the possibility of sales through clearings will also provide the possibility of sales for bills of exchange. As a permanent justification of clearing, the "no trade" alternative is fallacious for all countries taken together. But the argument does point to the necessity of international collaboration, since for one country in isolation the change to free payments may be difficult or impossible; *cf.* p. 411, above.

balance of trade were passive, this could not be brought to bear on the aggregate of its trading partners to secure the payment of old debts *unless* that country could deal with them collectively, and this is never the case.   On the other hand, whether the total balance of trade for a given country is active or passive, *if it can isolate its dealings* with that country or those countries with which it does have a negative balance, it can threaten to stop current payments.

Aside from the adventitious position of the current-account debtor, there are other circumstances underlying the imposition of clearings.   If a country knows that another is dependent upon it for new loans, it can secure bilateral agreements.   Nearly every country enjoys comparative advantages in the production of certain commodities which may be very important for near neighbors, and which can be made the basis of a demand for bilateralism.   A large country may constitute so large a portion of another country's selling outlets as to induce the smaller nation to accede to a clearing convention and the acceptance of imports of inferior quality, or at higher prices, than would be elsewhere available.   Finally, to these forms of economic pressure should be added the outright use of international power politics.

4. *How Bilateral Arrangements May Be Utilized*

Having once come by or strengthened a position of discriminating monopoly (in selling or buying) through dividing its trading partners into non-communicating groups, a country *may* employ its advantage more or less justifiably from the angle of international well-being.   One of the more "legitimate" ends, which has already been mentioned, is the inducing or forcing of payment of outstanding claims.   In a world-wide depression, however, this process of saddling current trade with the incubus of old debts cannot have had another effect than the progressive economic deterioration of debtor countries and the protracting of depression.   Even aside from this pragmatic angle, the ethics of permitting the fortunate debtor-on-current-account countries to enforce their claims while export surplus countries, such as the United States, are impotent in the situation, are doubtfully justifiable.

Eloquent chapters have been written concerning the use of bilateral clearing and compensation to reduce the trading partner to a state of economic bondage. The history of German trade relations with the Balkans shows how discriminating exchange rates, discriminating prices, discriminatory availability of exports, sudden switching of purchases, forced loans through debt balances on the clearings, and the like, can be used not merely to turn the terms of trade adversely to other countries but to penetrate economically and politically into other nations' affairs, set fellow-countrymen against one another, and aggrandize the war potential of the master of bilateral trade.

IV. IMPENDING OCCASIONS FOR RESORT TO BILATERALISM

If bilateralism can be curbed, the opportunity for the use of under- and over-valuation and of multiple exchange practices will be narrowly limited—aside from state trading—to the not-too-frequent cases of "natural" monopoly and monopsony. In open multilateral trade, incorrect or non-equilibrating rates of exchange can much more easily be identified than in a welter of mutually inconsistent clearing rates; and in open multilateral trade the mere absence of the gratuitous discrimination inhering in the very nature of bilateral balancing makes the overt types of discrimination much easier to detect. Consequently, the successful operation of the International Monetary Fund, in establishing equilibrium exchange rates and in bringing to pass equilibrium in the balance of payments of one country by recommending measures which are not at the expense of other countries' balances of payments, is effectively conditioned by the suppression of bilateralism. But there may be many interests vested in this institution.

1. *The Position of England on Current Account*

Quite aside from the question of the liabilities arising from the war, England faces a protracted period of struggle to maintain the volume of imports and exports necessary even to a moderately high standard of living. The physical destruction of war will have to be made good; the rationalization of British industry will require heavy investments, perhaps partly from foreign sources; the "social budget" cannot be reduced without sacrificing human values; and meanwhile England has lost much of her foreign investments and many of her market connections. But no nation has more to gain from a flourishing and free multilateral trade than the United Kingdom, nor more to lose by all-round restrictionism. Consequently, the counsel given by some of her younger economists in the direction of recourse to the whole gamut of discriminatory trade devices must signify a clear abandonment of international cooperation.[7]

The pretext for such a course, that the United States cannot be relied upon to maintain full employment and hence that England cannot permit herself to be vulnerable to foreign depressions, cannot be maintained. Discriminating monopoly can indeed, under certain conditions, raise the total value of a country's exports, or, in the face of depression, partly offset the decline which would otherwise occur. The simple exclusion of imports by quotas or exchange control can likewise protect domestic employment. But all of this is achieved with an inevitable toll upon the longer-run economic prospects of the country.

If quotas, exchange control, and the like are employed simply as protectionist devices, the shrunken volume of imports debases English consumption standards, no matter how successful the full employment program at home; and it is difficult to see any necessity for making those policies dependent upon a reduction of imports.

On the other hand, if discriminating rates and prices or clearings are successfully employed to sustain or force an increase in the value of exports, retaliatory measures abroad are almost certain to make the gain temporary. Finally, the distortions in the geographic distribution and commodity composition of trade resulting from bilateral clearing mean that even a temporary gain in volume of

---

[7] *See* E. F. Schumacher, *Export Policy and Full Employment*, Fabian Research Series, No. 77, London, 1943; Thomas Balogh, "The International Aspects of Full Employment," Ch. V in *The Economics of Full Employment*, Oxford University Institute of Statistics, London, 1944.

trade entails a long-run cost in profitability. The *volume* may continue at a deceptively satisfactory level; but the forced diversion from cheapest sources and best outlets lowers the *utility* of the foreign exchange of goods and produces more or less "concealed unemployment" in the domestic economy.

Thus the insulation of the British economy from foreign depressions by protectionist or beggar-my-neighbor policies can at best secure short-lived advantages entailed by long-run drawbacks. Needless to say, the same argument applies to the United States and our own unemployment.

2. *The Empire Blocked Balances*

With regard specifically, however, to the vast accumulation of blocked balances owed to her dependencies, particularly to India, England is victim of a recurrence of the old "war debts problem" with heightened intensity. Service and amortization can be provided only by reduced imports or increased exports. But the rehabilitation of her economy and the political necessity of maintaining living standards of the masses forbid a reduction of imports; and British exports may encounter strong competition from the United States, from Western Europe, and perhaps, over a longer term, also from Russia and other newly industrialized countries. In this dilemma it is not unnatural that the thinking of some groups should turn toward bilateralism as a device for insuring that payment for imports into the British Isles can be made in the products of British industry without sacrifice of the terms of trade.

A sound case can indeed be made for exchange control (but *not* bilateralism) to govern capital movements and to concentrate imports for a transitional period upon articles of mass consumption and industrial reconstruction. There is, furthermore, reason for making a certain fraction of the service and amortization of sterling blocked balances available only for purchases in England, thus entailing concessions by the creditors as to price or quality as a *quid pro quo* for the gradual unfreezing of the debt, and the payment of the remaining fraction of the sums in free exchange.

It would be possible to devise a scheme by which the annual

rate of amortization of blocked balances, beginning at a modest level to allow for England's limited capacity to export immediately after the war, would rise the more rapidly the greater the concession made by the particular creditor country as to total principal eventually to be paid. Depending upon the same concession, the schedule could also embrace progression as the fraction of the annual amortization to be paid in free foreign exchange compared to the fraction paid in sterling for use only in the purchase of *British* exports. This scheme would imply the funding of all blocked balances not involved in the first year's payments.

Once the debt payments were thus by a compromise solution put upon a permanent plan, and adjusted to Britain's capacity to pay, there would be no occasion for her to resort to bilateral clearings in order to force concessions of like character. Thus the world would be spared that purely gratuitous restriction of current trade, for the sake of payments on old debts, which characterized the Great Depression. If, by an offer of mediation, the United States government could contribute to the adjustment of the Empire blocked-balance problem, it would have made a contribution to peaceful economic intercourse in the future comparable in importance to its role in the international monetary and banking proposals.

3. *The Transfer of Reparations*

In addition to the general pressure to expand exports and the special circumstance of the British blocked balances, another element of the post-war situation which may throw international trade into bilateral channels is the collection of reparations. The statement and actual taking of reparations "in kind" enjoys a vogue nowadays which can only be explained as a delusion. It would lead too far afield to argue this in all its aspects, but the matter is relevant to the present theme.

The only absolute assurance that reparations will be raised and transferred is direct occupation and economic control of the paying country. Plans of the United Nations apparently contemplate such a program for Germany. But the occupation of an enemy country is both personally hazardous to the officers of the foreign powers and expensive, and the administration of an entire economy in which hostility and even sabotage may be encountered at every step may, after months or a few years, prove to be very discouraging. It is not inconceivable that those countries which aside from reparations would have an *import* balance from Germany—and throughout the two decades before the war this included the countries of Western Europe which, outside Russia, will be the chief reparation claimants—may suddenly hit upon a forced clearing with Germany as an easy, economical, and safe way of collecting reparations. This was the ubiquitous resort of these countries in the 'thirties to collect on debts outstanding at the time of introduction of German exchange control; a recurrence to the familiar device may again appear to be natural.

It is scarcely necessary to point out that such a procedure would be highly unjust, since it would force those reparation-claimant countries with favorable balances on current account with Germany either to collect by direct action—occupation and independent administration of the German economy—or to forsake the effort to realize upon their claims together. And this is true whether reparations are levied in kind or in money.

But it is necessary to add that, were bilateral clearings introduced as a method of forcing the transfer of reparations, the spread of bilateralism throughout Europe and the world would also follow. Every partner country which found its inflow of foreign exchange cut off by the imposition of a clearing would, as in the 'thirties, seek to maintain its foreign trade by itself resorting to bilateral arrangements with its partners. The permeation of clearings throughout South America and elsewhere would then receive the same impetus from the outside, in addition to indigenous forces, as it experienced in the decade before the present war.

4. *Trade with Russia*

Unlike the situation during the Great Depression, when the chief complication presented by the foreign trade of the Soviet Union was the undercutting of capitalist economies through the dumping of agricultural exports, the difficulties presented in the period after the war will fall on the side of Russian imports. In many markets Russia may rapidly develop into so important a position on the demand side as to play a dominant role. Quite without subversive design, and as an altogether natural result of her buying position and the anxiety of each industrial nation to share largely in her imports, she may be willing and even induced by outsiders to conclude bilateral trade agreements. On her side this may appear as a legitimate bargaining tool; and, on the side of ambitious suppliers, an agreement to receive an equal amount of Russian goods for the privilege of an "assured" position in the imports of the Soviet Union may be attractive.

In fact, of course, whatever the originating motives on either side, bilateral clearing with Russia would deliver her trading partners—on the assumption that her imports in important categories bulk large in the total demand—into the hands of a powerful discriminating monopoly (or, more accurately, monopsony). The monopsony would rest upon the two facts of state trading and the importance of Russian imports; and the possibility of discriminations, as argued on pages 419 and 420 above, would rest upon a segmenting of the market through bilateral clearing. Instead of an "assured" position, the trading partners could be exploited as to the terms of trade and could be subject to various pressures through threats of switching to other sources of supply. Conversely it is not precluded that in particular instances the Soviet Union itself might be the object of these policies, which bilateralism always permits.

In the interest of the individual exporter *vis-à-vis* the Russian state trading monopoly, as well as the interest of Russia in a flourishing multilateral trade and in a peaceful world, it is essential that bilateralism should not develop in Russian trade. Most of the proposals brought forward to date are altogether impotent to prevent this outcome. A pledge on the side of the state trading monopoly to "be guided by commercial principles," while perhaps a legitimate part of trade agreements with Russia, does nothing to realize this end; and, besides, discriminating monopsony cannot itself be denied the character of a "commercial principle." In some quarters implicit faith is put in global purchase commitments by Russia. Even if the problem were one of inducing Russia to purchase a certain minimum from the outside world, this proposal is naive in its assumption that Russian policy as to autarky *versus* articulation in the world economy could be influenced by mere minimum purchase agreements.

The only really effective method to protect the relatively defenseless trader in capitalistic countries confronting the Russian purchasing Leviathan would be an international agreement allocating Russian imports by countries. This suggestion has been made by Gerschenkron but in rather too modest and cautious a manner.[8] The device, as any system of market allocation resting upon relative shares in some base period, must suffer from a certain arbitrariness, and must be made subject to occasional revision. Yet it would effectively prevent the bargaining, through which exports of individual countries to Russia are determined, from becoming exclusively bilateral. Multilateral agreement, however painfully achieved, would work toward a genuinely multilateral pattern, and this would establish the best guarantee against discrimination either by or against the Soviet Union. In the course of time, with the progress of peaceful trade with the Soviet economy and with a gradual improvement of world trade in volume and in multilateral character, the governance of Russian trade by international agreement might be terminated.

5. *An Aggressive Export Policy on the Part of the United States*

The traditional and presumably permanent policy of the United States is opposed to discriminatory foreign trade practices in general and to exchange control and bilateral payment arrangements in particular. Yet we must be on guard lest our zeal in pressing exports and foreign loans for the sake of domestic employment lead directly or indirectly to these practices.

An effort to sustain exports at the $14.5 billion annual level

---

[8] Alexander Gerschenkron, *Economic Relations with the U.S.S.R.*, The Committee on International Policy, New York, 1945, pp. 37–41.

achieved in our war effort could scarcely be successful without risk of this sort.[9] If we accept the Department of Commerce projection of imports, $6.3 billion annually, for a virtual full employment economy with a gross national product of $175 billion, the export balance to be covered by gold imports, gifts, and loans would run close to $8 billion each year. The Department of Commerce estimate of imports at full employment rests upon the assumption of unchanged tariffs. If the level of our tariffs were substantially lowered, our imports would undoubtedly expand. Sometimes it is argued that this expansion would be slight because of the inelasticity of demand by the United States for imported goods. A recent study by Hans Adler argues that, when imports are separated into dutiable and non-dutiable, tariffs appear to keep out those commodities which are most elastic with reference to price.[10] But even making allowance for this fact, it would be difficult to imagine an expansion of imports, through tariff reductions, by as much as a billion dollars, and hence exports at the 1944 level would still involve an export balance of $7 billion or more.

For a time after the war, perhaps two or three years, it would not be unreasonable if substantial export balances from this country were financed by gifts and by our taking gold. On humanitarian grounds and even for our own illuminated long-run self-interest we should give generously toward the relief and reconstruction of foreign countries devastated by war. Furthermore we can reasonably, for a limited time, provide exports for these purposes to countries able to make payment in gold from existing stocks or new production.

Over a longer term, however, neither gifts nor gold imports

---

[9] The testimony of Lauchlin Currie before a House subcommittee (see "Trade Policies after Victory," *Foreign Commerce Weekly*, October 28, 1944, pp. 3–7, 37–38) seems to imply as desirable, but does not explicitly espouse as the objective for the post-war period, the continuance of war-time levels of exports. Memoranda in various government agencies frequently take this level as the one implied by domestic full employment.

[10] *See* J. Hans Adler, "United States Import Demand During the Inter-war Period," *American Economic Review*, June, 1945.

can be justified. Rather than demoralize foreign countries and international standards of solvency and probity by gifts or gifts concealed as loans, it would be preferable—if this were the only workable alternative—to expend the sums as domestic consumption or production subsidies to provide a national income necessary to full employment. And again—if this were the only workable alternative—it would be preferable to have recourse to these same domestic expenditures rather than secure employment through exports paid for only in gold. For in the latter event we should be acquiring an asset of complete worthlessness to ourselves, so that we might as well have made a gift; while the outside world as a whole is "worse off," relatively to the gift situation, by the amount of real resources devoted to gold production.

Gifts and gold are thus very shabby "solutions" of the problem of ordering our post-war international trade to maintain our domestic employment. Foreign loans by the United States are better, and they are just as much better as some yield is better than none. Given the present state of banker and popular psychology, it is probably most necessary to emphasize the extent to which American foreign loans can contribute to foreign productivity, to the profitable use of our capital and manpower, and to peaceful economic intercourse and progress for all nations. There can be little doubt that the extent of these beneficial capital movements would far exceed the amount of foreign loans on purely private initiative. It is not within the power of the private investor to judge the long-range productivity of investments within foreign economies where the success of the individual project is conditioned by its articulation in a very inclusive plan of national development. Nor can the private investor be expected to assume the added political risks of foreign investment without some offsetting guarantees by his own government.

Nevertheless it is also necessary to point to limits to a program of supporting our domestic employment through foreign loans—limits indeed which are additional to the requirement that even to be a *loan* the foreign use of the funds must provide for the service and amortization of the debt. An effort to maintain a "full employment" level of exports of $14.5 billion by loans of anything approaching $7 billion annually—ruling out the gifts and gold "solutions"—appears to be not only practically difficult to conceive in view of our previous maximum on foreign loans of $1.2 billion in 1928 but also dangerous from the viewpoint of the present analysis—the development of trade along bilateral and discriminatory lines.

The first danger lies within ourselves. As the volume of our new annual foreign lending increased, opposition to "spending" abroad against "spending" at home would increase, probably in a geometric progression. Parallel to this the demand would be more and more insistent that we assure the accrual of these expenditures to the demand for *our own* products by means of *tied loans*. In practical politics this would mean that loans would tend to depart farther from the *general* loan, contemplated, in the main, by the proposed International Development Bank, toward the tied loans made by the Export-Import Bank. Not only would multilateralism yield to bilateralism and a restrictive element be fastened upon trade; but also, intensifying the adverse effects, loans would shift from a broad developmental character to a narrow *ad hoc* type promising less in the aggregate and in the longer run.

The second danger would arise from the probable reaction of foreign countries to an enormous program of American foreign lending. To protect their domestic and foreign markets from the wave of American goods, the natural recourse would be to a heightening of tariffs, reducing of quotas, and the retaining or introducing of bilateral agreements. A mere government embargo upon our loans would afford a given country no immunity from the dislocations produced by our exports, since American loans elsewhere would increase the productive capacity of *other* countries and their export capacity.

The foregoing argument does not signify that universal disaster would attend an orderly development of capital-poor countries by means of American capital exports. On the contrary, this is a natural and mutually beneficial development which should be facilitated, as will be argued more fully presently. It does imply, however, that large American loans signify large American exports which in some products and for some areas will undercut the markets of other countries.   The problem is one of adverse initial impact, adjustment, and eventual equilibrium.   For this reason we cannot assume that immediately after the war the United States can switch its exports in undiminished volume from war to peacetime goods without adverse effects upon the export capacity and hence the economic viability of such a country as England.   If, instead of loans of $7 billion, we were to export capital to a half or third of this magnitude, the strain of adjustment would be vastly diminished; our exports would then be absorbed into the productive apparatus of foreign economies without at the same time competing too severely with their output.

The achievement of full employment is a process of adjustment. Exports from the United States contribute to our employment, it is true.   But, even if we finance our exports by loans, there is a point past which we are thrusting the adjustments necessary to our full employment upon the shoulders of other nations.

V. The Means of Preventing Bilateralism

We have seen that bilateralism involves interferences with foreign trade which are not only particularly restrictive but also restrictive in ways which are purely gratuitous so far as concerns the legitimate ends of government regulation.   We have seen also that very powerful forces will exist after the war tending to thrust trade into bilateral channels.   What steps can be taken to prevent this unfortunate turn of events?

1. *Proscription of Bilateral Trade Agreements*

The legitimate purposes of exchange control, such as the prevention of capital flight, stabilization of exchange rates, and the selective control of imports, do not require bilateral clearing or barter arrangements.   As an earlier section has shown, the real *raison d'être* of bilateralism is discriminating monopoly.   Now there are not lacking apologists for bilateralism on precisely these grounds, the application invariably being made for the benefit of countries needing to develop or restore their industries.   But this position cannot be defended.   In the first place, if the economically weak are accorded the use of this weapon there is no dividing line in an array of nations according to their wealth or power at which it is possible to call a halt. In fact, the practice, once admitted, is bound to spread as it did in the 'thirties; and as soon as the relatively strong countries also resort to discriminatory monopoly, the weaker countries will find themselves in an *absolutely* weaker position than if this course had not been set. Their relative position is no better, and they share in a world trade which is now smaller.

Secondly, it is difficult or next to impossible for one country to withdraw from a system of clearings, for at no single juncture will it believe that, by "letting down the bars" to free multilateral trade, it can derive sufficient foreign exchange to meet its import needs. Even Austria, which over the years 1933–1935 managed to remove other elements of exchange control, could not do away with them.

For these reasons the International Monetary Fund proposed at Bretton Woods is deficient upon a crucial issue. As it now stands, the Fund does indeed pledge signatory countries not to "impose restrictions on the making of payments and transfers for current international transactions" (Art. VIII, Sec. 2, a) and not to "engage in any discriminatory currency arrangements or multiple currency practices" (Art. VIII, Sec. 3); and these presumably include bilateral clearings. But provision is made for a transition period of somewhat indeterminate length during which these practices are permitted; and there is no clause preventing a country from construing the exchange control permitted in Article VII, for purposes of rationing a scarce currency, so as to include also the use of bilateral clearings. Clearings should simply have been categorically proscribed as of the date when the Fund agreement would go into effect. Lacking such a clause in the Fund, there would be every reason for providing in a Multilateral Commercial Policy Agreement, which has an importance paramount with the monetary arrangement, that all clearings shall be terminated as of a definite date not many months after the signing of the pact. Bilateralism, like military armaments, is something which in the nature of the case cannot be abandoned by individual nations *seriatim*, but only in concert and simultaneously.

2. *Strengthening of Weak Balance-of-Payments Countries*

While the only way effectively to abolish the gratuitous restriction and the inevitable discrimination of bilateralism is to proscribe the practice, it would be folly to stop with a merely negative action. Clearings arise and persist not only from a desire to secure for a nation the adventitious gains of monopoly but also from desperation resting upon deep-seated economic difficulties.

One of these may be an improper rate of exchange—usually one too high for equilibrium in the balance of payments. The experience of the 'thirties, however, reveals that there are at least three circumstances which make it impossible to rely upon individual countries for the correction of improper rates. One is the perennial temptation to engage in the "exporting of unemployment" by reducing the foreign value of the country's currency below its true or equilibrium value. Another is the attending temptation for other countries damaged by this undercutting to follow suit, whereas international equilibrium requires the correction of the original excessive devaluation. A third is reliance upon drastic devaluation in some cases where the elasticities of demand for exports and imports would indicate that no improvement in the balance of payments can be expected from minor exchange rate adjustment.[11] In all of these cases the *only* real guarantee against a purposeless devaluation cycle is an international monetary authority with power to veto inappropriate devaluation.

Complementing this veto, however, the authority should be able to bring pressure upon an individual country to make internal adjustments necessary to correct balance-of-payments disequilibrium. For the weak currency countries this will characteristically mean the curbing of inflationary price tendencies, resting perhaps upon inflationary fiscal or wage policies. For strong currency countries it will mean a checking of deflation, a lowering of import duties, or encouragement of long-term foreign loans. Pressure

---

[11] As, for example, inelasticity of home demand for foreign goods and inelasticity (in both cases with respect to price) of foreign demand for home goods, except for drastic devaluations.

can be exerted, as proposed in the International Monetary Fund, through withholding use of the authority's capital resources or by expulsion from the multilateral monetary organization. At the same time, the short-term emergency credits of the authority provide a means of tiding over seasonal or transitional balance-of-payments difficulties and the losses of reserves which continue while corrective action is being taken.

But currency difficulties cannot be cured fundamentally on the basis of an insecure national economy. The experience of the Great Depression has left an indelible impression that for countries dependent upon one or perhaps two or three export staples a safe international position requires a diversification of the country's economy. During the years 1929–1933, over 50 per cent of the gold lost from monetary reserves throughout the world came from extra-European raw-material exporting countries, and a very large part of the remainder came from European countries in the same category. If bilateralism is to be avoided in the future, the United States must provide large amounts of capital for the industrialization of backward countries as well as for the rehabilitation and rationalization of industry in countries wasted by war. As indicated in an earlier paragraph, capital exports of $2 or $3 billion *per annum*—two or three times the magnitude of our largest outflow hitherto—could be expected as a part of a high-income economy in the United States, provided the political risks of foreign investment in the uncertain post-war world were assumed through guarantees by an international bank.

3. *Establishment of an International Trade Authority*

We have suggested that bilateral trading will present itself as a powerful but dangerous weapon—if the economic battle is to be fought out by each nation on its own—in the cases of Britain's export problem, her blocked balances, the collection of German reparations, and conducting of trade with Russia. To these should be added the universal desire of backward countries to "manage their economies" away from dependence upon raw-material exports. The temptation in these cases to resort to manipulation of foreign trade is particularly strong, since the more orthodox remedies such as borrowing from abroad may be regarded—whether rightly or wrongly—as fraught with the danger of foreign exploitation and even intervention.

Thus the dangers of bilateralism are very real in the post-war scene. To cope with these dangers a strong and concerted international effort will be necessary. It has been stressed throughout this paper that bilateralism is, in many respects, the most objectionable form of restraint placed on international trade. But to say this does not minimize the damage inflicted on foreign trade by other devices from the arsenal of protectionism and discrimination.

Quite the opposite is true. The struggle against bilateralism in international trade will only be successful if it is conducted as a part of a general attack upon restriction and discrimination. In a world where international trade remains in the fetters of high tariffs, low quotas, arbitrary exchange allocations, and monopolistic exploitation by international cartels, the eventual success of the struggle against bilateralism would be unlikely.

The proscription of bilateralism, it has been suggested, should be included therefore in a general international agreement on commercial policies; that is to say, in an agreement by which import quotas would be abolished, tariff rates radically reduced, restrictive practices of international cartels suppressed, and equality of trading opportunity restored by a general application of most-favored-nation treatment.

The final purpose, however, cannot be accomplished by a single conference or simply by one act of international agreement. The next, equally essential, step would be the initiation of an international trade organization. By transforming the words of the agreement into the reality of international trade such an organization could carry the struggle against bilateralism to a successful termination. It is probably impossible to prevent bilateral transactions altogether. But a strong international organization, acting in close cooperation with the International Monetary Fund, will help redeem the promise of Bretton Woods, the creation of a healthy and expanding system of non-discriminatory multilateral trade.

19

INTERNATIONAL RELATIONS BETWEEN STATE-CONTROLLED NATIONAL ECONOMIES*

By Jacob Viner‖

This paper deals with some aspects, primarily some "politico-economic" aspects, of the probable pattern of international relations in a world of sovereign nation-states in which all or most of the national economies are "state controlled." By a state-controlled economy, I mean one in which the major decisions of what is to be produced, exported, imported, lent abroad, borrowed abroad, etc., are exercised by the state (or agencies thereof), as distinguished from a "free enterprise" economy, where the decisions are predominantly in private hands and are made on the basis primarily of calculations of private profit. State control may take the form of merely bureaucratic control, or of direct operation of business activities, or of intermediate types of governmental intervention. The only type of governmental intervention which is not intended to be included in the concept of state control, not a very prevalent type, is governmental interference with private enterprise with the purpose and effect of making it conform more closely with the principles of free competition.

I do not here use the now popular term of planned economy because there is no common understanding among users of the term as to how much—or for that matter what kind—of govern-

* *American Economic Review*, Volume XXXIV, Supplement (March 1944), pages 315–329. Reprinted by the courtesy of the *American Economic Review* and the author.

‖ Princeton University.

‡ The following article is reprinted without significant change from the original text.

mental control of the economic process it implies. It is essential for my argument that by a state-controlled economy be understood one in which the extent of state control goes much farther than it did, say, in the United States, England, France, Sweden, or Canada, in the twenties or even in the thirties, although what I have to say has implications for any substantial degree of substitution of decisions of state for decisions of (small or moderate-scale) private enterprisers. But there is one point which recurs in the recent literature on national planning on which something needs to be said here. To assuage the fears of those who find a menace to peace or prosperity or freedom in the extension of state-power over economic activity, exponents of national planning sometimes say that "the real issue" is not how much economic interference by governments but what kind of interference and for what purpose. I must insist that both questions raise real issues, that the kind and the purpose of the interference depend in large part on the degree of interference and that this paper is largely concerned with the kind of interference which tends to result in the international sphere when the degree of interference is substantial.

I have already dealt elsewhere and at some length with the technical economic problems arising for free-enterprise economies in their trade relations with national economies whose foreign trade is state controlled,[1] and I will not deal with these problems in this paper.

Whatever differences in the pattern of international relations should be expected to exist as between, on the one hand, a world of free-enterprise economies and, on the other hand, a world of state-controlled economies would be mostly the consequence of the

---

[1] "Trade Relations Between Free-Market and Controlled Economies," *League of Nations Publications, II. Economic and Financial*, 1943, II, A. 4. Acknowledgment of my authorship and an appropriate disclaimer on behalf of the League of Nations of responsibility for the specific contents of the memorandum can be found in Dr. A. Loveday's Preface. In the case of this paper, also, the views expressed are to be taken as the purely personal views of the writer, and as not in any way involving in responsibility for them any institution or agency with which he may now be or may at any time in the past have been connected.

differences in the types of behavior in the field of international relations, as between private enterprise, on the one hand, and governments conducting or directing economic activity, on the other hand. Both theoretical analysis of the nature and mode of operation of private enterprise as compared to government activity and historical evidence disclose certain differences in the two types of behavior.

1. Private enterprise, as such, is normally nonpatriotic, while government is automatically patriotic. The only important exceptions to this rule are to be found in the behavior of certain hermaphroditic corporations, which in form are more or less routine instances of profit-seeking private business, but in mode of operation are only with some difficulty distinguishable from governmental agencies. Such were some of the chartered trading companies of the Mercantilist period. In more recent times, such is the Bank of England, and such was the British East Africa Company, which, set up as a corporation to earn dividends for its shareholders, sank much of its proprietors' capital in the extension of territory for the British flag to fly over. Giant private corporations in general tend to acquire institutional objectives other than their proper ones of maximizing their shareholders' profits. These objectives occasionally have or seem to have a patriotic character, but it may generally be safely assumed in such cases that they have not been adopted by the corporations on their own initiative or of their own free will but have been accepted under government coercion, real or imagined or anticipated. Perhaps I should explain that for present purposes I will take "patriotic" activity to mean the deliberate utilization of privately-owned resources by the owners, at financial cost to themselves, to serve national ends of power, prestige, or prosperity.

It follows that the pattern of international economic relations will be much less influenced by the operation of national power and national prestige considerations in a world of free-enterprise economies than in a world of state-operated national economies. This "denationalized" character of private business is of course an ancient phenomenon. It was probably carried furthest during the golden age of freedom of "free enterprise" from governmental control in the middle of the nineteenth century.   It was carried far, however, even during the Mercantilist period, which, in the matters dealt with in this paper, is closest to our present age and trends of all past periods.   Under Mercantilism, there were important branches of industry and commerce where the state held a tight rein, or even established state monopolies.   But there was also a residual area, even in the international field, in which the legally recognized and protected freedom from state interference went further than anything we are now familiar with.   Even as far back as Magna Carta the effects of foreign merchants were protected against seizure or confiscation in case of war against their state. As I read the evolution of international law under modern capitalism, as revealed from before 1600 to 1914 in the detailed provisions of international treaties, one of its outstanding characteristics was its attempt to build a legal protection for property and for private enterprise from the power activities of foreign states both in times of peace and in times of war.   This protection was even extended to the property interests of nationals of one's own state which served enemy states and to the property interests of nationals of enemy states, sometimes with what, from a patriotic point of view, would seem to be fantastic results, as, for instance, when in the eighteenth century British insurance companies were free to insure the French owners of French merchant vessels against the risk of loss from capture by British naval vessels, or when during the Crimean War the British foreign minister lamented the absence of legal barriers against the London money market necessary to prevent them from financing the Russian military activities against Great Britain.

2. If international business is conducted by private enterprise it will for the most part be conducted on a substantially competitive basis.   The difficulty of organizing monopoly is ordinarily too great to make its achievement on a durable basis and with a high degree of monopoly power possible except by virtue of governmental aid in the form of special franchises, concessions, legal sanctions against breach of monopoly agreements, or biases, deliberate or fortuitous, in the tax system against small-scale enterprise.   Even

when business achieves a high degree of monopoly power in the domestic field, competition from foreign sources and protective measures by foreign governments will often prevent it from attaining an appreciable degree of monopoly power, whether as buyer or as seller, in the foreign trade field. A government engaged in economic activity, on the other hand, even if it is only moderately centralized and administers its affairs with only moderate efficiency, will achieve monopoly power almost effortlessly and automatically within at least the range of operations subject to its jurisdiction. Even if government is itself loose and decentralized, or disinclined to engage directly in commercial enterprise, it can delegate to specially chartered companies, as in the Mercantilist period, the task of exploiting its potential monopoly power. Whatever potential monopoly power, whether as buyer or seller, therefore, is inherent in the economic position of a national area, is much more likely to be largely exploited if government assumes the task, than if it is left to the unassisted initiative of private enterprise.

3. The process of competition—provided, as is generally the case, the competition is not completely "free" in the technical sense —will in the normal course of events give rise to a constant stream of allegations of chicanery, misrepresentation, gouging, unfair discrimination, and others of the less attractive manifestations of the mercantile art. If the alleged perpetrators of such practices in the international field, as also those who feel themselves injured thereby, are private individuals or firms, the resultant ill-feeling may put a strain on the maintenance of friendly relations, and if the individuals or groups concerned are influential may find expression in diplomatic complaints by the government of the aggrieved individuals. Where either perpetrators or victims are governments, however, and even more so if both parties are governments, the sense of grievance will result much more directly in an issue between governments, and the fact that a government, or governments, is involved will give the incident a much greater potency in inflaming public opinion in the countries concerned. The process of substitution of government business for private business is in the international field, therefore, also a process of transformation of private quarrels into inter-governmental quarrels.

This transformation of private quarrels into governmental quarrels is dangerous for peace. This is not only because resort to force is an immediately available instrument of persuasion for governments, and not only because the boiling point of patriotic public opinion is lower where governments are immediately involved in controversies than where either they are not formally involved at all or are involved only because of their intercession on behalf of individual nationals. There have been developed, in the course of centuries, detailed and elaborate codes and routine judicial procedures whereby disputes on commercial matters between nationals of different states can obtain adjudication in the courts of one or the other of the states upon the initiative of the complainant and on precisely the same terms as if both parties to the dispute were nationals of that state. These codes and procedures are, of course, incomplete in their coverage, and full enjoyment of the national standard of justice of the defendant's country may often leave the complainant with the feeling that all he got thereby was the addition of insult and legal expenses to the original injury. The situation in the private field is nevertheless incomparably better in this respect than in the field of intergovernmental relations. Here there is no code—except for the code of war! Except for mutual agreements, of very limited scope and effectiveness, for resort to arbitration or impartial adjudication, the only available procedures are diplomatic process, which in such cases is liable to be little more than a mechanism whereby threats and mutual recriminations can be transmitted in the most polite language; resort to political or economic reprisals; and, in extreme cases, or in cases where the aggrieved country appears to itself to be clearly the stronger, resort to force. The modern tendency to substitute *jure gestionis* for *jure imperii* (or the commercial code for the power code) where governments engage in business is not a real exception to the proposition laid down here, partly because the *jure gestionis* is by the nature of things applicable only to a very limited range of government activities in the economic sphere, and partly because there is a *jure gestionis* to apply only where private enterprise is still predominant.

A close parallel can be drawn between the logical pattern of the political and military power relationships of states to each other, on the one hand, and, on the other hand, the economic power relationships of business firms to each other when they are operating in a framework of bilateral-monopoly-plus-duopoly. When governments are also conductors of economic enterprise in the international field, what results is a pattern of intergovernmental relationship in which economic, political, and military bilateral-monopoly-plus-duopoly are all wrapped up in one package of international dynamite. There is then in international economic relations the same impossibility as in the field of private duopoly or bilateral monopoly of attaining stable equilibrium except by the Draconian methods either of smashing all the large units into atoms or of merging all the large units into one. In the private economic field the instability of equilibrium is of itself of no large consequence except to the pure theorist whose conventional diagrams are thereby rendered meaningless. In the international field where the monopolists are governments, however, the impossibility of reaching stable economic equilibrium has grave significance, for it involves as a corollary the persistence of economic factors working powerfully against the attainment of stable political equilibrium. Transfer of international business from private to governmental hands thus involves not only the economic costs of substitution of monopolistic for competitive procedures, but also the grave political disadvantage of the absence of any code or of any agency to enforce a code if one existed. Moreover, even if agencies could be established to enforce a code of rules, no one seems as yet to have discovered even the elements of a possible pattern for such code which would have some logic, be reasonably fair to most parties under most circumstances, be simple enough to be administrable, and be acceptable to countries which feel themselves to be possessed of relatively strong bargaining power.

To sum up the argument so far, I have tried to establish the propositions that the substitution of state control for private enterprise in the field of international economic relations would, with a certain degree of inevitability, have a series of undesirable consequences, to wit: the injection of a political element into all major international economic transactions; the conversion of international trade from a predominantly competitive to a predominantly monopolistic basis; a marked increase in the potentiality of business disputes to generate international friction; the transfer of trade transactions from a status under which settlement of disputes by routine judicial process is readily feasible and in fact is already well-established to a status where such procedure is not now routine, where a logical, administrable, and generally acceptable code does not seem to be available, where, therefore, *ad hoc* diplomacy is the best substitute available for the nonexistent law or mores, where diplomacy will by inherent necessity be such that the possibility of resort to force in case of an unsatisfactory outcome of the diplomatic negotiations will be a trump card in the hands of the powerful countries, and where weak countries will have to rely for their economic security primarily on their ability to acquire powerful friends, who will probably be acquirable, if at all, only at a heavy political or economic price.

I am aware, of course, that the foregoing, in its tacit assumption that all types of state-controlled economy would, in their international economic relations, follow the same evil pattern of behavior, will sound like irrelevant abstraction or even like willful paradox to many.   Socialists in particular, who have been brought up in or converted to the belief that a world of socialist states would be a world in which international relations, in the political as well as in the economic field, would be relatively frictionless as compared to anything we have known in the past, and that peace, harmony of interests, and mutual collaboration would come almost automatically in a socialist world, will be moved to strong protest. I am not able myself, however, to find any logical basis for confidence that if only state-controlled economies were equalitarian and democratic—which, I take it, would make them "socialist"— that would of itself take the curse off state control.   A fairly extensive search of socialist literature, moreover, has not disclosed to me much beyond mere dogmatic assertion on this point.

Since the issue is clearly an important one, this relative failure of socialists to explore it more thoroughly seems to call for explanation. As I see it, the explanation lies primarily in the circumstances in which the socialist movement had its origin and its early development. When socialism is but an aspiration, socialist movements are by psychological necessity utopian in character. The efficient missionary does not dwell on the possible existence of familiar plagues even in his promised land. The socialist doctrine, as we shall see, contended that in a capitalist world capitalism was the source of war, and much of the emotional appeal of socialism came from the success of its advocates in associating the idea of the overthrow of capitalism with the idea of the abolition of war. That the same method of argument used by the socialists to show that in a capitalist world capitalism was the cause of war might be used with comparable plausibility to show that in a socialist world socialism would be the cause of war, it would be demanding too much of a propagandist movement to see and to acknowledge. As Engels once pointed out to Marx—surely gratuitously—"true socialism is a movement which . . . theoretical impartiality, 'the absolute calm of thought,' would drain of its last drop of blood, its last trace of energy and elasticity."

It is—or was until the rise of Hitler—orthodox socialist doctrine that war arises out of the conflict of economic interests between the ruling classes of different countries. Under capitalism, in particular, the workers, as a class, have no fatherland, have nothing to gain from victorious war. Wars are fought by them, but never for them. The socialists, nationalist or imperialist, or merely objective, who questioned this doctrine, risked excommunication. As samples of conventional formulations of the doctrine, I cite, from the very many available, two statements, one by an English "liberal," J. A. Hobson, who in these matters was accepted as a guide by the avowed socialists, and the other from an authoritative Soviet source, so as to include both poles of socialist belief:

The apparent oppositions of interest between nations, I repeat, are not oppositions between the interests of the people conceived as a whole; they are expositions of class interests within the nation. The interests of America and Great Britain and France and Germany are common.   The interest between certain groups of manufacturers or traders or politicians or financiers may be antagonistic at certain times within these groups, and those antagonisms, usurping the names of national interest, impose themselves as directors of the course of history; that is the actual difficulty with which we are confronted. . . .[2]

The capitalistic structure of the various States and their competition on the world market, the chase after profits and super-profits are creating among them irreconcilable contradictions which unavoidably will lead to international conflicts—so long as capitalism exists.[3]

This doctrine of the purely economic causation of war and of its special affinity with capitalism and its associated class structure was not confined to socialists.   After the last war, in fact, it was the prevailing doctrine taught in American colleges, especially in the history and political science departments.   As I know to my cost, to question its validity before the properly indoctrinated undergraduate "Liberal Clubs" of the time was to disclose oneself as either incurably naïve or a hireling of the capitalists.   It is my impression that economists for the most part escaped the contagion. But this may have been because they were void of any ideas or knowledge with respect to the history of international relations rather than because they were less susceptible than professional historians to uncritical acceptance of gross distortions of history. Even when expounded by historians, the doctrine was in no case that I am aware of the product of genuine and reasonably objective historical research.   For the most part, no research of any kind or quality was involved, and the doctrine was a belated and corrupt example of that "conjectural or theoretical history," that *histoire raisonnée*, which is a legitimate substitute for the objective scrutiny of recorded facts only, if ever, when the relevant facts are not ascertainable even at the cost of great effort and toil.

I do not mean to assert that when historians and political scientists, "liberals" and socialists, expounded this doctrine they

---

[2] J. A. Hobson, "The Ethics of Internationalism," *International Journal of Ethics*, XVII (1906–07), 28.

[3] Communist Academy, Moscow, *Encyclopedia of State and Law*, 1925/1926, p: 749. i, as cited in *International Conciliation*, No. 386, January, 1943, p. 24.

did so wholly in abstract terms. The doctrine was basically a priori, but it was often dressed up in alleged facts. There was accumulated in fact, at the cost of what must have been for some persons a considerable effort in getting things wrong, a set of conventionalized accounts of the origin and motivation of some notorious episodes in the history of modern imperialism, which provided a stock ready at hand of stage properties available for all who wished to present the melodrama of peace murdered for profit by the evil capitalist. I am particularly fond of a statement of the doctrine in historical terms by Harold Laski, because in a single paragraph he cites almost every one of the stock episodes in the repertoire:

No one now denies that the British occupation of Egypt was undertaken in order to secure the investments of British bondholders; and that the South African War was simply a sordid struggle for the domination of its gold-mines. The French invasion of Mexico under Napoleon III was an effort to protect the interest of French investors in that ill-fated state. Nicaragua, Haiti, San Domingo, to take only the most notable cases, have all been reduced to the position of American provinces in the interest of American capitalists. The Russo-Japanese war was, in the last analysis, the outcome of an endeavour by a corrupt Government to defend the immense timber-concessions in Manchuria of a little band of dubious courtiers. The savage cruelties of the Congo; the struggle between British and American financiers for the control of Mexican oil; the fight between Germany and the Entente for the domination of pre-war Turkey; the reduction of Tunis to the position of a French dependency; the Japanese strangulation of Korean nationalism; all these are merely variations upon an identical theme. Men have sought a specially profitable source of investment. They have been able to utilize their Government to protect their interest; and, in the last analysis, the Government becomes so identified with the investor, that an attack on his profit is equated with a threat to the national honour. In those circumstances the armed forces of the state are, in fact, the weapon he employs to guarantee his privilege.[4]

Of all this long series of positive assertions as to historical fact, there is not one which would withstand even the most cursory inspection. Historical episodes always seem to grow more complex as one learns more about them, and I am sure that no one simple pattern of interpretation will fit any two of these episodes.

---

[4] H. J. Laski, "The Economic Foundations of Peace," in Leonard Woolf, *The Intelligent Man's Way to Prevent War* (London, 1933) pp. 507–508.

But of almost all of these episodes this at least is true, that if you exactly reverse the role of the capitalist vis-à-vis his government assigned to him by Laski, you will be much closer to the truth than he is.   In almost all of these cases, the capitalist, instead of pushing his government into an imperialistic enterprise in pursuit of his own financial gain, was pushed, or dragged, or cajoled, or lured into it by his government, in order that, in its relations with the outside world and with its own people, this government might be able to point to an apparently real and legitimate economic stake in the territory involved which required military protection against unfair treatment or general misgovernment by the local authorities or against encroachment by other powers.   In perhaps two or three of these cases, illegitimate profits of investors, even in terms of bourgeois morality, were notoriously involved.   But seekers of illegitimate profits are likely to try to find a foothold in any large-scale operation, and will sometimes succeed.   I know of only one case, of these cases, in which there is even plausible evidence that the act of imperialist aggression originated in a desire to promote the special financial interests of a small number of wealthy men.   The one exceptional case was the case of the Congo.   Here private profit was clearly the major, if not the sole, objective.   But the profiteer and the imperialist statesman were here the identical person, King Leopold of Belgium, and the moral to be drawn from this case would seem to be the general moral I am trying to expound; namely, that it is dangerous to peace for governments as governments to engage in international business transactions.

If, following an example which is not respectable but has nevertheless been set by ultrarespectable historians and other scholars, I were to venture to make sweeping historical generalizations on the basis of scanty and conflicting evidence, I would be tempted to counter the scandal theory of the role of capitalists in aggressive imperialism with another theory in which the particular capitalists directly involved are pictured as for the most part the passive instruments of "peaceful penetration" and in which capitalists as a class operate much more as "appeasers" than as "war-mongers" even when the wars in question are righteous wars.   That this theory would at least fit recent events fairly well I am sure many here would agree.   But even in the Mercantilist period, when the relations between military power policy and commercial policy were especially close, much of the "commercial" enterprise which was internationally aggressive in character was initiated by governments; those businessmen who were not given by government a special vested interest in these aggressive activities were on the whole hostile to them; it was not the middle or bourgeois classes who were the ruling classes; and the aristocrats, who were the rulers, were then, as in later times, impatient with the craven character of the moneyed classes and their preference for peace even as against successful wars.

While I suspect that Marx himself would not have hesitated to resort to the "scandal" theory of imperialism and war when convenient for propaganda purposes, I am sure that he would basically have despised it for its vulgar or unscientific character.   In any case, the neo-Marxians have developed, alongside and conflicting with the scandal theory, another more sophisticated theory of imperialism and war which seems to my meager acquaintance with the Marxian system of thought to be much more in harmony with its inner logic.   This other doctrine, instead of imputing imperialism to the profit-seeking machinations of a few unscrupulous capitalists, explains it as a natural and inevitable product of the *modus operandi* of the capitalist system as a whole.   This theory has been expounded in terms of the famous three "surpluses"—of capital, of population, and of goods—held to arise inevitably out of the capitalist process, and to be susceptible of liquidation only by the acquisition by force or threat of force of industrially backward areas, which can supply hitherto unexploited fields for the employment of surplus capital, new markets for goods, and opportunities for settlement of the redundant workers of the older countries.

This theory, which, like the scandal theory, is accepted by many who are not, as far as they are aware, socialists, is certainly not without plausibility.   There is no a priori reason why war should *not* arise from the search of more profitable fields than are available at home for the employment of capital, or from the desire for settlement colonies as a relief from population pressure at home, or from rivalry in obtaining privileged access to undeveloped export markets. Considerations of this character have, in fact, undoubtedly played a considerable role in the history of modern imperialism. These considerations, of themselves, fall far short, however, of accounting adequately for the prevalence of imperialism and war, either today or in any past period. Debtor countries alike with creditor countries, countries with declining population trends alike with countries conscious of acute population pressure, countries without commercial interests alike with actively trading countries, have engaged in imperialist ventures. Moreover, there is nothing in this theory, except perhaps its assumption of an embarrassing abundance of capital in the aggressive countries, which justifies any special association of the three surpluses as causes of war with modern capitalism or any disassociation of them from the socialist state, or from any other form of nation-state.

In the socialist state, moreover, such considerations should be expected to be given more weight, and to exercise more direct and more forceful influence on policy, than in a capitalist society where free enterprise prevails. In the first place, the socialist state, with its unified and centralized administration, would be technically better equipped to harness the national resources to national policy than would a loosely-organized capitalist democracy. In the second place, the equalitarian element in the socialist doctrine, while it might create an ideological barrier against making demands on poorer countries, would provide a moral basis not available to capitalist countries for aggression against richer countries reluctant to share their riches with other countries. The equalitarian logic of socialism has no natural stopping place at national boundaries. Third, in the full-fledged socialist state an aggressive foreign policy directed toward economic objectives could not be checked at home by an opposition believing or asserting that the profits of the aggression would go exclusively to a small privileged class. One of the disadvantages of the socialist state in this connection, as compared to the capitalist state, would be the absence of an antipatriotic socialist opposition. Fourth, there would not be in the socialist state a powerful middle class with property interests to protect against risks of all kinds, including the risks of war.

The socialist, I suppose, would deny that the internationalist, pacifist, antipatriotic elements in the programs of socialist parties were wholly or even largely to be explained by the minority and opposition status of these parties—and, I would add, to the middle-class education of their leaders—and would contend that they would be as prominent in the policy of a socialist state as in the party program of a socialist opposition.   Perhaps so, but I see no reason whatsoever for such optimism.   Anti-imperialism, in fact, was by no means peculiar to the socialists, but was borrowed by them from the bourgeois idealism of the capitalist world.   Except for the tendency to stress the evil role of the wicked capitalist, socialist internationalism was not distinguishable from the economic internationalism of those "lackeys of capitalism," the English classical school of economics, or of those "direct spokesmen of industrial capitalism," Cobden, Bright, and the rest of the Manchester School, including its Continental offshoots.   Lenin himself cited as a "profoundly true and important utterance" Kautsky's statement that:

> Modern Socialist consciousness can arise only on the basis of profound scientific knowledge.   Indeed, modern economic science is as much a condition for Socialist production, as, say, modern technology, and the proletariat can create neither the one nor the other . . . ; both arise out of the modern social process. The vehicles of science are not the proletariat but the *bourgeois intelligentsia*.[5]

This seems sound doctrine to me, and it is in keeping with it that I contend: that economic internationalism as doctrine is a product of bourgeois capitalism, and is consistent with it and with no other as yet known type of economic organization on a national basis; that the socialists, insofar as they adopted it, appropriated it from their fellow bourgeois intelligentsia; that the socialists found it an appealing doctrine, in part, because of its appeal to and its consonance with a bourgeois world in which the economic interests and ideas of the middle classes tended to prevail.   Even if under

---

[5] Lenin, *What Is To Be Done?* (New York, 1935; written in 1902, p. 40).

capitalism socialists tended to be internationalist and pacifist, that provides no assurance that in a world of socialist states socialists would not be unqualified national patriots.

It may perhaps make what I have said more persuasive and more palatable to socialists if I quote from a prominent socialist, Harold Laski, who normally follows the strictest tenets of the faith to the letter, words to very much the same effect. It is true that Laski here takes a position quite different from his customary one. But on these matters Laski in conflict with his usual doctrines is much more persuasive than Laski consistent with himself:

> A state is conceivable which is organized for the common welfare, in which the equal interest of men in its results is recognized as its essential principle. There is no a priori reason why such a state, if it were confronted by the prospect of a great addition to its common welfare, which it believed, for one reason or another, to be desirable or necessary, might not, if it thought the circumstances propitious, embark upon war in order to obtain that addition. It is even possible that such a state might embark upon war with a patriotism more extravagant, a loyalty more profound, than one in which its authority was exploited by a few. For the very fact that all citizens might share equally in the benefits expected would provide an incentive to victory far more intense than is likely in a state where these are confined to a small number of bondholders or a single industry battling for the domination of a market. The division of the world, that is to say, into a system of socialist states which retained the substance of sovereign authority would not, of itself, solve in a final way the problem of war. Until we recognize that an interdependent economic world, whatever the internal organisation of its constituent parts, is incompatible with a system of political units which bear no relation to that inescapable unity, we shall have left untouched the central cause of war.[6]

In the sixteenth and seventeenth centuries, writers on statecraft sometimes recommended to sovereigns resort to war as an effective means of diverting the attention of their subjects from their domestic troubles. As Dudley Digges put it in 1604: "forreigne warre [was] a sovereigne medecine for domesticall inconveniences." Even in the United States considerations of this sort have been said to have been a factor leading to the War of 1812 with England, and later, Seward appears to have advised President Lincoln to pick a war with some European power selected almost at random on the

---

[6] H. J. Laski, *op. cit.*, p. 502.

chance that it would stop the sectional conflict between North and South from coming to a head. Socialists might perhaps argue that in socialist states there would be no "domesticall inconveniences" from which the peoples would need to be diverted by "forreigne" wars, but I am not aware that they ever have used this argument.

A somewhat similar argument, however, has in recent years been stressed by socialist writers. Readiness of peoples to go to war, they claim, is the result, indirectly, of general dissatisfaction with the economic conditions, with the poverty, unemployment, monopoly exactions, inherent in unplanned capitalist economies. War, they assert, also arises more directly out of the restrictionist tariff and trade policies of capitalist states seeking means of escape at the expense of other countries from depression and unemployment. Under socialism, and only under socialism, they argue, is there a real possibility of international collaboration to increase production and trade, and thus to provide an economic basis for friendly international relations.

The argument has been most systematically developed by G. D. H. Cole:

. . . as long as national production is left unregulated, or is regulated only indirectly by means of tariffs and similar devices, there is no possibility of economic collaboration between States in any form which is not principally restrictive in its effects. . . . States cannot, save in very exceptional cases, come under present conditions to agreements designed positively to encourage trade between them except by taking measures definitely to exclude trade with some other country. Restrictive collaboration is possible, and does occur: direct planning for an increased volume of international trade is practically excluded under present conditions.

Economic planning under capitalism, however, cannot be expected to lead to nonrestrictive international collaboration:

The danger is that, if a planned economy is introduced under Capitalism, it will become the prey of powerful vested interests, which will thwart the intention of promoting a distribution of the national man-power in the interests of the maximum welfare, and, instead of aiming at the conclusion with other national groups of agreements designed to encourage international exchange, will resume the imperialist policies characteristic of the later stages of capitalist development, and press these policies with the added strength derived from the closer relationship between the State and the economic order which national planning necessarily involves. If this happens, national planning, so far from serving as a force for the liberation of international exchange and the increase of world production, may easily turn into an instrument for the drastic restriction of both.[7]

Cole thus argues that national planning under capitalism is more likely to increase than to decrease the economic friction between nations. Using "national planning" to mean what Cole means by it, namely, the assumption by the state of a major role in the conduct of business and the substantial elimination of the free competitive market, I wholly agree with his conclusion, though not with his method of reaching it. But in fairness to advocates of extensive national planning on a nonsocialist—i.e., nonequalitarian —basis, it should be pointed out that Cole does not present their argument that such planning, by promoting prosperity, would promote contentment and peace. The relationship between internal prosperity and international attitudes does not seem to me, either on a priori or on historical grounds, to be at all as simple or as one-directional as this, but I am not prepared to explore this important question further at this time. Cole unquestionably, however, would not claim for national planning under Naziism or under Fascism any greater peace-fostering tendency than for national planning under capitalism. What, therefore, is the peculiar aspect of socialistic economic planning which makes it, according to Cole, the sole economic pathway to peace? Here we encounter again the familiar argument that under socialism, and only under socialism, are there no special vested interests in aggressive foreign policy. Of the counter-argument that a nation unified by socialism might find a united national interest in aggression he makes no mention. Moreover, when he says elsewhere that "the economics of a planned world would resemble in the character and volume of international trade the imaginary world of the laissez-faire economists"[8] either he is thinking of a world planned as a unit

---

[7] G. D. H. Cole, *Studies in World Economics* (London, 1934), pp. 177, 183–184.
[8] G. D. H. Cole, *Principles of Economic Planning* (London, 1935), p. 282.

without reference to national boundaries, or else he has failed to grasp the point that the trade relations between state-controlled national economies, whether socialist or not, would be governed not by the cosmopolitan competitive principles and the economic pacifism of the Manchester School but by the principles of duopoly and of bilateral monopoly and of the full exploitation of national power for national profit.

I have stated my reasons for believing that the extension of state control over national economies would, of itself, not be conducive to peaceful relations between nations, but, on the contrary, would make international economic intercourse, and national restrictions on such intercourse, a breeding ground for deep and dangerous international friction.   I have argued that, insofar as, in the past, war has resulted from economic causes, it has been to a very large extent the intervention of the national state into economic process which has made the pattern of international economic relationships a pattern conducive to war.   I have given reasons for expecting that socialism on a national basis would not in any way be free from this ominous defect.   It may seem, therefore, that I have argued, in effect, that economic factors can be prevented from breeding war if, and only if, private enterprise is freed from extensive state control other than state control intended to keep enterprise private and competitive.   This is my conviction, *for a world of autonomous nation-states*.

War, I believe, is essentially a political, not an economic, phenomenon.   It arises out of the organization of the world on the basis of sovereign nation-states.   Sovereign states will find occasion for friction and for war with other states in all the types of contact, and of state-suppression of contact, across national boundaries, economic and noneconomic.   This will be true for a world of socialist states as for a world of capitalist states, and the more embracing the states are in their range of activities the more likely will be serious friction between states.   If states reduce to a minimum their involvement in economic matters, the role of economic factors in contributing to war will be likewise reduced.   Only, however, if mankind shall establish, or evolve, or have imposed on it, a world political order in which some form of world-authority will have the power and the will to restrain the activities of nation-states, whether economic or not, when they are such as to threaten the maintenance of peace, and perhaps also to enforce upon the nation-states positive action conducive to international collaboration, will mankind have any reasonable prospect of freedom from the recurrent threat of war.   The greater the movement toward state control of economies, whether on a socialist basis or not, the more will this be true.

The emergence in recent years of nation-states which were certainly not free-enterprise states, which assumed the socialist label, and which conformed in their economic, if not in their political, organization much more to the orthodox socialist than to the bourgeois capitalist pattern, but which were avowedly and unashamedly advocates and practitioners of the use of national economic and military power for aggressive purposes, has brought even some socialists to the same conclusion.   I have already quoted Laski to this effect.   I will quote from another English socialist, Barbara Wootton: "the notion that you must get socialism first, after which all things international will be added unto you, is a notion which ignores the lessons of experience."[9]

There still remain the questions whether the extension of state control over national economies makes the establishment of an agency or agencies for world-government more difficult, and, given such agency, whether its prospects of effective life would be reduced by the increase of state control over the national economies of the member states.   In general I am inclined to give affirmative replies to these questions.   But I do not have strong convictions with respect to them and do not have at my command any objective technique for acquiring them.   On these questions, I seek, but as yet have failed to find, light from the political scientists.

---

[9] Barbara Wootton, "Socialism and Federation," *Federal Tracts No. 6* (London, 1941), p. 13.

INTERNATIONAL INVESTMENT AND THE
BALANCE OF PAYMENTS

20

BALANCE OF PAYMENTS PROBLEMS OF COUNTRIES RECONSTRUCTING WITH THE HELP OF FOREIGN LOANS*

By J. J. Polak‖

INTRODUCTION

It seems pertinent at the present time to reconsider the problems connected with investment financed by large-scale capital import.   For one thing, we may expect that there will be, at the end of the war, a serious disequilibrium in the distribution of the world's stock of capital goods, owing to the heavy and unequal toll the war has taken from this stock in the form of destruction, undermaintenance, lack of replacement and diversion to war industries.   The movement of capital towards the worst stricken areas would tend to restore more rapidly than would be possible otherwise a situation nearer to a state of economic—and for that reason of political—equilibrium.   It is therefore probable, and no doubt desirable, that the after-war period should see large-scale international movements of capital.   It is important that in this period of foreign lending there should not be a repetition of the errors committed during the similar period after the first World War.   For this purpose it is necessary that there should be a better understanding of the interrelations between capital import, domestic expansion, and commodity imports than that which was commonly shown by the statesmen and financial experts of the 'twenties.

* *Quarterly Journal of Economics*, Volume LVII (February 1943), pages 208–240. Reprinted, without change from the original text, by the courtesy of the *Quarterly Journal of Economics*, and the author.   Copyrighted, 1943, by the Harvard University Press.

‖ International Monetary Fund, Washington, D.C.

A second reason flows from the strong feeling that the depression which started in 1929 was one of the most important single causes of the war which started in 1939.   Hence all causal lines leading up to that depression deserve full attention.   One of these lines, it seems clear, was foreign lending which went on at an unprecedented level during the five years 1924 to 1928.   On the foreign exchange provided by these loans was based a high level of spending in the borrowing countries—spending for investment in some, spending for consumption in others.   Signs of economic strain became noticeable in these countries as soon as the flow of foreign loans tended to decline.   On the other hand, these signs were taken as a warning by the creditors, who consequently became more hesitant about granting long-term loans, or to renew short-term ones; and this in turn increased the difficulties of the debtor countries.   This vicious circle ended in financial collapse in 1931.

What was the initial factor which started this process?   Was it that well-founded doubts concerning the basic soundness of the use made of the funds they had lent arose in the creditors' minds? Had Central Europe and South America—to mention two of the leading borrowing areas of this period—been "lent up" to such an extent that attractive investment projects were no longer available, and did investment decline for this reason?   Or did the initial causes of the reduced flow of capital lie outside the borrowing countries, and were the debtor countries innocent victims of the stock exchange frenzy in New York?   It would be a hard task to give a precise answer to these questions and to attribute the correct weight to each of the factors mentioned.   But the task would not only be difficult; the exact reproduction of this particular historical instance would also be of limited value in planning for the future. It seems a wiser procedure to take the alleged causes one by one, to analyze theoretically for each of them whether it is likely to lead to such a course of events as was in fact observed, and to suggest measures of policy which might prevent this factor, at least, from exercising a disturbing influence in similar circumstances in the future.   In this paper the alleged cause chosen for analysis is the international flow of capital.

THE PROBLEM

Let us first depict the situation of the country that will be the recipient of a stream of capital after the war. It starts out on the road of reconstruction with a severe shortage of capital in comparison with its pre-war situation. As a result, there is no means of fully employing the working population at anywhere near conventional real wage rates (which may be already far below pre-war). It is assumed that wages do not fall below a certain standard and that there is consequently severe unemployment. Incomes being low, there is little saving and this is in large part absorbed by the state to finance the payment of doles. The situation is bad and contains little prospect of improvement. Without new capital, productivity cannot be raised, nor can exports, which might serve to pay for the higher imports which would accompany higher incomes, be increased. Without higher incomes a sufficient part of national production cannot—except at extreme hardship to the population—be set aside for the expansion of capital. There is a deadlock.

To break this deadlock, foreign credits are essential. They widen the countries' "international margin," thus making an expansionist economic policy possible. Investment goods can be acquired either by purchase abroad or by increased production at home. With their help, production both for home demand and for export can be expanded and employment can thus be increased further. We assume this beneficial stream of foreign funds to become suddenly available, as a result, let us say, of the realizations of certain political conditions. The level of investment in the country rises rapidly as public bodies, industrial companies, and banks are able to borrow abroad, and at the same time the home capital market eases.

The crucial problem attending foreign lending is the solvency of the debtor country on international account. With this problem we shall be concerned throughout. We can therefore formulate our central problem as follows: Given the flow of foreign lending, be it constant or changing over time, and given, further, the service payments to be made on the loans, how far and in what directions can national investment be expanded in order that, neither during the period of the construction of capital goods nor during the long subsequent period of their "operation," the country's balance of payments will be endangered?

ASSUMPTIONS AND METHOD

We shall approach the problem under certain simplifying assumptions. The first set of assumptions concerns the world abroad. It will be assumed that economic conditions abroad are substantially stable—owing to the fact, for example, that business cycle policies are successfully applied. The degree of protection abroad is assumed not to be increased. The implications of these assumptions for the borrowing country are the following:

(*a*) Capital will not suddenly be withdrawn or its inflow stopped, because of an excessive boom in the lending countries.

(*b*) As more exportable products become available at a sufficiently low price, a market can be found for them.

(*c*) Exports will not suddenly decline owing to a depression in the lending countries.

These assumptions may not be realistic. They serve, however, to separate responsibilities. If these conditions are fulfilled, the borrowing country should be held responsible for adopting a national economic policy which will enable it to maintain the service of the debt. If they are not—if, as in the 'twenties, wide fluctuations and increasing protection occur in the creditor countries—it will be practically impossible for the debtor countries to fulfill their obligations, however wise an investment and consumption policy they have followed. It may further be noted in anticipation that these assumptions by no means assume all troubles away.

The second set of assumptions refers to conditions in the borrowing country:

(i) Of every additional amount of income a certain constant fraction (the marginal propensity to consume) is spent on consumption.

(ii) Of every amount spent, on consumption or investment, a

certain constant fraction (the marginal propensity to import) is spent abroad. For simplicity, it is assumed that the same fraction applies for consumption goods and investment goods. It might be objected that these imports will lead to an expansion abroad, and thus to higher exports of the country under consideration. It can be shown,[1] however, that the net effects of these repercussions on the country's balance of payments is quite small in comparison with the amount originally spent on imports: less than ten per cent under reasonable assumptions. To take care of these repercussions a "corrected marginal propensity to import" might be employed which would be slightly below the propensity to be obtained from direct observation.

The assumption of a constant and in fact relatively small marginal propensity to import (somewhere, say, between 0 and 0.5 and at any rate far below unity) implies that:

(iii) The country has ample excess capacity for the production of commodities and services which, for technical or economic reasons, cannot be exported. If there were no excess capacity, the marginal propensity to import would of necessity be equal to unity. If this capacity could also turn out "exportable" products it would not be clear why, given the assumptions, in particular (b) above, these products would not, in fact, be exported, that is, why the capacity would be *excess* capacity. Thus, the assumption comes down to this:

(iiia) There is excess capacity in sheltered industries: building, utilities, service industries.

(iiib) There is excess capacity in industries producing commodities which are of such a quality, design, etc., that, though they are bought by the home population, they are not exportable. This would apply to many industries in relatively backward countries which produce simple articles of clothing for domestic use, etc.

(iiic) There is excess capacity in industries enjoying a certain degree of protection.

---

[1] Cf. Appendix, p. 492.

(iii*d*) The part of total expenditure directed toward the industries mentioned in (*a*), (*b*) and (*c*) is very substantial.

Although it requires a rather laborious exposition, it would seem that assumption (iii) is, in fact, realistic.

(iv) Finally, it is assumed that the supply of resources is sufficiently elastic to permit us to disregard changes in prices. Thus, if investments are made in order to produce commodities for exports, it is assumed that these investments are not so large as to push up wages and prices and to actually destroy the country's competitive position.

The method applied to solve the problem at hand is that of the multiplier. The author is fully aware of the valid objections which can be raised against this method in general. The marginal propensity to consume is *not* a constant; neither is the marginal propensity to import. The magnitude of both depends on a host of special circumstances. The geometrical progression over time produced by dynamical multiplier analysis is artificial and probably rather unrealistic. Yet, even if all this be granted, the multiplier analysis seems extremely appropriate for the subject under consideration. Investment increases, money income expands, consumption and imports rise. The multiplier gives us a quantitative, though of course very approximate, description of this process.

The problem at hand lends itself to a treatment in three parts: investment, operation, and the joint effect over time of investment, operation and the changes over time in the width of the stream of capital. The step-by-step derivation of the various conclusions is given in mathematical shorthand in the Appendix. No higher mathematics is, in fact, involved; but it may be convenient to have two separate expositions—one in words and one in formulae—rather than a mixture of the two.

INVESTMENT

The first sub-problem is this: foreign loans promise a certain amount of foreign exchange per unit of time. What level of investment[2] per unit of time would require this given amount of

---

[2] Throughout this paper, investment, consumption, exports, imports, etc. are conceived of as additions to the level prevailing before capital imports started.

foreign exchange to pay for the imports caused directly and via the multiplier?

It will be clear that a flow of foreign capital of, say, one per unit of time provides foreign exchange for a flow of investment substantially above one, unless the marginal propensity to consume be as high as unity. For the final resting place of all additional money originally put into circulation as payment to the factors of production turning out investment goods is either in domestic saving[3] or with the central bank for the acquisition of foreign exchange for the purpose of buying imports.[4] If the marginal propensity to consume is equal to unity, all money put into circulation will eventually, and a very large part of it will in fact quite quickly, drain away as payment for imports. In that marginal case, the rate of investment cannot exceed the rate of foreign lending. But in the normal case, with the marginal propensity smaller than one, imports will run lower than investment. Taking arbitrary, but perhaps not unreasonable, values for the two propensities mentioned, a level of investment of about one and one-half to two times the level of capital inflow could be maintained.[5] We shall call the actual ratio of the rate of investment over the initial rate of capital inflow the "expansion ratio."

It would seem that the existence of such an expansion ratio was not clearly realized when, in the 'twenties, the reconstruction programs for various European countries, such as Austria and Hungary, were worked out in such a way that the foreign loan should equal the expected budget deficit of the state. As such a deficit is in its immediate effects comparable with investment, this equality is equivalent to an expansion ratio of one. As a result of this apparent misconception, the loans floated tended to be too large, and the burden of the service unduly heavy.

The desirability is often stressed, in connection with recon-

---

[3] Savings on the dole are included in this; the somewhat artificial procedure of the rigid Keynes school of deducting this item from investment is not followed.

[4] The payment of a service on the debt during the period of investment is provisionally neglected.

[5] Based on a marginal propensity to consume of about $\frac{3}{4}$ and a marginal propensity to import of about $\frac{1}{4}$.

struction investment, that the capital goods produced should be as far as possible of such a nature that they require little imports. It is useful, therefore, to analyze a case where assumption (ii) above, namely, that consumption expenditure and investment expenditure induce an equal proportional outlay on imports, is dropped.   It will readily be seen that the counsel mentioned rapidly loses in importance as the marginal propensity to consume approaches unity.   When it reaches this limit, any money spent at home instead of for imports will eventually "leak away" to pay for imports all the same.   However, at the reasonable magnitudes assumed above for the two propensities, an import ratio for the investment goods .10 higher (lower) than that for consumption goods will decrease (increase) the maximum expansion ratio by about 10 per cent; from, say, 2 to 1.8 or 2.2, respectively—a change of quite considerable magnitude.

The process of expanding investment by an amount greater than the foreign assets acquired works, in a price economy, in part through the lending policy of the banks.   The firms or the governmental entities which obtain foreign loans will normally sell the foreign exchange proceeds to the national banking system; they will use the deposits so obtained to finance their investments on the home market.   To the extent that these investments lead, directly or indirectly, to imports, the banking system will have to part with a fraction of the loan proceeds sold to it in exchange for a reduction in its deposits.   But as the sale of foreign exchange to importers compensates the previous purchase of foreign exchange only in part, there will be a net improvement in the reserve position of the banks, since reserves and deposits show a net increase by the same absolute amount.   This will enable the banks to offer easier credit terms.   Since the starting point was assumed to be one of great scarcity of capital, it is likely that the banks will, by a sufficient cheapening of credit, be able to induce additional new investment.

It is worth observing that there is no guarantee that the amount of additional investment which the banks are, on the basis of their reserve position, willing to finance will be equal to the amount for which the available foreign exchange reserves can cover the imports. That is, there is a possibility, a risk, that the ratio

$$\frac{\text{investment financed by foreign loans} + \text{investment financed by the banks}}{\text{foreign loans}}$$

will exceed the maximum expansion ratio. The amount of investment the banks are willing to finance depends on two things: the amount of imports for which they have had to sell foreign exchange and their reserve ratio. Now it is likely that at least part of the imports induced will be effected with a certain delay, so that, at least for a period of months, it might seem to the banks as if a very large proportion of the entire foreign loan were a permanent addition both to their assets and to their deposits. If they considered a reserve ratio of foreign assets to deposits of, say, 20 per cent to be sufficient, they would be willing to expand their loans and their deposits by four times the foreign loan minus whatever proportion of its proceeds had already been used to finance additional imports.

Obviously, such an expansion, possibly far in excess of the maximum expansion ratio, would quickly lead to disastrous consequences. In the course of time, demands would be forthcoming for foreign exchange to pay for induced imports in excess of the stock of foreign assets in the hands of the banks. Unless they could obtain additional loans from abroad, the banks would suddenly have to curtail credit severely; they would, indeed, have to force upon their customers a period of disinvestment, or at least greatly reduced investment, in order to pay off the distress loans, which, it may be hoped, they obtained abroad to finance the excessive imports temporarily. Thus an expansion of investment limited only by the reserve ratio of the banking system quite possibly will lead to an adjustment of the level of investment to the level of capital imports through severe oscillations. Only on the basis of an estimate of the expected import needs (i.e. an estimate of the marginal propensities to consume and to import) will it be possible to gauge an expansion ratio that can be maintained.

OPERATION

The execution of an investment project yields capital goods. These are installed with a view to being operated. We shall have to consider how this operation affects the country's foreign exchange position. For this purpose it seems necessary to consider three different types of operation, which, for convenience, we shall associate with three types of product. The net export surplus resulting from operation will be derived for each group.

(1) *Goods*[6] *additionally sold for export or sold on the domestic market in place of goods previously imported.* Of these goods the entire value added in the country represents an addition to the country's export surplus. This addition is not, however, a net one. The export value added—or the import value deducted—represents an increase of income of equal magnitude,[7] which will lead to a set of consecutive waves of imports in the ordinary multiplier fashion. These imports will be smaller than the total value of the goods exported or substituted for imports, unless the marginal propensity to consume is equal to unity. But they may easily absorb some 50 per cent of this value, the net export surplus of group (1) in that case being of the order of half the value added in the country.[8]

(2) *Goods sold on the home market replacing similar goods previously sold on the home market, and goods sold abroad replacing similar goods previously sold abroad.* Investment for this purpose—or with this result—is indeed very likely to occur after the war, when capital goods in many fields of production are in a rundown condition and the state of technical knowledge is, in the field of peace production, unusually far ahead of the application of this knowledge. A burst of investments both by existing and by new firms for the production of commodities already currently produced, or for commodities of a similar nature, is likely to develop. Investment for this purpose may result in somewhat lower prices owing to economies in production, or a somewhat higher one, if the product is of improved quality. The volume of output may be larger or smaller than that previously produced with the old capital structure. But there is no reason to expect an increase except to the extent that demand

---

[6] "Goods" includes services.

[7] We disregard in this connection incomes paid abroad and any possible consumption of capital.

[8] On the basis of the propensities assumed in footnote 5 on page 465.

has increased owing to higher incomes in other industries. This rise in demand has already been considered when we analyzed the successive waves of increased consumption in reaction to an expansion of investment, or to operation of type (1); and we shall refer to it again under (3) below. But the fact of a renewal of capital does not in itself produce this expansion of the volume of output.[9] Again it is possible that the new operation which is substituted for the old one requires more, or less, labor per unit of output; but here, too, nothing much can be said in general. On the plane of abstraction, then, where thoughts on this subject of necessity have to dwell in order to arrive at any statements of general validity, it may be said that operation of the investments of the second type does not constitute net operation, and that, by the same token, the net export surplus of this operation equals 0.

(3) *Goods sold on the home market in addition to those previously sold, and in excess of the increase in demand owing to the rise of incomes.* For instance, investments may be made to produce durable consumers goods which are sold by an extension of consumers instalment credits. Or a municipality may invest money in public utilities or slum clearance projects, which it operates at a loss without covering this loss out of taxation. This kind of "operation at the expense of saving" may, of course, occur in a far more general way without any direct connection with a particular investment or commodity, when the saving zeal of the community declines, i.e. when the average propensity to consume increases. This, however, would lie beyond the lines of causation we are following here, except perhaps when the reduced inclination to save is the result, on the part of the individual consumers or on the part of the government in its functions as fisc and as savings campaigner, of the successful course of the program of reconstruction.

Obviously, operation of type (3) requires as much imports as operation of type (1), but it does not yield any foreign exchange

---

[9] To the extent that the old capacity was too small to take care of all orders, so that exports could not be produced in sufficient quantity to satisfy demand, or part of demand had to be met out of imports, the investment would, of course, come under the first category.

in return.   The export surplus is a negative figure, of the order, perhaps, of fifty per cent of the value of the output of type (3) goods.

It is easily seen from the foregoing that it depends on the relative proportions in which operation is divided between groups (1) and (3) whether it will result in a net export surplus or a net import surplus.   With the approximate numerical values mentioned earlier—operation (1) yielding a net export surplus of 50 per cent of the value of its output, and operation (3) a net import surplus of the same relative magnitude—there will be a net export surplus due to total operation, if the share of (1) is greater than that of (3), and a net import surplus in the reverse case.   It follows that —using the same numerical assumptions—there can be no net export surplus if the share of operation of type (3) exceeds 50 per cent of the value of total operation and if the share of operation of type (2) is zero; and in general whenever the share of (3) is more than $\frac{1}{2}$ [100 per cent—the share of (2)].   As the share of (2) would, in general, seem likely to be quite large, this puts rather stringent limits on the maximum share of (3) under which operation as a whole will not result in a foreign exchange deficit.[10]

It is now necessary to link the value of output to that of the preceding investment.   For that reason output has to be measured —which it did not until this point—over a specific period of time, for which we take one year, and the concept of the rate of turnover of capital has to be introduced, namely, the value of annual output divided by the value of capital used to produce this output.   It will be clear that, given the magnitude of the capital investment of group (1), it is desirable, from the point of view of foreign exchange, to maximize output and thus the rate of turnover; and also, given the possible output of a certain good in group (1), it is desirable to minimize the investment required in order to keep the cost of the service of the debt down.   On the other hand, given the investment of group (3), it is desirable, from the same point of view, to mini-

---

[10] The limits become, of course, narrower as the marginal propensity to consume and the marginal propensity to import increase.   With the former at .9 and the latter at .4, the share of (3) has to be less than 13 per cent of [100 — the share of (2)].

mize output, i.e. to minimize the rate of turnover; but if the future output is given, it is desirable, for the same reason as it is for group (1), to minimize the investment required, i.e. to maximize the rate of turnover.[11] For operation of group (2), furthermore, the rate of turnover should be maximized, if output is given.

It may be said, therefore, with rather general validity, that the rate of turnover of the investment projects undertaken should, if possible, be large. This conclusion is obviously only a special case of the general economic law that production processes should be less roundabout when capital is scarce than when it is more abundant. This would seem to imply a rather strong case against investment in transportation and public utilities in countries in need of reconstruction.[12] One special factor should, however, be taken into account. Transportation may be the one factor lacking to make exports possible—for instance, when there are no facilities for moving exportable crops from the interior of the country. In such a case, though the railroad which makes transport possible may charge only a moderate rate and thus show a low rate of turnover, the rise in the value of the crop should, in fact, be calculated in its economic yield.

SERVICE COSTS

There will appear a debit item in the country's balance of international payments on account of the service of the foreign loans, consisting of interest, amortization and other costs (maintenance of loan offices abroad, etc.). It will be evident from the preceding analysis that the net export surplus resulting from

---

[11] There is a similar difference between investment of type (1) and of type (3) as regards the construction period of the investment goods. Operation of type (1) should start as quickly as possible, operation of type (3) as late as possible, while the construction period of type (2) would be indifferent. It is to be noted that these judgments are based on the narrow criterion of maximizing the country's foreign exchange holdings.

[12] The rate of turnover of capital was, in the United States in 1937, about 1 in most manufacturing industries, 2.5 in trade, and only .2 in transportation and public utilities.

operation of investment of type (1) will usually suffice to cover this debit item, whereas investments of type (2) and (3), showing a zero and a negative operation export surplus, respectively, will not provide funds to cover the service costs.   In this connection it is important to note that total investment can be considerably larger than the amount of foreign loans on which the service has to be paid.   Thus, if the expansion ratio is equal to two and the service costs are of the order of 10 per cent of the foreign loans, they would be of the order of only five per cent of the total investment.   It will readily be seen that whether the net export surplus of operation will be sufficient to pay these service costs depends only in a minor degree on the service conditions of the loan, and to a far greater degree on the distribution of total investment over groups (1), (2) and (3).   If all investment is of the nature of group (1), a net export surplus in the order of 50 per cent of total investment will annually be available[13] from which the debt service could easily be paid.   If, on the other hand, all investment is of the nature of group (3), there is a net import surplus of the order of 50 per cent of total investment, compared with which an additional debit item of five per cent of total investment fades into insignificance.

The above should not lead to indifference concerning the height of the service changes at which foreign loans can be obtained. Though not the only, and perhaps not the most important, factor determining the country's foreign exchange position, these charges do have to be taken into account.   But the analysis should shatter any confidence that the only or indeed the main danger attending an investment policy built on foreign loans is the debt service of the latter, and that, if the service is reasonably low, investment can safely go ahead.   Quite the contrary is true.   Even if the debt service is *nil*, operation may lead to a current deficit on international account, if too large a proportion is directed to type (3), whereas, if investment is distributed differently, operation may be so remunera-

---

[13] Again taking for the two propensities the numerical values assumed earlier and making the further assumption that the rate of turnover of capital equals 1. Cf. p. 471, footnote 12.

tive, in terms of foreign exchange, that any conceivable can easily be paid.

CHANGES IN THE FLOW OF CAPITAL

In the preceding sections we have shown two ways in which investment with the help of foreign loans can go astray: either the rate of investment exceeds the rate of capital inflow times the maximum expansion ratio, or investment is directed in such a way that the net export surplus of operation, if any, is insufficient to cover the service costs of the debt. We shall now analyze how these two partial findings are affected by changes in the rate of capital inflow.

It would be difficult to assign a definite theoretical pattern over time to the rate of capital inflow. Capital imports are attracted by a relatively high rate of interest. As reconstruction proceeds, industries will no longer be able to pay these high rates. This tendency may or may not be offset by changes in the confidence of the lenders, who may feel comforted by the borrowing country's economic rehabilitation, but may, perhaps, be increasingly frightened by its mounting indebtedness. The only general assumption which may perhaps be made is that borrowing for reconstruction is a proposition as temporary as reconstruction itself, so that it may be expected to decline, at least after a certain period, and finally to vanish, or even to evolve into the export of capital.

If the rate of capital inflow is constant, a constant rate of investment with a constant distribution over groups (1) to (3), and constant operation of this investment, can be indefinitely maintained, if each of them is within the limits outlined in the preceding sections. If the rate of capital inflow is increasing, the original rate of investment and its operation can be maintained *a fortiori*. If the rate is declining, the two cannot, of course, be maintained, if both are exactly at the maximum limit. However, if either investment or operation leaves a certain surplus of exchange, it may not be necessary for the country to bring about a change in the trend of its economic life in order to avoid a foreign exchange shortage in response to a decline in the rate of capital

DIAGRAM I

THE CHANGE IN FOREIGN EXCHANGE BALANCES OVER TIME
UNDER VARIOUS SPECIFIC NUMERICAL ASSUMPTIONS

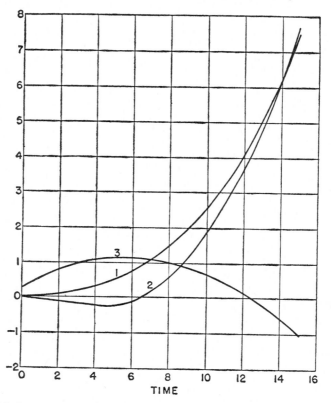

Unit: capital import in year 0 = 0.65 (=1/1.53); this results in investment = 1 for lines 1 and 2, and 0.65 for line 3.

import. Whether this possibility will be available depends, of course, on the relative magnitude of the various factors mentioned earlier in comparison with the magnitude of the decline of the rate of capital inflow. This complicated relation, for which a general formula is devised in the Appendix, is perhaps most conveniently summarized in a graphic way.

Diagram I shows the foreign exchange reserves of a hypothetical country executing a reconstruction program with the help of foreign loans. In two of the cases represented—portrayed by lines 1 and 2—it is assumed that investment is of the magnitude 1 in each year. The assumptions underlying lines 1 and 2 differ only in this respect, that the amount annually borrowed abroad is assumed gradually to decline to zero in the course of ten years in the former and in five years in the latter case.[14]

Both lines, it will be seen, begin at zero in the year 0. But line 1 gradually increases and remains constantly above the horizontal axis, whereas line 2 drops under the axis, remains there for the first six years, then gradually rises in the positive region, and finally, after the fourteenth year, exceeds line 1.[15] It is clear from a comparison of these two lines that, with all other things equal, the reconstruction project of our country would be feasible if it was assured of foreign loans for ten years, the annual amount of the loans gradually declining during that period, but that the same program would almost immediately lead to a foreign exchange deficit if undertaken on the basis of a stream of foreign assets declining to zero in five years. In the latter case the country would be faced by a foreign exchange deficit persisting for six years and attaining a maximum of about one-third of the amount of foreign exchange borrowed during the first year.[16]

It is conceivable that the country would have been able to obtain an emergency credit for this period. Such a credit would, our analysis shows, have been a sound one, for it could have been entirely paid back in the course of the seventh year. This sound position in the long run is due, in the cases represented by lines 1 and 2, to the fact that the allocation of the capital to groups (1), (2) and (3) is such that, with the assumed values for the other coeffi-

---

[14] The further numerical assumptions are found in the table on page 484.

[15] No importance should be attached to this excess, however, since it may well be due to the fact that the income which would be earned on the positive balances shown in the first case, and the costs of the negative balances during seven years in the second case, have not been taken into consideration.

[16] The lowest value shown for line 2 is −0.23 times annual investment. Since the expansion ratio is about 1.5, the minimum exceeds one-third of the amount borrowed abroad in the first year.

cients, the net export surplus of operation is more than sufficient to pay the service of the debt. The capital invested in a certain year thus yields a net balance of foreign exchange for all years to come. Under our assumptions this net export surplus is 15 per cent of the total capital annually invested or, with an expansion ratio of 1.5, 22½ per cent of the capital imported in the first year. Deducting 10 per cent service on this capital, there remains a net balance of 12½ per cent. Consequently, after eight years of investment at a given annual rate, the stock of capital so obtained produces each year sufficient foreign exchange to continue the same rate of investment. And if, as happened in case 2, the amount obtained in foreign loans is insufficient to pay all the foreign exchange required for the unrestricted continuation of investment, this deficit can always be made good from the net balances produced by the operation of the investment in later years.

Lines 1 and 2 thus show that, if all other things are equal, the rate of decline of the rate of capital import determines whether the country will face serious foreign exchange difficulties. Line 3 pictures a somewhat different case. Here the rate of capital import is constant: each year loans of the same amount are obtained abroad. Moreover, the expansion ratio has been chosen smaller than in cases 1 and 2, namely, at 1 instead of 1.53. Yet this moderate investment program under such favorable conditions of capital import comes to grief, and this for one reason only. The relative proportion of groups (1), (2) and (3) in the allocation of investments is assumed to be slightly different, namely:

Cases	Percentage of Capital Assumed Invested in Production of		
	Type (1)	Type (2)	Type (3)
1 and 2	50	40	10
3	40	40	20

This shift is sufficient to reduce the net export surplus of operation to five per cent of total investment and of the annual capital import (expansion ration = 1), as against a service of ten per cent. Thus, though there is a foreign exchange balance for the first ten years, which during a number of years exceeds the level of the annual rate of capital import, the eventual development is downward, and from the thirteenth year onward an ever-increasing foreign exchange deficit contrasts with the positive balances accumulated in cases 1 and 2.

There is one thing which this diagram shows most strikingly, namely, that the basic soundness of the various economic policies cannot be judged from the ease or strain of the country's foreign exchange situation.   It may be useful to imagine the considered opinion which would be given by the international financial expert who had observed the course of events during the first five years. Country 1, he might well find, after a prolonged critical period was tending towards a somewhat more secure position.   Country 2 was still prosecuting its extravagant[17] course of economic development which was leading it straight into bankruptcy; this amply explained the fact that the country's capacity to borrow abroad had declined steadily ever since she started reconstruction and was now, after five years, reduced to zero.   But look at the constructive economic, financial and social policy of country 3!   Indeed, the creditors who did not hesitate to lend to this island of prosperity the same amount year after year did show sound economic judgment.   *E tutti quanti.*

LAGGED PAYMENTS FOR IMPORTS

One important factor affecting the country's foreign exchange position still needs to be discussed.   In calculating the lines drawn in Diagram I, it has been assumed that incomes were spent immediately to the extent that they were not saved, and that the resulting imports had to be paid for immediately in foreign exchange. This, however, was a simplification.   The process summarized by the multiplier takes time.   Between any two consecutive instal-

---

[17] Remark by the statistician of country 2: "But country 3 has a greater proportion of type 3 production than we have."   Retort by the financial expert: "Luxury is all right for those who can afford it."

ments of "secondary" income payments a certain income period elapses.[18]   It is probable, moreover, that there is a certain time lag between an increased demand for imports and the actual increase of imports, the discrepancy being temporarily absorbed by changes in stocks.   It is possible, finally, that imports may be purchased on short credit, in which case the moment when foreign exchange will be needed is still further delayed.[19]   It follows that one "primary" payment of income will be followed by a number of foreign exchange payments for imports at various intervals of time.   We shall consider here only the weighted average of these lags, which may be quite a considerable period of time—say six months.

How this lag affects the foreign exchange situation can easily be deduced.   When there is a constant stream of investment of, say, I per annum, inducing a constant stream of imports of μI per annum, with a lag of six months, there will at every moment of time be an import value of $\frac{1}{2} \mu I$, which has in part not yet been demanded, in part temporarily sold from existing stocks and in part, if already imported, not yet been paid for.   If the stream of investment is not constant but increasing, the reserve of foreign exchange still to be drawn upon increases at the same rate.

In our case we have assumed a constant stream of new investment income plus an increasing stream of operation income being paid.   Consequently there will be a reserve for imports in addition to the balance of foreign exchange as calculated, which will also increase over time and which, all other things being equal, will be approximately proportional to the length of the period by which payments for imports lag behind the payment of "primary" incomes.   This growing reserve which can be used to fill a foreign exchange deficit, as shown by line 2 in Diagram I, will normally be of quite decisive magnitude.   In the case represented by line 2, for instance, the reserve yielded by a lag of only one month, which

[18] Professor Machlup has analyzed in detail how this income period should be measured.   Cf. his "Period Analysis and the Multiplier Theory," *Quarterly Journal of Economics*, September, 1939.

[19] Exports may, of course, also be sold on credit; this possibility has not been taken into account.

is certainly far below what might be expected in reality, would just about wipe out the entire foreign exchange deficit shown.

QUALITATIVE CONCLUSIONS

The foregoing analysis may be of use for two purposes, namely:

(1) In a *qualitative* sense, to provide a general understanding of the various factors at work during a period of reconstruction, or in general a period of capital expansion based on foreign loans, and to indicate the general outline of policies to be adopted in order to ensure that this economic process will develop without foreign exchange difficulties;

(2) In a *quantitative* sense, to arrive at a judgment, on the basis of certain measurements or estimates of the coefficients involved, concerning the failure or success of reconstruction in various countries in the past and to indicate specific quantitative changes of these coefficients which would help to make future reconstruction programs successful.

The first half of this application of our findings follows directly from what has been said above, and may be summarized as follows:

1. A country's investment program may lead to a shortage of foreign exchange owing to either of the three following main reasons or a combination of these reasons:[20]

(*a*) The rate of investment is too high in view of the initial rate of capital inflow;

(*b*) Investment is wrongly distributed, too small a proportion being directed towards the production of exportable goods;

(*c*) The rate of capital inflow declines too rapidly.

2. The first object of government policy should therefore be to keep total investment within the bounds set by the initial rate of capital inflow—if this rate itself is given—and the institutional properties of the national economy, the marginal propensities to

---

[20] Here the marginal propensities to consume and to import, the rate of service payments, the lag of payments for imports behind income and the rate of turnover of capital are taken as given. Changes in these magnitudes will be discussed below.

consume and to import. It has been shown that the adherence of the banking system to a rigid reserve ratio may easily lead to too large an expansion of investment, given the rate of capital inflow. The optimum rate of investment, i.e. a rate large enough to leave no substantial unused balances of foreign exchange, yet not so large as to induce demand for foreign exchange in excess of these balances, can be determined only on the basis of an appraisal of the magnitude of the propensities mentioned and would, for that reason, be a matter to be decided by the Government rather than by the banking system.

3. To prevent a failure on account of cause (*b*), and at the same time to offset any exchange shortages due to the operation of causes (*a*) and (*c*), the Government will have to see to it that a considerable part of investment is directed towards industries of type (1); and by directing both investment and savings it will have to see to it that only a very small part of total investment will eventually be operated as type (3), that is, for the production of goods sold at home at the expense of current savings.

4. The control of foreign borrowing is neither an efficient nor a sufficient device to prevent a failure of the reconstruction program on account of either (*a*) or (*b*). If the total amount of borrowing abroad is kept down below the maximum which could be obtained, the possible investment program is necessarily reduced, but the success of the smaller program would not seem to be in any way more likely than that of a larger one.[21] If the Government should not attempt to influence total borrowing abroad but should, for example, specify[22] that enterprises could borrow abroad only for investment of type (1), the probability of success would have been

---

[21] If the country's reserve of unused resources is small, it may, however, be desirable to keep investment down to a moderate rate, in order to prevent a rise in prices and consequent high imports. If these limiting factors do not prevail, there would seem to be no reason to assume that when the rate of capital import is reduced and, as a result, interest rates rise, investment of type (1) will be less discouraged than that of types (2) and (3).

[22] This policy seems to have been favored by the German Reichsbank in the 'twenties.

increased but little.   For the ability of the country as a whole to pay
the service on its foreign loans does not depend on which industry
is financed abroad and which at home, but on whether the operation of all industries together yields a sufficiently large net export
surplus.   And the foreign exchange troubles are not created by the
fact that expenditure for "unproductive" purposes is financed by
loans from abroad, but by the fact that such expenditure is made
at all.   If the expenditure itself is not controlled, there is no point
in prohibiting the financing of it with the help of foreign credits;
quite to the contrary, the foreign exchange thus obtained, assuming that it would not otherwise have been lent to the country,
should be regarded as an incidental advantage.[23]

5. The rate of change of the rate of capital inflow will probably
be beyond the capital importing country's control.   To the extent
that this is the case, the soundness of its investment program is
also beyond its control.   Therefore, for the success of the program
to be assured, it will be necessary for the borrowing country to
know what it can count upon.   If it does not have such assurances
for a number of years in advance, it will be obliged, for reasons of
safety, to keep its investment at a low level and to maintain a large
part of the foreign assets received in a liquid form.

6. Investment projects which will show a high rate of turnover
of capital are less likely to lead to a foreign exchange shortage than
those with a low rate of turnover.[24]

7. The success or failure of the investment program depends
in a large degree on the consuming habits of the population.   These
habits are, as it were, summarized in the marginal propensity to

---

[23] It is, of course, possible that expenditure of the nature mentioned would not
have been made but for a foreign loan, namely, when the national investing public
would be unwilling to grant loans for "unproductive" investment.   It should be
realized, however, that there is no direct connection between the capacity of the
debtor to pay the service of a loan and the "productiveness" of the purpose for
which the borrowed money is spent.   Public authorities may borrow for con-
sumptive purposes and yet have sufficient income from taxes for the loan to be a
very safe investment.

[24] Cf. however, above, page 471.

consume and the marginal propensity to import. If both are high, in particular if the marginal propensity to consume is near unity, the risk of a foreign exchange shortage becomes very great indeed.

8. Such a shortage may, however, remain concealed for a considerable time, owing to the time lag of payments for imports behind income. By increasing this lag, e.g. by arranging short-term import credits, the Government can substantially ease the foreign exchange problem, not only in the short run but also, if the newly constructed industries are sufficiently remunerative in terms of foreign exchange, permanently.

9. The rate of service to be paid on the foreign loans is only one factor out of the many mentioned which determine whether the country will have a positive or negative balance of foreign assets as a result of the investment program. A zero rate of service by no means dispels the country's foreign exchange troubles.

Quantitative Conclusions

We could arrive at qualitative conclusions on the basis of a general formulation of the problem combined with no more than a rough general idea of the order of magnitude of the various coefficients involved. In order to be able to give quantitative conclusions, however, we must have a more exact knowledge of the magnitude of these coefficients. For most of them this is indeed extremely difficult, as each poses complicated problems of definition, to say nothing of statistical measurement. It would be a considerable achievement to determine any of these coefficients with a margin of error of as little as ten per cent. The question is whether this degree of precision is sufficient to permit quantitative conclusions which are of any value.

In certain cases, where the calculation depends on only a few of the coefficients, quantitative conclusions are indeed possible. Such a case is the determination of the maximum expansion ratio. If we could determine statistically—which would not seem impossible—that the marginal propensity to consume was between 0.7 and 0.8 and the marginal propensity to import between 0.2 and

0.3, the expansion ratio would be found to lie between about 1.5 and 2.2. This finding, though by no means very precise, would be sufficiently so to be of use as a rough indication.

Similarly, it is possible to estimate with reasonable accuracy whether an expansion of investment, distributed in a given way over groups (1), (2) and (3) on the basis of relatively short credits, would in due time yield the foreign exchange to repay these loans; but the length of this period—whether it would be, say, three or eight years—cannot be determined, if the coefficients are subject to a considerable margin of error, with the precision that may be required in practice.[25]

The possibilities become much more restricted when we try to obtain results involving a greater number of coefficients. We might hope that the general pattern of the lines drawn in Diagram I (representing the total stock, positive or negative, of foreign assets at the country's disposal in each year) would be relatively insensitive to small changes in the underlying numerical values of the coefficients. If that were so, rough estimates of these values might yield a roughly outlined but still recognizable shape for the lines. Unfortunately, it is not so. The calculated balance of foreign assets is highly sensitive to relatively small changes in the coefficients.[26] This is clearly shown by the following table giving the change in the foreign exchange deficit shown by line 2 in the fifth year, if alternatively each of the coefficients is increased by ten per cent of its assumed value and if the lag of payments for imports behind primary income, which was assumed to be zero, is changed to one month. Under the values assumed, the balance would be −0.23 in the fifth year, which is the lowest value shown for line 2 in the Diagram.[27]

---

[25] Cf. Appendix, formulae (27) and (28).

[26] In fact, it was found that the result of the calculation was substantially affected by what seemed to be innocuous rounding-off in the process of calculation.

[27] It will be remembered that the unit of measurement is the annual rate of investment assumed in the case represented by line 2.

CHANGE IN FOREIGN EXCHANGE BALANCE SHOWN BY LINE 2 IN DIAGRAM I AT THE END OF THE FIFTH YEAR AS A RESULT OF A TEN PER CENT INCREASE IN VARIOUS COEFFICIENTS

Coefficient	Value Assumed[1]	Value Assumed Plus 10%	Approximate Change in Balance Calculated[2]
Marginal propensity to consume.............	0.70	0.770	−0.85
Marginal propensity to import..............	0.30	0.330	−0.52
Expansion ratio..........................	1.53	1.68	−0.13
Ratio of turnover of capital.................	1.00	1.10	+0.22
Investment of type (1) ⎫	50	55[3]	+0.40
Investment of type (2) ⎬ as per cent of total...	40	44[3]	−0.15
Investment of type (3) ⎭	10	11[3]	−0.21
Service charges as per cent of capital import.....	10	11	−0.09
Annual rate of change of capital.............	−0.20	−0.18	+0.16
Lag of payments for imports in months........	0	1	+0.21

[1] The values assumed for 1–4 and 8 are thought to be roughly realistic. Arbitrary possible values have been assigned to the other coefficients.

[2] Calculated on the basis of partial derivatives given in the Appendix.

[3] When one of these ratios is increased, the other two are at the same time decreased (both in the same proportion).

This quite substantial deficit would become almost five times as large if the marginal propensity to consume were 0.77 instead of, as assumed, 0.70; it would be changed into a large positive balance if this propensity were 0.63, or if the marginal propensity to import were 0.27 instead of 0.30. If we go through the last column of this table, it is seen that a ten per cent change in one of the coefficients produces in nearly all cases a change at least as large as the value of the deficit. It follows that a margin of error of only a few per cent in all the coefficients concerned would be sufficient to render doubtful the existence of a deficit, as against a surplus, of foreign exchange after five years.[28]

This finding clearly precludes general quantitative conclusions, with respect to either the interpretation of history or advice for the future. It does, however, lead to one more important conclusion

[28] In considering the reliability of the much larger surpluses in later years, it should be noted that most of the partial derivatives too increase rapidly with time.

of a qualitative nature. In an economy which is not entirely guided by the state, a reconstruction plan covering many years can be outlined only tentatively, and its eventual effects on the country's balance of payments situation can be forecast only on the basis of inaccurately known coefficients, which means, as we have seen, that they cannot really be forecast at all. We have also seen that the long-run soundness of the program cannot be judged from the observation of a foreign exchange surplus or deficit in the first few years. A deficit may, but need not, prove to be temporary; and the same is true of a surplus. It follows that the execution of a program of this nature has to be followed as carefully as possible by analytical observation. But this alone is not sufficient. Our findings clearly point to the further need of a great measure of patience and indulgence on the part of the lending countries. Small deviations of the coefficients from their expected values may profoundly change the outcome. They will have to be met, if they are more than temporary, by adjustments of the plan which will necessarily require time. In the meantime, if the changes of the coefficients are for the worse, additional credits will be necessary if the whole plan is not to break down.

In general, the correct attitude for creditor countries financing reconstruction would seem to be that of the investment banker who sees his client through a long period of possible trouble, rather than that of the investor who buys a share and tries to sell it when the enterprise seems to be less successful than he expected. The uncertainties of a country—not to mention a continent—embarking upon a great investment program are far greater than those of an individual starting a new enterprise. The latter can take the economic milieu in which he intends to work as given; he can exactly calculate his costs and make reliable estimates of his selling possibilities. A reconstruction plan of a large scope, however, changes the whole economic milieu in a way which it is impossible to forecast with any great degree of precision; and these very dangers will seriously affect the outcome of the plan. These great and unpreventable uncertainties call for a most interested banker's attitude on the part of the creditor countries.

Appendix

Variables

All capital symbols indicate annual values.

The year to which capital symbols refer is indicated by a letter or figure between brackets, e.g. $P_1(t)$; but for symbols not occurring with other subscripts, time is sometimes indicated as a subscript, e.g. L_t. Wherever formulae do not refer to a particular year, the indication of time is omitted.

All coefficients (small symbols) are assumed to be independent of time.

I = Investment = $I_1 + I_2 + I_3$.

I_1 = Investment to produce P_1.

I_2 = Investment to produce P_2.

I_3 = Investment to produce P_3.

L = Long term capital import.

M = Imports, directly and indirectly due to I.

$P = P_1 + P_2 + P_3$.

P_1 = Output of type (1) $\left.\right\}$

P_2 = Output of type (2) $\left.\right\}$ cf. text.

P_3 = Output of type (3) $\left.\right\}$

S = Service of long-term foreign debt.

X = Export surplus owing to P. (X_1 refers to P_1, etc.)

Z = Foreign exchange balance at end of year.

c = Marginal propensity to consume.

k = Rate of change of long-term capital import, defined as $(L_t - L_{t-1})/L_0$.

m = Marginal propensity to import; defined as Imports/Value of output.

$o = P/I$ = Rate of turnover of capital. ($o_1 = P_1/I_1$, etc.)

$q = I/L_0$ = Expansion ratio.

$s = S/L$.

t = Time in years.

$x_1 = P_1/P$.

$x_2 = P_2/P$.

$x_3 = P_3/P$.

θ = Lag of payments for imports behind "primary" income payments, in years.

Derivation of Formulae

1. Investment I leads to direct import mI and national income $(1 - m)I$. Of this $c(1 - m)I$ is spent, viz. $mc(1 - m)I$ abroad and $mc(1 - m)^2I$ at home. This again creates income at home, etc.

$$\therefore M = I[m + cm(1 - m)\{1 + c(1 - m) + c^2(1 - m)^2 \cdots \}]$$

$$= \frac{Im}{1 - c(1 - m)} \qquad m, c < 1 \quad (1)$$

We define
$$\mu = \frac{m}{1 - c(1 - m)} \tag{2}$$

It will be seen that $\mu < 1$ as $m, c < 1$

The maximum value for the expansion ratio, q, follows from (1) and (2):

$$q \le 1/\mu \tag{3}$$

2. The derivation of X_1 and X_3 is symmetrical with that of M. There is only a difference of sign, X being defined as an export surplus.
Hence:

$$X_1 = P_1(1 - \mu) \tag{4}$$
$$X_2 = 0 \tag{5}$$
$$X_3 = - P_3\mu \tag{6}$$
$$X = X_1 + X_2 + X_3 = x_1 o_1 I_1 - (x_1 o_1 I_1 + x_3 o_3 I_3)\mu \tag{7}$$

It follows that, if $0 < \mu < 1$

$$\left. \begin{array}{l} \dfrac{\partial X}{\partial o_1} > 0 \\[2mm] \dfrac{\partial X}{\partial o_2} = 0 \\[2mm] \dfrac{\partial X}{\partial o_3} < 0 \end{array} \right\} \; P \text{ variable, } I \text{ constant} \tag{8}$$

3. $S = sL = \dfrac{sI}{q}$ 　　　　　　　　　　　　　　　　　　(9)

For the net export surplus of operation to take care of the service of the debt it is necessary that
$$X - S > 0. \tag{10}$$

Clearly:
$$X - S = P\left[x_1 - (x_1 + x_3)\mu - \frac{s}{q}(o_1 x_1 + o_2 x_2 + o_3 x_3) \right]$$
$$\therefore \frac{\partial X}{\partial o_j} > 0 \quad j = 1, 2, 3. \quad I \text{ variable, } P \text{ constant} \tag{11}$$

The apparent divergence between (8) and (11) for $j = 2, 3$ is discussed in the text (p. 470).
We assume from here on:
$$o_1 = o_2 = o_3 = o \tag{12}$$

The condition expressed by (10) may then be written

$$o\{x_1 - (x_1 + x_3)\mu\} - \frac{s}{q} > 0 \tag{13}$$

If q is at its maximum according to (3), the following lower limit is found for x_1:

$$x_1 > (x_3 + s/o) \cdot \frac{m}{(1-c)(1-m)} \tag{14}$$

For reasonable values for m and c, it is likely that

$$\frac{m}{(1-c)(1-m)} > 1;$$ from this it follows that

$$x_1 > \tfrac{1}{2}(1 - x_2) \tag{15}$$

4. To determine the balance of foreign exchange at the end of year t, $Z(t)$, it is necessary to sum the various factors affecting it from 0 to t:

$$Z(t) = \sum_{j=0}^{t} L(j) - \sum_{j=0}^{t} S(j) - \sum_{j=0}^{t} M(j) + \sum_{j=0}^{t} X(j) \tag{16}$$

5. The formula for the change of capital import over time is

$$L_t = L_0(1 + kt) \tag{17}$$

However, when $k < 0$, it is perhaps unreasonable to assume that L would become negative, i.e. that the country would actually start exporting long-term capital, in particular if there is a foreign exchange deficit even without long-term capital export. Therefore, in lines 1 and 2 in Diagram I, it is assumed that long-term capital movements cease altogether after the rate of capital import has declined to 0. ($kt \leq -1$). Under these assumptions, the following equations are easily verified:

		Region I	Region II	
		$kt > -1$	$kt < -1$	
L_t	$=$	$L_0(1 + kt)$	0	(18)
$\sum\limits_{j=0}^{t} L_j$	$=$	$L_0\left(1 + \tfrac{1}{2}kt\right)(t+1)$	$\tfrac{1}{2}L_0\left(1 - \tfrac{1}{k}\right)$	(19)
$\sum\limits_{j=0}^{t} S_j = s\sum\limits_{j=0}^{t}(t+1-j)L_j =$		$\tfrac{1}{2}sL_0\left(1 + \tfrac{1}{3}kt\right)$ $(t+1)(t+2)$	$\tfrac{1}{6}sL_0\left(1 - \tfrac{1}{k}\right)$ $\left(3t + 4 + \tfrac{1}{k}\right)$	(20)

I is assumed to be constant over time. Hence

$$\sum_{j=0}^{t} M_j = I\mu(t+1) \tag{21}$$

It is assumed that it takes one year for an investment project to be terminated. The first results of operation are therefore in year 1, and the sum of these results is:

$$\sum_{j=0}^{t} X(j) = \sum_{j=1}^{t} X(j) = \tfrac{1}{2} o I t (t+1)\{x_1 - (x_1 + x_3)\mu\} \tag{22}$$

Combining equation (19) to (22) we obtain, by substituting I/q for L:
Region I:

$$Z(t) = I \cdot (t+1) \left[-\mu + \frac{1}{2} \, to \, \{x_1 - (x_1 + x_3)\mu\} \right.$$
$$\left. + \frac{1}{6q} \{ -skt^2 + t(3k - 3s - 2sk) + 6(1 - s)\} \right] \tag{23 I}$$

Region II:

$$Z(t) = I \cdot (t+1) \left[-\mu + \frac{1}{2} \, to \, \{x_1 - (x_1 + x_3)\mu\} \right.$$
$$\left. + \frac{1}{6q \cdot (t+1)} \left(1 - \frac{1}{k}\right) \left\{3 - s\left(3t + 4 + \frac{1}{k}\right)\right\} \right] \tag{23 II}$$

The sign of $Z(t)$ depends on the form between [ ]. This form is shown in Diagram II with its three components. Line I represents the effect of investment, Line II of operation, Line III the joint effect of capital inflow and the return flow of the service of the debt, and Line IV represents the sum of the three components. Lines III and IV show two different continuations from the fifth year on; in the heavy line account is taken of the fact that t moves from Region I to Region II, whereas the dash-line continues as if t were still in Region I; i.e. it is assumed that long-term capital import is followed by long-term capital export. It is interesting to note that even under the latter assumption the balance of foreign exchange becomes rather quickly positive (at about $t = 9$).[29]

In order to make a comparison with the earlier results, (23 I) may usefully be written:

$$Z(t) = I \cdot (t+1) \left[\left\{-\mu + \frac{1-s}{q}\right\} + \frac{1}{2} t \left(o\{x_1 - (x_1 + x_3)\mu\} - \frac{s}{q}\right) \right.$$
$$\left. + \frac{k}{6q} \{ -st^2 + t(3 - 2s)\} \right] \tag{23 I'}$$

---

[29] In fact the dotted line intersects the heavy line at

$$t = \frac{3}{s} - \frac{1}{k} - 1, \text{ i.e. in our case at } t = 33.$$

DIAGRAM II

The Factors Determining the Sign of the Balance of Foreign Exchange After *t* Years

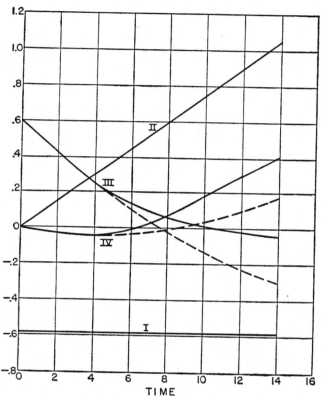

I = Component due to investment
II = Component due to operation
III = Component due to inflow of capital and return flow of debt service
IV = I + II + III
       All components as shown are divided by $(t + 1)$.
       Value of coefficients as in table on page 491.
       Unit: Annual rate of investment = 1.

We easily recognize in this the partial conditions for $\mathcal{Z}(t) > 0$ derived earlier, namely (3)[30] and (13). The last of the three terms composing the part between [ ] of (23 I'), which is proportional to k, represents the influence of the change in the rate of capital inflow.

6. If we want to consider the possibility that all import items are lagged by θ years, we would have to sum the terms with μ up to $(t - \theta)$ instead of up to t. If we designate the balance of foreign assets taking account of θ in the year t as $\mathcal{Z}(t,\theta)$, it follows from (21) and (22) that

$$\mathcal{Z}(t,\theta) - \mathcal{Z}(t) = I\left[\theta\mu + \frac{1}{2}o(x_1 + x_3)\mu\{t(t+1) - (t-\theta)(t-\theta+1)\}\right] \quad (24)$$

$$\therefore \frac{\partial \mathcal{Z}(t,o)}{\partial \theta} = \mu I\left\{1 + o(x_1 + x_3)\left(t + \frac{1}{2}\right)\right\} \quad (25)$$

7. It is perhaps of little use to write down $\dfrac{\partial \mathcal{Z}(t)}{\partial p}$, where p is any of the parameters introduced, as a function of t. The following table gives these derivatives for an assumed value of t, viz. $t = 5$, based on (23 I). Column (2) shows $\partial \mathcal{Z}(5)/\partial p$

p	$\dfrac{\partial \mathcal{Z}(5)/\partial p}{I}$	Sign of $\partial \mathcal{Z}(5)/\partial p$	Value assumed for p	Value calculated for $\dfrac{\partial \mathcal{Z}(5)/\partial p}{I}$
(1)	(2)	(3)	(4)	(5)
o	$15\{x_1 - (x_1 + x_3)\mu\}$	+	1.0	2.2
$x_1{}^*$	$150\{1 - \mu x_2/(1 - x_1)\}$	+	0.5	7.94
$x_2{}^*$	$150\{\mu - x_1/(1 - x_2)\}$	±	0.4	−3.67
$x_3{}^*$	$-150(1 + \mu x_2)/(1 - x_3)$	−	0.1	−20.58
k	$6(3 - 7s)/q$	+	0.2	8.24
s	$-7(3 + 5k)/q$	−	0.1	−9.15
m	$-\{150(x_1 + x_3) + 6\}(1 - c)\{1 - c(1 - m)\}^{-2}$	−	0.3	−17.30
c	$-\{150(x_1 + x_3) + 6\}m(1 - m)\{1 - c(1 - m)\}^{-2}$	−	0.7	−12.11
q†	$150[\{x_1 - (x_1 + x_3)\mu\} - 6\mu]/q$	±	1.53	−0.86
θ	$\mu\{1 + 5.5o(x_1 + x_3)\}$	+	0	2.54

* In deriving $\dfrac{\partial \mathcal{Z}}{\partial x_i}$ it is assumed that $\dfrac{\partial x_j}{\partial x_i} = -\dfrac{x_j}{1 - x_i}$ $(i, j = 1, 2, 3; i \neq j)$.

† Derived on the assumption that L_0 is constant and I is variable.

---

[30] Condition (3) would be $q < \dfrac{1 - s}{\mu}$ if we had taken account of the service of the debt in the year of investment.

expressed in the parameters after division by I. In column (3) the sign of the derivative is given if the parameters are not known numerically but are taken within reasonable limits (e.g. $1 > e$, $m > 0$). The next column gives an assumed value for the parameters, and in column (5) $\partial \mathcal{Z}(5)/\partial p$ is calculated numerically on the basis of these values.

8. There is little to be said about the signs of the derivatives, except for that of $\partial \mathcal{Z}/\partial q$. It seems useful to write this derivative[31] as a function of t:

$$\frac{\partial \mathcal{Z}(t)}{\partial q} = (t + 1)\left[\frac{1}{2}ot\{x_1 - (x_1 + x_3)\mu\} - \mu\right]/q \tag{26}$$

It follows from (26) that $\partial \mathcal{Z}(t)/\partial q$ will always be > 0 for high values of t provided

$$x_1 > (x_1 + x_3)\mu \tag{27}$$

Hence, if condition (27) is fulfilled, it will be desirable, independently of the amount of long-term capital available, to expand investment, provided the necessary additional relatively short credits can be obtained for the period

$$0 < t < \frac{2\mu}{o\{x_1 - (x_1 + x_3)\mu\}} \tag{28}$$

With the numerical values chosen above, the upper limit for t would be about eight years. It should be noted that the period for which additional borrowing is necessary does not depend on q.

A "Corrected Marginal Propensity to Import"

It was mentioned in the text[32] that the expansion caused abroad by additional imports purchased by the country under consideration might be taken into account by substituting a "corrected" value for the marginal propensity to import. This value, m_c, may be derived as follows.

We assume that the parameters c', m' and μ' describe properties of the rest of the world comparable with c, m and μ in our country. Then, according to (1), an export of 1 from the rest of the world produces the following chain of imports into $(+)$ and exports from $(-)$ our country:

$$1 - \mu' + \mu\mu' - \mu(\mu')^2 \cdots = (1 - \mu')\{1 + \mu\mu' \cdots (\mu\mu')^n\}$$
$$\underset{n \to \infty}{=} \frac{1 - \mu'}{1 - \mu\mu'} \qquad (\mu, \mu' < 1) \tag{29}$$

If no account is taken of the working of the multiplier abroad, only the first

---

[31] The derivative is the same for (23 I) and (23 II).

[32] Supra, page 463.

term of the geometrical series (i.e. 1) is taken into consideration. To compensate for this, m_c should be smaller than m in the following ratio:

$$\frac{m_c}{m} = \frac{1 - \mu'}{1 - \mu\mu'} \tag{30}$$

Now if the country under consideration is small in comparison with the world, m' will be very small, e.g. of the order of 0.05. Unless c' is very near to 1, u' will also be rather small and m_c/m will not be much below unity. On the assumptions that $c = c' = 0.70$, $m = 0.30$, $m' = 0.05$ it is found that

$$\frac{m_c}{m} = \frac{1 - 0.15}{1 - 0.15 \times 0.59} = 0.93$$

It is interesting to observe that even when c and $c' \rightarrow 1$, m_c/m approaches a limit little below unity. If $c = c' = 1 = \epsilon$, where ϵ is a very small positive value, we find

$$\underset{\substack{\epsilon \rightarrow 0 \\ n \rightarrow \infty \\ \epsilon n \rightarrow 0}}{Lim} \frac{m_c}{m} = \frac{1 - \mu'}{1 - \mu\mu'} \{1 - (\mu\mu')^n\}$$

$$= \frac{\epsilon(1 - m')/m'}{\epsilon(m + m' - 2mm')/mm'} \{1 - (\mu\mu')^n\}$$

$$= \frac{m(1 - m')}{m + m' - 2mm'} \tag{31}$$

If $m = 0.30$, $m' = 0.05$ this limit value for m_c/m works out at 0.89.

THE FUTURE OF WORLD TRADE

21

THE FUTURE OF INTERNATIONAL TRADE*

By D. H. Robertson‖

1. The question to which I am seeking an answer is—What is the future of international trade? Will it ever play again the same dominant part in the economic life of the world that it played in the nineteenth century?

Let me put the question another way. Consider two well-known sets of facts. Ever since the war, and especially since 1931, the course of international trade has been throttled by an incredible maze of obstacles and restrictions, culminating in that startling bid for economic self-sufficiency, the German four-year plan. Yet in 1929 the volume of world trade was greater by more than a quarter than in 1913; even in the trough of 1932 it did not sink below three-quarters of its 1929 level: and it has now come near to regaining that level. Which of these two sets of facts represents the true mind of the world for the future—the apparent determination of Governments, egged on by their citizens (for it is no use pretending it is all the fault of the Governments), to strangle international trade, or the obstinate determination of trade not to be strangled? or are the two sets of facts reconcilable in terms of some intelligible trend, some fumbling purpose to which the nations will one day learn to give fruitful effect?

2. Forgive me if I go back to the beginning. The case for a large volume of international trade rests on the different endow-

---

* A lecture delivered to the Liverpool Economic and Statistical Society on October 13, 1937, and printed (with the embodiment of some criticisms) in the *Economic Journal*, Volume XLVIII (March, 1938), pages 1–14; reprinted in D. H. Robertson, *Essays in Monetary Theory* (1940). Reprinted here without change from the original text, by the courtesy of Staples Press Limited and the author.

‖ Trinity College, Cambridge, England.

ment of nations in respect of natural resources, human quality and skill, and acquired equipment.   Where these differences are great, it is to the immediate economic advantage of all parties that a large volume of trade should take place.   The fact that Utopia *can* grow wheat, even the fact that she can grow more wheat per acre or more wheat per man than Ruritania, is not in itself an argument against her importing wheat from Ruritania if she can turn her resources to the production of other things in which her advantage over Ruritania is greater still.   The volume of profitable trade depends on the width of these gaps in the *comparative* advantages of different countries for the production of different things.

Let us first put ourselves back in the first decade of this century, endow ourselves with ordinary economic foresight but not with prevision of the war and its consequences, and ask ourselves what the future then seemed to hold in store as regards these gaps in Comparative Advantage.   It was, I think, fairly evident that they were tending to become narrower.   The sharpness of the outline between the granaries and the workshops of the world, to put it briefly, was already becoming blurred.   In the first place, it was becoming plain that proficiency in the arts of mechanised industry could not remain for ever the monopoly of the nation, or even of the group of nations, that had first learnt to use them.   Secondly, electricity was already promising to release the factory from the pull of the coalfields and pointing both to a different, and to a less intense, localisation of manufacturing industry.   Thirdly, to turn to the other side of the picture, the exploitation of virgin soils in the new countries appeared to be reaching its limit, and agriculture there too to be coming up against its old enemy, the law of diminishing returns.   Thus the long-term prospect seemed to be that of a world in which the international exchange of goods would play a smaller part relatively to total production, and would be conducted on terms progressively more disadvantageous to the teeming industrial populations of western Europe.

3. Now let us demand of ourselves a great feat of the imagination, and picture ourselves living indeed in 1937, but in a world in which there has been no war.   Have the forces which we descried

at work thirty years ago worked themselves out as we expected in reducing the advantages of international specialisation, or have they been modified in any way? Has any new force made its appearance?

As regards the first two forces, there is no doubt, I think, as to the answer. The diffusion of industrial capital and of industrial skill has proceeded even more rapidly than most people would have prophesied. In particular it has become evident that the simpler processes of textile manufacture can be carried on with approximately equal efficiency by almost any kind of population in almost any part of the world. The oil-engine and the hydro-electric plant have continued to press home their assault on the sovereignty of coal. From this side the narrowing of the gap of comparative advantage has proceeded apace.

4. When we turn to the other side, the conclusion is not so clear. There are three far-reaching factors to be taken into account, and it is by no means evident how their net effect is likely to work out. The first and most obvious is the astonishing achievements of science in the domain of agriculture. These achievements fall into two main groups, the mechanisation of agricultural operations and the improvement of the breeds of animals and plants; I have neither the time nor the knowledge to appraise them in any detail. Their most spectacular effect has been to cheapen the cost of the products of agriculture in terms of the products of industry, so that one of the tendencies which we thought we saw at work thirty years ago— the tendency of the terms of trade to turn against the manufacturing countries—has been dramatically reversed. To step for the moment into the real world (since for the hypothetical warless world which we have agreed to explore we dare not invent figures), the price of Britain's imports in terms of her exports was in 1931 some 30 per cent., and is even now some 20 per cent., lower than in 1913.[1] But for the purpose of our main problem what we want

---

[1] These figures, it is true, reflect not only the relative movement of *costs* in agriculture and industry, but also the relative change in ability to control production by monopolistic methods.

to know is not how much scientific progress has cheapened the products of the earth, but whether it has increased or diminished the economic advantages of international specialisation. And in spite of some confusing cross-currents, there seems at first sight to be no doubt about the answer. It is on the side of the large prairie wheat-factory, not of the fragmented country-side of the Old World, that the tractor and the combine weight the scales. It is in outlandish regions in the cold north or the drought-ridden desert rather than on the rich soils of temperate zones that the Mendelian plant expert confers his richest gifts. And it is not only in the field of the production of raw things but also of their transport that science, on the whole, still seems to fight on the side of regional specialisation and long-distance trade. Man has learnt to control temperature, and therefore the good fairies of ripening and the demons of decay; meat that is no worse than chilled can at last voyage safely from the Antipodes, and the most telegonous fruits appear in our shop-windows at the most unlikely seasons.

True, nothing in this world works only one way; and scientific invention, which can thus confer its blessing on the localised producer, can also suddenly turn round and smack him in the face. In the warless world in which we are still moving in thought, we can perhaps forget about Buna rubber; but we can hardly think away synthetic fertilisers and artificial silk. Air and wood are more widely diffused over the globe than nitrate deposits or fibrous annuals, as water is more widely diffused than coal; at the bid of science a Chile yesterday, a Texas or Bengal to-morrow, may wake up to find its occupation gone.

5. Furthermore—and this is the second of the far-reaching factors to which I alluded a few minutes ago—there hangs over the populations of the new countries, or some of them, a cloud of which they were scarcely aware thirty years ago. It is being increasingly borne in upon them that their vast specialisations of the late nineteenth century were to a certain extent bogus specialisations, founded on reckless mining of the soil, on natural but disastrous ignorance of the cyclical misbehaviour of sun and cloud, on improvident sacrifice of the leisurely tree to the crop which is

here to-day and gone to-morrow. Behind the restriction schemes of Secretary Wallace and the financial junketings of Mr. Aberhart looms the enormous spectre of the Dust-Bowl. The same charge of living on capital lies, of course, ultimately against specialisations founded on the exploitation of mineral wealth, though the pigeon takes longer to come home to roost,—*how much* longer the South African in particular does well from time to time to ask himself. But whether it work slow or fast, we have here a factor tending, like the diffusion of manufacturing skill, and on the whole *unlike* the factor of agricultural improvement, to limit the advantage of international specialisation and the growth of international trade.

6. Thus even for the peaceful 1937 of our imaginings, the picture is already somewhat complex and confusing. But perhaps we can fairly sum the argument, so far as it has yet gone, by saying that on the balance the tendencies which we descried thirty years ago towards the curtailment of long-distance trade have received a moderate check. It is true that the oversea populations have become cleverer at twisting and hammering things; but they have also become cleverer at their old game of growing things: so that if the gap of Comparative Advantage has been encroached upon from one side, it has also been widening out on the other.

Is that, still barring war and the mentality begotten by war, a picture which, however sketchy, is complete as far as it goes, or have we left something vital out? Yes, I am afraid the answer is that, apart altogether from war and the rumour of war, we have left out something of great importance—the third of the far-reaching factors which I mentioned some minutes ago. When we try to introduce it, the picture becomes more complex still; and I think on the whole the balance of the argument changes.

The specialisations of the nineteenth century were not simply a device for using to the greatest effect the labours of a given number of human beings; they were above all an engine of *growth*. Their most spectacular effect was to hold at bay for a century the devil which Malthus had unchained, so that, just as the Red Queen was five times as rich as Alice *and* five times as clever, so the inhabitants of these islands in the pre-war decade managed, according to a commonly quoted though obviously not very reliable computation, to be four times as well off as their ancestors of a hundred years before *and* four times as numerous.   And then, just as we were wondering whether the devil of population pressure could be kept at bay much longer, we looked over our shoulders, and lo and behold!—he was gone.   But he has left a curious smell behind, and we are none of us quite sure whether it is brimstone or roses. So far as the future of international trade is concerned, there is at present a strong disposition among thoughtful persons to believe that the brimstone predominates.

It is important, though it is not always quite easy, to make out exactly what these thoughtful persons are saying.   Let us try to give definiteness to the problem by supposing that the populations of the whole world, at any rate outside Soviet Russia and Eastern Asia, become stationary within the next few years, and continue practically stationary for, let us say, the next half-century.   Naturally we shall not expect the aggregate either of world production or of world trade to grow as fast as they did while population was still increasing smartly; we should expect production to grow, for instance, by an annual average of say 2 per cent. instead of 3 per cent.   But are there any reasons to expect that in such circumstances world *trade* will grow more slowly than world *production*, and indeed perhaps will cease growing at all?

Yes, say the thoughtful persons who smell brimstone, there are such reasons.   As people become richer they spend a smaller proportion of their income on food of any kind, and a smaller proportion still on the simpler and cheaper kinds of food.   Now, as long as the industrial populations were still increasing at a brisk rate, it was possible to rely on a constantly expanding market for the simpler foodstuffs.   Anything which cheapened their cost of production in the overseas countries was an unequivocal blessing to their farming populations; even falling prices were compatible with rising profits and increasing employment on the land.   But if the increase in aggregate world output has to be absorbed entirely in the form of increased consumption of goods per head, that is no longer true.   The combine and the tractor and the researches which produced Marquis wheat and P.O.J. 2878 have come in a sense too late. For they bring with them now not only lowered costs, but glutted markets, and a formidable problem of occupational transfer for the farming populations of the overseas lands. And even if that problem could be solved quickly and without friction, which is not the case, it seems likely that it would be solved in ways that tend to close rather than to widen the gap of Comparative Advantage, and so to limit the scope for international exchange.

7. There is, say the thoughtful persons, one outstanding reason why this process of readjustment should lead to a relative decline in international trade. The Great Specialisation of the nineteenth century was not simply an exchange of industrial products for agricultural products. Following Mr. Hartley Withers, we may visualise it as in part an exchange of capital goods for pieces of paper called securities, followed at a later date by an exchange of other pieces of paper, called interest-coupons, for agricultural products. Thus the volume of trade was kept at a high level by two closely-connected facts—first, the fact that the new countries keenly desired a type of goods, which we may think of for short as steel rails and girders, which the older countries were peculiarly fitted to supply, and secondly, the fact that the old countries did not demand immediate payment for these goods, but were willing in effect to supply them on tick, so that the volume of trade was continuously larger than it would have been had it depended solely on the opportunities for simultaneous barter.

Now this process of foreign investment, so the argument runs, was bound up with the growth of population rather than of production. In whatever exact form a stationary population elects to take its rising standard of life, it is not likely to be a form which entails the same hectic construction of railways and harbours and bridges in distant lands as did the clamour for bread and shirts which rose in the last century from the growing millions in the factory towns. Thus three consequences will follow, all of them damaging to the volume of international trade. In the first place, the imports of overseas countries will tend to be confined to what they can pay for out of their current output. In the second place, their demand will shift away from those things in which the gap of Comparative Advantage between agriculture and manufacture is widest—for when all is said and done there is stronger reason why steel should be forged in Sheffield than why cotton should be spun in Oldham or saucers baked in Staffordshire. And thirdly, so far as the overseas countries still *do* desire to borrow and to import capital goods, they will tend to make their interest payments in subsequent years not by expanding their exports but by curtailing their imports—a method equally satisfactory, perhaps, to the foreign creditor, who is concerned only to receive his money, but by no means equally satisfactory to those whose livelihood is bound up with the processes of international trade.

Now I think myself that there is at present a little too much disposition to smell brimstone rather than roses in the wake of the vanished devil of population pressure. It would seem as though we ought to be able to make the roses predominate if we really wish. But as regards the problem immediately in hand, the probable behaviour of the volume of international trade in the next half-century, I think there is much force in the argument which I have just tried to set forth, and that it goes a long way to cancel the argument on which I laid stress earlier—the argument, namely, that the progress of agricultural improvement has lowered agricultural costs more in the new than in the old countries, and so on the face of it favoured a still higher degree of international specialisation.

8. Let us now enlarge the range of our enquiry by asking a further question. Granted that we must learn to accommodate ourselves permanently to a smaller relative volume of international trade, does it also follow that we must learn to accommodate ourselves permanently to a more restrictionist trade policy throughout the world? Or is the tangle of restrictionism in the midst of which we live the result not of the deep-seated economic forces which we have so far been attempting to analyse, but of the factors which we have been deliberately trying to think out of the way—of the war and its unhappy aftermath?

The logical connection between trade *shrinkage* and trade

restriction is not, I think, immediately self-evident. The mere fact that the balance of advantage is on the side of having a smaller relative volume of international trade than in the past is not *in itself* an argument for taking steps to make that volume smaller still, for the benefit of particular groups of producers, any more than it is an argument for trying to keep the volume uneconomically large, for the benefit of the owners of ships or dockyards. It is good fun for the Protectionist to be able to catch the Free Trader out, as he sometimes can, adopting the posture of a defender of vested interests and the *status quo*—shedding over laid-up ships and closed bill-brokers' offices those tears which he would condemn as unmanly weakness if they were allowed to flow over derelict wheat-fields and idle cotton-mills. But to cry *Tu quoque* is not the same thing as to prove one's case. Why should the fact that the scope for advantageous exchange between nations is narrowing be an argument for putting increased obstacles in the way of such exchange as still remains advantageous? Is it not rather an argument for sweeping away those obstacles which exist?

Something like a rational answer to this question can perhaps be put forward on these lines. A narrowing of the gap of Comparative Advantage will not only diminish the volume of advantageous foreign trade, but will tend to produce a state of affairs in which there is a relatively large volume of foreign trade trembling, as it were, on the margin of advantageousness, and liable to be blown to one side or the other of that margin by small changes in the wind of circumstance. If, having been for some time just outside the range of profitableness, it is suddenly blown just within that range, great dislocation and distress will be caused to those who have laid their plans on the expectation of its remaining outside that range; and at the same time the benefit conferred on the community as a whole will be relatively small. To take an extreme example, the exchange of ice for coal between North Polia and Infernia not only yields a large measure of benefit to consumers, but is also likely to remain very stable, since a violent change in climatic conditions would be needed to disturb it. But the exchange of black shirts and red shirts between Fascia and Bolschevia is liable to ebb and flow in the most confusing fashion in accordance with minute technical changes; to eliminate it altogether would confer a great boon of security upon the shirt-makers of the two countries, at a cost to the shirt-wearers negligible compared with the sums of which they are already being mulcted for the benefit of their respective party funds.

It is very difficult to make up one's mind how much weight *ought to be* attached to this argument in any particular case. We must not overlook the fact that specialisation by different countries even in what look to the outsider like very similar branches of the same industry may bring great advantages, owing to the economies of production on a large scale, and may remain fairly stable over decades. But I think we can be certain that great weight *will* be attached to this argument from stability whenever it can be made to seem at all plausible to do so. And we can therefore affirm as a fact, so to speak, of natural history, that a relative shrinkage of world trade due to a narrowing of the gap of Comparative Advantage *is* likely to be associated with a further shrinkage due to policy, since it tends both to make more prominent the evils of instability and insecurity and to lower the real cost to the community of attempting to mitigate them.

9. So far as the prospective relative shrinkage of world trade is due to the agricultural revolution and the flight of the Malthusian devil, the connection with increased restrictionism appears to be of a somewhat different kind. For, as we have seen, the agricultural revolution has not diminished the relative advantage of the overseas countries in the production of food, but rather increased it. To the urban populations, therefore, the cost of agricultural protectionism, in the sense of the benefits now within their reach which it forces them to forgo, is not less but greater than it was. But since they have benefited absolutely from the agricultural revolution, they are not too acutely aware of this; and it proves politically feasible, in various countries in various degrees, to extract from them the sacrifices necessary to accord to the home agricultural populations some protection against that instability of livelihood which results from the recurrent tendency to world-wide agri-

cultural glut. Indeed, it proves feasible in some countries to go further, and to hold in check, perhaps indefinitely, that migration from the soil which the agricultural revolution and the flight of the Malthusian devil prescribe. Thus it becomes possible to indulge in a certain measure those deep non-economic instincts—in part military, in part social, in part aesthetic,[2] in part apparently sheerly mystical—which instruct all of us, in greater or less degree, that a country whose agriculture is "too small" (whatever exactly that may mean) is a country not fit to live in.

10. Now once more the prime object of my enquiry is not how far these developments of policy are justifiable, but how far they were in any case to be expected as a bye-product of fundamental economic change, as distinct from being merely the spawn of war and the atmosphere of war. It is, I think, quite extraordinarily difficult to determine. One cannot lay one's finger on this duty, that quota, that piece of exchange control and say that one is due to the check to the growth in population, the second to currency disturbance and the third to political ambition or military precaution. As our British tariff conspicuously illustrates, the arguments by which a measure is defended do not always bear much relation to the pressures which have led to its imposition; and the reasons for which it remains in force may differ widely both from the real and from the avowed reasons for its original introduction. But it may perhaps serve to throw some light on the prospects for the future if we attempt to distinguish three phases in the progressive orgy of restrictionism in which the world has in fact indulged since the end of the Great War. The first, taking principally the old-fashioned form of tariff protection, may be said to have arisen fairly directly out of the war itself: for its chief motive force was the desire of individual industries in numerous countries to perpetuate the natural protection which they had enjoyed, with the end of the submarine and the blockade, during war-time. Sir Arthur Salter

---

[2] My own ideal agricultural policy would make the payment of a subsidy on the production of wheat conditional on the sowing of a handsome quota of poppies in among it.

has vividly described how the great difficulty in making head-way against the "cumbrous, complex and provocative" tariff system which thus grew up in the twenties lay not in any "real conflict between divergent national interests and national policies," but in the fact that "there were no genuine national policies conceived as a whole but only a series of national systems improvised under pressure."[3]   It would be difficult, I think, to argue that this system, at any rate as it actually developed, represented any real or rational attempt on the part of the world to adjust itself to long-term changes in the underlying conditions of international economic relations.

The second wave of restrictionism, extending far beyond mere tariff protection into the jungles of quantitative regulation of imports and control of exchange dealings, was of course associated with the rush for cover from the depression of 1929 and the financial crisis of 1931.   In the case of every country the primary and ostensible object of the intensified restrictionism was the protection of its balance of payments, endangered, as the case might be, by the collapse of the market for its exports, by a drying up of the long-term loans on whose continuance it had based its economic life, by a flooding of its market with dumped imports, by a withdrawal of short-term loans which had been incautiously woven into the fabric of its monetary system—or by some combination of these various misfortunes.   Now since in every country this wave of restrictionism had its immediate origin in a crisis of currency and exchange, there has been a tendency to hope that it would recede automatically as, by one expedient and another, the various countries got their currency and exchange position into some sort of order; and the Tripartite Monetary Mouse of October 1936 was loudly acclaimed as heralding a return towards what seems in retrospect the economic liberalism of 1929.   This has turned out to be an over-optimistic view; for, apart from the special troubles of the French, and from that darkening of the political atmosphere to which I will come in a moment, the truth seems to me to be that,

---

[3] *World Trade and its Future*, p. 39.

so far as one can now distinguish between them, the post-1929 restrictions, whether justifiable or not, were more in the nature of a genuine reaction to a long-period change in underlying conditions than was the hugger-mugger tariff-building of the nineteen-twenties. For it was in the crisis of 1929–33 that the world first woke up to the long-term problems created by the agricultural revolution and by the precariousness of the whole system of foreign lending.   Whatever measure of recovery has been achieved since, these problems still remain unsolved; and the refusal of the post-1929 restrictions to disappear is therefore less surprising, if not less annoying, than is sometimes pretended.

In the third and latest era of restrictionist policy, we must, I think, detect a different strain.   For though in a sense it dates from the fall of the dollar and the breakdown of the World Economic Conference in 1933, and thus represents an intensification of the crisis policies of 1929–31, in another and deeper sense it is, it has lately been suggested,[4] more instructive to connect it with two slightly earlier events, the Japanese seizure of Manchukuo and the inauguration of the Ottawa System of Empire trade.   Each of these events, however different otherwise in character, represented the deliberate use of political power for the attainment of exclusive economic advantage, and in turn foreshadowed the sacrifice of economic well-being to the consolidation of political power.   With the closure of Germany for rearmament and repair, with the breakdown of the world peace system in the face of aggression, with the exhibition of the inconvenience which even half-hearted economic sanctions could inflict, with the tardy re-arming of the British Empire, the Economics of Crisis have tended to pass insensibly into the Economics of War.   And in the Economics of War the subtleties of Comparative Advantage become a foolish irrelevance.   *A* must grow, not what he is most fitted to grow, but what will save most shipping space.   *B* must make, not what he is most fitted to make, but what can be made most easily out of local sawdust and mud.

---

[4] PEP *Report on International Trade*, p. 223.

Confusingly enough, this final efflorescence of economic nationalism has been accompanied by a striking expansion of world trade, and even by a slight tendency towards the relaxation of certain trade restrictions. But we must not, I think, be too much uplifted by these facts. For in the first place the rise in the price of raw materials on which the trade recovery has been largely based has increased the economic pressure on the hungry Powers, and reinforced their motives for achieving ultimate self-sufficiency. And secondly, a temporary Governmental thirst for deadly metals is not a very firm foundation on which to base our hopes of freer trade.

11. We have now, I think, at last, however summarily, taken all the elements of the confused story into account. What kind of picture emerges? It is, I am afraid, neither a very clear nor a very cheerful one. But it seems to be a picture of a world in which a volume of international trade, relatively diminished as compared with pre-war or even pre-crisis days, will continue to be conducted by mechanisms more cumbrous, in the face of hindrances more severe, than then prevailed. In some degree, whatever political appeasement may achieve, these restrictive policies will continue inevitably to be coloured by the Economics of War. But in some degree they will be based on conceptions of national advantage, expressed in terms like "stability" and "balance," which would not be unintelligible or unworthy even in a world where peace was assured. So vague, however, are these concepts, so difficult of measurement are the advantages claimed, that there will be constant danger of the whole system degenerating into a struggle of interested groups, and constant need for initiative and endeavour to prevent the volume of international trade from being constricted beyond what is necessary or reasonable.

What particular courses of action does it behove a wise man, who wishes to keep his feet upon the earth, to advocate in this situation? That is what I wish to learn. For my own part, I can only pass on, in my own grouping, the thoughts which I have picked up from better instructed persons than myself—I have in mind particularly Sir Arthur Salter, and the anonymous authors of that remarkable production, the PEP *Report on International Trade*, on which I have already freely drawn. I propose therefore to end by flinging down, without argument, six propositions to serve as bones of contention.

(1) We should do our best to widen and exploit such gaps in Comparative Advantage as remain. The broad dichotomy between agriculture and manufacture does not exhaust the truth; there is agriculture and agriculture, manufacture and manufacture. In agriculture, the deflecting menace of war obstructs, perhaps fatally, the full exploitation of the economically obvious specialisation—durable foods from the prairies, perishable foods from the home acres: but subject to its pressure, we must do what we can. In manufacture there is still room for specialisation between the simple and the complex, the low grade and the high, the goods for consumption and the machine that makes the goods. If, say the PEP experts, manufacturing industries abroad are assisted to grow on sound lines with active participation by United Kingdom manufacturers, the inevitable decline in the export of directly competitive goods should be accompanied by increasing exports of capital and other specialised goods. How much is there in this idea?

But I think the event may show that sooner or later we must go further, and reconsider in some measure that wholesale lopping off of manufactured imports from Europe which constituted, together with the depreciation of the pound, our main contribution to the international beggar-my-neighbour of 1931. For the wise-acres who sneer at three-cornered trade have not appreciated, I think, the full dimensions of the world agricultural problem. For reasons already emphasised, we are not in a position to make up to the primary producers overseas for the loss of those European sales which gave them pounds with which to buy from us—pounds which they can no longer obtain because the European manufacturer is hindered by our tariffs from earning them by the sale of his goods in our markets.

(2) National complexes about the balance of payments, while less acute than they were, still exist among creditors and debtors

alike; they are not wholly irrational, and we must take account of them. Thus we must be prepared for a time to see foreign investment largely take the form of the export of machinery and the like, financed by credit of a few years' duration, rather than of the old long-term untied loan; though the opportunities for that may return some day. In a different field, here is another interesting suggestion of the fertile PEP. In the old days, they point out, the balancing of imports and exports was not left so wholly to chance as we are sometimes taught to believe. For the merchant who sold British goods abroad frequently did a two-way trade, providing a market for the wares of his customers. This the big manufacturing firm, who has learnt to dispense with the merchant's services, fails to do; and the opportunities for trade are curtailed accordingly. There is room, suggests PEP, for a new type of trading company to fill the gap.

(3) We must be thankful for small mercies. Bilateral agreements are better than nothing to start with; so perhaps even are the despised exchange clearings with which the Continent of Europe is honeycombed. Groups for the mutual expansion of trade would be better still. Our rigid insistence on the maintenance of our most favoured nation rights hampers their formation; it is also, in view of the Ottawa system, something of an impertinence.

(4) In the light of what is now known about the nutrition of the people, it is not tolerable that we should chatter for ever, as I have been chattering, about there being too much food in the world, though too much of *some* foods there may from time to time be. The recent report of the League of Nations Committee on Nutrition has given some striking illustrations of how far, even in the richest countries in the most prosperous years, the diet of large sections of the people falls below what is reasonable. If increases in direct taxation are needed to implement a nutrition policy which shall reap the fruits of modern dietetic knowledge and at the same time go some way towards reconciling the conflicting claims of Wiltshire, New Zealand and the Argentine, sooner or later they will have to be forthcoming.

(5) A detached matter, but one of great importance. It is our bounden duty to contribute to political appeasement by the reversal of the policy of discrimination in favour of British goods in the Colonial Empire—a policy which has been indifferent economics, bad morals, and shocking diplomacy—though it may not be an economist's business to say so. The recent stirrings of Government policy in this direction are much to be welcomed, though it does not look as if Lancashire is going to allow them to go very far.[5]

(6) To relax import control in booms and tighten it in slumps is a bright thought as far as it goes: the trouble is that it is likely to occur to other people as well, and that spoils half the fun. The truth is, commercial policy is not enough. Unless we can work towards international control of the cyclical movement of trade, sooner or later we shall all be back in the gutter playing beggar-my-neighbour. But that is another story.

---

[5] Since the lecture was delivered, the quota system in Malaya has been further extended.

22

THE PROSPECTS FOR FOREIGN TRADE IN
THE POST-WAR WORLD*

By Jacob Viner‖ ‡

The growth of the doctrine and practice of national economic planning and the experiences and experiments of the Great Depression have led many persons to look with an unfriendly eye on foreign trade, with its intractability to the disciplines of national Five-Year Plans. Even British economists reared in the free-trade tradition have come to write down the benefits that flow from foreign trade and to attach so much weight to its risks and inconveniences and disorderliness as seen from the point of view of the national planner that they welcome any natural tendencies toward autarky and either definitely advocate positive reinforcement by government for such tendencies or condemn it in such mild and hesitant terms as for practical purposes to amount to the same thing.[1]

The actual shrinkage in the ratio of foreign trade to total production over the past few generations would of itself have sufficed to raise the question as to whether forces have not been at

---

* *Transactions of the Manchester Statistical Society:* an address given at the Annual Meeting, June 19, 1946. Reprinted by the courtesy of the Manchester Statistical Society and the author.

‖ Princeton University.

‡ The following article is reprinted without significant change from the original text.

[1] Cf. J. M. Keynes, "National Self-Sufficiency," *Yale Review*, June, 1933, pp. 755–769 (also published in *New Statesman*, July 8th and 15th, 1933); D. H. Robertson, "The Future of International Trade," *Economic Journal*, March, 1938, pp. 1–15. It is perhaps unnecessary to point out that there was a very substantial degree of difference as between these two articles in the assurance with which *the autarkic* approach was supported.

work to reduce the importance of international specialization in production as a means of augmenting national income, and still more, national welfare in general.   German economists had earlier given their answer the dignity of a historical law, the "law of the diminishing importance of foreign trade."   It is not clear, however, that they had much evidence to present in support of the existence of this law beyond what could be inferred from the fact that for most countries and for the world at large the ratio of the value of foreign trade to total production had for a long time been declining.   But as meanwhile total production was increasing by leaps and bounds, a decline in the ratio of foreign trade to total production, assuming no change significant for present purposes in the economic character of foreign trade, could be quite consistent with a great increase in its importance.   Also, as will be expanded upon later, the decline in the relative volume of foreign trade may have been neither fortuitous nor the consequence of the victory of the fittest in the struggle between international trade and domestic trade but may instead have been the logical consequence of deliberate policy whose economic merits could not be settled merely by a demonstration that it had, in part at least, attained its objective.   And even if the potential capacity of international specialization to yield economic benefit has been undergoing a secular decline, and if the relative shrinkage in the volume of foreign trade has been the consequence wholly or mainly of the shrinkage of its serviceability to economic welfare, the question would still remain as to whether it was sensible deliberately to suppress it further because the consequent injury from so doing would not be so great as was once the case.

It is the purpose of this paper to examine in general terms the nature of the historical forces which have been influencing the volume of foreign trade, their significance for the question as to whether there has been a decline in the potential capacity of foreign trade to yield economic benefit, and their bearing on the issue of what direction commercial policy should take in the post-war period.

It is offered as an explanation of the downward trend in the

ratio of foreign trade to total production that technological progress
has operated to narrow the range of comparative differences in
costs of production at least of manufactures, and has thus lessened
the scope for economic gain from international specialization, at
least in the manufacturing field.   Technical skills, it is claimed,
are now more widely distributed and technical knowledge is more
communicable throughout the world than was formerly the case.
Modern productive processes, also, are said to require less skill of
the mass of labourers involved, so that, in the words of Keynes:
"most modern processes of mass-production can be performed in
most countries and climates with almost equal efficiency,"[2] and in
the words of Robertson, more cautious only in that they are un-
qualifiedly applied to textiles alone: "in particular, it has become
evident that the simpler processes of textile manufacture can be
carried on with approximately equal efficiency by almost any kind
of population in almost any part of the world."[3]

Perhaps so, although it is certainly not borne out by the available statistics of labour inputs or fuel-inputs or capital-inputs per
unit of output for manufactures even as between the United States
and Canada, to say nothing of the United States and England, or
England and India, or Switzerland and China.   It leaves it a
mystery why countries with low money wages and low materials
costs should insist on the necessity of import duties to keep themselves from being undersold by other countries.   It is true that the
facilities for the diffusion of technical knowledge and for the spread
of skills are much more abundant than used to be the case.   But
there are now so much more knowledge and skill to be communicated and so many more persons to whom it needs to be communicated that, if reliable measurement were possible, perhaps it would
turn out that relative to the greater number of persons involved
the degree of diffusion is less rather than greater than it once was.
Even leaving "backward" peoples out of account, I am not con-
vinced that there is more levelling of industrial knowledge and

[2] *Op. cit.*, p. 760.
[3] *Op. cit.*, p. 2.

skills to-day in the textile industry or in manufacturing at large than there was a century ago. The engineers move about more freely than they did then—or do they? But if the tales they tell in meetings of their profession are true, their task is often more to design processes suitable to the capacities and the attitudes of the workers and to the special climatic and other conditions in a particular region than to show these workers how to use the processes originated in another region.

The belief that there is even a moderate approach to "equal efficiency" in manufactures throughout the world, or even throughout the north temperate zone, rests largely, I suspect, on some optical illusions. It is certainly true now, as it was not 50 years ago, that a wide range of countries can produce, if they will, locomotives, complicated machinery, worsteds, shoes, delicate instruments, of comparable quality. What is not true, however, is that they can produce them at anything like comparable real costs. The United States and Japan were in the 1930's both able to produce automobiles and chemicals and typewriters, and in the lower price ranges these were of comparable quality. But despite the very much lower wage rates in Japan it required a stiff amount of tariff protection to keep these American products from completely dominating the Japanese market. The fact that the products of different countries may look alike does not mean that the processes by which they were manufactured would also look alike if put under the scrutiny of the trained engineer or economist. The fact also that when the similar products of different countries are sold in the same market they tend to be sold at similar prices does not mean that their costs of production, even their *money* costs of production, were at all similar. The similarity of *delivered* prices may conceal wide differences in money costs of production at the factory, and underneath the differences in money costs at the factory may lie even wider differences in wage rates, and in prices of raw materials. If the differences of "efficiency" between countries in manufactures are small, why is it that it tends to be the high-wage countries who command the export markets? After all, manufactures do move in volume in foreign trade, despite high wage-rates in the exporting countries, despite transportation costs, despite extra marketing costs for the foreign product because of local differences in language, specifications, and fashions, and despite import duties often exceeding 50 per cent. of the factory price.   Since national deficiencies in efficiency are largely remediable if enough effort is made to remedy them, to minimize them invites costly complacency.   Intellectually, it involves implicit denial that the patently great differences in national levels of education, in the extent, character, and attitudes of labour organization, in nutrition and health, in social legislation and political organization, in the supply and quality of business enterprise, have much economic significance.

It is frequently claimed also that the substitution of electric for steam-power and of hydro-power and petroleum for coal, and the growth in relative consumption of the products of the light industries requiring less power, have lessened the dependence of industry on nearby supplies of coal and have thus facilitated a wider distribution of industry.   I suspect that this is largely a rationalization of what has been happening to England's coal-based industry. England specialized in industries relying heavily on coal, and *these* industries, notably the lighter branches of the steel industry, have become somewhat less tied to particular localities by the weakening of their dependence on coal.   The great development in power-technology, however, has not been so much the development of sources of mechanical power alternative to coal but the cheapening of mechanical power in general and its consequent substitution for man-power and animal-power.   The sources of mechanical power taken as a whole are much less widely distributed than man-power and animal-power.   The development of mechanical power, at least if a long retrospective view is taken, seems clearly to have widened instead of narrowed the range of average differences in comparative costs between countries.   This development, even more clearly, has increased the productive capacity of the world, and in doing so has increased the economic area in which differences in comparative costs can provide a potential field of operation for profitable regional specialization.

The growth in technical knowledge, it is also said, by extending the possibilities of substitution of one raw material for another, lessens the dependence of any one area on the outside world. The experience of Germany, as of Sweden, during the recent war does, of course, show that it is technically more feasible now than formerly for a country to maintain an approximation of its normal modern range of consumption even if imports are cut off. For some countries at least, it is consequently more nearly possible to survive in the absence of any imports than was the case in earlier times. But the growth of knowledge of the potentialities of raw materials also works in the opposite direction, namely, to make it profitable to substitute new imported for old domestic primary products. Wool and hemp and leather, the older staple raw materials of the textile industry, are less regionally concentrated in their production than cotton, rayon, and nylon. This is true also of animal fats as compared to copra, palm-seeds, cottonseed, and groundnuts, and of mud, wood, stone, and iron as building materials as compared to cement, glass, the lighter metals, and plastics.

It is only in manufactures that a case of any plausibility can be made for an historical trend toward the ironing out of differences in efficiency, and it is only in the exchange of manufactures for manufactures and on the assumption that primary products could not enter into foreign trade that the existence of such a trend would necessarily involve the contraction of the field for profitable foreign trade. For even if there were everywhere exact equality in efficiency in manufactures, there would still be large scope for gainful exchange of the manufactures of countries relatively inefficient in the production of foodstuffs and raw materials for the primary products of countries relatively efficient in agriculture and mining. The gain from foreign trade results from the existence of comparative differences in efficiency. Such comparative differences will exist as between manufactures and primary products even if there is absolute equality of efficiency for manufactures provided there is inequality for non-manufactured products. All that would then be true would be that there was no profitable basis for the exchange of manufactures for manufactures. In any case, notwithstanding these alleged historical trends of technology and despite the un-doubted trend toward the relative—as well as absolute—increase of the barriers against imports of manufactures, the statistics of world trade, at least since 1913, show no tendency for the propor-tion of foreign trade which consists of the exchange of manufactures for manufactures to decline.[4]

I find echoes in the recent literature of an old argument, pre-sented over a century ago by an English economist, Robert Torrens, to the effect that with growing density of population specialization in the production of agricultural products is checked by the opera-tion of the law of diminishing returns, with the result that all countries are forced largely to produce their own raw materials and their own manufactures.[5]

If migration and natural growth of population tended every-where to bring the ratio of labor resources to natural resources to the same level, this reasoning, granted certain other assumptions, would be sound. The old industrial countries would find that per unit of effort engaged in the production of manufactures for export they were getting in exchange over the years a smaller

---

[4] Cf. Albert O. Hirschman, *National Power and the Structure of Foreign Trade*, University of California Press. Berkeley, California, 1945, p. 126.

[5] Robert Torrens, *Essay on the Production of Wealth*, London, 1821, pp. 288–289. The relevant passage is worthy of quotation in full: "As the several nations of the world advance in wealth and population, the commercial intercourse be-tween them must gradually become less important and beneficial . . . the species of foreign trade which has the most powerful influence in raising profits and in-creasing wealth, is that which is carried on between an old country in which raw produce bears a high value in relation to wrought goods, and a new country where wrought goods possess a high exchangeable power with respect to raw produce. Now, as new countries advance in population, the cultivation of infe-rior soils must increase the cost of raising raw produce, and the division of labour reduce the expense of working it up. Hence, in all new settlements, the increas-ing value of raw produce must gradually check its exportation, and the falling value of wrought goods progressively prevent their importation; until at length the commercial intercourse between nations shall be confined to those peculiar articles, in the production of which the immutable circumstances of soil and climate give one country a permanent advantage over another."

quantity of primary products, and it would after a time become advantageous for them to divert productive resources from the production of manufactures for export to the domestic production of foodstuffs and raw materials. But population-growths and technological progress have been uneven as between industrial and agrarian countries, and it is by no means clear that the net result of all the factors at work has been to lessen the extent to which it is profitable under existing conditions for old industrial countries to depend on imports for their foodstuffs and raw materials. It is probably true, however, that many countries have remained as specialized in the production of primary products as they are only or mainly because of remediable backwardness in technology and scarcity of capital. For such countries systematic promotion of industrialization is wise. If industrialization makes great progress in the countries still largely devoted to primary production continued specialization in manufactures will become increasingly difficult for the older countries, and Torrens' forecast will become true. During the past century, however, it is not clear that any important country which had been a net exporter of primary products, with the exception of the United States, had ceased to be so as the result of industrialization, and the regions of the world still capable of great expansion of primary production if capital and technical knowledge are made available to them are so extensive as to make Torrens' proposition a hazardous basis for forecast even as to the next century.

Keynes has noted that as per-capita wealth and income rise, housing, personal service, and local amenities, which are much less available for international exchange than tangible commodities, take on a more important role in consumers' expenditures. But with greater wealth comes a greater absolute capacity to profit from exchange, domestic or international. Greater wealth tends also to develop the demand for greater variety, and this tends to increase on the average the distance between point of consumption and point of production. Transportation costs, moreover, tend to be smaller in proportion to value for quality goods than for the staples of low-income consumption, and cost to be less of a factor in determining the direction of consumer expenditures, and thus the cost of carriage from a distant source which is often referred to as a "natural protection" for home industry becomes less of a barrier to import for a rich than for a poor country. While it is by no means certain, therefore, that growth of per-capita wealth tends to lessen even the *relative* importance of foreign trade, there is no reason whatsoever for questioning that it operates to increase its absolute importance.

I have now considered all of the important historical trends in the patterns of production and of consumption which are supposed to have operated in the past century to lessen the importance of foreign trade. I believe I have succeeded in showing, at the least, that if these factors had alone been at work it would not be clear that the ratio of world trade to world production would have fallen and that even if their net effect had been to reduce the relative importance of foreign trade they would nevertheless have tended to increase its absolute importance, its absolute contribution to economic welfare.

Since the 1870's, the ratio of world trade to world production has, however, been in fact declining, but it is not difficult to find an adequate explanation aside from "natural" or unplanned changes in the conditions of production or in human tastes. From the end of the Napoleonic Wars to the 1870's, there was a marked downward trend in tariffs, but from then on there was almost everywhere—in Great Britain not until World War I—a pronounced upward trend which has continued without significant break to the present day. In the 1930's there were added to the ordinary import duties even more effective barriers to trade in the form of import quotas and exchange controls. Given the rising trend of these deliberate obstacles to foreign trade, it seems otiose to seek in "natural factors" the important causes of the decline in the relative importance of foreign trade which simultaneously occurred. Given the extent of these trade barriers in recent years, there seems more occasion for wonder at the strength of the natural forces which have enabled foreign trade to surmount these barriers as well as it has done.

In considering the potential capacity of foreign trade to contribute to economic welfare, it is important that attention be given to the potential trade, to the trade which has been suppressed by legislative and administrative barriers, as well as to the trade which has survived these barriers. But in appraising the importance cf even the actual trade, judgment will be warped if it is not valued higher than its ratio to total production. In the United States the export trade, including exports of services, does not provide a market for more than 10 per cent. of American production. Many Americans are led thereby to the conclusion that foreign trade cannot be a matter of vital importance to the American economy. It is proper, of course, to point out in rebuttal that this 10 per cent. is only what remains after the American tariff and the trade barriers of other countries have done their work. But even for the actual trade, the 10 per cent. figure is misleading as a measure of its importance. It is impossible to determine what figure would correctly represent its importance, but it is possible to demonstrate by reasoning that it would be significantly larger than 10 per cent.

The 10 per cent. overall figure conceals a wide range of ratios of value of exports to value of total output for different American industries, and the ratio reaches as high as 50 per cent. for some industries. This is in the short-run important. The uneven impact of shutting off of American exports on different American industries would mean catastrophe for some industries, with serious repercussions on other industries not directly concerned with export, so that the adverse effect on industry as a whole would be greater than if the impact were evenly distributed. But in the long run these divergencies of impact would be evened out through transfer of productive resources from the more hard-hit industries to other parts of the productive economy, and industry as a whole would share more-or-less evenly the adjustment to the elimination of exports.

A sounder method of appraisal of the long-run economic importance of existing foreign trade for the United States, or for any country with high import barriers, is to put emphasis on the imports rather than the exports. The American imports which are left free of duty are all imports which for one reason or another are regarded as of special value to the American economy. Some are "key products,"—products required in small volume only but vital as ingredients in the productive processes of important industries, and not producible at home. For the United States, some of the non-ferrous metals and some chemicals are representative of this category. Others are commodities which bulk large in the imports, but are not producible at all or in quantity in the United States, and are highly valued by the American public as raw materials for processing or as consumers' goods. Natural rubber, coffee, silk, cocoa, jute, bananas, are examples of this category. Still others are commodities which are readily producible at home, but at costs greatly exceeding the costs of the imported goods. Carpet wool, long-staple cotton, various hides and skins, belong either in this or in the previous category. Still another category, destined to be of growing importance, embraces urgently wanted commodities which are procurable from domestic sources only by serious encroachment on an exhaustible stock. Actual and potential examples are petroleum, copper, wood-pulp, lumber. In all these cases, the fact that they are admitted free of duty—or at low rates of duty—demonstrates, given the American prejudice against imports, that they are regarded as worth more to the economy as a whole than their monetary value alone would indicate. For all but the marginal units of such imports, the units which are just on the margin of being worth importing, there is for the United States a "consumers' surplus," an excess of what buyers would willingly pay rather than go without over what has to be paid. There is also "consumers' surplus," of course, in connection with the domestic consumption of goods produced at home. But given the strong political bias against import the fact that these imports are left free of duty reflects a judgment that, per dollar of money costs, they are on the average worth more than the commodities produced at home for domestic consumption. In the case of the imports which enter in spite of heavy duties part of the national "consumers' surplus" is appropriated as customs revenue accruing to the national treasury, and thus becomes visible and measurable. But even here there is considerable "consumers' surplus" which is not less important because it remains invisible.

In recent years there have been operating additional factors of "political" as distinguished from "natural" origin which throw difficulties in the way of a flourishing foreign trade. The increasing participation of governments in industry operates as a brake on imports in several ways. When a community spends its income through government instead of on private initiative, such intangibles as education, public health, parks, and swimming pools, and also, I fear, the writing of intra-office memoranda and the design and distribution of official forms, take an enlarged proportion of the national income, and these services must for the most part be produced locally. Governments as purchasers, whether of office supplies or furniture, or munitions, or cloth for uniforms, almost universally apply a supplementary tariff, in the form of an administrative preference to domestic sources of supply, over-and-above the ordinary import duties to which the purchases of private individuals and officials alike are legally subject. When governments nationalize old industries or set up new industries for public operation, they not only tend to add this supplementary tariff but to set it at whatever level is necessary totally to suppress imports as long as they have unused capacity and to expand capacity as long as with full operation of existing plant there still is a market for imports. Given the natural proclivities of governments, they are especially unlikely to tolerate imports which by their cheapness or their attractiveness of design or quality cast an embarrassing reflection on the efficiency or the taste of government enterprise.

Governments everywhere also—except perhaps in the United States—are undertaking the responsibility of maintaining "full employment," and are finding that the inherent uncertainties and irregularities of foreign trade present difficulties for the formulation of comprehensive economic plans and seem likely also to interfere with their execution according to plan. Given the general tendency these days to underestimate the contribution which foreign trade makes to the average level of economic well-being and to overestimate the contribution it makes to the instability of that level, there is great likelihood that many countries will seek a solution of this problem by cutting down imports to the bare essentials.

This is a gloomy picture I have painted of the post-war prospects for foreign trade, and yet I do not think I have erred on the side of pessimism. I have said nothing of the lingering effects of the devastation of war, of the dismantling of German and Balkan and Japanese productive resources, of the threat of civil war and revolution looming over a large part of the world's surface.

There is only one ground for hope that these forebodings will prove to have been wrong that I can see, and that is if the major countries of the world can be brought to agree to follow in concert policies with respect to foreign trade drastically different from those which they seem committed to follow if they act singly. The United States has been urging such agreement upon the United Nations, so far with every appearance of success. If the verbal agreements get translated into binding contractual arrangements, there will be ground for hope that foreign trade will again flourish and expand. If the American program should be rejected or should be allowed to peter out into a collection of polite and empty resolutions, it seems to me that, once the emergency scarcities of the reconstruction period have been met and the accumulated pools of gold and of hard currencies have been spent, foreign trade will shrink to a fraction of its former proportions and what will be left will in the main be conducted in terms of hard bargaining between state foreign-trade monopolies.

All of this, I believe, has very special significance for the United Kingdom, for its prosperity and its very existence, politically and economically, depend more than that of any other of the great industrial countries on its ability to pay by means of exports for a large proportion of the foodstuffs and raw materials which its economy requires.

I am very much aware that one strong current in English public opinion, supported by some English economists, holds that the American program not only fails adequately to meet the special needs of England but threatens to present fatal obstacles to their being successfully met. It contends that England will be unable to pay for the imports it must have unless she is free to use her bargaining power as a great importer to negotiate bilateral arrangements with supplying countries under which they will agree to take British exports in quantities and at prices sufficient to provide England with the means to pay for the volume of imports she needs. They maintain also that acceptance of the American proposals would mean that England would be tied to a dangerous extent to the American economy with its extreme cyclical swings. They urge that instead England should pursue a policy which insulates her economy from the repercussions of American booms and depressions.

I cannot do more here than indicate briefly what the general nature of my reply to these contentions would be if there were time fully to expound it. The American proposals meet more urgent British than American needs. The English critics of the proposals, I fear, seriously overrate and misinterpret England's "bargaining-power." It is not the urgent necessity of import but the willingness to take or to do without imports in large quantities according to the terms offered which gives great bargaining power. It is the United States, and perhaps Soviet Russia, which have great bargaining-power in this sense, not England. Temporarily, it is true, countries whose economies have long been geared to the British export market can reject the terms England may lay down only at cost of severe hardship for themselves. It is easy to draw up a fairly impressive list of countries which are more-or-less in this situation to-day. But the experience with Germany of many European countries in the 1930's under this method of trade-bargaining has made this situation unpalatable to the lesser partners in such bargains even when the terms offered are generous ones. Even with the countries whose dependence on the British market is today most marked, and even though England has no doubt been a generous bargainer, the bargaining has been harder than the English public has been made aware of. In some at least of these countries, in Sweden, in Denmark, and elsewhere also, it is common knowledge that there is fear of the long-run economic consequences of too great dependence on the British market, and determination to reduce that dependence through shift to new export products, the cultivation of new markets for the old export commodities, and industrialization to lessen the need for imports. An export market in Britain which would seem highly attractive under multilateralism loses much of its charm when it can be entered only on terms reached by bilateral bargaining of the kind which prevailed in the 1930's or which England would be obliged to resort to in a bilateralistic post-war world.

The American economy is an unstable one. Its behaviour from 1929 to 1933 was the result, however, of a combination of stupid mistakes of omission and commission which were without parallel in earlier American history and which are highly unlikely to be matched in the future, in degree at least, if not in kind. It is my belief that, whatever party is in power, no American Government will again permit unemployment to grow to mass proportions without taking strong remedial actions. The American trade proposals involve pledges that these remedial actions shall not take the form of the export of the unemployment elsewhere. It is in the spirit, though not yet in the letter, of the American proposals, moreover, that the menace of mass-unemployment should be met by concerted international action of a positive kind. It is quite in order for Englishmen to make concrete proposals for such action as would be likely to be effective in maintaining or restoring employment without involving extraordinary restrictions on foreign trade, if they believe that the American program is wanting in this regard.

England's problem is a specially difficult one, and the American proposals admittedly do not suffice to provide a guarantee that it can be satisfactorily resolved. But such a guarantee, I fear, is not obtainable by any other route. The nearest thing to a guarantee that I can see would be assurance: 1.—that there shall be good export markets for good British products, well-made, well-designed, and offered at reasonable prices; 2.—that the raw materials and foodstuffs England needs shall be available at competitive prices in open markets; and 3.—that England shall obtain, or maintain, a social and economic organization under which her labour power and other productive resources can be effectively converted into goods saleable in the world's markets at remunerative prices. The third condition England must take care of on her own. The American proposals are the nearest thing available to-day to an assurance that the first and second conditions can be met. If these proposals fail of acceptance, I see little chance that these conditions can be met by any other means on the scale which England's import requirements makes necessary.

I believe myself that the American proposals, commercial and financial, need further extension, especially in the direction of making provision, perhaps through a new international employment stabilization fund endowed with great capital resources, for concerted international action to cope through international investment with any threatened world depression. But in the light of American history and traditions in the field of international economic relations, the American proposals constitute a much more impressive offer of American economic co-operation with the outside world in general, and with England in particular, than anyone could have predicted or expected only a few years ago. There is no reason whatever why England should not freely propose amendment of particular details which in her opinion do not meet her special needs or are otherwise regarded as faulty, and why she should not demand amplification of the program where such seems expedient. A rejection of the program as a whole would be for England a tragic mistake. A further extension of it along lines making fuller provision for English needs and English fears, but not conflicting with its objectives of multilateralism and of reduction of trade-barriers, is not beyond the negotiating powers of England's able and hard-bargaining diplomats.

23

SOME FACTORS AFFECTING THE FUTURE OF INTERNATIONAL TRADE AND INTERNATIONAL ECONOMIC POLICY*

By Gottfried Haberler‖ ‡

I

The future volume and intensity of world trade, the extent to which international division of labor and specialization between countries will contribute to the output of goods and services of the world community of nations, will depend on numerous, complex, and partly interrelated factors. We may group them in the following manner: First, we have the fundamental technological factors relating to the methods of production, transportation, and communication. These factors determine to what extent the trading nations can, if they choose, benefit from international trade and division of labor, and how much countries will lose if they exclude themselves wholly or partly from participation in world trade, as a consequence either of a pre-meditated policy or of bungling. Second, we may list as a determining factor the volume of employment and economic activity, especially in the leading industrial countries. If these countries, particularly the United States, are able to maintain a high and stable level of employment, the volume of international trade will be higher, other things being equal,

---

* By permission from *Economic Reconstruction* [Chapter XVIII], edited by Seymour E. Harris, copyrighted, 1945, by McGraw-Hill Book Company, Inc., and by permission of the author.

‖ Harvard University.

‡ Squared brackets in the present text indicate all substantial additions to or alterations of the original text.

than if violent fluctuations were allowed to develop or if a depressed or semidepressed situation were allowed to persist.

The third complex of determining factors, which probably will be the most crucial and strategic one, is the political factor. To what extent will the leading countries be willing to specialize and rely on imports for the satisfaction of their needs? To what extent will international economic policies be an adjunct of military and power politics? Will it be possible to build up an international monetary system which permits a high volume of international trade? Will international investment be resumed to a sufficient degree? Will the leading countries be able to extricate themselves from the shackles of the planned war economy, or to what extent will central planning be carried over into the peace economy? If a high degree of central planning is continued, will it be possible technically, politically, and psychologically to integrate and adjust the various national plans internationally so as to take advantage of the potentialities of increasing output by international division of labor to an extent comparable to the degree to which this can be achieved under a comparatively free, competitive price economy?

The general tendency of the international economic policies, their liberal and expansive or restrictive, protective and autarchic spirit will depend to some extent upon the first two factors mentioned. The greater the benefits of international division of labor, which the basic technological factors permit, the greater the inducement to use them. The higher the level of economic activity and employment, the less insistent the demand for protection on the part of underemployed producers and the weaker the temptation to increase employment by shutting out foreign competition. The drift toward protectionist and autarchic policies of the past sixty or seventy years has been sharply accelerated by each depression. The movement away from free trade exhibits not only a secular trend, but also cyclical oscillations. Depressions and wars bring an outburst of protectionism—higher tariffs and other impediments to trade, which are only incompletely removed during the following peace or prosperity period.

To a large extent, however, the spirit of international economic policy is independent of the two factors mentioned. To a large extent it is a function of the general attitude toward state intervention and planning, administrative potentialities, and all the spiritual and material forces behind these factors. Some importance may also be attributed to the teaching of economists and the prevailing economic theories.

In the following pages some of these factors and recent changes that they may have undergone will be examined.

II

Let us first consider briefly the technological factor. Have there been any fundamental changes in the technique of production or transportation tending to bring about a radical change in the importance of international trade for many countries? The answer seems to be that there have been, of course, great changes, but not large enough to change the picture radically. For most countries, international division of labor could still make a substantial contribution to their economic well-being—a contribution which would hardly be less than it was twenty or thirty years ago.

There may be a few real—and there are certainly many apparent—exceptions to that generalization. Many countries have learned to do without certain things they used to get from abroad. For other things, they have developed expensive substitutes. Industrially backward countries, to be sure, have made great strides on the road toward industrialization and diversification. But the highly industrialized countries have not stood still either. The distance between the leading industrial nations and the raw-material-producing countries, in the tropical and temperate zones, is probably as great if not greater than it was thirty years ago.

It has been said (*e.g.*, by Keynes) that the modern development of the chemical industry has reduced the scope for profitable international division of labor. It is now possible to produce out of local dust and dirt (as Prof. Robertson once put it) all sorts of things which formerly had to be imported. This development probably more than offset the countervailing effect of the exhaustion of scarce natural resources in certain countries. Thus it has reduced the dependence of certain countries on international trade for minimum civilian and military requirements. In other words, the standard of living which could be maintained with no trade or little trade is higher than it was thirty years ago. But it does not follow that the improvement in that standard, which can be secured by utilizing to the full international division of labor, is less than it was. If the national income which can be produced without the help of foreign trade has been raised by the advance in the "synthetics industries," the volume of production which can be obtained with the help of trade has also been pushed up. The tremendous progress in the field of transportation (air transport, etc.) and the improved methods of mass production, presupposing as they do large markets, have contributed to making trade more profitable.

III

That the volume of international trade should rise and fall together with the rise and fall in national income and output of the trading countries is self-evident and has never been denied. It is true in the secular as well as in the cyclical sense. The upward trend in output and income the world over has been reflected in a rising trend in the volume of world trade. And the cyclical ups and downs in output and employment are closely paralleled by cyclical fluctuations in the volume of trade. Of course the rate of growth and decline in the two series need not be and is not the same. But the parallelism, especially with regard to recent short-term cyclical fluctuations, is very striking.[1] The reason is obvious: A part of the increased national expenditure is directed toward imported goods. Demand for foreign raw materials as well as for foreign finished goods increases (falls off) with a rise (fall) in national income.

---

[1] Cf., for example, August Maffry, "Foreign Trade in the Post-war Economy," *Survey of Current Business*, November, 1944; and Randall Hinshaw, "American Prosperity and the British Balance-of-payments Problem," *Review of Economic Statistics*, February, 1945. See also Imre De Vegh, "Imports and Income in the United States and Canada," *Review of Economic Statistics*, 1941, p. 130.

In the case of cyclical fluctuations in national income which are due to fluctuations in employment and unemployment, the mechanical influence on imports is strengthened by influences via policy. In depressions the demand for protection from competing imports becomes irresistible. Moreover, in depressions disturbances in the balance of payments of many countries are apt to occur, which in turn lead to the imposition of exchange control and other impediments to trade. The experience of the Great Depression in the thirties has made a deep impression on economists, businessmen, and politicians, especially in Great Britain. The fear that the United States will not be able to avoid severe depressions[2] is the chief professed reason for the reluctance of the British to play ball with the United States in setting up a stable exchange system and a liberal and multilateral trading system.

IV

The most important determining factor of postwar international trade will be international economic policy—international monetary as well as commercial policy. Commercial policy is, of course, no longer confined to tariff policy but has a most formidable armory of weapons at its disposal ranging from quotas, licenses, exchange control, informal pressure upon, or directives to, users of foreign goods, to partial or comprehensive government import monopolies.

In the capitalistic world the general tone of international trade policy, its degree of liberalism or restrictiveness, is (as explained before) strongly influenced by the state of business activity. But it is by no means uniquely determined thereby. Some of the other independent or semi-independent factors we shall discuss in the following pages.

The general outlook is profoundly different today from what it was at the close of World War I, and the probability of a speedy

---

[2] The explicit or implicit assumption that the severity of world depression of the thirties was due almost entirely to the instability of the American economy and economic mismanagement in the United States is greatly exaggerated. The depression had several important focuses outside the United States, one of them, for example, in Germany.

return to more liberal practices much smaller than it was in 1919. The economic ravages of the war are infinitely greater than they were twenty-five years ago. The objective chance of a durable peace based on a tolerably reasonable settlement following the present war seems to be decidedly less bright than it was after World War I; at any rate, the confidence of the world in the durability of the coming peace is likely to be less. This does not create an atmosphere favorable for the adoption of more liberal trade policies. But there are other factors pointing in the same direction on which the economist is more competent to pass judgment.

There is first the fact that economic planning and state interference in the economic process are much more widespread over the world than they were twenty-five years ago. The world has rapidly moved toward socialism between the two wars and had even before the present war reached the stage of collectivism in such important countries as Russia and Germany.[3] There can be no doubt that even without war and occupation the surrounding countries in eastern and southeastern Europe and Asia would have been rapidly assimilated to the economic system of the two collectivist giants. In western Europe and in the Western Hemisphere the movement toward central planning has been slower and the resistance greater; at any rate it has not yet gone so far as in central and eastern Europe. But the trend is unmistakably in the same direction.

Now it is clear that national planning and government direction of production and prices of the type and intensity now practiced almost everywhere require regulation of international trade. It

---

[3] The difference between the German and Russian planned economy is hardly greater than one would expect in view of the cultural differences between the two countries and in view of the fact that Germany was rich and industrially highly developed, while Russia was poor and industrially backward. In Russia the middle and entrepreneurial classes were wiped out and the new economic system built from scratch to the accompaniment of incredible suffering and bloodletting. In Germany the transition was comparatively orderly, efficient, and somewhat more gradual; and the middle and entrepreneurial classes (excepting the Jews) were not wiped out but tamed and utilized by the Nazi state for its purposes.

is true that theoretically it may be a different type of regulation from the old-fashioned restrictive protectionism. The theorists of socialism like Dickinson, Lange, and Lerner are fully alive to the advantages of international division of labor, and in their Utopias there is planned but "free" trade along the lines of comparative cost.[4] Unfortunately, international socialism is not likely to spring out of Mr. Lange's or Mr. Lerner's head as Pallas Athene sprang out of the head of Zeus. Whatever the final outcome, there will certainly be a long transition, a lot of muddling, with different countries advancing at a different pace (or even in different directions). This stage of development is obviously not conducive to bringing about a large volume of international trade.

To this should be added the fact that administrative skill and efficiency have increased greatly during the past twenty-five years. Today in many countries administrative tasks can be undertaken with a degree of efficiency which twenty years ago would have been entirely out of the question.

Parallel with these changes in institutions and policies has gone a change in economic thinking. We need not decide here which is cause and which effect, whether the chicken or the egg comes first. Probably economic thinking and economic ideas are led by economic events as much as they lead them.[5]

This change in economic thinking away from liberalism and free trade toward planning and protection has been especially marked in Great Britain, not so much in the United States. What holds of Great Britain holds also of Germany and other European countries, even of some of the smaller ones (e.g., the Netherlands), although economists in smaller countries are more likely to have a

---

[4] Cf., for example, Lerner's *Economics of Control*, Chs. 26–29.

[5] Witness the fact that the Great Depression has made a large part of economics "depression economics." If the Supreme Court follows the election, is it surprising that economists move with the business cycle? [Moreover, unfortunately cycles in economic thinking follow the business cycle with a considerable lag. This is illustrated by the fact that depression economics continued well into the war and post-war boom.]

vivid appreciation of the advantages of freer trade.[6]   In the following pages we shall discuss the most important issues involved in this ideological evolution.

V

The new British protectionism and imperial economic nationalism—whose most vocal publicists and theorists are Thomas Balogh, E. F. Schumacher,[7] and Paul Einzig—admit, of course, the theoretical validity of the classical argument for free, multilateral trade.[8] Only the crudest protectionists have ever failed to preface their arguments in favor of protectionist policies by an expression of respect to the free-trade doctrine in the abstract.   But the "new" doctrine is more refined than old-fashioned protectionism although almost every single element in the argument can be traced far back in the history of the theory of international trade.

------

[6] Not much economic literature has come out of Germany since the outbreak of the war, and it has probably dried up progressively as the war went on.   But so long as it was possible to follow German thinking and writing somewhat, the tenor in the field under consideration here was surprisingly similar to that in recent British writings.   Even under the Nazis, German economics was strongly influenced by British literature, just as many of the younger Keynesians have undoubtedly been deeply impressed by the apparent success of Nazi economic policies, especially in the field of international trade.   This influence is, for example, strongly in evidence in the essays on *The Economics of Full Employment: Six Studies in Applied Economics*, prepared at the Oxford University Institute of Statistics, Oxford, 1944.   These essays were written by the theoretical mentors and coaches of Sir William Beveridge and contain the ideas on which his *Full Employment* program is based.

[7] It is a pity that the great majority of British economists has been silenced for the time being—at least as far as the public is concerned—by the fact that they are engaged in war work for the government.   [After the end of hostilities this situation has fortunately changed.   English economists like Benham, Harrod, Hicks, Jewkes, Meade, Paish, Robbins, Robertson have returned to academic life and regained their liberty to write on matters of economic policy.   This has completely changed the tenor of the discussion and has revealed that the protectionists and economic nationalists are a small minority, at least among academic economists.]

[8] *Cf.*, for example, the opening article in the series "Principles of Trade," *The Economist*, Jan. 1, 1944.

Let us discuss now the most important cases of which it is said that drastic regulation of exports and imports cannot be dispensed with.   It should be clearly understood from the beginning that the practical issue is never the retention or abolition (or even sharp reduction) of the existing tariff walls.   Virtually everybody admits that a sudden elimination of existing tariffs is out of the question, although it may not be too much to hope for gradual reduction over a period of years, if wars and serious depressions could be avoided.   The practical issues are whether the more drastic impediments to trade such as quotas, exchange control, clearing and payment agreements, bulk purchases, and discriminatory tariffs can and should be eliminated or in some cases replaced by uniform nondiscriminatory duties—not immediately after the end of hostilities, but during a period of transition of, say, 4 to 5 years. Today a free trader is an individual who believes that tariff protection is sufficient and that duties should be fairly stable and should be subject to the most-favored-nation principle, *i.e.*, should be nondiscriminatory.[9]

Let us begin with the case of the chronically scarce dollar. The fear of "the overwhelming competitive power of American industry" and "the irrepressible tendency of the American balance of payments to be active" and "to suck in gold," is a strong motive for the reluctance in influential British quarters to accept the Bretton Woods agreements and to renounce the utilization of drastic trade regulations.   This theory has been accepted by the London *Economist* in a surprisingly extreme form.   In the second of two articles on "The Dollar Problem" (Dec. 4, 1943, pages 750–751), which were devoted to a discussion of the well-known Department of Commerce study, *The United States in the World Economy*, *The Economist* came to the following conclusion:

---

[9] It should go without saying that a prohibitive or a very high duty can be more restrictive than a large quota or a mild exchange control.   This, however, does not alter the fact that quotas and exchange control are much more disturbing elements in the price mechanism of a capitalist economy than duties.   *Cf.* J. Viner, *Trade Relations between Free Market and Controlled Economies* and G. Haberler and Martin Hill, *Quantitative Trade Controls*.

Indeed, it may very well be that the much-abused American tariff is more of an irritant than a real obstruction to the flow of trade. It is almost certainly true that any reduction in the tariff that is at all likely to be politically practicable would be wholly inadequate to solve the problem of the dollar. It may be, in fact, that the problem should not be regarded as the fruit of aberrations of policy . . . , but that it should be looked upon as the result of a set of economic circumstances never contemplated by the textbooks—namely, the existence of a country which, all policy apart, needs so little from the rest of the world, while the rest of the world requires so much from it, that an equilibrium of accounts can be brought about by no means available to a free, or even a tolerably free, market.

This is indeed an amazing statement and it is a sad experience to find it in the columns of *The Economist*. When writing the quoted passage the author of the article seems to have completely forgotten the most elementary principles of international trade.[10] It is on the same level as the view which used to be so popular in the United States, that America needs high protection, for otherwise she would be flooded by imports because of the incomparably high living standard of American labor and the consequential high cost of production of the American economy. The lack of synchronization of policy and public opinion in the field of international trade in the United States and England is deplorable. When American industry and public opinion become ready to apply the elementary principles of trade, important circles in Great Britain seem to have all but forgotten them.[11] Even in the land

---

[10] One wonders whether it was the same person who wrote the previously quoted series, "The Principles of Trade" which appeared in *The Economist* of Jan. 1 to Feb. 19, 1944.

[11] The following sentence, two paragraphs farther down in the quoted article, cannot fail to heighten one's amazement: "It would be a mistake to reach a conclusion of hopelessness. There may be hitherto unrevealed factors that will help to solve the problem—for example, an inflationary rise in costs in the United States unaccompanied by any fall of the dollar or any enhancement of tariffs." The writer seems to be entirely unaware of the fact that what he calls a "hitherto unrevealed factor" is nothing but the textbook case and he does not suspect that there may be a mechanism or a rule of the game to bring about that result; nor does he mention that for "inflationary rise in costs" he could substitute "appreciation of the dollar" or "depreciation of sterling." He even missed the terms of trade argument which he could have used with advantage for his case at that point;

of Adam Smith, Ricardo, J. S. Mill, and Marshall it is not only necessary to explain again and again to laymen and politicians but also to remind certain economists that trade is governed by comparative not by absolute advantage and cost.[12]

There are, however, more refined versions of the theory of the chronic dollar scarcity. A well-known one can be found in Mr.

---

that is, he failed to point out that an "inflationary rise in cost" in the United States, although it would correct the balance of payments, would imply a deterioration in the terms of trade for Britain and other countries.

[12] [The fallacy of an absolute dollar shortage has been propounded also by Dr. Thomas Balogh in "The United States and the World Economy" (*Bulletin of Institute of Statistics*, Oxford, October 1946, p. 321). Dr. Balogh was at that time naturally much impressed by the gloomy forecasts emanating from Washington concerning an impending depression in the United States and he swallowed hook, line and sinker the then current "projections" of excess saving which in the meantime have turned out to be entirely wrong. But the point here at issue is this: Dr. Balogh goes on to say that even if by "prodigious investment activity in the United States" a depression could be avoided, this would still not solve the dollar problem because by these very investments "the competitive power" of the United States would increase "faster than productivity rises elsewhere." Moreover, he thinks that even if savings were reduced and "United States business activity were maintained by social reform or 'non-productive' government expenditure" the dollar problem would still not be solved, because "given the initial startling superiority of the United States and the aggressiveness of its managerial leadership—it is likely that technical progress will be faster in the United States than in other countries." (*loc. cit.*)

The passage is not quite clear, but the meaning seems to be that there is grave danger that the United States will outcompete and undersell the rest of the world all along the line for an indefinite period to come. This is a great tribute to the productive power of capitalism and the free enterprise system but it is poor economics nonetheless. It conflicts with the basic principles of international trade, namely the comparative cost theorem.

For further discussion, see my article "Dollar Shortage" in *Foreign Economic Relations of the United States: in Practice and in Theory*, ed. S. E. Harris (Harvard University, Cambridge, Mass., 1948)].

Professor Samuelson, in his paper "Disparity in Postwar Exchange Rates" (in *Foreign Economic Policy for the United States*, ed. S. E. Harris, 1948), says that, "if one interprets the classical theory of comparative advantage in a narrow sense, a chronic unbalance will appear to be an impossibility," (p. 406). But then he continues that "from a broader view of the pure theory . . . such a chronic con-

Kindleberger's article, "International Monetary Stabilization," in *Postwar Economic Problems*.[13] It runs in terms of low price and income elasticity of American demand for imports, coupled with a high income elasticity of demand abroad for American exports and an absolute superiority of American industry in the production of durable goods over foreign competitors. The theory is not stated in precise terms and the exposition is marred by formal blemishes.[14] This makes it difficult to give a detailed criticism. It is certainly possible to make assumptions with respect to these elasticities which would preclude the existence of a stable or perhaps even any exchange equilibrium between two countries.

---

dition can exist. . . . It is simply not true that the theory of comparative cost proves that one country cannot continue to 'undersell' another in every commodity," (p. 407).

Lest the unwary reader gets the impression that the generally accepted principles of international trade are after all compatible with the assumption of an incurable, chronic unbalance, he should be warned to read Professor Samuelson's paragraph carefully. Then he will notice that the "broader view of pure theory" merely means the assumption of an unlimited credit line. All Professor Samuelson asserts is that the law of comparative cost does not prevent any country from continuously running into debt and from defaulting from time to time, provided it always can find somebody willing to 'lend.' Is there an economist, classical or otherwise, who would deny that?

Professor Samuelson then adds: "If one assumes only simple barter to be possible, then *ex definitione* goods can be exchanged only against goods. . . . The question has been begged but not proved." Barter is here, evidently, nothing but another expression for the assumption that a country may have to live within its foreign means, i.e., that it is not able to go on borrowing and defaulting. Now it may be unrealistic to assume that there must be an end to that process. But this is really irrelevant. For the problem on hand is precisely what would happen, if borrowing were no longer possible. What Professor Samuelson calls the "narrow view" is inherent in the problem, and on that assumption, as he himself says, a chronic unbalance becomes an impossibility.

This does, of course, not settle everything. The question remains what kind of equilibrium is likely to emerge. And this leads to the issue of the terms of trade. (See footnote 15 below.)

[13] Edited by Seymour E. Harris, pp. 375*ff*.

[14] *E.g.*, the author identifies marginal propensity to import and income elasticity of demand for imports; *op. cit.*, p. 380.

Nevertheless, it is safe to say that, for countries with many actual and potential competing export and import goods (such as the great industrial countries), the assumption of the nonexistence of a stable equilibrium is entirely unrealistic.[15] The question of the price elasticities will be taken up below.

VI

The next case must be taken more seriously.   It is the case of the cyclical dollar scarcity or of the disturbing influence of American slumps.   The American economy, so the argument goes, is

---

[15] [Even Joan Robinson, who can hardly be said to present the classical theory in the most favorable light comes to the conclusion that an equilibrium in the balance of payments can be always reached either by a change in the exchange rate or, what is analytically the same, by an adjustment of relative wages. "It may be objected [to the classical theory]," she says, "that in some concatenations of elasticities of demand and supply a rise in wages (or an appreciation in the exchange rate) may increase a surplus of exports, or a fall increase a surplus of imports, instead of wiping it out, but it can be shown that, from a formal point of view, this objection is not fatal to the classical analysis." After further analysis, she concludes that "the classical analysis can be vindicated." ("The Pure Theory of International Trade" in *Review of Economic Studies*, Vol. XIV, 1946–47, pp. 100–102.)

It is true she qualifies this admission by such clauses as "from a formal point of view" and "on its [*i.e.*, the classical theory's] own assumptions" and by the statement that "the hidden hand will always do its work [*i.e.*, there is always an equilibrium] but it may work by strangulation [*i.e.*, the equilibrium may require a standard of living below the existence level]." (*loc. cit.*) But since she deals with the purest of pure theory and makes no attempt to make realistic assumptions with respect to number of countries, range of actual and potential export and import goods, etc., these qualifications need not be taken seriously.

It is, of course, also true that the high level of abstraction on which she writes her brilliant essay does not prevent her from making sweeping applications of her theory to the real world, which could be justified only by making additional quantitative assumptions. This is in the best tradition of the early classical writers (notably Ricardo) though not in the Cambridge tradition of Marshall, who did not derive his qualified optimism from an unrealistic two-country, two-commodity case. But no harm is done, for the ideological roots of Mrs. Robinson's practical conclusions (as distinguished from the presentation of the classical theory) are too clearly visible.]

subject to specially violent cyclical fluctuations. Whenever there is a depression in the United States, American import demand drops precipitously and American producers attempt to push exports in order to find some offset for the contracting home market, thus spreading the depression to other countries. Owing to the economic weight of the United States and the comparatively large marginal propensity to import, the disturbance wrought abroad is very serious.

It is intimated that the United States will not be able in the future to stabilize its economy with any greater success than in the past.[16] On the other hand, it is assumed with implicit confidence that Great Britain, the members of the British Empire, and the countries in western Europe which are expected and invited to join the sterling bloc, will succeed in maintaining full employment all the time. Hence it will be essential for Britain and "like-minded countries," *i.e.*, for "full-employment countries," to keep their hands free to use all the trade weapons necessary to ward off deflationary influences from outside, *i.e.*, from the United States. In

---

[16] [This whole literature has, of course, been strongly influenced by the many gloomy forecasts and "projections" made in the United States during and immediately after the war which predicted a bad depression soon after the end of hostilities. These forecasts which were all based on a crude Keynesian theory were not borne out by the facts. That does, of course, not mean that there will be no depressions in the United States but there are good reasons to believe that a catastrophic slump like the one of the 1930's can and will be prevented.

In the meantime it has been clearly demonstrated that maintenance of full employment alone does not solve the balance-of-payments problem as was widely assumed in the economic literature which grew up during the Great Depression. It is even possible to argue that a depression in the United States, at least if it does not get too severe, is a more desirable condition from the British point of view than high prosperity, for two reasons: (a) It is easier to get American loans when the American economy is depressed and (b) the terms of trade move in favor of the industrial countries in depressions.

This is true, however, only under two conditions, first, that Great Britain is able to maintain full employment, in the face of an American depression and second that a sharp rise in American protectionism (like in 1930) is prevented. It follows that a trade agreement with the United States which effectively binds American duties is of the utmost importance for Great Britain.]

order to accomplish that purpose, discriminatory trade policies against the prospective mischief-maker are indispensable, while it is quite safe to practice multilateral trading methods within the "full-employment bloc." Therefore the "full-employment bloc" must reserve the right to use quotas, exchange control, bilateral (or intra-empire) clearing and payment agreements. The Bretton Woods agreements (and still more so the proposed commercial policy convention) would limit the freedom of action far too much and should therefore not be ratified.[17]

Now the idea that unregulated international trade and a regime of stable exchanges have the disadvantage of exposing a country to deflationary influences from abroad (inflationary influences are easier to ward off) is a very old one. But while it was formerly possible to reply that (apart from the long-run benefits of international division of labor) occasional expansionary influences from abroad were at least a partial offset to the disadvantage of being occasionally exposed to deflationary influences, that argument does not carry weight any more against the conviction that full employment will be maintained anyway by domestic measures and that, therefore, expansionary influences from abroad are not needed.

It does not seem very useful to speculate which countries are likely to succeed best in maintaining economic stability, because it is impossible to attain any confidence to such speculations.[18] It is probably true that in the past economic fluctuations in the United States were more violent than in Great Britain, and fluctuations in

---

[17] It has also been proposed that ratification should be contingent upon a formal declaration by the big powers, especially the United States, in which they "pledge themselves to stabilize national income at full-employment levels." It is not quite clear whether the political naivety of these proposals is genuine or simulated. In any case it should be clear that there is no government which would not promise, in all sincerity, to do all in its power to maximize employment and national income.

[18] In passing it may be mentioned that stability as such is important, not necessarily stability at full or a very high level of employment. Instability at a higher average level would be more disturbing than stability at a somewhat lower level.

Britain were more violent than fluctuations in France, etc. But there are plenty of cases in which foreign countries managed to produce their own depressions without American help!

It will be more fruitful to consider what could be done if a big country, say, the United States, in fact experiences a slump. What could other countries do to insulate themselves as far as possible against deflationary influences from America? We exclude domestic deflation because it would spell unemployment, which is precisely what we wish to avoid.[19] With this limitation the first rule is that credit must not be tightened in the face of an unfavorable balance of payments and an outflow of international reserves (including gold and international credit facilities of all kinds). This alone will, however, not be sufficient to maintain activity. It will offset the secondary effects of a deterioration in the current balance.[20] The primary effect, the decline of activity in the export industries themselves (and in industries suffering from intensified competition on the part of the industries in the depressed country) is not yet eliminated. To offset the primary effect too, it would be necessary to stimulate domestic expenditures by about the

---

[19] In case somebody answered that monetary deflation need not involve unemployment, if only prices and wages were sufficiently flexible downward, the answer is twofold: First, it is very doubtful whether a sufficient flexibility of prices and wages is politically possible and, if it were enforced, it would have many undesirable consequences. Second, waiving the difficulties just mentioned, it could work only if the same elasticity conditions are fulfilled which are required to make a policy of devaluation a success. *Cf.* now *Economic Stability in the Post-war World*, League of Nations, 1945, where the whole problem is discussed in considerable detail. See especially Ch. XVII of that report.

[20] By "secondary effects" is meant here effects via credit policy, not effects on consumption expenditures by way of the multiplier. It should be observed that champions of a gold standard with a broad gold base, like Prof. Hayek, recommend the elimination of the secondary effect. (*Cf.* his *Monetary Nationalism and International Stability, passim.*) This effect constitutes for him an "unneutral" behavior of money due to the erection of a multiple credit structure upon the gold base. Professor Hayek would, however, not approve of a policy of offsetting the primary effect and its multiplier consequences.

amount that aggregate expenditures have fallen in consequence of the deteriorated trade balance.[21]

If and when these offsetting policies are successful in preventing the spread of the depression, they intensify the outflow of reserves. What can be done about that? The ideal solution (apart from a domestic expansion policy in the depressed country which would effectively eliminate the trouble at its root) would be the existence of international reserves sufficiently large to enable the countries concerned to outride the storm. International monetary cooperation should, and through credit extension always could, make reserves large enough to achieve that end. How much would be required depends on numerous circumstances: on the comparative size of the countries involved; on the rapidity with which an export surplus in the depressed country makes its expansionary influence felt; on the severity and length of the depression. There is no space here to attempt a quantitative analysis, but it would seem that the depression of 1937–1938 could have been handled that way, while the depression of 1929–1932 would have required very large sums.[22]

If international reserves (including credit facilities provided by the Bretton Woods International Monetary Fund) prove insufficient to fill the gap, the adverse balance must be corrected by one method or another. This calls for important policy decisions

---

[21] It is, of course, misleading to discuss the problem entirely in terms of broad aggregates. In many cases it will be difficult to direct offsetting expenditures sufficiently in the direction required, i.e., toward the export industries. Obviously highly specialized raw-material-producing countries will be in an unfavorable position in this respect. Lack of space prevents a more thorough discussion of the problem in the present chapter, but it is obvious that multiplier effects on consumption can be more easily offset by appropriate spending policies or tax remissions. (For further details see the above-mentioned League of Nations report.)

[22] The earlier depression was, of course, complicated by the disturbing upward revision of the American tariff of 1930. Such a policy would always wreck international cooperation. It should not be forgotten, however, that other countries raised their tariffs too and did worse things. Not all of these steps can be condoned as having been forced by prior balance of payments troubles.

which give rise to divergent opinions. Still excluding deflation, the choice is between an alteration in the exchange rate,[23] exchange control of different types, and import restriction by tariffs, quotas, etc.

There can be hardly a doubt that from the liberal point of view, which wishes to minimize government interference in the international division of labor, devaluation would be the best solution. The question is, will it work?

VII

The attitude of many theoretical and practical economists toward exchange depreciation has undergone remarkable changes in the past 25 years. The traditional gold-standard position of the twenties gave way to an attitude favorable for exchange depreciation in the early thirties. Largely under the influence of Keynes, many economists and publicists, especially in England, regarded exchange depreciation as an easy cure for many different ills.[24] Now the pendulum has swung again in the opposite direction, not quite so far as under the gold standard, but almost as far and too far, in the writer's opinion.

The reasons for that latest reaction are manifold: During the first depression the currency depreciation was abused and overplayed; it will not work if all or many countries are ready to follow or to retaliate if any one country tries to steal a march on the others by depreciating its currency; all countries now have more powerful weapons of control at their disposal. Consequently, conservative

---

[23] Assuming a *tertium comparationis* (gold or currencies of "third" countries), this may take the form either of a depreciation of the currency of the deficit (full-employment) countries or an appreciation of the currency of the depressed surplus country.

[24] For a well-balanced discussion see S. E. Harris, *Exchange Depreciation*, 1936. The extreme recommendation to leave exchanges entirely free to the forces of the market and to refrain from any attempt to keep them stable was made by only a few. See, *i.e.*, C. R. Whittlesey, *International Monetary Issues*. Why a system of free exchanges did not and could not work is well explained in Nurkse, *International Currency Experience*, p. 117.

as well as radical economists have become skeptical. The conservative frequently rejects exchange depreciation in the illusion that an immutable gold standard is a practical alternative; the radical rejects it because he prefers quotas and exchange control.

The conditions under which a change in the exchange rate is an efficient method for correcting disequilibriums in the balance of payments are as follows:

1. Competitive exchange depreciation must be avoided and the depreciation should not be greater than is necessary to equilibrate the balance of payments. This is generally accepted and it is to be hoped that the proposed international monetary fund will effectively eliminate the danger of competitive depreciation.

2. Much more important is the danger of speculative capital movements being induced by expected changes in the exchange rate. Especially for smaller countries this is a very serious matter. Even if frequent changes are avoided, the mere fact that rates are no longer sacrosanct as under the gold standard may be sufficient to create a disposition to capital flight which would necessitate indefinite maintenance or reimposition of exchange control for the purpose of regulating capital movements. However, if and so long as such controls are maintained anyway, which may well be the case, the matter loses much[25] of its importance.

3. The third condition is that demand of the countries concerned for each other's exports should be sufficiently elastic with respect to price.[26] This matter of elasticity of international demand is of great importance, not only for the problem under

---

[25] Not all, because controls must be tightened if the propensity to move capital is strong.

[26] The elasticity with respect to income is also important. If it is high, a mild depression will be sufficient to correct an adverse balance. Since we rule out depression (unemployment) as a means of correcting a balance of payments deficit, income elasticity is not so important for us in the present context. But it is of some importance because, even without unemployment, real income will change with the terms of trade. In large industrial countries this is likely to be a negligible factor—a fraction of a fraction—but for small and internationally highly specialized countries it may be of some importance.

discussion, but for many others as well. We discuss it in the next and final section of this paper.[27]

VIII

If a country reduces its export prices by depreciation (or deflation), the value of its exports will rise the more elastic the foreign demand for its export goods in general; the value of its imports will fall the more elastic its own demand for foreign goods. It follows that the more elastic the demand, the easier it will be to correct the balance. If the elasticity were less than unity, a depreciation would increase the deficit, but in that case an appreciation would improve it. The situation would be most difficult to handle, if the relevant elasticities were in the neighborhood of unity. For in that case a correction either cannot be brought about at all through price changes or can be brought about only at the expense of disturbingly sharp changes in the terms of trade.

It is clear that it is a matter of utmost importance to know what the relevant elasticities actually are. This is important not only for the numerous questions connected with the balance-of-payments mechanism, such as the transfer of capital, reparations,[27a] etc., but

---

[27] As we remarked above, these elasticity conditions are also relevant for the case of a deflation with flexible factor prices, *i.e.*, deflation without unemployment.

[27a] It is instructive to compare the present discussion on the dollar shortage and American aid with the controversies on German reparations which took place during the 1920's. Then it was customary to distinguish between the problem of collecting reparations within Germany and the problem of transferring them. Nobody could doubt that Germany was able to raise the sums requested under the Dawes and Young plan, because they did not amount to more than a small fraction of the German national income. Therefore the discussion dealt mainly with the transfer aspect.

Today we can make a similar distinction between, let us say, the primary burden of eliminating a balance of payments (dollar) deficit and the secondary burden. The primary burden consists of the necessity of getting along without an import surplus financed by American aid. The secondary burden corresponds to the transfer problem; it reduces to the question of how the terms of trade would be influenced by an attempt to equilibrate the balance of payments and how a change in the terms of trade would affect the real national income.

That the primary burden is intolerably heavy can no longer be maintained

also for commercial policy: If the elasticities are small, it becomes possible for countries to influence their terms of trade by export and import duties and other devices; in other words, to exploit other countries monopolistically or monopsonistically. Of course, what matters in these cases is not so much the total or average elasticities, but the elasticities of demand of individual countries and for individual commodities and the opportunity of dealing separately with single countries and commodities by means of the numerous discriminatory devices of commercial policy, currency manipulation, and exchange control. In the present chapter we shall, however, confine ourselves to making some remarks on the question of the over-all elasticities.

Until recently it was fairly generally assumed that the elasticities of international demand are great. This assumption was made in many cases implicitly or possibly without clear realization that it might be otherwise; Marshall, however, took a strong position, fully conscious of the complexity of the problem and its important implication. In a famous passage he said:

It is practically certain that the demand of each of Ricardo's two countries for the goods in general of the other would have considerable elasticity *under modern industrial conditions*,[28] even if E and G were single countries whose sole trade

---

at this time (October 1948) for any one of the Western European countries. (Immediately after the end of hostilities the situation was, of course, different.) For that reason, discussion should be concentrated on the "secondary" burden, the terms of trade and the underlying elasticities.

I wish Professor Samuelson were right when he says that "economists have become so sophisticated as to put to the background of the discussion anything but the secondary burden," in *Foreign Economic Policy for the United States* (ed. S. E. Harris, 1948), p. 400. But I cannot agree that it requires a great degree of sophistication to see that. A little common sense and some knowledge of a few basic magnitudes would be quite sufficient.

For further discussion, see H. S. Ellis, "The Dollar Shortage in Theory and Fact" (*The Canadian Journal of Economics and Political Science*, Vol. 14, Aug. 1948); G. Haberler, "Dollar Shortage?" in *Foreign Economic Policy for the United States*, and "Some Economic Problems of the European Recovery Program," in *American Economic Review*, Vol. 38, Sept. 1948.

[28] Italics in the original.

was with one another. And if we take E to be a large and rich commercial country, while G stands for all foreign countries, this certainly becomes absolute.[29]

Nowadays the opposite assumption has become popular.[30] My
impression is, however, that many or most of those who make it
fail to realize sufficiently all factors involved. They argue as if
the elasticity of reciprocal demand of countries for each other's
products depends only on the elasticity of consumers' demand. In
fact, it depends also on the supply conditions. The import-
demand curve for each commodity can be derived by deducting,
for each price, domestic supply from domestic demand.[31] Hence,
even if the final consumers' demand for an imported article were
entirely unresponsive to price changes, the import-demand curve
of the country would have some elasticity, so long as there is
domestic supply which is not absolutely inelastic. Moreover, the
existence of potential export and import goods increases the
elasticity of the aggregate curve.[32]

It follows that the time factor is of importance. In the short
run, the elasticities will be less than if we allow time for supply to
adjust itself. Moreover, tariffs and other impediments to trade
reduce the elasticities of international demand, by reducing the
number of potential export and import goods. What is, however,
more important than the existence of tariffs at, say, prewar levels,
is the imposition of new duties to prevent increases in imports and
the existence of quantitative import controls. These practices are
calculated to make imports and exports very inelastic with respect
to price.

But apart from the last two complications (widespread quota
protection and *ad hoc* imposition of duties whenever imports rise),
I am inclined to believe that Marshall's statement is still correct

----

[29] *Money, Credit and Commerce*, pp. 171 and 354. *Cf.* also F. D. Graham, "The
Theory of International Values," *Quarterly Journal of Economics*, Vol. 46, 1932.

[30] *Cf.*, for example, Kindleberger, *op. cit.*

[31] For prices at which the former exceeds the latter the curve becomes, of
course, an export-supply curve.

[32] Of course, all that has been explained by Marshall, *op. cit.*

for all the larger countries with a great variety of actual and potential exports and imports.

Only recently attempts have been made to measure statistically elasticities of demand for imports.[33] These studies seem to lend support to the now fashionable assumption of low elasticities or even to point in the direction of these elasticities being in the neighborhood of one. These investigations are very ingenious and constitute a promising beginning. But for various reasons which cannot be discussed at this point, they are not yet sufficiently refined and trustworthy to upset the theoretical presumption that, except perhaps in a very short run, the elasticity of reciprocal international demand is likely to be great.

The only question which, it seems to us, can be seriously asked, is whether in a depression the elasticity of demand may be temporarily lower than usual. There are reasons for believing that this might be so.[34] But it is probably only a question of waiting somewhat longer for an appreciable effect.[35] This only underlines the

[33] See especially the excellent pioneering study by Randall Hinshaw, "American Prosperity and the British Balance-of-payments Problem," *Review of Economic Statistics*, February, 1945. Other papers on the same subject are in process of publication by various journals.

[34] See my notes "Currency Depreciation and the International Monetary Fund," in *Review of Economic Statistics*, November, 1944, pp. 178 and 191, reprinted in *Foreign Economic Policy for the United States* (ed. S. E. Harris, 1948, pp. 384–396). Thomas Balogh believes that demand elasticities for imports are low in depressions. (See his paper "The International Aspects of Full Employment" in *The Economics of Full Employment*, p. 142.) He concludes that currency depreciation is no suitable weapon to ward off deflationary effects from abroad, if they are due to slump conditions in foreign countries. However, a few pages later (p. 163) he says that an appreciation of the currency of the depressed country (which is assumed to have an active balance) "could, in fact, work. [It] could largely neutralize the effects of a slump in one country on the world, or would at least reduce or wipe out the surplus resulting from the reduction of effective home demand on the balance of payments." Why an appreciation would work, but a depreciation would be ineffective, is not explained.

[35] Another more serious matter is that a depressed country is likely to interfere with the process of adjustment by imposing import restrictions. But that has

desirability of large international reserves with the help of which countries can wait for the forces of adjustment to correct the situation.[36]

IX

The allotted space is running out and leaves room for only a few concluding remarks. Clearly quantitative studies are needed. But I think it could be shown that, given moderately skillful management, the large liquid resources now available to most countries, supplemented by the lending facilities of the proposed international agencies, should be sufficient, after the lapse of a transitional period of a few years, to operate a multilateral trading system without recourse, except in rare cases, to exchange control, quotas, bilateral clearings, and the like. Of course, such a system can be mismanaged and misused.[37] Large liquid resources may tempt countries to go on a spending spree or simply keep them from taking the necessary corrective measures in time. It would be too much to expect that this will not happen. But if it happens only occasionally and not to the leading countries, the world system should be able to absorb such shocks. That wholehearted cooperation, at least by the leading capitalistic countries, a minimum of political security, and the absence of acute fear of war are indispensable conditions should be self-evident. Nobody can tell now whether

nothing to do with the elasticity of demand, although Thomas Balogh mentions it as the chief reason for the elasticity being low (*op. cit.*, p. 142), thereby admitting that apart from this extraneous, political factor they may not be so low after all.

[36] Balogh (*op. cit.*, p. 161) argues that the full-employment countries will not wish to accumulate indefinitely debit balances with the country or countries that are unable to avoid cyclical depressions. But there is no reason why the balances should not be reduced during the years between depressions, in other words why the value of the currency of the full-employment countries should not be kept at an average level low enough to assure *long-run* equilibrium in the balance of payments.

[37] But surely the only practical alternative (which is not the gold standard but Schachtianism at least of the mild kind now proposed in Great Britain) would be also misused for other than its avowed purposes.

these conditions eventually will be fulfilled. But it is certainly worth trying.[38]

---

[38] [At this writing (Spring 1948) it is clear that the "noble experiment" which was made with the founding of the International Monetary Fund, the International Bank for Reconstruction and Development, and the proposed International Trade Organization has failed. Moreover, the chances are not too good that a success will be achieved in the near future. The reasons are manifold. The fact that the economic dislocations resulting from the war were greater than expected is probably the least important reason. More important is that no real peace has been established. In this respect the evil forebodings expressed in Section IV of the present paper have been proved to be only too well founded. However, the most important cause of the failure of the International Monetary Fund to make any headway towards the reconstruction of freer multilateral trade is the inability of the governments of most countries to end inflation and to restore internal monetary equilibrium and order. Especially the persistence of suppressed inflation in some key countries, notably in Great Britain, makes it impossible to restore equilibrium in the exchange markets and prevents "the establishment of a multilateral system of payments in respect of current transactions . . . and . . . the elimination of foreign exchange restrictions which hamper the growth of world trade." *Articles of Agreement, International Monetary Fund*, Art. I (IV).]

CLASSIFIED BIBLIOGRAPHY OF ARTICLES ON INTERNATIONAL ECONOMICS

The articles and essays included in the following bibliography cover a considerably broader field than the articles selected for reprinting in the text of this book. The text is limited to studies in the *theory* of international economics, whereas the bibliography, as its title indicates, covers the entire subject matter customarily regarded as international economics. This difference in coverage largely explains why the classification adopted for the bibliography differs somewhat from the classification employed for the readings themselves.

Anyone who has attempted to compile a bibliography in such a broad and diversified field as the present one knows that many articles which are clearly a part of his subject seem to defy any system of classification whatever. It is, therefore, probably unnecessary to warn the reader that the classes and subclasses presented below are by no means mutually exclusive; many articles would fit almost equally well into several different categories. Under such conditions the best that can be hoped is that the system of classification adopted involves a minimum amount of duplication and therefore requires a minimum amount of cross-referencing. But some cross-referencing is unavoidable in any event, and the reader who is interested in a special branch of international economics will seldom find that all of the articles relevant to this special branch can be found in one class or subclass of our bibliography.

One problem which had to be solved at an early stage was whether the system of classification should be functional or geographical. Since both systems appeared to have many defects, the system finally adopted was essentially a compromise: the major classifications are functional or topical, but within several of the major classes are geographical subclasses. In the section dealing with monetary aspects of international economics (II), for instance, there is a subsection devoted to the monetary problems of particular countries or regions. In deciding whether a particular article should be placed in a topical or a geographical subsection, we have usually given priority to the topical subsection. Thus, for example, articles dealing with fluctuations in the external value of the Canadian dollar and illustrating the principles of free-market exchange rates have, for the most part, been included in II-E (Currency Depreciation and Fluctuating Exchange Rates). On the other hand, articles devoted to a more general discussion of Canada's external monetary problems have usually been included in the geographic subsection, II-F, even though fluctuations in the external value of the Canadian dollar may be a part of the monetary problems discussed therein. In general, the articles included in the geographical subsections each cover a number of different functional topics with reference to a single country or region. Even articles which deal with only a single topic, such as exchange controls or fluctuating exchange rates of a particular country, however, have sometimes been included in the appropriate geographic subsection rather than the topical section; this has been done whenever the particular article was primarily descriptive in character, and when no broad principles of international economics were illustrated. From these remarks it should be apparent that a reader interested in a given problem for a particular country will usually find it profitable to examine both the geographical and the functional subsections of the bibliography.

The bibliography covers the entire inter-war period from 1919 to 1939, as well as the period of the second World War and the post-war years through 1947. Although this span of almost thirty years is clearly somewhat long for such an undertaking, it appeared to the editors that there was no later starting point which could have been adopted without omitting some important studies. The economic disturbances following the first World War were the source of a number of developments in international economics which are not only important in themselves but also highly useful for comparison with the post-war economics of today.

The extent to which the bibliography is complete or selective varies from one periodical to another. In the case of the English-language journals dealing primarily with economics, such as *The American Economic Review*, *The Economic Record*, and *The Canadian Journal of Economics and Political Science*, for example, an attempt has been made to obtain a complete coverage of all articles in international economics. For the foreign-language journals, on the other hand, and for English-language journals dealing with political, diplomatic, and social problems as well as with economics (e.g., *Annals of the American Academy of Political Science*, *The London Economist*, *Foreign Affairs*), the bibliography is necessarily highly selective. To have attempted a complete coverage of all such periodicals would have lengthened the bibliography unduly, without, in the opinion of the editors, adding much to its usefulness. This is particularly true of Russian journals which, in the field of international economics, are inferior to Russian books dealing with the same subject. Government publications, except for a few isolated pamphlets, have been omitted from the list.

Articles in French, German, and Italian periodicals have been listed in the language in which they were written, whereas articles in other foreign languages have been translated into English.

The editors gratefully acknowledge the valuable assistance which they have received from Mr. Philip W. Bell, Princeton University, Mr. Bernard Goodman, University of Oregon, Mr. Albert O. Hirschman, Board of Governors of the Federal Reserve System, and Mr. J. M. Letiche, University of California (Berkeley).

HOWARD S. ELLIS
LLOYD A. METZLER

July 1948

OUTLINE OF THE BIBLIOGRAPHY

I. PRICE THEORY AND INTERNATIONAL TRADE

I-A. THE LAW OF COMPARATIVE ADVANTAGE, THE GAINS FROM TRADE, AND RELATED TOPICS

Includes only articles in which the primary emphasis is on the international aspects of price theory. Applications of international price theory to particular problems, such as the problem of tariffs, will be found in other sections. See especially VI-B.

ADARKAR, B. P., High wages and international prices, *Manchester School*, III (1932) 21–28.

BEACH, W. E., Some aspects of international trade under monopolistic competition, *Explorations in Economics*, New York, McGraw-Hill, 1936, 102–107.

BENHAM, F., The terms of trade, *Economica*, VII, new series (1940) 360–376.

BREGLIO, A., Divisione del lavoro e scambio internazionali, *Giornale degli Economisti*, LXX (1929) 221–255.

BURNS, A. F., A note on comparative costs, *Quarterly Journal of Economics*, XLII (1928) 495–500.

COE, V. F., The gains of trade, *Canadian Journal of Economics and Political Science*, I (1935) 588–598.

COLM, G., Das Gesetz der komparativen Kosten—das Gesetz der komparativen Kaufkraft, *Weltwirtschaftliches Archiv*, XXXII (1930) 371–405.

CONDLIFFE, J. B., The value of international trade, *Economica*, V, new series (1938) 123–137.

DUNCAN, A. J., Marshall's paradox and the direction of shift in demand, *Econometrica*, VI (1938) 357–374.

ELLIOTT, G. A., Price ceilings and international trade theory, *Canadian Journal of Economics and Political Science*, VIII (1942) 186–196.

ELLSWORTH, P. T., Comparative costs, the gains from trade, and other matters considered by Professor Viner, *Canadian Journal of Economics and Political Science*, V (1939) 234–242.

———, A comparison of international trade theories, *American Economic Review*, XXX (1940) 285–289.

ENKE, S., Monopolistic output and international trade, *Quarterly Journal of Economics*, LX (1946) 233–249.

FEIS, H., What determines the volume of a country's international trade, *American Economic Review*, XII (1922) 238–245.

*GRAHAM, F. D., The theory of international values re-examined, *Quarterly Journal of Economics*, XXXVIII (1923) 54–86.

———, The theory of international values, *ibid.*, XLVI (1932) 581–616.

———, (Chairman) Round table on the theory of international trade, *American Economic Review*, XXX (1940 supplement) 219–222.

HABERLER, G., The theory of comparative costs, once more, *Quarterly Journal of Economics*, XLIII (1929) 376–381.

———, Die Theorie der komparativen Kosten und ihre Auswertung für die Begründung des Freihandels, *Weltwirtschaftliches Archiv*, XXXII (1930) 349–370.

*HECKSCHER, E. F., The effect of foreign trade on the distribution of income, *Ekonomisk Tidskrift*, XXI (1919, II) 1–32. (Translated by Svend and Nita Laursen.)

HOFFMAN, M. L., Cost theory and the theory of international trade, *American Economic Review*, XXVIII (1938) 742–746.

INMAN, J., The terms of trade, *The Manchester School*, VI (1935) 37–50.

JANES, C. V., The terms of trade, *Economic Record*, VII (1931) 64–70.

*LEONTIEF, W. W., The use of indifference curves in the analysis of foreign trade, *Quarterly Journal of Economics*, XLVII (1933) 493–503.

LERNER, A. P., The diagrammatical representation of cost conditions in international trade, *Economica*, XII (1932) 346–356.

———, The diagrammatical representation of demand conditions in international trade, *ibid.*, II, new series (1934) 319–334.

LORIA, A., On a passage of Professor Taussig's International Trade, *Quarterly Journal of Economics*, XLVI (1931) 187–188.

TAUSSIG, F. W., Reply, *ibid.*, 188–189.

LÖSCH, A., Eine neue Theorie des internationalen Handels, *Weltwirtschaftliches Archiv*, L (1939) 308–328.

LOVASY, G., International trade under imperfect competition, *Quarterly Journal of Economics*, LV (1941) 567–583.

MANOILESCO, M., Arbeitsproduktivität und Aussenhandel, *Weltwirtschaftliches Archiv*, XLII (1935) 13–43.

MARSH, D. B., The scope of the theory of international trade under monopolistic competition, *Quarterly Journal of Economics*, LVI (1942) 475–486.

MAZZEI, J., Deduzioni dalla teoria dei costi comparati a favore dell'autarchia, *Rivista Italiana di Scienze Economiche*, XI (1939) 251–297.

MERING, O., Ist die Theorie der internationalen Werte widerlegt?, *Archiv für Sozialwissenschaft und Sozialpolitik*, LXV (1931) 251–268.

NORTON, J. E., International trade and prices, *Quarterly Journal of Economics*, XXXIII (1919) 368–373.

OHLIN, B., Ist eine Modernisierung der Aussenhandelstheorie erforderlich?, *Weltwirtschaftliches Archiv*, XXVI (1927, II) 97–115.

———, Die Beziehung zwischen internationalem Handel und internationalen Bewegungen von Kapital und Arbeit, *Zeitschrift für Nationalökonomie*, II (1930) 161–199

---

* Reprinted in the present volume.

PORZSOLT, L., On the economic consequences of foreign trade, *Ekonomisk Tidskrift,* XLVII (1945) 17–33.

ROBERTSON, D. H., Note on the real ratio of international interchange, *Economic Journal,* XXXIV (1924) 286–291.

————, Changes in international demand and the terms of trade, *Quarterly Journal of Economics,* LII (1938) 539–540.

ROTHSCHILD, K. W., The small nation and world trade, *Economic Journal,* LIV (1944) 26–40.

SAMUELSON, P. A., Welfare economics and international trade, *American Economic Review,* XXVIII (1938) 261–266.

*————, The gains from international trade, *Canadian Journal of Economics and Political Science,* V (1939) 195–206.

SIMPSON, K., A re-examination of the doctrine of comparative cost, *Journal of Political Economy,* XXXV (1927) 465–479.

VINER, J., The doctrine of comparative costs, *Weltwirtschaftliches Archiv,* XXXVI (1932) 356–414.

WALKER, E. R., The theory of international trade, *Economic Record,* VI (1930) 89–101.

————, Comparative costs in international trade, *ibid.,* XIII (1937) 47–57.

*WILLIAMS, J. H., The theory of international trade reconsidered, *Economic Journal,* XXXIX (1929) 195–209.

YNTEMA, T. O., The influence of dumping on monopoly price, *Journal of Political Economy,* XXXVI (1928) 686–698.

YOUNG, A. A., Marshall on consumers' surplus in international trade, *Quarterly Journal of Economics,* XXXIX (1925) 144–150.

————, Supplementary note, *ibid.,* 498–499.

ZAPOLEON, L. B., International and domestic commodities and the theory of prices, *Quarterly Journal of Economics,* XLV (1930) 409–459.

I-B. HISTORY OF THE THEORY OF INTERNATIONAL TRADE

This section is limited, for the most part, to articles dealing with the history of the doctrines presented in I-A.   Additional articles discussing the history of the monetary theory of international trade will be found in II, particularly in II-E.

BLOOMFIELD, A. I., The foreign-trade doctrines of the Physiocrats, *American Economic Review,* XXVIII (1938) 716–735.

CABIATI, A., La dottrina dei "costi comparati" e i suoi critici, *Rivista di Storia Economica,* IV (1939) 1–31.

FAY, C. R., Adam Smith, America, and the doctrinal defeat of the Mercantile System, *Quarterly Journal of Economics,* XLVIII (1934) 304–316.

FETTER, F. W., The term "favorable balance of trade," *Quarterly Journal of Economics,* XLIX (1935) 621–645.

JOHNSON, E. A. J., British mercantilist doctrines concerning the "exportation of work" and "foreign-paid incomes," *Journal of Political Economy,* XL (1932) 750–770.

LA NAUZE, J. A., The substance of Adam Smith's attack on mercantilism, *Economic Record,* XIII (1937) 90–93.

---

* Reprinted in the present volume.

Mason, E. S., The doctrine of comparative cost, *Quarterly Journal of Economics*, XLI (1926–27) 63–93.

Meusel, A., Das Problem der Äusserhandelspolitik bei Friedrich List und Karl Marx, *Weltwirtschaftliches Archiv*, XXVII (1928, I) 77–103.

Packard, L. B., International rivalry and free trade origins 1660–78, *Quarterly Journal of Economics*, XXXVII (1923) 412–435.

de Roover, R., What is dry exchange? A contribution to the study of English mercantilism, *Journal of Political Economy*, LII (1944) 250–266.

di Tucci, R., Le idee d' un ignoto mercantilista piemontese del secolo decimoltavo, *Giornale degli Economisti*, LXX (1929) 80–88.

Viner, J., Angell's "Theory of International Prices," *Journal of Political Economy*, XXXIV (1926) 597–623.

———, Balance of trade, *Encyclopaedia of the Social Sciences*, II, New York, Macmillan, 1930, 399–406.

———, English theories of foreign trade before Adam Smith, *Journal of Political Economy*, XXXVIII (1930) Pt. I, 249–301; Pt. II, 404–457.

———, International trade theory, *Encyclopaedia of the Social Sciences*, VIII, New York, Macmillan, 1932, 200–208.

———, Professor Taussig's contribution to the theory of international trade, *Explorations in Economics*, New York and London, McGraw-Hill, 1936, 3–13.

White, H. D., Haberler's "Der Internationale Handel"; Ohlin's "Interregional and International Trade," *Quarterly Journal of Economics*, XLVIII (1934) 727–741.

II. MONETARY ASPECTS OF INTERNATIONAL TRADE

II-A. The Balance of Payments and the Concept of International Equilibrium

Includes general discussions of the balance of payment and the meaning of international equilibrium. For studies of the balancing process under particular types of monetary conditions and for particular types of disturbances, see II-B, II-D, II-E, II-F, III-A, IV-A, and IV-B.

Aftalion, A., Les théories dominantes du change, *Revue d'Economie Politique*, XL (1926) 769–795.

Angell, J. W., International finance, *Political Science Quarterly*, XLI (1926) 29–39.

———, Equilibrium in international trade: the United States, 1919–26, *Quarterly Journal of Economics*, XLII (1928) 388–433.

———, Equilibrium in international payments: the United States, 1919–35, *Explorations in Economics*, New York, McGraw-Hill, 1936, 13–25.

Anonymous, The balance of international payments of the United States, *Review of Economic Statistics*, XIV (1932) 118.

Baracs, J., Exchange stability and unproductive foreign credits, *Social Research*, V (1938) 328–349.

Baster, A. S. J., The international acceptance market, *American Economic Review*, XXVII (1937) 294–304.

Bell, H. H., Short-run equilibrium in the balance of payments, *Southern Economic Journal*, VIII (1941–42) 366–379.

BELLERBY, J. R., Some international aspects of monetary policy, *American Economic Review*, XV (1925) 60–66.

BLOOMFIELD, A. I., The mechanism of adjustment of the American balance of payments: 1919–1929, *Quarterly Journal of Economics*, LVII (1943) 333–377.

———, Ellis, H. S.; Lerner, A. P.; Mikesell, R.; Wood, E.; Domestic versus international economic equilibrium: discussion, *American Economic Review*, XXXVII (1947 supplement) 581–594.

BRONFENBRENNER, M., The Keynesian equations and the balance of payments, *Review of Economic Studies*, VII (1940) 180–184.

BRYCE, R. B., A note on banking policy and the exchanges, *Review of Economic Studies*, IV (1937) 214, 240–243.

CANNAN, E., The application of the apparatus of supply and demand to units of currency, *Economic Journal*, XXXI (1921) 453–461.

CONDLIFFE, J. B., Some problems of international economic equilibrium, *Index*, VIII (1933) 226–237.

DAVIDSON, D., Theoretical thoughts concerning the debates on foreign exchange, *Ekonomisk Tidskrift*, XXVI (1924) 11–34.

———, The controversy over foreign exchange and monetary policy, *ibid.*, XXXVII (1935) 63–78.

DONALDSON, J., The international balances: some theories and policies, *Annals of the American Academy of Political Science*, CLXX (1933) 152–161.

ELLIS, H. S., The problem of exchange systems in the postwar world, *American Economic Review*, XXXII (1942 supplement) 195–205.

FEIS, H., The mechanism of adjustment of international trade balances, *American Economic Review*, XVI (1926) 593–609.

FELLNER, W., Die quantitative Selbstregulierung der Zahlungsbilanz, *Archiv für Sozialwissenschaft und Sozialpolitik*, LXIX (1933) 590–628.

FREI, L., Crisis in the balance of payments of capitalist countries, *Vneshniaia Torgovlia*, (1933, No. 20) 14–16.

FRISCH, R., Forecasting a multilateral balance of payments, *American Economic Review*, XXXVII (1947) 535–551.

GIBSON, J. D., The Canadian balance of international payments: a study of methods and results, *Canadian Journal of Economics and Political Science*, VI (1940) 282–288.

HABERLER, G., Comments on "National central banking and the international economy," *International Monetary Policies*, Postwar Economic Studies, No. 7, Washington, D. C., Board of Governors of the Federal Reserve System, 1947, 82–102.

HALL, R. O., Some neglected relationships in the balance of payments, *American Economic Review*, XXXI (1941) 81–86.

HANSEN, A. H., The situation of gold today in relation to world currencies, *American Economic Review*, XXVII (1937 supplement) 130–140.

HARRIS, S. E., External aspects of a war and a defense economy: the British and American cases, *Review of Economic Statistics*, XXIII (1941) 8–24.

IVERSEN, C., The importance of the international margin: some lessons of recent Danish and Swedish monetary policy, *Explorations in Economics*, New York, McGraw-Hill, 1936, 68–83.

KNOX, F. A., Canadian war finance and the balance of payments, 1914–18, *Canadian Journal of Economics and Political Science*, VI (1940) 226–257.

————, Some aspects of Canada's post-war export problem, *ibid.*, X (1944) 312–327.

KORANYI, K., Zahlungsbilanz—Kaufkraft und Wechselkurs, *Weltwirtschaftliches Archiv*, XXVI (1927, II) 260–292.

LEWIS, C., The international balances, *Annals of the American Academy of Political Science*, CLXX (1933) 162–169.

MAGEE, J. D., The correctives of the exchanges, *American Economic Review*, XXII (1932) 429–434.

MAHR, A., Zur Theorie der Wechselkurse, *Weltwirtschaftliches Archiv*, XXVI (1927, II) 223–259.

MCKINLEY, G. W., The residual item in the balance of international payments, *American Economic Review*, XXXI (1941) 308–316.

NOYES, C. R., Stable prices versus stable exchanges, *Econometrica*, III (1935) 129–146.

*NURKSE, R., Conditions of international monetary equilibrium, *Essays in International Finance*, No. 4, Princeton, New Jersey, Princeton University Press, 1945.

————, Domestic and international equilibrium, *The New Economics*, (S. E. Harris, ed.), New York, Alfred A. Knopf, 1947, 264–292.

OHLIN, B., Equilibrium in international trade, *Quarterly Journal of Economics*, XLIII (1928) 184–188.

————, International price relations, *Index*, V (1930) 156–163.

OU, P.-S., International payments in national income, *Quarterly Journal of Economics*, LX (1946) 289–298.

*PAISH, F. W., Banking policy and the balance of international payments, *Economica*, III, new series (1936) 404–423.

PIGOU, A. C., Disturbances of equilibrium in international trade, *Economic Journal*, XXXIX (1929) 344–356.

ROBINSON, J., Banking policy and the exchanges, *Review of Economic Studies*, III (1936) 226–229.

SMITH, D. T., and HARRIS, S. E., The balance of payments in 1934 and the international economic position of the United States, *Review of Economic Statistics*, XVII, new series (1935) 28–33.

TRIFFIN, R., National central banking and the international economy, *International Monetary Policies*, Postwar Economic Studies, No. 7, Washington, D. C., Board of Governors of the Federal Reserve System, 1947, 46–81.

WHALE, P. B., International short-term capital movements, *Economica*, VI, new series (1939) 30–39.

WILLIAMS, J. H., The adequacy of existing currency mechanisms under varying circumstances, *American Economic Review*, XXVII (1937 supplement) 151–168.

II-B. THE PROCESS OF ADJUSTMENT UNDER THE GOLD STANDARD

See also I-A, II-C, II-F, III-A, IV-A, and IV-B.

BELLERBY, J. R., and ISLES, K. S., Wage policy and the gold standard in Great Britain, *International Labor Review*, XXII (1930) 137–154.

---

* Reprinted in the present volume.

BERNSTEIN, E. M., Exchange rates under the gold standard, *Journal of Political Economy*, XLVIII (1940) 345–356.

BOWSER, H. R., The gold percentage, *Review of Economic Statistics*, XV (1933) 82–96.

BRESCIANI-TURRONI, C., Egypt's balance of trade, *Journal of Political Economy*, XLII (1934) 371–384.

CARR, R. M., The role of price in the international trade mechanism, *Quarterly Journal of Economics*, XLV (1931) 710–719.

CURRIE, L., Money, gold, and income in the United States, 1921–32, *Quarterly Journal of Economics*, XLVIII (1933) 77–95.

DONALDSON, J., Gold and international trade, *Annals of the American Academy of Political Science*, CLXV (1933) 181–195.

———, Foreign exchange and gold policies, *ibid.*, CCXI (1940) 18–26.

EGLE, W., The spreading of the gold points as a means of controlling the movement of foreign short-term balances, *Journal of Political Economy*, XLVII (1939) 857–866.

EINZIG, P., The gold points of the exchanges today, *Economic Journal*, XXXVII (1927) 133–139.

———, Present and future gold export points, *ibid.*, 480–483.

———, International gold movements, *ibid.*, XXXVIII (1928) 662–665.

———, Gold points and central banks, *ibid.*, XXXIX (1929) 379–387.

———, Some theoretical aspects of forward exchanges, *ibid.*, XLVI (1936) 462–470.

———, Some theoretico-technical aspects of official forward exchange problems, *ibid.*, XLVIII (1938) 249–255.

———, The forward price of gold, *ibid.*, 748–751.

FLANDIN, P. E., The problem of the gold standard, *International Affairs*, XII (1933) 460–480.

GIDEONSE, H. D., The United States and the international gold standard, *Annals of the American Academy of Political Science*, CLXXI (1934) 118–126.

GILBERT, D. W., The economic effects of the gold discoveries upon South Africa: 1886–1910, *Quarterly Journal of Economics*, XLVII (1933) 553–597.

GILBERT, J. C., The present position of the theory of international trade, *Review of Economic Studies*, III (1935) 18–34.

———, The mechanism of interregional redistributions of money, *ibid.*, V (1938) 187–194.

GRAHAM, F. D., Achilles' heels in monetary standards, *American Economic Review*, XXX (1940) 16–32.

GREGORY, T. E., Britain and the gold standard, *Foreign Affairs*, XI (1932–33) 268–278.

HARDY, C. O., Gold and credit, *Annals of the American Academy of Political Science*, CLXV (1933) 197–201.

HAWTREY, R. G., The gold standard and the balance of payments, *Economic Journal*, XXXVI (1926) 50–68.

HOFFMAN, M. L., A note on the working of the gold standard, *Economica*, V, new series (1938) 84–89.

JOHNSON, E. A. J., Gerard de Malynes and the theory of the foreign exchanges, *American Economic Review*, XXIII (1933) 441–455.

JONES, J. H., The gold standard, *Economic Journal*, XLIII (1933) 551–574.

KEMMERER, E. W., The gold exchange standard, *Economic Essays in Honour of Gustav Cassel*, London, George Allen and Unwin, Ltd., 311–326.

KINDLEBERGER, C. P., Speculation and forward exchange, *Journal of Political Economy*, LXVII (1939) 163–181.

KNOX, F. A., The international gold standard reinterpreted, *Canadian Journal of Economics and Political Science*, X (1944) 502–507.

LAUGHLIN, J. L., The gold exchange standard, *Quarterly Journal of Economics*, XLI (1927) 644–663.

LAYTON, W. F., British opinion on the gold standard, *Quarterly Journal of Economics*, XXXIX (1925) 184–195.

LUTZ, F., A note on gold movements in the present international monetary system, *Review of Economic Studies*, V (1937) 66–72.

MOONEY, J. D., Stabilizing the exchanges, *Foreign Affairs*, XVI (1937–38) 222–230.

NADLER, M., The partial abandonment of the gold standard, 1931–1932, *Annals of the American Academy of Political Science*, CLXV (1933) 202–206.

OHLIN, B., Gold policy and the distribution of the world's gold, *Index*, IV (1929) 3–9.

PASVOLSKY, L., The gold standard before and after the war, *Annals of the American Academy of Political Science*, CLXV (1933) 171–175.

REYNAUD, P., France and gold, *Foreign Affairs*, XI (1932–33) 253–267.

RIST, C., Gold and the end of the depression, *Foreign Affairs*, XII (1933–34) 244–259.

ROBERTS, G. E., Speculation, gold, and bank policy, *Review of Economic Statistics*, XI (1929) 197–202.

SPRAGUE, O. M. W., Prerequisites to monetary stabilization, *Foreign Affairs*, XV (1936–37) 303–310.

SUBERCASEAUX, G., The modern gold standard with illustrations from South America, *American Economic Review*, XXI (1931) 249–259.

TOCKER, A. H., The monetary standards of New Zealand and Australia, *Economic Journal*, XXXIV (1924) 556–575.

TRIFFIN, R., International versus domestic money, *American Economic Review*, XXXVII (1947 supplement) 322–324.

WALKER, C. H., The working of the pre-war gold standard, *Review of Economic Studies*, I (1934) 196–209.

WHALE, P. B., The working of the prewar gold standard, *Economica*, IV, new series (1937) 18–32.

———, A note on the working of the gold standard: a reply, *ibid.*, V, new series (1938) 90–92.

WILLIAMS, J. H., The crisis of the gold standard, *Foreign Affairs*, X (1931–32) 173–187.

II-C. THE PRODUCTION AND MONETARY USE OF GOLD AND SILVER

Includes such topics as estimates of the world's gold and silver production in relation to demand, as well as the gold trade and production of particular countries. See also II-B and II-F.

ANONYMOUS, The future of gold, *Economist*, CXXVII (1937) 151–152.

———, The postwar gold problem, *ibid.*, CXXXIX (1940) 704–705.

BALOGH, T., The import of gold into France, *Economic Journal*, XL (1930) 442–460.

————, Some theoretical aspects of the gold problem, *Economica*, IV, new series (1937) 274–294.

BERRIDGE, W. A., The world's gold supply, *Review of Economic Statistics*, II (1920) 181–199.

————, The world's gold supply again considered, *ibid.*, XVI (1934) 141–147.

————, Some facts bearing on the silver program, *ibid.*, 231–236.

BOWEN, H., Gold maldistribution, *American Economic Review*, XXVI (1936) 660–666.

BRATTER, H. M., Silver—some fundamentals, *Journal of Political Economy*, XXXIX (1931) 321–368.

————, The silver episode, *ibid.*, XLVI (1938) Part I, 609–652; Part II, 802–837.

BROWN, P. S., The anomalous course of South African gold mining since 1925, *Journal of Political Economy*, XLVI (1938) 176–201.

BROWN, W. A., JR., Gold: master or servant?, *Foreign Affairs*, XIX (1940–41) 828–841.

————, Comments on gold and the monetary system, *American Economic Review*, XXXI (1941 supplement) 38–51.

BULLOCK, C. J., Gold, *Review of Economic Statistics*, XVI (1934) 148–152.

CANNAN, E., The future of gold in relation to demand, *Economic Journal*, XLIV (1934) 177–187.

————, The future of gold in relation to demand, *South African Journal of Economics*, II (1934) 119–129.

DAVIDSON, D., The gold question, *Ekonomisk Tidskrift*, XXIII (1921) 38–47.

EDIE, L. D., Gold economies and stable prices, *Journal of Political Economy*, XXXVII (1929) 1–30.

EINZIG, P., Some new features of gold movements, *Economic Journal*, XL (1930) 56–63.

————, Recent changes in the London gold market, *ibid.*, XLI (1931) 61–66.

ELLISTON, H. B., The silver problem, *Foreign Affairs*, IX (1930–31) 441–456.

FOSSUM, P. R., The relation of gold production to the prices of agricultural products, *American Economic Review*, XXI (1931) 281–282.

FROMAN, L. A., Bimetallism—reconsidered in the light of recent developments, *American Economic Review*, XXVI (1936) 53–61.

GARDNER, W. R., Central gold reserves, 1926–1931, *American Economic Review*, XXII (1932) 56–65.

GAY, E. F., The gold problem, *Foreign Affairs*, IX (1930–31) 195–203.

GRAHAM, F. D., The fall in the value of silver and its consequences, *Journal of Political Economy*, XXXIX (1931) 425–470.

————, and WHITTLESEY, C. R., Has gold a future?, *Foreign Affairs*, XVI (1938–39) 578–598.

GREGORY, T. E., The economic significance of gold maldistribution, *The Manchester School*, II (1931) 77–85.

HAMILTON, E. J., American treasure and the rise of capitalism, *Economica*, IX (1929) 338–357.

————, Imports of American gold and silver into Spain, 1503–1660, *Quarterly Journal of Economics*, XLIII (1929) 436–472.

HANSEN, A. H., Gold in a warring world, *The Yale Review*, XXIX, new series (1939–40) 668–686.

HARDY, C. O., The price level and the gold problem: retrospect and prospect, *American Economic Review*, XXXI (1941 supplement) 18–29.

HARRIS, S. E., American gold policy and allied war economics, *Economic Journal*, L (1940) 224–230.

——, Gold and the American economy, *Review of Economic Statistics*, XXII (1940) 1–12.

HAYEK, F. A. VON, A regulated gold standard, *The Economist*, CXX: 2 (1935) 1077–1078.

HAYES, H. G., Bimetallism before and after 1834, *American Economic Review*, XXIII (1933) 677–679.

HORNE, R., Silver, *International Affairs*, X (1931) 55–75.

KAHN, W. B., Trends in gold production and monetary stocks, *Foreign Affairs* XIV (1935–36) 702–705.

KEYNES, J. M., Fine gold vs. standard gold, *Economic Journal*, XL (1930) 461–465.

——, The supply of gold, *ibid.*, XLVI (1936) 412–418.

KIRK, J., Silver: a study in monetary instability, *Economic Journal*, XLI (1931) 384–394.

KITCHIN, J., The position of gold, *Review of Economic Statistics*, III (1921) 257–263.

——, Gold production: a survey and forecast, *ibid.*, VI (1924) 73–76.

——, Gold production: a survey and forecast, *ibid.*, VIII (1926) 114–119.

——, Gold production: a survey and forecast, *ibid.*, XI (1929) 64–67.

——, Gold production and consumption, *ibid.*, XIV (1932) 126–131.

KOTZE, R., The gold mining position, *South African Journal of Economics*, I (1933) 133–146.

——, Notes on Dr. W. J. Busschau's "The theory of gold supply," 132–135. *South African Journal of Economics*, V (1937) 132–135.

BUSSCHAU, W. J., Reply to discussion on "Theory of gold supply" by Kotze, *ibid.*, 136–144.

LEAVENS, D. H., The distribution of the world's silver, *Review of Economic Statistics*, XVII (1935) 131–138.

——, Bullion prices and the gold-silver ratio, 1929–45, *ibid.*, XXVIII (1946) 160–164.

LEHMANN, F., The gold problem, *Social Research*, VII (1940) 125–150.

LESLIE, R., Gold, 1936–37, *South African Journal of Economics*, V (1937) 229–242.

LESTER, R. A., Gold imports: cost and benefits, *American Economic Review*, XXXI (1941) 340–341.

HARDY, C. O., Professor Lester's questions on gold: a reply, *ibid.*, 560–562.

NEISSER, H. P., Professor Lester's questions on gold: a reply, *ibid.*, 562–563.

LIMEBEER, A. J., Gold mining industry and the gold standard, *South African Journal of Economics*, III (1935) 145–157.

MACHLUP, F., Eight questions on gold: a review, *American Economic Review*, XXXI (1941 supplement) 30–37.

MICHELL, H., The impact of sudden accessions of treasure upon prices and real wages, *Canadian Journal of Economics and Political Science*, XII (1946) 1–17.

MORTARA, G., Movimenti internazionali dell'oro nel decennio 1927–1936, *Giornale degli Economisti*, LII (1937), 793–806.

NEF, J. U., Silver production in central Europe, 1450–1618, *Journal of Political Economy*, XLIX (1941) 375–591.

NEISSER, H. P., The price level and the gold problem, *American Economic Review*, XXXI (1941 supplement) 1–17.

NICHOLS, J. P., Silver diplomacy, *Political Science Quarterly*, XLVIII (1933) 565–588.

OHLIN, B., Gold policy and the distribution of the world's gold, *Index*, IV (1929) 3–9.

PAISH, F. W., Causes of changes in gold supply, *Economica*, V, new series (1938) 379–407.

PHINNEY, J. T., Gold production and the price level: the Cassel three per cent estimate, *Quarterly Journal of Economics*, XLVII (1933) 647–679.

REEDMAN, J. N., Exchange depreciation and the future of gold, *South African Journal of Economics*, V (1937) 254–268.

———, The future of gold reconsidered, *ibid.*, VII (1939) 135–148.

———, Gold and postwar currency standards, *ibid.*, IX (1941) 379–399.

RIST, C., La question de l'or, *Revue d'Economie Politique*, XLIV (1930), 1489–1518.

ROUGH, B., The gold situation, *Economic Record*, VIII (1932 supplement) 70–75.

SALTER, A., The silver problem, *Political Science Quarterly*, XLVI (1931) 321–334.

SHIRRAS, G. F., The future of gold and Indian currency reform, *Economic Journal*, XXXVII (1927) 237–246.

———, Gold and British capital in India, *ibid.*, XXXIX (1929) 629–636.

———, The position and prospects of gold, *ibid.*, L (1940) 207–223.

SNYDER, C., The stabilization of gold: a plan, *American Economic Review*, XIII (1923) 276–285.

TUCKER, R. S., Gold and the general price level, *Review of Economic Statistics*, XVI (1934) 8–16, 25–27.

———, Price fluctuations and the gold supply, *Journal of Political Economy*, XLII (1934) 517–530.

DEL VECCHIO, G., Oro ed argento in relaziono con gli odierni problemi monetari, *Giornale degli Economisti*, XLIX (1919) 37–42.

WARREN, G. F., Some statistics on the gold situation, *American Economic Review*, XXIV (1934 supplement) 111–129.

WHITTAKER, E., Gold-mining taxation in relation to national planning in South Africa, *American Economic Review*, XXVIII (1938) 688–701.

WHITTLESEY, C. R., The gold dilemma, *Quarterly Journal of Economics*, LI (1937) 581–603.

II-D. EXCHANGE CONTROLS

Includes articles on the theory of exchange controls as well as empirical studies of the exchange controls of particular countries. Further articles on the subject, in which exchange controls are treated only incidentally to a discussion of a country's general monetary position, will be found in II-F. See also VI-D and VI-E.

ANONYMOUS, Trade under exchange clearings, *Economist*, CXIX: 1 (1934) 225–226.

———, South American exchanges, *ibid.*, 275–276.

———, Some consequences of exchange clearing, *ibid.*, CXXIII (1936 banking supplement) 11–12.

———, Britain's exchange clearings, I, *ibid.*, CXXXV (1939) 317–318.

———, Britain's exchange clearings, II, *ibid.*, 374–375.

———, Retreat from convertibility, *ibid.*, CLI (1947) 450–452.

AVISON, T. L., The Canadian Foreign Exchange Control Board, *Canadian Journal of Economics and Political Science*, VI (1940) 56–60.

BALOGH, T., The drift towards a rational foreign exchange policy, *Economica*, VII, new series (1940) 248–279.

————, Foreign exchange and export trade policy, *Economic Journal*, L (1940) 1–26.

BELSHAW, H., Import and exchange control in New Zealand, *Economic Record*, XV (1939) 173–186.

BLOOMFIELD, A. I., Postwar control of international capital movements, *American Economic Review*, XXXVI (1946 supplement) 687–709.

BOGGIO, G., Contingentamenti e cambi specifici, *Rivista Italiana di Scienze Economiche*, XI (1939) 970–996.

CIANO, J. L. D., The pre-war "black" market for foreign bank notes, *Economica*, VII, new series (1940) 378–392.

DEMARIA, G., I rapporti di cambio manovrato in regime di autarchia corporativa, *Giornale degli Economisti*, LIII (1938) 1–16.

————, Sulla teoria dei "clearings" complementari nel quadro dell'autarchia di approvvigionamento, *ibid.*, I, new series (1939) 225–250.

ELLIS, H. S., Exchange control in Austria and Hungary, *Quarterly Journal of Economics*, LIV (1939) Part II of issue, 1–185.

————, Exchange control in Germany, *ibid.*, LIV (1940) Part I of issue, 1–220.

*————, Bilateralism and the future of international trade, *Essays in International Finance*, No. 5, Princeton, New Jersey, Princeton University Press, 1945.

————, Exchange control and discrimination, *American Economic Review*, XXXVII (1947) 877–888.

GOICHBARG, A., Clearing agreements in world trade, *Vneshniaia Torgovlia*, (1934, No. 14) 12–14.

GUNDRY, H., Some features of wartime finance and exchange control in the Southwest African karakul trade, *South African Journal of Economics*, XIII (1945) 318–325.

HEUSER, H. K., The German method of combined debt liquidation and export stimulation, *Review of Economic Studies*, I (1934) 210–217.

HOLDEN, G., Rationing and exchange control in British war finance, *Quarterly Journal of Economics*, LIV (1940) 171–200.

————, A correction, *ibid.*, 694–695.

JANES, C, V., History of exchange control in Australia, *Economic Record*, XVI (1940) 16–33.

LEGUIZAMON, G. E., An Argentine view of the problem of exchange restrictions, *International Affairs*, XII (1933) 504–517.

LOW, A. R., Exchange control in New Zealand, *Economic Record*, XVI (1940) 218–235.

MASON, F., A cursory glance at exchange regulations, *Manchester School*, III (1932) 52–57.

MEYER, F., Devisenbewirtschaftung als neue Währungsform, *Weltwirtschaftliches Archiv*, XLIX (1939) 415–472.

MITNITZKY, M., Germany's trade monopoly in eastern Europe, *Social Research*, VI (1939) 22–39.

OHLIN, B., Mechanisms and objectives of exchange control, *American Economic Review*, XXVII (1937 supplement) 141–150.

POLK, J., Freezing dollars against the Axis, *Foreign Affairs*, XX (1941–42) 113–130.

RITTER, K., Germany's experience with clearing agreements, *Foreign Affairs*, XIV (1935–36) 465–475.

* Reprinted in the present volume.

Rona, F., Objectives and methods of exchange control in the United Kingdom during the war and post-war transition, *Economica*, XIII, new series (1946) 259–277.

Schumacher, E. F., Multilateral clearing, *Economica*, X, new series (1943) 150–165.

Scroggs, W. O., What is left of the gold standard?, *Foreign Affairs*, XIII (1934–35) 154–156.

Tocker, A. H., Exchange control in New Zealand, *Economic Record*, VIII (1932) 112–115.

Tsipkin, N., Methods of German foreign exchange dumping, *Vneshniaia Torgovlia*, (1934, No. 1–2) 42–45.

———, Exchange dumping as a weapon of commercial policy, *ibid.*, (1934, No. 13) 11–15.

White, H. G., Jr., Blocked commercial balances in American foreign policy, *American Economic Review*, XXIX (1939) 74–91.

Whittlesey, C. R., Exchange control, *American Economic Review*, XXII (1932) 585–604.

Novick, D., Comment on "exchange control," *ibid.*, XXIII (1933) 85–86.

———, Governmental controls and the theory of international trade and finance, *Quarterly Journal of Economics*, LI (1936) 90–105.

II-E. Currency Depreciation and Fluctuating Exchange Rates

Includes discussions of the supply and demand for foreign exchange, of the theory of exchange-rate stability, and of the experiences of particular countries with fluctuating exchange rates. See also II-F, IV-A, and VI-B.

Allely, J. S., Some aspects of currency depreciation, *Canadian Journal of Economics and Political Science*, V (1939) 387–402.

Amonn, A., Das Ziel der Währungspolitik, *Zeitschrift für Volkswirtschaft und Sozialpolitik*, I (1921) 401–430.

Angell, J. W., International trade under inconvertible paper, *Quarterly Journal of Economics*, XXXVI (1922) 359–412.

Anonymous, The foreign exchanges in 1934, *Economist*, CXX: 1 (1934) 18–19.

———, Foreign exchanges in 1935, *ibid.*, CXXII (1936) 18–19.

———, Devaluation in retrospect, *ibid.*, CXXV (1936 banking supplement) 6–7.

Baster, A. S. J., A note on Australian exchange, *Economic Journal*, XL (1930) 466–471.

Bickerdike, C. F., The instability of foreign exchange, *Economic Journal*, XXX (1920) 118–122.

———, Internal and external purchasing power of paper currencies, *ibid.*, XXXII (1922) 28–38.

Bloomfield, A. I., Foreign exchange rate theory and policy, *The New Economics* (S. E. Harris, ed.), New York, Alfred A. Knopf, 1947, 293–314.

Bresciani-Turroni, C., Il deprezzamento del marco e il commercio estero della Germania, *Giornale degli Economisti*, LXV (1924) 457–485.

———, La crisi della "stabilizzazione monetaria," *ibid.*, LXVII (1926) 1–48.

———, The purchasing power parity doctrine, *L'Egypte Contemporaine*, XXV (1934) 433–464.

Brisman, S., Some reflections on the theory of foreign exchange, *Economic Essays in Honour of Gustav Cassel*, London, George Allen and Unwin, Ltd., 1933, 69–74.

BROWN, A. J., Trade balances and exchange stability, *Oxford Economic Papers*, No. 6 (April 1942) 57–76.

BUCKLEY, H., Sir Thomas Gresham and the foreign exchanges, *Economic Journal*, XXXIV (1924) 589–601.

BULLOCK, C. J., Devaluation, *Review of Economic Statistics*, XVI (1934) 41–44.

BUNTING, F. H., The purchasing power parity theory reëxamined, *Southern Economic Journal*, V (1938–39) 282–301.

CABIATI, A., Il ritorno all' oro, *Annali di Economia*, II (1925) 183–275.

———, La bilancia dei pagamenti ed il commercio dei cambi in regime di moneta deprezzata, *Giornale degli Economisti*, LXVII (1926) 417–438.

CANNAN, E., Professor Cassel on money and foreign exchange, *Economic Journal*, XXXII (1922) 506–513.

CASSADY, R., JR., and UPGREN, A. R., International trade and devaluation of the dollar, 1932–1934, *Quarterly Journal of Economics*, L (1936) 415–435.

CASSEL, G., Some leading propositions for an international discussion of the world's monetary problem, *Annals of the American Academy of Political Science*, LXXXIX (1920) 259–267.

———, The restoration of the gold standard, *Economica*, III (1923) 171–185.

CONDLIFFE, J. B., Exchange rates and prices, *Index*, X (1935) 2–17.

COPLAND, D. B., The stabilization of sterling, *Economic Record*, VIII (1932 supplement) 2–19.

D. D., Ricardo and the theory of the foreign exchange rate, *Ekonomisk Tidskrift*, XXIII (1921) 21–23.

DEHEM, R., Emploi et revenus en économie ouverte: théorie et applications à l'évolution belge et britannique de 1919 à 1939, *Bulletin de l'Institut de Recherches Economiques* (Louvain, Belgium), XII (1946) 41–115.

VAN DORP, E. C., Abnormal deviations in international exchanges, *Economic Journal*, XXX (1920) 411–414.

DOUGALL, W. R., Exchange rates and Australian prices, *Economic Record*, VII (1931) 125–127.

EDELBERG, V., and KRISHNASWAMI, A., Measuring the power of undervalued currency to stimulate exports, *Review of Economic Studies*, V (1937) 1–17.

MALENBAUM, W., The power of undervalued currency, *ibid.*, V (1938) 143–151.

———, A reply, *ibid.*, 152–157.

———, Measuring the power of undervalued currency to stimulate exports, II, *ibid.*, V (1938) 195–217.

MALENBAUM, W., The power of undervalued currency—further considerations, *ibid.*, 218–233.

ELLIS, H. S., The equilibrium rate of exchange, *Explorations in Economics*, New York and London, McGraw-Hill, 1936, 26–34.

ELLSWORTH, P. T., Export, import, and domestic prices in the United States, 1931–36, *Review of Economic Statistics*, XIX (1937) 192–202.

FANNO, M., Inflazione monetarie e corso dei cambi, *Giornale degli Economisti*, LXIII (1922) 341–363, 481–511, 562–583, 609–620; LXIV (1923) 245–272.

FEILER, A., The pressure for monetary depreciation, *Social Research*, I (1934) 61–82.

FETTER, F. W., The Bullion Report reëxamined, *Quarterly Journal of Economics*, LVI (1942) 655–665.

Fox, B., Gold prices and exchange rates, *Review of Economic Statistics*, XVII (1935) 72–78.

Frei, L., The devaluation of the dollar, *Vneshniaia Torgovlia*, (1933, No. 10) 6.

———, The condition of basic foreign exchanges, *ibid.*, (1934, No. 22) 19–22.

———, The world exchange and credit crisis, *ibid.*, (1934, No. 1–2) 21–26.

Garnsey, M. E., Postwar exchange-rate parities, *Quarterly Journal of Economics*, LX (1945) 113–135.

Dupriez, L. H., Postwar exchange rate parities: comment, *ibid.*, 299–308.

Salera, V., Exchange rate parities: comment, *ibid.*, 622–623.

———, Reply, *ibid.*, 624–630.

Gignoux, C. J., Le problème monétaire mondial et la théorie du professeur Cassel, *Revue d'Economie Politique*, XXXVI (1922) 600–614.

Gilbert, D. W., Foreign trade and exchange stabilization, *American Economic Review*, XXVI (1936) 272–279.

Graham, F. D., International trade under depreciated paper: the United States, 1862-79, *Quarterly Journal of Economics*, XXXVI (1922) 220–273.

———, Self-limiting and self-inflammatory movements in exchange rates: Germany, *ibid.*, XLIII (1929) 221–249.

———, Fundamentals of international monetary policy, *Essays in International Finance*, No. 2, Princeton, New Jersey, Princeton University Press, 1943.

———, and Whittlesey, C. R., Fluctuating exchange rates, foreign trade and the price level, *American Economic Review*, XXIV (1934) 401–416.

Haberler, G., The choice of exchange rates after the war, *American Economic Review*, XXXV (1945) 308–318.

Hall, N. F., and others, eleven articles on currency devaluation in the following countries: United Kingdom, Denmark, Norway, Sweden, South Africa, Australia, New Zealand, Japan, Chile, Czechoslovakia, Belgium, United States, *Weltwirtschaftliches Archiv*, XLIII (1936) 1–318.

Harris, S. E., Auswirkungen der Währungsabwertung, *Weltwirtschaftliches Archiv*, XLIV (1936) 252–293.

———, Measures of currency overvaluation and stabilization, *Explorations in Economics*, New York and London, McGraw-Hill, 1936, 35–45.

Horsefield, J. K., Currency devaluation and public finance, 1929–37, *Economica*, VI, new series (1939) 322–344.

Janes, C. V., Some aspects of the sterling-group proposals, *Economic Record*, VIII (1932 supplement) 58–69.

Keilhau, W., The valuation theory of exchange, *Economic Journal*, XXXV (1925) 221–232.

Lachapelle, G., Les théories du professeur Cassel sur la monnaie et le change, *Revue d'Economie Politique*, XXXVII (1923) 549–561.

Lehfeldt, R. A., Statistics of extremely depreciated currencies, *Economic Journal*, XXXII (1922) 557–560.

Li, C.-M., The effect of depreciated exchange upon merchandise movements, *Quarterly Journal of Economics*, XLIX (1935) 495–502.

———, The theory of international trade under silver exchange, *ibid.*, LIII (1939) 491–521.

*Machlup, F., The theory of foreign exchanges, Pt. I, *Economica*, VI, new series (1939) 375–397; Pt. II, *ibid.*, VII, new series (1940) 23–49.

Mawas, A., Le "Bullion Report" Anglais de 1810, *Revue d'Economie Politique*, XXXIV (1920) 41–58.

Metzler, L. A., Exchange rates and the International Monetary Fund, *International Monetary Policies*, Postwar Economic Studies, No. 7, Washington, Board of Governors of the Federal Reserve System, 1947, 1–45.

Mikesell, R. F., The determination of postwar exchange rates, *Southern Economic Journal*, XIII (1947) 263–275.

Mises, L. von, Die geldtheoretische Seite des Stabilizierungsproblems, *Veröffentlichungen des Vereins für Sozialpolitik*, CLXIV (1923) 1–75.

Mortara, G., Alcuni confronti internazionali in materie di rivalutazione monetario, *Giornale degli Economisti*, LXVIII (1927) 613–617.

Ohlin, B., The equilibrium rate of exchange, *Ekonomisk Tidskrift*, XXIII (1921) 29–37.

———, European currency situation, "special phases of European conditions," *Annals of the American Academy of Political Science*, CXXXIV (1927) 151–159.

———, Can the gold block learn from the sterling block's experiences?, *Index*, XI (1936) 51–65.

Pigou, A. C., Some problems of foreign exchange, *Economic Journal*, XXX (1920) 460–472.

———, The foreign exchanges, *Quarterly Journal of Economics*, XXXVII (1922) 52–74.

Polak, J. J., European exchange depreciation in the early twenties, *Econometrica*, XI (1943) 151–162.

———, Exchange depreciation and international monetary stability, *Review of Economic Statistics*, XXIX (1947) 173–182.

Pose, A., La théorie de la parité des pouvoirs d'achat et les faits, *Revue d'Economie Politique*, XL (1926) 987–1013.

Reddaway, W. B., The new exchange rates, *Economic Record*, XII (1936) 187–194.

Remer, C. F., International trade between gold and silver countries: China, 1885–1913, *Quarterly Journal of Economics*, XL (1926) 597–643.

*Robinson, J., The foreign exchanges, *Essays in the Theory of Employment*, 2nd. ed., Oxford, Basil Blackwell., 1947, 134–155.

Rogers, J. H., The problem of international monetary stabilization, *Annals of the American Academy of Political Science*, CLXXXVI (1936) 34–40.

Roy, R., Balance des comptes et relations de change, *Econometrica*, XIV (1946) 257–284.

Scroggs, W. O., Depreciated currencies and world trade, *Foreign Affairs*, XI (1932–33) 513–516.

Seligman, E. R. A., Bullionists, *Encyclopaedia of the Social Sciences*, III, New York, Macmillan, 1930, 60–64.

Silberling, N. J., Financial and monetary policy of Great Britain during the Napoleonic Wars, *Quarterly Journal of Economics*, XXXVIII (1924) Pt. I, 214–233; Pt. II, 397–439.

---

* Reprinted in the present volume.

SILVERSTEIN, N. L., Effects of the American devaluation on prices and export trade, *American Economic Review*, XXVII (1937) 279–293.

SILVERSTOLPE, G., The periodic fluctuations of the rate of exchange, *Ekonomisk Tidskrift*, XXIII (1921 supplement) 125–137.

————, The foreign exchange problem, *ibid.*, (1921 supplement II) 69–92.

SMITH, L., The suspension of the gold standard in raw material exporting countries, *American Economic Review*, XXIV (1934) 430–449.

SMITH, N. S., Japanese competition and international trade theory, *Economic Journal*, XLVI (1936) 424–430.

SPRAGUE, O. M. W., The effect of depreciated exchange on foreign trade, *Annals of the American Academy of Political Science*, XCIV (1921) 51–54.

STAFFORD, J., The abandonment of the gold standard, *Manchester School*, II (1931) 92–99.

STUART, C. A. V., Metallic and non-metallic standards of money, *Economic Journal*, XXXIII (1923) 143–154.

TAMAGNA, F. M., The fixing of foreign exchange rates, *Journal of Political Economy*, LIII (1945) 57–72.

TERBORGH, G. W., The purchasing power parity theory, *Journal of Political Economy*, XXXIV (1926) 197–208.

TOCKER, A. H., Exchange policy and economic recovery in New Zealand, *Economic Record*, XII (1936) 86–91.

TRIFFIN, R., La théorie de la surévaluation monétaire et la dévaluation belge, *Bulletin de l'Institut de Recherches Economiques*, Louvain, Belgium, IX (1937–38) 19–52.

UPGREN, A. R., Devaluation of the dollar in relation to exports and imports, *Journal of Political Economy*, XLIV (1936) 70–83.

VARGA, E., The end of the Gold Block and the currency problem in the period of general crisis, *Mirovoe Khoziaistvo i Mirovaia Politika*, (November 1936) 17–30.

VEREIN FÜR SOZIALPOLITIK, Verhandlung über die theoretische und ökonomischetechnische Seite des Währungsproblems, *Veröffentlichungen des Vereins für Sozialpolitik*, CLXX (1925) 242–346.

WHALE, P. B., The theory of international trade in the absence of an international standard, *Economica*, III, new series (1936) 24–38.

WHITE, H. G., JR., Foreign exchange rates and internal prices under inconvertible paper currencies, *American Economic Review*, XXV (1935) 259–272.

WIJNHOLDS, H. W. J., Some observations on foreign exchange rates in theory and practice, *South African Journal of Economics*, XV (1947) 235–247.

WILLIAMS, J. H., Foreign exchange, prices, and the course of international trade, *Annals of the American Academy of Political Science*, LXXXIX (1920) 197–210.

————, Monetary stabilization from an international point of view, *American Economic Review*, XXV (1935 supplement) 156–170.

WYNNE, W. H., The French franc, June 1928–February 1937, *Journal of Political Economy*, XLV (1937) 484–516.

YOUNG, J. P., Exchange rate determination, *American Economic Review*, XXXVII (1947) 589–603.

ZAGOROFF, S. D., The external depreciation of the dollar and its effect upon the price level in the United States, *Journal of Political Economy*, XLII (1934) 641.

II-F (1). International Monetary Problems of Particular Countries: *Countries of the Western Hemisphere*

See also II-A, II-C, II-D, II-E, III-A, III-B, III-D, and VI-D.

Anonymous, The dollar, *Economist*, CXXV (1936 supplement) 18–19.

——, The dollar problem, I, *ibid.*, CXLV (1943) 717–718.

——, The dollar problem, II, *ibid.*, 750–751.

——, Bretton Woods, V, The dollar problem, *ibid.*, CXLIX (1945) 220–221.

Bloomfield, A. I., Operations of the American exchange stabilization fund, *Review of Economic Statistics*, XXVI (1944) 69–87.

Blyth, C. D., Some aspects of Canada's international financial relations, *Canadian Journal of Economics and Political Science*, XII (1946) 302–312.

Bogart, E. L., The United States as a creditor nation and the development of the export trade, *Annals of the American Academy of Political Science*, XCIV (1921) 37–42.

Chandler, H. A. E., International aspects of Federal Reserve policy, *American Economic Review*, XVI (1926 supplement) 316–324.

Edie, L. D., The rate of increase of the monetary gold stock of the United States, *Journal of Political Economy*, XXXVI (1928) 560–568.

Frei, L., Exchange policy of the U.S.A., *Vneshniaia Torgovlia*, (1942, No. 11–12) 6–13.

Goldenweiser, E. A., Effects of further gold imports on our banking situation, *American Economic Review*, XIII (1923) 84–91.

Goldstein, A., International aspects of Federal Reserve policy, *Review of Economic Statistics*, XVII (1935) 60–71.

Gregory, T. E., Twelve months of American dollar policy, *Economica*, I, new series (1934) 121–146.

Harris, S. E., British and American exchange policies (American experience), *Quarterly Journal of Economics*, XLVIII (1934) 686–726.

——, A year of banking and monetary policy, *Review of Economic Statistics*, XVI (1934) 72–79.

——, Dollar scarcity: some remarks inspired by Lord Keynes' last article, *Economic Journal*, LVII (1947) 165–178.

James, F. C., The return to gold, *Annals of the American Academy of Political Science*, CLXXI (1934) 138–143.

Keynes, J. M., The balance of payments of the United States, *Economic Journal*, LVI (1946) 172–187.

Knox, F. A., Canada's balance of international payments, 1940–45, *Canadian Journal of Economics and Political Science*, XIII (1947) 345–362.

Mikesell, R. F., United States international financial policy, *Canadian Journal of Economics and Political Science*, XII (1946) 313–320.

Nettels, C., The origins of paper money in the English colonies, *Economic History*, III, No. 9 (1934) 35–56.

Rogers, J. H., Federal Reserve policy in world monetary chaos, *American Economic Review*, XXIII (1933 supplement) 119–129.

Schneider, F., Jr., Federal Reserve policy: its international implications, *Foreign Affairs*, VII (1928–29) 543–555.

Taussig, F. W., The present and future of the international trade of the United States, *Quarterly Journal of Economics*, XXXIV (1919) 1–21.

TAYLOR, A. E., America's international accounts, *Annals of the American Academy of Political Science*, CCXI (1940) 9–17.

WHITTAKER, E., Too much gold—America's problem, *South African Journal of Economics*, V (1937) 215–216.

WILLIAMS, J. H., Latin America's foreign exchange and international balances during the war, *Quarterly Journal of Economics*, XXXIII (1919) 422–465.

———, The future of our foreign trade: a study of our international balance in 1919, *Review of Economic Statistics*, II (April 1920 supplement) 1–28.

———, Argentine foreign exchange and trade since the Armistice, *ibid.*, III (1921) 47–56.

———, The balance of international payments of the United States for the year 1920, with a statement of the aggregate balance July 1, 1914–December 31, 1920, *ibid.*, 169–212.

———, The balance of international payments of the United States for the year 1921, *ibid.*, IV (1922) 201–214.

———, The balance of international payments of the United States in the year 1922, *ibid.*, V (1923) 279–291.

YOUNG, R. A., The United States and gold, *Annals of the American Academy of Political Science*, CLXV (1933) 210–218.

———, Gold, capital movements, and the dollar, *ibid.*, CLXXI (1934) 107–117.

II-F (2). INTERNATIONAL MONETARY PROBLEMS OF PARTICULAR COUNTRIES: *The British Commonwealth of Nations, Excluding Canada*

See also II-C, II-D, II-E, III-A, III-B, III-D, and VI-E.

ANONYMOUS, Financial observations on the exchange equalization fund, *Vneshniaia Torgovlia*, (1933, No. 1) 12.

———, The eternal triangle, *Economist*, CXIX: 2 (1934) 782–783.

———, The exchange triangle, *ibid.*, CXXIII (1936) 492–493.

———, Sterling exchange policy, *ibid.*, CXXVI (1937) 69–70.

———, Tripartite agreement in action, *ibid.*, CXXIX (1937) 644–645.

———, The free market in sterling, I, *ibid.*, CXXXVIII: 1 (1940) 337–338.

———, The free market in sterling, II, *ibid.*, 381–382.

———, Ten years off gold, *ibid.*, CXLI: 1 (1941) 346–347.

———, The defence of the pound, *ibid.*, CXLIII (1942 banking supplement) 10.

———, Sterling after the loan, *ibid.*, CL (1946) 102–103.

———, Britain's balance of payments, *ibid.*, 1009–1010.

BASTER, A. S. J., A note on the sterling area, *Economic Journal*, XLVII (1937) 568–574.

BERNSTEIN, E. M., British policy and a world economy, *American Economic Review*, XXXV (1945) 891–908.

BLOOMFIELD, A. I., The British balance-of-payments problem, *Essays in International Finance*, No. 6, Princeton, New Jersey, Princeton University Press, 1945.

BONAR, J., Ricardo's ingot plan: a centenary tribute, *Economic Journal*, XXXIII (1923) 281–304.

BRUNYATE, J. B., Report of Royal Commission on Indian Currency and Finance, *Economic Journal*, XXXVI (1926) 659–665.

CANNAN, E., South African currency, *Economic Journal*, XXX (1920) 519–530.

CARPENTER, C. C., The English specie resumption of 1821, *Southern Economic Journal*, V (1938–39) 45–54.

CARTER, C. F., and CHANG, T. C., A further note on the British balance of payments, *Economica*, XIII, new series (1946) 183–189.

CASSEL, G., Monetary reconstruction, *International Affairs*, XI (1932) 658–677.

CLAUSEN, G. M., The British colonial currency system, *Economic Journal*, LIV (1944) 1–23.

COMSTOCK, A., The British Exchange Equalization Account, *American Economic Review*, XXIII (1933) 608–621.

COPLAND, D. B., Australian banking and exchange, *Economic Record*, I (1925) 17–28.

———, Notes on Australian exchange, *Economic Journal*, XXXV (1925) 645–649.

———, The Australian problem, *ibid.*, XL (1930) 638–649.

———, New Zealand's economic difficulties and expert opinion, *ibid.*, XLII (1932) 371–379.

CRUMP, N., Finance and reconstruction, *International Affairs*, XX (1944) 43–53.

DAUGHERTY, M. R., The currency-banking controversy, *Southern Economic Journal*, IX (1942–43) Pt. I, 140–155; Pt. II, 241–251.

EINZIG, P., The unofficial market in sterling, *Economic Journal*, XLIX (1939) 670–677.

FRANKEL, S. H., The situation in South Africa 1929–32, *Economic Journal*, XLIII (1933) 93–107.

GIBLIN, L. F., The Australian balance of payments, *Economic Record*, IX (1933) 296–297.

GREGORY, T. E., New Zealand's economic difficulties and expert opinion: a comment, *Economic Journal*, XLII (1932) 649–656.

HALL, N. F., The British Exchange Equalization Account, *Economist*, CXVIII: 2 (1934 supplement). 8 pp.

HARRIS, S. E., British and American exchange policies (British experience), *Quarterly Journal of Economics*, XLVIII (1934) 471–510.

———, The official and unofficial markets for sterling, *ibid.*, LIV (1940) 655–664.

HENDERSON, H. D.; ROBBINS, L.; and SALTER, A.; British monetary policy, a symposium, *Economist*, CXXV (1936) 297–298.

HURST, W., Holland, Switzerland, and Belgium and the English gold crisis of 1931, *Journal of Political Economy*, XL (1932) 638–660.

KEYNES, J. M., Professor Jevons on the Indian exchange, *Economic Journal*, XXXIII (1923) 60–65.

———, The committee on the currency, *ibid.*, XXXV (1925) 299–304.

———, The Gold Standard Act (1925), *ibid.*, 311–313.

———, The British balance of trade, 1925–27, *ibid.*, XXXVII (1927) 551–565.

———, The prospects of the sterling exchange, *Yale Review*, XXI, new series (1931–32) 433–447.

LESLIE, R., South Africa and the gold standard, *Economic Journal*, XLIII (1933) 88–92.

NORTON, J. E., The Bank of England and the money market, *Political Science Quarterly*, XXXVI (1921) 433–453.

PAISH, F. W., The British Exchange Equalisation Fund, *Economica*, II, new series (1935) 61–74.

———, The British Exchange Equalisation Fund in 1935, *ibid.*, III, new series (1936) 78–83.

————, The British Exchange Equalisation Fund, 1935–37, *ibid.*, IV, new series (1937) 343–349.

PUMPHREY, L. M., The Exchange Equalization Account of Great Britain 1932–1939: exchange operations, *American Economic Review*, XXXII (1942) 803–816.

SALTER, A., Conditional stabilization, I, *Economist*, CXXI: 1 (1935) 3–4.

————, Conditional stabilization, II, *ibid.*, 57–58.

SAYERS, R. S., The question of the standard in the eighteen-fifties, *Economic History*, II, No. 8 (1933) 575–601.

————, The question of the standard, 1815–44, *ibid.*, III, No. 10 (1935) 79–102.

THOMAS, P. J., Indian currency in the depression, *Economic Journal*, XLVIII (1938) 237–248.

WILSON, R., Australian exchange on London, 1893–1931, *Economic Record*, VII (1931) 121–125.

————, The Australian balance of payments, 1928–29 to 1931–32, *ibid.*, VIII (1932 supplement) 47–58.

II-F (3). INTERNATIONAL MONETARY PROBLEMS OF PARTICULAR COUNTRIES: *France*

See also II-C, II-E, III-A, III-B, III-D, and VI-E.

ANONYMOUS, The franc and its background, *Economist*, CXXIII (1936) 17–18.

AFTALION, A., Les expériences monétaires récentes et la théorie du revenu, *Revue d' Economie Politique*, XXXIX (1925) 813–841.

————, Les experiences monétaires récentes et la théorie psychologique de la monnaie, *ibid.*, 1009–1031.

————, Théorie psychologique du change (suite et fin) *ibid.*, XL (1926) 945–986.

————, L'histoire du change en France de 1915 à 1926 et la théorie psychologique du change, *ibid.*, XLIV (1930) 211–225.

ANSIAUX, M., The Belgian exchange since the war, *Economic Journal*, XXX (1920) 196–208.

BOUNIATIAN, M., Ma théorie des crises et les critiques de M. Aftalion, *Revue d'Economie Politique*, XXXVIII (1924) 656–673.

HANSEN, A. H., The international monetary situation, *Yale Review*, XXVI, new series (1936–37) 24–36.

HAWTREY, R. G., Stabilization of the franc and French foreign trade—a comment, *Economic Journal*, XLIV (1934) 729–730.

KEYNES, J. M., The French stabilization law, *Economic Journal*, XXXVIII (1928) 490–494.

LAYTON, W., The end of the gold bloc: a new opportunity for international cooperation, *International Affairs*, XVI (1937) 23–44.

MARJOLIN, R., Reflections on the Blum experiment, *Economica*, V, new series (1938) 177–192.

PIROU, G., La piastre et le franc, *Revue d'Economie Politique*, LII (1938) 42–64.

RIST, L. and SCHWOB, P. A., Vingt-cinq ans d'évolution dans la balance des paiements française, *Revue d'Economie Politique*, LIII (1939) 528–550.

DE SANCHEZ, J. A. M., Stabilizing the franc, *Foreign Affairs*, VII (1928–29) 64–71.

SCHWOB, P. A., Reflections on the consequences of the stabilization of the franc on French foreign trade, *Economic Journal*, XLIV (1934) 509–512.

———, French monetary policy and its critics, *Economica*, II, new series (1935) 277–297.

HAWTREY, R. G., French monetary policy, *ibid.*, III, new series (1936) 61–71.

———, A reply to Mr. Hawtrey, *ibid.*, 72–77.

WOLFF, R., Liaison entre prix et monnaie, *Revue d'Economie Politique*, XLVIII (1934) 1691–1763.

II-F (4). INTERNATIONAL MONETARY PROBLEMS OF PARTICULAR COUNTRIES: *Other European Countries and Europe as a Whole*

See also II-C, II-D, II-E, III-A, III-B, III-D, and VI-E.

AGGER, E. E., The proposed new central gold bank of Germany, *American Economic Review*, XIV (1924) 463–474.

ANDERSON, B. M., JR., The European financial situation and possible remedies, *American Economic Review*, XIII (1923) 65–67.

ANONYMOUS, International (London) Economic Conference, *Vneshniaia Torgovlia*, (1933, No. 11) 1–2.

———, Survey of the international monetary conference, *ibid.*, (1933, No. 13–14) 32–33.

BACHMANN, G., The gold standard in Switzerland, *American Economic Review*, XIX (1929) 198–205.

BORTKIEWICZ, L., Valutapolitik auf neuer Grundlage, *Bankarchiv*, XIX (1920) 98 ff.

BRESCIANI-TURRONI, C., Studi sul deprezzamento del marco tedesco, *Giornale degli Economisti*, LXV (1924) 219–247.

DAVIS, J. S., World banking and currency: a review of recent developments, *Review of Economic Statistics*, II (1920) 209–238.

———, World currency and banking: the first Brussels financial conference, *ibid.*, 349–380.

ECKER, L. L., The Hungarian thrift-crown, *American Economic Review*, XXIII (1933) 471–474.

EINAUDI, L., and MORGENSTERN, O., Il controllo dei cambi esteri in Austria (1931–1934) *Rivista di Storia Economica*, II (1937) 312–343.

GRAMPP, W. D., The Italian lira, 1938–45, *Journal of Political Economy*, LIV (1946) 309–334.

HAHN, A., Handelsbilanz—Zahlungsbilanz Valuta, Güterpreise, *Archiv für Sozialwissenschaft und Sozialpolitik*, XLVIII (1920–21) 596–614.

HAMILTON, E. J., Monetary disorder and economic decadence in Spain, 1651–1700, *Journal of Political Economy*, LI (1943) 477–493.

KOCH, K., Paper currency and monetary policy in Sweden, *Economic Essays in Honour of Gustav Cassel*, London, George Allen & Unwin Ltd., 1933, 343–356.

LESTER, R. A., The gold-parity depression in Norway and Denmark, 1925–28, *Journal of Political Economy*, XLV (1937) 433–465.

CHRISTENSON, C. L., and LESTER, R. A., Criticism and discussion, *ibid.*, 808–815.

———, International aspects of wartime monetary experience, *Essays in International Finance*, No. 3, Princeton, New Jersey, Princeton University Press, 1944.

Lotz, W., Valutafrage und öffentliche Finanzen in Deutschland, *Veröffentlichungen des Vereins für Sozialpolitik*, CLXIV (1923) 100–118.

Lutz, F. A., The Marshall Plan and European recovery, *Essays in International Finance*, No. 9, Princeton, New Jersey, Princeton University Press, 1948.

Mortara, G., La rivalutazione della lira e il commercio con l' estero, *Giornale degli Economisti*, LXIX (1928) 350–359.

Moulton, H. G., Economic conditions in Europe, *American Economic Review*, XIII (1923) 48–64.

Nadler, M., European currencies and the gold standard, *Journal of Political Economy*, XXXII (1924) 567–581.

Ohlin, B., Sweden's monetary policy: twelve months of paper currency, *Index*, VII (1932) 268–277.

Penson, J. H., The Polish mark in 1921, *Economic Journal*, XXXII (1922) 163–170.

Redlich, F., Payments between nations in the eighteenth and early nineteenth centuries, *Quarterly Journal of Economics*, L (1936) 694–705.

Rosselli, C., Rivalutazione e stabilizzazione della lira, *La Riforma Sociale*, XXXVII (1926) 157–171.

Rossi-Ragazzi, B., Il valore esterno della lira prima e dopo gli "allineamenti monetari," *Rivista Italiana di Scienze Economiche*, XI (1939) 42–61.

Shann, E. O. G., The world economic conference, *Economic Record*, IX (1933) 161–175.

Smith, L., The zloty, 1924–35, *Journal of Political Economy*, XLIV (1936) 145–183.

Southard, F. A., Jr., Some European currency and exchange experiences: 1943–1946, *Essays in International Finance*, No. 7, Princeton, New Jersey, Princeton University Press, 1946.

Tagliabue, G., Le alterne vicende della lira dal 1913 ad oggi e la fase culminante della politica monetaria italiana, *Revista Internazionale di Scienze Sociali*, III (1927) 177–195.

Weber, A., Deutschlands finanzielle Leistungsfähigkeit jetzt und künftig, *Archiv für Sozialwissenschaft und Sozialpolitik*, XLIX (1922) 265–297.

II-F (5). International Monetary Problems of Particular Countries:
All Other Countries

See also II-C, II-D, II-E, III-A, III-B, III-D and VI-E.

Allen, G. C., The recent currency and exchange policy of Japan, *Economic Journal*, XXXV (1925) 66–83.

Kreps, T. J., The price of silver and Chinese purchasing power, *Quarterly Journal of Economics*, XLVIII (1934) 245–287; 565–571.

Leavens, D. H., The silver clause in China, *American Economic Review*, XXVI (1936) 650–659.

Liu, T.-C., China's foreign exchange problems: a proposed solution, *American Economic Review*, XXXI (1941) 266–279.

Mikesell, R. F., Financial problems of the Middle East, *Journal of Political Economy*, LIII (1945) 164–176.

Tamagna, F. M., The financial position of China and Japan, *American Economic Review*, XXXVI (1946 supplement) 613–627.

II-G. International Monetary Organizations

Includes the proposals for an International Clearing Union, discussions of the International Monetary Fund, the Bank for International Settlement, and related subjects. See also II-A, II-D, IV-A, and IV-B.

Anonymous, The currency plans, *Economist*, CXLIV (1943) 556–557.

———, Postwar currency, *ibid.*, CXLV (1943) 261–262.

———, Bretton Woods, *Economic Record*, XX (1944) 141–151.

———, The joint currency scheme, *Economist*, CXLVI (1944) 560–561.

———, The monetary agreements, *ibid.*, CXLVII (1944) 207–208.

———, Bretton Woods, I, *ibid.*, 138–139.

———, Bretton Woods, II, Britain's debts, *ibid.*, CXLIX (1945) 109–110.

———, Bretton Woods, III, A debt settlement, *ibid.*, 151–152.

Beckhart, B. H., The Bretton Woods proposal for an International Monetary Fund, *Political Science Quarterly*, LIX (1944) 489–528.

Bernstein, E. M., A practical international monetary policy, *American Economic Review*, XXXIV (1944) 771–784.

———, Monetary stabilization: the United Nations program, *Economic Reconstruction* (S. E. Harris, ed.), New York, McGraw-Hill, 1945, 336–352.

———, Scarce currencies and the International Monetary Fund, *Journal of Political Economy*, LIII (1945) 1–14.

Böök, K., Postwar monetary problems against the background of the Keynes and White plans, *Ekonomisk Tidskrift*, XLV (1943) 134–146.

Bourneuf, A., Professor Williams and the Fund, *American Economic Review*, XXXIV (1944) 840–847.

———, Lending operations of the International Monetary Fund, *Review of Economic Statistics*, XXVIII (1946) 237–247.

Brown, W. A., Jr., The repurchase provision of the proposed International Monetary Fund, *American Economic Review*, XXXV (1945) 111–120.

Condliffe, J. B., Exchange stabilization and international trade, *Review of Economic Statistics*, XXVI (1944) 166–169.

Dikanssci, M., Preparation for the postwar period and international agreements, *Vneshniaia Torgovlia*, (1943, No. 9) 26–30.

Dulles, E. L., The Bank for International Settlements in recent years, *American Economic Review*, XXVIII (1938) 290–304.

Ellis, H. S., Can national and international monetary policies be reconciled?, *American Economic Review*, XXXIV (1944 supplement) 385–395.

Feis, H., Restoring trade after the war, *Foreign Affairs*, XX (1941–42) 282–292.

Fraser, L., The international bank and its future, *Foreign Affairs*, XIV (1935–36) 453–464.

Frei, L., Projects for the solution of postwar exchange problems, *Vneshniaia Torgovlia*, (1944, No. 1) 15–29.

———, The International Monetary Fund, *ibid.*, (1944, No. 4–5) 24–30.

———, The international conference on quotas of exchange and finances, *ibid.*, (1944, No. 9) 15–32.

GRAHAM, F. D., Keynes v. Hayek on a commodity reserve currency, *Economic Journal*, LIV (1944) 422–429.

KEYNES, J. M., Keynes v. Hayek on a commodity reserve currency: rejoinder, *ibid.*, 429–430.

HABERLER, G., Currency depreciation and the International Monetary Fund, *Review of Economic Statistics*, XXVI (1944) 178–181.

HAINES, W. W., Keynes, White, and history, *Quarterly Journal of Economics*, LVIII (1943) 120–133.

HALASI, A., International monetary cooperation, *Social Research*, IX (1942) 183–203.

HALM, G. N., The International Monetary Fund, *Review of Economic Statistics*, XXVI (1944) 170–175.

HAMMARSKJÖLD, D., From Bretton Woods to full employment, *Index*, supplement A (December 1945) 24 pp.

HANSEN, A. H., World institutions for stability and expansion, *Foreign Affairs*, XXII (1943–44) 248–255.

———, A brief note on "fundamental disequilibrium," *Review of Economic Statistics*, XXVI (1944) 182–184.

HARRIS, S. E., The contributions of Bretton Woods and some unsolved problems, *Review of Economic Statistics*, XXVI (1944) 175–177.

HAYEK, F. A. VON, A commodity reserve currency, *Economic Journal*, LIII (1943) 176–184.

HOLLOWAY, J. E., The Bretton Woods Conference, and the International Monetary Fund, *South African Journal of Economics*, XII (1944) 205–222.

JACK, L. B., Proposals for international exchange stabilization, *International Labor Review*, XLVIII (1943) 157–173.

JACOBSSON, P., The International Bank and monetary policy, *Index*, IV (1929) 7–16.

JAMES, F. C., The Bank for International Settlements, *Annals of the American Academy of Political Science*, CXLIX (1930) 74–81.

KEYNES, J. M., The objective of international price stability, *Economic Journal*, LIII (1943) 185–187.

———, The International Clearing Union, a speech delivered before the House of Lords, London, May 18, 1943. Reprinted in *The New Economics* (S. E. Harris, ed.), New York, Alfred A. Knopf, 1947, 359–368.

———, The International Monetary Fund, a speech delivered before the House of Lords, May 23, 1944. Reprinted in *ibid.*, 369–379.

KINDLEBERGER, C. P., International monetary stabilization, *Postwar Economic Problems* (S. E. Harris, ed.), New York, McGraw-Hill, 1947, 375–395.

LACHMANN, L. M., Notes on the proposals for international currency stabilization, *Review of Economic Statistics*, XXVI (1944) 184–191.

LADENBURG, H., Plan for a postwar clearing bank, *Social Research*, IX (1942) 510–529.

LUTZ, F. A., International monetary mechanisms: the Keynes and White proposals *Essays in International Finance*, No. 1, Princeton, New Jersey, Princeton University Press, 1943.

MACGIBBON, D. A., International monetary control, *Canadian Journal of Economics and Political Science*, XI (1945) 1–13.

MIKESELL, R. F., The key currency proposal, *Quarterly Journal of Economics*, LIX (1945) 563–576.

*———, The role of the international monetary agreements in a world of planned economics, *Journal of Political Economy*, LV (1947) 497–512.

MORGAN, E. V., The plans for an international clearing system, *Economica*, X, new series (1943) 297–301.

———, The joint statement by experts on the establishment of an International Monetary Fund, *ibid.*, XI (1944) 112–119.

MORGAN, S., Constructive functions of the international bank, *Foreign Affairs*, IX (1930–31) 580–591.

NEISSER, H. P., An international reserve bank, comments on the American and British plans, *Social Research*, X (1943) 265–279.

NEWCOMER, M., Bretton Woods and a durable peace, *Annals of the American Academy of Political Science*, CCXL (1945) 37–42.

POOLE, K. E., National economic policies and international monetary cooperation, *American Economic Review*, XXXVII (1947) 369–375.

RASMINSKY, L., International credit and currency plans, *Foreign Affairs*, XXII (1943–44) 589–603.

ROBERTSON, D. H., The postwar monetary plans, *Economic Journal*, LIII (1943) 352–360.

ROBINSON, J., The international currency proposals, *Economic Journal*, LIII (1943) 161–175.

SMITH, J., JR., The Bank for International Settlements, *Quarterly Journal of Economics*, XLIII (1929) 713–725.

STERN, E. H., The agreements of Bretton Woods, *Economica*, XI, new series (1944) 165–179.

DE VEGH, I., The International Clearing Union, *American Economic Review*, XXXIII (1943) 534–556.

VINER, J., Two plans for international monetary stabilization, *Yale Review*, XXXIII, new series (1943–44) 77–107.

WALLICH, H. C., The path from Bretton Woods, *Economic Reconstruction* (S. E. Harris, ed.), New York, McGraw-Hill, 1945, 366–377.

WHALE, P. B., Notes on the International Bank and the creation of credit, *Economica*, X (1930) 130–136.

WHITE, H. D., Postwar currency stabilization, *American Economic Review*, XXXIII (1943 supplement) 382–387.

———, The monetary fund: some criticisms examined, *Foreign Affairs*, XXIII (1944–45) 195–210.

WILLIAMS, J. H., Currency stabilization: the Keynes and White plans, *Foreign Affairs*, XXI (1942–43) 645–658.

———, Currency stabilization: American and British attitudes, *ibid.*, XXII (1943–44) 233–247.

———, International monetary plans: after Bretton Woods, *ibid.*, XXIII (1944–45) 38–56.

---

* Reprinted in the present volume.

————, The postwar monetary plans, *American Economic Review*, XXXIV (1944 supplement) 372–384.

III. INTERNATIONAL CAPITAL MOVEMENTS

III-A. THE THEORY OF CAPITAL TRANSFERS AND THE PROBLEM OF REPARATIONS

Includes theoretical discussions of the mechanism of capital transfer as well as empirical discussions of reparation payments following two world wars. Articles dealing with reparations have been separated from articles dealing with war debts; the latter will be found in III-B.

A. F., The mythology of reparations, *Economic Journal*, XXXVIII (1928) 426–433.

ANGELL, J. W., The reparations settlement and the international flow of capital, *American Economic Review*, XX (1930 supplement) 80–88.

  BROWN, W. A., JR., German reparations and the international flow of capital—discussion, *ibid.*, 89–92.

AULD, G. P., The reparation problem today, *Foreign Affairs*, II (1923–24) supplement to No. 3.

————, The Dawes and Young Loans: then and now, *ibid.*, XIII (1934–35) 6–25.

BALOGH, T., Some theoretical aspects of the Central European credit and transfer crisis, *International Affairs*, XI (1932) 346–369.

BERGMANN, C., Germany and the Young plan, *Foreign Affairs*, VIII (1929–30) 583–597.

BIELSCHOWSKY, G., War indemnities and business conditions, *Political Science Quarterly*, XLIV (1929) Pt. I, 334–361; Pt. II, 528–547.

BOYDEN, R. W., The Dawes Report, *Foreign Affairs*, II (1923–24) 583–597.

BRAND, R. H., The reparation problem, *Journal of the Royal Institute of International Affairs*, VIII (1929) 203–226.

BRITISH ECONOMIST, The reparation problem, *International Affairs*, XXI (1945) 325–330.

BROCK, F. H., Is Professor Ohlin's theory of the transfer of purchasing power meaningless?, *Ekonomisk Tidskrift*, XXXII (1930) 59–65.

BRONFENBRENNER, M., International transfers and the terms of trade: an extension of Pigou's analysis, *Studies in Mathematical Economics and Econometrics* (O. Lange, F. McIntyre, and T. O. Yntema, ed.), Chicago, University of Chicago Press, 1942, 119–131.

CABIATI, A., Caratteristiche dell' esportazione di capitali in regime di valuta sana, *La Riforma Sociale*, XXXIX (1928) 15–33.

CLOUGH, S. B., What about reparations this time?, *Political Science Quarterly*, LIX (1944) 220–226.

COMSTOCK, A., Reparation payments in perspective, *American Economic Review*, XX (1930) 199–209.

CURRIE, L., Domestic stability and the mechanism of trade adjustment to international capital movements, *Explorations in Economics*, New York, McGraw-Hill, 1936, 46–56.

DAVIDSON, D., The problem of transferring the German reparations, *Ekonomisk Tidskrift*, XXXI (1929) 82–86.

————, A new phase in the German reparations problem, *ibid.*, XXXIII (1931) 11–32.

DULLES, J. F., The reparation problem, *Economic Journal*, XXXI (1921) 179–186.

EINAUDI, L., Prestiti esteri e bilancia dei pagamenti internazionali, *La Riforma Sociale*, XXXVIII (1927) 97–112.

ELLIOTT, G. A., Transfer of means-of-payment and the terms of international trade, *Canadian Journal of Economics and Political Science*, II (1936) 481–492.

FISHER, P., Reparation labor—a preliminary analysis, *Quarterly Journal of Economics*, LX (1946) 313–339.

FRIEDRICH, C. J., Reparation realities, *Foreign Affairs*, VII (1928–29) 118–131.

GIDEONSE, H. D., Comment on reparation payments, *American Economic Review*, XX (1930) 691–695.

GILBERT, S. P., The meaning of the "Dawes Plan," *Foreign Affairs*, IV (1925–26) supplement to No. 3, i-xii.

GRAHAM, F. D., Germany's capacity to pay and the reparation plan, *American Economic Review*, XV (1925) 209–227.

GUILLEBAUD, C. W., The economics of the Dawes report and the London agreement, *Economic Journal*, XXXIV (1924) 540–555.

HABERLER, G., Transfer und Preisbewegung, *Zeitschrift für Nationalökonomie*, I (1930) 547–560.

HARRIS, C. R. S., Reparation: the Young Report, *Journal of the Royal Institute of International Affairs*, VIII (1929) 458–480.

*KEYNES, J. M., The German transfer problem, *Economic Journal*, XXXIX (1929) 1–7.

*OHLIN, B., The reparation problem, a discussion: I, transfer difficulties, real and imagined, *ibid.*, 172–178.

————, The reparation problem, a discussion: II, a rejoinder, *ibid.*, 179–182.

RUEFF, J., Mr. Keynes' views on the transfer problem: I, a criticism, *ibid.*, 388–399.

OHLIN, B., Mr. Keynes' views on the transfer problem: II, a rejoinder, *ibid.*, 400–404.

————, Mr. Keynes' views on the transfer problem: III, a reply, *ibid.*, 404–408.

KNAPP, J., The theory of international capital movements and its verification, *Review of Economic Studies*, X (1943) 115–121.

KOCH, K., Some problems of definition and terminology in the theory of international capital movements, *Ekonomisk Tidskrift*, XLI (1939) 311–324.

KUCZYNSKI, R. R., A year of the Dawes plan, *Foreign Affairs*, IV (1925–26) 254–263.

LAMONT, T. W., The final reparations settlement, *Foreign Affairs*, VIII (1929–30) 336–363.

LEONTIEF, W. W., Note on the pure theory of capital transfer, *Explorations in Economics*, New York, McGraw-Hill, 1936, 84–91.

LOUCHEUR, L., The essentials of a reparations settlement, *Foreign Affairs*, II (1923–24) 1–9.

LUTZ, H. L., Inter-Allied debts, reparations, and national policy, *Journal of Political Economy*, XXXVIII (1930) 29–61.

MACHLUP, F., Die Theorie der Kapitalflucht, *Weltwirtschaftliches Archiv*, XXXVI (1932) 512.

* Reprinted in the present volume.

McFadden, L. T., The reparations problem and the Bank for International Settlements, *Annals of the American Academy of Political Science*, CL (1930) 53–64.

*Metzler, L. A., The transfer problem reconsidered, *Journal of Political Economy*, L (1942) 397–414.

Muhs, K., Zum Gutachten der Dawes Kommission, *Jahrbuch für Nationalökonomie und Statistik*, CXXII (1924) 295–318.

Ohlin, B., The German reparations problem, *Ekonomisk Tidskrift*, XXXII (1930) 59–65.

——, The reparations problem, *Index*, III (1928) No. 27, 19 pp.; No. 28, 39 pp.

——, Is the Young plan feasible?, *ibid.*, V (1930) 34–44.

P. M., La stabilité des monnaies Européennes et le problème des transferts, *Revue d'Economie Politique*, XL (1926) 1127–1143.

Palyi, M., The mechanism of international capital transfer under the gold standard, *Economic Record* III (1927) 266–272.

——, Der Zahlungsbilanz—Ausgleich bei einseitigen Wertübertragungen, *Archiv für Sozialwissenschaft und Sozialpolitik*, LVI (1929) 302–338.

Parmentier, J., The reparations problem after London, *Foreign Affairs*, III (1924–25) 244–252.

Pigou, A. C., The effect of reparations on the ratio of international interchange, *Economic Journal*, XLII (1932) 532–543.

Pugliese, M., Note sui transferimenti internazionali di capitale, *Giornale degli Economisti*, LXVII (1926) 378–406.

Quigley, H., The industrial aspect of reparations, *Journal of the Royal Institute of International Affairs*, VIII (1929) 154–168.

Robertson, D. H., and Viner, J., Indemnity payments and gold movements, *Quarterly Journal of Economics*, LIII (1939) 312–317.

Röpke, W., Zum Transferproblem bei internationalen Kapitalbewegungen, *Jahrbuch für Nationalökonomie und Statistik* CXXXIII (1930), 225–240.

Rosenstein-Rodan, P. N., How much can Germany pay?, *International Affairs*, XXI (1945) 469–476.

Rueff, J., Les idées de M. Keynes sur le problème des transfers, *Revue d'Economie Politique*, XLIII (1929) 1067–1081.

Schacht, H., German trade and German debts, *Foreign Affairs*, XIII (1934–35) 1–5.

Schiff, E., Direct investments, terms of trade, and balance of payments, *Quarterly Journal of Economics*, LVI (1942) 307–320.

Stamp, J., The economic consequences of the peace, *Foreign Affairs*, XIII (1934–35), 104–112.

Stresemann, G., The economic restoration of the world, *Foreign Affairs*, II (1923–24) 552–557.

Suviranta, B., Finland's war indemnity, *Index*, (March 1947 supplement) 44 pp.

Taussig, F. W., Germany's reparation payments, *American Economic Review*, X (1920 supplement) 33–49.

Tyler, R., The Eastern reparations settlement, *Foreign Affairs*, IX (1930–31) 108–117.

Varga, S., Bemerkungen zu den Problemen von Aufbringung und Transfer, *Economic Essays in Honour of Gustav Cassel*, London, George Allen and Unwin, Ltd., 1933, 649–663.

---

* Reprinted in the present volume.

Viner, J., German reparations once more, *Foreign Affairs*, XXI (1942–43) 659–673.

Walker, G., The payment of reparations, *Economica*, XI (1931) 213–236.

Whittlesey, C. R., Internationale Kapitalbewegungen bei gebundener und freier Währung, *Weltwirtschaftliches Archiv*, XLIV (1936) 437–472.

Williams, J. F., Reparations, *International Affairs*, XI (1932) 183–202.

Williams, J. H., Reparations and the flow of capital, *American Economic Review*, XX (1920 supplement) 73–79.

———, German foreign trade and the reparations payments, *Quarterly Journal of Economics*, XXXVI (1922) 482–503.

Y, La question des réparations depuis la paix, *Revue d'Economie Politique*, XXXV (1921) 673–712.

Young, A. A., The United States and reparations, *Foreign Affairs*, I: 3 (1922–23) 35–47.

———, War debts, external and internal, *ibid.*, II (1923–24) 397–409.

III-B. War Debts and the Balance of International Indebtedness

Contains, in addition to articles on war debts, several articles on the debtor-creditor position of various countries. See also II-A, II-F, III-A and III-D.

Alexander, M. W., The economic significance of the inter-ally debts, *Annals of the American Academy of Political Science*, CXX (1925) 51–58.

Alpha, Reparations and the policy of repudiation: an American view, *Foreign Affairs*, II (1923–24) 55–83.

Andrew, A. P., Should the debt settlements be revised?, *American Economic Review*, XVIII (1928 supplement) 235–243.

Angell, J. W., The payment of reparations and inter-ally debts, *Foreign Affairs*, IV (1925–26) 85–96.

———, The effect of the debt settlements on the trade balance of the United States, *Annals of the American Academy of Political Science*, CXXVI (1926) 38–41.

Auld, G. P., The British war debt: retrospect and prospect, *Foreign Affairs*, XVI (1937–38) 640–650.

Bogart, E. L., An examination of the reasons for revision of the debt settlements, *American Economic Review*, XVIII (1928 supplement) 245–258.

Boswell, J. L., Some neglected aspects of the world war debt payments, *American Economic Review*, XXI (1931) 236–248.

Bullock, C. J., The United States as a creditor nation, *Review of Economic Statistics*, XIV (1932) 178–180.

Dickens, P. D., Criteria for determining the creditor-debtor position of a country, *Journal of Political Economy*, XLVII (1939) 846–856.

Dulles, J. F., The Allied debts, *Foreign Affairs*, I (1922–23) 116–132.

Elliston, H. B., Reparations, debts, and the future, *Foreign Affairs*, VI (1927–28) 671–674.

Fisher, I., Stabilization of Europe, *American Economic Review*, XIII (1923) 76–80.

———, Europe's big debts, *Yale Review*, XIII (1923–24) 449–466.

Gottlieb, L. R., Indebtedness of principal belligerents, *Quarterly Journal of Economics*, XXXIII (1919) 504–530.

Haensel, P., Some recent publications on inter-allied indebtedness and reparations, *Economic Journal*, XXXIX (1929) 63–70.

HOLLANDER, J. H., American public opinion and war debts, *Economic Essays in Honour of Gustav Cassel*, London, George Allen and Unwin, Ltd., 1933, 293–300.

HOLT, L. W., Reduction of New Zealand debt in London, *Economic Record*, XV (1939) 245–248.

LEFFINGWELL, R. C., War debts, *Yale Review*, XII (1922–23) 22–40.

MOULTON, H. G., War debts and international trade theory, *American Economic Review*, XV (1925) 700–706.

———, The American stake in the war debts, *Yale Review*, XXII, new series (1932–33) 78–96.

PASVOLSKY, L., Balance sheet of the war debts, *Foreign Affairs*, XI (1932–33) 146–147.

PATTERSON, E. M., The effect of the debt situation upon Europe's relations with the United States, *Annals of the American Academy of Political Science*, CXXVI (1926) 27–33.

POLK, J., The future of frozen foreign funds, *American Economic Review*, XXXII (1942) 255–271.

RATHBONE, A., Making war loans to the Allies, *Foreign Affairs*, III (1924–25) 371–398.

SALTER, A., War debts, *International Affairs*, XII (1933) 147–167.

TROUTON, R., Cancellation of inter-allied debts, *Economic Journal*, XXXI (1921) 38–45.

WINSTON, G., The present phase of the war debts, *Yale Review*, XIX, new series (1929–30) 267–279.

WOOD, G. L., War debts of British dominions, *Economic Record*, VII (1931) 112–114.

———, Reparations and war debts, *ibid.*, VIII (1932 supplement) 33–46.

WOODRUFF, J. D., Allied debts, 1702–1914, *Journal of the Royal Institute of International Affairs*, V (1926) 134–149.

III-C. ECONOMIC EFFECTS OF INTERNATIONAL INVESTMENT

Includes studies of the effects of industrializing undeveloped regions as well as studies of the economic consequences of foreign lending on both the borrower and the lender. See also III-A and III-D.

ANONYMOUS, Export trade and the problem of international long-term credit, *Vneshniaia Torgovlia*, (1944, No. 4–5) 2–11.

BALOGH, T., Some theoretical problems of postwar foreign investment policy, *Oxford Economic Papers*, No. 7 (March 1945) 1–20.

BRYCE, R. B., International aspects of an investment program, *Postwar Economic Problems* (S. E. Harris, ed.) New York, McGraw-Hill, 1943, 361–373.

BUCHANAN, N. S., International investment: some postwar problems and issues, *Canadian Journal of Economics and Political Science*, X (1944) 139–149.

———, Deliberate industrialization for higher incomes, *Economic Journal*, LVI (1946) 533–553.

BALOGH, T., Note on the deliberate industrialization for higher incomes, *ibid.*, LVII (1947) 238–241.

BELSHAW, H., Observations on industrialization for higher incomes, *ibid.*, 379–387.

CAIRNCROSS, A. K., Did foreign investment pay?, *Review of Economic Studies*, III (1935) 67–78.

DONALDSON, J., International industrial relations: migration of enterprise and policies affecting it, *American Economic Review*, XXI (1931 supplement) 150–160.

FEILER, A., International movements of capital, *American Economic Review*, XXV (1935 supplement) 63–73.

FEIS, H., Political aspects of foreign loans, *Foreign Affairs*, XXIII (1944–45) 609–619.

FETTER, F. W., The need for postwar foreign lending, *American Economic Review*, XXXIII (1943 supplement) 342–346.

FRANKEL, H., Industrialization of agricultural countries and the possibilities of a new international division of labour, *Economic Journal*, LIII (1943) 188–201.

HINCHCLIFFE, A. H. S., The international industrial situation and British problems, *International Affairs*, XXI (1945) 355–362.

HINSHAW, R., Foreign investment and American employment, *American Economic Review*, XXXVI (1946 supplement) 661–671.

JAMES, F. C., Benefits and dangers of foreign investments, *Annals of the American Academy of Political Science*, CL (1930) 76–84.

KINDLEBERGER, C. P., Planning for foreign investment, *American Economic Review*, XXXIII (1943 supplement) 347–354.

KURIHARA, K. K., Foreign investment and full employment, *Journal of Political Economy*, LV (1947) 459–464.

LARY, H. B., The domestic effects of foreign investment, *American Economic Review*, XXXVI (1946 supplement) 672–686.

NURKSE, R., Ursachen und Wirkungen der Kapitalbewegungen, *Zeitschrift für National-ökonomie*, V (1934) 78–96.

ORCHARD, J. E., The social background of Oriental industrialization: its significance in international trade, *Explorations in Economics*, New York, McGraw-Hill, 1936, 120–130.

PALYI, M., Foreign investment, *Encyclopaedia of the Social Sciences*, VI, New York, Macmillan, 1931, 364–378.

PELTZER, E., Industrialization of young countries and the change in the international division of labor, *Social Research*, VII (1940) 299–325.

*POLAK, J. J., Balance of payments problems of countries reconstructing with the help of foreign loans, *Quarterly Journal of Economics*, LVII (1943) 208–240.

RAHMER, B. A., Note on the industrialization of backward areas, *Economic Journal*, LVI (1946) 657–661.

REMER, C. F., Investments in kind, *Explorations in Economics*, New York, McGraw-Hill, 1936, 92–101.

ROSENSTEIN-RODAN, P. N., The international development of economically backward areas, *International Affairs*, XX (1944) 157–165.

STAUDINGER, H., The United States and world reconstruction, *Social Research*, VIII (1941) 283–296.

UPGREN, A. R., International capital financing, *Economic Reconstruction* (S. E. Harris, ed.), New York, McGraw-Hill, 1945, 353–365.

VINER, J., International finance in the postwar world, *Journal of Political Economy*, LV (1947) 97–107.

WHITTLESEY, C. R., Foreign investment and the terms of trade, *Quarterly Journal of Economics*, XLVI (1932) 444–464.

---

* Reprinted in the present volume.

————, Foreign investment and national gain, *American Economic Review*, XXIII (1933) 466–470.

WINSTON, A. P., Does trade "follow the dollar"?, *American Economic Review*, XVII (1927) 458–477.

WU, Y.-L., A note on the post-war industrialization of "backward" countries and centralist planning, *Economica*, XII, new series (1945) 172–178.

III-D (1). INTERNATIONAL INVESTMENT IN OR BY PARTICULAR COUNTRIES:
Countries of the Western Hemisphere
See also II-F.

BLOOMFIELD, A. I., The significance of outstanding securities in the international movement of capital, *Canadian Journal of Economics and Political Science*, VI (1940) 495–524.

BRUÈRE, H., Constructive versus dollar diplomacy, *American Economic Review*, XIII (1923) 68–76.

COLLINGS, H. T., The foreign investment policy of the United States, *Annals of the American Academy of Political Science*, CXXVI (1926) 71–79.

CUMBERLAND, W. W., Investments and national policy of the United States in Latin America, *American Economic Review*, XXII (1932 supplement) 152–172.

DOMERATZKY, L., American industry abroad, *Foreign Affairs*, VIII (1929–30) 569–582.

DULLES, A. W., The protection of American foreign bondholders, *Foreign Affairs*, X (1931–32) 474–484.

DULLES, J. F., Our foreign loan policy, *Foreign Affairs*, V (1926–27) 33–48.

————, The securities act and foreign lending, *ibid.*, XII (1933–34) 33–45.

EDWARDS, G. W., American policy with reference to foreign investments, *American Economic Review*, XIV (1924 supplement) 26–35.

————, Government control of foreign investments, *ibid.*, XVIII (1938) 684–701.

FEIS, H., The export of American capital, *Foreign Affairs*, III (1924–25) 668–686.

GARDNER, W. R., The future international position of the United States as affected by the Fund and Bank, *American Economic Review*, XXXV (1945 supplement) 272–288.

GOLDSTEIN, A., Federal Reserve aid to foreign central banks, *Review of Economic Studies*, II (1935) 79–98.

JOLLIFFE, M. F., The movement of capital to and from the United States in 1935 and 1936, *Quarterly Journal of Economics*, LIII (1938) 150–159.

KEYNES, J. M., The Anglo-American financial arrangement, a speech delivered in the House of Lords, December 18, 1945. Reprinted in *The New Economics* (S. E. Harris, ed.), New York, Alfred A. Knopf, 1947, 380–395.

KREUSER, O. T., Some inter-American financial problems, *Annals of the American Academy of Political Science*, CCIV (1939) 165–168.

LABASTILLE, F. M., Methods of extending credit facilities for the export of automobiles, *American Economic Review*, XXII (1932) 208–218.

LASSWELL, H. D., Political policies and the international investment market, *Journal of Political Economy*, XXXI (1923) 380–400.

MORROW, D. W., Who buys foreign bonds?, *Foreign Affairs*, V (1926–27) 219–232.

MOULTON, H. G., The limitations of foreign credit, *Journal of Political Economy*, XXIX (1921) 791–805.

PALYI, M., Die Zahlungsbilanz der V. S. von Amerika als Gläubigerland, *Veröffentlichungen des Vereins für Sozialpolitik*, CLXXIV (1928) 223–300

POLK, J. and PATTERSON, G., The British loan, *Foreign Affairs*, XXIV (1945–46) 427–440.

ROBINSON, H. M., Are American loans abroad safe?, *Foreign Affairs*, V (1926–27) 49–56.

ROSENSON, A., The Anglo-American financial agreement, *American Economic Review*, XXXVII (1947) 178–187.

SCHOEPPERLE, V., Future of international investment: private versus public foreign lending, *American Economic Review*, XXXIII (1943 supplement) 336–341.

SCROGGS, W. O., The American investment in Germany, *Foreign Affairs*, X (1931–32) 324–326.

———, The American investment in Latin America, *ibid.*, 502–503.

———, The American investment in Canada, *ibid.*, XI (1932–33) 716–719.

SLICHTER, S. H., Foreign trade and postwar stability, *Foreign Affairs*, XXI (1942–43) 674–689.

SOUTHARD, F. A., JR., American industry abroad since 1929, *Journal of Political Economy*, XLI (1933) 530–547.

WALLICH, H. C., The future of Latin American dollar bonds, *American Economic Review*, XXXIII (1943) 321–335.

WHITE, H. G., JR., Foreign trading in American stock-exchange securities, *Journal of Political Economy*, XLVIII (1940) 655–702.

WINKLER, M., Investments and national policy of the United States in Latin America, *American Economic Review*, XXII (1932 supplement) 144–151.

———, War and American foreign investments, *Annals of the American Academy of Political Science*, CXCII (1937) 74–81.

YOUNG, R. A., An American foreign investment policy, *Annals of the American Academy of Political Science*, CLXXIV (1934) 47–53.

III-D (2). INTERNATIONAL INVESTMENT IN OR BY PARTICULAR COUNTRIES:
The British Commonwealth of Nations, Excluding Canada

See also II-F.

ANONYMOUS, Debtors and their debts, *Economist*, CXIX: 2 (1934) 1151–1152.

BOURDILLON, B. H., Colonial development and welfare, *International Affairs*, XX (1944) 369–380.

KINDERSLEY, R. M., A new study of British foreign investments, *Economic Journal*, XXXIX (1929) 8–24.

———, British foreign investments in 1928, *ibid.*, XL (1930) 175–183.

———, British foreign investments in 1929, *ibid.*, XLI (1931) 370–384.

———, British foreign investments in 1930, *ibid.*, XLII (1932) 177–195.

———, British overseas investments in 1931, *ibid.*, XLIII (1933) 188–204.

———, British overseas investments in 1932 and 1933, *ibid.*, XLIV (1934) 365–379.

———, Britain's overseas investments in 1933 and 1934, *ibid.*, XLV (1935) 439–455.

———, British overseas investments in 1934 and 1935, *ibid.*, XLVI (1936) 645–661.

———, British overseas investments in 1935 and 1936, *ibid.*, XLVII (1937) 642–662.

———, British overseas investments, 1937, *ibid.*, XLVIII (1938) 609–634.

———, British overseas investments, 1938, *ibid.*, XLIX (1939) 678–695.

LANDSBERG, E., South Africa's imports of capital and the balance of payment, 1932–36, *South African Journal of Economics*, V (1937) 285–305.

SAMUEL, A. M., Has foreign investment paid?, *Economic Journal*, XL (1930) 64–68.

STEWART, R. B., Great Britain's foreign loan policy, *Economica*, V, new series (1938) 45–60.

WILSON, R., Australian capital imports, 1871–1930, *Economic Record*, VI (1930) 281–285.

———, Australian capital imports, 1871–1930, *ibid.*, VII (1931) 33–63.

III-D (3). INTERNATIONAL INVESTMENT IN OR BY PARTICULAR COUNTRIES:
Continental Europe
See also II-F.

BRESCIANI-TURRONI, C., Alcuni effetti economici dei prestiti esteri in Germania negli anni 1924–1929, *Giornale degli Economisti*, LXX (1929) 994–1067.

DE BUDAY, K., Foreign loans in Central Europe, *Annals of the American Academy of Political Science*, CLXXIV (1934) 22–30.

FEDERECI, L., La teoria dei prestiti esteri e la pratica italiana, *Giornale degli Economisti*, LXX (1929) 645–688.

KRIZ, M. A., Postwar international lending, *Essays in International Finance*, No. 8, Princeton, New Jersey, Princeton University Press, 1948.

LAMER, M., Die Wandlungen der ausländischen Kapitalanlagen auf dem Balkan, *Weltwirtschaftliches Archiv*, XLVIII (1938) 470–524.

LAVES, W. H. C., German governmental influence on foreign investments, 1871–1915, *Political Science Quarterly*, XLIII (1928) 498–519.

MIRY, R., Die direkte Investition belgischer Kapitalien in Auslande, *Weltwirtschaftliches Archiv*, L (1939) 243–264.

ROBINSON, N., Problems of European reconstruction, *Quarterly Journal of Economics*, LX (1945) 1–55.

ROOSEVELT, N., Salvaging the debts of Eastern Europe, *Foreign Affairs*, XII (1933–34) 134–140.

ROSENSTEIN-RODAN, P. N., Problems of industrialization of Eastern and South-eastern Europe, *Economic Journal*, LIII (1943) 202–211.

STALEY, E., Private investments and international politics in the Saar, 1919–20: a study of politico-economic "penetration" in a postwar plebiscite area, *Journal of Political Economy*, XLI (1933) 577–601.

III-D (4). INTERNATIONAL INVESTMENT IN OR BY PARTICULAR COUNTRIES:
All Other Countries
See also II-F.

CALLIS, H. G., Capital investment in Southeastern Asia and the Philippines, *Annals of the American Academy of Political Science*, CCXXVI (1943) 22–31.

MACMURRAY, J. V. A., Problems of foreign capital in China, *Foreign Affairs*, III (1924–25) 411–422.

WEINRYB, B. D., Industrial development of the Near East, *Quarterly Journal of Economics*, LXI (1947) 471–499.

594 CLASSIFIED BIBLIOGRAPHY OF ARTICLES

III-E. AGENCIES FOR INTERNATIONAL LOANS AND GIFTS

Includes discussions of such agencies as the International Bank for Reconstruction and Development, the Export-Import Bank of Washington, D. C., the Lend-Lease Administration, and the United Nations Relief and Rehabilitation Administration. Studies of the Bank for International Settlement are in II-G.

ADAMS, H. C., International supervision over foreign investments, *American Economic Review*, X (1920 supplement) 58–67.

ANONYMOUS, World capital bank, *Economist*, CXLV (1943) 527–528.

——, The International Bank, *ibid.*, CXLVII (1944) 355–356.

——, The United Nations Relief and Rehabilitation Administration, *International Labor Review*, XLIX (1944) 145–159.

CONDLIFFE, J. B., Implications of lend-lease: economic problems in the settlement, *Foreign Affairs*, XXI (1942–43) 494–504.

FISHER, A. G. B., The constitution and work of UNRRA, *International Affairs*, XX (1944) 317–330.

KEYNES, J. M., The Bank for Reconstruction and Development, opening remarks at the first meeting of the Second Commission of the Bank, July 3, 1944. Reprinted in *The New Economics* (S. E. Harris, ed.), New York, Alfred A. Knopf, 1947, 396–400.

DE KOCK, M. H., The International Bank for Reconstruction and Development, *South African Journal of Economics*, XII (1944) 223–232.

MYERS, M. G., The League loans, *Political Science Quarterly*, LX (1945) 492–526.

PATTERSON, G., The Export-Import Bank, *Quarterly Journal of Economics*, LVIII (1943) 65–90.

PIERSON, W. L., Export-Import Bank operations, *Annals of the American Academy of Political Science*, CCXI (1940) 35–40.

PITIGLIANI, F., I sindicati di investimento internazionali, *Revista Internazionale*, I (1929) 25–41.

ROSTOW, E. V., Two aspects of lend-lease economics, *American Economic Review*, XXXIII (1943 supplement) 376–381.

SMITHIES, A., The International Bank for Reconstruction and Development, *American Economic Review*, XXXIV (1944) 785–797.

STALEY, E., The economic implicatons of lend-lease, *American Economic Review*, XXXIII (1943 supplement) 362–376.

DE VEGH, I., Peace aims, capital requirements, and international lending, *American Economic Review*, XXXV (1945 supplement) 253–261.

VILLASEÑOR, E., The inter-American bank: prospects and dangers, *Foreign Affairs*, XX (1941–42) 165–174.

WEYL, N., and WASSERMAN, M. J., The International Bank, *American Economic Review*, XXXVII (1947) 92–106.

WHITTLESEY, C. R., Five years of the export-import bank, *American Economic Review*, XXIX (1939) 487–502.

WU, Y.-L., International capital investment and the development of poor countries, *Economic Journal*, LVI (1946) 86–101.

IV. INTERNATIONAL ASPECTS OF BUSINESS CYCLES

Includes developments related to the theory of employment as well as more orthodox discussions of the subject.

IV-A. THE INTERNATIONAL SPREAD OF BUSINESS CYCLES

Includes articles dealing explicitly with the way business cycles are transmitted from one country to another and those discussing the influence of external fluctuations upon a country's internal economy. See also II-A, II-B, II-E, II-F, and IV-B.

BELSHAW, H., Stabilization in a dependent economy, *Economic Record*, XV (1939 supplement) 40–60.

BENHAM, F., Full employment and international trade, *Economica*, XIII, new series (1946) 159–168.

BRYCE, R. B., The effects on Canada of industrial fluctuations in the United States, *Canadian Journal of Economics and Political Science*, V (1939) 373–386.

BULLOCK, C. J., and MICOLEAU, H. L., Foreign trade and the business cycle, *Review of Economic Statistics*, XIII (1931) 138–159.

CABIATI, A., Il ciclo produttivo in regime di moneta avariata, *Giornale degli Economisti*, LXVII (1926) 645–671.

DAVIS, J. S., World currency expansion during the war and in 1919, *Review of Economic Statistics*, II (1920) 8–20.

FANNO, M., Credit expansion, savings and gold export, *Economic Journal*, XXXVIII (1928) 126–131.

FORCHHEIMER, K., The "short cycle" in its international aspects, *Oxford Economic Papers*, No. 7 (March 1945) 1–20.

HARRIS, S. E., International economics: introduction, *The New Economics* (S. E. Harris, ed.), New York, Alfred A. Knopf, 1947, 245–263.

HAWTREY, R. G., London and the trade cycle, *American Economic Review*, XIX (1929 supplement) 69–77.

HILGERDT, F., Foreign trade and the short business cycle, *Economic Essays in Honour of Gustav Cassel*, London, George Allen and Unwin, Ltd., 1933, 273–292.

KISCH, C. H., The part played by central banks in international affairs, *Journal of the Royal Institute of International Affairs*, IX (1930) 366–375.

DE KOCK, M. H., World monetary policy after the present war, *South African Journal of Economics*, IX (1941) 113–137.

MORGENSTERN, K., Internationalvergleichende Konjunkturforschung, *Zeitschrift für die gesamte Staatswissenschaft*, LXXXIII (1927) 261–290.

MORGENSTERN, O., On the international spread of business cycles, *Journal of Political Economy*, LI (1943) 287–309.

NOYES, C. R., The gold inflation in the United States, 1921–1929, *American Economic Review*, XX (1930) 181–198.

NURKSE, R., International monetary policy and the search for economic stability, *American Economic Review*, XXXVII (1947 supplement) 569–580.

OHLIN, B., International trade and monetary policy, *Index*, X (1935) 154–165.

POLAK, J. J., The international propagation of business cycles, *Review of Economic Studies*, VI (1939) 79–99.

ROBINSON, J., The United States in the world economy, *Economic Journal*, LIV (1944) 430–437.

*SALANT, W. A., Foreign trade policy in the business cycle, *Public Policy*, II (C. J. Friedrich and E. S. Mason, eds.), Cambridge, Mass., Graduate School of Public Administration, 1941, 208–231.

SILVERMAN, A. G., Some international trade factors for Great Britain, 1880–1913, *Review of Economic Statistics*, XIII (1931) 114–124.

SIMKIN, C. G. F., Insulationism and the problem of economic stability, *Economic Record*, XXII (1942) 50–65.

THOMAS, P. J., India in the world depression, *Economic Journal*, XLV (1935) 469–483.

TOCKER, A. H., Effects of the trade cycle in New Zealand, *Economic Journal*, XXXIV (1924) 128–134.

WOYTINSKY, W. International measures to create employment: a remedy for the depression, *International Labor Review*, XXV (1932) 1–22.

IV-B. THE PROPENSITY TO IMPORT AND THE FOREIGN TRADE MULTIPLIER

Includes statistical studies of the demand for imports as well as theoretical studies of imports, exports and national income.

ADLER, J. H., United States import demand during the interwar period, *American Economic Review*, XXXV (1945) 418–430.

————, The postwar demand for United States exports, *Review of Economic Statistics*, XXVIII (1946) 23–33.

CHANG, T.-C., International comparison of demand for imports, *Review of Economic Studies*, XIII (1945–46) 53–67.

————, The British demand for imports in the interwar period, *Economic Journal*, LVI (1946) 188–207.

BARNA, T., The British demand for imports: a comment, *ibid.*, 662–664, with a reply by T.-C. CHANG.

————, A note on exports and national income in Canada, *Canadian Journal of Economics and Political Science*, XIII (1947) 276–280.

HINSHAW, R., American prosperity and the British balance of payments problem, *Review of Economic Statistics*, XXVII (1945) 1–9.

————, and METZLER, L. A., World prosperity and the British balance of payments, *ibid.*, 156–170.

KAHN, R. F., The relation of home investment to unemployment, *Economic Journal*, XLI (1931) 173–198.

LEONTIEF, W. W., Exports, imports, domestic output and employment, *Quarterly Journal of Economics*, LX (1946) 171–193.

METZLER, L. A., Underemployment equilibrium in international trade, *Econometrica*, X (1942) 97–112.

MUNZER, E., Exports and national income in Canada, *Canadian Journal of Economics and Political Science*, XI (1945) 35–47.

---

* Reprinted in the present volume.

NEISSER, H., Government net contribution and foreign balance as offset to savings, *Review of Economic Statistics*, XXVI (1944) 216–220.

———, The significance of foreign trade for domestic employment, *Social Research*, XIII (1946) 307–325.

POLAK, J. J., The foreign trade multiplier, *American Economic Review*, XXXVII (1947) 889–897.

HABERLER, G., Comment, *ibid.*, 898–906.

POLAK, J. J., and Haberler, G., A restatement, *ibid.*, 906–907.

ROBERTSON, D. H., Mr. Clark and the foreign trade multiplier, *Economic Journal*, XLIX (1939) 354–356.

CLARK, C., Mr. Clark and the foreign trade multiplier: comment, *ibid.*, 356–358.

DYASON, J., A note on the multiplier in Australia, *Economic Record*, XV (1939) 114–118.

HORNER, F. B., The multiplier in Australia: a further comment, *ibid.*, 211–222.

JASTRAM, R. W., and SHAW, E. S., Mr. Clark's statistical determination of the multiplier, *Economic Journal*, XLIX (1939) 358–365.

SHACKLE, G. L. S., The multiplier in closed and open systems, *Oxford Economic Papers*, No. 2 (May 1939) 135–144.

STOLPER, W. F., The volume of foreign trade and the level of income, *Quarterly Journal of Economics*, LXI (1947) 285–310.

DE VEGH, I., Imports and income in the United States and Canada, *Review of Economic Statistics*, XXIII (1941) 130–146.

VINING, R., Regional variation in cyclical fluctuation viewed as a frequency distribution, *Econometrica*, XIII (1945) 183–213.

———, Location of industry and regional patterns of business-cycle behavior, *ibid.*, XIV (1946) 37–68.

———, The region as a concept in business-cycle analysis, *ibid.*, 201–218.

WARMING, J., International difficulties arising out of the financing of public works during depression, *Economic Journal*, XLII (1932) 211–224.

V. THE STRUCTURE OF WORLD TRADE

For the most part the articles in this section are empirical in nature, dealing with such subjects as the past and probable future development of international trade, the tendency toward bilateralism, trade problems of "international" commodities, the composition of exports and imports, etc.

V-A. GENERAL DISCUSSION

CANADIAN ECONOMIST, Economic reconstruction in Europe, *International Affairs*, XX (1944) 527–541.

DENNISON, S. R., The theory of industrial location, *Manchester School*, VIII (1937) 23–47.

EDMINSTER, L. R., Control of exports of raw materials: an international problem, *Annals of the American Academy of Political Science*, CL (1930) 89–97.

EMENY, B., The distribution and control of natural resources, and America's world position, *Annals of the American Academy of Political Science*, CCXVIII (1941) 58–65.

FISHER, A. G. B., Some essential factors in the evolution of international trade, *Manchester School*, XIII (1943–44) 1–23.

——, Tertiary production as a postwar international economic problem, *Review of Economic Statistics*, XXVIII (1946) 146–151.

FOX, A. M., International trade during the depression, *American Economic Review*, XXVII (1937 supplement) 12–28.

GLENDAY, R., The future of export trade, *International Affairs*, XVIII (1939) 641–660.

*HABERLER, G., Some factors affecting the future of international trade and international economic policy, *Economic Reconstruction* (S. E. Harris, ed.), New York, McGraw-Hill, 1945, 319–335.

HARMS, B., Der Begriff der Weltwirtschaft, *Weltwirtschaftliches Archiv*, XXIII (1926, I) 131–159.

——, Strukturwandlungen der Weltwirtschaft, *ibid.*, XXV (1927, I) 1–58.

HILGERDT, F., The approach to bilateralism: a change in the structure of world trade, *Index*, X (1935) 175–188.

HIRSCHMAN, A. O., The commodity structure of world trade, *Quarterly Journal of Economics*, LVII (1942–43) 565–595.

INSTITUT FÜR WELTWIRTSCHAFT UND SEEVERKEHR, Die Welthandelsentwicklung und das Problem der deutschen Ausfuhrpolitik, *Weltwirtschaftliches Archiv*, XXXVI (1932) 24–58.

LIEFMANN, R., Theorie des weltwirtschaftliches Reichtumsausgleiches, *Weltwirtschaftliches Archiv*, XIX (1923) 501–539.

LÖSCH, A., The nature of economic regions, *Southern Economic Journal*, V (1938–39) 71–78.

MACGREGOR, D. H., Trade of large and small countries, *Economic Journal*, XXXV (1925) 642–645.

NEULING, W., Entwicklungstendenzen im Welthandel der Letzten 50 Jahre, *Weltwirtschaftliches Archiv*, XXXVII (1933) 360–380.

REDFIELD, W. C., Competition for raw materials, *Annals of the American Academy of Political Science*, CL (1930) 85–88.

*ROBERTSON, D. H., The future of international trade, *Economic Journal*, XLVIII (1938) 1–14.

SOLLOHUB, W. A., The plight of foreign trade, *American Economic Review*, XXII (1932) 403–413.

VICTOR, M., Das sogenannte Gesetz der abnehmenden Aussenhandelsbedeutung, *Weltwirtschaftliches Archiv*, XXXVI (1932) 59–85.

*VINER, J., The prospects for foreign trade in the post-war world, *Manchester School*, XV (1947) 123–138.

ZINGALI, G., La bilancia alimentare pre-bellica, bellica, e post-bellica di alcuni stati d'Europa, *Giornale degli Economisti*, LXVI (1925) 517–533.

V-B (1). THE TRADE OF PARTICULAR COUNTRIES: *Countries of the Western Hemisphere*

See also II-F, VI-C, VI-D and VI-E.

AKAGI, R. H., Future of American trade with Manchukuo, *Annals of the American Academy of Political Science*, CCXI (1940) 138–143.

---

* Reprinted in the present volume.

BEAN, L. H., Export prospects for southern farm products, *Southern Economic Journal*, VI (1939–40) 1–19.

BURROWS, H. R., International trade with special reference to the British Commonwealth and the USA, *South African Journal of Economics*, VI (1938) 134–150.

CHANDLER, C. L., United States commerce with Latin America at the promulgation of the Monroe Doctrine, *Quarterly Journal of Economics*, XXXVIII (1924) 466–486.

CLARK, L. B., Competing for Latin American markets, *Annals of the American Academy of Political Science*, CCXI (1940) 164–172.

FEILER, A., America in world trade, *Social Research*, I (1934) 248–250.

HANSEN, A. H., and UPGREN, A. R., Some aspects, near-term and long-term, of the international position of the United States, *American Economic Review*, XXXI (1941 supplement) 366–372.

JOHNSON, F., Trade with the belligerents, *Annals of the American Academy of Political Science*, CCXI (1940) 117–122.

KILDUFF, V. R., Economic factors in the development of Canadian-American trade, *Southern Economic Journal*, VIII (1941–42) 201–217.

KLEIN, J., The competitive situation in South American trade, *Review of Economic Statistics*, III (1921) 11–18.

KRAMER, R. L., Recovery of American foreign trade, *Annals of the American Academy of Political Science*, CXCIII (1937) 99–109.

———, Trends in United States foreign trade, *ibid.*, CCXI (1940) 3–8.

KREPS, T. J., Import and export prices in the United States and the terms of international trade, 1880–1914, *Quarterly Journal of Economics*, XL (1925–26) 708–720.

———, Export, import, and domestic prices in the United States, 1926–30, *ibid.*, XLVI (1931–32) 195–250.

LITMAN, S., The past decade of the foreign commerce of the United States, *American Economic Review*, X (1920) 313–331.

LOCKWOOD, W. W., Future of the China trade, *Annals of the American Academy of Political Science*, CCXI (1940) 130–137.

———, American-Japanese trade: its structure and significance, *ibid.*, CCXV (1941) 86–92.

NADLER, M., The postwar international economic position of the U. S., *Annals of the American Academy of Political Science*, CCXXVIII (1943) 92–100.

NORRIS, R. T., The physical volume of American foreign trade with leading countries, 1920–1932, *Review of Economic Statistics*, XVIII (1936) 89–96.

PATTERSON, E. M., The United States and the world economy, *Economic Essays in Honour of Gustav Cassel*, London, George Allen and Unwin Ltd., 1933, 479–490.

ROORBACH, G. B., Some recent tendencies in the development of the foreign trade of the United States, *Review of Economic Statistics*, II (1920) 125–137.

WILLIAMS, J. H., The foreign trade balance of the United States since the Armistice, *American Economic Review*, XI (1921 supplement) 22–39.

WILLIAMSON, H. F., Prophecies of scarcity or exhaustion of material resources in the United States, *American Economic Review*, XXXV (1945 supplement) 97–109.

ZIMMERN, W. H., Lancashire and Latin America, *Manchester School*, XIII (1943–44) 45–60.

V-B (2). The Trade of Particular Countries: *The British Commonwealth of Nations*
See also II-F, VI-C and VI-E.

ALISON, C. A., The second Russian five-year plan and the Australian primary producer, *Economic Record*, IX (1933) 108–112.

ANONYMOUS, Ten years of trade, *Economist*, CXIX: 2 (1934) 767–769.

BELSHAW, H., New Zealand in the postwar world: reconstruction problems of a vulnerable economy, *Canadian Journal of Economics and Political Science*, XI (1945) 388–401.

BEVERIDGE, W. H., British exports and the barometer, I, *Economic Journal*, XXX (1920) 13–25.

————, British exports and the barometer, II, *ibid.*, 209–213.

BUTTERWORTH, G. N., and CAMPION, H., Changes in British import trade, 1924–36, *Manchester School*, VIII (1937) 48–55.

CLAY, H., The place of exports in British industry after the war, *Economic Journal*, LII (1942) 145–153.

————, Britain's declining rôle in world trade, *Foreign Affairs*, XXIV (1945–46) 411–428.

CONDLIFFE, J. B., The international position as it affects New Zealand, *Economic Record*, XV (October 1939 supplement) 17–24.

DACEY, W. M., British reconversion and trade, *Foreign Affairs*, XXIII (1944–45) 247–255.

DANIELS, G. W., Overseas trade of the United Kingdom in recent years as compared with 1913, *Manchester School*, II (1931) 1–9.

FISHER, A. G. B., The Commonwealth's place in the world economic structure, *International Affairs*, XX (1944) 32–41.

FLUX, A. W., British export trade, *Economic Journal*, XXXVI (1926) 551–562.

FORRESTER, R. B., Britain's access to overseas markets, *Economic Journal*, XLII (1932) 517–531.

KAHN, A. E., The British balance of payments and problems of domestic policy, *Quarterly Journal of Economics*, LXI (1947) 368–396.

LEWIS, E. M. R., and MILLER, K. W., Notes on the balances of payments of the British and French Empires with non-sterling countries, *Economic Record*, XVI (1940) 114–118.

MACDOUGALL, G. D. A., Britain's bargaining power, *Economic Journal*, LVI (1946) 27–37.

————, Britain's foreign trade problem, *ibid.*, LVII (1947) 69–113.

McNAIR, W. A., New Zealand's trade with the East, *Economic Record*, V (1929) 83–98.

McPHEE, E. T., Review of the Australian export trade, 1904–08 to 1926–27, *Economic Record*, IV (1928 supplement) 105–113.

MURPHY, M. E., Trends and conflicts in the British economy, *American Economic Review*, XXXVI (1946 supplement) 628–641.

ROBERTSON, C. J., Monoexport in Africa, *South African Journal of Economics*, VIII (1940) 1–18.

ROBERTSON, D. H., The problem of exports, *Economic Journal*, LV (1945) 321–325.

SCHUSTER, G., Empire trade before and after Ottawa, *Economist*, CXIX: 2 (1934 special supplement) 1–20.

SUTCH, W. B., Changes in New Zealand's import structure, *Economic Record*, XIX (1943) 203–211.

TAUSSIG, F. W., The change in Great Britain's foreign trade terms after 1900, *Economic Journal*, XXXV (1925) 1–10.

V-B (3). THE TRADE OF PARTICULAR COUNTRIES: *Continental Europe*

See also II-F, VI-C and VI-E.

ANONYMOUS, The foreign trade monopoly and the struggle for independence, *Vneshniaia Torgovlia*, (1933, No. 8) 5–8.

———, Russia's trade, I, *Economist*, CXLIV (1943) 453–454.

———, Russia's trade, II, *ibid.*, 520–521.

———, Russia's trade, III, *ibid.*, 582–583.

HILLMANN, H. C., Analysis of Germany's foreign trade and the war, *Economica*, VII, new series (1940) 66–88.

HIRSCH, J., Amerikas Wirtschaftsüberlegenheit und die Möglichkeiten des wiederausgleiches Deutschland, *Weltwirtschaftliches Archiv*, XXIV (1926, II) 130–164.

HOOVER, C. B., The future of the German economy, *American Economic Review*, XXXVI (1946 supplement) 642–649.

LEDERER, E., European international trade, *Annals of the American Academy of Political Science*, CLXXIV (1934) 107–115.

MOLODOWSKY, N., Germany's foreign trade terms in 1899–1913, *Quarterly Journal of Economics*, XLI (1926–27) 664–683.

ROBINSON, N., German foreign trade and industry after the First World War, *Quarterly Journal of Economics*, LVIII (1943–44) 615–636.

SCHLOTE, W., Zur Frage der sogenannten "Enteuropaeisierung" des Welthandels, *Weltwirtschaftliches Archiv*, XXXVII (1933) 381–411.

TAYLOR, A. E., The commercial importance of Russia, *American Economic Review*, XII (1922) 447–459.

WAGENFÜHR, R., Die Bedeutung des Aussenmarktes für die deutsche Industrie wirtschaft (1870–1936), *Sonderhefte des Instituts für Konjunkturforschung*, No. 41 (1936) 1–71.

V-B (4). THE TRADE OF PARTICULAR COUNTRIES: *All Other Countries*

See also II-F, VI-C and VI-E.

BISSON, T. A., American trade and Japanese aggression, *Annals of the American Academy of Political Science*, CCXI (1940) 123–129.

CHRISTIANS, W. F., and STARKEY, O. P., The Far East as a source of vital raw materials, *Annals of the American Academy of Political Science*, CCXV (1941) 80–85.

GREGORY, T. E., Japanese competition in world markets, *International Affairs*, XIII (1934) 325–342.

LEDERER, E., Japan in world economics, *Social Research*, IV (1937) 1–32.

LOCKWOOD, W. W., Postwar trade relations in the Far East, *American Economic Review*, XXXIII (1943 supplement) 420–430.

MUND, V. A., The trade problem of the Pacific, *American Economic Review*, XXVII (1937 supplement) 43–48.

MURRAY, K. A., Some regional economic problems of the Middle East, *International Affairs*, XXIII (1947) 11–19.

ORCHARD, J. E., Oriental competition in world trade, *Foreign Affairs*, XV (1936–37) 707–719.

SAYERS, R. S., Japan's balance of trade, *Economica*, II, new series (1935) 51–60.

UPGREN, A. R., Southeastern Asia and the Philippines as a market, *Annals of the American Academy of Political Science*, CCXXVI (1943) 9–21.

V-C (1). TRADE PROBLEMS OF PARTICULAR COMMODITIES: *Minerals and Mineral Products*

See also VI-C, VI-D and VI-E.

BAIN, H. F., World mineral production and control, *Foreign Affairs*, XI (1932–33) 706–710.

BEHRE, C. H., JR., and WANG, K.-P., China's mineral wealth, *Foreign Affairs*, XXIII (1944–45) 130–139.

BIDWELL, P. W., The battle of the metals, *Foreign Affairs*, XVIII (1939–40) 719–734.

EASTHAM, J. K., Rationalization in the tin industry, *Review of Economic Studies*, IV (1936) 13–33.

FINLAY, J. R., Copper, *Foreign Affairs*, IV (1925–26) 123–133.

JOESTEN, J., The scramble for Swedish iron ore, *Foreign Affairs*, XVI (1937–38) 347–350.

LEITH, C. K., The international aspect of the mineral industry, *Annals of the American Academy of Political Science*, CL (1930) 98–104.

———, The mineral position of the nations, *Foreign Affairs*, IX (1930–31) 133–148.

———, Mineral resources and peace, *ibid.*, XVI (1937–38) 515–524.

PETTENGILL, R. B., The United States foreign trade in copper: 1790–1932, *American Economic Review*, XXV (1935) 426–441.

RAWLES, W. P., Provisions for minerals in international agreements, *Political Science Quarterly*, XLVIII (1933) 513–533.

RICHTER, F. E., The copper industry in 1927, *Review of Economic Statistics*, X (1928) 33–39.

WARSKOW, H. T., Tin: an international metal, *Foreign Affairs*, V (1926–27) 482–489.

V-C (2). TRADE PROBLEMS OF PARTICULAR COMMODITIES: *Foods and Food Products*

See also VI-C, VI-D and VI-E.

BERNHARDT, J., The transition from government control of sugar to competitive conditions, *Quarterly Journal of Economics*, XXXIV (1919–20) 720–736.

BOOTH, J. F., The economic problems of Canadian agriculture in the war and postwar period, *Canadian Journal of Economics and Political Science*, VIII (1942) 446–459.

BRANDT, K., The reconstruction of European agriculture, *Foreign Affairs*, XXIII (1944–45) 284–294.

BRITNELL, G. E., The war and Canadian wheat, *Canadian Journal of Economics and Political Science*, VII (1941) 397–413.

BURTON, F. W., Wheat in Canadian history, *Canadian Journal of Economics and Political Science*, III (1937) 210–217.

DAVIS, J. S., Wheat, wheat policies, and the depression, *Review of Economic Statistics*, XVI (1934) 80–88.

ENFIELD, R. R., The world's wheat situation, *Economic Journal*, XLI (1931) 550–565.

GRIFFIN, H. L., Public policy in relation to the wheat market, *Canadian Journal of Economics and Political Science*, I (1935) 482–500.

HUMPHRIES, A. E., The international aspects of the wheat market, *International Affairs*, X (1931) 84–102.

LINDBERG, J., Food supply under a program of freedom from want, *Social Research*, XII (1945) 181–204.

McDOUGALL, F. L., The international wheat situation, *International Affairs*, X (1931) 524–538.

————, International aspects of postwar food and agriculture, *Annals of the American Academy of Political Science*, CCXXV (1943) 122–127.

ORR, J. B., The role of food in postwar reconstruction, *International Labor Review*, XLVII (1943) 279–296.

PATTON, H. S., The war and North American agriculture, *Canadian Journal of Economics and Political Science*, VII (1941) 382–396.

SCHNEIDER, F., JR., Sugar, *Foreign Affairs*, IV (1925–26) 311–320.

UKERS, W. H., The world trade in tea, *Index*, XI (1936) 159–168.

WALL, J. E., The world food situation, *International Affairs*, XXIII (1947) 307–316.

WALLACE, H. A., American agriculture and world markets, *Foreign Affairs*, XII (1933–34) 216–230.

WHEELER, L. A., Agricultural surpluses in the postwar world, *Foreign Affairs*, XX (1941–42) 87–101.

WRIGHT, C. M., Butter as a world staple, *Index*, X (1935) 254–269.

V-C (3). TRADE PROBLEMS OF PARTICULAR COMMODITIES: *Cotton and Wool*

See also VI-C, VI-D and VI-E.

BEAN, L. H., Changing trends in cotton production and consumption, *Southern Economic Journal*, V (1938–39) 442–459.

BERGLUND, A., The effects of international trade conditions and foreign agricultural developments on southern agriculture, *Southern Economic Journal*, II (1936) 61–68.

BLACK, J. D., The outlook for American cotton, *Review of Economic Statistics*, XVII (1935) 68–78.

CAMPION, H., American raw cotton policy, *Manchester School*, V (1934) 32–53.

CRONJÉ, F. J. C., The influence of raw wool prices on wool consumption, *South African Journal of Economics*, XV (1947) 147–148.

DANIELS, G. W., and JEWKES, J., The crisis in the Lancashire cotton industry, *Economic Journal*, XXXVII (1927) 33–46.

NAWROCKI, Z., The prospects of the British cotton industry, *Economic Journal*, LIV (1944) 41–46.

PEARSE, A. S., The cotton industry of Japan, China, and India, and its effect on Lancashire, *International Affairs*, XI (1932) 633–657.

WALLACE, H. A., The world cotton drama, *Foreign Affairs*, XIII (1934–35) 543–556.

WHITE, B. S., JR., The shrinking foreign market for United States cotton, *Quarterly Journal of Economics*, LIV (1939–40) 255–276.

V-C (4). TRADE PROBLEMS OF PARTICULAR COMMODITIES: *Fuels*

See also VI-C, VI-D and VI-E.

CLARKE, R. W., The influence of fuel on international politics, *Journal of the Royal Institute of International Affairs*, II (1923) 107–118.

EASTMAN, M., International aspects of the British coal crisis of 1926, *Journal of Political Economy*, XXXVI (1928) 229–239.

FEIS, H., Order in oil, *Foreign Affairs*, XXII. (1943–44) 616–626.

LEE, W. A., The international aspect of the coal problem, *International Affairs*, XI (1932) 473–492.

MAULDON, F. R. E., The problem of Australian coal, *Economic Record*, IV (1928) 177–192.

POGUE, J. E., The outlook for the oil industry, *Review of Economic Statistics*, X (1928) 31–32.

———, Oil in the world, *Yale Review*, XXXV, new series (1945–46) 623–632.

REGUL, R., Energiequellen der Welt, *Sonderhefte des Instituts für Konjunkturforschung*, No. 44 (1937) 1–78.

SLADE, E. J. W., The influence of oil on international politics, *Journal of the Royal Institute of International Affairs*, II (1923) 251–258.

V-C (5). TRADE PROBLEMS OF PARTICULAR COMMODITIES: *Other Commodities*

See also VI-C, VI-D and VI-E.

ANONYMOUS, Empires and raw materials, *Economist*, CXXI: 2 (1935) 793–794.

———, The problem of raw materials, *ibid.*, CXLIII (1942) 577–578.

BAUER, P. T., Future competition between natural and synthetic rubber, *Manchester School*, XIV (1946) 40–64.

CHAPMAN, D., The establishment of the jute industry: a problem in the location of industry?, *Review of Economic Studies*, VI (1938) 33–55.

FEIS, H., Raw materials and foreign policy, *Foreign Affairs*, XVI (1937–38) 574–586.

GLESINGER, E., Forest products in a world economy, *American Economic Review*, XXXV (1945 supplement) 120–129.

HOHMAN, E. P., American and Norwegian whaling: a comparative study of labor and industrial organization, *Journal of Political Economy*, XLIII (1935) 628–652.

ORTON, W., Rubber: a case study, *American Economic Review*, XVII (1927) 617–635.

RIVE, A., The consumption of tobacco since 1600, *Economic History*, I, No. 1 (1926) 57–75.

V-D. TRANSPORTATION AND COMMUNICATION

ADLER, J. H., British and American shipping policies: a problem and a proposal, *Political Science Quarterly*, LIX (1944) 193–219.

ANONYMOUS, Merchant fleets of the world, *Economist*, CXXI: 1 (1935) 167–168.

BERGLUND, A., The war and the world's mercantile marine, *American Economic Review*, X (1920) 227–258.

———, Our merchant marine problem and international trade, *Journal of Political Economy*, XXXIII (1925) 642–656.

BRIGDEN, J. B., Australian oversea shipping, *Economic Record*, VI (1930) 173–190.

CHAMBERLIN, J. P., Control of international transportation and communication, *Annals of the American Academy of Political Science*, CL (1930) 25–32.

COOPER, J. C., Some historic phases of British international civil aviation policy, *International Affairs*, XXIII (1947) 189–201.

DAY, E. E., The American merchant fleet; a war achievement, a peace problem, *Quarterly Journal of Economics*, XXXIV (1919–20) 567–606.

DEIMEL, H. L., JR., United States shipping policy and international economic relations, *American Economic Review*, XXXVI (1946 supplement) 547–560.

———, and PERRY, H. S., Postwar merchant marine problems, *Annals of the American Academy of Political Science,* CCXXX (1943) 54–62.

DEWEY, R. L., The Merchant Marine Act of 1936, *American Economic Review*, XXVII (1937) 239–252.

DIEBOLD, W., JR., A merchant marine second to none?, *Foreign Affairs*, XXI (1942–43) 711–720.

———, Shipping in the immediate postwar years, *Journal of Political Economy*, LIII (1945) 15–36.

DRURY, H. B., World peace and the rivalry of merchant marines, *Annals of the American Academy of Political Science*, CL (1930) 33–39.

FOENANDER, O. DE R., The shipping enterprise of the Australian Commonwealth Government, *American Economic Review*, XIX (1929) 605–618.

GREGG, E. S., Vicissitudes in the shipping trade, 1870–1920, *Quarterly Journal of Economics*, XXXIV (1919–20) 603–617.

———, The failure of the Merchant Marine Act of 1920, *American Economic Review*, XI (1921) 601–615.

HARBORD, J. G., America's position in radio communication, *Foreign Affairs*, IV (1925–26) 465–474.

HICHENS, W. L., Anglo-Japanese competition in the shipping trade, *International Affairs*, XVIII (1939) 661–678.

HILL, N., Shipping subsidies as an international problem, *International Affairs*, XII (1933) 327–343.

HONDELINK, E. R., Transport problems in Europe, *International Affairs*, XXI (1945) 512–521.

HUTCHINS, J. G. B., One hundred and fifty years of American navigation policy, *Quarterly Journal of Economics*, LIII (1938–39) 238–260.

KEYLIN, A. D., Postwar problems of merchant marine, *Vneshniaia Torgovlia*, (1944, No. 2–3) 16–25.

KRAMER, R. L., War and our merchant marine, *Annals of the American Academy of Political Science*, CCXXX (1943) 48–53.

LACHMANN, K., The shipping problem at the end of the war, *Social Research*, X (1943) 52–75.

LAND, E. S., Building an American merchant marine, *Annals of the American Academy of Political Science*, CCXI (1940) 41–48.

LEONARD, W. N., Some problems of postwar air transportation, *American Economic Review*, XXXVII (1947 supplement) 462–477.

LEWIS, W. A., The interrelations of shipping freights, *Economica*, VIII, new series (1941) 52–76.

LOENING, G., Ships over the sea: possibilities and limitations of air transport in war, *Foreign Affairs*, XX (1941–42) 489–502.

McCONNELL, B. P. M., The race for aerial trade routes, *Yale Review*, XXVII, new series (1937–38) 348–365.

MACLAY, J. S., The general shipping situation, *International Affairs*, XXII (1946) 488–500.

MARX, D., JR., Strategy and American shipping policy, *Yale Review*, XXXIV, new series (1944–45) 684–698.

———, The determination of postwar ocean freight rates, *American Economic Review*, XXXVI (1946 supplement) 561–574.

MILLER, B. O., The protective tariff and the American merchant marine, *Southern Economic Journal*, IV (1937–38) 211–225.

PAGE, F. H., The future of the skyways: a British view, *Foreign Affairs*, XXII (1943–44) 404–412.

PERRY, H. S., The United States shipping industry, *Annals of the American Academy of Political Science*, CXCIII (1937) 88–98.

———, The wartime merchant fleet and postwar shipping requirements, *American Economic Review*, XXXVI (1946 supplement) 520–546.

VISHNEPOLSKY, S. A., Four years of crisis in world shipping, 1929–1933, *Vneshniaia Torgovlia*, (1933, No. 17) 2–4.

WARNER, E. P., International air transport, *Foreign Affairs*, IV (1925–26) 278–293.

———, Atlantic airways, *ibid.*, XVI (1937–38) 467–483.

———, Airways for peace, *ibid.*, XXII (1943–44) 11–27.

WRIGHT, Q., The international regulation of the air, *American Economic Review*, XXXV (1945 supplement) 243–248.

V-E. INTERNATIONAL ECONOMIC ASPECTS OF POPULATION AND MIGRATION

A. J. B., Population trends and power, *International Affairs*, XXI (1945) 79–86.

ANGUS, H. F., The future of immigration into Canada, *Canadian Journal of Economics and Political Science*, XII (1946) 379–386.

ANONYMOUS, Population and social problems, *International Labor Review*, XXXIX (1939) 291–318.

BEVERIDGE, W., The fall of fertility among European races, *Economica*, V (1925) 10–27.

BLADEN, V. W., The population problem, *Canadian Journal of Economics and Political Science*, V (1939) 528–547.

———, On population, *ibid.*, VIII (1942) 273–288.

BRIGDEN, J. B., The limits of Australian immigration, *Economic Record*, I (1925) 145–147.

CARR-SAUNDERS, A. M., Fallacies about over-population, *Foreign Affairs*, IX (1930–31) 646–656.

———, Migration policies and the economic crisis, *ibid.*, XII (1933–34) 664–676.

CHARLES, E., The new population problem, *Economist*, CXXIII (1936) 718–719.

CONDLIFFE, J. B., Population movements and international trade, *Index*, XI (1936) Pt. I, 122–129; Pt. II, 138–146.

FAIRCHILD, H. P., The Immigration Law of 1924, *Quarterly Journal of Economics*, XXXVIII (1923–24) 653–665.

———, Immigration and the population problem, *Annals of the American Academy of Political Science*, CL (1930) 7–12.

FORSYTH, W. D., Population growth—some comparisons, *Economic Record*, XVII (1941) 248–252.

HARROD, R. F., Modern population trends, *Manchester School*, X (1939) 1–20.

HUNTINGTON, E., Agricultural productivity and pressure of population, *Annals of the American Academy of Political Science*, CXCVIII (1938) 73–92.

IRWIN, J. O., World population, *Manchester School*, VIII (1937) 63–68.

JEWKES, J., The population scare, *Manchester School*, X (1939) 101–121.

KUCZYNSKI, R. R., Population growth and economic pressure, *Annals of the American Academy of Political Science*, CL (1930) 1–6.

———, Economic causes of population movement, *Index*, XI (1936) 223–233.

———, World population problems, *International Affairs*, XX (1944) 449–457.

LANDRY, A., La révolution démographique, *Economic Essays in Honour of Gustav Cassel*, London, George Allen and Unwin Ltd., 1933, 357–367.

LASKER, B., Displacement of population in Eastern Asia, *Annals of the American Academy of Political Science*, CCXXXIV (1944) 13–21.

LEVMORE, B. W., A stimulus for American industry: non-professional refugees, *Annals of the American Academy of Political Science*, CCIII (1939) 162–167.

LORIMER, F., Population trends in the Orient, *Foreign Affairs*, XXIII (1944–45) 668–674.

McFALL, R. J., Is food the limiting factor in population growth?, *Yale Review*, XV (1925–26) 297–316.

MACMAHON, E. C., The attitude of immigration countries, *Annals of the American Academy of Political Science*, CL (1930) 13–24.

MADGWICK, R. B., Immigration, *Economic Record*, XII (1936) 71–82.

MEARS, E. G., Financial aspects of American immigration, *Economic Journal*, XXXIII (1923) 332–342.

NOTESTEIN, F. W., Population and power in postwar Europe, *Foreign Affairs*, XXII (1943–44) 389–403.

NOYES, C. R., The weather chart of population, *Yale Review*, XII (1922–23) 813–825.

OSTROLENK, B., The economics of an imprisoned world—a brief for the removal of immigration restrictions, *Annals of the American Academy of Political Science*, CCIII (1939) 194–201.

SHIRRAS, G. F., The population problem in India, *Economic Journal*, XLIII (1933) 56–73.

SPENGLER, J. J., Population movements, employment, and income, *Southern Economic Journal*, V (1938–39) 129–157.

TAEUBER, I. B., Population displacement in Europe, *Annals of the American Academy of Political Science*, CCXXXIV (1944) 1–12.

TAIT, D. C., International aspects of migration, *Journal of the Royal Institute of International Affairs*, VI (1927) 25–46.

———, The international organization of migration, *International Labor Review*, XXI (1930) 202–216.

TAYLOR, P. S., Some aspects of Mexican immigration, *Journal of Political Economy*, XXXVIII (1930) 609–615.

THOMPSON, W. S., and WHELPTON, P. K., Levels of living and population pressure, *Annals of the American Academy of Political Science*, CXCVIII (1938) 93–100.

WALDECK, C., The great new migration, *Foreign Affairs*, XV (1936–37) 537–546.

Wickens, C. H., Australian population: its nature and growth, *Economic Record*, I (1925) 1–16.

Wood, G. L., The immigration problem in Australia, *Economic Record*, II (1926) 229–239.

Younge, E. R., Population movements and the assimilation of alien groups in Canada, *Canadian Journal of Economics and Political Science*, X (1944) 372–380.

V-F. International Comparisons of Prices, Productivity, etc.

Anonymous, Consumi e prezzi nel confronto internazionale fra i salari reali, *La Riforma Sociale*, XXXVII (1926) 538–552.

Daniel, A., Regional differences of productivity in European agriculture, *Review of Economic Studies*, XII (1944–45) 50–70.

Fox, B., International price relationships for selected raw materials, *Explorations in Economics*, New York, McGraw-Hill, 1936, 109–119.

Gilles, R. C., International comparison of wholesale prices, *Review of Economic Statistics*, XXII (1940) 150–156.

Michell, H., Notes on prices of agricultural commodities in the United States and Canada, 1850–1934, *Canadian Journal of Economics and Political Science*, I (1935) 269–279.

Read, T. T., The world's output of work, *American Economic Review*, XXIII (1933) 55–60.

Rostas, L., Industrial production, productivity, and distribution in Britain, Germany, and the United States, *Economic Journal*, LIII (1943) 39–54.

Rothbarth, E., Causes of the superior efficiency of U. S. A. industry as compared with British industry, *Economic Journal*, LVI (1946) 382–390.

Saunders, C. T., Man-power distribution, 1939–45: some international comparisons, *Manchester School*, XIV (1946) 1–39.

Sawkins, D. T., International comparisons of the cost of living, *Economic Record*, XI (1935) 13–19.

Stone, R., National income in the United Kingdom and the United States of America, *Review of Economic Studies*, X (1942–43) 1–27.

Tarshis, L., Real wages in the United States and Great Britain, *Canadian Journal of Economics and Political Science*, IV (1938) 362–376.

VI. COMMERCIAL POLICY

VI-A. General Discussion

Includes a number of studies of the politico-economic aspects of commercial policy as well as discussions of reciprocity, the most-favored-nation principle, economic regionalism, self-sufficiency, etc.

Anonymous, The principles of trade, I, *Economist*, CXLVI (1944) 4–5.
———, The principles of trade, IV, the multilateral approach, *ibid.*, 94–95.
———, The principles of trade, V, planned expansion, *ibid.*, 136–137.
———, The principles of trade, VI, the regional solution, *ibid.*, 169–170.
———, The principles of trade, VII, prices and markets, *ibid.*, 204–205.
———, The principles of trade, VIII, the new liberalism, *ibid.*, 232–233.

ASHLEY, W., A retrospect of free-trade doctrine, *Economic Journal*, XXXIV (1924) 501–539.

MITCHELL, A. A., A retrospect of free-trade doctrine: a comment, *ibid.*, XXXV (1925) 214–220.

BAILEY, S. H., The political aspects of discrimination in international relations, *Economica*, XII (1932) Pt. I, 89–115; Pt. II, 160–179.

———, Reciprocity and the most-favored-nation clause, *ibid.*, XIII (1933) 428–456.

BALOGH, T., The League of Nations on post-war foreign trade problems, *Economic Journal*, LIV (1944) 256–261.

BASCH, A., European economic regionalism, *American Economic Review*, XXXIII (1943 supplement) 408–419.

BEALS, C., A self-sufficient Latin America, *Yale Review*, XXIV, new series (1934–35) 479–497.

VON BECKERATH, H., Some international aspects of capitalism and its present crisis, *Southern Economic Journal*, III (1936–37) 115–142.

BENHAM, F., The muddle of the thirties, *Economica*, XIII, new series (1946) 1–9.

BIDWELL, P. W., Trade, tariffs, the depression, *Foreign Affairs*, X (1931–32) 391–401.

———, Trading with dictators, *Annals of the American Academy of Political Science*, CCIV (1939) 59–65.

———, Controlling trade after the war, *Foreign Affairs*, XXI (1942–43) 297–311.

BISTRITSKY, V., On the functions of capitalistic and soviet trade, *Sovietskaya Torgovlya*, III (1934) 64–83.

BRESCIANI-TURRONI, C., Solidarita economica e concorrenza commerciale fra gli stati, *Giornale degli Economisti*, L (1920) 361–395.

BROSSARD, E. B., Commerical policies and tariffs in their relation to world peace, *Annals of the American Academy of Political Science*, CL (1930) 154–161.

BRYCE, R. B., Basic issues in postwar international economic relations, *American Economic Review*, XXXII (1942 supplement) 165–181.

BUKHARIN, N., Imperialism and communism, *Foreign Affairs*, XIV (1935–36) 563–577.

CABIATI, A., Organizzazione scientifica del lavoro e il "dumping," *Giornale degli Economisti*, XLIX (1919) 76–91.

———, Betrachtungen über das Dumping, *Zeitschrift für Nationalökonomie*, VI (1935) 1–27.

CHALMERS, H., The postwar drift in European commercial policy, *American Economic Review*, XIV (1924 supplement) 14–25.

———, Current trends in foreign commercial policy, *Annals of the American Academy of Political Science*, CL (1930) 126–145.

———, The depression and foreign trade barriers, *ibid.*, CLXXIV (1934) 88–106.

CLARK, G., The dangerous fallacies of imperialism, *Annals of the American Academy of Political Science*, CLXXXVI (1936) 6–15.

CONDLIFFE, J. B., Vanishing world trade, *Foreign Affairs*, XI (1932–33) 645–656.

———, The economic war, *Annals of the American Academy of Political Science*, CCXVIII (1941) 20–25.

———, Economic power as an instrument of national policy, *American Economic Review*, XXXIV (1944 supplement) 305–314.

COPLAND, D. B., The theory of marketing, with special reference to primary products, *Economic Record*, IV (1928 supplement) 2–17.

CRICK, W. F., Free trade and planned economy, *South African Journal of Economics*, XV (1947) 40–46.

CULBERTSON, W. S., Raw materials and foodstuffs in the commercial policies of nations, *Annals of the American Academy of Political Science*, CXII (1924 supplement) 133 pp.

DIETRICH, E. B., Foreign trade blocs, *Annals of the American Academy of Political Science*, CCXI (1940) 85–91.

EDMINSTER, L. R., International trade and postwar reconstruction, *American Economic Review*, XXXIII (1943 supplement) 303–321.

ELLIS, H. S., Removal of restrictions on trade and capital, *Postwar Economic Problems* (S. E. Harris, ed.), New York, McGraw-Hill, 1943, 345–359.

FEILER, A., Current tendencies in commercial policy, *American Economic Review*, XXVII (1937 supplement) 29–42.

———, International trade under totalitarian governments, *Social Research*, V (1938) 424–441.

FEIS, H., The trade policies of a neutral: some conjectures on the alternatives, *Explorations in Economics*, New York, McGraw-Hill, 1936, 131–144.

———, The conflict over trade ideologies, *Foreign Affairs*, XXV (1947) 217–228.

FELLNER, W., The commercial policy implications of the Fund and Bank, *American Economic Review*, XXXV (1945 supplement) 262–271.

FIRTH, G. G., Article seven—a program for prosperity?, *Economic Record*, XVIII (1942) 1–15.

FISHER, A. G. B., International problems of economic change, *International Affairs*, XVII (1938) 147–167.

GRAMPP, W. D., The third century of mercantilism, *Southern Economic Journal*, X (1943–44) 292–302.

GREGORY, T. E., Economic nationalism, *International Affairs*, X (1931) 289–306.

HABERLER, G., Chairman, Problems of international economic policy (Abstracts of conference discussions by K. L. Anderson, A. Basch, I. de Vegh, H. Heuser, F. Hilgerdt, M. L. Hoffman, F. Machlup, A. R. Upgren, E. S. Shaw.), *American Economic Review*, XXXII (1942 supplement) 206–211.

———, The political economy of regional or continental blocs, *Postwar Economic Problems* (S. E. Harris, ed.), New York, McGraw-Hill, 1943, 325–344.

HAMILTON, W., The control of strategic materials, *American Economic Review*, XXXIV (1944) 261–279.

HAMMOND, M. B., Economic conflict as a regulating force in international affairs, *American Economic Review*, XXI (1931) 1–9.

HAUSER, H., The most-favored-nation clause: a menace to world peace, *Annals of the American Academy of Political Science*, CLVI (1931) 101–106.

HEATON, H., Heckscher on mercantilism, *Journal of Political Economy*, XLV (1937) 370–393.

HECKSCHER, E. F., The origin of protectionism, *Ekonomisk Tidskrift*, XXII (1920) 25–65.

———, The continental bloc then and now, *ibid.*, XLIII (1941) 1–17.

HILGERDT, F., The case for multilateral trade, *American Economic Review*, XXXIII (1943 supplement) 393–407.

HINSHAW, R., Keynesian commercial policy, *The New Economics*, New York, Alfred A. Knopf, 1947, 315–322.

Hoselitz, B. F., Socialist planning and international economic relations, *American Economic Review*, XXXIII (1943) 839–851.

Istel, A., "Equal access" to raw materials, *Foreign Affairs*, XX (1941–42) 450–465.

Kalecki, M., Multilateralism and full employment, *Canadian Journal of Economics and Political Science*, XII (1946) 322–327.

Keynes, J. M., National self-sufficiency, *Yale Review*, XXII, new series (1932–33) 755–769.

Kotok, E. I., International policy on renewable national resources, *American Economic Review*, XXXV (1945 supplement) 110–119.

Langer, W. L., A critique of imperialism, *Foreign Affairs*, XIV (1935–36) 102–119.

Lenin, V. I., From pronouncements by Lenin on trade and cooperation, *Voprosy Sovietskoi Torgovli*, IV (1940) 11–28.

Lingelbach, W. E., Commercial policies as causes of international friction, *Annals of the American Academy of Political Science*, CL (1930) 117–125.

Lippmann, W., Self-sufficiency: some random reflections, *Foreign Affairs*, XII (1933–34) 207–215.

Mackintosh, W. A., Trade barriers as an obstacle to prosperity, *Annals of the American Academy of Political Science*, CLXXXVI (1936) 1–5.

Martin, W., The tariff truce, *Index*, V (1930) 45–49.

Mertens, A., A defense of the most-favored-nation clause, *Annals of the American Academy of Political Science*, CLVI (1931) 107–109.

Miller, W. L., Government aid in foreign trade, *Political Science Quarterly*, XXXVI (1921) 211–225.

Muhlbach, W., Tariff devices to meet a problem of depreciating currencies, *Journal of Political Economy*, XXXIII (1925) 293–317.

Nayman, G., Lenin and Stalin on trade during the transition period, *Sovietskaya Torgovlya*, I (1934) 26–57.

Ohlin, B., A road to freer trade, *Index*, IV (1929) 2–9.

Opie, R., A British view of postwar trade, *American Economic Review*, XXXIII (1943 supplement) 322–331.

Paish, G., The world breakdown, *Annals of the American Academy of Political Science*, LXXXIX (1920) 219–226.

Palyi, M., International aspects of problems of production and trade, *American Economic Review*, XXV (1935 supplement) 45–62.

Parks, W., Postwar international commodity trade: public problems and policies, *Political Science Quarterly*, LX (1945) 241–266.

Patterson, E. M., Government support of economic interests abroad, *Annals of the American Academy of Political Science*, CCVI (1939) 56–61.

Porri, V., Colonie ed independenza economica, *La Riforma Sociale*, (1920) 14–59.

Rasminsky, L., Anglo-American trade prospects: a Canadian view, *Economic Journal*, LV (1945) 161–178.

S., New complications in commercial policy, *Foreign Affairs*, XIII (1934–35) 68–81.

Salter, A., The future of economic nationalism, *Foreign Affairs*, XI (1932–33) 8–20.

Schrecker, C., The growth of economic nationalism and its international consequences, *International Affairs*, XIII (1934) 208–225.

Schüller, R., Commercial policy between two wars—personal observations of a participant, *Social Research*, X (1943) 152–174.

612 CLASSIFIED BIBLIOGRAPHY OF ARTICLES

SHEPARDSON, W. H., Nationalism and American trade, *Foreign Affairs*, XII (1933–34) 403–417.

SIMONS, H. C., Postwar economic policy: some traditional liberal proposals, *American Economic Review*, XXXIII (1943 supplement) 431–445.

———, Trade and the peace, *Postwar Economic Problems* (S. E. Harris, ed.), New York, McGraw-Hill, 1943, 141–155.

SMITH, J. G., Economic nationalism and international trade, *Economic Journal*, XLV (1935) 619–648.

SMITHIES, A., Multilateral trade and employment, *American Economic Review*, XXXVII (1947 supplement) 560–568.

SNYDER, R. C., Commercial policy as reflected in treaties from 1931 to 1939, *American Economic Review*, XXX (1940) 787–802.

———, The most-favored-nation clause and recent trade practices, *Political Science Quarterly*, LV (1940) 77–97.

SOULE, G., The United States and Britain's economic policy, *Annals of the American Academy of Political Science*, CCXL (1945) 55–63.

STALEY, E., Communication on Taussig's letter to Wilson in 1918 on "International allotment of important commodities," *American Economic Review*, XXXIII (1943) 877–881.

THOMAS, N., The basis of international cooperation, *Annals of the American Academy of Political Science*, CL (1930) 179–191.

TROTSKY, L., Nationalism and economic life, *Foreign Affairs*, XII (1933–34) 395–402.

VARGA, E., The economic evaluation of world commerce, *Vneshniaia Torgovlia*, (1934, No. 20–21) 16–18.

———, Features of the internal and foreign policy of the capitalist countries during the epoch of the general crisis of capitalism, *Mirovoe Khoziaistvo i Mirovaia Politika*, June 1946, 8–17.

VINER, J., Dumping, *Encyclopaedia of the Social Sciences*, V, New York, Macmillan, 1931, 275–278.

———, The most-favored-nation clause, *Index*, VI (1931) 2–17.

*———, International relations between state-controlled national economies, *American Economic Review*, XXXIV (1944 supplement) 315–329.

WEBB, S., The end of laissez faire, *Economic Journal*, XXXVI (1926) 434–441.

WHITTLESEY, C. R., The cost of self-sufficiency, *Annals of the American Academy of Political Science*, CXCVIII (1938) 15–21.

WILLIAMS, T. O., Tariffs and economic nationalism, *South African Journal of Economics*, II (1934) 43–54.

WINSLOW, E. M., Administrative protectionism: a problem in commercial policy, *Explorations in Economics*, New York, McGraw-Hill, 1936, 179–189.

WRIGHT, P. G., The bearing of recent tariff legislation on international relations, *American Economic Review*, XXIII (1933) 16–26.

YOUNG, J. P., Problems of international economic policy for the United States, *American Economic Review*, XXXII (1942 supplement) 182–194.

* Reprinted in the present volume.

VI-B. Theory of Tariffs and Other Commercial Restrictions

See also I-A.

Anderson, K. L., Tariff protection and increasing returns, *Explorations in Economics*, New York, McGraw-Hill, 1936, 157–168.

——, Protection and the historical situation: Australia, *Quarterly Journal of Economics*, LIII (1938–39) 86–104.

Samuelson, M. C., The Australian case for protection reëxamined, *Quarterly Journal of Economics*, LIV (1939–40) 143–151, with comments by K. L. Anderson.

Balogh, T., A note on the economics of retaliation, *Review of Economic Studies*, XI (1944) 86–90.

de Beers, J. S., Tariff aspects of a federal union, *Quarterly Journal of Economics*, LVI (1941–42) 49–92.

Beghi, P. M., Dei contingentamenti, *La Riforma Sociale*, XLVI (1935), 165–180.

Bladen, V. W., Tariff policy and employment in depression, *Canadian Journal of Economics and Political Science*, VI (1940) 72–78.

Brigden, J. B., The Australian tariff and the standard of living, *Economic Record*, I (1925) 29–46.

Benham, F. C., The Australian tariff and the standard of living: a reply, *ibid.*, II (1926) 20–42.

——, The Australian tariff and the standard of living: a rejoinder, *ibid.*, III (1927) 102–116.

Benham, F. C., The Australian tariff and the standard of living: a restatement, *ibid.*, 239–248.

Brisman, S., Protective tariffs and the value of money, *Ekonomisk Tidskrift*, XXVII (1925) 191–198.

Comitavo del Gruppo Libero-Scambisto Italiano per la Riduzione delle Tariffe doganali, *La Riforma Sociale*, XXXIV (1923) 225–234.

Copland, D. B., A neglected phase of tariff controversy, *Quarterly Journal of Economics*, XLV (1930–31) 289–308.

——, A note on tariff theory, *Economic Record*, X (1934) 83–87.

Crawford, J. G., and Wolstenholme, S. H., Some effects of the Australian tariff, *Economic Record*, XIII (1937) 246–248.

Denis, H., A note on the theory of tariffs, *Review of Economic Studies*, XII (1944–45) 110–113.

Elliott, G. A., Protective duties, tributes, and terms of trade, *Journal of Political Economy*, XLV (1937) 804–807.

——, The relation of protective duties to domestic production, *Canadian Journal of Economics and Political Science*, VI (1940) 296–298.

Enke, S., The monopsony case for tariffs, *Quarterly Journal of Economics*, LVIII (1943–44) 229–245.

Gifford, C. H. P., Protection and the price level in Australia, *Economic Record*, X (1934) 46–49.

de v. Graaff, J., A note on the relative merits of tariffs and subsidies, *South African Journal of Economics*, XV (1947) 149–150.

HÄFNER, K., Die Politik der mengenmässigen Einfuhrregulierung, *Weltwirtschaftliches, Archiv*, XL (1934) 18–59.

————, Zur Theories der mengenmässigen Einfuhrregulierung, *ibid.*, XLI (1935) 190–223.

HECKSCHER, E. F., Protective tariffs and the value of money, *Ekonomisk Tidskrift*, XXVII (1925) 126–137.

KALDOR, N., A note on tariffs and the terms of trade, *Economica*, VII, new series (1940) 377–380.

KREIDER, C., Valuation for customs, *Quarterly Journal of Economics*, LVI (1941–42) 157–159.

LEHFELDT, R. A., Tariffs and the distribution of foreign trade, *Economica*, VII (1927) 275–285.

LERNER, A. P., The symmetry between import and export taxes, *Economica*, III, new series (1936) 308–313.

LOVASY, G., Schutzzölle bei unvollkommener Konkurrenz, *Zeitschrift für Nationalökonomie*, V (1934) 336–355.

LOVEDAY, M. A., The Australian tariff: a criticism, *Economic Record*, VI (1930) 272–278.

MACGREGOR, D. C., The provincial incidence of the Canadian tariff, *Canadian Journal of Economics and Political Science*, I (1935) 384–395.

MACKENROTH, G., Zollpolitik und produktionsmittelversorgung, *Weltwirtschaftliches Archiv*, XXIX (1929, I) 77–105.

MARSH, D. B., Fiscal policy and tariffs in postwar international trade, *Canadian Journal of Economics and Political Science*, IX (1943) 507–531.

MYERS, J. H., Tariffs and prices: a diagrammatic representation, *American Economic Review*, XXXI (1941) 553–557.

OHLIN, B., Protection and non-competing groups, *Weltwirtschaftliches Archiv*, XXXIII (1931) 30–45.

————, Protektionismus und Volkseinkommen, *ibid.*, XLI (1935) 295–315.

PAISH, G., How tariffs affect prosperity, *Annals of the American Academy of Political Science*, CLVI (1931) 84–100

REDDAWAY, W. B., Some effects of the Australian tariff, *Economic Record*, XIII (1937) 22–30.

————, Further comments on the Australian tariff, *ibid.*, 249–250.

REEDMAN, J. N., Some notes on the theoretical aspects of import quotas, *South African Journal of Economics*, IV (1936) 425–435.

ROBBINS, L., Economic notes on some arguments for protection, *Economica*, XI (1931) 45–62.

*ROBINSON, J., Beggar-my-neighbour remedies for unemployment, *Essays in the Theory of Employment*, 2d. ed., Oxford, Basil Blackwell, 1947, 156–170.

ROLPH, E. R., The burden of import duties, *American Economic Review*, XXXVI (1946) 788–812.

MORGAN, J. N., The burden of import duties: comment, *ibid.*, XXXVII (1947) 407–409.

* Reprinted in the present volume.

————, Burden of import duties with fixed exchange rates, *ibid.*, XXXVII (1947) 604–632.

RUEFF, J., Une erreur économique du protectionnisme: L'argument de la balance commerciale, *Revue d'Economie Politique*, XLVII (1933) 403–416.

SANDWELL, B. K., Centre and circumference in a tariff-protected area, *Canadian Journal of Economics and Political Science*, I (1935) 379–383.

*DE SCITOVSZKY, T., A reconsideration of the theory of tariffs, *Review of Economic Studies*, IX (1942) 89–110.

SOMMER, L., Freihandel und Schutzzoll in ihrem Zusammenhang mit Geldtheorie und Währungspolitik, *Weltwirtschaftliches Archiv*, XXIV (1926, II) 33–72.

*STOLPER, W. F., and SAMUELSON, P. A., Protection and real wages, *Review of Economic Studies*, IX (1941) 58–73.

THRELFELL, R. L., The relative merits of tariffs and subsidies as methods of protection, *South African Journal of Economics*, XIV (1946) 117–131.

VINER, J., The Australian tariff, *Economic Record*, V (1929) 306–315.

WICKSELL, K., An example of the tariff problem, *Ekonomisk Tidskrift*, XXVII (1925) 23–42.

VI-C. CARTELS, COMMODITY AGREEMENTS, AND STATE TRADING

See also VI-D and VI-E.

ANONYMOUS, Foreign trade monopoly in trade agreements with foreign governments, *Vneshniaia Torgovlia*, (1933, No. 8) 12.

————, The control of raw products, *Economist*, CXIX: 2 (1934) 912–913.

————, International cartels, *ibid.*, CXLVII (1944) 724–725.

BAUER, P. T., Rubber and foreign exchange, *Economic Journal*, L (1940) 231–239.

————, The working of rubber regulation, *ibid.*, LVI (1946) 391–414.

BLACK, J. D., and TSOU, S. S., International commodity arrangements, *Quarterly Journal of Economics*, LVIII (1943–44) 521–552.

BRADY, R. A., The role of cartels in the current cultural crisis, *American Economic Review*, XXXV (1945 supplement) 312–320.

COLE, G. D. H., Planning international trade, *Foreign Affairs*, XII (1933–34) 231–243.

DAVIS, J. S., International commodity agreements in the postwar world, *American Economic Review*, XXXII (1942 supplement) 391–403.

————, International commodity agreements in the postwar world, *Postwar Economic Problems* (S. E. Harris, ed.), New York, McGraw-Hill, 1943, 305–321.

————, Experience under intergovernmental commodity agreements, 1902–45, *Journal of Political Economy*, LIV (1946) 193–220.

DOMERATZKY, L., Cartels and the business crisis, *Foreign Affairs*, X (1931–32) 34–53.

DUBANSKY, M., Franco-German potassium cartels, *Vneshniaia Torgovlia*, (1933, No. 6) 10.

EDWARDS, C. D., International cartels as obstacles to international trade, *American Economic Review*, XXXIV (1944 supplement) 330–339.

FRUMKIN, M., Lenin and the monopoly of foreign trade, *Mirovoe Khoziaistvo i Mirovaia Politika*, (May 1936) 89–109.

---

* Reprinted in the present volume.

HALEY, B. F., The relation between cartel policy and commodity agreement policy, *American Economic Review*, XXXVI (1946 supplement) 717–734.

HAMILTON, W. H., Cartels, patents and politics, *Foreign Affairs*, XXIII (1944–45) 582–593.

———, The economic man affects a national role, *American Economic Review*, XXXVI (1946 supplement) 735–744.

HAUSMANN, F., World oil control, past and future: an alternative to "international cartellization," *Social Research*, IX (1942) 334–355.

HEXNER, E., American participation in the international steel cartel, *Southern Economic Journal*, VIII (1941–42) 54–79.

———, International cartels in the postwar world, *ibid.*, X (1943–44) 114–135.

HOSELITZ, B. F., The cartel report, *Canadian Journal of Economics and Political Science*, XII (1946) 172–175.

———, International cartel policy, *Journal of Political Economy*, LV (1947) 1–27.

JAMES, C. L., The international control of raw sugar supplies, *American Economic Review*, XXI (1931) 481–497.

KLEIN, J., International cartels, *Foreign Affairs*, VI (1927–28) 448–458.

KOVOLENKO, A. S., International regulation of world trade in wheat, *Vneshniaia Torgovlia*, (1943, No. 12) 14–19.

KREIDER, C., The Anglo-American cotton-rubber barter agreement, *Southern Economic Journal*, VII (1940–41) 216–224.

KREPS, T. J., Cartels, a phase of business *haute politique*, *American Economic Review*, XXXV (1945 supplement) 297–311.

LATTIMER, J. E., The British bacon agreement, *Canadian Journal of Economics and Political Science*, VI (1940) 60–67.

LIEFMANN, R., Internationale Kartelle, *Weltwirtschaftliches Archiv*, XXV (1927, I) 260–294.

MACGREGOR, D. H., Recent papers on cartels, *Economic Journal*, XXXVII (1927) 247–254.

MASON, E. S., The future of international cartels, *Foreign Affairs*, XXII (1943–44) 604–615.

———, International commodity controls: cartels and commodity agreements, *Economic Reconstruction* (S. E. Harris, ed.), New York, McGraw-Hill, 1945, 217–233.

MEAKIN, M. W., The international aspect of nationalization, *Journal of the Royal Institute of International Affairs*, IX (1930) 79–89.

MOND, A., International cartels, *Journal of the Royal Institute of International Affairs*, VI (1927) 265–283.

NOTZ, W., International private agreements in the form of cartels, syndicates and other combinations, *Journal of Political Economy*, XXVIII (1920) 658–679.

RABINOVICH, P., Fifteen years of monopoly in foreign trade, *Vneshniaia Torgovlia*, (1933, No. 8) 8.

ROWE, J. W. F., The artificial control of raw material supplies, *Economic Journal*, XL (1930) 401–421.

———, Artificial control schemes and the world's staples, *Index*, X (1935) 75–89.

SEHLBERG, N., Indirect protection, *Index*, IV (1929) 9–16.

STALIN, J., On foreign trade monopoly, *Vneshniaia Torgovlia*, (1933, No. 8) 3.

STAUDINGER, H., The future of totalitarian barter trade, *Social Research*, VII (1940) 410–433.

TERRILL, R. P., Cartels and the international exchange of technology, *American Economic Review*, XXXVI (1946 supplement) 745–767.

TOWER, W. S., The new steel cartel, *Foreign Affairs*, V (1926–27) 249–266.

VINER, J., National monopolies of raw materials, *Foreign Affairs*, IV (1925–26) 585–600.

WALTERS, A., The international copper cartel, *Southern Economic Journal*, XI (1944–45) 133–156.

WHITTLESEY, C. R., The Stevenson Plan: some conclusions and observations, *Journal of Political Economy*, XXXIX (1931) 506–525.

VI-D. COMMERCIAL POLICIES OF THE UNITED STATES

BECKETT, G., The problem of reclassification in the reciprocal trade agreements, *Journal of Political Economy*, XLVIII (1940) 199–209.

———, Effect of the reciprocal trade agreements on the foreign trade of the United States, *Quarterly Journal of Economics*, LV (1940–41) 80–94.

BERGLUND, A., The Tariff Act of 1922, *American Economic Review*, XIII (1923) 14–33.

———, The Tariff Act of 1930, *ibid.*, XX (1930) 467–479.

———, The Reciprocal Trade Agreements Act of 1934, *ibid.*, XXV (1935) 411–425.

BERNHARDT, J., The flexible tariff and the sugar industry, *American Economic Review*, XVI (1926 supplement) 182–191.

BIDWELL, P. W., The new American tariff: Europe's answer, *Foreign Affairs*, IX (1930–31) 13–26.

———, Tariff reform: the case for bargaining, *American Economic Review*, XXIII (1933 supplement) 137–146.

———, Our invisible tariff, *Foreign Affairs*, XVI (1938–39) 774–787.

———, Chairman, Round table on problems of American commercial policy, *American Economic Review*, XXX (1940 supplement) 118–123.

———, Our economic warfare, *Foreign Affairs*, XX (1941–42) 421–437.

———, A postwar commercial policy for the United States, *American Economic Review*, XXXIV (1944 supplement) 340–353.

———, Imports in the American economy, *Foreign Affairs*, XXIV (1945–46) 85–98.

———, and UPGREN, A. R., A trade policy for national defense, *ibid.*, XIX (1940–41) 282–296.

BLACK, J. D., The McNary-Haugen movement, *American Economic Review*, XVIII (1928) 405–427.

CASTLE, W. R., A critique of the trade agreements program, *Annals of the American Academy of Political Science*, CXCVIII (1938) 48–52.

CLAPP, E. J., Foreign trading zones in our seaports, *American Economic Review*, XII (1922) 262–271.

COOPER, L. W., The tariff and organized labor, *American Economic Review*, XX (1930) 210–225.

COPLAND, D. B., Some reciprocal effects of our anti-trust laws with special reference to Australia, *Annals of the American Academy of Political Science*, CXLVII (1930) 117–124.

CULBERTSON, W. S., Equality of treatment among nations and a bargaining tariff, *Annals of the American Academy of Political Science*, XCIV (1921) 160–175.

CUMBERLAND, W. W., Our economic policy toward Latin America, *Annals of the American Academy of Political Science*, CL (1930) 167–178.

DEIMEL, H. L., Jr., Commercial policy under the trade agreements, *Annals of the American Academy of Political Science*, CLXXXVI (1936) 16–23.

DICKEY, J. S., Our treaty procedure versus our foreign policies, *Foreign Affairs*, XXV (1947) 357–377.

DIEBOLD, W., JR., Oil import quotas and "equal treatment," *American Economic Review* XXX (1940) 569–573.

EDMINSTER, L. R., The trade agreements program and American agriculture, *American Economic Review*, XXVI (1936 supplement) 129–140.

ELLSWORTH, P. T., American tariff policy in a changing world, *Annals of the American Academy of Political Science*, CCVI (1939) 62–67.

———, An economic foreign policy for America, *American Economic Review*, XXXI (1941 supplement) 301–319.

FAULKNER, H. U., The development of the American system, *Annals of the American Academy of Political Science*, CXLI (1928) 11–17.

FEIS, H., After tariffs, embargoes, *Foreign Affairs*, IX (1930–31) 398–408.

———, A year of the Canadian trade agreement, *ibid.*, XV (1936–37) 619–635.

———, On our economic relations with Britain, *ibid.*, XXI (1942–43) 462–475.

FETTER, F. W., Congressional tariff theory, *American Economic Review*, XXIII (1933) 413–427.

FOURNIER, L. T., The purposes and results of the Webb-Pomerene law, *American Economic Review*, XXII (1932) 18–33.

GIDEONSE, H. D., The relation of American foreign-trade policy to new-deal domestic policy, *American Economic Review*, XXX (1940) 87–97.

GOLDENBERG, H. C., The Canada-United States trade agreement, 1935, *Canadian Journal of Economics and Political Science*, II (1936) 209–212.

GORDON, M. S., International aspects of American agricultural policy, *American Economic Review*, XXXVI (1946) 596–612.

GRADY, H. F., The new trade policy of the United States, *Foreign Affairs*, XIV (1935–36) 283–296.

———, Reciprocal agreements for trade expansion, *Annals of the American Academy of Political Science*, CCXI (1940) 58–64.

GREGG, E. S., A case against discriminating duties, *Journal of Political Economy*, XXX (1922) 404–411.

HANOV, United States foreign trade and commercial policy, *Vneshniaia Torgovlia*, (1933, No. 4) 6–8.

HENCHIN, A., and ROZIN, M., The direction of United States commercial policy, *Vneshniaia Torgovlia* (1934, No. 9–10) 17–20.

JONES, E., The Webb-Pomerene Act, *Journal of Political Economy*, XXVIII (1920) 754–767.

KREIDER, C., The effect of American trade agreements on third countries: retrospect, *American Economic Review*, XXXI (1941) 780–793.

LANDRY, R. S., The Federal Trade Commission and "unfair competition" in international trade, *American Economic Review*, XXXV (1945) 575–584.

MacBRIDE, H. L., Export and import associations as instruments of national policy, *Political Science Quarterly*, LVII (1942) 189–213.

McCLURE, W., The commercial policy of the United States in the light of current world developments, *Annals of the American Academy of Political Science*, CL (1930) 146–153.

MACKINTOSH, W. A., Reciprocity, *Canadian Journal of Economics and Political Science*, VI (1940) 611–620.

NOTZ, W., Ten years' operation of the Webb law, *American Economic Review*, XIX (1929) 9–19.

PASVOLSKY, L., Some aspects of our foreign economic policy, *American Economic Review*, XXXI (1941 supplement) 320–337.

PATTERSON, E. M., United States in the world economy, 1940: a summary, *American Economic Review*, XXXI (1941 supplement) 338–343.

PATTON, H. S., Reciprocity with Canada: the Canadian viewpoint, *Quarterly Journal of Economics*, XXXV (1920–21) 574–595.

PETTENGILL, R. B., The United States copper industry and the tariff, *Quarterly Journal of Economics*, XLVI (1931–32) 141–157.

ROGERS, J. H., The position of the United States in world affairs, *Annals of the American Academy of Political Science*, CXLIX (1930) 82–87.

ROSTOW, E. V., American security and foreign economic policy, *Yale Review*, XXXIV, new series (1944–45) 495–523.

SAYRE, F. B., How trade agreements are made, *Foreign Affairs*, XVI (1937–38) 417–429
——, Does American labor stand to win or lose by trade agreements?, *Political Science Quarterly*, LIV (1939) 175–186.

SCHULTZ, T. W., Which way will farmers turn?, *Foreign Affairs*, XXIII (1944–45) 627–634.

SIEGFRIED, A., European reactions to American tariff proposals, *Foreign Affairs*, VIII (1929–30) 13–19.

SMITH, J. G., Development of policy under the trade agreements program, *Quarterly Journal of Economics*, L (1935–36) 297–312.

SMITH, M. A., The United States flexible tariff, *Explorations in Economics*, New York, McGraw-Hill, 1936, 169–178.
——, Reciprocal trade agreements and the South, *Southern Economic Journal*, IV (1937–38) 303–313.

SNOW, C. D., American foreign trade problems, *American Economic Review*, XIV (1924 supplement) 5–13.

SOUTHWORTH, C., The newsprint industry and the tariff, *Journal of Political Economy*, XXX (1922) 681–697.

STERNBERG, F., The United States in the future world economy, *Social Research*, XI (1944) 285–304.

STEVENS, R. B., Lowering our tariff wall by trade agreements, *Annals of the American Academy of Political Science*, CCXI (1940) 76–84.

STEVENSON, P. J., American trade faces barriers abroad, *Annals of the American Academy of Political Science*, CCXI (1940) 51–57.

TASCA, H. J., Fundamental aspects of the trade agreements program, *Annals of the American Academy of Political Science*, CCXI (1940) 65–71.

TAUSSIG, F. W., The Tariff Act of 1922, *Quarterly Journal of Economics*, XXXVII (1922–23) 1–28.
——, The United States Tariff Commission and the tariff, *American Economic Review*, XVI (1926 supplement) 171–181.
——. The tariff bill and our friends abroad, *Foreign Affairs*, VIII (1929–30) 1–12.
——, The Tariff Act of 1930, *Quarterly Journal of Economics*, XLV (1930–31) 1–21.

————, Necessary changes in our commercial policy, *Foreign Affairs*, XI (1932–33) 397–405.

————, and WHITE, H. D., Rayon and the tariff, the nurture of an industrial prodigy, *Quarterly Journal of Economics*, XLV (1930–31) 588–621.

THOMAS, E. P., Inter-American trade problems, *Annals of the American Academy of Political Science*, CCIV (1939) 147–154.

————, Has the trade agreements program succeeded?, *ibid.*, CCXI (1940) 72–75.

UNDERWOOD, O. W., The tariff as a factor in American trade, *Foreign Affairs*, I: 3 (1922–23) 25–34.

UPGREN, A. R., Triangular trade, *Journal of Political Economy*, XLIII (1935) 653–673.

VARGA, E., Anglo-American rivalry and partnership: a Marxist view, *Foreign Affairs*, XXV (1947) 583–595.

VINER, J., The most-favored-nation clause in American commercial treaties, *Journal of Political Economy*, XXXII (1924) 101–129.

————, The commercial policy and the foreign trade of the United States, *Index*, IV (1929) 3–17.

WALLACE, B. B., Tariff bargaining, *Foreign Affairs*, XI (1932–33) 621–633.

WATKINS, M. W., Scarce raw materials, *American Economic Review*, XXXIV (1944) 227–260.

WHITTLESEY, C. R., Import quotas in the United States, *Quarterly Journal of Economics*, LII (1937–38) 37–65.

WILLIS, H. P., A tariff policy for the future, *Annals of the American Academy of Political Science*, CLVI (1931) 93–101.

ZAPOLEON, L. B., Farm relief, agricultural prices, and tariffs, *Journal of Political Economy* XL (1932) 73–100.

VI-E (1). COMMERCIAL POLICIES OF OTHER COUNTRIES: *The United Kingdom*

ANONYMOUS, Achieving a balance, *Economist*, CLI (1947) 390–392.

————, When the dollars run out, *ibid.*, 504–505.

BACKMAN, J., and FISHMAN, L., British war-time control of copper, lead, and zinc, *Quarterly Journal of Economics*, LV (1940–41) 210–238.

————, and ————, British war-time control of aluminum, *ibid.*, LVI (1941–42) 18–48.

BEACHAM, A., The proposal for a coal subsidy, *Review of Economic Studies*, VII (1939) 59–72.

BENN, W., The Safeguarding of Industries Act: orders under Part II, *Economic Journal*, XXXII (1922) 408–414.

BRANDIS, B., British overseas trade and foreign exchange, *Political Science Quarterly*, LVIII (1943) 191–216.

BROSTER, E. J., A proposal for a scientific tariff, *Economic Journal*, XLI (1931) 313–316.

DIETRICH, E. B., The new model trade agreements, *Journal of Political Economy*, XLII (1934) 595–612.

————, British export credit insurance, *American Economic Review*, XXV (1935) 236–249.

DMITRIEVICH, D., The development of England's export policy under the conditions of war, *Vneshniaia Torgovlia*, (1942, No. 1–2) 18–22.

FAY, C. R., Corn prices and the corn laws, 1815–1846, *Economic Journal*, XXXI (1921) 17–27.

————, Price control and the corn averages under the corn laws, *Economic History*, I: 1 (1926) 149–154.

FISHMAN, L., Wartime control of tin in Great Britain, *Journal of Political Economy*, LIV (1946) 413–435.

HANOV, The commercial policy of England, *Vneshniaia Torgovlia*, (1933, No. 13–14) 21–24.

JAMES, G., British preferential export taxes, *American Economic Review*, XIV (1924) 56–63.

KAWAKAMI, K. K., Britain's trade war with Japan, *Foreign Affairs*, XII (1933–34) 483–494.

KENDALL, M. G., Control of market supplies of agricultural produce, *Manchester School*, X (1939) 122–133.

LITOVA, The Anglo-Japanese commercial war, *Vneshniaia Torgovlia*, (1933, No. 15) 11–13.

MORGAN, D. J., Commentary on "Great Britain's trade policy," *Social Research*, XII (1945) 370–374.

REES, J. F., The phases of British commercial policy in the eighteenth century, *Economica*, V (1925) 130–150.

ROBERTS, S. G., The Wheat Act of 1932, *Manchester School*, IV (1933) 41–54.

SALTER, A., England's dilemma: free trade or protection?, *Foreign Affairs*, X (1931–32) 188–200.

SCHÜLLER, R., Great Britain's trade policy, *Social Research*, XI (1944) 268–284.

STEWART, R. B., Anglo-Argentine trade agreements, *Canadian Journal of Economics and Political Science*, II (1936) 16–26.

WORSWICK, G. D. N., British raw material controls, *Oxford Economic Papers*, No. 6, (April 1942) 1–42.

VI-E (2). COMMERCIAL POLICIES OF OTHER COUNTRIES: *Other Members of the British Commonwealth of Nations, Including Canada*

AMERY, L. E., The Imperial Economic Conference: before the meeting at Ottawa, *International Affairs*, XI (1932) 678–699.

ANONYMOUS, Ottawa Section, *Economist*, CXXVII (1937) 262–271.

BELSHAW, H., Guaranteed prices for New Zealand exports, *Economic Record*, XIII (1937) 168–188.

BINNS, K. J., and PEARSON, A. G., Australian-Japanese trade relations, *Economic Record*, XII (1936) 276–281.

BRIGDEN, J. B., Australian tariff policy, *Economic Record*, IX (1933) 202–213.

CAMPBELL, R. M., Empire free trade, *Economic Journal*, XXXIX (1929) 371–378.

CLARK, S. D., The Canadian manufacturers' association and the tariff, *Canadian Journal of Economics and Political Science*, V (1939) 19–39.

COOPER, J. I., Some early French-Canadian advocacy of protection: 1871–1873, *Canadian Journal of Economics and Political Science*, III (1937) 530–540.

COPLAND, D. B., The economics of insulation, *Economic Record*, XV (October 1939 supplement) 25–31.

DYASON, E. C., BAWRA, *Economic Record*, IV (1928 supplement) 51–67.

FEIS, H., The future of British imperial preferences, *Foreign Affairs*, XXIV (1945–46) 661–674.

FISHER, A. G. B., New Zealand wheat: a new sliding-scale experiment, *Economic Record*, IV (1928) 306–313.

——, Sliding scales in depression: New Zealand wheat, *ibid.*, VIII (1932) 262–269.

FOWKE, V. C., Dominion aids to wheat marketing, 1929–1939, *Canadian Journal of Economics and Political Science*, VI (1940) 390–402.

GIBLIN, L. F., Reports of the tariff board, *Economic Record*, VI (1930) 102–115.

——, The tariff: its costs and effects, *Annals of the American Academy of Political Science*, CLVIII (1931) 119–132.

——, The reports of the wheat commission, *Economic Record*, XI (1935) 1–12.

GLICKMAN, D. L., The British imperial preference system, *Quarterly Journal of Economics*, LXI (1946–47) 439–470.

HALL, N. F., "Trade diversion," an Australian interlude, *Economica*, V, new series (1938) 1–11.

HODSON, H. V., Before Ottawa, *Foreign Affairs*, X (1931–32) 589–599.

——, Imperial economic policy, *International Affairs*, XIV (1935) 531–550.

JACOBSON, M., Crisis of the Ottawa empire agreements, *Vneshniaia Torgovlia*, (1934, No. 23) 14–16.

JONES, R. L., The Canadian agricultural tariff of 1843, *Canadian Journal of Economics and Political Science*, VII (1941) 528–537.

MACDONNELL, F. M., After the Ottawa Conference, *Foreign Affairs*, XI (1932–33) 331–346.

McDOUGALL, F. L., The Empire Marketing Board and Empire economic affairs, *Economic Record*, IV (1928 supplement) 139–147.

McFADYEAN, A., International repercussions of the Ottawa Agreements, *International Affairs*, XII (1933) 37–59.

MILLS, R. C., The tariff board of Australia, *Economic Record*, III (1927) 52–81.

NEALE, E. P., New Zealand customs tariff policy in the face of fluctuating exchanges, *Economic Record*, IX (1933) 41–48.

——, The report of the New Zealand tariff commission, *ibid.*, X (1934) 253–260.

——, Recent trade policy in New Zealand, *ibid.*, XIV (1938) 83–87.

PATTON, H. S., Observations on Canadian wheat policy since the World War, *Canadian Journal of Economics and Political Science*, III (1937) 218–233.

PLANT, A., The anti-dumping regulations of the South African tariff, *Economica*, XI (1931) 63–102.

PRATO, G., La controversia doganale e la preferenza imperiale in Inghiltérra, *Annali di Economia*, III (1927) 351–369.

REEDMAN, J. N., Exchange policy and import control, *South African Journal of Economics*, VIII (1940) 372–387.

RICHARDS, C. S., Subsidies, quotas, tariffs, and the excess cost of agriculture in South Africa, *South African Journal of Economics*, III (1935) 365–403.

RODWELL, H. R., Economic aspects of Empire tariff preference, *Economic Record*, VIII (1932) 1–15.

ROSE, W. J., A "made to measure" tariff, *Economic Record*, XXI (1945) 212–222.

SAUNDERS, S. A., The reciprocity treaty of 1854: a regional study, *Canadian Journal of Economics and Political Science*, I (1936) 41–53.

SHARP, M. W., Allied wheat buying in relationship to Canadian marketing policy, 1914–1918, *Canadian Journal of Economics and Political Science*, VI (1940) 372–389.

SKEOCH, L. A., Changes in Canadian wheat policy, *Canadian Journal of Economics and Political Science*, IX (1943) 565–569.

STUART, N. F., Some tariff board reports, *Economic Record*, XV (1939) 87–91.

SUTCH, W. B., The Ottawa Agreement and after, *Economic Record*, XV (October 1939 supplement) 32–44.

WADIA, P. A., The true basis of protection for India, *Economic Journal*, XXXIV (1924) 193–199.

WESTCOTT, F. J., An approach to the problem of tariff burdens on Western Canada, *Canadian Journal of Economics and Political Science*, IV (1938) 209–218.

WILSON, R., The export trade and imperial preference, *Annals of the American Academy of Political Science*, CLVIII (1931) 86–94.

WOOD, G. L., The reciprocal tariff, *Economic Record*, I (1925) 150–151.

———, Wheat pools with special reference to Australia, *ibid.*, IV (1928 supplement) 18–37.

ZIMMERN, A., The "open-door" and reciprocity in the British Empire, *Index*, VIII (1933) 123–133.

VI-E (3). COMMERCIAL POLICIES OF OTHER COUNTRIES: *Continental Europe*

ABEZGANS, B., Export trade and policy of fascist Germany, *Vneshniaia Torgovlia*, (1934, No. 17–18) 20–23.

ANONYMOUS, Soviet-United States trade relations, *Vneshniaia Torgovlia*, (1933, No. 23–24) 1–3.

B. R., Commercial and political relations of the USSR and the capitalist countries, *Mirovoe Khoziaistvo i Mirovaia Politika*, (March 1934) 51–71.

BAUDIN, L., France and international economic policy, *International Affairs*, XXII (1946) 187–198.

BIDWELL P. W., Latin America, Germany, and the Hull program, *Foreign Affairs*, XVII (1938–39) 374–390.

BONN, M., The Austro-German customs union, *International Affairs*, X (1931) 460–476.

BORISOFF, B., Trade agreements between the USSR and capitalistic countries, *Vneshniaia Torgovlia*, (1934, No. 24) 4–7.

CZECHOWICZ, P., Die Exportpolitik und das Problem der Exportfähigkeit der USSR, *Weltwirtschaftliches Archiv*, XXXV (1932) 475–513.

DAVIDOV, J., Soviet-Japanese economic relations, *Mirovoe Khoziaistvo i Mirovaia Politika* (September 1938) 50–64.

DAWSON, W. H., The Pan-European movement, *Economic Journal*, XXXVII (1927) 62–67.

DIETRICH, E. B., French import quotas, *American Economic Review*, XXIII (1933) 661–674.

FAY, H. VAN V., Commercial policy in post-war Europe: reciprocity versus most-favored-nation treatment, *Quarterly Journal of Economics*, XLI (1926–27) 441–470.

FISHER, A. G. B., The German trade drive in south-eastern Europe, *International Affairs*, XVIII (1939) 143–170.

FRISELLA-VELLA, G., La politica commerciale doganale italiana nel dopoguerra, *La Riforma Sociale*, XXXIX (1928) 34–51.

HUBER, J. R., Effects of German clearing agreements and import restrictions on cotton, 1934–1939, *Southern Economic Journal*, VI (1939–40) 419–439.

MENKINSKY, E., Problems of postwar export policy, *Vneshniaia Torgovlia*, (1944, No. 10) 16–22.

MORTARA, G., Per l' independenza economica dell' Italia, *Giornale degli Economisti*, LXVII (1926) 593–606.

OHLIN, B., A European customs union?, *Index*, IV (1929) 5–9.

OHOTNIKOV, T., On the nature and functions of soviet trade, *Sovietskaya Torgovlya*, III (1934) 84–94.

ROSENGLOTZ, A. P., In the struggle for economic independence of the Soviet Union, *Vneshniaia Torgovlia*, (1934, No. 3) 3–5.

SCHIFF, E., Dutch foreign-trade policy and the infant-industry argument for protection, *Journal of Political Economy*, L (1942) 280–290.

SCHWEITZER, A., The role of foreign trade in the Nazi war economy, *Journal of Political Economy*, LI (1943) 322–337.

TAUSSIG, F. W., The tariff controversy with France, *Foreign Affairs*, VI (1927–28) 177–190.

V. P-N., Imports and the struggle of the Soviet Union for economic independence, *Vneshniaia Torgovlia*, (1934, No. 1–2) 6–12.

WELK, W. G., League sanctions and foreign trade restrictions in Italy, *American Economic Review*, XXVII (1937) 96–107.

VI-E (4). COMMERCIAL POLICIES OF OTHER COUNTRIES: *All Other Countries*

MACKINTOSH, H. S., Politics and economics in Latin America, *International Affairs*, XXI (1945) 331–342.

REMER, C. F., Economic reconstruction in the Far East, *American Economic Review*, XXXVI (1946 supplement) 603–612.

STERNBERG, F., Japan's economic imperialism, *Social Research*, XII (1945) 328–349.

YUMOTO, T., Wandlungen der japanischen Devisen- und Zollpolitik, *Weltwirtschaftliches Archiv*, XXXVIII (1933) 170–194.

VI-F. INTERNATIONAL ORGANIZATIONS DEALING WITH PROBLEMS OF COMMERCIAL POLICY

Includes discussions of the International Trade Organization, the Food and Agriculture Organization, proposed buffer-stock agencies, etc.

ANONYMOUS, Hot Springs: a summary, *Economist*, CXLIV (1943) 751.

———, The United Nations conference on food and agriculture, *International Labor Review*, XLVIII (1943) 139–156.

———, World food plans, *Economist*, CL (1946) 402–403.

———, Trade talks: the points at issue, *ibid.*, 630–631.

———, Prelude to Geneva, *ibid.*, CLI (1947) 444–445.

BIDWELL, P. W., and GERSCHENKRON, A., International Trade Organization: discussion, *American Economic Review*, XXXVII (1947 supplement) 554–559.

BLACK, J. D., The international food movement, *American Economic Review*, XXXIII (1943) 791–811.

FLEXNER, J. A., Food policies of the United Nations, *American Economic Review*, XXXIII (1943) 812–824.

CLASSIFIED BIBLIOGRAPHY OF ARTICLES 625

GERSCHENKRON, A., Russia and the International Trade Organization, *American Economic Review*, XXXVII (1947 supplement) 624–642.

HEXNER, E., World industrial committees, *Southern Economic Journal*, XII (1945–46) 348–356.

KNORR, K. E., The functions of an International Trade Organization: possibilities and limitations, *American Economic Review*, XXXVII (1947 supplement) 542–553.

MIKESELL, R. F., The I.T.O. Charter, *American Economic Review*, XXXVII (1947) 351–368.

PIQUET, H. S., Functional international organization, *Annals of the American Academy of Political Science*, CCXL (1945) 43–50.

RIEFLER, W. W., A proposal for an international buffer stock agency, *Journal of Political Economy*, LIV (1946) 538–546.

VINER, J., Conflicts of principle in drafting a trade charter, *Foreign Affairs*, XXV (1947) 612–628.

WILCOX, C., Organization to liberate world trade, *Annals of the American Academy of Political Science*, CCXLVI (1946) 95–100.

——, The London Draft of a charter for an International Trade Organization, *American Economic Review*, XXXVII (1947 supplement) 529–541.

INDEX OF AUTHORS
CITED IN THE BIBLIOGRAPHY